D0871851

A HISTORY OF MUSIC IN AMERICAN LIFE

Volume III

THE MODERN ERA, 1920 - Present

RONALD L. DAVIS was born in Cambridge, Ohio and raised in Dallas. He attended the University of Texas at Austin, where he received his B.A. in anthropology and his M.A. and Ph.D. in American history. He has taught cultural history at Kansas State College at Emporia, Michigan State University, and since 1972 has been Professor of History at Southern Methodist University in Dallas. He has written *A History of Opera in the American West* (1965), *Opera in Chicago* (1966) and edited *The Social and Cultural Life of the 1920s* (1972). He is the director of the DeGolyer Institute for American Studies and the SMU Oral History Program on the Performing Arts.

A HISTORY OF MUSIC IN AMERICAN LIFE
Volume III

THE MODERN ERA,
1920 - Present

by
Ronald L. Davis

ROBERT KRIEGER PUBLISHING COMPANY
MALABAR, FLORIDA
1981

Original edition 1981

Printed and Published by
ROBERT E. KRIEGER PUBLISHING CO., INC.
Krieger Building, Krieger Drive
Malabar, FL 32950

Printed in the United States of America

Library of Congress Cataloging in Publication Data

Davis, Ronald L
  A history of music in American life.

  Includes bibliographies.
  CONTENTS: v. 1. The formative years, 1620-1865.—v. 2.
The gilded years, 1865-1920.—v. 3. The modern era, 1920-
present.
  1. Music—United States—History and criticism.
I. Title.
ML200.D3   780'.973   79-25359
ISBN 0-89874-002-9 (v. 1)

In Memory
of

BLANCHE M. MARTS
my own incredible Auntie Mame,
who showed me the meaning of
beauty and adventure

and

WALTER PRESCOTT WEBB
who loved the arts
as he loved the West,
and who affected many lives,
including mine

Introduction

Although immigrants came to the New World singing, frontier America had little time for the serious arts. Music, perhaps the most sensuous of Western Civilization's aesthetic expressions, was particularly neglected by a country whose cultural ideals emphasized hard work, material and social success, and emotional restraint. The Protestant ethic, reinforced by the wilderness experience, led the Puritans and other religious zealots to consider music a waste of time unless specifically contributing to the task at hand. The power of music to affect human emotions caused the Calvinist denominations especially to view it with more suspicion than fondness and therefore to restrict its role even in worship. An infant nation admiring reserve and control was far more comfortable with intellectual pursuits than with an art form prone to excite the senses.

With adolescence came an early nostalgia for vanishing innocence and a tendency to mistake sentimentality for honest feelings. As gentility was sought in the urban centers of the East, theaters and concert life slowly appeared as appendages of an aspiring commercial class who needed public arenas in which to display their newly acquired wealth and refinement. Serious music became prized as a demonstrable link with established civilization, an exotic and edifying experience that could be appreciated only with effort. Since men were consumed with economic and political matters, art in the young nation fell increasingly under the domination of women. Gradually the notion grew that serious music was not masculine. While music was essential for a sophisticated image, it was at the same time threatening to manhood if pursued in more than a cursory way. "I do not think," conductor Walter Damrosch would write, "there has ever been a country whose musical development has been fostered so almost exclusively by women as America."

Fawned over by the leisured classes, art music in the United States remained separate from life itself—an adornment imported from Europe for social purposes rather than an extract from the American experience. Until World War I serious music in America was dominated by immigrants and foreigners—first British, later Italian and especially German. Successful concert artists doted on the spectacular. John Philip Sousa at the turn of the century observed that life in the United States was more hurried than almost

VII

anywhere else; being restless, American audiences demanded variety and more in the way of showmanship.

By the middle of the nineteenth century vernacular music had been largely turned over to the minorities. Black entertainers, when outside the restrictions of the genteel tradition, often devised spontaneous expressions that were original, uniquely American, and frequently voiced the repressed emotions of whites as well as blacks, creating an idiom that would eventually develop into a national music. Even white performers in blackface could be less inhibited, less self-conscious, and therefore more honest about the issues and feelings that bothered or inflamed them. Later, with the advent of vaudeville and the rise of the commercial music business, the Jew came to dominate popular music in America, a phenomenon that continued at least until the end of the big studio era in Hollywood.

Meanwhile serious musicians were consistently being told they could not hope to win acceptance unless they had studied and been acclaimed in Europe. Since there were few symphony orchestras and no provincial opera houses in the United States, singers and conductors either went abroad to gain experience or turned to mass media, out of necessity spanning the gulf between vernacular music and the cultivated tradition. Eugene Ormandy, long the mainstay of the Philadelphia Orchestra, was first given a chance to conduct at the Roxy Theater in New York, one of the original movie palaces. Soprano Rosa Ponselle came to grand opera from vaudeville, whereas baritone Robert Merrill had worked in movie houses, the "borscht circuit," and radio before winning his Metropolitan Opera contract. Even then Merrill sought the best of both worlds—grand opera *and* popular entertainment— and was once fired from the Metropolitan for canceling performances to make a film in Hollywood. Beverly Sills, who made a sensational debut at the Metropolitan in Rossini's *The Siege of Corinth* after performing the same role at La Scala, began her professional career as Bubbles Silverman singing "Rinso White" commercials on radio. And American-born Klara Barlow, who made a hasty entrance into the Met as Isolde early in 1974, had been a cigarette girl in New York's Latin Quarter for a time.

While maturity and world leadership have brought increased sophistication, Americans have remained basically a vernacular people. The minstrel show, burlesque, vaudeville, Hollywood films, radio, and television have been the entertainment forms revered by the multitude, for whom musical comedy is high art. Symphony orchestras, opera, and recitals for most Americans suggest the unapproachable, the exalted, the tedious. Dynamic personalities—a Callas or a Bernstein—can occasionally break through this general reticence, but seldom does the music itself have such power. If the New Orleans opera company offers a nude Thais, as it did in 1973, *that* will make the national news. But barring the extreme, art music in the United States remains in the background—ardently supported by a select few, noticed in passing by the great majority.

American popular music, on the other hand, is heard around the world. Berlin, Kern, Porter, Rodgers, and the other giants of Tin Pan Alley wrote standards that are still performed wherever there is a piano or a dance orchestra. *South Pacific, My Fair Lady, Hello, Dolly!* and *Fiddler on the Roof* have played with immense success in London, Tokyo, and Tel Aviv, as well as year after year in dinner theaters and stock productions across the United States. Discos in Madrid or Rome or Mexico City throb with contemporary American hits, while Willie Nelson and Waylon Jennings have made their way from Texas to the Orient via Nashville, making those decades when American music was dismissed almost without a hearing seem quaint and long ago.

Yet there are those around who remember well when music that was considered any good at all came from Europe, and native works still have difficulty finding their way into American concert halls and opera houses. Music's dramatic struggle to take root in the United States has been far more than a story of art at war with barbarism, more than the determination of the creative spirit to triumph in the face of diffidence and even ridicule. When viewed collectively, the nation's history has been written in music, as vividly as it has been chronicled in words. So have its values and aspirations, its tensions and fears, its joys and yearnings for self-expression, along with the never-ending search for both personal and collective identity. What the historian has phrased in words, the musician has captured with notes, preserving the spirit and dimension of American life with accuracy and insight.

Dallas, Texas   RONALD L. DAVIS
March 28, 1980

Acknowledgments

A fourteen-year writing project carries with it innumerable frustrations and counterbalancing rewards. High among the latter has been the opportunity to meet an assortment of helpful, talented people. My gratitude literally extends from coast to coast, and one of the frustrations has been a temptation to rewrite portions of the story long ago completed when subsequent conversations with performers and musicians have opened up nuances too tantalizing to ignore. But as that great legend of popular song Ruth Etting told me in a long distance telephone conversation a matter of days before her death in Colorado, "There comes a point at which time stops." Certainly there comes a point at which any writer must stop, even though he knows there is more to tell and often wants desperately to go on.

I must first thank David D. Van Tassel of Case Western Reserve University, who initially suggested a broader topic as the logical successor to my previous books on opera in Chicago and opera in the American West. Van Tassel later admitted he had in mind a brief paperback survey of American music with emphasis on interpretation. Obviously I misunderstood and went my own direction, preferring to write a longer version with the undergraduate cultural history student and the curious layman in mind. A grant from the Graduate Council of Humanities at Southern Methodist University enabled me to begin my research in 1966, and I soon found gracious assistance in SMU's Fondren Library, especially from Dorothy Bosch, Margaret Hamzy, and Esther Smith. Much of the material needed was furnished through Inter-Library Loan, and there were many trips to the University of Texas at Austin, where a competent staff turned tedious work into an adventure. Most of the photographs in these three volumes came from the Hoblitzelle Theatre Arts Collection in Austin, and a special thanks goes to W. H. Crain and the dedicated personnel in the Humanities Research Center on the University of Texas campus.

Robert W. Richmond of the Kansas State Historical Society read the entire manuscript and offered constructive criticism at a formative stage of the writing, while my colleagues Luis Martin and R. Hal Williams provided encouragement when I needed it most. Richard B. Allen at the William Ransom Hogan Jazz Archive of Tulane University made useful notations on the jazz chapters and earlier opened a mass of invaluable material for my use. Lee Breeden read the introductory volume from a musician's viewpoint, as did Ann Burk some time later. Eleanor Solon typed and retyped the whole manuscript, read galley proofs, and labored over index cards above and beyond the call of duty. My appreciation to her is boundless. Mary Plunkett and JoAnn Brown also read galley proofs, volunteering fresh eyes when they were especially welcome.

Two sections of the work, "Sentimental Songs in Antebellum America" and "Early Jazz," have appeared in the *Southwest Review*, and as always Margaret Hartley proved a dream editor. Valcour Lavizzo edited the final copy, rescuing me from any number of foolish errors.

I owe a special debt to Clifford L. Snyder, who has aided my writing ventures repeatedly over the years and was instrumental in the completion of this one. Also I have been fortunate in having the cooperation of Robert E. Krieger and his production staff.

Personal gratitude must be expressed to Joe B. Frantz, Anne Russ, Bruce H. Beard, Robert R. Wade, Frank and Jane Moffit, and William and Elaine Sweet, all of whom gave supportive strokes between chapters.

R.L.D.

Illustrations

Contents

SYMPHONY ORCHESTRAS, CONCERT LIFE, AND A DEMOCRATIC SOCIETY

Major Henry Lee Higginson, urging a wealthy relative to endow Harvard University liberally, warned of the necessity "to save ourselves and our families and our money from the mobs." Generous as his patronage had been, Higginson's attitude toward the Boston Symphony Orchestra was basically elitist. He fought unionization of the orchestra, arguing that regimentation would be ruinous for art. Major Higginson essentially saw the Boston Symphony as a personal gift for the enrichment of his community, and he would suffer little compromise. By the time of his death in 1919, however, the benefactor's finances were so shaken that it was impossible for him to provide an endowment for the orchestra, aside from his music library. E. B. Dane served for a number of years as the symphony's "angel," but in the fall of 1923 it was revealed that the average annual deficit since Higginson's retirement had been approximately $100,000. The capacity of the philanthropists was rapidly being overcome, and economic reorganization was imminent. Boston, like other American cities, would shortly have to devise a broader base of support for the arts.

The quality of the Boston Symphony Orchestra had deteriorated badly since the imprisonment of Karl Muck, and the psychological effects of the Muck affair on the largely German orchestra was disastrous. French composer Henri Rabaud, who conducted during the 1918-1919 season, proved an ineffectual leader, but under Pierre Monteux, 1919-1924, the decline became even more striking. Some of the orchestra's ablest musicians were lured to Philadelphia and New York by better salaries; over twenty more, including the concertmaster, left when a general strike failed to establish a union in 1920. Suddenly the Boston Symphony was but a skeleton of its former self, its concerts seeming especially prosaic in light of the precision achieved by Muck a few years before. Attendance dwindled alarmingly, as a listlessness overtook the enterprise. Clearly reform was necessary if the once great orchestra was to be saved from disorganization and collapse.

There was little inclination to invite another German conductor, yet the announcement that Serge Koussevitzky would replace Monteux at the close of the 1923-1924 season was greeted with surprise and enthusiasm. Koussevitzky was unknown to American audiences except for distant, although good reports. Russian by birth and educated at the Moscow Conservatory, Koussevitzky was first known to the world of music as a virtuoso on the double bass. He founded a new orchestra in Moscow in 1909 and shortly won recognition as one of Russia's best conductors. He was appointed director of the Russian State Orchestra in Petrograd by the provisional government after the March, 1917 revolution, but found it expedient to leave Russia in 1920, following the solidification of the Bolshevik regime. The conductor took up residence in Paris, formed another orchestra, and within four years had earned a reputation far beyond the French capital. His programs were interesting, with novelties from many countries. He became a favorite guest conductor in England and also filled engagements in Berlin, Warsaw, Rome, Lisbon, Barcelona, and Madrid.

Koussevitzky was approaching his fiftieth year when he was selected to head the flagging Boston Symphony Orchestra. He had by then attained full mastery of his art, was a genius of interpretation, and enjoyed great international prestige. He was a fascinating personality, a leader of unsurpassed authority, who offered exciting impressions and artistic finish. His task was to bring the Boston Symphony Orchestra back to its former brilliance and lead it to new heights, and he proved more than worthy of the challenge. Koussevitzky would remain with the Boston Symphony for twenty-five years, providing the orchestra with an uninterrupted stability during which it could develop and absorb the innovative policies of its conductor.

The new conductor arrived in Boston amid much excitement and a tremendous press barrage. His first concert, on October 10, 1924, was covered by most of the major eastern newspapers and hailed as an unqualified triumph. Koussevitzky quickly made his authority felt, issued orders in French, German, and Russian, and by the end of his second season had made twenty-two replacements in the Boston Symphony's personnel. His imperious ways were considered sadistic by some, secured the respect of others. His programs were heavy on contemporary composers living in Paris, and he excelled in the emotionalism of Tchaikovsky and the rich hues of Rimsky-Korsakoff. He was more roundly catholic in his tastes than either of his predecessors, while his interpretative abilities were unsurpassed. The famous "Koussevitzky tone" was distinguished by color and oceanic depth.

By the time he arrived in Boston, Koussevitzky had already established himself as a prophet of modern music, having given thrilling performances in Europe of Scriabin, Moussorgsky, and Stravinsky. Although he was not yet acquainted with a large number of American works, he cautiously tested this ground during his initial Boston season. On February 20, 1925, he startled patrons by introducing the modernistic Symphony for Organ and Orchestra by twenty-four year-old Aaron Copland, whom the conductor had met in Paris. There were other American selections on Koussevitzky's early programs, but Copland's was decidedly the most advanced. The rest were by conservative, older composers more palatable to Boston audiences. Over the next two decades the Boston Symphony Orchestra would perform no less than sixty-six new American works, playing altogether 162 native works under Koussevitzky's direction by April, 1944. The musician was fastidious in his selections. The loud, aggressive compositions of Varese, Antheil, Ornstein, and Cowell had little interest for him, nor did the strong individualism of Charles Ives or Carl Ruggles. But the conductor's devotion to creative American talents grew with his tenure in Boston, and a Koussevitzky premiere became looked upon as a very special event indeed, the American composer's dream. "It is easy to foresee," Copland predicted, "that the story of Serge Koussevitzky and the American composer will some day take on the character of a legend. Here at least is one legend that will have been well founded."

Koussevitzky abolished from his programs the weekly star soloist that Rabaud and Monteux had featured in an effort to lure audiences to Symphony Hall. In place of soloists Koussevitzky enthroned modern composers. Above all, he restored an aura of fascination to conducting. His suave mannerisms, his flair for showmanship, even his dictatorial air the public found enchanting. While the conductor exerted his power over the Boston Symphony, inspired its players to outdo themselves, instituted painstaking rehearsals to thrash his musicians into discipline, and put vibrancy back into the orchestra, he also enveloped the podium in glamor. Through the years Koussevitzky loomed greater and greater, yet was imbued with the personality and foresight to involve the public and press as he lifted the Boston Symphony Orchestra to glory.

In Philadelphia the charismatic Leopold Stokowski continued to turn concertgoing into an adventure, particularly for the young. He emphasized the purely sonic side of music and became the recognized master of amplitude and color. "He approached orchestral music much as Franz Liszt must have approached piano music," Herbert Kupferberg suggests, "as a virtuoso who knew how to draw the utmost expressivity from his instrument, and to make the greatest possible effect upon his hearers." The Philadelphia Orchestra along with the Boston Symphony became the finest sounding symphonic organizations in the nation, on a par with any in the world. By 1925 Stokowski was conducting twenty-nine pairs of Friday and Saturday concerts at the Academy of Music, plus occasional programs on other evenings. Virtually every solo artist of importance appeared as a guest with the Philadelphia Orchestra. The director reseated his musicians, experimentally allowed his violinists to bow independently, and in 1929 passed the concertmaster's position around in alphabetical order. Audiences found much of his unconventional programming incomprehensible, but Stokowski riveted their attention nonetheless. His hands, wrists, and arms became interpretive clues to his orchestra and public alike, while the grace of his batonless conducting became the subject of enthusiastic discussion. By avoiding the commonplace and the routine, Stokowski galvanized concert life in Philadelphia into an exhilarating experience.

He instituted a new series of children's concerts in 1921, which he often conducted himself. The children's concerts gave full reign to Stokowski's sense of the spectacular. When the orchestra played Saint-Saens' *Carnival of the Animals*, he insisted on having a live menagerie on stage, including several baby elephants. For Prokofiev's *Peter and the Wolf* he wanted a real wolf, but finally settled for a large dog. In 1925 Stokowski and his orchestra made a pioneer electrical recording for RCA Victor, and on Sunday afternoon, October 6, 1929, the Philadelphia Orchestra became the first symphonic group to make a commercially sponsored radio broadcast.

Each year following World War I, Stokowski would return from his summer in Europe with a suitcase full of new works he wanted to perform. Schoenberg, Ravel, Satie, Delius, Elgar, Sibelius—he was intrigued with them all. "It is rather difficult to deal with Stravinsky, however," the conductor told a reporter in 1920, "because he has some strange notions and is inclined to be more than a trifle grasping in financial dealings." Yet on March 3, 1922, Stokowski gave the American premiere of the composer's *Le Sacre du Printemps* and presented Stravinsky's *Song of the Nightingale* the next year. *Le Sacre du Printemps* was fairly well received at first, but when Stokowski kept playing it, the public balked. "If you can relax yourselves for forty minutes from your narrow, comfortable life, with its ice cream, its steam heat, and its Prohibition," the conductor lectured an audience, "the *Sacre du Printemps* can be a magnificent experience....It is not comfortable music, but it is tremendous music, magnificent music and important music—the most important, perhaps, of this generation."

Stravinsky himself came to Philadelphia in 1925 to conduct a concert of his own music—*Fireworks, Scherzo Fantastique*, the *Petrouchka Suite*, the *Firebird Suite*, and the *Song of the Nightingale*. He was warmly received. Other modern composers were greeted with less enthusiasm. As early as 1921 members of the audience hissed Malipiero's *Ditirambo Tragico*, and similar reactions accompanied several other new works during the next few years. But Stokowski played what he wanted. In 1924 the Philadelphia Orchestra, whose repertoire boasted many modern pieces, introduced the radical sounds of Edgard Varese to the Philadelphia public. Novelties like Falla's *El Amor Brujo*, Hindemith's *Nusch-Nusch Dances*, and Schoenberg's *Kammersymphonie* did not preclude a full complement of Beethoven, Brahms, Wagner, and Tchaikovsky. Stokowski transcriptions of Bach's organ pieces appeared frequently on programs, while Sibelius' Symphony No. 5 in E-flat, Mahler's *Das Lied von der Erde*, and Rachmaninoff's *The Bells* all had American premieres in Philadelphia.

The cult of the conductor remained in vogue in symphony halls throughout the 1920s. In New York, Willem Mengelberg first appeared with the Philharmonic in 1921 and quickly jerked the orchestra back to life. Behind the scenes Mengelberg was a finicky German drillmaster, but to the public he was a magnetic personality full of appeal. The conductor allowed himself to be pampered and caressed like a Hollywood star, and audiences loved him for it. He commanded the respect of his musicians, who responded with rejuvenated performances. Mengelberg established the fad of the guest conductor, and as rivalry between the Philharmonic and the New York Symphony Society quickened in the early twenties, both orchestras attempted to bring the world's foremost conductors to the city. The Symphony Society presented Bruno Walter, Vladimir Golschmann, Otto Klemperer, and Fritz Busch, while the Philharmonic offered Wilhelm Furtwangler, Fritz Reiner, Arturo Toscanini, and Sir Thomas Beecham. Walter Damrosch had resigned his post with the Symphony Society to devote himself entirely to radio work. He went on the air with his "Music Appreciation Hour" in 1924 and became the first music executive of the National Broadcasting Company two years later. His programs would continue until 1942.

By the time Damrosch retired from conducting, both the New York Symphony Society and the New York Philharmonic faced rising wage scales and were beset with financial problems. Talk of consolidating the orchestras began as early as 1910, and on March 30, 1928, a merger was formally announced, symbolized in the union of names—the Philharmonic-Symphony Society. Arturo Toscanini, who had made his debut as guest conductor with the New York Philharmonic on January 14, 1926, was chosen principal conductor of the amalgamated forces. Willem Mengelberg was appointed his Associate. The director was entrusted with the selection of personnel, twenty of whom were drawn from the former Damrosch group. Since Toscanini initially was present for only about half of the season, Mengelberg was still much in the limelight, along with guest conductors like Arthur Honegger, Fritz Reiner, and occasionally Damrosch.

For nearly a decade Toscanini stood at the helm of the New York Philharmonic-Symphony Society, evoking a frenzied hero worship more characteristic of the sports arena than of dignified concert halls. After 1929, when the conductor retired from La Scala, Toscanini changed his primary focus from opera to orchestral music. And his career would center from that point on mainly in America. Toscanini's sound was lean and crisp, sacrificing some beauty for absolute clarity. Like Koussevitzky and Stokowski, his regime was autocratic, and even more than his Boston and Philadelphia counterparts, Toscanini was ever the temperamental *artiste*. But his interpretations were of an inspired originality, and he possessed artistic integrity in everything he did. For the public the wiry Italian could do no wrong. Tickets for his concerts were invariably at a premium, regardless of the program he selected. In 1929 the New York Philharmonic began its series of Sunday afternoon broadcasts, turning the orchestra into a national institution.

Unfortunately Frederick Stock, who took over the direction of the Chicago Symphony Orchestra after the death of Theodore Thomas, never attained the celestial stature of Toscanini, Stokowski, or Koussevitzky. His was not the sort of personality to court the news media or woo the public with spectacle and displays of temperament, and his fame suffered. While his programs seldom scaled Olympian heights, Stock was a forceful conductor and a sensitive interpreter. He was a genuine musician who gave solid performances, and under his leadership the Chicago Symphony remained among the major American orchestras, touring widely throughout the Midwest. Next to Koussevitzky, Stock was most consistently hospitable to American music, responsible for an impressive list of premieres. As competition for good musicians increased in the 1920s, Chicago like the eastern orchestras faced extensive difficulties with unions. More orchestras, the opportunities for work in the better motion picture theaters, and the rising cost of living prompted musicians unions to become more aggressive in their demands. Management, dominated by philanthropists, was equally loath to grant more generous contracts. As a result, labor-management conflicts at times threatened the dissolution of the Chicago Symphony Orchestra, as well as others.

The Cleveland Orchestra, soon one of the nation's most promising, gave its first concert in Gray's Armory on December 11, 1918, a month after the Armistice. Nikolai Sokoloff, a Russian-American violinist formerly with the Boston Symphony, conducted. He presented a mixture of French and Russian works, characteristic of him, with Victor Herbert's *American Fantasy* for accent. Sokoloff at one time was a student of Charles Martin Loeffler, while his conducting had been greatly influenced by Artur Nikisch, the flamboyant interpreter of romantic and neoromantic music. He proved to be an intelligent man, full of zeal, a great person but not a great conductor. During its opening season the Cleveland Orchestra played twenty-seven concerts. The primary moving force behind the symphony was Adella Prentiss Hughes, a Vassar graduate and a leading light in the prospering city's cultural life. Possessing a will of iron, the young woman had returned home in 1891, after a grand tour of Europe, determined to bring music and refinement to her native city. She eventually talked Cleveland's industrial aristocracy into supporting a resident orchestra. There had been several earlier attempts, and the Cleveland Municipal Orchestra had been overcome by problems as recently as World War I. But the orchestra initiated by Sokoloff proved permanent. In the early years its subscribers tended to be highly conservative and easily shocked. Performances of Scriabin and Bax in 1927 brought reproof even from the critics and the suggestion that programs be arranged "more in conformity with general demand and appreciation," with "less of this ultramodern experimentation."

The Minneapolis Symphony Orchestra began earlier, in 1903, under the direction of Emil Oberhoffer, a tawny-haired Bavarian who had arrived in St. Paul in the early nineties with one of the many Gilbert and Sullivan troupes then playing the country. Perhaps because the company met with financial embarrassment, Oberhoffer and his wife decided to remain in the Twin Cities. The Minneapolis Symphony became the eighth major orchestra in the United States (two of them in New York), a rather remarkable achievement for a city ranking eighteenth in population. Oberhoffer's programs were fairly conservative, and in the orchestra's second decade Tchaikovsky's stock was particularly high. Between 1911 and 1922 the *Pathetique* was performed fifteen times in Twin Cities concerts and repeated again and again on the road. On its maiden tour in 1907, the orchestra visited neighboring Moorhead, Grand Forks, and Duluth and was soon traveling widely over Kansas and the Midwest, rarely at full strength. After ten years of touring the Minneapolis Symphony had brought music to a hundred and seventy communities, most of which had never heard an orchestra before.

Meanwhile Oberhoffer had gained greater control over his orchestra and solidified its position in the Twin Cities. His repertoire was becoming increasingly sophisticated. But following a particularly successful 1921-22 season, the conductor left the Minneapolis Symphony and never returned. After a series of guest conductors the genial Belgian Henri Verbrugghen came from Australia to head the orchestra in 1923. Verbrugghen was a small man physically, who loved Beethoven, chamber music, and horses. He collected old musical instruments, smoked vile French tobacco, and sported a waxed mustache. It was said he "looked like a Frenchman, spoke like an Englishman, and acted like an American." Verbrugghen was a conductor of far greater stature than Oberhoffer and was paid accordingly—$25,000 a year. "In contrast to Oberhoffer, who never quite shook off the ambiguous role of village genius," John Sherman, historian of the Minneapolis Symphony Orchestra, writes, "Verbrugghen came from afar, trailing an impressive banner of accomplishment behind him."

In 1930, during Verbrugghen's eighth season, Northrop Auditorium on the campus of the University of Minnesota became the Minneapolis Symphony's permanent headquarters. There had been signs that the conductor's grip on the orchestra had loosened. He seemed tired and to have aged tremendously. At times he appeared to conduct with little regard for how the orchestra was playing. Critics began to deplore the Symphony's fall from grace. On October 26, 1931, Verbrugghen was rehearsing the brass section in the basement beneath Northrop's stage. It was unseasonably warm, and the conductor appeared exhausted. He called for a trumpet passage at a point where the score indicated none. Verbrugghen put down his baton and sat in a nearby chair, presumably to study the score. The musicians waited, then grew concerned. Verbrugghen stared at the music, finally rose, and with help walked out of the room. "I can't see," he was heard to say. "Everything is going black." The conductor, at fifty-eight, had suffered a cerebral hemorrhage and was hospitalized immediately.

The season continued under another series of guest conductors, one of whom was a rising young musician from the East named Eugene Ormandy. He would shortly become the orchestra's director. Born in Budapest, Ormandy had learned his trade not in the European concert halls or provincial opera houses, as most of his contemporaries had, but in American movie theaters and radio studios. He came to the United States in 1921, at the age of twenty-two, and took a job in the violin section of the pit orchestra of the Capitol Theater on Broadway, a movie palace run by S. L. Rothafel, the celebrated "Roxy." The Capitol maintained an eighty-five piece orchestra which accompanied silent films and performed light classics and occasional symphonic works as well. The musicians played four shows a day, seven days a week. Ormandy stayed at the Capitol for two and a half years, earning about sixty dollars a week. He was soon concertmaster there. One day the young violinist arrived at the theater just in time for a two o'clock show, only to be informed that the scheduled conductor for the afternoon had taken ill. "Roxy says you have to conduct," the doorman told him. Eventually Ormandy was made associate director of the orchestra. During the late twenties he was working in radio, conducting the Jack Frost Melody Moments, the Dutch Masters Hour, the McKesson-Robbins and Endicott Johnson programs for a fee of $500 a week.

In the summer of 1929 Ormandy directed the New York Philharmonic at Lewisohn Stadium and the next summer led the Philadelphia Orchestra at Robin Hood Dell. By then he was among the principal conductors of the Columbia Broadcasting network. When illness delayed Toscanini in returning from Europe in the fall on 1931. Ormandy took over the maestro's guest assignment with the Philadelphia Orchestra. That same autumn he appeared for the first time with the Minneapolis Symphony. His success was complete. The sounds he drew from the orchestra were unlike anything the Twin Cities had heard before. The Minneapolis Symphony Orchestra seemed reborn; suddenly it sang. Under the direction of this thirty-two year-old bundle of energy, the ensemble had acquired vigor, unanimity, and a compelling rhythmic impulse. The orchestra had expounded music before, now it dramatized it. According to Sherman, Eugene Ormandy's initial concert in Minneapolis "could be compared to an explosion, but an explosion that operated in reverse, consolidating rather than shattering."

After Ormandy was made director of the Minneapolis Symphony, he continued to give performances of intelligence and compelling quality. Despite the downward economic trend of the Depression, the conductor planned ambitious programs, among them the Verdi *Requiem*, Mahler's *Resurrection* Symphony, Bruckner's Seventh and Beethoven's Ninth Symphony, all involving huge forces and intensive preparation. He chose his programs carefully, striving to balance what he wanted to play with what audiences might like to hear. His aim was to offer about two-fifths classical music, two-fifths semi-modern, and one-fifth modern. He brought in guest soloists ranging from Fritz Kreisler to Nelson Eddy to Feodor Chaliapin. Under Ormandy the Minneapolis Symphony Orchestra recorded widely and encompassed much of the same geography on tours as in earlier years, although the number of out-of-town concerts dwindled. The conductor's contract permitted him frequent absences for guest appearances in the East, where he wanted to retain a foothold.

During the 1932-33 season the guaranty fund in Minneapolis took a $64,000 drop from the previous year's figure. Consequently the fund campaign for the next season began early, and the question solicitors put to prospective donors was blunt: "Do you want the Minneapolis Symphony Orchestra to continue?" The Twin Cities press took up the cry, "The Symphony Must Be Saved!" Abandonment of the orchestra would be unthinkable, civic leaders agreed. There was a Symphony Tag Day, and the Third Minnesota Infantry Band paraded weekly in behalf of the orchestra. The schools were enrolled in a "last desperate attempt" to attain the $145,000 goal. After four months of sales talk and cajolery, workers netted $106,700—enough to assure the cities a symphony for one more season. Two years later the annual guaranty sank to a low of $100,700.

But the Minneapolis Symphony was not the only American orchestra beset by financial problems during the Great Depression. The Philadelphia Orchestra was just as severely hit. The progressive income tax had taken its toll, and by 1933 two of the Philadelphia Orchestra's principal backers— Edward Bok andAlexander Van Renssellaer—were gone. Hard times meant a decline in contributions and ticket sales, while season subscriptions in 1932 were down by fifteen percent. Orchestra members accepted a ten percent reduction in salary that year, and in 1933—over bitter protest—took another cut of nine percent. Leopold Stokowski, elevated to musical director in 1931, continued to make somewhere between $200,000 and $250,000 a year, about three times the salary of the President of the United States.

Stokowski and the Orchestra's board had been at odds for some time over programming and deficits. On March 21, 1931, the conductor had given Alban Berg's opera *Wozzeck*, just six years after the premiere of the Berg shocker at the Staatsoper in Berlin. The production was staged in association with the Philadelphia Grand Opera Company, featuring a young baritone named Nelson Eddy in the cast. The excitement the opera caused recalled that surrounding the Mahler Eighth Symphony in 1916, but conservative guarantors were disturbed by its naturalistic theme. Hardly had the *Wozzeck* commotion died down than Stokowski revealed plans for presenting Stravinsky's *Oedipus Rex*. Along with the salary cut in 1932, an announcement was made that "programs will be almost entirely devoted to acknowledged masterpieces. The directors feel that in times such as the present, audiences prefer music which they know and love, and that performances of debatable music should be postponed until a more suitable time." Stokowski objected strongly, but the board insisted that subscriptions were down by $100,000 and that changes had to be made.

In 1933 the conductor decided to supplement the children's concerts, which admitted no one over twelve, with a series of youth performances for age group thirteen to twenty-five. The youth concerts suddenly became the center of controversy when Stokowski, who had recently returned from a summer trip to Russia, made public his intention of playing the *Internationale*, the Communist anthem, together with the *Star-Spangled Banner*. The young people would be invited to sing both. There was an immediate clamor from the American Legion. For days the argument dragged on in the press and pulpit, until at last a compromise was reached. The *Internationale* would be played, but sung *in French*. Concert time found the atmosphere tense, with police on the alert and a full covey of reporters on hand. The singing, however, came off without incident.

Less controversial was Stokowski's hiring in 1930 of the Philadelphia Orchestra's first woman player, a twenty-two year-old harpist who remained for eleven years. In 1934 he led a 100-piece orchestra at Yankee Stadium, New York, in a benefit for Jewish refugees from Nazi Germany. But that fall friction between the conductor and the Philadelphia Orchestra's board of directors grew more heated, eventually throwing the musical world into something of an uproar. By 1935 the disappearance of many large individual contributors from the board denied Stokowski much of his principal support. Power passed to a new group of board members, who questioned whether or not the Orchestra could afford Stokowski under present economic conditions and survive. Friction between the fiery conductor and the new directors climaxed over tours he was planning to Europe and South America. To frighten the board and bring them around, Stokowski handed in his resignation. To his surprise, the directors accepted it.

The end of the long love-hate relationship between Leopold Stokowski and the Philadelphia Orchestra began at the conclusion of the 1935-36 season. Technically he would share the podium in Philadelphia for another five years, but during the 1936-37 season he conducted only six out of twenty-two weeks. "I finally left Philadelphia," Stokowski said, "because I saw that certain persons had the power to try to stop progress—or not so much progress as the evolution of music." The conductor soon participated in three Hollywood films—*The Big Broadcast of 1937, 100 Men and a Girl* with fifteen year-old Deanna Durbin, and Walt Disney's classic *Fantasia*. Stokowski's career would be a long and distinguished one, and he would be associated with several of the nation's major symphonic organizations. But never again was he to have so long and glamorous a tenure as the one he had enjoyed in Philadelphia.

With the acceptance of Stokowski's resignation, the Philadelphia Orchestra's board of directors brought in Eugene Ormandy from Minneapolis as resident conductor. "We have realized for some time," a spokesman for the Minneapolis Symphony board said, "that we could not retain his services permanently." Economic considerations had undoubtedly played a major role in the selection of the new conductor, for Ormandy's salary was much less than his illustrious predecessor's. Ormandy was an instant success with Philadelphia audiences and drew good reviews from the critics. For a number of years the shadow of Stokowski's reputation clouded a bit the young director's achievement in Philadelphia, although by 1941, when he took full command, this Alger hero of American music had clearly risen to the task.

As a former violinist, Ormandy was particularly skilled at obtaining what he wanted from his string sections. The board had insisted that programming be arranged with greater box office appeal and that rehearsals be reduced by limiting the presentation of unfamiliar works. Ormandy was basically no reformer; he willingly accepted audiences as he found them. The conductor frankly admitted that he liked to send people out of the concert hall humming or whistling the last number played. He was cautious toward contemporary music and careful to balance the new works he performed with popular favorites. He was far more concerned with public relations than Stokowski had ever been and cheerfully took popular taste into account in program planning. When he made changes in the orchestra, he made them slowly.

Ormandy returned to Minneapolis to open the 1936-37 season there, but the Twin Cities orchestra spent the remainder of the year in the hands of guest conductors. In January, 1938, Dimitri Mitropoulos arrived from Athens as the Minneapolis Symphony Orchestra's new permanent conductor. The Greek musician first came to America in 1936, invited by Koussevitzky to direct some concerts of the Boston Symphony. He made a tremendous impression and won the wholehearted support of Koussevitzky. Mitropoulos was brought out to Minneapolis for a guest appearance early in 1937. The board thought he might be their man—as indeed he was for more than a decade. Mitropoulos had originally planned to become a priest and was eventually known in musical circles as the "monk in conductor's clothing." His ascetic look was enhanced by hollow cheeks, deeply set eyes, and a bald head, while his private life was notably cloistered.

"Oberhoffer was the poet," Sherman concludes, "Verbrugghen the scholar, Ormandy the dramatist. Dimitri Mitropoulos was the mystic and missionary." The new conductor looked upon concerts as a holy rite whereby the public was not so much entertained as taken to the mountain top. For Mitropoulos symphonic performances were an act of faith and filled a spiritual need. Yet his concerts created excitement, and his initial appearance in Minneapolis nearly prompted a riot. "Wild-eyed spectators cheered and shouted bravos," Sherman recounted, "clapped strangers on the back, and otherwise acted as if they were under the influence of strong stimulants." Yet the Greek conductor aimed for the transcendental in music and proved himself a tonal alchemist. Under his direction the Minneapolis Symphony Orchestra took on a spiritual fury and an ethereal richness. His readings were highly personal, sometimes overaccented. His tempos for the most part were brisk, even flagellated in moments of high tension. Mitropoulos' program policy was seldom hampered by precepts of variety and balance. It was unpredictable, often reflecting the conductor's individual tastes and areas of interest he was currently exploring. Rarely did his programs cater to the public.

Koussevitzky, Mitropoulos' American mentor, continued as one of the most colorful figures in serious music. The conductor's cape, his inexplicable accent, his amazing malapropisms, and his Dostoevskian rages all became legendary. Yet Koussevitzky could be the diplomat, capable of promising and then breaking his promise without causing undue hostility. Talk around the Boston Symphony Orchestra during the 1930s was not of change, but of a wholesome sense of permanency. Replacements in membership were few. The orchestra's seasons went their way, supported by an adoring public and brightened by the director's unfailing inspiration. While Koussevitzky encouraged a generation of native composers, he responded best to the modern European school, composers like Stravinsky, Ravel, Honegger, and Prokofieff especially. Yet his Beethoven could be grandiose, his Brahms profound, his Mendelssohn angelic, his Tchaikovsky poignant. The Boston Symphony under Muck had undoubtedly been the first great virtuoso orchestra in the United States, but Koussevitzky transformed that combination from a "German" to a "French" orchestra without peer. Whereas the Philadelphia Orchestra under Stokowski produced sounds of spectacular beauty, its range was more limited. Stokowski excelled in the darker, more exotic tones, while his mood was openly voluptuous and erotic. Koussevitzky's orchestra possessed a transparency that came from precision. "I have never met a man who loved music more passionately than Serge Koussevitzky," Aaron Copland wrote. "But when he thinks of music he doesn't conjure up a pristine and abstract art—he thinks rather of a living, organic matter brought into being by men who are thoroughly alive."

With Koussevitzky every concert was an experience—partly because of the great orchestra he fashioned, partly because of his own overwhelming personality. He approached music intuitively and, like Stokowski, conducted with more emotion than intellect. His instinct for phrasing and building dramatic effects was incredible, and his sense of rhythm was meticulous. On the one hand a marvelous technician, Koussevitzky at the same time expressed his individuality with every movement of his hand. During his tenure the Boston Symphony had fewer soloists than any comparable orchestra in the world and practically no guest conductors, for Koussevitzky was a jealous star, who hated sharing the limelight. His performances of works for which he felt a closeness possessed electricity and unrivaled imagination; only when attempting compositions holding no real fascination for him did he sometimes lean toward the pedestrian. For twelve-tone music he showed almost no patience at all.

A concert by the Boston Symphony Orchestra was transmitted by radio in 1927. Seven years later the incorporated orchestra secured title to Symphony Hall, assessed at $800,000, thereby owning its own home. The Berkshire Music Festival at Tanglewood, Massachusetts, began in 1937, with Koussevitzky and the Boston Symphony playing a leading role. The Festival included summer concerts and a school where students, teachers, and professional musicians could mingle, study, and exchange ideas. In December, 1942, the Boston Symphony, the last major American orchestra still outside the musicians union, became unionized.

With the rise of fascism in Europe, Toscanini endeared himself to the American public more than ever by his courageous stand against Mussolini. The conductor's dislike for the dictator was both political and personal. In the fall of 1931 a shower of paper slips was thrown from the balcony of Carnegie Hall, carrying the words, "Liberty is essential to Art—*Evviva Arturo Toscanini!*" Later that season the musician was forced to miss a number of concerts as a result of an ailing arm and shoulder. The taxing schedule calling for four concerts a week was becoming too strenuous for one who placed such formidable demands on himself as Toscanini. He was tired and wanted free of long contracts. His farewell appearance with the New York Philharmonic took place on April 29, 1936, during a Beethoven-Wagner program with Jascha Heifetz as soloist. The concert was assumed to be the end of the sixty-nine year-old maestro's American career and occurred amid great frenzy. Tickets went on sale with a ten dollar top. On the day of the performance a thousand people waited in line for standing room, when only 140 could be admitted. Carnegie Hall was packed. Mounted police and fifty foot patrols maintained order.

The conductor was not about to return to Italy with Mussolini in power. He accepted performances in Salzburg and guest appearances here and there in Europe during the summer of 1936. Americans continued to buy his records, while Toscanini seemed eager for news from the United States. The next year he surprised the musical world by accepting the directorship of the NBC Symphony, created especially for him. The orchestra was set up exclusively as a broadcasting and recording organization, and Toscanini was enthusiastic about the prospect of reaching millions of people with his music rather than a few thousand. The country was combed for the finest instrumentalists available. The process of elimination was long and rigorous. Once selected, the orchestra was whipped into shape and refined by Artur Rodzinski and Pierre Monteux. On Christmas evening, 1937, Toscanini made his return to America by conducting the NBC Symphony in a program of Mozart and Brahms. An estimated audience of 20,000,000 listened, while Studio 8-H in Radio City was filled with invited guests. All in all, the orchestra had cost the National Broadcasting Company approximately $250,000, but it proved to be a great orchestra.

For seventeen seasons Toscanini directed the NBC Symphony, until his retirement in 1954. He never seemed to lose his touch, although he did mellow a bit. Always he remained the objectivist, the conductor of supreme clarity and sweeping force. From 1939 until 1946 Toscanini did not see Italy, but looked upon the United States as home. He traveled to South America with his orchestra in 1940 and toured the United States. His programs consisted mostly of the composers he loved. Yet he was so stirred by the Russian fight against Germany that he asked to conduct the American premiere of Shostakovich's Seventh Symphony, which had largely been written during the seige of Leningrad. On May 25, 1944, he directed a benefit concert for the Red Cross at Madison Square Garden that netted more than $100,000. In February, 1946, Toscanini presented *La Boheme* in two broadcasts, fifty years after he had conducted the opera's premiere in Italy. Later he offered *Fidelio*, *La Traviata*, *Otello*, *Aida*, and *Falstaff*—all of which exist in near-definitive recordings. His last concert was a heartbreaking occasion. It took place about a week after his eighty-seventh birthday. He died three years later. "[T]o me," baritone Robert Merrill concedes, "Arturo Toscanini will always stand alone. He was the perfect artist, always painting a masterpiece, balancing, blending all into one immense canvas."

It has been said that throughout his career Toscanini left a trail of demoralized orchestras behind him. Certainly this was true of the New York Philharmonic when the conductor departed in 1936. The orchestra had responded to Toscanini with sensitivity and fine performances, but under his successor, the young Englishman John Barbirolli, the Philharmonic's playing deteriorated badly. Barbirolli was relatively inexperienced when he took over the orchestra in 1937, although he had made a good impression the season before. Perhaps anyone would have looked pale after the Italian maestro; in his later career Barbirolli certainly evolved into a conductor of the first rank. However the youth was not the man to replace Toscanini. When Barbirolli's contract expired in 1940, it was not renewed. A period of guest conductorships followed. The parade of talent was often dazzling, yet the constant reshuffling was unsettling for the orchestra. The Philharmonic chafed, fretted, and at times nearly overturned its temporary leader. A crisis was averted in 1943, when Artur Rodzinski was appointed musical director.

The gruff, short-tempered Rodzinski was known as a "difficult" conductor, but was recognized as an iron disciplinarian. He had served as the first guest conductor in the history of the Cleveland Orchestra and replaced Sokoloff as that organization's permanent director in 1933. Rodzinski brought vigor and a substantially expanded repertory to the Cleveland Orchestra. He strengthened the ensemble and led the orchestra into its golden age and national prominence. For five of his ten years in Cleveland, Rodzinski presented intimate operatic performances as well as concerts in Severance Hall, an offering duplicated nowhere else in the country. The opera series began on November 30, 1933, with Wagner's *Tristan und Isolde*.

The next season there were six pairs of operatic performances, plus eighteen pairs of subscription concerts. The Cleveland Orchestra staged Shostakovich's one year-old *Lady Macbeth of Mtsensk* on January 31, 1935, the first performance outside the Soviet Union. The production, headed by Anna Leskaya, was sung in Russian by a predominantly Russian cast. Rodzinski also produced *Der Rosenkavalier*, with Lotte Lehmann, as well as *Parsifal*, *Tannhauser*, and *Elektra*. But the opera project shortly ran into financial trouble. The Great Depression was no time to begin anything so costly as an opera company. The series was reduced to four productions, then two, and finally abandoned—much to Rodzinski's disgust. The conductor remained with the Cleveland Orchestra through the 1942-43 season, resigning his post there to accept the position with the New York Philharmonic.

Under Rodzinski the Philharmonic regained much of its former glory, presenting a number of big works for orchestra, chorus, and soloists that placed tremendous strain on the budget. In February, 1947, the temperamental Rodzinski walked out on his $56,000-a-year New York position amid great controversy, claiming managerial interference in programming. He had made similar charges in Cleveland, Philadelphia (where he served for a time as Stokowski's assistant), and Los Angeles, where he conducted from 1929 to 1933, right before going to Cleveland.

The Los Angeles Philharmonic, which received its financial impetus largely from mining entrepreneur W. A. Clark, had given its first concert in October, 1919, under Walter Henry Rothwell. Rothwell continued as the orchestra's director until his sudden death in 1927; Emil Oberhoffer was summoned from Minneapolis to finish out the season. Scandinavian conductor George Schneevoigt headed the Los Angeles symphony for two years, then resigned because of poor health. Rodzinski came in, built the orchestra up, and was succeeded by Otto Klemperer. Klemperer stayed through 1940, when he was stricken with a serious illness. Guest conductors kept the orchestra together for three seasons, until Alfred Wallenstein was engaged as musical director in 1943. Under Wallenstein the Los Angeles Philharmonic enjoyed a long, steady growth.

The Cincinnati Symphony Orchestra, the nation's fourth oldest, continued to thrive. After the Kunwald affair, Cincinnati officials chose Eugene Ysaye as conductor—a friend of the Allies, as well as a distinguished musician. He stayed until 1922. Fritz Reiner then took over the orchestra for nine years with tremendous success. In 1931 Eugene Goossens was engaged as musical director, remaining with the Cincinnati Symphony through the 1946-47 season, at which point he became conductor of the orchestra in Sydney, Australia.

Pianist Rudolph Ganz assumed the leadership of the St. Louis Symphony in 1921, showing musical taste and a willingness to explore new areas. Under Ganz the repertoire was enlarged, while the St. Louis public gained an awareness of modern trends in orchestral writing. Ganz resigned after six seasons and was followed by four years of guest conductors. The St.

Louis Symphony's advance was sporadic until 1931, when the French-trained Vladimir Golschmann was appointed permanent director. The next quarter century found the orchestra and its conductor developing enormously, distinguished by refinement and plasticity.

By 1940 the American people's exposure to serious music had vastly increased. Not only were there more orchestras playing longer seasons, but technology had added means by which good music could filter down to the uninformed citizen. Gradually a larger segment of the American public was becoming aware of symphonic music, although the process was a slow one to be sure. By 1926 phonograph albums presenting larger orchestral works had come into existence and were met with growing enthusiasm, as the quality of recorded sound improved. In 1937 Victor announced that its sale of serious music exceeded that of 1930 by 535 percent. Radio soon came to provide the public with a wide variety of semi-classical and classical music, while motion pictures, even in the silent days, used a great many serious compositions, although not always in a serious way. Dramatic situations on the screen called for appropriate music—to heighten suspense, add a touch of sentiment, or otherwise underline the mood of the moment. The storm section of the *William Tell* Overture became the stereotyped accompaniment for climaxes, *Hearts and Flowers* synonymous with heartbreak, the *Light Cavalry Overture* an indication of suspense, and *Rustle of Spring* the companion of bucolic scenes. As the movies advanced from the nickelodeon days to the "cathedral" era, the music associated with them improved, some of it original. As early as 1915 the New York showing of D. W. Griffith's *The Birth of a Nation* offered music especially written by Joseph Carl Breil, performed by a full orchestra. A year later Victor Herbert was commissioned to write an original score for the picture *The Fall of a Nation*. Other productions borrowed themes from *Tristan und Isolde, Salome*, and *Eugen Onegin* for background music. With the arrival of sound, film producers came to prefer their own composers, with a special talent for atmospheric music. The first Academy Award for scoring went to Max Steiner in 1935, for his original music for *The Informer*. Hollywood staff composers would eventually include such distinguished writers for the screen as Alfred Newman, Miklos Rosza, Dimitri Tiomkin, and Victor Young, although Aaron Copland, Louis Gruenberg, Roy Harris, Virgil Thomson, Douglas Moore, and Marc Blitzstein all composed for the movies at one time or another.

Popular concert series, usually featuring the lighter classics, paralleled the growth of many of the major orchestras. The Boston "Pops," for instance, has existed nearly as long as the Boston Symphony, although its concerts were not always so successful. The "Pops" was begun in 1885 partly as an evangelistic gesture, partly as an economic supplement for members of the orchestra. In pre-union days the "Pops" Orchestra was paid less than the Boston Symphony, but the popular series extended the season of the Boston musicians up to ten weeks. The "Pops" had a long line of early conductors, but the orchestra did not reach a sustained development until Arthur Fiedler became its conductor in 1930. Fiedler shrewdly combined musical ability, sensitivity to public taste, and good showmanship, turning the Boston "Pops" into one of the most noted orchestras in the country. Members of the Philadelphia Orchestra decided in 1930 to organize an eight-week series of summer concerts at Robin Hood Dell, a natural amphitheater in rustic Fairmount Park. They hired conductors and soloists, without any involvement by the orchestra association. Alexander Smallens became the principal conductor, although Eugene Ormandy, unknown in Philadelphia at the time, was guest conductor for three concerts the first summer and seven the second. Later Dimitri Mitropoulos became a major conductor of the Robin Hood Dell series.

Closely related to the history of the Los Angeles Philharmonic is the Hollywood Bowl. Outdoor music in the Hollywood hills initially went through an erratic evolution, but the Bowl concerts associated with the Los Angeles Philharmonic began with an Easter sunrise service in 1921. That summer a series of Symphonies under the Stars was presented with Alfred Hertz as conductor of the Philharmonic. Hertz and Emil Oberhoffer shared the Bowl's podium for two more summers. Then followed a list of some 150 guest conductors, during which time orchestral concerts were occasionally interspersed with opera and other special features. In 1945 Leopold Stokowski was appointed musical director of the Hollywood Bowl, demanding the right to select his own orchestra. For three years the connection with the Los Angeles Philharmonic was broken. At the end of the second season of a three-year contract Stokowski abruptly left the Bowl. Eugene Ormandy assumed the directorship of the concerts there in 1948. The Hollywood Bowl programs not only brought quality music and distinguished artists to southern California, but ticket prices were kept reasonable. The charm of the setting attracted hosts of people who ordinarily did not attend concerts. Many of the casual visitors found themselves enjoying the music despite noisy latecomers and patrons of the hotdog and popcorn stands.

Orchestra management had long been aware that a sure method of enticing the occasional concertgoer was to offer a celebrated soloist, particularly an artist who had received a great deal of attention from the press. Paderewski or Fritz Kreisler could add luster to a program and bring out a substantial crowd almost anywhere in the 1920s. Rudolf Serkin made a successful debut with the New York Philharmonic under Toscanini in 1936 and was quickly accepted as one of the leading pianists in the country. Pianists were especially popular as guest artists, and by 1940 Artur Rubinstein, Robert Casadesus, and Jose Iturbi could all be counted on to fill a concert hall. But the public was often fascinated still by the personality rather than the music of a performer. Yehudi Menuhin made a sensational debut at Carnegie Hall in 1927 and was immediately numbered among the nation's musical darlings—in no small measure because he was eleven years old at the time. Marian Anderson, the gifted black contralto, became a legend in 1939, when the Daughters of the American Revolution barred her from singing a concert in Constitution Hall. The news media carried the story from coast to coast. Eleanor Roosevelt resigned from the DAR in protest, as the furor spread. Secretary of the Interior Harold Ickes finally invited Miss Anderson to sing from the steps of the Lincoln Memorial, which she did on Easter Sunday to a crowd of 75,000. The contralto's name was suddenly a household word, while her concerts were packed.

From the 1920s on, colleges and universities played an increasingly important role in stimulating musical activity and whetting the appetite of young people for good music. University symphony orchestras grew in number and proficiency, while most colleges came to have a resident string quartet and eventually a professional concert series. Music schools like Juilliard and Curtis Institute not only provided frequent programs on a high level, but were able to maintain a more experimental outlook than most professional groups, offering an abundance of new music and works by unknown composers. Gradually the larger high schools began to develop symphonic bands, which ultimately added an awareness of the lighter classics, if not deep appreciation.

During the Depression thousands of musical performances were given under the auspices of the federal government, primarily in an effort to put unemployed musicians to work. Prompted by a suicide, the Musicians' Emergency Fund was created in 1931, while in upstate New York unemployed instrumentalists were assigned to the newly formed Buffalo Symphony Orchestra by the Mayor's Committee on Unemployment. In 1935 the Federal Music Project was initiated under the Works Progress Administration, with the former Cleveland Orchestra conductor Nikolai Sokoloff as director. Eventually 15,000 musicians were employed by the government in work that ranged from playing in WPA orchestras and dance bands to teaching music classes in rural schools and collecting folk songs. By March, 1938, thirty-four symphony orchestras under the Federal Music Project employed 2,533 musicians. Some one hundred million Americans, many of whom had never heard a live orchestra or string quartet before, were now given an opportunity to hear concerts either free or at nominal prices. Concerts were given in schools, hospitals, parks, and public auditoriums, sometimes with Sokoloff conducting. But the Federal Music Project also stimulated American compositions and gave jobs to music teachers, who found themselves with a sudden loss of pupils. Sokoloff insisted on standards, employed only professional musicians, resisted much bureaucratic pressure, and probably maintained the highest level of achievement of any of the New Deal's arts projects. Standards were undoubtedly higher in metropolitan centers, where more applicants were available, than in the smaller cities and rural areas. Sir Thomas Beecham even conducted several programs with the New York City Symphony, one of the orchestras under the aegis of the Works Progress Administration.

In September, 1939, the Federal Music Project was renamed the WPA Music Program and transferred from federal to state control. Sokoloff, anticipating the change, had resigned shortly before and was succeeded by Earl Vincent Moore, director of the School of Music at the University of Michigan. The project's more ambitious programs were severely curtailed. Moore was forced to accept a social service philosophy of the arts, while most of the musicians who stayed with the state projects were incapable of the quality of performance Sokoloff had demanded. With the call to arms after Pearl Harbor and the employment opportunities in defense plants, the Music Program soon lost most of its musicians, although it was not officially terminated until July, 1943.

The major orchestras also lost players to the armed forces. The Philadelphia Orchestra, for example, lost thirteen men during the war years, although replacements were found without noticeably damaging the sound. By 1944 the membership included six women. Touring became a problem during the war, with trains crowded and rolling stock put to military use. The Philadelphia Orchestra, heretofore the most traveled of American symphony orchestras, abandoned its long tours, restricting itself to Washington, Baltimore, New York, and Harrisburg. Audiences were invited to be more casual in their dress, but most of the subscribers came essentially as before. The 1942 season in Philadelphia opened with an all-Russian program, in tribute to the Soviet defense against Germany's invasion, but the wartime programs did not basically differ from those given earlier. There was no talk in World War II of dropping Wagner, although more American works were heard than usual. During the 1942-43 season, twenty-five of the Philadelphia Orchestra's concerts were broadcast by shortwave overseas to the armed forces. The orchestra also visited local USO clubs to play light works, and for a time a restaurant area under the vestibule of the Academy of Music served as a Stage Door Canteen. Wartime attendance at the Academy, as elsewhere, ran close to capacity.

The ensemble stability of the Minneapolis Symphony was more severely damaged by shifting membership during the war than the Philadelphia Orchestra's. In Minnesota the shortage of manpower became a real problem; eventually eight of Mitropoulos' musicians were women, most of them in the string sections. The war also brought an entertainment tax, and touring became more of a scramble than ever before. Not only were there discomforts and makeshift accommodations, but at times the orchestra found it practically impossible to meet the next engagement by any means of transportation. And yet Mitropoulos continued to give quality concerts and introduce new music. Paul Hindemith arrived in the Twin Cities for a performance of his Symphony in E-flat, Bela Bartok's violin concerto was heard in 1943 with Yehudi Menuhin as soloist, while Shostakovitch's *Leningrad* Symphony proved the sensation in Minneapolis it did nationally.

Symphony orchestras across the land freely contributed their services to the war effort, sometimes with considerable concessions to artistic standards.

The Houston Symphony, for instance, played a concert in City Auditorium early in the war to sell bonds—in conjunction with a wrestling match! Conductor Ernst Hoffmann and his orchestra sat on the stage in formal dress, while the athletes performed in a ring in the center of the auditorium. During the main bout, the symphony performed a funeral march. At the conclusion of the match, one of the contestants leaped on the platform, knocked the fragile conductor from the podium, and proceeded to lead the orchestra himself—much to the delight of the crowd of 4000 looking on.

Among the casualties of the war was the American record industry. Shellac, then fundamental in the manufacture of records, became sufficiently scarce that the production of new recordings was curtailed drastically. Then in 1942, James C. Petrillo, president of the American Federation of Musicians, imposed a ban on all recordings. The use of recorded music on radio stations and jukeboxes, Petrillo argued, was having a disastrous effect on the employment of live musicians. He wanted record manufacturers to contribute a royalty on every recording sold to a fund for unemployed musicians. In the end Petrillo essentially got what he wanted, but the dispute lasted from 1942 until 1944 (with a brief revival in 1948), during which time neither RCA Victor nor Columbia made any records. Symphonic music was an innocent bystander in the feud, since the union's concern was mainly over popular music, but Petrillo's ban was total.

The war ultimately meant gains for music in America as well as losses. European composers like Stravinsky, Schoenberg, Bartok, Hindemith, and Milhaud all fled from the Nazi and Fascist regimes by making their home in the United States. Conductors did the same. When Max Reiter, founder of the San Antonio Symphony, arrived in the United States from Austria in 1939, he discovered the East coast so glutted with refugee conductors that he went to Texas looking for work. He appeared in San Antonio, traditionally the most musical city in the state, armed with letters of introduction from Toscanini and Bruno Walter and was invited by local musicians to conduct them in a concert in the city's Sunken Garden Theater. With the success of this performance the San Antonio Symphony took residence in the cavernous Municipal Auditorium and quickly became the first orchestra in Texas to achieve major symphony status. The organization received a great financial assist in 1944, when Otto Koehler—head of the San Antonio Brewing Association, a German, and an ardent music lover—added forty thousand dollars to the symphony fund. Although Max Reiter was a musician of high standards, he clearly saw the orchestra as a civic enterprise and was not beyond catering to the taste of his public. In the early years especially he might follow a Brahms symphony with an arrangement of "Old Man River" or "Star Dust," and he often sprinkled his programs with light classics like "Jazz Pizzicato"—much as Theodore Thomas and Walter Damrosch had done in the East a half century before. Concert audiences in San Antonio have characteristically been casual and relaxed, but genuinely appreciative of good music. The orchestra under Reiter frequently played to crowds of men in shirtsleeves and women holding fretful babies. "A symphony concert in San Antonio," an observer maintained in 1946, "looks more like a baseball game or a revival meeting than like the polite gathering in New York's Carnegie Hall."

George Szell, the master builder of the Cleveland Orchestra, was another refugee from Austria. Like Reiter, he came to the United States in 1939, not certain whether he was about to launch a new career or simply marking time until he could resume his conducting activities in Europe. Szell began teaching in New York City and first heard the Cleveland Orchestra on February 6, 1940, at a concert in Carnegie Hall. Within the year his American career had quickened noticably. The Chicago Symphony engaged him for its summer concerts at Ravinia Park in 1941, where he returned for another five summers. He appeared as guest conductor with several major orchestras and in 1942 made his debut at the Metropolitan Opera.

Meanwhile the Cleveland Orchestra had named Vienna-born Erich Leinsdorf to replace Artur Rodzinski. In January, 1944, however, Leinsdorf was called to active duty with the United States Army. He returned to Severance Hall in the autumn of 1945 to complete the third year of his contract, but withdrew from the Cleveland Orchestra at the end of that season. Szell had been selected as his replacement the previous January. The new director was forty-nine years old at the time and had spent thirty-three of those years conducting. He would remain in Cleveland until his death in 1970, lifting the level of the orchestra there to rival any in the country. Szell's relationship with the Cleveland Orchestra was one of the happiest in American music. The orchestra was fortunate in having only four musical directors in fifty-two seasons, and only one of those was in residence for less than a decade. Sustained leadership certainly seems to have been a key factor in the Cleveland Orchestra's impressive growth. After a period of guest conductors, which included Pierre Boulez, Lorin Maazel was chosen as Szell's successor.

The Chicago Symphony Orchestra held the unique distinction of playing its first fifty-one years under only two permanent conductors. When Frederick Stock died in the fall of 1942, a week deep in the season, his associate director, Hans Lange, continued the programs Stock had outlined. For the next four years Desire Defauw, from Brussels, Belgium, served as the orchestra's musical director, although Defauw's merits became a subject of heated controversy. In 1947 his contract was not renewed. Artur Rodzinski, having just left the New York Philharmonic in anger, took over the Chicago Symphony for one year. Brilliant as his performances were, Rodzinski's idiosyncracies proved too much, and he was forced to leave after the one season. Since then the development of the Chicago Symphony Orchestra has been sporadic—controversial under the direction of Rafael Kubelik, reaching greatness under Fritz Reiner, declining under Jean Martinon, and ascending again under Georg Solti.

Koussevitzky retired from the Boston Symphony Orchestra in 1949, leaving behind the Koussevitzky Music Foundation, which the musician had established in memory of his wife. The Foundation would aid living composers by commissioning new orchestral works and chamber music. Charles Munch succeeded Koussevitzky, shortly emerging as perhaps the most important French conductor of his generation. Munch was particularly noted for his Berlioz performances and remained with the Boston Symphony until 1962, when Erich Leinsdorf became music director. Under Leinsdorf the symphony maintained its claim as "The Aristocrat of Orchestras," although criticism of the new conductor's machinelike interpretations grew sharp. Leinsdorf stayed through the Tanglewood Festival in 1969 and was followed by William Steinberg. Seiji Ozawa later took over the orchestra, conducting a series of televised concerts.

Eugene Ormandy continued at the helm of the Philadelphia Orchestra, refining the sublime sound for which that orchestra had so long been noted. With the end of the war the ensemble resumed extensive touring, and Ormandy began to program more new works. In 1947 the conductor received the National Music Council Award of Honor in recognition of the American premieres he had directed. The orchestra's income from record royalties became increasingly important, while the number of women players had risen by 1968 to eight, five of whom had husbands also in the orchestra. The 1960s, however, found the Philadelphia Orchestra, like other American orchestras, plagued by seriously deteriorating labor relations. A contract negotiated in 1963 assured the symphony members year around employment, including four weeks of paid vacation. Three years later no one in the orchestra was making less than $12,400 a year, counting record fees, and many were receiving more. Yet union demands persisted—to the point that the orchestra's very existence was threatened. Particularly unpleasant was an eight-week strike in 1966, dramatically pointing out the financial dilemma faced by symphony orchestras across the country.

Whereas the Philadelphia Orchestra had lured Ormandy away from the Minneapolis Symphony, his Minnesota replacement, Dimitri Mitropoulos, was captured by the New York Philharmonic. After the Rodzinski turmoil in New York, Bruno Walter agreed to serve as musical adviser and principal conductor of the Philharmonic for two seasons. When Walter held firm in his refusal to assume the full burden of the orchestra, Mitropoulos was invited in. For one year, 1949-50, he shared the New York podium with Leopold Stokowski, then was named musical director. The Mitropoulos era was colorful, brilliant, erratic. The conductor was particularly successful with contemporary works, although his results with the standard repertoire were frequently less happy. Opera had always been Mitropoulos' first love, and he was anxious to turn more of his efforts in that direction. A heart attack in 1955 meant that the musician would have to cut back on all commitments, so that his duties at the Philharmonic were shared in 1956-57 with two "chief guests," Paul Paray and Leonard Bernstein. The next season Bernstein was engaged as codirector.

Bernstein had burst forth as the golden boy of American serious music on Sunday afternoon, November 14, 1943, when he stepped before the New York Philharmonic as an eleventh-hour substitution for the indisposed Bruno Walter. He was twenty-five years old at the time. Born in Lawrence, Massachusetts, Bernstein was the son of Russian immigrants. He began piano lessons at the age of ten and majored in music at Harvard. He studied composition with Walter Piston and Edward Burlingame Hill and as a student staged the first Boston performance of Marc Blitzstein's *The Cradle Will Rock*. When he graduated in 1939, he went to New York and lived for a while with Adolph Green in an apartment in Greenwich Village. With Mitropoulos' help, Bernstein entered Curtis Institute in Philadelphia, where he studied conducting with Fritz Reiner. He was also a member of Koussevitzky's conducting class during one of the Berkshire Music Festivals.

In the early autumn of 1943 the young musician was virtually unknown. He was a freshly appointed assistant conductor for the New York Philharmonic and played for a Jennie Tourel recital in Town Hall. The next day he was called upon to fill in for Walter. On Monday morning he awoke to find himself famous. His studio in Carnegie Hall was jammed with reporters and aglow with flashbulbs. The *New York Times Magazine* shortly called him "a sort of mixture of Mozart, Toscanini, Horatio Alger hero and Frank Sinatra." An engagement with the Pittsburgh Symphony the next year launched a guest conducting marathon. Bernstein traveled 50,000 miles that season and conducted eighty-nine concerts with orchestras all over the United States.

He returned to the New York Philharmonic as a full-fledged guest conductor and in 1945 became director of the New York City Symphony. He remained with that orchestra for three years, programming works by Shostakovich, Bartok, Hindemith, Milhaud, and Chavez and reviving Stravinsky's *Oedipus Rex*. In December, 1953, he became the first American-born, American-trained conductor to direct an opera at La Scala in Milan. The occasion was a staging of Cherubini's *Medea* with Maria Callas. On November 14, 1954, he launched his *Omnibus* series on television, with a lecture on Beethoven, and firmly established himself as a nationally known personality. He took control of the New York Philharmonic in 1958, and despite complaints about his "show business approach," the orchestra began to thrive. Performances were consistently sold out. Bernstein, according to critic Harold Schonberg, is essentially a throwback to the romantic age. "He employs considerable fluctuation of tempo, often slows down for second subjects, underlines melodies, is constantly using a full palette of expressive devices that are generally scorned today." He conducted the opening night performance at Philharmonic Hall in Lincoln Center in 1962, but left the orchestra at the end of the 1968-69 season to devote more time to composing. He was eventually replaced by Pierre Boulez.

The number of symphony orchestras in the United States has blossomed enormously since World War II. In 1972 there were twenty-eight major orchestras—that is, with budgets in excess of $250,000—and seventy-two metropolitan orchestras. Not only are there more orchestras, but the length of their seasons has increased and in almost every case the scope of the major organizations has grown to reach a larger public. Two of the most promising new conductors are Oriental. The Los Angeles Philharmonic in recent years made amazing progress under the direction of Zubin Mehta, from India. Mehta showed a flair for the exotic and even insisted upon coming to Los Angeles that ushers wear Indian dress. Later he became the conductor of the New York Philharmonic. The San Francisco Symphony, which grew tremendously under Pierre Monteux, continued its advance under the leadership of Seiji Ozawa, from Japan. The young American conductor Thomas Schippers added vitality to the Cincinnati Symphony, while the St. Louis Symphony continued to thrive under the leadership of Walter Susskind. The Utah Symphony, directed since 1947 by Maurice Abravanel, became as significant a part of Salt Lake City's cultural life as the Mormon Tabernacle Choir, although the orchestra travels over the entire state. The Minneapolis Symphony, which continued on a high level under Mitropoulos' replacement, Antal Dorati, recently changed its name to the Minnesota Orchestra, to better reflect its statewide operations. When Max Reiter died in 1950, he was succeeded as conductor of the San Antonio Symphony by Texas-born Victor Alessandro. In addition to its regular, "pop," and youth concerts in San Antonio, the orchestra initiated the Rio Grande Valley International Music Festival in 1960, playing performances each March in cities like McAllen, Harlingen, Edinburg, and Brownsville. The Honolulu Symphony Orchestra, a metropolitan orchestra, flies throughout the islands to bring music to a widely dispersed population. George Barati, its longtime conductor, insisted that the orchestra play wherever there was an interest—in large halls or small, in windstorms, under a burning sun.

Most of the nation's orchestras, however, have a municipal basis and are underwritten as much as a civic duty as for the cultural benefits to be gained. Deficits are primarily covered by donations from business firms, banks, and wealthy, civic-minded individuals who have been convinced that a symphony orchestra is essential to complete the image of a metropolis. There is the vague feeling that a symphony orchestra is important for children and a more tangible one that wives of promising young executives will not venture beyond the Alleghenies if they regard the community their husband is contemplating a cultural wilderness. A symphony, most guarantors feel, is a necessary investment in city building; music is often a secondary consideration. As the Dallas *Morning News* critic John Rosenfield once insisted, "The postwar orchestra is supported like the hospital the donor never expects to visit, the college he will never attend, the library he will never patronize, and the orphanage that is not for him or his." In Texas at least, the patron is frequently a product of a folk heritage in which men—of the "he-man" variety—leave the arts to their women and even pride themselves in cultural illiteracy. When the Dallas banker R. L. Thornton was asked to head a "Save Our Symphony" campaign in 1951, the dedicated community leader not only agreed, but contributed a healthy sum to the $200,000 donation drive himself. "I think a symphony is a good thing for the town, and I'm for it," Thornton characteristically announced. "I'll do anything for it but go to hear it."

In Dallas serious music developed from a far narrower foundation than in San Antonio, where a large Mexican and German population proved beneficial. The growth of the Dallas Symphony Orchestra has been deliberate and serves as a prime example of civic boosterism in music. During the late 1880s Hans Kreissig, a young German musician who had been conducting a touring orchestra, became stranded in Texas and decided to make Dallas his home. He earned his living as a piano teacher, and in 1900 gathered together what local talent he could find and organized the Dallas Symphony Club. The ensemble initially consisted of twenty-one members—all violinists! Undaunted, Kreissig announced three concerts for the first season. Five years later a more formal attempt was made to establish a symphony by Walter Fried, who came to Dallas to teach violin after studying conducting in Germany. Although Fried would become director of the orchestra again in 1918, he temporarily stepped aside in 1911, when Carl Venth—a former concertmaster of the Metropolitan Opera and founder of the Brooklyn Symphony—appeared in the city.

Maintaining a symphony orchestra proved expensive for promoters, but Dallas leaders were increasingly coming to feel that a symphony was something a growing town could not be without. From 1925 to 1938 Paul Van Katwijk, head of the department of music at Southern Methodist University, kept the orchestra together, often working with inadequate musicians and limited rehearsal time. Gradually the symphony backers began to realize that artistic excellence required sufficient financing. In 1938 Jacques Singer was chosen director of the Dallas Symphony and given instructions to build the organization into a major orchestra. But four years later, with the war effort darkening, officials decided to suspend operations.

The modern Dallas Symphony was launched in 1945 with the appointment of Antal Dorati as conductor. Dorati, who previously had won an outstanding reputation as a conductor of ballet, immediately showed himself a personable, energetic musician interested in building the symphony into an orchestra of major importance. Whereas the budget before the war had averaged between thirty and forty thousand dollars a year, Dorati's achievements called for an underwriting of several hundred thousand dollars. The conductor broadened the standard Romantic repertoire to include unusual portions of Schumann and Mendelssohn and introduced both classical and modern compositions, not always to the pleasure of conservative Dallas audiences. On one of the programs under Dorati the orchestra played Stravinsky's *Le Sacre du Printemps*, touching off a fairly heated controversy. The piece brought insults against Dorati, threats to cancel season tickets, and proposals to withdraw financial support. After the press and sophisticated townspeople pointed out at some length that the Stravinsky work had been an accepted masterpiece in larger cities for a good twenty-five years, the disturbed symphony patrons calmed down, and some even boasted later that they had heard the "progressive" composition.

When Dorati accepted the offer in 1949 from the Minneapolis Symphony, he was replaced by thirty-two year-old Walter Hendl, formerly associate conductor of the New York Philharmonic. For seven seasons the symphony under Hendl's direction presented competent programs with new and unusual compositions, but the excitement of a great orchestra clearly was not present. Since 1958 the Dallas Symphony has met with varying success under the leadership of Paul Kletzki, Georg Solti, Donald Johanos, Anshel Brusilow, and Eduardo Mata. Financial support has remained adequate, although by no means copious. Like other American orchestras, the Dallas Symphony has recently attempted to reach a greater public through "pop" concerts. One such program was sponsored in 1967 by a leading chain of supermarkets, which sold tickets at its stores exclusively. The price was held to $1.98, for which the buyer received S & H Green Stamps.

With Dorati's success in Dallas, Houston—Dallas' great rival— evidenced alarm; civic leaders were determined not to be outdone. In 1948 Efrem Kurtz was made director of the Houston Symphony, with orders to improve the orchestra—fast. The organization had begun in 1913, with Julian Paul Blitz, a Dutch cellist, as conductor. Twenty years later Blitz was succeeded by Frank St. Leger of the Chicago Opera. Under the leadership of Ernst Hoffmann, 1936-47, the symphony expanded its membership to seventy-seven musicians and increased its concerts from ten to forty a season, in addition to offering free, outdoor summer programs. Kurtz set out to convert the orchestra into a well disciplined, highly professional ensemble. He discharged approximately half of the old members, while others resigned. In their place the conductor hired fifty-three musicians from all over the country, adding them to the thirty-two still remaining from the Hoffmann days. Kurtz announced an immensely enlarged concert schedule and arranged for women players to wear gowns designed in Paris. By 1950 the Houston Symphony was supported by an annual budget of $35,000, the largest of any orchestra in the South and Southwest. A gift of $20,000 a year came from Hugh Roy Cullen, but much of the money was provided by contributions of $10 or less.

Since 1950 improvements in the orchestra have been even more remarkable. A succession of superlative conductors—including Sir Thomas Beecham, Leopold Stokowski, Sir John Barbirolli, and Andre Previn—have earned the Houston Symphony national recognition. On tour under Barbirolli in 1964, the orchestra performed a concert at Philharmonic Hall in New York City, winning a prolonged ovation. Two years later the symphony moved into a new permanent home, when the resplendent Jesse H. Jones Hall for the Performing Arts opened, complete with teak walls, cherry-red carpets, a sculpture by Richard Lippold, and a chrome fireplug outside. While Houston definitely has the foremost orchestra in the state today, Dallas can ease her civic pride with the knowledge that she has the better opera company.

Besides the municipal orchestras, hundreds of community orchestras have sprung up across the nation since World War II. Virtually every city in the country now supports some kind of symphonic group, as do many of the smaller towns and even the larger suburbs. In the cities these orchestras are constituted primarily by resident professional musicians and music teachers, while in the smaller towns membership consists mainly of local teachers, students, and interested townspeople who play on a volunteer basis. The Topeka Civic Symphony, for instance, includes housewives, Washburn University faculty members and students, a few high school students, clergymen, music teachers, psychiatrists, a physicist, and a printer. Since 1946 the orchestra has been under the direction of Everett Fetter, longtime chairman of the Washburn music department and a student of Monteux. The first viola is also the hottest trumpet player in the area and a real jazz enthusiast. The orchestra originally performed in the high school auditorium, but has recently moved to the new Washburn Fine Arts Center. A typical program for the symphony would include the standard classics mixed with modern works and occasionally musical comedy numbers. The orchestra is periodically joined by the symphony chorus, which holds practice sessions once a week. "These are not groups for people who play or sing badly," state archivist Robert Richmond maintains, "but neither does one have to be a Jascha Heifetz, a Robert Merrill or an Al Hirt to participate. These organizations are waiting for anyone who wants to use, to improve his talent, who wants to work but have fun doing it."

A "grassroots" concern for homegrown music has been a definite part of the post-war cultural boom, as greater interest in the arts spread beyond the metropolitan areas. America has not only become more sophisticated, but with the vast reshuffling of population, differences between village and urban life have been reduced. Every community of any size contains people who have studied music and have a healthy appreciation for serious art. Although most of the community orchestras started on a shoestring and are comprised of enthusiastic amateurs, their contribution to the nation's cultural life and musical growth is substantial. At the same time that mass communication has brought more "good" music to the inlands than ever before, a regional independence has also issued forth, while the notion that all serious music comes from the big city has lost ground.

America's major orchestras, however, have become among the finest in the world. No longer need the old cultural inferiority complex be present in the United States. With the exception of Bernstein, Thomas Schippers, and a few others, the foremost conductors still come mainly from Europe, but orchestra members are now mostly American-born. Ensemble playing has advanced tremendously, while the symphonic repertory has grown in variety and quality. As audiences have become more knowledgeable, conductors have increasingly concerned themselves with keeping programs fresh and dynamic, avoiding overuse of the established war horses. Far more than opera, American orchestras have found their way into community life, although their concerts are usually as much social events as musical. Historian John Mueller compares an American symphony concert with a dinner party, where the motives for attendance are mixed.

And yet there is little question that more people enjoy "good" music than ever before. With increased leisure time, there has been a gradual rise in the nation's awareness of art and general maturity. The music education program in the public schools has borne considerable fruit, as well as cultural events series and music appreciation courses in the colleges. Children's concerts and concerts for workers are paying off. Long-playing records, high fidelity equipment, FM radio stations, television specials, quality motion pictures, and even Muzak have played an important part in conditioning the American public to serious compositions. But symphony orchestras have also become aware of modern promotion and publicity methods and have learned to fashion these to their own needs.

Much of the orchestras' efforts to court a larger public has not been by choice. Financial needs have demanded fundamental changes. The days when a Henry L. Higginson, an H. H. Flagler, an Edward Bok, or a Taft family could keep a symphony orchestra going almost singlehandedly were gone long ago. The progressive tax structure and other economic reforms cut into the ability of the very wealthy to underwrite civic enterprises of all sorts. Since the income from ticket sales is substantially below their cost of operation, symphony orchestras across the country have been forced to widen their base of support. To do so, they have found it essential to establish a closer and more informal relationship with the general public.

Fund-raising drives have become an annual event with the larger orchestras, to which thousands of citizens, business firms, and organizations contribute. The upper income groups still make up the bulk of the orchestras' patronage, although over eighty-five percent of the donations are in amounts of less than $100. While attendance on the whole has gone up, rising prices and increased demands from the unions have meant that operating deficits have continued to soar. The expenditures of the New York Philharmonic amounted to less than $3000 in 1850; by 1965-66 the orchestra's total outlay was roughly $3,000,000. Financial matters for most symphony orchestras are in the hands of a board of directors, as a rule dominated by members of the social register. The board frequently attempts to restrict spending and occasionally offers other obstacles to the orchestra's artistic development. Sometimes the board's control is manifest in conservative programming and may result in the alienation of the musicians, which in turn leads to greater labor conflicts and perhaps even loss of public support.

Nonprofit cultural organizations, to be sure, lead a precarious existence under a private enterprise economy. Municipal subsidy has helped some, as well as assistance from charitable foundations. In 1966 the Ford Foundation created an $82,500,000 trust fund for the benefit of the nation's symphony orchestras, dwarfing all previous aid to the arts. Money was to be raised by the participating orchestras on a two-for-one matching basis. But foundation grants are generally available only to furnish impetus toward a specific goal. The funds awarded are intended to stimulate other sources and are usually not renewable. Federal support for the arts has been small, and the arts projects under the WPA suggest that government funding, when accompanied by regimentation and bureaucratic control, is of limited value, if aesthetic considerations are the primary concern.

To curb deficits and keep their boards happy American symphony orchestras must continually be mindful of the box office. A conductor with magnetism can usually fill concert halls, whereas a less showy personality with greater talent may not. Merely being a fine musician is not enough, nor has it ever been in the United States. The successful conductor must be able to project his personality to the public and create an intangible "chemistry" with audiences. The public can still be moved by the way a conductor moves his hands, an upward stare of transfiguration in celestial passages, or a lock of hair falling across his forehead at crucial moments in a performance. The guest conductor vogue continues as a means of adding variety to programs and offering enticements to subscribers.

Solo artists, however, still serve as the major lure, and again the public favors personalities with glamor and distinction. Pianists remain the most popular. The Philadelphia Orchestra played to its largest home attendance up to that time on January 23, 1943, when 3500 people crowded into the Academy of Music to hear blind pianist Alec Templeton. Texas-born Van Cliburn returned from Moscow in 1958, having won first prize at the International Tchaikovsky Competition, and immediately endeared himself to the American public. The cherubic Cliburn became the embodiment of the small town boy who took music lessons from his mother, practiced his scales dutifully, and gained world renown. For matrons across the land he was the symbol of what their son could have been, had he not preferred the gridiron over the keyboard. For American males he was a reflection of a gentler side they had never developed. Violinists can occasionally establish themselves on the concert circuit as romantic virtuosos, but since the prime of Pablo Casals cellists have had more difficulty. "Nobody comes to hear cellists these days," one manager said.

Many of the star performers have won adulation through highly controlled publicity campaigns. Columbia Artists Management, National Concert and Artists Corporation, and Hurok Attractions, which dominate the concert field, are large-scale businesses that operate out of New York and employ the most efficient corporation methods. They can make or break an artist's career and largely determine who will appear where. Like businessmen in other fields, concert managers are interested in success. They will focus on the personalities that somehow command public attention and are well aware that the fewer the stars, the brighter they shine. The system is extremely artificial and often ruthless. For the young performer a New York recital is essential. Success at Carnegie Hall, Town Hall, or Lincoln Center, coupled with aggressive management, can lead to engagements on community concert series across the country. A few of the newcomers may someday enter the stellar ranks, yet hundreds of others, with as much or more talent, will fall by the wayside. Instrumentalists for the most part have a tougher time establishing themselves than singers, although the concert field is—by design—crowded and achieving fame is seldom easy. "I enjoy being a musician," one orchestra member insisted. "I wouldn't discourage my children from being musicians—but I wouldn't want my daughter to marry one."

The American public is normally as little interested in new artists as they are in new music. They have to be told who is important and who the virtuoso is. And this is what the concert managers willingly do—with perhaps a bit more finesse than P. T. Barnum did for Jenny Lind in the mid-nineteenth century. Audiences are less swayed by showy pieces and cheap theatrics than they once were, but they are rarely attracted to music they have not heard before. They still wait to be told what music is good and worth listening to. The conductor remains the principal arbiter of taste. A popular figure on the podium can make practically anything acceptable to the public; a less winsome personality had best steer a more conservative path in programming. The general interest is more in an old repertory with new interpretations than in brand new music. When the public reaches out, it seems to prefer reaching back into the past for rarely heard pieces, rather than making forays into the contemporary storehouse. Harpsichordist Wanda Landowska, for instance, was able to create a fairly lively interest in baroque music after World War II, while recent compositions remained suspect.

America's concern for serious music has taken giant strides since the circuslike performances of Jullien and Gilmore. An affluent public now spends hundreds of millions of dollars on phonograph records, can frequently identify the theme from Tchaikovsky's Sixth Symphony after a few measures, and attends concerts in numbers that would have been unthinkable to Theodore Thomas and Walter Damrosch. Temples for the performing arts like Lincoln Center in New York and the John F. Kennedy Center in Washington, D.C. have been built, while the Eighty-ninth Congress established a National Foundation for the Arts and Humanities. There is a National Symphony, currently under Antal Dorati, and the Little Orchestra Society can fill New York's Town Hall eight times a year playing strictly music that is unfamiliar to most of the audience. More musicians are working at better wages than ever before, and yet the financial structure and centralization of the nation's concert life denies Americans much promising talent and excludes a vast repertory that is simply not commercial. The question recurs whether or not the United States has produced a truly educated musical audience. For a growing few serious music has developed into a genuine tradition, has become an integral part of life. For many others it is just "culture"—an ideal that is vague and distant, respected yet awesome, and irrelevant to the routine of existence.

CHAPTER

II

THE DIFFUSION OF

GRAND OPERA

The 1920s was the age of the flivver and the flapper, the Charleston and the raccoon coat, Babe Ruth and Bobby Jones, the zenith of the Ziegfeld *Follies* and George White's *Scandals*. Prohibition was the law, but the rumrunner, the speakeasy, and the racketeer were closer to reality. Grand opera was still the prerogative of the few, and the Chicago Grand Opera, at least, found attendance in 1920 down from what it had been in the decade before, when social opulence was more in vogue. "Aw, I don't like opera," a wealthy stockbroker told a reporter for the *Musical Leader*. "What's it all about anyway? I've spent fifteen hundred dollars on opera. My wife has to have new dresses all the time, and I've got to dress and hang around at the back of a box, twiddle my thumbs, when I could be at the club having a nice quiet game." A Chicago banker, asked why he attended the opera so infrequently, replied, "I only go when Mary's there," referring, of course, to the effervescent Mary Garden, "because you know—hm! ha!—she really is good to gaze upon." One woman put it this way: "I don't like going Saturday afternoon because there is always a show like the *Scandals* or *Follies* in town; my husband doesn't like going out nights, and my husband likes *Scandals*." *Musical Leader*, a Chicago publication, was forced to conclude that the public knew little or nothing about art and cared less. Chicago "is a plain butcher and broker business city," the journal insisted. "The merchants have no interest in anything save their counter-jumping and the wares upon their shelves; the stockbrokers and grain dealers know nothing except that which pertains to their own individual profits." Much the same could have been said about virtually any city in the country.

At the Metropolitan in New York, however, Gatti-Casazza continued his long tenure as general manager with remarkable success, offering some forty-eight productions a season and showing a profit every year of the 1920s except the last. Caruso's mantle came to be fairly evenly shared by Beniamino Gigli and Giovanni Martinelli, although Giacomo Lauri-Volpi was a contender at times. Amelita Galli-Curci made her debut at the Metropolitan in the 1921-22 season, opening as Violetta. The biggest sensation that year was created by Maria Jeritza, another newcomer, who audaciously sang Tosca's *"Vissi d'arte"* lying flat on her stomach. Gatti claimed the ovation that followed was the loudest he had ever heard. Jeritza later scored successes as Thais, Fedora, Elisabeth, Jenufa, Maliella in *Jewels of the Madonna*, Minnie, Carmen, and Richard Strauss' Helena, a role she had created in Vienna. For *Cavalleria Rusticana* she had the head carpenter add two more steps to the entrance of the church so that when Santuzza was cast aside, she could roll down them with sufficient abandon. But Jeritza, a tall blonde, could also be stunning and graceful. For the American premiere of Puccini's *Turandot*, November 16, 1926, seven months after the work's initial staging at La Scala, under Toscanini, she produced not only amazing tones, but handled the endless train on her gown with what seemed to be perfect ease.

Feodor Chaliapin made an impressive return to the Metropolitan in 1921 as Boris Godunov, eventually adding King Philip II in *Don Carlos*, Mephistopheles in *Faust*, and Massenet's *Don Quichotte* to his New York repertoire. Lucrezia Bori became one of Gatti's most valuable assets, commanding a respect from her following that bordered on worship, while Rosa Ponselle developed into the backbone of the company's Italian dramatic wing. In successive seasons Ponselle won cheers for La Gioconda, Selika in Meyerbeer's *L'Africana*, Norma, Spontini's *La Vestale*, Donna Anna, and Fiora in *L'Amore dei tre re*. Olin Downes said she possessed "probably the most beautiful voice of any soprano of her generation." Ponselle's sister, Carmela, sang at the Met briefly, including Amneris in *Aida* during 1925-26, but her operatic career was limited.

Other singers introduced by Gatti were more durable: Toti Dal Monte, Lauritz Melchior, Elisabeth Rethberg, Ezio Pinza, and several Americans. The young California baritone Lawrence Tibbett arrived inconspicuously in 1923, but won his first great success the next season as Ford in Verdi's *Falstaff*, opposite veteran Antonio Scotti in the title role. In 1927 Tibbett was assigned the lead in the world premiere of Deems Taylor's *The King's Henchman*, the first full-length American opera produced at the Metropolitan in nearly ten years. He made a success of it and for the next decade remained the top choice any time the management had a native work in mind. Eighteen year-old Marion Talley, from Kansas City, made a much-heralded Metropolitan debut in 1926, as Gilda. A special train brought in 200 hometown admirers, but there was general excitement over the discovery of an American soprano. During the performance her father, a telegraph operator, was permitted to sit in the wings and send out gushing reports. A capacity house went wild, while the Missouri girl's debut made the front page of newspapers across the country. The reviews, however, for the most part were savage. Pretty though she was, Miss Talley had little imagination and no flair. Three years later she sang "Hymn to the Sun" in *Coq d'or* and received absolutely no applause. At that point she gave up opera for the movies.

Another American singer, who made a far greater mark both in Hollywood *and* opera, was Grace Moore. She came to the Metropolitan on February 7, 1928, as Mimi in *La Boheme*, after appearances in *Hitchy-Koo* and *The Music Box Revue*. The daughter of a prosperous Tennessee merchant, Moore had attended a fashionable girls' school and was blessed with a peach-blossom complexion and a naturally beautiful voice. Her acting, on the other hand, was rudimentary. One critic claimed it consisted of an expression that was smiling and another that was not. She fared best later as Tosca and Louise. From the beginning she had an eye for publicity, and her love affairs became notorious. Gladys Swarthout, born in Peoria, Illinois, made her Met debut as La Cieca in 1929 and scored a hit in Rimsky-Korsakov's *Sadko* later that season. Swarthout had appeared in small roles earlier with the Chicago Civic Opera and while there had won the attention of Mary Garden. Lore has it that during rehearsals one day at the Chicago Auditorium a cry of "Swarthout!" went up. "Where's Swarthout?" It was Mary Garden. Young Gladys appeared before Mary meek and trembling, fearing she had done something wrong. Garden threw her shawl to the girl and predicted then that she would be the next great Carmen. Radiant and charming, Swarthout eventually did become the leading Carmen of her day and, like Grace Moore, enjoyed a reasonably successful interlude in the movies.

Physical productions were less important at the Metropolitan in the 1920s than they would later become. A typical performance during the decade might offer Rethberg as Aida, wearing a striped robe that looked roughly like an advertisement for Aunt Jemima pancakes. But Gatti did freshen the repertoire with novelties: Catalani's *Loreley* with Muzio in 1921; Rossini's *Guglielmo Tell* with Martinelli in 1922, for the first time since 1895; Giordano's *La Cena delle beffe*; Cornelius' *Der Barbier von Bagdad*; Falla's *La Vida Breve*; and Stravinsky's *Le Rossignol* in 1925; Puccini's *La Rondine* with Bori and Meyerbeer's *Le Prophete* with Martinelli in 1927; Respighi's *La Campana sommersa* in 1928; and Verdi's *Luisa Miller* with Ponselle, Lauri-Volpi, and Giuseppe De Luca in 1929. While Tullio Serafin conducted much of the Italian wing, Artur Bodanzky took care of the major German works. As new singers came in, old ones said farewell. Chaliapin left quietly at the close of the 1928-29 season; the next year was the last for Galli-Curci.

But by the end of the 1929-30 season things were beginning to come apart for Gatti-Casazza. His private life had experienced a rupture that year when he and Frances Alda were divorced. Gatti quickly married the Metropolitan ballerina Rosina Galli. Although divorce no longer carried quite the social stigma it had before World War I, many of the company's influential backers frowned upon the manager's remarriage, especially since his bride was many years his junior. Then too, for the first time in twenty years the Metropolitan Opera failed to show a profit. The loss for 1929-30 was only $14,743, but it was an ominous straw in the wind that shortly became a gale. Gatti's $1,100,000 reserve fund began melting away, as hard times set in. The 1930-31 deficit was $322,000, and within three years the reserve was entirely gone. External conditions and internal circumstances joined in signaling far-reaching changes. The days when the Metropolitan's Diamond Horseshoe could be the private arena for the display of the wealthy had at last come to an end. Henceforth the box office would have to be taken much more into account.

In Chicago the shift had already taken place. As Harold and Edith Rockefeller McCormick approached their final season of patronage at the Chicago Opera Association, they asked Mary Garden to take charge as general director. Garden thereby became the first woman ever to head an opera company, elevated to that post early in 1921, less than five months after American women gained the constitutional right to vote. Interviewed during an intermission of Monna Vanna, one of her favorite vehicles, the newly appointed director indicated that a number of changes were forthcoming. "First of all," she said over a cup of tea, "this is to be an American company, run from top to bottom by Americans." She insisted she would give fewer operas and thus better ones. Her aim was to give 50 percent Italian operas, 35 percent French, and 15 percent English. She would like to give German opera, but not until it could be sung in the original language, for she abominated translations. "I have heard Wagner butchered by poor translations," she explained. "I want to give opera in English, but it must be American opera, written by Americans, and sung in the language it is written in. I hope we can have at least one new American opera every year." Would a woman be able to handle the backstage bickering that had broken out during the current season? "I am a fighter," she replied. "I am an Anglo-Saxon, and we love, by gosh! nothing better than a fight. And count me as a fighter. I am right there in the fray; but the Latin races must be treated with kindness and consideration, and I would pat their cheeks."

According to Mary Garden, Harold McCormick approached her, reminding her that his term of patronage had only one more year to go. "We want to go out in a blaze of glory," he told her, "and we need your name." With attendance off, he undoubtedly felt it would take someone with Mary's flamboyance and understanding of the public to restore the box office to its former level. Garden would continue as an artist as well as director and would accept no salary for her managerial duties, only for the performances in which she herself starred. But she would take the position, she told the board, only on the condition that "you don't give me a business manager with whiskers." She assumed her new office curiously determined to make this "an American opera company" run by "American businessmen," and she said so time and again. "Young American singers used to knock at the doors of the American opera companies," she maintained in New York, "only to have them opened by foreigners, who would say: 'Not at home.' Now they will be welcomed by an American, and that is as it should be." Interestingly enough, Mary herself was legally British.

George M. Spangler, for thirteen years convention manager of the Chicago Association of Commerce, was appointed by the board as the opera company's new business manager. "In making this appointment," the official statement read, "Mr. Spangler was chosen as the man who by American business methods is best fitted to wipe out the annual deficit of the company, amounting last season to $350,000." It was Spangler's belief that to make opera pay, the art had to be popularized. His approach was not limited to the upper social strata, but aimed at the city as a whole. "It's their support, not their dress suits, we want. Even if they wear overalls, they're welcome." It had been McCormick's hope that when his term of patronage was up, the Association of Commerce would assume the financial burden. The appointment of Spangler was the first step in this direction. The board's feeling was that if Spangler could reduce the deficit enough, the Association of Commerce would then be kindly disposed to serve as the company's principal guarantor.

The following summer director Mary Garden—the "directa," as she insisted upon being called—scouted for talent in Europe. Right beside her was George Spangler, who fruitlessly tried to keep expenses down as much as possible. He was working against impossible odds, he discovered, for thrift had never been a Garden virtue. The diva insisted that Harold McCormick had told her the deficit for the coming season might run as high as $600,000. Therefore, when Spangler balked at an expense, Garden would turn to him and ask, "Have we reached the six hundred thousand dollar mark yet?" Once she signed a young artist who would gladly have come to Chicago for $200 a performance. "Why two hundred dollars per performance?" the directress asked in amazement. "You are worth six hundred dollars!" And $600 it was.

By fall Mme. Directa had lined up the largest array of operatic talent in Chicago's history, promising artists fees that were more than generous. The final roster listed seventeen sopranos, nine contraltos and mezzo-sopranos, thirteen tenors, eight baritones, nine bassos, and five conductors—just about twice as many singers in each category as the company actually needed or would be able to use. Three days after the season opened, George Spangler was asked by the board of directors to resign. No one cared to comment on why.

Meanwhile Mary Garden was moving fast and furiously. She showed up in Chicago that fall carrying a swagger stick and wearing her hair bobbed. She was also thinner. "And, in case anyone may want to know why I wear short skirts," she told a reporter, "it is to get about more easily and quickly. I will move in streaks until the beginning of our season." She also claimed the French psychotherapist Emile Coue—who made "Every day in every way I am getting better and better" a 1920s proverb—had cured her of bronchial pneumonia, colds, buzzing in the head, irritability, and depression.

Her season opened with Lucien Muratore and Marguerite D'Alvarez in *Samson and Delilah*. Edith Mason made her debut with the company as an enchanting Butterfly, and Claire Dux was introduced as Mimi. Galli-Curci was currently dividing her time between Chicago and the Metropolitan, while Rosa Raisa remained the mainstay of the company's dramatic section. Mary Garden, despite her duties as director, sang sometimes as often as three times a week, doing all the operas she enjoyed most: *Carmen, Le Jongleur de Notre Dame, Louise, Monna Vanna, Pelleas et Melisande, Thais*, and even *Salome*.

On December 30, 1921, the Chicago Opera staged the world premiere of Sergei Prokofieff's *The Love for Three Oranges*. The production was sung in French translation and cost in the neighborhood of $100,000. Its sets and costumes were the most sumptuous the company had ever used. The composer's modernistic score was too advanced for the public, however, and most of the critics found it difficult. "I detected the beginnings of two tunes," the *Tribune*'s Edward Moore observed. "For the rest of it Mr. Prokofieff might well have loaded up a shotgun with several thousand notes of varying lengths and discharged them against the side of a blank wall." The opera received but two performances, both of which the composer conducted.

Meanwhile, all was not well backstage. A feud had been raging practically from the moment the season began. Garden claims in her autobiography that she began receiving anonymous letters, then knives, revolvers, and once a box of bullets by mail. The crux of the problem was that the directress had hired too many singers, with not enough roles to go around. Johanna Gadski, the great Isolde, waited for two weeks for rehearsals to begin, but eventually was handed a check for $7500 and told her services would not be needed. When mutterings about her husband's questionable war record were offered as partial explanation, the soprano brought suit against the company for $500,000. Before long D'Alvarez, Muratore, Tito Schipa, and many more were in a huff, had been dismissed, or had left. Other singers were brought over from Europe, sang once, and were sent back home. Garden and Giorgio Polacco, her principal conductor, quarreled, and at one point she supposedly took him by the shoulders and threw him bodily out of her dressing room.

And yet from an artistic standpoint the season was a spectacular success. Productions were well rehearsed and star-studded. Attendance was up over the previous year, but costs were staggering. Two works had been lavishly prepared, including new sets and costumes, but were never staged. When the deficit was figured, it totaled $1,100,000. Harold McCormick, true to his promise, covered everything over $100,000. Mary Garden may not have turned the Chicago Opera Association into an American company, but she certainly gave the city the most sumptuous lyric theater it has ever witnessed. Yet it was obvious that this sort of spectacle could not bear repeating, especially with the McCormick underwriting no longer available. Mme. Garden resigned her post as general director at the close of the season. "I am an artist," she declared, "and I have decided that my place is with the artists, not over them." Reflecting on her season as the Chicago Opera's "directa" for her autobiography, Mary said breezily, "If it cost a million dollars, I'm sure it was worth it."

In the spring of 1922 the company was reorganized into the Chicago Civic Opera. Although the new organization would continue in much the same vein artistically as its predecessor (gradually becoming more Italianate), its financing was revolutionized, a move necessitated by fundamental changes in the nation's economic structure. McCormick's support had represented a dying era, a time of giant fortunes relatively unhampered by taxation. With the decline of massive wealth went the days of great guarantor support for the arts. The burden now had to be spread out over several hundred, eventually several thousand, people. Conscious efforts had to be made to democratize the arts, a process that had begun earlier. Through the years the operatic public in the United States had slowly broadened; now the dissemination was speeded up, in part to enlarge the base of support.

The original plan for financing the Chicago Civic Opera was for 500 guarantors each to pledge $1000 a year for five years. All through the 1921-22 season a fund drive had been in progress. By early summer the entire $500,000 a year had been pledged. To secure this amount, however, it had been necessary to accept contributions of $500 and even $100. Rather than the 500 guarantors initially envisioned, by the time the goal was reached, the list of patrons numbered 2200. All of the properties, costumes, scenery for ninety operas, and contracts of the Chicago Grand Opera Association were turned over to the new company as a gift from the McCormicks.

If anything was admired more than business in America during the 1920s, it was business efficiency. Every effort was made to put the Chicago Civic Opera on a strict business basis. The company's president was Samuel Insull, who had carved an empire out of public utilities. Born in England into humble circumstances, Insull came to this country at twenty-three as Thomas Edison's private secretary. Proving himself a financial wizard, he shortly became Edison's business manager, and in 1892 was placed in charge of the Edison Company in Chicago. With this as a foothold, he rapidly assimilated his public utilities kingdom. Although his first love was always business, Insull had become stage-struck as a youth and was especially a devotee of the opera. Upon taking over the direction of the Chicago Civic Opera, he attempted to run it as he would any other business; the keynote was thrift. "I am not in any sense an authority on Grand Opera," he once said, "except as to what it costs." Administratively he saw little difference between a company whose product was art and one of his utilities companies. "One cannot ignore the dollar without getting into trouble," he declared.

Equally dedicated to a policy of efficiency was Charles G. Dawes, the Chicago Civic Opera's vice president. Dawes was also heading President Harding's national Bureau of the Budget at the time, where his duty was to scrutinize each governmental expenditure and eliminate waste. His goal was to cut government spending to a minimum, and his views on the financing of the Chicago Opera were but a carbon copy of his outlook on the federal budget. Together Dawes and Insull worked out a strict accounting system for the Civic Opera, geared toward cutting out unnecessary extravagance. "No contract will be signed by any general director or business manager or any other individual from this day on," Insull assured. "Every contract in the future must bear the signature of the chairman of the finance committee and one member of the Board of Directors. We will spend our own money."

Insull was also strong in his belief that opera should belong to the people, not just the social elite. When the revamped Chicago company opened its season in November, 1922, with an *Aida* that featured Raisa and Charles Marshall, the *Tribune* announced: "It would seem that grand opera made safe for democracy, Chicago brand, means grand opera indeed, fine opera, brilliant opera, even grandiose opera." Raisa, like Mary Garden, was one of those Chicago regulars who never sang with the Metropolitan, although she had created the role of Turandot at La Scala. She was to Chicago roughly what Ponselle and Jeritza became to the Metropolitan, doing many of the same roles: Norma, Gioconda, Maliella, Tosca, Selika, Donna Anna, Minnie, Rachel in *La Juive*. Other artists—like Muzio, Chaliapin, Dal Monte, and Galli-Curci—the two companies shared, although Galli-Curci left Chicago in anger at the end of the 1923-24 season. The Chicago Symphony Orchestra director, Frederick Stock, conducted his first opera with the company in 1923—*Siegfried*, the only Wagner in the repertoire that year.

There was an aggressive contingent during this period that battled for opera in English, an issue that became closely linked with the jingoism of the decade. Insull's attempt to make the Chicago Opera a sound business led the management at times to engage in fairly tasteless commercialism, including some contemporary advertising methods. A simple announcement of *Faust*, listing cast and conductor, would no longer do. Instead a *Tribune* advertisement read:

> ## HE SOLD HIS SOUL
> ## TO BE YOUNG AGAIN
>
> *but he had to pay. In the end "Faust"*
> *belonged to The Devil. He took his fill*
> *of the fleshpots of the world and*
> *Mephistopheles took him.*

The 1924-25 season, however, closed with a deficit of $400,000, although attendance did seem to be advancing faster than expenses.

Many of the novelties presented by the company were French specialties for Mary Garden, works like Massenet's *Cleopatre*, *Werther*, and *Sapho*. Two new roles added by Garden in the late 1920s, Katusha in Alfano's *Resurrection* and Honegger's *Judith*, became favorite vehicles of hers. Rimsky-Korsakov's *Sniegurotchka* with Edith Mason, *La Cena delle beffe* and *Loreley* both with Muzio, and Humperdinck's *Konigskinder* with Claire Dux were other items of interest staged by the Chicago forces. There was a brief flurry of native opera. W. Franke Harling's *A Light from St. Agnes* in 1925 contained a number of jazz effects and a libretto by actress Minnie Maddern Fiske. The jazz motif presented something of a problem, since most of the jazz musicians hired to augment the orchestra could not read the score, while the regular orchestra members were equally baffled by the jazz technique. Charles Wakefield Cadman's *A Witch of Salem* received its world premiere by the company in December, 1926, with Charles Hackett singing the lead.

The Chicago Civic Opera continued to maintain its independent character throughout the 1920s. Singers like English soprano Eva Turner and the American mezzo Coe Glade performed there, yet were never heard at the Metropolitan. Charles Marshall was a great Otello for Chicago at a time when the Metropolitan had none. He was also a notable Tristan. The company had its own conductors, production ideas, and supporting singers—such stalwarts as Jose Mojica, who looked strikingly like Rudolph Valentino, and Virgilio Lazzari, who did not sing with the Met until considerably later.

The company gave its final performance in the Chicago Auditorium on January 26, 1929. Gounod's *Romeo and Juliet*, the first opera sung there forty years before, was also the last, this time featuring Edith Mason and Charles Hackett. The next season opened in Insull's new Civic Opera House on Wacker Drive, six days after the collapse on Wall Street. The idea was to house the opera on the lower level of a forty-five-story office building, allowing the office rental to cover the annual deficit. Many objected to moving the opera out of the Auditorium, where acoustics were far superior to those in the new house, and there were even some who saw the skyscraper at 20 North Wacker Drive as no more than a monument to Insull himself. "Insull's Throne" the new building came to be called, and if viewed from the back, it actually looked like a giant seat with huge armrests on either side. The theater inside was long and narrow, minimizing communication between the performers and the audience. "When I looked into that long black hole," Mary Garden recalled, "I said, 'Oh, no!'" And Edgar Lee Masters wrote, "All this was a material expression of the superman, Insull."

A third major American opera company appeared on the scene in 1923, the San Francisco Opera Association. Its founder, Gaetano Merola, had studied at the Royal Conservatory in Naples, his home city, and served briefly as an assistant conductor with the Metropolitan. He had been Oscar Hammerstein's chorus master at the Manhattan, had conducted the premiere of Victor Herbert's *Naughty Marietta*, and had worked for Hammerstein in London. Later he presided over operettas for the Shuberts, including *Maytime*, before he was hired by Fortune Gallo as conductor of the itinerant San Carlo Opera Company. Merola had visited San Francisco many times, first in 1906 as Nordica's pianist. He dearly loved the city and in 1921 decided to settle there. He found friends among the bay area's extensive Italian community and particularly enjoyed the restaurants in the heavily Neapolitan North Beach district. For some time he had nursed the idea of producing opera, but the notion took definite form during a Stanford vs. University of California football game. Invited to the tournament by friends, the musician was impressed with the marching bands and felt that the acoustics in Stanford Stadium were suitable for opera. He was reminded of the Verona Arena and the Baths of Caracalla in Rome, where grand opera was staged regularly with great success. He left the game determined to secure financial backing for a trial season.

Merola cashed in his own Italian bonds and obtained most of the remaining funds from North Beach friends, none of whom were especially wealthy. San Francisco had enjoyed a long, albeit sporadic, tradition of opera and possessed a cosmopolitan, European atmosphere that was unique. With financial support in view, Merola went East to engage singers. San Francisco Symphony members were contracted, and a chorus was selected and trained. A stage was constructed at the north end of Stanford Stadium, with redwood trees set decoratively on either side. Seating capacity was 17,000, while ticket prices were scaled from one to five dollars. A special train was arranged to take patrons down to Palo Alto. The season opened on June 3, 1922, with *I Pagliacci*. *Carmen* and *Faust* were also given; Giovanni Martinelli was heard in all three productions.

The Stanford experiment was a disaster financially, but successful enough artistically that negotiations began for a series of indoor performances in San Francisco. A plan was conceived whereby seventy-five persons would contribute $1000 each, although in the end some 2700 "founders" donated fifty dollars apiece to create a revolving fund. Remarkably enough, this fund served as a guarantee for the San Francisco Opera for over a decade. By the fall of 1923 the company was scheduled for ten performances of eight operas. Only the principals, which included Martinelli, Gigli, and De Luca, were imported. More than 95 percent of the company's personnel were San Francisco residents; all of the minor roles, too, were sung by Californians. Merola himself acted as artistic director, while Armando Agnini, the conductor's nephew, served as stage director. Scenery that first year was rented; most of the props were borrowed from the homes of subscribers.

The San Francisco Opera was christened on September 26, 1923, in the reconditioned Civic Auditorium, with a production of *La Boheme* featuring Martinelli and Queena Mario. The performance went remarkably well, considering there had been no time for a dress rehearsal. Seven of the operas given that season were Italian: *Rigoletto*, *Tosca*, *Pagliacci*, *Mefistofele*, *Andrea Chenier*, and Puccini's *Trittico*. *Romeo and Juliet* was the single French offering. During the next eight years the standard Italian works continued to dominate. *Aida* was given most frequently, produced seven times within the company's initial nine seasons. The only novelties staged (Mascagni's *L'Amico Fritz*, Vittandini's *Anima Allegra*, and Giordano's *La Cena delle beffe*) were works that the Metropolitan had given with reasonable success a season or so earlier. Met stars like Jeritza, Pinza, Rethberg, and Tibbett repeatedly headed the roster, although Merola occasionally borrowed artists from the Chicago Civic, most notably Muzio and Tito Schipa. Productions for the most part looked like copies of those offered in New York. Alfred Hertz, then conductor of the San Francisco Symphony, was a guest on the podium in 1927 for *Tristan und Isolde*, the company's first Wagner, but the decade closed with the San Francisco Opera Association largely a satellite of the Metropolitan.

Although the Metropolitan continued to represent the light for San Francisco and other cities artistically, financially the New York company plunged deeper into the dark. The decline in box office income during 1930-31 was followed by a falling off in subscriptions of more than ten percent the next year. Gatti-Casazza maintained that the bulk of the subscribers who cancelled were from the wealthy classes. When Otto Kahn retired as chairman of the board, there were even rumors that the company would soon disband. Artists and staff were asked to take a ten percent salary cut, and a new source of revenue—radio broadcasts—was tapped. Since CBS had the prestigious Sunday afternoon Philharmonic broadcasts, NBC executives were anxious to acquire the Metropolitan as a counterattraction. Gatti had initially feared that the dignity of the house would suffer if the Met became associated with the new medium, but financial necessity forced him to change his mind. On Christmas Day, 1931, *Hansel and Gretel* was heard complete from the Metropolitan stage, and three years later the first sponsored performance was heard. Deems Taylor, the commentator for the early broadcasts, summarized the plot briefly in advance, then gave a running interpretation as the opera was being sung. This approach was shelved when the management began receiving complaints that "some idiot keeps talking" during the music. The arrival of radio was propitious, for it won new friends for opera at a time when they were desperately needed.

Despite substantial compensations from radio broadcasts, however, economic conditions at the Metropolitan remained grim. The 1932-33 season was shortened from twenty-four to sixteen weeks. More important, the assets of the Metropolitan Opera Company were "reorganized" into the Metropolitan Opera Association, a stockless, nonprofit organization. The company would now be underwritten by public funds. There was much talk about the "democratization of the Metropolitan" and of "broadening the base," as everybody was invited to become a Metropolitan patron. Since the reorganization gave the company the status of an educational institution, the amusements tax was dropped. Consequently ticket prices could be reduced without loss of income. The company launched an aggressive campaign for funds, using radio as the lifeline to make the appeal national. Many of the artists joined in the plea to "Save the Metropolitan," asking the public to "Give! Give! Give!"

Meanwhile Gatti continued offering the best performances possible. Lily Pons, the Met's golden girl for nearly three decades, was introduced as Lucia on January 3, 1931. She had been discovered in a provincial French opera house and was unveiled in New York quietly. Her reception was overwhelming. She went on to do Gilda, Olympia, Rosina, and rarities like *La Sonnambula* and *Linda di Chamounix*. When she sang *Lakme*, she wore a costume that left off at the rib cage and resumed at the hips, revealing a body that served as explanation. She was also charming. Pons quickly became the mainstay of the coloratura repertoire, singing during the lean years virtually with no understudy. "She wasn't just a star," baritone Robert Merrill said later. "She was a whole darned constellation!"

When Gigli left the company, rather than accept a salary cut, Tito Schipa was brought in from Chicago to fill his place. Richard Crooks, Rose Bampton, John Charles Thomas, and Helen Jepson all made Metropolitan debuts during the late Gatti years, while Bori, Rethberg, Martinelli, and De Luca remained pillars of strength. Jeritza withdrew after the 1931-32 season. Ponselle added her vigorously unconventional Violetta in 1931, did a disastrous Carmen four years later, and departed at the close of the 1936-37 season, when she married and moved to Baltimore. Ernestine Schumann-Heink made her farewell to opera on March 11, 1932, as Erda, at more than seventy years of age. Antonio Scotti retired the next season, and Serafin left to become director of the Royal Opera House in Rome.

Gladys Swarthout was making steady progress, taking over such roles as Preziosilla in *Forza* and Adalgisa in *Norma*, while Pinza was gaining polish as the Don. Tibbett was showing increasing evidence of growth, scoring a tremendous success in 1932 as Simon Boccanegra. He was also the backbone of Gatti's renewed attempt to discover the great American opera. Deems Taylor's *Peter Ibbetson* in 1931 came closest, with Tibbett, Bori, Edward Johnson, and Serafin conducting. The work opened the season two years later, the first American opera so honored. The world premiere of Louis Gruenberg's *The Emperor Jones*, based on Eugene O'Neill, took place on January 7, 1933, again with Tibbett in the lead and Serafin in the pit. The following year Howard Hanson's *Merry Mount* had its stage premiere, with Tibbett as Wrestling Bradford. In 1934-35 the American novelty was John Laurence Seymour's *In the Pasha's Garden*, Tibbett singing the Pasha. Even with a shortened season Gatti managed to crowd upwards to thirty-seven works into the repertory, including, in his final years as director, an Italian version of Mussorgsky's *The Fair at Sorochintzy*, Mascagni's *Iris* with Rethberg, Italo Montemezzi's one act *La Notte di Zoraima* with Ponselle, the initial Metropolitan staging of Strauss' *Elektra*, and the first *Don Pasquale* in twenty years, with Pinza, Bori, and Schipa.

Even though Melchior had begun to come into his own, Wagner performances were at a low ebb at the Metropolitan in 1931-32. The situation improved drastically the next year with the addition of Frida Leider and Maria Olszewska. Within another season Lotte Lehmann made her debut as Sieglinde, adding further strength to Wagner. Then on February 22, 1935, Kirsten Flagstad was introduced, during a broadcast matinee. It was one of those glorious moments in opera, the voice of a lifetime, coming almost without fanfare. Flagstad was virtually unknown outside her native Norway and was brought to the Metropolitan on a one-year contract. She was nearly forty at the time. During rehearsals Bodanzky turned over his baton to an assistant and went to the back of the auditorium to listen. After a few phrases he sent a messenger for Gatti. Before long word was racing through the house: "My God! Drop everything and come hear this voice!" The theater began filling as if for an actual performance. When she finished, even the orchestra members stood and cheered, as Bodanzky shouted, *"Brava, Flagstad!"* She was heard first as Sieglinde, then sang Isolde four days later to a sold out house. Her presence electrified those who worked with her; the result was Wagnerian performances such as had not been heard in the United States in more than thirty years.

Flagstad was Gatti-Casazza's last great discovery. He left the Metropolitan after the 1934-35 season. The loss of Otto Kahn had been a blow to his freedom. Many of the directors had become openly hostile; others argued that any operation that lost money was surely being mismanaged. In late April, Gatti boarded the *Rex* and sailed for Europe, "very downcast," his wife reported. "I have left the Metropolitan," he told stage director Herbert Graf, "because I feel convinced that opera can no longer be done the way I did it." For twenty-seven years Gatti-Casazza had remained something of a mystery man at the Met. He had been responsible for a total of 110 works not previously given there, about half of which were heard for only one season. He was remembered as "a true impresario in every way," "tops in the production of grand opera," a scholar that "artists and staff alike respected...and liked," with a trim beard that "made his handsome face more distinguished." Now he departed, never to be seen in New York again.

He was replaced as general manager by Herbert Witherspoon, a former bass, who had had brief administrative experience in Chicago. On May 10, 1935, Witherspoon paused for a word with his secretary. Suddenly the new manager doubled up; he was dead by the time doctors reached him. Edward Johnson, the former Met tenor, whom Gatti-Casazza had favored as his successor all along, was elevated to general manager. Under Johnson would evolve an even more democratic form of opera at the Metropolitan. It was clear from the start that Johnson did not have anywhere near the free hand that Gatti-Casazza had enjoyed. There was increasingly heavy pressure from the unions and constant worry over costs. While the personable Johnson found it difficult to discipline artists whom he had known for years, he did seem to grasp the new economic pattern within which the Met must operate. He was also handsome, white-haired, and considered one of the most eligible widowers around.

Johnson continued the Wagner renaissance. Marjorie Lawrence, a vivacious, blonde Australian, made her debut as the *Die Walkure* Brunnhilde early in Johnson's first season. She electrified audiences later in *Gotterdammerung* by leaping astride the horse Grane and riding triumphantly offstage. The American soprano Helen Traubel was introduced in 1937, during the world premiere of Walter Damrosch's *The Man without a Country*, but launched her Wagnerian performances two years later—as Sieglinde, opposite Melchior and Flagstad. Traubel's voice was more trumpetlike than Flagstad's, while the latter sounded fresher and more effortless. "Traubel's voice seemed to penetrate the orchestra," John Briggs recalls; "Flagstad's to soar above it."

But the Italian works were by no means neglected. Most of Ponselle's roles passed on to Gina Cigna, while Bidu Sayao, Jan Kiepura, Maria Caniglia, Jussi Bjoerling, Zinka Milanov, Jarmila Novotna, Alexander Kipnis, Licia Albanese, and Stella Roman were powerful acquisitions. Gigli was even welcomed back for a few performances. American singers became more important as the war clouds gathered over Europe, particularly Leonard Warren, Rise Stevens, and Eleanor Steber. Martinelli capped a career of twenty-five seasons during the 1937-38 season with an extraordinary Otello, and Tibbett held his own as Iago. Pinza graduated to Boris Godunov the following year, acclaimed as the Met's successor to Chaliapin. When Bodanzky died in 1939, young Erich Leinsdorf took over most of the German assignments. Mozart came in for a revival in 1940, when a long awaited *Marriage of Figaro* was heard, with Pinza, Rethberg, Brownlee, Sayao, and Stevens heading the cast. The revival deepened a year later with the entrance of Bruno Walter, who conducted a penetrating *Don Giovanni*, as well as a fine *Fidelio*. Walter had been made available by the curtailment of operatic activities in Europe, the first in a series of such conductors who added dimension to the Metropolitan offering in the forties.

The Metropolitan Opera Guild was formed by Mrs. August Belmont in 1937, "to develop and cultivate a wider public interest in opera." The Guild's growing membership helped project the Metropolitan Opera into a national institution. When the house was renovated in the summer of 1940, the democratization process was carried still further. The Diamond Horseshoe was eliminated, and the boxes were put on sale to anyone who could pay the price. The boxes in the grand tier were replaced by rows of seats. Title to the house at this point passed from a real estate company to the Metropolitan Opera Association itself. Largely because of the weekly broadcasts, the Metropolitan's appeal for funds in 1940 was answered from across the country, mostly in donations of one dollar, five dollars, or ten. Nearly a third of the million dollars collected was contributed by radio listeners. "If the Metropolitan Opera was to continue on the scale and with the standards of the past," Olin Downes put it plainly in the New York *Times*, "the public would have to contribute to its subsidy." Fortunately the 1940-41 season closed with the lowest deficit since 1936, a manageable $50,975. It had been as high as $113,530.

In Chicago Insull's Civic Opera began coming apart shortly after the crash on Wall Street. Curiosity about the new house stimulated better attendance during the 1929-30 season than had been the case for the past several years at the Auditorium, but large sections of unsold seats soon became characteristic. The 1930-31 season closed with the largest deficit since Insull took over. The Civic Opera House itself was also proving something of a disaster.

Nevertheless, despite the effects of the Depression, the Chicago company continued to stage interesting opera, at least for three more seasons. Mascagni's *Iris* was mounted for Edith Mason in the 1929-30 season; Raisa was heard in Zandonai's *Conchita*, and Vanni-Marcoux and Coe Glade teamed for *Don Quichotte*. The next year opened with the American premiere of Ernest Moret's *Lorenzaccio*. Moret was a pupil of Massenet, and his music proved it. Vanni-Marcoux, who had created the role in Paris ten years before, sang Lorenzo, while Charles Hackett and Jennie Tourel were in the cast. Muzio added a new part that season, Fiora in *L'Amore die tre re*, playing it as a Bernhardt or a Duse might. Mary McCormic returned after an absence of several years, and Lotte Lehmann sang with the company before appearing at the Metropolitan.

The most expensive novelty of the 1930-31 season was the world premiere of Hamilton Forrest's *Camille*, with Mary Garden in the title role and sets that cost in the neighborhood of $42,000. Forrest was born and raised in Chicago and at one time had worked as an office boy in Insull's utilities firm. His opera was staged largely because Garden wanted to do it. The score, as Mary herself said, "just screeched with modernism" and was anything but a success. Garden also sang Massenet's *Navarraise* for the first time in Chicago and closed the season with *Le Jongleur de Notre Dame*. She recalled that during the *Jongleur* performance she had said to herself, "I...have given twenty of the best years of my life to my work here in Chicago, and I've given everything to the people as well as I could, and now I think I'll go." When the curtain fell, she went to her dressing room, gathered her things together, returned to her hotel, and without saying good-bye to anyone, left the city. Upon arriving in Paris, she cabled Samuel Insull: "My career in America is done."

With the passing of Mary Garden, the golden era of Chicago opera was practically spent. During the 1931-32 season entertainment was the keynote, with the company reflecting some of the escapist sentiment of the time. Jan Kiepura made his American debut on opening night, while Leoni's *L'Oracolo* proved an exciting vehicle for Vanni-Marcoux and Schillings' *Mona Lisa* was given with Frida Leider. Artists were asked to take a salary cut of between ten and twenty percent, but financial conditions worsened. The fund-raising campaign did not go well; only about half of the amount needed was raised. By spring it was obvious the funds could not be found. The Chicago Civic Opera came to an end. Then, adding a sad denouement, Samuel Insull himself met disaster. In April, 1932, his utilities kingdom collapsed. Faced with charges of fraud and embezzlement, Insull fled to Paris and later Athens. In March, 1934, extradited from Greece, he was arrested in Istanbul and turned over to the United States for trial. His empire and his operatic dream were suddenly as dead as the age he embodied. Only the empty "throne" on Wacker Drive remained.

There was no Chicago opera season in 1932-33. In the summer of 1933 the Chicago Grand Opera Company was formed, with Paul Longone as general manager. Talk circulated for a while that the new company would stage its productions in the Auditorium, but eventually the Civic Opera House was selected, since the scenery, costumes, and properties of the local opera company were now tied to the new house. Longone put a season together quickly, and his company operated on a shoestring. The weekly outlay for the Chicago Grand Opera Company, for instance, averaged from $29,000 to $36,000, as compared with the $125,000 a week spent by the Civic Opera. Tickets were priced with a three dollar top. The company opened on December 26, 1933, with Jeritza as Tosca. Some of the old Civic Opera singers were back: Mason, Raisa, Glade. But Metropolitan artists came to dominate. Jeritza returned in 1934 for *Turandot* (which Raisa had done the year before) and *Salome*. Pinza was a sensation as Don Giovanni, Martinelli well liked in everything he did, and Melchior praised for Tristan (under the direction of the Chicago Symphony's Frederick Stock). Yet after two seasons the Chicago Grand Opera was forced to disband.

The Chicago City Opera Company was formed the following summer, again with Longone as general manager. It opened in the fall of 1935 on a budget cut to the bone. So great was the financial pressure that at six o'clock some evenings it seemed unlikely that the curtain would go up at eight. Performances were persistently ragged and underrehearsed. Many of the singers were grossly unqualified for their roles, for one of Longone's more dubious policies was his practice of allowing wealthy would-be singers to purchase productions, an arrangement he defended as helping to balance the budget. And there were bizarre attempts to make opera popular. For instance, night club entertainers Veloz and Yolanda were borrowed from the Empire Room of the Palmer House to head the ballet in *Carmen*. Shep Fields, the Empire Room's band leader, took the baton for their dances. During this same performance, Micaela was so bad that when Don Jose fired at her from offstage, one man in the audience lamented, "Too bad; they missed her."

Within these slipshod productions, however, there were individual performances of quality. Pinza had opened the season in *Mefistofele*. Marjorie Lawrence sang Brunnhilde opposite Melchior's Siegmund. Pons was heard as Lakme, and Jepson and John Charles Thomas joined for *Thais*. The big success that season was the first American staging of Respighi's *La Fiamma*, a year after the opera's world premiere in Rome. Raisa sang the lead.

Even *Time* magazine agreed that *La Fiamma* had been better than good, but added, "It was not enough to make subscribers forget what they had sat through before." John Charles Thomas also took part in the world premiere of Ethel Leginska's one act *Gale*, with Miss Leginska, formerly conductor of the Chicago Women's Symphony, serving in the pit. Friends of Leginska had put up five thousand dollars to see her opera produced, one thousand of which was to cover Thomas' fee. Indicating the extent to which chaos reigned at the Opera House that year, four days before the premiere of *Gale* nothing had been done toward its preparation. The first performance was really no more than a public rehearsal, as even Thomas did not know his part. His understudy claimed that Thomas sang only about half of the correct words that first night.

At the end of what *Time* called "undoubtedly the worst season of opera that a resident Chicago company has ever presented," the deficit was figured at something under $40,000, less than half what it had been the year before. Attendance for the year had been around 60 percent of capacity. Further financial reorganization followed.

Opera was becoming increasingly democratic. Throughout the 1936 season the Chicago management urged ticket holders to attend performances in business clothes. Formal dress was no longer expected. The Chicago City Opera had worked out a pact with the Metropolitan which enabled Met artists to participate in Chicago seasons, heralding a period when Chicago's productions essentially looked like copies of those given in New York. There were still independent touches. Louis Gruenberg's *Jack and the Beanstalk* received its world premiere by the Chicago forces in 1936, and *La Boheme* made news twice. Once was when a fifteen year-old Chicago high school junior named Betty Jaynes sang Mimi, opposite Martinelli. It was her first appearance in opera. As a matter of fact, *Boheme* was the only opera she knew. Even bigger news was the much discussed return of Galli-Curci in the role. The diva had not sung in opera for six years because of increasing vocal troubles resulting from goiter. An operation in the summer of 1935, it was said, had returned her voice to its former beauty and added weight. Her reappearance was set for November 24, 1936, almost exactly twenty years after her legendary American debut at the Auditorium. Her entrance was greeted by a seven minute ovation. There had been no time for a rehearsal. Galli-Curci was nervous; everybody was nervous. It was a sad occasion, and the soprano knew it better than anyone. She gave up further operatic plans.

When the company opened a year later, one observer said the most dressed-up people were the ticket takers. There were many small children in the audiences, for opera had now become a family affair rather than a grand social event. Met stars almost completely dominated, as they did again in 1938. With the death of Paul Longone, Henry Weber agreed to take over as musical director. He opened the 1939 season with Pinza as Boris. Elen Longone, the late director's widow, sang the role of Marina. Weber conducted. Metropolitan singers had begun trying out new roles in Chicago before undertaking them on home ground. Swarthout sang her first Carmen with the Chicago City Opera; Martinelli sang Tristan, a role he never did at the Met. Sometimes new artists were introduced in Chicago as a sort of warm-up, a few weeks before their scheduled Metropolitan debut.

In 1940 there was yet another reorganization, and the name Chicago Opera Company was taken. Henry Weber was appointed general director. The season that followed was outstanding in several regards. Most of the productions were polished and well integrated, for on the podium were giants. Artur Rodzinski conducted *Salome*; Fritz Reiner was brought in for *Der Rosenkavalier*. Italo Montemezzi came for his *L'Amore die tre re*, coaching Grace Moore for her first Fiora. But while the season was better than its predecessors, the deficit was higher. There were many complaints, enough that Weber resigned in the summer of 1941, convinced he could no longer produce quality opera.

While the Chicago Opera proceeded by fits and starts, the San Francisco company advanced along an amazingly stable path during the Depression and war years. Merola operated practically without deficit until 1931, and then the loss was a comfortable $18,000. Artistically the west coast company remained almost a branch of the Metropolitan. Merola did stage the American premiere of Ravel's five year-old *L'Enfant et les Sortileges* in 1930, but most of his novelties were repetitions of what had been given at the Met a season or so before. After years of negotiation and planning the War Memorial Opera House was completed in time for the 1932 season and opened with a gala production of *Tosca* that featured Claudia Muzio in the title role. The house, located in the Civic Center, was classic in design. It was acclaimed one of the finest and most fully equipped opera houses in the world and provided the San Francisco Opera with a home worthy of its best efforts. It was also the nation's first municipally owned opera house. As the *Examiner* said the morning after the opening: "It's come true at last, the dream of dreams—a magnificent Opera House for San Francisco, an Opera House that belongs to you and me and all the neighbors, and to every man and woman on the street, and every quiet little woman clearing away the breakfast dishes this very minute!"

Merola gave some excellent performances in the new Opera House. The first week of the 1935 season brought a complete cycle of Wagner's *Ring*, by far the company's most ambitious undertaking up to that time. Some $80,000 in depression money was spent to lure in such first-rate Wagnerians as Bodanzky, Melchior, and Flagstad. Another $40,000 was invested in scenery and props, including a lifelike dragon and a special cloud machine that projected photographs of real clouds on a backdrop. Many of the great characterizations of that era were presented on the War Memorial stage: Tibbett's Rigoletto, Pons' Lucia, Melchior's Tristan, Flagstad's Isolde, Albanese's Butterfly, Lawrence's Sieglinde, Rethberg's Countess, Bori's Magda, Lehmann's Marschallin, Stevens' Octavian, Moore's Fiora. The company evolved during the thirties from a cozy "family affair" toward an assured professionalism.

But there were inevitable disasters. One was a 1940 production of *Carmen* with a badly miscast Marjorie Lawrence. Another was a 1943 staging in English of Puccini's *The Girl of the Golden West*. The translation only intensified the triteness of the pseudo-western libretto, while Florence Kirk, the Minnie, towered a head taller than her Dick Johnson, Frederick Jagel. The audience literally laughed the opera off the stage. "They hissed the villain last night at the Opry House," Alfred Frankenstein reported, "as he twirled his black mustache and cried, 'Ya must and shall be mine, me proud and haughty beauty,' or words to that effect." A scheduled second performance of the work was canceled.

There were interesting touches. Nelson Eddy took time out from film-making to sing Amonasro with the company in 1935. Three years later, in an effort to break his dependence on the Metropolitan, Merola imported several singers directly from Europe. Ebe Stignani, the great mezzo, made her American debut. So did Alessandro Ziliani, the La Scala tenor, and Mafalda Favero, a light soprano. On the recommendation of Pierre Monteux, then conductor of the San Francisco Symphony, Janine Micheau and Georges Cathelat were brought over from Paris for the company's first *Pelleas et Melisande*. Merola planned to continue this fresh approach the next year, but the outbreak of hostilities in Europe made it impossible. For the duration of the war the San Francisco Opera was forced to rely on Metropolitan artists and a standard repertoire.

With the bombing of Pearl Harbor the management questioned whether or not the company could continue, but Merola became convinced that entertainment of every form was needed to help ease wartime tensions. Opera in San Francisco, therefore, went on, practically undaunted by the turmoil around it. Advance ticket sales proved extremely slow during the war, although over-the-counter sales hit an unprecedented high. Lines a block long at the box office became a nightly occurrence. Military personnel flocked to the Opera House, as the war in the Pacific centered more and more activity in San Francisco. Much to everyone's surprise the 1942 season closed with a profit, the first since the company's move into the new opera house. Two seasons later ticket sales were the best in the company's twenty-two-year history. Virtually every performance was sold out. The men declared a black tie edict shortly after the war began, but even in a supposed time of shortage the women, Frankenstein observed, seemed to find "some very fancy sackcloth among the ashes."

Patriotism was conspicuous at times, as the company's production of *The Daughter of the Regiment*, sung in French rather than Italian, demonstrated. On the nights the Donizetti opera was given, the stage of the War Memorial was flanked on either side by the flags of the Allied Nations. In the finale the banner of Free France, the Cross of Lorraine, was used in place of the usual French tri-color. At the end Lily Pons, singing the role of Marie, burst forth into a rousing "Marseillaise," beckoning the audience to join her.

The same was true when Pons sang the role at the Metropolitan. The war also meant that New York operagoers were denied Milanov for one year; Bjoerling spent the war years in Sweden, while Flagstad returned to Norway. On the other hand, Sir Thomas Beecham, Bruno Walter, and George Szell were made available to the Metropolitan as a result of the conflict. A brief flurry involving Ezio Pinza occurred on March 13, 1942, when the basso was taken into custody by the Federal Bureau of Investigation and charged with boasting of his friendship with Mussolini. The singer was interned on Ellis Island, but released once his denials were substantiated. Wagner was performed virtually unchallenged during the war, in sharp contrast to the World War I situation, but *Madama Butterfly* was not staged anywhere in the United States until after the Japanese surrender.

The personnel list for the Metropolitan's 1942-43 season showed fifty-one American-born singers, almost half the total listed. In the 1944-45 season, for the first time in the company's history, no singer of foreign birth was added to the roster, although fourteen more Americans were hired. Jan Peerce, Jennie Tourel, James Melton, Regina Resnik, Blanche Thebom, Richard Tucker, and seventeen year-old Patrice Munsel were among the native talent introduced at the Metropolitan during the war years. In 1942 Traubel became the first American Isolde since Nordica, and Steber advanced to the Countess in *Figaro* that same season.

Astrid Varnay, Swedish by birth, yet reared in America, won rave notices for her debut as Sieglinde, taking over when Lehmann fell ill, the day before the bombing at Pearl Harbor. Varnay was twenty-three at the time and had never appeared on any opera stage before. Six days later she stepped in for Traubel as the *Walkure* Brunnhilde, then went on to do Elsa and Elisabeth! While appearing in opera in Mexico during 1942, Marjorie Lawrence was stricken with polio and suddenly became unable to walk. She returned to the Metropolitan a season later to sing Venus in *Tannhauser*, a role for which she need not stand. Later she appeared as Isolde.

Since many of the singers lacked operatic experience during the war years, the conductors became all the more important. George Szell did a virtuoso job with *Salome*, despite an inadequate cast, demanding twenty-one hours of rehearsal. Beecham took over most of the French works and supervised a *Falstaff* in English. Mozart remained heavy in the Metropolitan repertoire, the 1941-42 season including *Figaro, Don Giovanni,* and *The Magic Flute*. The company opened on November 22, 1943, with *Boris Godunov* in Italian, a tribute to America's Russian allies.

Ticket prices were again lowered at the Met, and in recognition of the company's new status as a public institution, a detailed financial report was published. Artistic standards suffered considerably in the face of transportation problems and wartime priorities, and practically nothing was spent on new productions or novelties. The spring tour was limited to

Chicago and Cleveland in 1942, but expanded almost to normal the next year. Once the radio income was figured in, the 1944-45 receipts totaled $2,671,123, the highest in fifteen years. A net profit of $5872 was recorded.

Conditions in Chicago were not nearly so happy. Fortune Gallo, who for twenty-five years had managed the touring San Carlo Opera Company and actually made money, became the director of the Chicago company in 1941. Rumors circulated that after the expense of the season before no guarantors could be found, but Gallo assured his board that if they would take care of the boxes, he would fill the rest of the house. The new manager began preparations for the 1941 season with practically no financial assurance. Mostly for publicity purposes, Giovanni Martinelli was announced as the company's artistic director. Gallo gave eighteen operas in five weeks. He did everything possible to attract large audiences. He emphasized the star system, stuck to the standard repertoire, and on opening night even sent perfume through the ventilating system. While production standards dropped, attendance rose to over ninety percent of capacity.

Pearl Harbor was bombed a week before the season closed. Immediately there was the question of a 1942 season, although most people felt that giving one would be good for morale. The management emphasized that it already had the scenery and costumes needed for the operas that would be staged, so that no materials would be diverted from the war effort. The season opened the night before the Allied landing on North Africa, interestingly enough with Milanov as Aida. "The women took seriously the advice of periodicals and newspapers to keep up morale by looking their prettiest," the *Tribune* reported. Capacity houses again proved the norm. Large numbers of army and navy personnel were present at performances that year, and many women came unescorted. The Chicago ballet was unionized for the first time in 1942, forcing the management to pay higher salaries. Gallo made up for this by cutting rehearsals. The results were often sad. Metropolitan artists were still emphasized, with resident singers and members of the San Carlo Opera filling minor roles and occasionally assuming major ones. Nevertheless, Gallo closed the season with a deficit of only $25,000, a new low.

He resigned as general manager early the next year, intending to produce two operettas on Broadway and continue with his San Carlo Opera Company. Lack of leadership combined with transportation difficulties resulted in no season during 1943. The Chicago Opera Company was yet again reorganized, now with Metropolitan conductor Fausto Cleva as artistic director. Cleva offered a five-week season in 1944 that was more ambitious than satisfying. The chorus was none too young and the ballet downright makeshift. Staging for the most part was pedestrian, rehearsals limited. While most of the featured singers came from the Metropolitan, one unusual bit of casting proved surprisingly successful both with the critics and at the box office. Movie queen Jeanette MacDonald made her operatic debut with the company as Gounod's Juliet, adding Marguerite in *Faust* a little later. She looked radiant, acted the parts well, and sang better than anyone expected.

Her voice was slender, but sweet. Even Claudia Cassidy, the *Tribune*'s famed "hatchet woman of the Midwest," was pleased.

Cleva continued to head the Chicago Opera for two more uneven seasons. His stars frequently performed well, but production standards were generally haphazard. Criticism in 1945 was sharp. In an attempt to break out of the Metropolitan mold, the director went to Europe the following year, engaging a number of artists Chicago had never heard, most notably Ferruccio Tagliavini, Janine Micheau, and Italo Tajo. Performances in 1946 were more polished, as rehearsal time was increased. Dorothy Kirsten sang the first Butterfly since Pearl Harbor, and the company's repertoire was slightly more adventurous. While *Musical Courier* announced "the vastly improved condition of the Chicago Opera Company," Cleva's accounting department worried over poor attendance. Some of the best productions played to scant houses, with the result that the six-week season closed with a deficit of nearly $150,000. Since the company could produce no more opera until the debt was paid, it was forced to dissolve.

For eight years Chicago was virtually without resident opera. The city all but fell out of the opera habit. Yet the prosperous years following World War II found the art enjoying an international renaissance, aided in Europe by Marshall Plan dollars, stimulated in this country by the Metropolitan broadcasts, television, and especially the advent of longplaying records. Throughout the 1950s the glow of what would flicker into the cultural boom of the 1960s grew more luminous. All over the country interest in drama, art, and music began an upward surge. Sophisticates of a complex industrial society seemed to thirst for art and beauty in unprecedented numbers, as they searched for serenity in a disorderly world and reassurance that nobility still existed.

On the crest of this cultural rebirth, opera companies began springing up across the land. In Chicago the Lyric Theatre was formed by three young enthusiasts who were convinced the city had been too long without a resident company. Carol Fox, the daughter of a wealthy Chicago furniture manufacturer, originated the idea and became the company's general manager. She had just returned from studying voice herself in Europe. Her former vocal coach, Nicola Rescigno, who had conducted with Gallo's San Carlo troupe and with the Chicago Opera under Cleva, was asked to become the Lyric Theatre's musical director. Lawrence Kelly, a dynamic young real estate agent and insurance broker whose first love was opera, joined as managing director. Together the three incorporated the company and began looking for guarantors.

To convince critics and underwriters they knew what they were doing, the youngsters decided to stage a "calling card" performance. After months of work and planning a production of *Don Giovanni* was announced for February 5, 1954. It was a delight! Nicola Rossi-Lemeni was the Don; Eleanor Steber was Donna Anna, her first attempt at the role on any stage. Rescigno conducted an orchestra drawn mainly from the Chicago Symphony. With

Don Giovanni to their credit, Carol Fox left for Europe to engage artists for a regular fall season. What she came back with was incredible. Tito Gobbi, La Scala's leading baritone, agreed to sing for her. Giuseppe di Stefano, one of Italy's most celebrated tenors, was signed. So was Giulietta Simionato, the great Italian mezzo. But Fox was not through. She wanted soprano Maria Callas, the *prima donna absoluta* of Europe, and Callas she got..

Filled with the enthusiasm of youth, the three entrepreneurs raced ahead, little daunted by the obstacles that had spelled ruin for so many Chicago opera companies in the past. "Their necks were out so far they must at times have thought the chopping block inevitable," Claudia Cassidy wrote, and Kelly, thinking back on this first season a decade later, shook his head in disbelief. It was launched, he said, with "eighty-seven sets in the warehouse from the Insull regime, a great deal of hope, and even more guts."

On November 1, 1954, the company launched a three-week season with *Norma*, featuring Maria Callas in her American debut and Giulietta Simionato. Largely because of Callas, the season drew national and even international attention. Most of the leading music and news magazines sent reporters to cover the opening, while the major New York and California newspapers dispatched their chief critics. "It was a great night for Chicago," *Musical America* proclaimed. "It may prove an even greater night for opera in America." From the beginning it was evident that Fox, Kelly, and Rescigno planned to offer fresh talent in productions that bore little resemblance to what the Metropolitan was doing. Their company brought Chicago its first really new look in opera in over twenty years.

Enthusiasm mounted as the season progressed; the last two weeks were complete sellouts. Callas went on to sing *La Traviata* and *Lucia di Lammermoor*. She seemed to get better with each performance, as much an actress as a singer. Lucia was her zenith, and during the final curtain calls the aisles were clogged with young men pushing as close to the stage as possible. Even Claudia Cassidy came under her spell: "this creature called Callas is something special." Tito Gobbi was heard first in *The Barber of Seville*, opposite Simionato's Rosina. The ensembles bordered on perfection. "The era of singers is with us again," Cassidy effused. Baritone Gian Giacomo Guelfi made his American debut; di Stefano was heard with Steber and Gobbi in *Tosca*; Simionato sang Carmen; and Victorio Giannini's *The Taming of the Shrew* was given its first full-scale staging anywhere. Although the physical productions were consistently shabby, the performances were richly cast and remarkably executed. "How can it be," the *Daily News* asked, "that opera should have languished so long in Chicago and then suddenly burst forth on a level of total artistic perfection, stunning in its dramatic impact, dazzling in its vocal purity?"

Callas returned the next year, opening the season with Bellini's *I Puritani*, a work not heard in the United States for thirty years. At Callas' suggestion Renata Tebaldi was also contracted. The two sopranos were arch rivals and had feuded violently in public. But Callas ventured that it might be interesting to let Chicago audiences have the opportunity of comparing them. And so for two weeks running the Lyric Theatre offered Callas and Tebaldi on alternate nights, a record no other company in the world could match. Tebaldi was introduced as Aida. Then Callas sang Leonora in *Il Trovatore*. Tebaldi countered with Mimi. Callas concluded with Madama Butterfly. It was her first time to sing the role and her least satisfying portrayal. Yet the demand for tickets was so great that an extra performance was added; the house was sold out in an hour and thirty-eight minutes. Her final appearance was greeted by a prolonged ovation. Time and again Callas was called before the footlights, until tears came to her eyes. She left the stage emotionally spent. Then, on the way to her dressing room, a process server that the company had been protecting her from for weeks forced a court summons into her kimono. The legendary Callas temperament, heretofore unseen, was unleashed in full fury. "Chicago will be sorry for this!" she screamed and departed in a huff. It was a sad ending to a two-year love affair.

The rest of Lyric's 1955 season seemed anticlimactic, although there were some fine performances. Gobbi sang a masterful Rigoletto. Jussi Bjoerling was a sensation in everything he did. Teresa Stich-Randall, Carlo Bergonzi, and Anita Cerquetti were all heard in their American debuts. A seventy-seven year-old Tullio Serafin conducted a number of productions with aplomb. Carol Lawrence, soon headed for Broadway, led the *Faust* ballet. And unusual items like Monteverdi's *Il Ballo delle Ingrate* and Rafaelo de Banfield's *Lord Byron's Love Letter*, based on a text by Tennessee Williams, were staged. Audiences no longer came from the city's old social elite so much as from prosperous middle class business and professional people. Youth was also in notable abundance. In a mid-twentieth-century democracy dressing for the opera was not the elaborate affair it once was, but on the other hand attendance figures were higher than ever before. The company's underwriting came primarily from a multitude of small donations.

All through the 1955 season a struggle had been brewing backstage between Carol Fox on the one hand, Kelly and Rescigno on the other. Both factions eventually sought control of the Lyric Theatre, as the schism degenerated into a long, involved court battle. For several months neither side could negotiate for the coming season. The stalemate was broken when Carol Fox secured the necessary financial backing and was authorized to continue as general manager. The company was revamped under the name Lyric Opera of Chicago.

As before, the young directress placed the emphasis on singers, striking a careful balance between art and business. Tebaldi, Gobbi, and Simionato remained mainstays of the company for more than a decade, performing practically everything in their repertoire over the years. The Lyric's offering of fresh voices has been impressive. Anna Moffo, Walter Berry, Gre Brouwenstijn, Christa Ludwig, Eberhard Waechter, Renata Scotto, Ilva Ligabue, Sesto Bruscantini, Regine Crespin, Alfredo Kraus, Nicolai Ghiaurov, Elena Suliotis, and Katia Ricciarelli are but a few of the internationally esteemed singers who made their American debuts with the Chicago Lyric. Many others have been heard with the company well in advance of their Metropolitan appearances. Outstanding conductors have also been introduced—among them Georges Pretre, Antonio Votto, and Kiril Kondrashin, who had recently conducted for Van Cliburn in Russia. When *Prince Igor* was staged in 1962, Rudolf Nureyev was brought to this country for the first time, to head the Polovtsian dances.

There have been great performances. An uncut *La Forza del Destino* was heard in 1956, with Tebaldi, Tucker, Simionato, Ettore Bastianini, Rossi-Lemeni, and Georg Solti conducting. Two years later an inspired *Tristan und Isolde* was given under the direction of Artur Rodzinski, former conductor of the Chicago Symphony. Boito's *Mefistofele* was mounted in 1961 with Boris Christoff, Bergonzi, Ligabue, and Christa Ludwig. And an almost perfect staging of Donizetti's *La Favorita* was unveiled in 1964 for the American debut of Fiorenza Cossotto. There have also been interesting novelties: Cilea's *Adriana Lecouvreur* and Giordano's *Fedora* for Tebaldi, Verdi's *Nabucco* for Gobbi, Rossini's *La Cenerentola* for Teresa Berganza, Bizet's *The Pearl Fishers*, Janacek's *Jenufa*, Mussorgsky's *Khovanshchina*, Bartok's *Bluebeard's Castle*, Prokofiev's *The Flaming Angel*, Britten's *Billy Budd*, Rossini's *Semiramide* with Joan Sutherland and Marilyn Horne, Verdi's *I Due Foscari*, and Donizetti's *Maria Stuarda* with Montserrat Caballe. But there have been fiascos, like the 1958 *La Traviata* with Steber. Cassidy complained that the soprano had no feel for the part: "She plays a blonde hausfrau who has a bad time of it, sobs a lot, and eventually expires because the script says she must." Another miscalculation was a revival of *Thais* the following year, featuring a miscast Leontyne Price and sets dating back to the days of Mary Garden.

Visual productions have been a constant problem for the Lyric, since most of the company's sets initially were museum pieces left over from the Insull and Campanini eras. *The Marriage of Figaro* in 1957 was Carol Fox's first new production, and additions came slowly. The void was filled in part by borrowing costumes and scenery either from abroad or from other major American companies. Staging at the Lyric has often been perfunctory, lighting has been poor (sometimes to hide antiquated sets), and secondary casting has been consistently weak. Stars remained the strong point, although the chorus has proved a reliable asset and the orchestra has been generally good. An advance was made in the summer of 1957 when Pino Donati was added to the staff as musical assistant. Bruno Bartoletti was later made principal conductor. As his singing grew less frequent, Tito Gobbi became valuable as a stage director, supervising first a 1965 production of *Simon Boccanegra* in which he sang the title role.

Although Carol Fox has developed into an astute business woman, the Lyric Opera has had its share of financial difficulties. The company is not the national institution the Metropolitan is and does not enjoy the New York organization's coast to coast patronage. Like every American opera company, the Lyric has had problems with unions. A prolonged orchestra strike forced the cancellation of the 1967 season. On the brighter side, the Lyric received an unprecedented gift in 1958 from the Italian government—a $16,000 subsidy offered in gratitude for the company's stress on Italian singers and an Italianate repertoire. A year later the Ford Foundation announced an appropriation of $950,000 for the purpose of stimulating the composition and production of American opera. Under this grant the Lyric staged the world premiere of Vittorio Giannini's *The Harvest* in 1961. The work, despite the presence of Marilyn Horne, was not a success. "Just about everything happened in the Civic Opera house Saturday night except the great American opera," Cassidy wrote. "In general his [the composer's] first act is bad Puccini, the second frightful Copland, and his third ghastly Montemezzi." The ballet she judged "run of de Mille." Yet even with failures, the Lyric Opera of Chicago has maintained an attendance average of nearly ninety-seven percent.

Like Carol Fox, Gaetano Merola favored singers. With the war over the San Francisco impresario eagerly resumed his importation of young artists from Europe. Tito Gobbi was introduced in his American debut in 1948, a brash matinee idol at the time and far from the subtle artist Chicago would know later. On opening night, 1950, Renata Tebaldi and Mario Del Monaco made their American debuts in *Aida*. Both were established stars in Italy and were enthusiastically received in San Francisco. Del Monaco would sing a guest date at the Metropolitan on his return home from the west coast. Tebaldi would not appear in New York for another five years. Merola also enjoyed offering established singers in new and unusual roles. A prime example is the Violetta undertaken by Lily Pons in 1951, a controversial performance of a part the diva never attempted at the Metropolitan.

In the months preceding the 1949 season a controversy raged over the announcement that Kirsten Flagstad would appear with the San Francisco Opera in two performances each of *Tristan* and *Walkure*. Flagstad's return to Norway during the Nazi occupation had made her *persona non grata* in some circles in the United States. When she sang a concert in Philadelphia in 1948, a stink bomb had been thrown. Her engagement by Merola would mark her first American appearances in opera since the war. The city's reaction was sharply divided. Judge Milton Sapiro, of the Local Legion, insisted, "Her appearance would desecrate the War Memorial and the ideals it stands for. We wouldn't want a Benedict Arnold to sing in the Opera House. It would be better for the Opera Association to go out of business than hire a traitor of Norway." Yet ticket sales for the scheduled Flagstad performances were well ahead of any other operas in the repertoire. Despite continued opposition, her performances went on as planned. Her Isolde on September 30 was greeted by a standing ovation and no incident. A special third performance was added to meet the demand for tickets.

While Merola's ideas on casting came to be relatively progressive, his repertoire, mostly out of financial considerations, remained timid. His concern for staging was downright indifferent, with the result that stage pictures were often static and sometimes distressingly tasteless. Alfred Frankenstein had quipped earlier, about a production of *Don Giovanni*, that the interiors conveyed "the idea that Don Giovanni lived in a North Beach night club." In a 1949 staging of *Samson and Delilah* the critic found Delilah's abode to resemble Tarzan's tree hut, while the temple scene "looked like something left over after D. W. Griffith had finished *Intolerance* in 1916."

On August 30, 1953, Merola was conducting an outdoor concert, which included some *Madama Butterfly* arias. Suddenly he doubled up and fell from the podium. He had suffered a heart attack and was dead by the time doctors reached him. Kurt Herbert Adler, the San Francisco Opera's chorus master for ten years, was in stages elevated to general manager. The season about to begin had been planned by Merola and included the American debuts of Inge Borkh, Giulietta Simionato, Cesare Valletti, and conductor Georg Solti. But Adler was the chief architect of the 1954 season, and to it the Viennese director brought a freshness of approach that launched a new era for opera in San Francisco, in repertoire as well as staging. Mado Robin and Rosanna Carteri both made American debuts, while the services of a seventy-nine year-old Pierre Monteux were procured for the pit. The repertoire was highlighted by the American premiere of Cherubini's 1798 opera buffa *The Portuguese Inn* and the first fully staged presentation in this country of Honegger's *Joan of Arc at the Stake*, featuring Dorothy McGuire and Lee Marvin in speaking roles.

Over the next two decades Adler converted the San Francisco Opera into a cosmopolitan organization of independent flavor. The company was run on the highest professional level, while the staging of contemporary operas became more or less an annual event. Among the newer works to receive American premieres in San Francisco have been Sir William Walton's *Troilus and Cressida* in 1955, Francis Poulenc's *Dialogues of the Carmelites* in 1957, Carl Orff's *Die Kluge* in 1958, Richard Strauss' *Die Frau ohne Schatten* in 1959, Benjamin Britten's *A Midsummer Night's Dream* in 1961, and Gottfried von Einem's *The Visit of the Old Lady* in 1972. Underwriting from the Ford Foundation prompted the world premiere of Norman Dello Joio's *Blood Moon* in 1961, the first American opera staged by the company since *The Emperor Jones* in 1933. Older works like Cherubini's *Medea* in 1958 and Berlioz's *Les Troyens* in 1966 also received their initial American staging by the San Francisco forces, while novelties such as Zandonai's *Francesca da Rimini, Maria Stuarda* with Sutherland, and Meyerbeer's *L'Africaine* with Shirley Verrett have been heard with regularity. And the list of American debuts seems infinite: Elisabeth Schwarzkopf, Mattiwilda Dobbs, Leonie Rysanek, Birgit Nilsson, Leyla Gencer, Oralia Dominguez, Anselmo Colzani, Boris Christoff, Leontyne Price, Rita Streich, Giuseppe Taddei, Graciella Sciutti, Gabriella Tucci, Sena Jurinac, Eugenia Ratti, Sandor Konya, and dozens more.

The company's staging has become a model of vitality, fresh in terms of the modern theater. *Carmen* in 1959 had sets and costumes designed by Broadway's Howard Bay. A revival of *The Girl of the Golden West*, a work that had been a colossal failure earlier, proved enchanting in 1960. The second act curtain, at the conclusion of the famous poker scene, was among the most exciting ever witnessed at the War Memorial Opera House—Gobbi throwing a chair against the back wall and storming out, Kirsten laughing hysterically and allowing the cards to cascade to the floor. Gunther Rennert's production of *The Barber of Seville*, unveiled in 1963, consisted of a charming three-story set, while *The Visit of the Old Lady* served for the opera debut of film director Francis Ford Coppola, who had recently scored a huge success with *The Godfather*.

"In some ways," *Time* magazine argued in 1959, "San Francisco is now the finest opera company in the United States, often on a par with the Met in quality (if not in size), and consistently ahead of the Met in dash and daring." Certainly the company operates one of the most dynamic American opera houses, with profile and color of its own, and has developed a public that looks upon its venturesome offerings with favor. A spring season was added in 1961, which gives training to young artists and aspiring local talent. All of this costs money, yet San Francisco seems to have found the prestige and excitement worth the expense. The company launched its first public fund drive in 1955; the goal was then $100,000. The amount has been increased steadily over the years, but the total is always reached. The Los Angeles tour, begun in 1937, has helped the company financially, since the Auditorium there seats close to 6000 and is almost always filled. The operas staged in Los Angeles do not require extra rehearsal and have enabled the company to broaden its guarantor support into southern California as well.

About the time the San Francisco Opera began coming into its own, the Metropolitan was experiencing some dark moments. Both discipline and imagination were absent during the latter days of Edward Johnson's regime. Only a token amount was spent on scenic construction, with the result that the company's physical productions were always in shambles. Staging was bad and the repertoire less than dynamic. Although new artists began arriving from Europe after the war, the Met generally had fallen on lackluster times. Johnson remained charming and well liked and usually managed to avoid a financial loss, but a visionary he was not.

Some of the old glamor had returned by opening night, 1945. White ties and ermine were back, while President Truman's wife and daughter were prominent in the audience. Margaret Truman's vocal aspirations were already known, and she and her Secret Service escort would become familiar figures at the opera house over the next few years. American singers continued to play an important part in Metropolitan productions. Peerce, Steber, Warren, Stevens, and Tucker had grown in stature, while Robert Merrill, Dorothy Kirsten, Thomas Hayward, Jerome Hines, Frank Guarrera, Eugene Conley, and Jean Madeira all made debuts between 1945 and 1950. The conducting was often strong, and there were sometimes impressive casts—like the 1945-46 season's *Gioconda* with Milanov, Stevens, Tucker, Warren, and Pinza. Benjamin Britten's *Peter Grimes*, written on a commission from the Koussevitzky Foundation, was staged in 1948 and repeated the next year to celebrate Tibbett's silver anniversary. Mussorgsky's *Khovanshchina* was presented for the first time at the Metropolitan in 1949, in an English translation.

The sensation of these years, however, was a production of *Salome*, introduced on February 4, 1949, with the Bulgarian soprano Ljuba Welitch making her debut in the title role. Fritz Reiner conducted. Welitch had dyed her mop of hair flaming red for the part, rehearsed it wearing a plaid suit and galoshes. But from the moment the curtain went up, a packed house was gripped by the searing performance of a tigress. Rather than blasting its way through the role by force, Welitch's silvery voice floated effortlessly over the rampaging Strauss orchestra. After the scene with the head, pandemonium greeted the new star. For many it was the house's greatest night in memory.

The Metropolitan management was becoming more deeply involved in labor problems and for a time suspended plans for a 1948-49 season. At one point night club entrepreneur Billy Rose proposed to operate the Met for a year without loss, if "given a free hand and allowed to clean house." The offer was disregarded. The season opened three weeks later, but protracted negotiations with unions undoubtedly served as a factor in Johnson's decision to retire. The board persuaded him to stay until May, 1950, thereby rounding out fifteen years as general manager.

During the winter of 1949 Johnson was visited by Rudolf Bing, then manager of the summer opera festival at Glyndebourne, in England. It was a courtesy call, arranged by Bing's old friend, conductor Fritz Stiedry. After preliminary pleasantries Bing and Johnson settled down to discuss the difficulties of producing opera in a world of spiraling costs. Suddenly Johnson looked up at Bing in despair and said, "How would *you* like this job?" The two continued the conversation over the next forty-eight hours, and Bing returned to England with the promise that he would be given serious consideration as Johnson's replacement. He returned to New York for extended interviews with the board in May and was engaged for the position the next month. He would spend the 1949-50 season at the Metropolitan as a salaried "observer."

Bing's appointment was both bold and unconventional, for he was an unknown commodity in New York. Yet split as the Metropolitan was with factionalism, a neutral personality was not without certain advantages. Bing had grown up in Vienna, worked with opera in Darmstadt and Berlin, served as a concert manager and during the war was assistant to a London department store head. In addition to his duties at Glyndebourne, he had recently directed the Edinburgh Festival. He was slim, sharp-featured, polite, elegant, and rather aloof. He immediately became the focal point of much opera house gossip, and there was tension from the start. But Bing went about planning his first New York season as if the turmoil did not exist.

"What I found at the Metropolitan," Bing noted in his memoirs, "was *much* worse than I had expected, in every way—physical conditions, artistic integrity, sense of professionalism, support from the board were all well below anything I had lived with before." He spent the 1949-50 season charting his course and taking stock—"most of what I observed was a lesson in how not to organize an opera house." Bing was a great believer in organization and discipline and offended many with his candor and cutting remarks; but he steered the Metropolitan back to international prominence.

The ship he ran was a tight one indeed. He feuded early with Melchior and Traubel and dismissed Merrill for canceling out on the 1951 tour. "I find that artists are more often uneducated than genuinely temperamental," Bing once said with disdain, and such was the sort of icy remark for which he became notorious. When Antonietta Stella later threatened not to finish a performance of *Aida* unless allowed to take a solo bow after her Nile Scene, in violation of Bing's rule, the manager calmly looked at his watch and told the soprano she had exactly three minutes to make up her mind to sing. Otherwise he would suspend the performance, sue her for the evening's box office receipts, and file a protest with the American Guild of Musical Artists. "Incidentally," he added, "you now have only two minutes and a half."

Irritating though his ways could be, Bing was a skilled administrator and a man of taste. Above everything else he was determined to improve the looks and action on the Metropolitan stage, thereby enhancing musical qualities. He launched his New York career with a new production of Verdi's *Don Carlos*, a work that the Met had not done for nearly thirty years. It was an energetic performance that emphasized the ensemble. To transfuse the opera into exciting theater, Bing brought in the noted Shakespearean director Margaret Webster, whose staging had dignity and grandeur. Rolf Gerard's sets and costumes gave the production a freshness and a sense of style long absent from the Metropolitan's offerings. The cast included veterans Jussi Bjoerling, Robert Merrill, and Jerome Hines, while Cesare Siepi, Fedora Barbieri, Delia Rigal, and Lucine Amara were heard for the first time. Fritz Stiedry conducted. Webster stressed the notion that even singers could act, a revolutionary idea in those days, yet the production proved a musical delight as well. *Don Carlos* added up to the neatest total performance the Metropolitan had offered in decades and remained Bing's favorite production.

Later in his first season the new manager unveiled a spirited production of Johann Strauss' operetta *Die Fledermaus*, hoping to draw a broader audience to the Metropolitan. Howard Dietz prepared a colloquial English libretto, and the work was staged by Garson Kanin, author of the brilliant comedy *Born Yesterday*. English was the native language for most of the singers, while Eugene Ormandy was borrowed from the Philadelphia Orchestra to conduct, his first major effort with opera. *Fledermaus* had Broadway bounce and precision and became a centerpiece of Bing's initial season. Although there were complaints that it was beneath the opera house's dignity to stage so frivolous a production, the Strauss operetta was presented over twenty times that year, prompting Edward Johnson to refer to it as "Fledermice."

Even before taking over as general manager, Bing had stirred up a commotion, when he let it be known that he planned to bring Flagstad back to the Metropolitan. The opposition to the Norwegian soprano was every bit as strong in New York as it had been in San Francisco, although the charges against her were still vague. Flagstad did return on January 22, 1951, as Isolde, receiving nineteen curtain calls. She sang *Fidelio* under Bruno Walter's direction, but made her farewell a year later with six memorable performances of Gluck's *Alceste*.

To appease Traubel for the role of Isolde which she had lost to Flagstad, the American soprano was permitted to sing her first Marschallin, one of her few non-Wagnerian ventures ever. The season's most awaited new artist was Victoria de los Angeles, although Roberta Peters made an unexpected debut, replacing the indisposed Nadine Conner as Zerlina.

Within a few weeks Bing noted "one great weakness that seemed unlikely to be remedied without drastic action: conducting." The problem was never really solved. Bing quarreled with Reiner and Szell, but made much use of Monteux and Mitropoulos. Rudolf Kempe arrived from Germany in 1954, and Thomas Schippers made his debut with the company the next year, at the age of twenty-five. But much of the conducting at the Metropolitan remained uninspired; even strong productions often fell to assistant conductors after a few performances.

Bing's rejuvenation of the Met's set designs, on the other hand, continued throughout his twenty-two years as general manager. Mozart's *Cosi fan tutte* was a big hit in 1951, performed in English, with an English speaking cast, and directed by Alfred Lunt. Tyrone Guthrie staged a new production of *Carmen* that season, with Rise Stevens, emphasizing the earthier qualities of the characters, while Eugene Berman designed sets and costumes for *Rigoletto*, his first involvement with opera. He later created an excellent *Don Giovanni*. Hollywood's Joseph Mankiewicz came in 1952 to stage *La Boheme*, and Igor Stravinsky's *The Rake's Progress* was given, shortly after its premiere at the Venice Biennale. Actor Cyril Ritchard staged a spirited *Barber of Seville* in 1953, and Broadway director Jose Quintero supervised a *Cavalleria Rusticana/Pagliacci* double bill in 1958. The *Fledermaus* tradition was continued with a charming production of Offenbach's *La Perichole* in 1956, featuring Munsel, a less successful *Gypsy Baron* in 1959, and a disastrous *Martha* in 1960.

Bing persuaded Marian Anderson to make her opera debut early in 1955, as Ulrica in *Un Ballo in Maschera*. She was the first black artist to sing at the Metropolitan. The contralto was well past her prime and knew no opera from beginning to end. The short role of Ulrica served her well, particularly since the part required practically no acting. A delicate situation was handled with utmost tact, and Miss Anderson remembered her Metropolitan appearances as "a highlight of my life." Her success, and the respect she commanded, prepared the way for steady employment of other black singers: Mattiwilda Dobbs, George Shirley, Leontyne Price, Reri Grist, Grace Bumbry, Felicia Weathers, Martina Arroyo, Shirley Verrett.

American born Maria Callas was introduced at the Metropolitan on opening night, 1956, again as Norma. Her debut was surrounded by more glamor than the opera house had known in years. The diva was paid an inflated fee and even extended the privilege of taking solo bows. Bing later wrote, "her opening night was undoubtedly the most exciting of all such in my time at the Metropolitan." She also sang *Lucia di Lammermoor* and *Tosca* and added *La Traviata* the next season. Callas was the sort of performer about whom it was impossible to feel neutral. Listeners either loved her or hated her. She certainly had her vocal flaws, and the strain of her early singing days, when she was recklessly alternating Brunnhilde and Lucia, was already beginning to show. During a matinee performance someone threw a bunch of radishes on the stage. Fortunately Callas was so nearsighted she thought they were tea roses.

The soprano had sung amid some of the shabbiest sets in the Metropolitan warehouse. She had been promised a new production of Verdi's *Macbeth* for the 1958-59 season, in addition to more *Traviata*'s. The schedule Bing drew up required her to intersperse Lady Macbeth's dark, dramatic music with the florid role of Violetta. Callas objected. Bing offered to substitute *Lucia* for *Traviata*, an even greater contrast. The manager grew impatient, finally demanding that Callas let him know her plans by ten o'clock the next morning. When no reply came, he sent the singer a telegram of dismissal. To the press he explained that while the Metropolitan was "grateful for her artistry for two seasons," it was "nevertheless also grateful that the association is ended." *Macbeth* was produced with Leonard Warren in the title role and Leonie Rysanek as his lady.

Callas returned for two gala performances of *Tosca* in March, 1965. Ticket scalpers had a heyday. Standees began lining up outside the box office forty-eight hours in advance. The voice was smaller than most people remembered, the blemishes more exposed. But Callas played the part more deeply than before. "She did not sing well," Bing maintained, "but it made no difference whatever—never had there been such a *Tosca*. Nearly everything she ever did spoiled that opera for me; I never fully enjoyed any other artist in one of her roles after she did it. . . . She and Herbert von Karajan were the complete artists of my time at the Metropolitan."

Renata Tebaldi would remain the darling of the house for nearly two decades. She sang all of her great roles there and even talked Bing into staging her favorite vehicle, Cilea's *Adriana Lecouvreur*, twice, against his better judgment. "Tebaldi was always very sweet and very firm," the manager insisted; "I used to say she had dimples of iron." Leontyne Price and Franco Corelli made their debuts in 1961, in the same performance of *Il Trovatore*, immediately establishing themselves among the company's most valuable artists. Bing made no secret of his coolness toward Wagner, although this thawed considerably with the appearance of Birgit Nilsson in 1959. The Swedish soprano's voice was a marvel, as focused as a beam of light. She was introduced as Isolde, proving herself the most distinguished Wagnerian since Flagstad. In her first season she sang one performance of *Tristan* opposite three different tenors, all three ailing and therefore up to only one act each. "Fortunately," Bing told the audience in a brief curtain speech, "the opera has only three acts." The *Ring* cycle was restored for Nilsson. She made a *tour de force* of both *Salome* and *Elektra*, and for the first time at the Met doubled as Venus *and* Elisabeth in performances of *Tannhauser*. She was also heard in Italian opera—as Tosca, Aida, Amelia in *Ballo*, and especially Turandot. Puccini's last opera was unveiled in a new production in 1960, conducted by Stokowski, with Nilsson, Corelli, and Anna Moffo. It was one of the truly great productions in recent years.

Die Meistersinger in 1962 was another triumph, containing a second act set showing a street in Nuremberg that was at once expressive and realistic. *Falstaff* a year later was even more exciting, designed and staged by the young Italian director Franco Zeffirelli and conducted by Leonard Bernstein. Elisabeth Schwarzkopf came at last in 1964, singing eight Marschallins opposite the Octavian of Lisa Della Casa, acclaimed herself for her renditions of the Marschallin. Schwarzkopf was perhaps the Met's most glaring sin of omission. By the time she sang there her voice had to be handled carefully, although her Marschallin was radiant to look at, an emotional mixture of joy and pain.

While Bing's singers came from everywhere, American artists were not forgotten. George London, Rosalind Elias, Anna Moffo, Mary Costa, and Sherrill Milnes were but a few of the native voices to add luster to performances in the old house. Eileen Farrell was introduced in 1960 as Alceste and opened the season two years later as Maddalena in *Andrea Chenier*. She was buxom, plainspoken, but hers was another talent experienced at the Met too late. The American baritone Leonard Warren reached the high point of his career on March 1, 1960, with a new production of *Simon Boccanegra*. Three nights later, he died onstage during a performance of *La Forza del Destino*, in full view of the audience. His place in the opening night *Nabucco* the next season was taken by Cornell MacNeil.

The first world premiere of the Bing era was that given *Vanessa* in 1958 by Pennsylvania-born Samuel Barber. The original cast was headed by Steber, Elias, Nicolai Gedda, Giorgio Tozzi, and Regina Resnik as the almost mute Baroness. Mitropoulos conducted. The opera proved an interesting piece of theater with opportunities for real singing. An orchestral interlude and a quintet stood out as especially lovely. *Vanessa* was revived in 1964 with Mary Costa in the title role. One of the Met's more adventuresome efforts at contemporary opera was a 1958 staging of Alban Berg's *Wozzeck*. The work was generally well received and considered quite daring, although its world premiere had taken place in 1925. *Wozzeck* had been given twice before in the United States, but the Metropolitan's board of directors had haggled over the propriety of staging it for years. Gian-Carlo Menotti's *The Last Savage* was introduced by the company in 1963, after a lukewarm premiere in Paris. Bing maintained that his one complete success with modern opera was the revival of Britten's *Peter Grimes* in 1967. The conducting of Colin Davis and the stage direction of Tyrone Guthrie combined, the manager explained, "to convince even our more skeptical subscribers that they were in attendance at a great performance of a wonderful opera."

While the Metropolitan remains the foremost American stronghold of European grand opera, it has been less dynamic in both repertoire and casting than either the San Francisco Opera or the Lyric Opera of Chicago in recent years. Critics have suggested time and again that the New York company has become little more than a museum for the old operatic war horses. Many of the new ideas, to be sure, have been tried elsewhere first and are welcomed into the Metropolitan only after some of the freshness and excitement have gone. "With an unsubsidized company, the public is always right," Bing declared. "And that public loves what it knows—it is inalterably conservative. Europe can afford to do things the public doesn't necessarily want—it is an age-old tradition in Germany, for example—but we cannot afford to antagonize subscribers to that extent, no matter how heavily we may be subscribed at any one time. Subscribers are not ours till death do us part. They can get a divorce any time."

Expenses have soared at the Metropolitan, as everywhere else. The total budget when Bing took over hovered around two million dollars. By the 1966-67 season the figure was closer to fifteen million, and this has gone up alarmingly since. Box office receipts cover slightly more than seventy percent of the total costs, as ticket prices have steadily increased. The Vienna Staatsoper eliminates only thirty percent of its costs at the box office, Milan's La Scala only twenty percent. From twenty to twenty-five percent of the Met's annual deficit is made up by individual contributions. To break from established tradition—conventional operas, known singers, the accepted look—would mean that deficits would go still higher, and this the Metropolitan could not endure with its extended season and high standards. Consequently, the adventure of the new has been sacrificed.

All of this is made more critical by strong pressure from the unions. The management of the Metropolitan must deal with some fourteen separate unions. The autocratic Bing was determined not to be dictated to, and his fights with labor were notoriously stormy. The 1961-62 season was temporarily canceled when contract negotiations with the musicians' union became deadlocked. The great gold curtain might never have gone up that year had President Kennedy not intervened and sent his Secretary of Labor, Arthur Goldberg, to mediate. But the resolution was only temporary. The 1969-70 season opened three months late, after an even more exhausting stalemate. "I can't tell the American people how to handle their union situation," Bing said, "but this business of a bloody battle every year is such a *bore!*"

For its new productions the Metropolitan depends on private sponsorship and more recently donations from major business corporations. For the 1963-64 season American Export/Isbrandtsen Lines put up $110,000 for a new *Aida.* Eastern Airlines, from which the Met charters two planes for its spring tour, later gave $500,000 toward the cost of a *Ring* cycle. In 1963 the Ford Foundation awarded the company over three million dollars for the performance of contemporary works, while periodic gifts from the Metropolitan Opera Guild have made other productions possible.

In the summer of 1955, John D. Rockefeller III announced plans to transform a rundown section of upper Broadway into a center for the performing arts, with quarters for the Metropolitan, the Philharmonic, the New York City Opera, and other groups. Bing at first was not in favor of the move to Lincoln Center, although he was well aware of the shortcomings of the old house. But the Rockefellers insisted, and Bing finally yielded. "You can't fight the Royal Family," the manager said philosophically. Wallace K. Harrison, the architect of Radio City, was engaged to design the new Metropolitan Opera House. He made sketch after sketch, scale model upon scale model before the directors agreed upon a design. Time and again the date of opening night was pushed back, as costs mounted higher, ultimately coming to $45,700,000. Philharmonic Hall was completed first, but the acoustics there proved so inferior they had to be seriously modified. Fearing a similar disaster in the new opera house, Metropolitan officials thought it wise to try out the sound in advance. Without notice, a student matinee audience was transported by buses to Lincoln Center for a performance of *The Girl of the Golden West.* Reporters were barred. Before the music began technicians startled the students by firing blank cartridges to test the hall's reverberations. Fortunately all went well.

The old house closed with a gala farewell on April 16, 1966. Tickets had sold quickly, and scalpers enjoyed a brisk business. Since the old Metropolitan was slated to be torn down, pickets demonstrated outside the performance, in a fruitless campaign to "Save the Met." The program featured eleven conductors and sixty vocalists. Nilsson appeared, wearing the massive gold girdle-wreath that had been given her namesake, Christine Nilsson, on opening night eighty-three years before. She sang the Immolation Scene from *Gotterdammerung.* Milanov, who had sung her official farewell earlier in the week, was heard with Tucker in the final duet from *Andrea Chenier.* Then the gold curtains came down for the last time. The audience filed out slowly, many taking a backward glance. Souvenir hunters had already removed most of the metal plates designating seat numbers, and a student was seen in a balcony unscrewing a light bulb from one of the rosette lamps. Within a few weeks the wrecker's iron ball started swinging. Suddenly the Metropolitan was gone. "In the world's long history, it had been only a moment," John Briggs wrote. "But it had been a moment not without grandeur."

The first year at Lincoln Center brought one disaster after another. The uptown house opened, September 16, 1966, with the premiere of Samuel Barber's *Antony and Cleopatra*. The work cost a half million dollars to produce, starred Leontyne Price, and was designed and directed by Franco Zeffirelli. Since the new stage offered many technical advantages over the old one, the emphasis was on spectacle. Zeffirelli's Pyramid of Egypt burst open, and Cleopatra's barge glided toward the audience from a distance of 120 feet. The production almost overwhelmed Barber's music, although the score did include a few telling moments. Price seemed strangely out of place, stuck as she was for many minutes inside a huge golden sphinx. The whole season was overplanned. There was a total of nine new productions, four of them coming in the first week. The biggest success was an elaborate mounting of *Die Frau ohne Schatten*, with a cast headed by Rysanek, Ludwig, and Irene Dalis. Karl Bohm conducted. *La Gioconda* with Tebaldi showed the soprano's reworked voice to good advantage, while Marc Chagall's *Magic Flute* proved exciting. The painter had also provided two murals for the new house. Stagings of *La Traviata, Elektra, Lohengrin, Peter Grimes*, and Marvin David Levy's *Mourning Becomes Electra* were also introduced. It was the Metropolitan's most glittering offering in some time, but the season's budget went over its estimate by almost six million dollars.

There have been triumphs at the new Met. Herbert von Karajan came to conduct a new production of *Die Walkure* during the 1967-68 season and returned a season later for *Das Rheingold*. "Karajan was unquestionably the outstanding artistic phenomenon of my latter years at the Metropolitan," Bing wrote. The level of tension rose the moment he entered the house, for he set to work with an energy and professionalism not seen since Callas. The conductor paid attention to everything. The results were amazing, even though his reading of Wagner proved controversial. The 1969 strike interrupted the *Ring* cycle, which was resumed three years later under Erich Leinsdorf. Bing felt that the most important debuts of his later years were those of conductors: Bernstein, Georges Pretre, Zubin Mehta, Colin Davis, Alain Lombard. Yet singing was often exemplary. Joan Sutherland and Marilyn Horne joined for a lyric *Norma* in 1970. Tebaldi was heard for the first time as Minnie, and Zeffirelli designed a strong *Cavalleria/Pagliacci*. Massenet's *Werther* was given in 1971 with Corelli and Ludwig; *The Daughter of the Regiment* was borrowed from Covent Garden the following year for Sutherland and Luciano Pavarotti. Despite miscarriages along the way, the fresh point of view Bing had displayed in his first Metropolitan season—the originality and sparkle brought by designers and directors from the legitimate theater—continued through his last season, even if the repertoire itself remained limited.

Bing announced his retirement for the end of the 1971-72 season. There was another gala and much fanfare. Goeran Gentele, formerly of the Swedish Royal Opera was named his successor. Then tragedy struck. In July, 1972, eighteen days after taking over as general manager, Gentele was killed in an automobile accident in Sardinia. Two of his daughters died with him. He had appointed Rafael Kubelik as music director and Schuyler G. Chapin as assistant manager. Chapin was now elevated to acting general manager, the first American to head the company. A production of *Carmen*, conceived by Gentele and which the new manager was to have staged, opened the 1972-73 season. Leonard Bernstein conducted, using spoken dialogue in place of the customary recitatives. Marilyn Horne sang Carmen; James McCracken was Don Jose.

Horne made a charming Isabella in Rossini's *Italiana in Algeri* the next season, and Berlioz's *Les Troyens* was finally staged in the house, with Jon Vickers and Shirley Verrett. Caballe was heard in *Norma* and Verdi's *I Vespri Siciliani*, while contemporary works like Britten's *Death in Venice*, Berg's *Lulu*, and Weill's *Rise and Fall of the City of Mahagonny* were staged successfully. Beverly Sills made a belated Met debut in 1975 in the same opera that had brought her acclaim at La Scala a few years before, Rossini's *The Siege of Corinth*. Later in 1975 Anthony Bliss took over as executive director of the Metropolitan, aided by James Levine as music director and John Dexter as director of production. Under this arrangement Sutherland appeared in Massenet's *Esclarmonde;* Meyerbeer's *Le Prophete* was rediscovered, with Horne, James McCracken, and Renata Scotto; and Placido Domingo sang his first American Otello. Luciano Pavarotti became a vital force, while Scotto grew into the leading Italian dramatic soprano, eventually assuming all three soprano roles in Puccini's *Trittico*. Sylvia Saas made her United States debut in 1977 as Tosca, the same year that Scotto and Pavarotti joined for the first "live" telecast from the Metropolitan stage. The opera, *La Boheme*, was so well received that telecasts from the major American opera houses have since become an important part of the nation's cultural life.

With the Metropolitan's move to its new house, the company came into close proximity of its chief in-town rival, the New York City Opera, now just across the plaza from the Met. Founded by Laszlo Halasz, the New York City Opera Company was launched on February 21, 1944, with a performance of *Tosca*. For twenty-two years the company operated in the cramped, musty shambles of the New York City Center on Fifty-fifth Street. During that time it built up an amazing record for pioneering. Over half of the company's repertoire were contemporary operas, most of them world or American premieres. Among the best of the modern works have been Prokofiev's *Flaming Angel*, Shostokovich's *Katerina Ismailova*, Poulenc's *Carmelites*, Ginastera's *Bomarzo*, Weisgall's *Six Characters in Search of an Author*, Jack Beeson's *Lizzie Borden*, Robert Kurka's *Good Soldier Schweik*, and Britten's *Midsummer Night's Dream*. American operas have included Douglas Moore's *The Ballad of Baby Doe* and *The Wings of the Dove*, Robert Ward's *The Crucible* and *He Who Gets Slapped*, Carlisle Floyd's *Susannah*, Blitzstein's *Regina*, and Dello Joio's *Triumph of Saint Joan*. With the aid of the Ford Foundation, the company presented ten new American operas in five weeks during the spring of 1958. Eight more were added the next year.

But the New York City Opera has given its share of *Boheme*'s and *Traviata*'s and successfully mixed grand opera in the original language with lighter works in English translation. It has offered Gilbert and Sullivan and Broadway productions like *Show Boat, Street Scene,* and *Porgy and Bess.* More than any other American company the New York City Opera has given native singers a chance to develop: Dorothy Kirsten, Brenda Lewis, Phyllis Curtin, Norman Treigle, Frances Bible, Gilda Cruz-Romo, and scores more. Within recent years the company has raised its very own superstar in Beverly Sills, acclaimed from Milan to the Rio Grande Valley. American music and stage directors have also been given repeated opportunities. Since 1957 the company has been guided by Julius Rudel, one of its original conductors. Audiences at the City Opera tend to be younger than those at the Metropolitan, generally more responsive, and far more informal. Ticket prices are less than half what the Met charges.

The City Opera moved into the handsome, well-equipped New York State Theater at Lincoln Center in February, 1966, opening with Placido Domingo in Ginastera's *Don Rodrigo.* Since leaving City Center there have been appreciably fewer contemporary operas, although the company's biggest successes have been far from routine. Handel's *Julius Caesar* with Treigle and Sills brought raves from the critics. So did *Manon* and *Mefistofele.* But perhaps Rudel's unqualified triumph has been a cycle of Donizetti's rarely heard Tudor trilogy—*Roberto Devereaux, Maria Stuarda,* and *Anna Bolena*—staged in successive years for Sills. And yet while the New York City Opera is not quite as experimental as it once was, modern works are still important. Britten's *Albert Herring,* Hoiby's *Summer and Smoke,* Ginastera's *Beatrix Cenci,* Henze's *Young Lord,* and Robert Ward's *Hedda Gabler* have all been staged since the move to the new quarters.

Since World War II the proliferation of opera companies across the country has been fairly astonishing. Among the most imaginative has been the Opera Company of Boston, founded in 1965, under the leadership of Sarah Caldwell. The lady has proved a veritable dynamo; she not only serves as producer-manager, but occasionally conducts. The company staged the United States premiere of Nono's anti-Fascist satire *Intolleranza* in 1965 and the first American production of Schoenberg's *Moses and Aaron* a year later. When *The Rake's Progress* was given in 1967, Sarah Caldwell lifted Tom Rakewell out of the eighteenth century and put him in the "mod" world of contemporary London, replete with leather, pad, motorcycle, and Art Nouveau. *Bluebeard's Castle* and Kurka's *The Good Soldier Schweik* have been presented, and the world premiere of Gunther Schuller's *The Fisherman and His Wife,* with text by John Updike. More traditional works have regularly been mounted: the original version of *Boris Godunov,* Rossini's *Semiramide* with Sutherland and Horne, Berlioz's *Les Troyens.* And casting has often been interesting; Beverly Sills, for instance, sang her first Norma with the company in 1971.

Yet from the standpoint of singers, the Dallas Civic Opera has commanded even more attention. Formed in 1957 by Lawrence Kelly, the company enjoyed a great deal of financial backing from community leaders who felt the time had come for their city to display culture and plenty of it. Kelly had just lost out in the court battle with Carol Fox over control of the Chicago Lyric and was eager to show what he could do on his own. He brought with him an initial ace—an agreement from Maria Callas to sing during his first Dallas season. The company was therefore assured national publicity. But Kelly also brought Nicola Rescigno as musical director, Broadway's Jean Rosenthal as production manager, and Franco Zeffirelli as stage director, his first work in America.

A concert by Callas initiated the project on November 21, 1957. The next evening the company revealed a stunning production of Rossini's *Italiana in Algeri*, designed by Zeffirelli and featuring Giulietta Simionato. "For a couple of nights running," *Newsweek* wrote, "Dallas was the operatic capital of the United States." Callas returned in 1958 for *La Traviata*, produced by Zeffirelli, and an unforgettable *Medea*, staged by Alexis Minotis of the Greek National Theater. The first performance of *Medea* coincided with the famed Bing firing of Callas, and excitement ran high onstage and off. "Dallas," the Metropolitan manager noted in his memoirs, "was starting a short celebrity opera season with deficits for three weeks that approximated ours for thirty-one weeks." But Kelly gained civic support and international recognition. Initially the Dallas Civic Opera tried to orient itself along a close Milan-Dallas axis, while carefully avoiding anything that resembled what the Metropolitan was doing. La Scala's retiring chorus master, Noberto Mola, was even acquired by the Texas company in 1963.

During the summer of 1958 the entire *Medea* production was loaned to the Royal Opera, London, in exchange for an acclaimed Zeffirelli staging of *Lucia di Lammermoor*, which in Dallas starred Callas. Joan Sutherland made her United States debut with the company in 1960 in Zeffirelli's handsome Venice production of Handel's *Alcina*, an American premiere. Although the Dallas Civic Opera slowly built its own permanent repertory, several physical productions were borrowed from Europe over the next decade—*The Daughter of the Regiment* from Palermo in 1960, Lila de Nobili's *La Boheme* from Spoleto in 1961, *Fedora* from Milan in 1969. Besides Sutherland's United States debut, Dallas has enjoyed those of Montserrat Caballe, Jon Vickers, Teresa Berganza, Gwyneth Jones, Placido Domingo, Helga Dernesch, and the legendary Italian soprano Magda Olivero.

The company's 1963 season was dampened by the assassination of President John F. Kennedy in Dallas. Ironically, on the night after the tragedy a performance of Verdi's *Un Ballo in Maschera*, dealing with the slaying of a respected king, was scheduled. The season was rearranged, as the nation and the city adjusted to a tragedy too deep for understanding. Choristers and orchestra members stood around in shocked silence, while European performers tried to offer condolences. American singer Regina Resnik left the stage weeping after her final performance of *Carmen*; but the season was completed.

The Dallas Civic Opera management realized early that it would have to build an operatic tradition in the city, a task facing new opera companies across the country. The first student matinee was given in 1961, when Dallas financier H. L. Hunt underwrote a performance of *La Boheme*. To involve young people even more closely with the opera season, a poster contest was held in 1967 for children in grades five, six, and seven. The winning design became the program cover for that season. Gradually the company has become part of the city, although its place frequently seems like a tentative one. The enthusiast may grow optimistic about the appreciation of music in Texas after a capacity audience has given a standing ovation to an almost perfect production of Puccini's *Il Tabarro*, only to have these hopes dashed a few nights later when a similar audience bestows practically the same ovation on a positively wretched performance of *Rigoletto*. To attract the younger generation in 1970, the company brought in Bertrand Castelli, producer of the rock musical *Hair*, to stage *Carmina Burana*. Many found the production fresh and relevant, yet it cost the Dallas Civic Opera three of its older backers who withdrew something like $170,000. As a result the season finished with checks bouncing and bills going unpaid. The next year the company returned to Donizetti and Saint-Saens and let Beethoven provide the novelty.

Whereas most American opera companies, particularly the younger ones, have found modern opera hazardous, the Santa Fe Opera, like the Opera Company of Boston, has consistently thrived on it. The whole atmosphere at Santa Fe is conducive to experimentation. Located five miles north of the New Mexico city on director John Crosby's ranch, the company gave its first performance on July 3, 1957. The outdoor theater is extremely picturesque, built on a pinon-covered hillside, with the Sangre de Cristo mountains as a backdrop. When the original structure burned during the 1967 season, it was replaced by an open, redwood-faced pueblo seating 1450. The acoustics are close to perfect.

The Santa Fe Opera is a true repertory company in the European tradition. Although its featured singers are sometimes artists of some repute, one may play the lead this night and a subordinate role the next. The company offers an apprenticeship program for student singers, ballet dancers, directors, and conductors, along with its summer opera season. The young artists receive fifteen hours of instruction each week and a weekly living expense. In return they give twenty-five hours a week to the company— helping at rehearsals, playing bit parts, or serving as members of the chorus. Most of the company's productions are sung in English, which in the intimate theater comes across fairly well.

Audiences are offered a blend of contemporary works, rarely heard operas, and the standard classics. The company has given the world premiere of Marvin David Levy's *The Tower*, Carlisle Floyd's *Wuthering Heights*, Villa-Lobos' *Yerma*, and Luciano Berio's *Opera*. It has staged the American premiere of Berg's *Lulu*, Hindemith's *News of the Day* and *Cardillac*, Shostakovich's *The Nose*, Strauss' *Daphne*, Henze's *The Stag King* and *Boulevard Solitude*, Penderecki's *Devils of Loudun*, and Menotti's *Help! Help! the Globolinks*. For six summers Igor Stravinsky came to Santa Fe to supervise and conduct his operas, including the American premiere of *Persephone*. But traditional works are also mounted: the first American performance of Donizetti's *Anna Bolena* in over a century, Puccini's *Gianni Schicchi* with Jose Ferrer, Wagner's *The Flying Dutchman*, Mozart, Verdi, Bizet, Gilbert and Sullivan, Offenbach. Although contemporary operas offer much more of a production problem than the standard works, the Santa Fe Opera finds the burden and expense worthwhile. It was estimated, for example, that *Lulu* in 1963 required fifty hours of orchestra rehearsal, as opposed to twelve hours for *Madama Butterfly*. Yet *Butterfly* sold out for six performances, while *Lulu* could scarcely fill two.

Santa Fe, according to Mary Jane Matz, "represents the best in avant-garde operatic thinking in the United States." The company, however, enjoys certain advantages which most American opera producers do not. While its performances are highly professional, its mountings are not as costly as those of the larger houses. Then too, the company is able to capitalize on Santa Fe's large summer tourist trade as a guarantee of a substantial audience. In a vacation environment patrons seem less reluctant to try something new, in opera as other areas. And since so many tourists attend the Santa Fe Opera, financial aid comes from all over the country. Santa Fe is the only company besides the Metropolitan to receive national support.

The Central City Opera House Association, another summertime operation, is much more conservative. The old Colorado mining town is a haven for vacationers, who find attending its historic opera house an attractive way to spend an evening. The house was reopened in 1932, amid a calculated frontier atmosphere. Onstage was Dumas' *Camille*, featuring Lillian Gish and directed by Robert Edmund Jones. Outside there were ore-digging contests, fire runs, and Faro games. The company's first opera was given in 1940: Smetana's *The Bartered Bride*, sung in English, with Colorado native Josephine Antoine heading the cast. Frank St. Leger conducted. Since then two operas have generally been presented each summer, with young singers from the Metropolitan and the New York City Opera Company. The Central City Opera House seats only 794 people, so that productions take on a unique charm. The offering has covered a wide spectrum: *The Barber of Seville*, *Orpheus ed Eurydice*, *The Abduction from the Seraglio*, *Martha*, *Aida*, *Fidelio*, *The Tales of Hoffmann*, *Rigoletto*, *Die Fledermaus*, *Il Trovatore*, *Ariadne auf Naxos*, and several seasons of Gilbert and Sullivan. Although contemporary opera has been by no means Central City's long suit, the association did stage the world premieres of Moore's *The Ballad of Baby*

Doe in 1956 and Ward's *Lady from Colorado* in 1964, and mounted Floyd's *Of Mice and Men* in 1970.

The nation's oldest summer opera festival, the Cincinnati Summer Opera, is also the second oldest American opera company. Begun in 1921, in part to provide off-season employment for members of the Cincinnati Orchestra, the company received great initial support from the Taft family. An open-air theater was built in the Cincinnati Zoological Garden and a production of *Martha* was staged. Abandoned for a time during the Depression, operas were presented at the pavilion in the zoo each summer between 1935 and 1971. After a period of considerable floundering in the 1950s, Fausto Cleva was brought in as music director. Audiences found it pleasant to stroll through the greenery of the zoo before performances and became accustomed to listening to opera interlaced with the unsolicited barking of seals and the cackle of the hyena. But there were performances to remember—Schwarzkopf's very last Marschallin in 1967, Bellini's *Il Pirata* with Caballe in 1969. The pavilion in the zoo, however, became increasingly shabby, while the summer humidity was sometimes unbearable. Consequently the company moved into the refurbished Music Hall in 1972, where production standards were much improved.

If the summer opera festivals in the United States are diversified, winter seasons are no less so. Philadelphia has two opera companies—the Philadelphia Lyric Opera and the Philadelphia Grand Opera, an auxiliary of the Philadelphia Orchestra. Both of these give performances in the Academy of Music, sometimes on consecutive nights. The city prefers the standard repertoire, although the Grand Opera did give Mascagni's *L'Amico Fritz* in 1971, while the Lyric earlier staged in successive years the American premieres of Renzo Rossellini's *A View from the Bridge*, Bellini's *I Capuleti e I Montecchi* with Renata Scotto, and Donizetti's *Lucrezia Borgia* with Caballe.

More experimental is the Opera Society of Washington, D.C., formed in 1956, which collaborates with the National Symphony Orchestra. The company has undertaken with good success productions of *Ariadne auf Naxos, The Rake's Progress, Falstaff, Pelleas and Melisande,* Menotti's *Maria Golovin,* Haydn's *L'Infedelta Delusa,* Rossini's *Comte Ory,* Delius' *Koanga* and the world premiere of Ginastera's *Bomarzo.* The Opera Society relies on young professional singers and directors and utilizes the Washington Ballet. Since May, 1971, its home has been the Opera House in the John F. Kennedy Center for the Performing Arts.

The Baltimore Civic Opera benefitted from the direction of Rosa Ponselle, while the Opera Guild of Greater Miami, first under the management of Arturo Di Filippi and now under Robert Herman, in collaboration with the University of Miami, produces three operas a year in their original languages. The Florida company began in 1941, with a staging of *Pagliacci.* That production cost $1200, and Dr. Di Filippi sang the role of Canio. Twenty-five years later the company was spending over $100,000 per opera and employing singers like Sutherland, Corelli, and

Farrell. The Miami organization also offers a program of "family operas," using young singers in leading roles.

Resident opera returned to New Orleans during the summer of 1943, when an outdoor season of popular-priced operas was presented in City Park. Encouraged by the attendance at these performances, the New Orleans Opera House Association was formed, with Walter Herbert as musical director. An indoor season was launched in Municipal Auditorium the following fall. Despite vast financial difficulties, the company has generally presented six operas a year, spread over the fall, winter, and spring.

Interesting, in that it is presented within the framework of the Symphony Society, is the San Antonio Opera Festival. Added to extend the symphony season, the opera festival originally consisted of four productions given on two successive spring weekends. Victor Alessandro conducted until his death in 1976. While San Antonio prefers grand opera sung in the original language by name singers, the Kansas City Lyric Theater, initiated in 1957, has had good success with opera in English, a more experimental repertoire, and young performers. The Seattle Opera Association has engaged in some interesting casting since its inception in 1964, although its repertoire has remained fairly traditional. In Seattle Sutherland sang *Lakme* for the first time in her career in 1967, as well as all four heroines of *Tales of Hoffmann* three years later. Entertainer Edie Adams made her operatic debut with the Seattle company in 1972, singing the lead in Offenbach's *La Perichole*.

And so the pattern goes in urban areas from coast to coast. The opera companies in operation in 1945 have grown; dozens more have been organized. Most of the smaller civic opera groups tend to be conservative in their offering, but unusual items are presented from time to time. The New Orleans Opera House Association staged Verdi's *Attila* in 1969 for the first time in the United States since 1850; the Connecticut Opera Association offered Madga Olivero that same year in her first American performance of *Adriana Lecouvreur*; the San Antonio Symphony mounted Verdi's *Nabucco* before the Metropolitan revived interest in it and in 1970 staged Puccini's *La Rondine* for Moffo. The Houston Grand Opera Association added Massenet's *Don Quichotte* to its repertoire in 1969, while the San Diego Opera gave the world premiere of Henderson's *Medea* in 1972 with Irene Dalis in the title role. The Fort Worth Opera Association presented Donizetti's *L'Elisir d'amore* in 1973 with its setting changed from an Italian village around 1800 to the Texas panhandle of 1840. Dr. Dulcamara became a patent medicine vendor; Adina, a rich rancher's daughter; Nemorino, a lovesick cowboy.

Opera in the United States is probably more diversified than that presented anywhere else in the world. Besides the major companies and the civic opera groups, there are New York enterprises like the American Opera Society and the Little Orchestra Society that specialize in highly esoteric works for select listeners. There are the NBC Television productions and PBC "live" broadcasts, that attempt to reach a mass audience, and occasional offerings in Aspen and the Red Rocks Theater on the slopes of the Colorado

Rockies. And there is Grass Roots Opera, like that in Amarillo, Texas, which in 1971 staged *Tosca* and *Die Fledermaus*. The operas were sponsored by the Federated Music Clubs, with admission free. "Amarillo businessmen are behind it!" advertisements assured. "Y'ALL COME!"

From 1909 until 1955, Fortune Gallo's San Carlo Opera toured the United States, giving opera at low prices to cities large and small. The company was named for the opera house in Naples and was always self-supporting. The whole music business knew "Papa" Gallo, who arrived in this country from Italy with twelve cents in his pocket. He began working as a bill collector for the New York City gas company. His career in music began when he came upon a stranded Italian band and booked them into an empty Yorkville theater. The San Carlo Opera traveled by every means available and invariably had budget problems. When one conductor complained that there were only fifteen men in the orchestra and for *Traviata* he needed at least twenty-eight, Gallo supposedly told him: "That's all right. Have them play twice as loud, and I'll give them a bonus." Yet the San Carlo performances were seldom shoddy. Gallo's singers were adequate and well rehearsed, while the ensemble was sometimes more spirited than those of the big, important theaters. Some of his performers later became famous: Coe Glade, Dorothy Kirsten, Eugene Conley, Jean Madeira. Gallo also became director of two New York savings banks, and he knew how to get his money's worth. During one San Carlo performance the manager reputedly saw his harpist having a cigarette outside the theater. Gallo asked why he had left the pit.

"There is no harp part in this opera," the musician replied.

"Well, come inside and I'll write one," Gallo stormed. "I'm not paying anybody to walk the streets."

Besides its regular spring tour, the Met ran a special touring company for two seasons, the Metropolitan Opera National Company. The subsidiary was comanaged by singer Rise Stevens and former executive stage manager Michael Manuel. It made its first tour during the 1965-66 season, presenting low cost productions with young artists. The aim was to stimulate a nationwide taste for opera by bringing quality performances to cities that saw little or none otherwise. But the Met's overextension after the move to Lincoln Center forced the National Company's disbandment. More lasting has been the Goldovsky Opera Theatre, which began to tour during the 1964-65 season, visiting eighty-five American cities. The Goldovsky company offers scaled-down productions, with a small orchestra and chorus, but has nevertheless established a reputation for quality. The New York City Opera has undertaken a substantial amount of touring, especially throughout the Midwest, although it plays an extensive season in Los Angeles.

Opera workshops on college and university campuses, as well as private music schools, present several productions a year, many of them quite good and some worthy of national attention. The Juilliard School of Music, for instance, occasionally offers performances of works previously unknown to New York. The School of Music of Indiana University, Bloomington, stages an ambitious repertoire each year, including since 1949 an annual Palm Sunday production of *Parsifal*. The performance is attended by hundreds of people from all over the state, and a special *Parsifal* supper is served in the Union Building during a long intermission. Bob Jones University in Greenville, South Carolina, also has an impressive opera program, as do the University of Southern California, the University of Denver, and the University of Washington in Seattle. The opera workshop movement received great impetus around 1947, in part from the success of two works by Gian-Carlo Menotti, *The Medium* and *The Telephone*. The first was commissioned from the Alice M. Ditson Fund and was initially performed during the 1946 contemporary music festival at Columbia University. It made such a strong impression that it was taken to Broadway with a professional cast; *The Telephone* was added as a curtain raiser. Many composers began writing especially for opera workshops, which welcome contemporary pieces and offer the best possibilities for getting a new opera staged.

With all of the opportunities there are for hearing opera, it might appear that the art has at last become domesticated. Such an assumption would be too optimistic. Much of the nation's operatic experience is limited to a few centers, and even there a brief season exists somewhat in a vacuum. Most of the American opera companies are young, while the tradition they are building is scarcely more than surface. Each urban area has its opera lovers, but they exist as an exclusive cult. The millions go untouched. Even the Saturday afternoon Metropolitan broadcasts must wait until the autumn football schedule is over. Television, films, and amateur productions may bring a brush with opera to a broader public, but even the voice of Tebaldi coming from the mouth of Sophia Loren (as it once did in a film version of *Aida*) is not likely to attract a mass audience.

Most of the American opera public are professional people and students. Although the number is proportionately small, more blue collar workers are found at opera than at other cultivated art forms, a fact in part explained by immigration. While the opera cult is growing, the art's advance toward becoming mass culture is slow indeed. Americans still become self-conscious and pretentious when they approach opera, and it is viewed by the general public with a double-edged suspicion, symbolizing for them both pretentious art and effete society. Only occasionally will this bias be temporarily shattered by the presence of a commanding singer, but apathy is quick to return. Americans still tend to perceive opera with the head rather than the heart and miss much of the magic worrying over words they cannot understand. Cultivating a taste for a foreign art is a slow process. Obstacles easily get in the way, especially when the art costs as much as opera. In Europe, where there is vast government subsidy, ticket prices for the less expensive seats for opera would be roughly the price of movie admissions in the United States. Admission fees are simply too high in America to attract a casual public to opera. But Americans admire success in any area. If a singer or a specific opera production gains enough recognition that the mass media take notice, then the general public may become aware and even interested. This is the exception, however, not the rule. Limited though opera's support was in the United States at the turn of the century, the society leaders that kept the art going then were dependable. In a less aristocratic society audiences and patrons do not have the earlier commitment; they are more given to whims, more easily lured away. And yet the expense of producing opera continues to soar.

The spread of opera across the country has been a conspicuous part of the post-World War II cultural boom. The demand for tickets from each of the several opera companies and the sale of longplaying records has been encouraging. The problem is that a few people are doing all the buying. In Italy Fiat runs chartered buses to La Scala, while in this country we charter buses only for athletic events. Opera is simply not a very important part of our overall life, only for a fraction of the educated upper-middle class and a few recent immigrants. Therefore, while Americans are enjoying more opera than ever before, its future—even in prosperous times—remains precarious. The civic opera groups live from season to season, attempting one plan after another to achieve a firm financial base. Until opera filters down to a larger segment of the public, a solution to these economic straits will probably stay elusive. Unless it becomes an integral part of the American mainstream, grand opera will likely remain what it has always been in this free enterprise society—a regal but eternal pauper.

BALLET AND MODERN

DANCE

The last of the two American tours of Diaghilev's Ballet Russes came during the 1916-17 season. The company had caused a passing furor, but little more. Pavlova continued to dance in the United States extensively throughout World War I and into the early 1920s. She gave performances in cities and towns and villages across the country, sometimes as many as seven or eight a week, and spent a half year at the Hippodrome in New York. Her final American tour ended in 1926. The ballerina died at The Hague in January, 1931. More than anyone else she had sown the seeds of later balletic development in the United States.

Between Pavolova's last appearance and the advent of Colonel Wassily de Basil's Ballet Russe de Monte Carlo in 1933 there were few advances in building a classical dance tradition and no major company in existence giving American performances. Adolph Bolm's group traveled the country in 1927 with Ruth Page as its premiere danseuse, but the troupe was too small to offer the standard ballet repertory. Diaghilev died in Venice in 1929, leaving the world without any Russian ballet company that toured. Then in 1931 Colonel de Basil and Rene Blum, a Frenchman with a taste for culture, founded the Ballet Russe de Monte Carlo, under the patronage of the Prince of Monaco. Since the Russian Revolution the Monacan royalty had offered self-exiled Russian dancers security and ideal working conditions in the sophisticated atmosphere of Monte Carlo. The troupe that de Basil and Blum formed there became the heir to the Diaghilev legacy, soon emerging as the most important touring dance company in the world. For a brief time George Balanchine was ballet master, but Leonide Massine was shortly appointed chief choreographer, when Balanchine left to organize his own troupe. Alexandra Danilova was senior ballerina for the Ballet Russe, Irina Baronova one of several "baby ballerinas."

But the Monte Carlo company was much more conservative than Diaghilev's had been. Many of the exiles from Russia tried valiantly to maintain what they could of Tsarist traditions. Most Russian connoisseurs of the ballet, especially members of the nobility and upper classes, had viewed Diaghilev's modernism with disfavor, looking back with nostalgia to the Imperial Russian ballet they recalled from Moscow and St. Petersburg. The old-time balletophiles were quite influential in the dance world of the 1920s and early 1930s, while Diaghilev came to be regarded as a renegade. De Basil, his successor, however, was a former Tsarist colonel, and his attitude toward ballet was rooted in the past. It was this more traditional approach that the Ballet Russe de Monte Carlo brought to the United States under the management of Sol Hurok, another Russian and a balletophile.

The company opened at the St. James Theatre in New York on December 21, 1933. The venture was one of considerable financial risk, especially since the dancers were unknown to Americans, and the troupe's arrival had been preceded long in advance by a sensational publicity campaign. Its repertoire included *Les Sylphides, Prince Igor, Petrouchka,* and other productions from the Diaghilev days, as well as new ballets by Massine, among them the symphonic ballets for which he became noted. These utilized music from Tchaikovsky's Fifth, Brahms' Fourth, and Berlioz's *Symphonie Fantastique,* but there were also lighter Massine works, like the popular *Gaite Parisienne.* Baronova's adolescent beauty and amazing technical facility attracted much attention. The company's productions generally were well mounted, impressed a broad audience on the tour that followed the brief New York season, and launched a new era for ballet in America. Financially the enterprise proved nearly disastrous. But Hurok persisted, bringing the company back season after season for cross-country tours, until Ballet Russe became almost synonymous with the ballet in the mind of the American public.

In 1934 Massine created *Union Pacific,* on a scenario by Archibald MacLeish, the first ballet on an American theme given by a Russian company. The Ballet Russe de Monte Carlo added to its prestige the next year by appearing at the Metropolitan Opera House. But there were internal conflicts. Rene Blum withdrew in 1936 to form a company that would restrict itself almost exclusively to the principality of Monaco. Differences between de Basil and Massine had been growing over the years, with the result that the Ballet Russe split in 1938. De Basil headed one unit, Massine the other. The two resembled each other like twins. De Basil's troupe functioned under a number of names, the most familiar of which was the Original Ballet Russe, while Massine's company retained the parent name and established itself more permanently. Both directors attempted at first to maintain a predominantly Russian ensemble and repertory, but gradually included non-Russian elements as well. Even when English and Canadian dancers were added, they frequently masqueraded under pseudo-Slavic names. Slowly Americans infiltrated the *corps de ballet* and eventually came to hold minor positions. Although Massine offered such works as *The New Yorker,* *Saratoga,* and *Ghost Town,* his Ballet Russe remained essentially European in flavor, even after World War II forced the company to take up headquarters in New York.

Much of the company's support during the war came from the American Julius Fleischman. But by 1941 both segments of the Ballets Russes were showing signs of deterioration. Massine, as chief choreographer and leading dancer of the one, was wearing down, and increased managerial disagreements added to the burden. Consequently he left the company in 1942. With Massine's departure the policy of the Ballet Russe de Monte Carlo changed rapidly. This was first evident in the fall of 1942 when Agnes de Mille choreographed *Rodeo,* with music by Aaron Copland. Not only was the Russian company dealing with a pleasant piece of Americana, but it was presenting ballet of a new genre. *Rodeo* dealt with folk in common dress and casual parlance, thereby humanizing ballet for a wider public. The work was first given at the Metropolitan Opera House, where it was hailed by nineteen curtain calls. Its deliberate lightness of touch and unqualified success marked a turning point for ballet in America. The Ballet Russe soon invited other native choreographers to contribute to its offering, while the Russian artists and the classical repertory began losing ground. Gradually the prewar Ballet Russe seemed old-fashioned, as the old decors and costumes faded, but not until the company had roused Americans to the beauties and excitement of great ballet.

As the Ballet Russe de Monte Carlo was making its New York debut in 1933, two young Americans, Lincoln Kirstein and Edward M. M. Warburg, were rounding out plans for establishing the School of American Ballet. The school opened in January, 1934, in New York, under the direction of George Balanchine and Vladimir Dimitriew, formerly a tenor with the Maryinsky Theater. Its founders envisioned a school not only for training American dancers and choreographers, but also as a base from which a performing company might one day emerge. In the fall of 1934 a unit of the school presented four ballets, all by Balanchine, in Hartford, Connecticut. The American Ballet Company made its New York debut at the Adelphi Theater in March, 1935, with guest artists augmenting the school's second-year students. The engagement was successful enough to be extended from one week to two and brought an invitation from the Metropolitan Opera for the American Ballet to become its resident company, a union which did not prove satisfactory. Two years later the American Ballet again appeared as an independent organization, offering a program of three works by Stravinsky.

Balanchine served as a link between traditional Russian ballet and the modern American forms. He was educated in the Imperial schools, trained as a choreographer under Diaghilev, but was not afraid to experiment. He had initially planned to become a concert pianist, and his musical knowledge was exceptionally thorough for a dancer. Even his early work was full of subtlety, employing intricacies of rhythm and making use of counterpoint. Born in St. Petersburg, Balanchine left Russia in 1924, at the age of twenty. He was brought to the United States in September, 1933 by Kirstein and Warburg expressly to launch the School of American Ballet, which Balanchine planned to pattern after the Imperial schools of Russia. But the American Ballet reflected his advanced ideas from the beginning. Balanchine proved both a great choreographer and a sensitive teacher-director. He eagerly adapted Russian training methods to American temperaments and was enthusiastic about creating ballets for an American style as yet unformulated. Although his works remained formal in shape, Balanchine added color by borrowing colloquialisms from American square dances and syncopated steps from the popular theater.

A subsidiary of the American Ballet was the Ballet Caravan, which performed on tour. The smaller troupe devoted itself exclusively to the work of American choreographers, but was later combined with the parent organization. The San Francisco Opera Ballet was established by Adolph Bolm in 1933, becoming the San Francisco Ballet under William Christensen. In 1935 the Philadelphia Ballet was founded by Catherine Littlefield, who served both as chief choreographer and star dancer. While the Philadelphia company produced one of the first full-length stagings of *The Sleeping Beauty* in America (1937), its reputation rested mainly on contemporary ballets. Ruth Page and Bentley Stone formed a company bearing their names in 1937. The Page-Stone Ballet Company made its headquarters in Chicago, although it traveled extensively, bringing contemporary ballet to towns and cities across the nation. Ruth Page also served as ballet mistress and choreographer for the assorted Chicago opera enterprises and worked with the dance project of the Federal Theater in Chicago, begun in 1935 under the auspices of the Works Progress Administration. She created one of the pioneer American ballets, *Frankie and Johnny*, which was originally produced by the Federal Theater, later given by the Page-Stone Company, and eventually incorporated into the repertory of the Ballet Russe de Monte Carlo.

During the decades when the Russians dominated ballet in the United States, few Americans were able to win positions of leadership. William Christensen, Catherine Littlefield, and Ruth Page were the exceptions, but even they were wise enough not to attempt a conquest of New York. Instead they located in major theatrical centers outside the American stronghold of the Ballet Russe, affiliating themselves with existing opera houses, a pattern long prevalent in Europe.

Although Americans made slight inroads into ballet before World War II, they remained pivotal to the development of modern dance. In fact the balletic drought between Pavolova's last appearance and the reawakening of interest in the ballet prompted by the arrival of the Ballet Russe de Monte Carlo may actually have aided the advance of modernism, since the lack of an established tradition provided the second generation of American dancers the latitude in which to innovate. There were no established companies, and ballet choreographers were limited to special engagements and used dancers brought together for that occasion. They often performed in vaudeville houses and movie palaces under conditions that were far from ideal, but audiences were flexible in attitude and the larger theaters at least paid good money. When Massine came to the United States in 1928 as ballet master and premier danseur of the Roxy Theatre in New York, he found the environment abominable, gave four shows a day, yet amassed a fortune that made him financially independent for the rest of his career. For the experimentalists there was the freedom to gain confidence and try out new ideas, much as young Ruth St. Denis and Ted Shawn had done earlier.

The Denishawn dancers were still performing Oriental, Spanish, and Indian dances in vaudeville when Martha Graham, the most famous of the Denishawn students, arrived at the school in 1916. She had become fascinated with dance during her junior year in high school after seeing a performance by Ruth St. Denis. "Miss Ruth opened a door for me," Graham later wrote, "and I passed through it." Born in 1893 near Pittsburgh, Pennsylvania, Martha Graham was of Puritan and Presbyterian stock; her mother was a descendant of Miles Standish. As a child Martha was taken to California to live, and she grew up in a conservative family environment in Santa Barbara. Her father, a neurologist, insisted that he always knew when his daughters were lying because their muscles involuntarily betrayed them. Since he disapproved of the theater, Martha waited until after his death to persuade her mother to let her study dance in Los Angeles with Denishawn.

She was not a lovely or graceful young woman, as Isadora Duncan and St. Denis had been. She was shy, intense, awkward, older than most beginning dance students. Her body seemed unsuited to the flowing motions and delicate gestures that emanated from St. Denis. Ted Shawn suggested they turn her loose, expose her to a number of Denishawn techniques, and allow her to find one consistent with whatever gifts she possessed. Her teachers watched with concern as she went through form after form. Then one day a flame burst forth. It was not ballet or St. Denis' Hindu creations, but primitive dance that provided the spark—dance which sprang from "the bone of the land" and permitted the dancer to "objectify in physical form" the beliefs and feelings of the inner being.

Graham made her professional debut in vaudeville with the Denishawn company in 1919, dancing the title role in Ted Shawn's exotic Aztec ballet, *Xochitl*. She toured with the company for the next four years, which included a season in England in 1922. She left Denishawn a year later to become solo dancer in the *Greenwich Village Follies*. After two years she tired of the musical theater and in 1925 assumed direction of the dance department at the Eastman School of Music. Here she consciously set to work to develop her own technique, having gained from Shawn the courage to be herself without compromise.

Her experiments led her back to natural movement—walking, running, leaping. Whereas Isadora Duncan had sought a free movement that was lyrical and romantic, Martha Graham sought a more realistic expression of the human self. Not all of her movements were pretty; some even appeared tortured and grotesque. She once described the dance as "a graph of the heart." Slowly she began to fuse her own body and personality into a new dance element, embodying truth as she saw it.

When she gave her first New York recital in April, 1926, there were still echoes of Denishawn. But she freed herself the next year with a work entitled *Revolt* and by 1929 had substituted a percussive vigor, in which each motion was attacked with a sharp accent, for St. Denis' gentler approach. The Oriental shell had vanished, revealing a descendant of Puritanism, full of power, yet a Puritan who permitted her emotions to break forth. Graham was a small woman, about five feet three inches tall, with a bony face and dense dark hair. Her expression seemed perpetually haunted, and she looked like a person who saw visions. Her magic lay in making these visions come to life onstage.

In 1930 she joined with Massine in a New York staging of *Le Sacre du Printemps* under the direction of Stokowski. That same year she visited New Mexico, where she was impressed by the art of the American Indians. Upon returning to New York she created the deeply moving *Primitive Mysteries*, followed in 1935 by her masterful *Frontier*. Graham wanted to discover a dance that would be relevant to contemporary America, but hers was always a personal expression, coming deep from within the American she knew best, herself. *American Document* came in 1938. *Salem Shore* depicted a New England housewife waiting on the beach for her husband's return from sea, while *Letter to the World* was based on the life and poems of Emily Dickinson. In *Appalachian Spring* the pioneer wife, danced by Graham, was reserved in the eyes of her neighbors, but the audience was allowed to see her inner self.

By no means was all of Martha Graham's material taken from American sources. She began her mythological repertoire with *Tragic Patterns* in 1933 and was strongly drawn to ancient Greece, as she explored the rituals and emotions that bind all peoples and all ages into one human race. Here she pictured Greek demons as well as divinities. *Cave of the Heart* was based upon the legend of Medea, while *Errand into the Maze* dealt with the story of the Labyrinth and the Minotaur and with man's need to do battle with fear. There were also Biblical subjects in the Graham repertoire and many others. In dramatic dance portraits, like her Mary of Scotland in *Episodes* and her full-length Clytemnestra, the dance became heroic theater. Yet everything she did was colored by her own forceful temperament, so that it became distinctly personal.

Graham was peculiarly sensitive to her surroundings, and through the years her art was shaped and reshaped, colored and recolored. Her music was contemporary, much of it written to order. During the middle thirties she emerged as the symbol of modern dance. Yet she disturbed audiences and critics alike and set off quarrels that smoldered and flamed over more than three decades. But Graham would not dance what she did not believe. "I do not want to dance as a tree, a flower or a wave," she insisted; her goal was to enact "something of the miracle that is a human being." For those absorbed in the ballet renaissance ushered in by the Ballet Russe de Monte Carlo, Graham's approach was often a wrenching ordeal. Audiences that admired exquisite ballerinas as Swan Queens and Sugarplum Fairies found it difficult to accept the anguish and horror and hate of Graham's dance as art. Many were confused by the demands she placed on viewers, and some even declared she was destroying the dance and insulting the human race. A minority, however, found her style compelling, her dynamic strength hypnotic, her message stimulating, her effort realistic. The few recognized in her tremendous vitality a dance that expressed the essence of the American character, and for them she became a prophet.

The United States between the world wars was a disquieted nation—first socially and intellectually, later politically and economically as well. Change had come rapidly, too rapidly for easy acceptance. A Victorian calm of plush sofas and charming bric-a-brac had been shattered by war, disillusionment, industrial turbulence, questions of identity, financial disaster, and cynicism. The seas of confusion were made all the more threatening by innovations in the arts and the surfacing of new ideas. To a people breaking loose from its traditional moorings, the obscurity, the inelegance, the angularity, the functionalism of modern art were both abrupt and menacing. In place of beauty came starkness. Eero Saarinen and Charles Eames stripped home furnishings to the essential about the time Martha Graham was influencing the trend of modern dance, while painters, writers, and architects all seemed in the popular mind to be conspiring in a consortium of ugliness.

The anguish of the Great Depression was so intensely real that the public generally preferred escapism and sweetness in their entertainment and art. Martha Graham and the modernists gave them more anguish, more anxiety, more questions to ponder, and most chose to deal with the challenge by fleeing from it, turning instead to a sentimentality they wanted to believe was real. Some lost themselves in causes. Often the artists, too, could not resist the lure, flirting for a time with Fascism, Communism, or Socialism or fighting the cause of labor, race, and justice for the proletariat more than art. Modern dance sometimes turned into angry protest, its dancers making obtuse statements regarding the condition of the world and portraying little but gloom and doom. Militant crusaders spoke to the masses with such pieces as *Eviction, Hunger, Unemployment,* and *While Waiting for Relief,* put on mostly in trade union halls by young dancers burning with the desire to right the wrongs of the world. But those who saw themselves as the social conscience of their times did so at the expense of art, limiting themselves to the moment and to specific issues rather than universal ones.

Martha Graham remained the artist, communicating on the broader level. Although a world in uproar often condemned her work for its abstractness, her message was general enough to have lasting meaning. The agony and pain she depicted went beyond the difficult times at hand and stood apart from the melange of causes then in vogue. She refused an invitation by the Nazi Government to perform in Germany at the Olympic Games in 1936, objecting to Nazi anti-Semitism. But her highest concern was art—enduring art, stripped of the merely ornamental. Through the years her art changed many times in style and technique. She was constantly restudying the basis of movement, yet she held firmly to the principle that dance must speak to the mind, the emotions, and the body of the spectator, in terms that cannot be translated into words.

Early in her career Graham taught modern dance at Bennington College several summers, helping Bennington to become the fount of lively experiments in dance education. Later the Martha Graham School of Contemporary Dance in New York was the recognized mecca of modern dance for American and foreign dancers alike. Her students were far better grounded in analysis and the technical aspects of the dance than Isadora Duncan's had been. "Technically speaking," Agnes de Mille maintains, "Graham's is the single largest contribution in the history of Western dancing."

She was still performing in the 1960s, still the iconoclast, affronting audiences who sought dancing that was conventionally pretty. By then she had created a huge repertoire and made several trips abroad. What she lost in facility, she compensated for in artistic substance, as her creative impulse seemed to increase its range with the passing of time. She retired in 1970 at the age of seventy-six, after a half century on the stage. "It is a bitter thing with me not to be able to dance again," Graham told the press. "Dancing is a call. You either have to be a dancer or you don't. Free choice doesn't enter into it."

A colleague of Martha Graham's at Bennington and another product of Denishawn was Doris Humphrey. Like Graham, Humphrey was of New England stock and had been brought up in a devoutly religious home. Both of her grandfathers were ministers in the Congregational Church. Her father was a professional photographer, her mother a pianist, each of whom had developed an interest in theater arts. Born in Oak Park, Illinois, in 1895, Doris began dancing lessons in Chicago at the age of eight. She saw a performance by Anna Pavlova as a high school student and was bewitched. Upon graduation she continued her dance lessons, taught ballet for a while, and in 1913 made her professional debut on a concert tour of the Midwest sponsored by the Santa Fe Railroad. Four years later she went to Los Angeles to study at Denishawn, becoming a member of the company in 1918 and one of the school's teachers within another two years. She arrived in California wearing plain clothes and looking like the stereotype of the timid school marm. Yet she was tall and slender and moved like a nymph. St. Denis quickly recognized in her a student of no ordinary ability, encouraging her to choreograph as well as dance. Humphrey made a setting of MacDowell's sonata *Tragica* in 1924, but the music was taken away when St. Denis felt the dance was a strong enough composition to stand alone. Humphrey toured with Denishawn for ten years, except for two seasons in vaudeville with her own company. She went to the Orient with Denishawn in 1926 and was placed in charge of the school's New York branch the next year, when Ruth St. Denis and Ted Shawn went on the road with the Ziegfeld *Follies.* In the spring of 1928 Humphrey, with her longtime associate, Charles Weidman, gave her first independent concert in New York, leaving Denishawn the following autumn.

Doris Humphrey had gradually evolved her own ideas, sufficiently revolutionary that a breach with Denishawn was inevitable. She rejected the ethnologic dances of alien peoples and began looking for a dance rooted in her own background and experience. She attempted to clear aside all that had gone before and came up with a fundamental principle. The scope of all human movement, she concluded, runs the path between balance and unbalance, fall and recovery. A simple step or gesture can cause the body to depart from its equilibrium, producing certain compensatory movements, some instinctive and others conscious, to restore the balance. Inherent in this action is the stuff of which dance is made. Rhythm is found not in music, but in the body itself. Drama comes from the feeling experienced in the fall and the recovery from the fall, heightened by gesture. The closer a state of unbalance approaches the dangerous, the more exciting it becomes to watch, the recovery the more pleasurable. The discovery of this principle freed the dancer, since the arc between inaction and destruction provides a range of limitless possibilities.

Humphrey possessed a logical mind, and her approach to dance was highly scientific. She emerged as the most direct, analytical, and lucid of the modern dance pioneers, keenly aware that public acceptance was necessary if modern dance was to survive and develop. She was convinced that human nature is splendid and noble. She recognized man's impulse toward progress, his ambition and drive, his longing for adventure, versus his desire for stability and peace. This struggle for maintenance and increase is symbolized in the movement of the dancer, what Humphrey called "the arc between two deaths." At one extremity stands negation, motionlessness; at the other is destruction, the yielding to unbalance. Action is prompted by the conflicting needs for excitement and repose. The dancer's fall and recovery, Humphrey contended, reflects "the constant flux which is going on in every living body...all the time."

During her first seasons of independence she continued to explore herself and discover a dance style which mirrored that self. Her stimuli as a choreographer came from many sources. She created *Color Harmony, Water Study, Life of the Bee, The Shakers,* and many other works. She tested the possibilities of the fall-and-recovery principle and broadened her experiments with accompaniment. *Water Study* was concerned with the abstract representation of the rise and fall of waves and was performed without music. *Life of the Bee* had a buzzing background.

She established a dance company with Charles Weidman in the early 1930s. The troupe embarked on the first extended modern dance tour of the United States in 1935, traveling from Canada to Texas. The reception was often cool; in some towns people even walked out on performances. Humphrey and Weidman opened their own dance studio in New York; both taught at Bennington and later at the New School for Social Research and Columbia University. They also did much to raise the standards of dancing in Broadway musical comedy and the revue. Meanwhile Humphrey led a conventional personal life, the wife of a ship officer and the mother of one son.

While their compositions were often thoughtful and searching, Humphrey and Weidman did not seek to agitate their audiences politically, preferring to concentrate on stagecraft and a repertoire that was handsomely mounted and danced. Doris Humphrey's own dancing was marked by an intrinsic delicacy, a strong femininity, and a heroic lyricism. She was always forthright and devoid of affectation. Gifted as she was as a performer, her work was never merely a *tour de force.* Her primary interest lay in ensemble, which led her to create in the larger, more comprehensive forms. When she retired from dancing in the early 1940s, because of a hip injury, she continued to teach, eventually at the Juilliard School of Music, as well as choreograph. For Jose Limon she created the *Lament for Ignacio Sanchez Mejias* and *Day on Earth.* She died in 1958.

Charles Weidman had been a student of Humphrey's at Denishawn, although Ted Shawn himself was his major teacher. Born in Lincoln, Nebraska, in 1903, Weidman had initially wanted to become either an architect or a cartoonist. A concert by St. Denis and Shawn in 1915 focused his attention on the dance. He began studying dance in Lincoln, copying the Denishawn style and making sketches of the company's costumes. He entered the Los Angeles school in 1920, without completing his academic studies, and shortly made his professional debut opposite Martha Graham in *Xochitl.* The seventeen year-old Weidman was pressed into service and rushed to Tacoma, Washington, when Robert Gorham broke a toe and had to retire from the cast.

Weidman left Denishawn the same year as Doris Humphrey, but for him the break led to greater difficulties. He was not as sure of the direction he wanted to follow in his dance experiments as either Humphrey or Graham; he knew only the Denishawn method. "I just went into the studio and couldn't move," he said. Shawn had early recognized Weidman's gift for characterization and flair for comedy, and his forte ultimately became the dramatic dance, in which he successfully drew together pantomime and pure movement. No other American male dancer of his day could rival him as a performer. Even his humor had a certain spicy bitterness about it, while his serious works often possessed an angry, sardonic force. His approach was masculine, imaginative, distinguished by a skilled technique. His themes were homely and familiar. Perhaps his most impressive characterization for Denishawn was the crapshooter in *Danse Americaine*. He produced a long work for a concert at the Guild Theater in 1936—*American Saga*, based on the legend of Paul Bunyan. For *On My Mother's Side* he created a dance portrait of a favorite aunt, who does high kicks and has the time of her life. *Lynch Town*, on the other hand, strikes out at injustice and its mood is one of grim horror.

The Second World War interrupted Weidman's career, during which he served in the United States Army. After the war he formed a new company in New York and composed *A House Divided*, taking the role of Lincoln. His later years were spent mainly in teaching, both in New York and on highly extolled teaching tours.

Not all of the innovations in modern dance in America have come from native interpreters, however. Mary Wigman's dance was as essentially German as Isadora Duncan's was American and had the advantage of greater technical solidification. Wigman's first tour of the United States in 1930-31, under the management of Sol Hurok, was so well received that she and the impresario decided a branch of her school should be opened in New York. Hanya Holm, a member of Wigman's original dance group and the head teacher in her school at Dresden, was placed in charge. Holm was born in Worms, the daughter of a prosperous wine merchant from a family of Bavarian brewers. She had been strongly affected as a child by Pavlova's performances and decided then to become a professional dancer. Toward the end of World War I, she moved to Dresden and soon came under the influence of Wigman, the great dance revolutionary of Germany. Like the American pioneers, Wigman and Holm rejected sugary prettiness in favor of the beauty of inner illumination. They built their method largely by trial and error, but Holm arrived in America a top-notch technician. She brought with her the discipline, analysis, and scientific dance pedagogy of Central Europe. But she adapted the German ways to the particular characteristics of the dancers she taught in the United States, thereby bringing herself within the American modern dance tradition. From 1934 to 1940 she was a leading teacher at Bennington College, working with Graham, Humphrey, and Weidman. When Mary Wigman chose to remain in Germany, despite the rise of Nazism, the strong anti-Nazi feelings in the United States caused Wigman to be held in mild contempt. Consequently, in 1936 her school in New York became the Hanya Holm School of Dance. Beginning in 1941 Holm taught summer courses at Colorado College in Colorado Springs, where she also presented annual dance productions.

Hanya Holm's greatest contribution to modern dance in America has been in the use of space. The "birdlike swoop" became the hallmark of the Holm dancer. To her dance is life, and the reason for dancing is to know that one is alive. The impulse may be physical, mental, or emotional. While the inner self is disclosed in the Holm dance, there is also full-bodied action, as the dancer explores the drama of space. Holm's purpose is to "convey idea through form." Motion springs from the center of the body, not chaotically, but like spokes from the hub of a wheel.

Holm did not perform in America for six years after her arrival. She produced her first major work, *Trend*, in 1937, which proved an American masterpiece. She had stopped working on the concert stage by the close of World War II. Her least gift was as a performer; her strengths lay in teaching and choreography. Perhaps because she performed so little herself, she did not attempt to turn students into a miniature Holm, but was willing to discover and nurture the talent within each one. She received national acclaim as the choreographer of the Broadway musical *Kiss Me, Kate* and later worked on *My Fair Lady* and *Camelot*. She also directed the opera *The Ballad of Baby Doe*.

An independent influence on American modern dance came from Helen Tamiris. She did not stem from Denishawn, nor was she included in the Bennington group, but established herself in the late 1920s as one of the foremost nonconformists of dance in the United States. Born Helen Becker, of Russian parents, she had grown up in poverty on the streets of New York's East Side. But she liked to dance and at eight was enrolled in a dance class at the Henry Street Settlement. Her first job was in the ballet of the Metropolitan Opera, which also provided her with the opportunity of three free dance lessons a week. Changing her name to Tamiris, after reading a poem about a Persian queen, she studied Russian ballet briefly with Michel Fokine, before moving on to a Duncan studio. She worked for a while in Chicago night clubs, appeared in the fourth *Music Box Revue*, and in 1927 presented her first concert program, *Dance Moods*, at the Little Theater in New York. In her desire to be an American dancer, she created a program in which she attempted to capture the movements of the American black, the prize fighter, and the jazz age populace living in the America of the 1920s. To do this she discovered she needed a new dance vocabulary, one which she drew from a variety of sources.

After this initial New York success, Tamiris went to Europe, performing at Salzburg, Paris, and Berlin, where her jazz compositions and spirituals were hailed as uniquely American. She returned to the United States and in 1929 introduced a flood of lusty dances filled with social significance, in which she commented on relevant issues of the day with conviction, indignation, and defiance. Later she created a number of works for the Federal Theater Project. But she also produced more poetic pieces, like her *Walt Whitman Suite*, which abounded in energy and free beauty.

By the late 1930s Tamiris' period of protest was over. She produced *Liberty Song* in 1941, one of her most attractive pieces, based upon some songs from the American Revolution. *Liberty Song* was richly American, alive with affirmation, humor, power, and romance. She turned to the

Broadway stage after the Second World War, not cheapening her art, but applying the principles she had developed to the American Indian ballet in *Annie Get Your Gun* and the movements of the Boss Tweed ring in *Up in Central Park*. She gave up dancing herself in the mid-1950s, but continued as an active choreographer. "I resent very deeply," she said, "the attitude that the artist in our society must be a very special kind of person. It is a nineteenth-century hangover which brands the artist as an eccentric bearing no relationship to the general movement of life." To Tamiris dancing is simply part of living, and she has tried to provide Americans with a sturdy dance idiom that is peculiarly their own.

By the outbreak of World War II a third generation of American modern dancers was appearing on the scene. Among the most significant and original of this new generation was Jose Limon, Doris Humphrey's most famous protege. Born in Mexico, Limon moved to California in his youth. He became a soloist with the Humphrey-Weidman troupe before entering the armed forces during World War II. After the war he formed a company of his own, for which Humphrey was the artistic director and chief choreographer. Limon shortly developed into the nation's most distinguished male dancer in the modern field, also serving as a frequent guest artist with the Mexican National Ballet. He was a dancer of great technical skill, but one of warmth, power, and passion. His best known choreography is *The Moor's Pavane*, a dance treatment of the Othello story, although he often turned to his native Mexico for inspiration, including ancient Indian legends, and to religious themes. *The Traitor* was built around the personality of Judas and the betrayal of Christ. While Limon was a devoted disciple of Humphrey and Weidman, he was not enslaved to their method and was able to evolve movements and gestures that reflected his individual personality.

Valerie Bettis, Hanya Holm's most celebrated pupil, was the first modern dancer to compose works for traditional ballet companies. She was a vivid performer, full of vitality and dramatic intensity, gifted in a variety of roles. In *The Golden Round* she portrayed Lady Macbeth, in *As I Lay Dying* a woman who looks back on a life of tragedy, weariness, and a single illicit love affair which bore her a son. Besides her concert pieces, Bettis won acclaim as a dancer in musical comedy, as a choreographer for the musical theater and the screen, and as a dramatic actress. Also included in the third generation of modern dancers is Esther Junger, Katherine Dunham, and Pearl Primus.

Intensely theatrical though modern dance has been, a strong emphasis on dance education has always been present. Dance entered the public schools as a recreational activity, usually part of the physical education program. It was looked upon as a means for strengthening the body and developing coordination, helping students adjust to group activity, instilling a sense of poise, and encouraging a free expression of ideas and feelings. Dance taught discipline, yet at the same time offered a release. As dance made its way into the public schools, it became desirable for college students preparing themselves for teaching careers, particularly girls, to be given elementary instruction in modern dance. The first dance major to be offered was established in 1926 at the University of Wisconsin. Then came the dance programs formulated by Martha Hill at Bennington College and New York University. Ted Shawn began his school for male dancers, Jacob's Pillow, at Becket, Massachusetts, in 1933, followed by the Connecticut College School of Dance and summer programs across the country. Gradually modern dance instruction in some form was added to the curriculum of most public and private schools, colleges and universities, and academies such as the Juilliard School of Music.

Ballet remained more exclusive, since it required the mastery of a special vocabulary of movement before the individual could even begin to dance. Nor did professional ballet make many creative strides in the United States until after World War II. The American Ballet went out of existence in 1939. Ballet Caravan produced Eugene Loring's *Billy the Kid*, one of the most popular of all American ballets, in New York during the fall of 1938, but disbanded two years later. The Ballet Russe de Monte Carlo continued to function, despite growing difficulties, under the direction of Serge Denham. Alexandra Danilova remained loyal to the company, and its roster included such star performers as Alicia Markova, Mia Slavenska, and Frederic Franklin. But the Ballet Russe's glamor continued to wane. After the war it became primarily a touring company, offering aging productions of old favorites like *Swan Lake, The Nutcracker, Giselle*, and *Scheherazade*. By the early 1950s the Ballet Russe was avoiding New York altogether, except for Lewisohn Stadium.

Although the School of American Ballet kept going, Lincoln Kirstein had been in the army during the war, while George Balanchine worked for a time with the Ballet Russe de Monte Carlo. Then in 1946 Kirstein announced the formation of the Ballet Society. Performances of the Ballet Society were open to members only, and one of its problems was finding places to perform. In 1948 Kirstein's organization joined forces with the New York City Center of Music and Drama, and from that union the New York City Ballet was born. The company began with Maria Tallchief, an American ballerina of Osage Indian origin, formerly with the Ballet Russe de Monte Carlo, as prima ballerina. Balanchine was artistic director.

Within a few years the New York City Ballet had grown into the most important ballet company in the country and one of the finest in the world. Balanchine supplied most of the repertory, proving himself among the most prolific of all contemporary choreographers of the ballet. The repertory was broadened in 1949, when Jerome Robbins was added as associate director, while the dramatic wing was strengthened by the inclusion of works by Antony Tudor. Most of the company's dancers have come from the School of American Ballet. Tanaquil LeClercq even rose to the rank of ballerina. Other principal dancers include, or have included, Andre Eglevsky, Melissa Hayden, Michael Kidd, Patricia Wilde, Jacques d'Amboise, Todd Bolender, Violetta Verdy, Patricia McBride, Francisco Moncion, and Edward Villella.

Janet Reed retired in 1954, while Marie-Jeanne and Nora Kaye, the world's foremost dramatic ballerina, danced with the company for a few seasons. Jean Rosenthal designed the lighting, until her death in 1969, so imaginatively that scenery at times seemed almost unnecessary.

Rudolf Nureyev, on his first trip to the United States, went to see the New York City Ballet as soon as he could. He found it "an excellent company, with a tremendously varied selection of Balanchine ballets." Admission prices at the City Center were kept low, helping to build a fairly wide audience. Compared with the Metropolitan Opera at least, the company has been a relatively successful operation financially. During the 1962-63 season it came within less than $50,000 of meeting the annual expenditure of nearly $1,500,000 from the 223 performances given in New York and on a seventeen-week tour. Like the country's major opera houses, the New York City Ballet has benefited from Ford Foundation aid. City Center, however, was scarcely more desirable for dance than for opera, so that in 1966 the New York City Ballet also made the move into the more auspicious New York State Theater in Lincoln Center.

In 1978 Mikhail Baryshnikov joined the company, eager to work under Balanchine and Robbins. Baryshnikov, a Soviet dancer recently defected from the Bolshoi via Canada, had already won a reputation with the American Ballet Theatre and been nominated for an Academy Award for his supporting role in the film *The Turning Point*, which also established him as something of a national heartthrob. He made his debut with the New York City Ballet in Balanchine's *Jewels*, a performance critics agreed was overwhelming. More than any dancer of his generation Baryshnikov popularized ballet, aided in no small measure by the availability of public television.

The second most important American ballet company, the American Ballet Theatre, did not have a permanent home for many years and, therefore, lacked the stability attained by the New York City Ballet. The company was able to use the New York State Theater during the summer months, but in the winter, when the theater's resident companies were at home, it had to make do with the inadequate City Center Theater and abandon big productions. The American Ballet Theatre, now the official company of Kennedy Center in Washington, D.C., was formed in 1939 out of the nucleus of the Mordkin Ballet. Its founders were Richard Pleasant, a young American formerly on the executive staff of the Mordkin company, and Lucia Chase, a wealthy American widow and one of Mordkin's advanced students. The company has had a precarious existence from the beginning, since it has relied solely on private resources, mainly Lucia Chase's. Its backers hoped to offer new works and the best of the classical repertory, although initially the company evidenced something of a museumlike quality.

The American Ballet Theatre gave its first performance at Center Theatre in Rockefeller Center on January 11, 1940, presenting *Les Sylphides*, *The Great American Goof*, and *Voices of Spring*. The corps was well trained, the costumes fresh, the debut a distinct success. That same year the company introduced the work of England's Antony Tudor to American audiences and performed *Black Ritual*, the first ballet by Agnes de Mille. Pleasant and Chase originally divided the company into three wings. Anton Dolin was in charge of the classic ballets, Eugene Loring the American, and Tudor the English. Michel Fokine worked with the group for a time on revivals, and during the 1941-42 transcontinental tour, under Hurok's management, the American Ballet Theatre was advertised as "The Greatest in Russian Ballet."

But the foreign domination gradually relaxed. Agnes de Mille, whose work was always saturated with the American point of view, grew in stature, and in 1944 a young dancer with the company, Jerome Robbins, was allowed to try his hand at choreography. The result was *Fancy Free*, with music by Leonard Bernstein. Michael Kidd has also done some distinguished choreography for the company, as slowly the American Ballet Theatre built perhaps the most balanced repertory of any dance company anywhere. It has also developed more native dancers than any other American company, at first out of necessity, later maintaining schools in New York, Washington, D.C., Detroit, and Denver.

New York-born Nora Kaye became a star overnight in 1942, when she danced the principal role in Tudor's romantic *Pillar of Fire* with the American Ballet Theatre at the Metropolitan Opera House. She later developed into "The Duse of the Dance." Marina Svetlova, after three seasons with the Original Ballet Russe, danced with the company during the 1940s; so did Alicia Markova, Irina Baronova, and later Rosella Hightower. Alicia Alonso, whose *Giselle* eventually rivaled Markova's, came up through the ranks, as did John Kriza and Donald Saddler. Eric Bruhn was a mainstay of the Ballet Theatre, retiring in 1972, while Natalie Makarova became one of the company's principal ballerinas after she defected from Russia.

The American Ballet Theatre has always done a great deal of traveling. In the early days the company made grueling tours of one-night stands from coast to coast, since only New York, Chicago, San Francisco, and Los Angeles had sufficient interest in ballet for a company to stay any length of time. In most cities the troupe could saturate the public with only two or three performances. Travel during World War II was particularly difficult, although the war did permit the company to sink its roots deeply into American soil. Expenditures have been staggering. During its first decade and a half the American Ballet Theatre cost Lucia Chase in excess of $2,000,000. In the 1960s the company was traveling with fifty-eight dancers, plus thirty-eight musicians and technicians. Even if it played to capacity houses, the troupe still lost $10,000 every week of the tour. Grants from the Ford Foundation and the National Endowment for the Arts have helped keep the company dynamic.

The Joffrey Ballet was installed as the City Center's resident company after its successful debut in March, 1966. Says choreographer Robert Joffrey, "I look upon the ballet as total theater." His concept of the dance is an eclectic hybrid, breaking sharply with the rules, cliches, and conventions of the past.

Suicide, bigotry, and alienation all become possible subjects for the Joffrey dancers. The company's productions are often flashy, mod, far out, and mind-boggling, making contemporary American dance perhaps the least inhibited of the performing arts. Joffrey's most spectacular contribution to the repertory thus far is *Astarte*, a $60,000 multimedia presentation entailing a riot of sight and sound. Four projectors, a distorted movie screen, flashing lights, and screeching music are designed to take the audience beyond the proscenium. The lead male dancer, having spent his passion on the moon goddess Astarte, exits through a rear door of the theater, stripped to his shorts, in full view of the audience, while a camera shows his progress down Fifty-sixth Street.

Another newcomer is the Harkness Ballet, which cherishes the great traditions of the classical ballet, yet presses forward into new frontiers of dance as well. The company was begun in 1965 by Rebekah Harkness, the Standard Oil heiress and longtime ballet enthusiast. Since then it has built up an impressive repertory and toured throughout the United States. Harkness emphasizes youth and has given special attention to young American choreographers, composers, dancers, and designers.

The San Francisco Ballet continues to flourish and has become really two companies. The number one company dances with the opera in the fall, puts on performances of *The Nutcracker* at Christmas, has a short spring season and a two-month national tour. The number two company makes a short road tour of one-night stands in small towns and performs new works during a summer season. The San Francisco Ballet also maintains a school, which with about 400 students enrolled is one of the largest in the country. An exchange program between the west coast company and the New York City Ballet has enriched the San Francisco repertory with several Balanchine works.

Ruth Page long remained at the helm of the Chicago Opera Ballet, a company which makes annual tours and presents original pieces. Maria Tallchief now directs. The Philadelphia Ballet still operates, while the modern-minded National Ballet of Washington, D.C. gives upwards to one hundred performances a year. The Utah Civic Ballet performs over a seven-state area, in locations ranging from the vast amphitheater at Zion National Park to little Indian villages. The Cincinnati Civic Ballet is quite active; so are the Dallas Civic Ballet, under George Skibine, and the Atlanta Civic Ballet, the first such organization in the country. And there are smaller groups, like the Civic Ballet of St. Joseph, Missouri and the Anchorage Civic Ballet, which has graduated from the Elks Club to the West High School auditorium.

Visiting foreign companies have also contributed to America's interest in the ballet. The Paris Opera Ballet made a brief trip to New York in 1948, although French ballet was better represented by the Ballets de Paris, headed by Roland Petit. Petit's company has made several tours and given vivid performances; Leslie Caron was one of his dancers. The Royal Danish Ballet brought a different style to the classical repertory, placing emphasis on aerial actions. The national Ballet of Canada and the Royal Winnipeg Ballet have given frequent performances in the United States—the first especially concerned with the classics, the latter more involved with modern works.

The Sadler's Wells Ballet of London has made a number of successful American tours, the first during the fall of 1949. The company gave performances at the Metropolitan Opera House and in various other centers of the United States and Canada, under Hurok's management. The initial Sadler's Wells tour was highly publicized and received with great enthusiasm, gathering some $500,000 from ticket sales. Margot Fonteyn proved the company's brightest star, a ballerina in the truest sense, whose complete *Sleeping Beauty* was a marvel of taste and beauty. Frederick Ashton was the chief creator of ballets for the English company, introducing the United States to a more lyrical, romantic style than that of either the New York City Ballet or the American Ballet Theatre. Rather than a program of several shorter pieces, as had been customary in America, Sadler's Wells offered the novelty of full-length ballets filling an entire evening.

In 1954 the Sadler's Wells Ballet was granted a royal charter and officially became the Royal Ballet Company. Rudolf Nureyev, formerly leading dancer with the Kirov Ballet of Leningrad, joined the company in 1961, having made the decision to defect in search of artistic freedom. Nureyev, at twenty-three, immediately established himself as a celebrity in the West and became a favorite dance partner of Margot Fonteyn. The two made their joint New York debut in 1963, followed by a record-breaking tour. This success was repeated in the spring of 1967.

The popularization of ballet had long been of special interest to George Balanchine, and by the late 1930s he had begun to take seriously the possibilities of the Broadway musical stage and motion pictures. During the summer of 1937 he choreographed two elaborate dances for the *Goldwyn Follies*, his first large-scale work for film. Two years earlier Balanchine had revolutionized dancing in Broadway musical comedy by creating two ballets for the Rodgers and Hart musical *On Your Toes* and making them an integral part of the story and action. The most provocative of these was a thoroughly American number called "Slaughter on Tenth Avenue." What Balanchine had introduced to the musical theater, Agnes de Mille made an established fact in 1943, when she created the dances for Rodgers and Hammerstein's *Oklahoma!* De Mille made dancing a living part of the show itself. Her famous dream sequence carried the plot forward and said things words could not convey. She used ballet, modern dance, folk dance, and dramatic gesture, achieving both characterization and narrative. Late the next year, Jerome Robbins' *Fancy Free* was effectively expanded into a full-length musical, the smash hit *On the Town*. Robbins also did the choreography for *High Button Shoes* and *The King and I*. Then in 1957 he fused dancing and drama even more tightly in *West Side Story*, a story-ballet in which much of the action is nonrealistic dance pantomime.

Dance reached a creditable level in motion pictures with Fred Astaire, Gene Kelly, and Rita Hayworth. Astaire made dancing a natural expression of joy, achieving an artistic height in the 1940s with *Yolanda and the Thief*, opposite Lucille Bremer. Kelly was a different sort of dancer, more imaginative in some ways, but still basically a tap dancer. The "Shadow Dance" in *Cover Girl* and the fantasy duo with an animated cartoon mouse in *Anchors Aweigh* represented Kelly at his best, although *An American in Paris*, with Kelly and Leslie Caron, offered distinguished dancing throughout. Hayworth worked with both Astaire and Kelly, but did perhaps her finest dancing in *Down to Earth*. Ray Bolger, Cyd Charisse, Donald O'Connor, Gene Nelson, and Juliet Prowse all turned out notable performances for Hollywood, but not until *Seven Brides for Seven Brothers* in the mid-1950s, choreographed by Michael Kidd, did the movies use dance as an integral part of the plot itself.

By that time every major television station had at least a part-time choreographer on its staff. Practically every show of a variety or musical format presented dance of some type, and in special productions dancing often played a major role. When Mary Martin's *Peter Pan* was adapted for television in 1954, Jerome Robbins, who had choreographed the theater production, was brought in to stage the show. The industry was surprised to learn the next year that a ninety-minute version of the Sadler's Wells Ballet production of *The Sleeping Beauty*, with Fonteyn, commanded a fairly enthusiastic public response.

Although the audience for ballet is still relatively small, the art has gained a respectable following in recent years. World War II had a stimulating effect on ballet, as it did on opera and symphonic music, since money became more plentiful and the demand for entertainment of all kinds went up. The public interest in dance, however, is concentrated in a few large metropolitan areas and is dependable only among a select circle of *aficionados*, so that touring is economically hazardous. Traveling costs are prohibitively high, while operating expenses even at home preclude the possibility of ballet's becoming commercially profitable. Modern dance has not received the private subsidy that ballet has, although foundation support has been generous, at least for a few established enterprises. Nevertheless, most of the Ford Foundation money has gone to traditional ballet. Fund-raising for dance companies has not yet become as well organized as the campaigns for opera; there are no ladies' guilds and few subscription lists to be canvassed. Since most American dance groups operate on a shoe-string budget, their life is extremely tentative, their ability to withstand crises slight.

Although company budgets run high, dancers are generally the lowest paid of the performing artists, and employment is uncertain. In 1964 the New York City Ballet became the first company in the United States to offer its dancers a full-year contract. And yet for upper-middle class America, leotards and toe shoes have almost come to replace the piano as a cultural symbol in the upbringing of young girls. The manager of the Utah Civic Ballet estimates that one third of the little girls in Salt Lake City take ballet lessons at some time. There are over sixty dance schools in greater Washington, D.C., around seventy in Manhattan, not counting Arthur Murray or Fred Astaire studios. One New York teacher, observing the proliferation of dance schools, said, "They're like bookies—there's one in every basement." Of the millions of dance students in the country today, several thousand will become professionals, working in night clubs, movies, Broadway shows, and television. Only a few hundred will perform in concert or with ballet companies. Competition is keen, particularly for girls. Of every 100 students that enter a good dance school, perhaps one will have the chance of becoming a professional.

As might be expected, what has developed into the American ballet style is a hybrid. No longer is it possible to differentiate clearly between ballet and modern dance. Recent American choreographers have freely blended the two, adding pantomime and colloquial folk steps, both country and urban. Contemporary ballet may include the whole popular vocabulary—buck and wing, tap dancing, the jitterbug, rock 'n roll, all superimposed upon a classic base. The training of Agnes de Mille, Jerome Robbins, and Michael Kidd was not limited to the classical techniques. "These were theater brats," de Mille herself says, "who fought their way up through the entertainment field and showed in their style their mongrel experiences and heritage." This cross-fertilization, however, has given their work great vitality. "American dance," Benjamin Harkarvy, codirector of the Netherlands Ballet, maintains, "is the most advanced and richest in choreographic development in the world today."

Most of this came about because ballet began taking contemporary subjects for themes. The movements of the kings and birds and ghosts of classic ballet were simply different from those suitable for sailors, cowboys, crapshooters, and their molls. Unlike opera, the stress in both American ballet and modern dance has been on the native scene. While individual dancers and choreographers have gone their separate ways, the American spirit, her folkloric atmosphere, vigor, and frontier strength have colored their work nonetheless, until eventually a new idiom was created. Sometimes the American quality is subtle and elusive, sometimes concrete and direct.

Isadora Duncan proclaimed a great vision: "I see America dancing." Certainly ardent champions have worked to realize that dream, and exciting progress has been made. From the beginning modern dancers especially have alienated great segments of the public with their advanced ideas and experimental efforts. At the same time they have profoundly influenced ballet, the musical theater, and the popular entertainment media. While the position of formal dance in the United States is still precarious and peripatetic, America's contribution to the art in the past half century has been significant. If the dance enriches only a fragment of the nation's life through concerts and ballet performances, in more popular forms its impact has been deeper and more far-reaching.

CHAPTER

IV

TRADITIONAL COMPOSERS

Contemporary art music as an organized movement reached the United States at the close of World War I. It arrived in New York during the early 1920s and gradually spread through the rest of the country. By the end of the decade the new music, initially greeted with snickers and sarcasm, had been conceded a place in the repertoire and was being accepted with increasing enthusiasm. Many young American composers came under the influence of Stravinsky, Schoenberg, and the other early European modernists, yet a minority continued to work along more or less conservative lines. Some clung to essentially romantic concepts, while others had no desire to write in forms departing from traditional European standards.

Perhaps the best established of these fundamentally conservative composers was Deems Taylor, whose opera *The King's Henchman* was well received at the Metropolitan in 1927. Born in New York City on December 22, 1885, Taylor was educated at the Ethical Culture School and New York University. He first considered painting as a career, but showed an interest in composition at an early age. At six he wrote a piece in seven movements entitled "Love," "Hatred," "Sorrow," "Gladness," "Anger," "Joy," and "Fetig" (Fatigue), drawing some of the staves with four lines, others with six or more. Later he wrote a waltz for piano and violin, employing the two instruments because he could not play the piano well enough to manage both melody and accompaniment. He could be counted on to entertain with burlesques on grand opera at fraternity smokers, and while in college wrote the music for four comic operas. One of them, *The Echo*, was given a Broadway staging by Charles Dillingham. Victor Herbert saw the second of Taylor's student productions and was impressed with the boy's talent. "But," he said, "you know nothing of musical theory, do you?" The youth confessed he had had only ten months of piano lessons, at the age of ten. Aside from that he was self-taught. "You must study," Herbert continued. "Otherwise you will never get beyond this point."

Reluctantly financed by his father, Taylor went to work with Oscar Coon, a retired bandsman, on harmony and counterpoint. He sped through Richter's *Harmony* and Jadassohn's *Canon and Fugue* in three months, more and more convinced that he wanted to be a musician. Upon graduation from college, however, he went to work on the staff of the *Nelson Encyclopedia* and the *Encyclopaedia Britannica*. He was assistant editor of the *Western Electric News*, before becoming assistant editor of the New York *Herald Tribune*'s Sunday magazine. During 1916 and 1917 he was the *Tribune*'s war correspondent in France and for two years was associate editor of *Collier's Weekly*. From 1921 to 1925 he was music critic of the New York *World* and in August, 1927, became editor of *Musical America*. Later he was music critic for the New York *American* and *McCall's Magazine*. Despite his deepening interest in composition, Taylor realized that he would have to support himself in other ways. "I have tried teaching," he once said, "and found it an intolerable bore. No one would dream of hiring me as a conductor, and I am a dreadful pianist. So, long ago, I hit on a fourth choice: I would be subsidized. Therefore, for many years, I, the composer, have been supported by me, doing other things."

The Echo had died on the road after a ten-week run on Broadway. Taylor made later attempts at comic opera, but had no success. Then he read about a prize being offered by the National Federation of Music Clubs for the best symphony or symphonic poem by an American composer. "If I can't get anywhere in musical comedy," he decided, "I'll go highbrow." He sat down to write his first serious music, a symphonic poem for orchestra called *The Siren Song*. It was so poorly orchestrated that passages of it were unplayable. But Taylor submitted the piece in 1912 and won second prize. The judges awarded no first, since they could not justify the winner's rough orchestration for a top award. The selection was later reworked and in 1924 played by the New York Philharmonic Orchestra. Taylor was then music critic of the New York *World* and reviewed the piece himself. He claimed *The Siren Song* showed promise, aside from certain crudities, and said he hoped to hear many more works by the same composer.

Next came two choral selections: *The Chambered Nautilus*, a cantata for mixed chorus and orchestra, based on a poem by Oliver Wendell Holmes, and *The Highwayman*, a cantata for women's chorus and orchestra, written for the 1914 MacDowell Festival in Peterboro. Already Taylor evidenced an ability to sense public taste. His music was always warm, rich, melodious, full of lush harmony, explaining why he would become the most widely played American composer of the early 1920s. He wrote songs, piano pieces, and after the war *Through the Looking Glass*. Originally conceived for strings, wind, and piano, the suite was rescored in 1922 for full orchestra, shortly entering the repertoire of the country's leading orchestras. *Through the Looking Glass* was based on Lewis Carroll's tale and cemented Deems Taylor's reputation as a serious composer. In the 1920s the work was considered an American classic and performed in London and Paris. The piece is full of sparkle and humor, which helped make it an immediate hit. There are reminders of Wagner and Puccini and an unashamed lyricism.

The Portrait of a Lady, a rhapsody for strings, woodwinds, and piano, was followed by *Jurgen*, a symphonic poem commissioned by Walter Damrosch and performed by the New York Symphony Society in 1925. That same year Taylor wrote *Circus Day* for Paul Whiteman, orchestrated for jazz ensemble by Ferde Grofe and subsequently revised for symphony orchestra. Taylor also composed incidental music for eight plays, including the Theatre Guild's original production of Molnar's *Liliom*, and in 1924 wrote a complete score for the silent picture *Janice Meredith*. Out of his music for Gilbert Miller's production of *Casanova* and the Katharine Cornell vehicle *Lucrece* the composer later fashioned concert suites.

The strength of Taylor's achievements in other musical forms led to his commission in 1925 by the Metropolitan Opera for a work based on a libretto of his own choosing. Taylor resigned from the New York *World* in order to devote his entire attention to writing and asked Edna St. Vincent Millay to collaborate with him. The two first considered a setting of *Snow White and the Seven Dwarfs*, but eventually abandoned that idea in favor of a story from the Anglo-Saxon chronicle which they called *The King's Henchman*, similar in theme to *Tristan und Isolde*. Since Millay was in poor health that year, she stayed on her farm in upstate New York, mailing Taylor the libretto in installments. "It was not too easy," he later admitted, "to work on the first act without knowing what the second act would be." The opera was completed in slightly more than eight months. Taylor finished the orchestration in Paris during September, 1926. Rehearsals began the following month, and the first performance was given on February 17, 1927, before a house that had sold out weeks in advance.

Taylor's devotion to the theater and earlier experience equipped him well for writing opera. *The King's Henchman* had been heralded by much advance publicity, but the critics received it as enthusiastically as the public. It was acclaimed the best American opera to date, the work of "an expert craftsman." The score made frequent use of the Wagnerian *leit-motif*, but whatever its derivations, the music was warm, rich in melody, strong in choruses, and above all effective theater. The opera held the boards of the Metropolitan for three seasons.

A few days after the premiere the Metropolitan Board of Directors announced they had commissioned Taylor to write a second opera. Late that fall the composer informed an eager public that his new opera would be based on an American novel and that he himself would be the librettist. "I have found," he told an Associated Press reporter, "the most charming and compatible, the most accomplished and erudite of collaborators. We get along splendidly together." But the search for a suitable story continued for another two years. Finally Taylor found what he wanted in George Du Maurier's novel *Peter Ibbetson*. The composer did collaborate on the libretto with Constance Collier, reworking the play the actress had made from the book some years earlier for herself and the Barrymore brothers. The plot was an appealing dream story, but when Taylor's opera was produced in February, 1931, the critics failed to grant it the unanimous acclaim that had greeted its predecessor. The music was judged old-fashioned by many and said to reflect too closely idioms of the European masters, without adding anything new. Yet with the public *Peter Ibbetson* was an even greater success than *The King's Henchman*, remaining in the Metropolitan repertoire for four consecutive seasons. During the summer of 1931, the opera was staged at Ravinia, outside Chicago, and in 1938 was selected by the Italian Ministry of Education for broadcast over EIAR, one of the largest radio stations in Italy, in a special Italian version.

Taylor began a third opera, *Ramuntcho*, in the spring of 1934 and completed it four years later. The work, based on a novel by Pierre Loti, was produced by the Philadelphia Opera Company on February 10, 1942. The composer's later orchestral pieces include *Processional* (1941), *Marco Takes a Walk* (1942), *A Christmas Overture* (1944), and *Fanfare for the People of Russia* (1944). An operetta based on Defoe's *Moll Flanders* occupied his attention between 1947 and 1948, but was never finished. From it he drew a series of dances, put together in 1950 as a *Restoration Suite*.

Meanwhile Taylor continued his career as a writer, critic, and commentator. For a time he was music critic of the New York *American* and in 1931 was chosen narrator for the first Metropolitan Opera broadcasts. He was appointed musical consultant for the Columbia Broadcasting System in 1936 and at that time began his Sunday afternoon intermission talks on the New York Philharmonic-Symphony broadcasts. He remained at that post until 1943, becoming a familiar voice to radio audiences all over the United States and Canada. His approach was to balance technical explanation with humor and sidelights of human interest. These talks were later expanded into three books: *Of Men and Music*, *The Well-Tempered Listener*, and *Music to My Ears*. In 1940 the personable Taylor acted as commentator for Walt Disney's *Fantasia* and over the next decade worked on several other films. He died in 1966.

Composition, however, was always his primary interest. His style remained melodic, venturing no farther toward modernism than glimmers of French impressionism. "I sometimes wonder whether the appalling speed with which our mechanical civilization has advanced during the past thirty years hasn't lured a whole generation of composers into trying to keep up with it," Taylor once wrote. "I sense, among a vast number and variety of composers, an uneasy impulse to keep abreast of their times, a dread of being thought old-fashioned." Deems Taylor did not share that dread, even basked in the heritage of Wagner, Puccini, and Debussy. During the 1920s and 1930s he was considered dean of American composers, received wide press coverage, and achieved a material success unusual among serious musicians. But time eventually passed him by. Later generations knew him primarily for his commentary, for his music was seldom played. To the advanced guard he became anathema, the symbol of musical stagnation, while even his champions conceded he had served old wine in bottles that were none too new.

Younger than Taylor by a decade was Howard Hanson, one of the new generation of American composers who came into their own during the 1920s. Like Taylor, Hanson was fundamentally a traditionalist and stayed so throughout a long career, although showing growth and greater creativity as the years went by. Born in Wahoo, Nebraska, a Swedish community near Lincoln, on October 28, 1896, Hanson received his first musical training from his mother. He later attended Luther Academy in Wahoo, where he found a "very respectable little music department." Hanson's early life, according to Patricia Ashley, "was a curious mixture of smalltown American morality, Lutheran musical values, the educational strivings of a town past the frontier stages, and that combination of old-country and new-country nationalism which for decades characterized the Swedish-American community that stretched north and west from Chicago." Early he developed a sense of mission and the drive that would help him accomplish it. A local piano teacher once told the boy, "What Grieg has done for the Norwegians, you must do for the Swedes." And yet the community in which Hanson grew up had little patience with artists. "Why do you go into music?" his school superintendent asked. "You have brains!"

But the lad knew his mind. He played piano and organ in the various churches in town, sang in choir performances, played cello in a string quartet, and eventually became conductor of the Wahoo High School orchestra. He spent a year at the state university in Lincoln and at sixteen was off to New York and the Institute of Musical Art. To finance his studies he spent the summer of 1913 on a Chautauqua tour, playing one-night stands across the country. He soon gave up aspirations of becoming a concert pianist, however, in favor of the even more precarious path of the professional composer. The boy was something of an introvert at this time, devoting most of his time to his studies. He acquired a teaching fellowship at Northwestern University and received his Bachelor of Music degree from the Illinois institution in 1916. In the fall of that year, still not quite twenty years old, the lanky, tow-headed youth was invited to the College of the Pacific in San Jose, California, as Professor of Theory and Composition. He was named dean of the school's Conservatory of Fine Arts two years later.

It was while he was in California that Hanson did his first serious composing. He wrote some chamber music and three pieces for orchestra: *Symphonic Poem, Legend,* and a *Symphonic Rhapsody*. His work won the attention of Walter Henry Rothwell, then director of the Los Angeles Philharmonic. Rothwell invited the young composer to conduct the orchestra in a performance of his *Symphonic Rhapsody*. "I never hope to get in this world the thrill which I had in hearing the first chord of my own music from a great orchestra," Hanson later declared. In 1921 he became one of the three winners of the first American *Prix de Rome* competition. The prize enabled him to spend three years in Rome, as a fellow of the American Adademy there. He was able to listen much, study, and compose. All around him he found young musicians arguing the relative merits of atonality and polytonality and attempting to decide whether they should compose in three or four keys at once. Hanson experimented with the new idiom briefly, but gave it up after Alfred Hertz, longtime conductor of the San Francisco Orchestra, told him in Paris: "Young man, you don't have to write that other kind of music. You have *talent!*"

Fortunately Hertz's advice and Hanson's own inner urge coincided. He essentially turned his back on the sophisticated trends of his peers, considering them more mental exercises than an expression of the emotions and therefore at odds with his fundamental concept of music. His first symphony (the *Nordic*), written in 1922, shows the strong influence of Sibelius and was initially performed by the Augusteo Orchestra of Rome, with the composer conducting. Also written in Italy were a string quartet and two symphonic poems, *North and West* and *Lux Aeterna*. Hanson began the *Lament of Beowulf*, his first large choral work, although the piece was not finished until 1925. He found Rome fascinating, Paris interesting, but London disagreeable.

During his third year in Europe, Walter Damrosch invited Hanson to return home long enough to conduct the New York Symphony in the premiere of *North and West*. He was also guest conductor with the young Rochester Philharmonic for a performance of his *Nordic* symphony. It was then that the dapper Hanson, sporting a beard and high-button shoes, met George Eastman, who shortly offered him the directorship of the three year-old Eastman School of Music. Hanson assumed that position in 1924 and held it for forty years.

In a country with no patronage system, at a time before foundation grants, Hanson discovered in teaching and administration a satisfactory way of devoting himself exclusively to music and still keeping solvent. He proved an able administrator and a born teacher—intelligent, enthusiastic, with a disarming sense of humor. He shortly inaugurated regular American Composers' Concerts in Rochester, launched an annual Festival of American music in 1931, appeared frequently as guest conductor with orchestras throughout the United States, yet continued his own writing. "It is not good," he once said, "to be so introspective that you resent every minute taken from your composing.

He nonetheless managed to produce an impressive amount of music. Ultimately there would be six symphonies. The Second (*Romantic*) Symphony, commissioned by Koussevitzky in 1930 for the fiftieth anniversary of the Boston Symphony Orchestra, proved one of Hanson's most popular works. The composer recognized at the time that his style was "without the social standing of. . .neoclassicism," but held to the belief that "romanticism will find in this country rich soil for a new, young and vigorous growth." The *Romantic* symphony contains an idyllic, haunting quality and demonstrates that the composer has energy and a sure grasp on a varied orchestral palette. The Third Symphony was commissioned by the Columbia Broadcasting Company and was first performed on radio, September 19, 1937. The work is more polyphonic than Hanson's previous symphonies, harmonically purer. The composer considered the Fourth Symphony his best orchestral writing, and critics tend to agree. The piece, dedicated to the memory of Hanson's father, was awarded the Pulitzer Prize in 1944. *Sinfonia Sacra*, the fifth symphony, a bare fifteen minutes long, was first performed by the Philadelphia Orchestra on February 18, 1955. The Sixth Symphony, introduced by the New York Philharmonic under the composer's direction in 1968, is somewhat more linear and contrapuntal in texture than Hanson's earlier works, but is still within the bounds of traditional harmony and romantic lyricism.

Hanson's opera, *Merry Mount*, was produced at the Metropolitan on February 10, 1934, achieving a total of nine performances that season. The libretto by Richard L. Stokes, taken from Hawthorne's story "The Maypole of Merry Mount," centers around an austere Puritan leader named Bradford whose religious convictions are in conflict with his natural impulses. Bradford falls in love with a beautiful girl from the gay settlement of Merry Mount, struggles to save her soul, but loses his own. In the end drunken Indians sack the Puritan village. Bradford seizes the girl, marches into the flames with her, while the faithful chant the Lord's Prayer. Most critics found Hanson's choral writing best. Olin Downes thought the music at times "conventional and noisily effective," but otherwise deemed it neither original nor particularly good theater. *Merry Mount* represents the composer's most ambitious undertaking, and he later drew from it an orchestral suite. Hanson maintained "a lingering fondness" for the opera, but insisted that it needed to be "cut and tied together."

The composer wrote other choral works, including *Songs from Drum Taps* (1925), from Walt Whitman, *Hero Elegy* (1927), and *The Cherubic Hymn* (1950). The *Lament for Beowulf*, however, remained his finest. The symphonic poem *Pan and the Priest* appeared in 1926, while *Mosaics* (1958), *Summer Seascape* (1959), and *Bold Island* (1962) are also for orchestra. Among his later chamber music are a *Serenade* for flute, harp, and strings and a *Pastorale* for oboe and strings. He has written a number of pieces for piano and organ.

Hanson has remained a controversial figure through the years. Few would deny that he is a composer of dignity, but many have objected to his harking back to the nineteenth century and the early twentieth century writer Sibelius. Audiences have generally been more pleased with his music than critics. One forward-looking critic reviewed Hanson's Third Symphony, calling it "Sibelian bilge." The composer dropped him a note saying, "No, that's the Second." Hanson's technique has actually been quite eclectic, and his harmony especially is often highly personal. Much of his music was inspired by the sagas of northern Europe and the open spaces of western America. His best works are full of beauty and charged with emotional intensity.

The biggest problem for Hanson was finding the time to compose, and most of it was done at night, at the sacrifice of his personal life. "In the creative field," he stated, "it is necessary to fight for every bit of leisure." He did not marry until he was nearly fifty, then was surprised to learn that he did more composing than before. "One of the driving forces of composition is that it's so *hard!*" Hanson maintained. When people commented on how prolific he was, he shuddered: "If only they knew the time I take over deciding between, in a single instance, F-sharp and F-natural!"

Despite his own preference for music in the grand manner, Hanson insisted that the artist must have absolute freedom in creative expression. Each composer must write from the depths of his own soul. "Well-knit music that sounds like hell," he contended, "is still competent musicianship and deserves a hearing." He himself supervised the premieres of almost 2000 pieces by more than 700-odd American composers. Many of these works contained harsh dissonance, for which Hanson had little personal liking. He also introduced a number of American compositions abroad. In 1925 he stirred a convention of the Music Teachers' National Association with the plea:

> American music must be created by Americans and no amount of importation of the foreign article will create it for us. Our pioneer grandfathers conquered the West, in spite of untold suffering, to create a material prosperity. Their descendants must now prove that they can, in spite of obstacles, lead their country to the discovery of beauty; that they have not degenerated into lounge-lizards and jazz hounds, but that they too still have the blood of the pioneers in their veins, and the love of beauty in their souls.

Hanson devoted much of his life to that end, training two generations of young musicians and serving as the constant champion of his fellow American composers, regardless of their style. By 1951 he seemed pleased with the headway. "We hear constantly of the gigantic strides in scientific and technological progress in the United States in the twentieth century," Hanson said in a lecture on contemporary American civilization, "but I question whether that progress, though more startling in its implications, is intrinsically more amazing than our development in the world of music."

Hanson is the humanist, concerned not only with the relationship between the artist and his society, but with the more abstract relationship between human beings and their universe. His music has frequently reflected the inner struggle between the spiritual and the sensuous, which the composer considered part of the character development of every individual. He was convinced that musicians should be integral parts of the society in which they live. During the Depression he worked in an advisory capacity with the Federal Music Project. He became a musical consultant to the State Department in 1939 and later served as a member of the United States Commission for UNESCO.

In spite of his devotion to the growth of American music, Hanson was no chauvinist. Nor was he an advocate of a "nationalist" school as such. To him American music simply meant music written by Americans. In the face of repeated criticism, he himself held to a conservative path, writing music that was consistent with his experience and aesthetic viewpoint. Although Hanson was no innovator, his music cannot easily be dismissed. Viewed on its own terms, it possesses strength and a remarkable richness of texture. And while it owes much to the past, it nevertheless speaks to the present.

One of Hanson's colleagues at the Eastman School of Music was Bernard Rogers, another American composer who leans toward traditionalism. All four of Rogers' symphonies, in fact, were introduced by the Rochester Philharmonic under Hanson's direction. Rogers was born in New York City, February 4, 1893. He heard his first concert at sixteen, a revelation which turned his interest from painting to music. He was working as an office boy at the time, but began studying music at night. He later worked with Ernest Bloch in Cleveland, Frank Bridge in England, and Nadia Boulanger in Paris. He was awarded a Pulitzer traveling scholarship in 1918 and came to the attention of American concertgoers the next year with his tone poem *To the Fallen*, written in memory of the war dead. He held a Guggenheim fellowship from 1927 to 1929, was on the staff of *Musical America* for nine years, and joined the faculty of the Eastman School of Music in 1929, later becoming head of the Composition Department.

Hanson performed Rogers' *Soliloquy* (1922), for flute and string quartet, at one of his first American Composers Concerts. A number of the musician's early pieces reflect his interest in Oriental cultures. *Fuji in the Sunset Glow* (1926) and *Three Japanese Dances* (1928), both written for orchestra, were inspired by Japanese prints and mirror their economy, delicacy, and balance. *Fuji in the Sunset Glow*, one of his first purely impressionistic works, was introduced by Walter Damrosch and the New York Symphony Society. Rogers also proved gifted in depicting religious subjects. *The Raising of Lazarus* (1927) and *The Exodus* (1932) are cantatas, while *The Supper at Emmaus* (1937) is an orchestral selection based on Rembrandt's painting by that name. The composer blends his palette of tones in much the same way that the artist mixes his colors, and he is a master of exotic orchestration. Rogers likes to experiment with the possibilities of percussion instruments and unusual sound effects. Although he has written on native themes—for example, *Two American Frescoes* (1935), for orchestra, and *The Plains* (1940), for small orchestra—he feels that whatever national idiom develops in American music will come not from a conscious use of indigenous material, but from strong individual personalities.

Three orchestral works were inspired by World War II: *Sailors of Toulon* (1943), *Invasion* (1943), and *In Memory of Franklin D. Roosevelt* (1945). His operas include *The Marriage of Aude* (1931); *The Warrior* (1947), a one act version of the Samson and Delilah story, produced by the Metropolitan Opera Company; *The Veil* (1950); and *The Nightingale* (1955). Simplicity and directness have been among Rogers' major virtues, and while his music is often romantic and derivative, its honesty prevents it from becoming banal. The composer returned to Oriental themes for *Dance Scenes* (1953), again inspired by Japanese art, and *New Japanese Dances* (1962). Outstanding among his later religious works are *The Passion* (1944), an oratorio that many consider his finest effort, and *The Prophet Isaiah* (1962), for chorus, soloists, and large orchestra.

Rogers' music is difficult to categorize, for he has written in many styles. It is music conceived in great intimacy and a personal mode. Most of his mature life he has spent quietly in Rochester, absorbed in his teaching and his art. "The joyous creative energies, tempered by a sorrowful patience born of humility, are well known to Rogers," David Diamond, his most prominent student, wrote in 1947. "He has waited almost thirty years for the proper recognition of a dedicated creative life: years in which much personal sorrow has mellowed an almost childlike sensitivity and tenderness into an emotional and human largesse which few creative spirits are able to attain in their lifetime."

Whereas Howard Hanson stands as a clear example of American neoromanticism, Rogers has been more influenced by the French impressionists and the pastoral English composers like Holst and Vaughan Williams. Harvard's Walter Piston, on the other hand, best represents neoclassicism, for he is a formalist who codifies rather than invents and strives for balance in his construction. Piston is of Italian descent, born in Rockland, Maine, on January 20, 1894. There were no musicians in his family, and he grew up without even a piano in the home. He lived in Rockland until he was ten, and, like many composers, developed an earlier interest in art. After his family moved to Boston, he spent four years at the Massachusetts Normal Art School, where tuition was free, training to be a painter. There he met the girl who in 1920 would become his wife. It was while Piston was a student at the Mechanic Arts High School that he first became seriously interested in music. He began lessons on the violin, taught himself to play the piano, and managed to earn spending money playing in dance halls, restaurants, and theaters. He grew increasingly serious about music, even wrote a few tunes, but continued his studies in art.

When World War I came, Piston enlisted in the Navy Band. He did not know how to play any band instrument at the time, but went down to Oliver Ditson's Music Company and bought a saxophone. Then he stopped by the public library, checked out an instruction book, and taught himself to play by ear. Although he never saw the sea, his months in the service turned out to be valuable. The band room where he was stationed was full of instruments, and he learned to play a number of them. After the war Piston entered Harvard as a special student, enrolling in Archibald Davison's counterpoint class. Later he became a regular student and was appointed Davison's assistant. "The Harvard music department was a new world," Piston recalled, "where one was in daily contact with great music." But he also enjoyed liberal arts courses outside his field.

Upon graduation in 1924, Piston went abroad on a Paine Fellowship and began studying in Paris with Nadia Boulanger. She was an attractive young woman—highly intelligent, enthusiastic, with an exceptional capacity for inspiring those who worked with her. Piston had decided to become a composer. "If I become a violinist in an orchestra," he told himself, "I'll spend the rest of my life doing what someone else tells me to do." He quickly discovered that he lacked the training needed to become the kind of composer he wanted to be. He had learned the rules at Harvard, but only in a purely academic way. "Rules are not directions how to write music," Piston explains; "using rules is something like going to a gymnasium and lifting bars so that you will become strong." He began studying counterpoint all over again with Boulanger. On Wednesday afternoons, Mlle. Boulanger held a gathering of her students at her apartment. They discussed all sorts of topics and played different kinds of music. Boulanger did not attempt to teach her pupils a particular style, but helped them discover their own. "In my case," Piston said, "I did just what I wanted to and then we'd talk it over." Piston also remembers hearing concerts of modern music in Paris—especially Bartok, Stravinsky, Hindemith, Prokofiev, and Ravel. "Of course, in those days," he later maintained, "we wouldn't have gone to a Beethoven symphony if you paid us." Some of Piston's first compositions were performed in Paris—pieces that he considered "pretty close to Stravinsky, musically speaking."

After two years in Paris, Piston began thinking about earning a living. He returned home with his wife and was soon offered a position as assistant professor at Harvard. "The atmosphere of learning and the association with young people seemed right for me as a composer," he said. The mid-1920s was an exciting period for new music in the United States. Piston and several of his friends got together and formed the Arrow Press, for the printing of their own work. Most of them were writing only chamber music at the time, aware that the great conductors were not much interested in what young American composers were doing. Piston's trio for flute, clarinet, and bassoon was played at the first Copland-Sessions concert in a little theater off Broadway. Then Edward Burlingame Hill, chairman of the Music Department at Harvard, spoke to Koussevitzky about Piston, and the Boston Symphony Orchestra director asked to see him.

"Why you no write for orchestra?" Koussevitzky wanted to know.

"Because nobody would play it," Piston replied.

"Write, and I will play," the conductor promised.

And so Piston wrote, and Koussevitzky played. The composer first gained prominence in 1928 when the Boston Symphony performed his *Symphonic Piece*. A Suite for Orchestra followed the next year. But Koussevitzky continued to ask: "Now what are you writing? Where is the next?" Piston's Concerto for Orchestra was introduced by the Boston Symphony in 1934, and his First Symphony, commissioned by the League of Composers, was initially heard there in 1938.

Piston had already been labeled a twentieth-century classicist, since he adhered to traditional forms, but he did not consider himself such in the early days. "I was writing for a good symphony orchestra music that I knew would be playable," he insisted. "And it was." He was more attracted to modernism in the 1920s than he would be later on. Some of his early works were fairly difficult, changing meters and containing dissonant harmony. But his music was always well constructed and shortly became less complex. The neoclassic balance and alternation of themes was characteristic from the beginning. Clifford Taylor calls Piston "a formalist who attempts to establish the limitations of a creative vision before giving in to its impulses." The composer consistently endeavored for proportion and restraint, economy and clarity, so that his music has come to symbolize the stability of intelligent formulation, in a chaotic and often incomprehensible world.

Although Piston maintained a strong predilection for French culture, his work has not ignored America. Neither has he drawn exclusively from the past. Piston's Suite for Orchestra combined atonality with allusions to American popular idioms, particularly the blues. The first movement of his Second Symphony (1944) contains syncopated rhythms, while the second theme of the slow movement evidences traits of American popular song. Yet Piston has integrated these popular expressions into his musical texture, using them organically rather than decoratively. Time and again the composer has demonstrated that art music can relate to new cultural-aesthetic impulses, without abandoning familiar contexts.

Piston's great popular success came in 1938, with the ballet *The Incredible Flutist*, later arranged as a concert suite. The work was composed for the Boston "Pops" Orchestra and was first performed as a ballet by the Hans Wiener troupe in Providence, Rhode Island. The piece depicts a marketplace where a country circus has been set up. The flutist is the main attraction. The score is marked by Piston's usual breadth and simplicity, but is notably melodic. It is full of wit and gaiety, orchestral color and swirling sonority. In 1943 the suite was played in Moscow to celebrate the United States Independence Day.

Piston followed Edward Burlingame Hill as chairman of the Harvard Music Department, but later resigned that office to devote more time to composing. From 1948 until his retirement from Harvard in 1960, he was the Naumberg Professor of Music. He wrote four textbooks: *Principles of Harmonic Analysis* (1933), *Harmony* (1941), *Counterpoint* (1947), and *Orchestration* (1955), essentially reinterpreting Boulanger's French scholastic pedagogy. For several seasons he also conducted the Pierian Sodality

Orchestra at Harvard. Students found him a reserved, soft-spoken man, who enjoyed a good game of chess. He is remembered often quoting the maxim, "Life is short and art long," to point out his belief that the composer must keep learning.

Certainly Piston continued to learn, moving closer to his ideal of perfect balance. Elliott Carter, one of his most distinguished students, argues that his work before 1946 can be divided into two chronological groups, that written before *The Incredible Flutist* and that written after. The first, Carter feels, was occupied with integrating and assimilating modern techniques, while the second was dominated by Piston's urge toward directness and simplicity. The difference, however, is more a matter of emphasis than a sudden, well-defined change. By 1945 Piston was considered among the major contemporary American composers. "He has not exploded into stellar prominence like a surprising nova," Nicolas Slonimsky maintained, "but took his place inconspicuously, without passing through the inevitable stage of musical exhibitionism or futuristic eccentricity."

Piston wrote a Concerto for Violin and Orchestra in 1940 and would eventually complete nine symphonies. The Third Symphony (1948) was awarded a Pulitzer Prize, as was the Seventh (1961), commissioned by the Philadelphia Orchestra. He composed a Concerto for Viola in 1958 and added a Second Concerto for Violin two years later. A Concerto for Two Pianos and Orchestra appeared in 1959 and a large composition called Variations for Cello and Orchestra was introduced in 1966. The composer wrote a *Lincoln Center Festival Overture* in 1962 for the opening of the new Philharmonic Hall and continued to produce a vast amount of chamber music. Like Haydn, Piston seemed to hit his stride as he got older.

There are those who consider Piston's music inordinately conventional, and he has clearly been no experimental pathfinder. He has remained primarily an instrumental composer, who likes to give every orchestra member something interesting to do in the course of each piece, even if his part is a subordinate one. His music is tremendously lyrical and invariably achieves a high level of technical proficiency. It is cool, yet by no means antiromantic. Personally and artistically Piston is an aristocrat. His work is refined and noble, without being decadent or pompous, and possesses integrity and character. Although his forms are never static, Piston keeps control over large expanses of sound. His compositions are ultimately tonal and without loose ends. "Piston's music is sane and unneurotic," Klaus George Roy concludes; "he does not hand on to us his problems, but his solutions."

While the avant-garde moderns were busily exploring fantastic new sounds and techniques, Walter Piston lived modestly on Belmont Hill, overlooking Cambridge and Harvard, composing in his own way. Young people, he once claimed, "all seem to go through a certain natural evolution. First they are all burned up, the way we were back in the twenties: they want to destroy the past. Then they grow up and say, 'Perhaps the past doesn't have to be destroyed after all. I guess I won't destroy it.'" Later they begin to realize they do not know what the past is, since they have never studied it. Finally, as they mature, "they look inside themselves to see what they have to say, and they find they have great need for a deep knowledge of their musical heritage." Piston discovered a need for that heritage early, yet rejected a tangibly national music in favor of abstract themes and universal forms.

Less noted than either Hanson or Piston is Leo Sowerby, another twentieth-century academic composer, who for many years taught at the American Conservatory in Chicago. Although Sowerby's music lacks Hanson's color and Piston's craftsmanship, it is marked by freshness and vigor. His organ works are particularly viable, while his melody and harmony have been compared with Brahms. Born in Grand Rapids, Michigan, May 1, 1895, Sowerby was the son of an English father and a Canadian mother. He began taking piano lessons at the age of seven and continued with the same teacher until he finished grammar school. Later he studied piano and theory in Chicago, where he attended Englewood High. He graduated from the American Conservatory there and in 1917 joined the army. He was first stationed at Camp Grant, Illinois, was soon made bandmaster, and eventually served in England and France. From 1921 to 1924 he held a fellowship at the American Academy in Rome. He returned to the United States, was appointed to the faculty of the American Conservatory, where he taught composition and orchestration, succeeded his own teacher as head of the composition department, and for thirty-five years was organist and choirmaster of St. James Episcopal Church. In 1962 he became the first director of the newly formed College of Church Musicians at the Washington Cathedral, in Washington, D.C.

Sowerby was eighteen when critic Glenn Dillard Gunn included his violin concerto on a program of American music presented in Chicago. That was his first publicly performed piece, and the critics "landed on my concerto with all fours," the composer remembers, insisting that the youth "displayed no musical ability." Four years later Eric DeLamarter directed an entire program of his works in Orchestra Hall, and again the critics trounced him. But Frederick Stock, conductor of the Chicago Symphony, heard the concert and liked Sowerby's music well enough to ask the red-headed boy to write a piece for his orchestra. The result was *A Set of Four*, played by the Chicago Symphony while Sowerby was a private at Camp Grant. This time the critics were much kinder, and the composer's commanding officer was sufficiently impressed to promote him to the rank of third-class musician.

Between 1919 and 1921 Sowerby wrote his First Symphony, several chamber selections, and an organ piece, *Requiescat in Pace*, in memory of his fallen comrades in France. During the excitement over Gershwin's *Rhapsody in Blue*, he produced two works for Paul Whiteman's "symphonic-jazz" concerts—*Monotony* and *Sinconata. The Irish Washerwoman* had been written earlier in a popular idiom, but he returned to more serious composition in 1925 with *The Vision of Sir Launfal*, for chorus and orchestra. *A Medieval Poem,* for organ and orchestra and dedicated to Howard Hanson, followed the next year, while a Second Symphony was completed in 1927. Sowerby's tone poem *Prairie,* based on a poem by Carl Sandburg, appeared in 1929, proving one of his most virile works and probably his best known. There are two piano concertos, two more symphonies, a later violin concerto, and a Concerto for Organ and Orchestra, introduced by E. Power Biggs and the Boston Symphony in April, 1938.

Sowerby adheres to a strict formal design in his compositions and stays within the bounds of traditional tonality. His harmony, however, frequently belongs to the twentieth century. "I have been accused by right-wingers of being too dissonant and cacophonous," Sowerby confesses, "and by the leftists of being old-fashioned and derivative." Oscar Sonneck agreed with the first opinion and once commented that the American composer should be added to Bach, Beethoven, and Brahms, forming a fourth B—"Sour B!" Much of the musician's later work has been ecclesiastical music, a field in which he has particularly distinguished himself. He received a Pulitzer Prize in 1946 for a choral work based on St. Francis of Assisi's *Canticle of the Sun.* His oratorio *Christ Reborn* appeared in 1953, followed four years later by *The Throne of God,* a poem for mixed voices. There are also several shorter anthems and countless songs, only a few of which have been published.

Aside from his war experiences, Sowerby led a secluded life. Like most traditional composers, he devoted years to teaching and was basically academic by temperament. In art, as well as learning, the university or academy is looked upon as the upholder of tradition. Such institutions have the duty of transmitting established rules and an inherited knowledge from one generation to another. It is therefore understandable that professors who write music tend to do so in modes that may be considered conventional or classical.

But not all traditionalists are academicians. Some like Deems Taylor have supported their composition by other means, usually music criticism; others at least recently have benefited from foundation grants. Samuel Barber, surely the best known and most performed contemporary romantic composer, has been successful enough as a writer that teaching has rarely been necessary. Barber's music is quiet, elegant, cosmopolitan, whole-heartedly traditional. Not all of it is equally conservative, and probably no single work could actually have been written in the nineteenth century. Yet the composer has remained faithful to a lyric tonality that has won him continued popularity.

Barber represents a younger generation of American composers who arrived on the scene in the 1930s. Born in West Chester, Pennsylvania, March 9, 1910, he is the nephew of Louise Homer, the Metropolitan contralto. Barber wrote his first melody at age seven, although his parents made no attempt to develop a possible prodigy. They tried to encourage him to play sports and engage in the activities of a normal American boy. But Samuel was interested in other things. When he was about eight, he left a note on his mother's dressing table. "To begin with," he said, "I was not meant to be an athelete, I was meant to be a composer. and will be, I'm sure . . . Don't ask me to try to forget this . . . and go and play football.—*Please*—Sometimes I've been worrying about this so much that it makes me mad! (not very)."

Barber's father was a physician and for twenty-five years president of the West Chester school board. Although Dr. Barber loved music, he wanted his son to go to Princeton and study medicine. Sam's mother's family was more musical. The boy received a great deal of encouragement from both Louise and Sidney Homer, whom he frequently visited during summer vacations. His Uncle Sidney was himself the composer of a number of songs, and Louise Homer would include some of her nephew's early pieces on her recital programs in 1927. At ten Sam wrote an opera to a libretto by the family's Irish cook, and he continued taking piano lessons through high school. The youth was shy and moody with strangers, enjoyed reading and walking in the country, and withdrew more and more into his inner life as he got older. While still in high school, he began studying at the Curtis Institute of Music in nearby Philadelphia. He was appointed organist of the Westminster Presbyterian Church in West Chester and invested some of his earnings in a subscription to the concerts of the Philadelphia Orchestra, then under Leopold Stokowski.

He became a fulltime student at Curtis Institute in 1926, adding voice and composition to his studies. He learned counterpoint and harmony from Rosario Scalero, an Italian who had trained in Germany. Scalero insisted that student exercises must be expressive, and he carefully fostered any signs of individuality. Early in 1928 Barber read a notice on the bulletin board at Curtis Institute, announcing the Bearns Prize of $1200 for the best composition submitted to the judges designated by Columbia University. He sent in a violin sonata and won, using the money to make his first trip abroad. He visited Scalero and his family, who were staying in a village in the Italian Alps, then he progressed to Venice, Vienna, Salzburg, and Munich, where he heard *Parsifal*. The youth spent the next four summers in Italy, but returned to Philadelphia each fall to continue his work in piano, composition, and voice.

Barber's feeling for form is evident in his very early pieces. He won a second Bearns Prize in 1933 for his *Overture to The School for Scandal*, first played by the Philadelphia Orchestra at Robin Hood Dell, under Alexander Smallens. *Dover Beach*, for voice and string quartet, was written in the fall of 1933. *Music for a Scene from Shelley*, based on some lines from *Prometheus Unbound*, was introduced by the New York Philharmonic-Symphony in March, 1935. Barber's instrumental music owes much to the continuity of its lyric flow, while his understanding of the human voice is apparent from the outset. It is music that wears its heart on its sleeve—a sleeve cut from a nineteenth-century pattern. Yet the heart is none the less true, so that the music still has meaning. Barber's appeal, according to Wilfrid Mellers, "depends on qualities that his music shares with Tchaikowsky and Puccini.

It matters because it is heartfelt, never secondhand: and its awareness of adolescence strikes deep into the American experience."

Barber left Curtis Institute in the spring of 1933. He wanted to compose, but knew that he would have to earn money elsewhere. He tried singing professionally and teaching. Singing did not prove financially profitable, whereas teaching involved him so deeply that there was no time for his own work. His dream was to devote himself completely to writing. "Give me a place to live *in the country* and a peaceful room with a piano in which to work," he said time and again in letters, "and I ask for nothing more." He spent 1933-34 in Vienna, where he composed and studied conducting, and the next fall settled in New York. He supported himself by singing on the radio while he wrote a Cello Sonata and *The Virgin Martyrs*, for women's voices. In 1935 he received both a Pulitzer Scholarship and the American Prix de Rome. The latter included a stipend of $2500 and free living quarters in Rome. That winter he wrote several songs, among them "Rain Has Fallen" and "Sleep Now" to poems by James Joyce, and finished his First Symphony. The symphony was initially heard in Rome, May, 1936, and was played at the Salzburg Music Festival the next year. It received its American premiere in Cleveland in 1937.

The composer returned to the United States for a brief visit with his family in February, 1936, but by April was back in Rome. He received another Pulitzer Scholarship and completed a String Quartet. Some three years before he had met Arturo Toscanini at his villa on an island in Lake Maggiore. Toscanini was again in Italy during the summer of 1937, preparing programs for his coming season with the National Broadcasting Company Orchestra. The conductor wanted to do an American work, but was undecided about the composer. Artur Rodzinski, who had directed Barber's Symphony in One Movement both in Cleveland and New York, urged Toscanini to play something by the young man from Pennsylvania. On November 5, 1938, Toscanini conducted Barber's First Essay for Orchestra and his Adagio for Strings (arranged from the slow movement of the String Quartet), the first American works performed by the NBC Symphony. The Toscanini broadcast promptly put the twenty-eight year-old Barber in the front rank of American composers, while the Adagio—a relatively simple piece, purely romantic, showing Barber's lyrical qualities at their best—immediately became one of the composer's most popular selections.

Barber took an apartment in Paris during the early fall of 1939, planning to finish a violin concerto he had started in Switzerland. He had barely gotten settled in France when Americans were warned to leave. He boarded a ship for home and arrived in New York as German troops were invading Poland. His Concerto for Violin and Orchestra was introduced by Albert Spalding and the Philadelphia Orchestra in February, 1941. The war experience, coupled with his father's death, had a maturing effect on the composer. After 1939 the traditional characteristics of his music became mingled with more modern idioms. He grew more venturesome in his use of dissonance and in his handling of tonality. His lyric line became more chromatic and angular, while his dramatic leaps were contracted into shorter themes, more jagged and biting. Barber's later music has a tendency to avoid the obvious, and nowhere is this demonstrated better than in his choice of rhythms, which are varied and active.

The composer taught orchestration briefly at Curtis Institute and wrote a Second Essay for Orchestra, far more contemporary in sound than the First. He was inducted into the United States Army in 1942 and, because of defective vision, was assigned to Special Services. Later he was transferred to the Air Force where he was given time to compose. He wrote a *Commando March*, which the Army Air Force Band played, and was commissioned to write a symphony dedicated to the AAF. To prepare himself Barber flew with pilots on their trips and was particularly impressed with the night flights. The heroism of the aviators, the tragic implications of an existence so detached from ordinary life, the sense of being alone in the universe moved the composer deeply. He tried to incorporate this emotional content into his Second Symphony. The symphony was first performed by Koussevitzky and the Boston Symphony Orchestra on March 3, 1944, with a number of highranking officers in attendance. Many were bewildered by a work full of irregular rhythms and dissonance. A few days after the premiere Corporal Barber received a note from a Chinese serviceman who said he had heard the symphony and disliked it intensely. The enlisted man explained that he had applauded, however, for he felt all corporals should be encouraged.

When he was mustered out of the service in September, 1945, Barber returned to Capricorn, the home he and his friend and schoolmate Gian-Carlo Menotti had bought together two years before. The house was near Mt. Kisco, about an hour's drive from New York City, located on a wooded knoll overlooking Croton Lake in the distance. A low, rambling structure, the house contained separate wings converging upon a large living room. Each composer had his own quarters, including a work room with piano, on opposite sides of the house, so that they could write at the same time without disturbing one another. Capricorn became a meeting place for artists, musicians, poets, and writers. But for Samuel Barber it was the fulfillment of his dream to have "a place to live in the country and a peaceful room with a piano in which to work." He wrote his *Capricorn* Concerto, for chamber orchestra, in 1944, experimenting with irregular rhythms and colors in a Stravinsky-like manner.

He treated American folk idioms in *Excursions* (1944), four selections for piano. The Cello Concerto (1945) is broader in scope, the dissonant elements easily absorbed into traditional shapes. *Cave of the Heart* (1946), the ballet Barber wrote for Martha Graham, deals with the relationship between Medea and Jason at the end of their tragic stay in Corinth. The music is taut, intense, a fusion of old and new elements. The composer later recast some of this material into a symphonic suite entitled *Medea's Meditation and Dance of Vengeance*, introduced by the Philadelphia Orchestra in 1947. Not until his

Piano Sonata (1949), however, did Barber truly break with neoromanticism and employ a twelve-tone technique. While the form of the sonata is more or less traditional and its themes are sharply defined, its texture is almost entirely chromatic and dissonant. Emotionally the piece is more profound than many of the composer's earlier works.

For the nostalgic *Knoxville: Summer of 1915*, commissioned by soprano Eleanor Steber in 1948, Barber deliberately looks back to his early lyric style, returning to conventional key relationships. Based on a prose text by James Agee, the piece opens tenderly. A child is lying in the grass on a summer evening, as his family sits on the porch, rocking and watching things go by— people, a horse pulling a buggy, a loud auto, a quiet auto. This mood is suddenly interrupted by a passing streetcar. The tranquility returns, and the child gazes at the stars and thinks about his various loved ones talking "of nothing in particular ..., of nothing at all." The music swells into a passionate outburst at the words "By some chance, here they are, all on this earth; and who shall ever tell the sorrow of being on this earth." Then the child offers a prayer: "May God bless my people, my uncle, my aunt, my mother, my good father, oh, remember them kindly in their time of trouble; and in the hour of their taking away." In a while the child is put to bed. As the lyrics end, the child yearns for an identity, while the orchestra continues with a gentle, rocking postlude.

Barber often comes across better with the intimate statement than with the large gesture. *Nuvoletta* (1947), for voice and piano, is set to a passage from James Joyce's *Finnegans Wake* in a somewhat surrealistic manner. The *Hermit Songs* (1953) are drawn from translations of ten medieval Irish poems by anonymous monks and scholars. On a bigger scale is *Prayers of Kierkegaard* (1954), for mixed chorus, soprano, and orchestra and ranging in harmonic style from the modal to the classical to the atonal. Here Barber treats the Man-God relationship much like a child-parent relationship, while his music has a gentle distinction that is free from the inflated bombast of his earlier symphonic works. *Andromache's Farewell* (1963), for soprano and orchestra, was written for the New York Philharmonic's first season at Lincoln Center.

The composer had long wanted to write an opera, but was unable to locate a suitable libretto. Edward Johnson had offered Barber $5000 to compose a work for the Metropolitan, but the musician had declined when he discovered he would not have complete freedom in the choice of his subject. Eventually he found his librettist in his own home. In 1956 Gian-Carlo Menotti wrote the text for *Vanessa*, a four act opera that Barber set to music the following year. It appeared at the Metropolitan in a lavish production on January 15, 1958. The work received the Pulitzer Prize, and the public reception was warm. Critic Winthrop Sargeant thought the score "both complex and highly charged with emotional meaning" and insisted that Barber had "demonstrated that serious grand opera is still a living thing." Emily Coleman of *Theatre Arts* pronounced it the best American work yet heard at the Metropolitan. "Unclassified nationally," she added, "it ranks with the four or five finest written anywhere in the last quarter century." Critics later expressed reservations. Neither the characters nor the setting are very clearly defined. The music, in Eric Salzman's opinion, merely "increases the sense of a vague nostalgia and a brooding, melancholy regret that seems to permeate the piece." The opera is frankly romantic, but Mellers claims it fails because Barber attempts to deal with a hermit theme in an adult way. "The failure of Barber's art to grow up," the English musicologist concludes, "becomes a liability only when he seeks to give it more weight than it can bear."

Yet *Vanessa*'s success was auspicious enough that manager Rudolf Bing commissioned Barber to write *Antony and Cleopatra*, the opera which opened the new Metropolitan Opera House in Lincoln Center. This time Winthrop Sargeant felt the composer's "sensitive, retiring temperament" seemed "out of its element in a spectacle of such grandiose proportions." Despite appealing moments, the dramatic scale of the work was simply not filled out with "music of sufficient power and eloquence." All in all, Sargeant regarded *Antony and Cleopatra* inferior to *Vanessa* in every way. Irving Kolodin thought the new opera took up "in sureness of procedure and certainty of direction" where *Vanessa* left off, but agreed the spectacle and pageantry did not serve Barber well. Franco Zeffirelli's libretto gave the composer no opportunities for musical elaboration. Not until the third act, when Cleopatra has retired to her monument, was Barber's music able to triumph over the action, especially in the aria beginning "Give me my robe." "Wagner visits the scene," Kolodin maintained, "and also Mahler, but the personality that prevails is Barber's own."

Most of the composer's later music shows a synthesis of elements, although the romantic leaning remains strong. His First Piano Concerto, which won the Pulitzer Prize in 1963, is strongly lyrical, an enchanting poem as fresh as it is lovely. Barber has constantly searched for new means of creating beauty, and the totality of his work is like a living organism, growing and deepening as the composer perfected his art. He tends to work slowly, paying much attention to thematic material. His orchestration is tasteful and varied, and he has a keen ear for instrumental colors. The best of his music, like Barber himself, tends to be somewhat withdrawn and private, although it is seldom static. His conservatism is not purely academic, Mellers insists, for it is Barber's wish "to conserve, not merely a musical tradition, but also the emotional aura of his youth." His work mirrors a sophisticate longing for innocence, a twentieth-century American nostalgic for the past, as he attempts to come to grips with the present.

Barber first heard of Gian-Carlo Menotti when his composition teacher, Scalero, told him one day in 1928 that a talented young Italian was coming to study at Curtis Institute. Since Menotti could speak French but no English and Barber could speak French, Scalero hoped the two might become friends. Menotti was a year younger than Barber, born in Cadegliano, Italy, July 7,

1911. He had grown up listening to opera at La Scala, in Milan. Barber dutifully took the gangly foreigner under his wing, and a lifelong friendship began. Whereas Barber was melancholy and reserved, Menotti was volatile and cheerful. Barber was intense and organized; Menotti was haphazard and somewhat irresponsible. The newcomer spent his first Thanksgiving and Christmas in America with Barber's family at West Chester. To him the quiet Quaker town was "exotic." Barber, on the other hand, spent several summers with the Menotti family near Milan, and the two boys traveled and hiked over Europe together.

Even as a student Menotti wrote music with amazing facility, and he was irritated by rules and regulations. He spent five years at Curtis mastering theory and counterpoint, thereby reversing the nineteenth-century custom of Americans going abroad to study. His great love was opera, and he began his first success, *Amelia Goes to the Ball*, when he was twenty-two. The work was initially staged by the opera department at Curtis, under Fritz Reiner, but was subsequently performed at La Scala and the Metropolitan. Menotti, as later, wrote his own libretto, and the piece is full of charm and sparkling humor. The success of *Amelia* led the National Broadcasting Company to commission *The Old Maid and the Thief*, first heard over radio in April, 1939. Again the composer demonstrated skill and craftsmanship.

The Island God was produced by the Metropolitan in 1942, and *The Medium* (1946) and *The Telephone* (1947) both played on Broadway for several seasons to sold-out houses. *The Consul* (1950) is a tragic look at the dehumanized world of bureaucracy and, like the composer's earlier works, proved exceptionally good theater. The Christmas fantasy *Amahl and the Night Visitors* (1951), *Maria Golovin* (1958), and *Labyrinth* (1963) were all written for television. Other operas include *The Saint of Bleecker Street* (1954), *The Last Savage* (1963), and *Martin's Lie* (1964). In addition Menotti has written two ballets, a concerto for piano and orchestra, a *Pastorale* for string orchestra and piano, a symphonic poem, a concerto for violin and orchestra, and a cantata (*The Death of the Bishop of Brindisi*, 1963).

But the operas stand as Menotti's finest contribution. He has a knack for choosing timeless themes in topical settings and, like Barber, has a love for melody. He has transplanted the conventions of European opera to America and at the same time successfully bridged the gap between the opera house and Broadway. His music is derivative, showing the influence of Puccini, Verdi, Debussy, Richard Strauss, and others, but he has used this heritage with a freedom and flexibility and a sense of contemporary values that has given it new significance. Mellers contends that Menotti effectively "brings Puccini up to date." By taking his cue in part from Hollywood, he has "created an operatic stylization that seems almost as natural—and therefore acceptable to a popular democratic audience—as realistic drama." The composer finds that English has a great variety of inflections and accents and lends itself well to opera. While he has never become an American citizen, Menotti has lived principally in this country. The technicality has not negated his being considered America's leading operatic composer.

Robert Ward, another major composer of opera, studied composition with Hanson and Rogers at the Eastman School of Music and later at the Juilliard Graduate School. He is convinced that a reaction against the great musical revolution is in order and has commonly written in a language that recalls the nineteenth century, using harmonic combinations as simple as the triad. At thirty he expressed his credo: "My generation will have the task of reworking materials which the revolution has given us, while at the same time reapplying the basic principles which have again been clarified."

Born in Cleveland, Ohio, on September 13, 1917, Ward began writing songs and orchestral works in the late 1930s. He composed an andante and scherzo for strings, an *Ode*, a *Yankee Overture*, and his First Symphony before entering the United States Army during World War II. He was also on the faculty of Queens College. In the service he was bandleader of the Seventh Infantry Division and wrote music for an all-soldier show. After the war he composed the boisterous *Jubilation* Overture, three more symphonies, a sonata for violin and piano, a concerto for piano and orchestra, and *Night Fantasy*, for band. His growth as an artist has been essentially assimilative, marked by an individuality that is both consciously and intuitively eclectic. Even in his earliest pieces he demonstrated a skill for keeping the orchestra moving and has consistently preferred writing on the larger scale.

Like Menotti, Ward has become best known for his operas. *He Who Gets Slapped*, freely adapted from Leonid Andreyev's play, was produced by the New York City Opera Company in 1959. *The Crucible*, based on the drama by Arthur Miller, followed two years later. Commissioned by the New York Opera under a Ford Foundation grant, *The Crucible* received the New York Music Critics' Circle Award and a Pulitzer Prize. Ward's vocal writing, like his other music, is melodious and natural, yet is charged with dramatic force.

Among the more inventive American composers still using traditional forms has been Elliott Carter. While his early works show little of the originality and daring that would come later, by the 1950s Carter had gained recognition as one of the most original composers in American serious music, particularly in his use of vigorous, unique, and asymmetrical rhythms. Born in New York City, December 11, 1908, he studied at Harvard with Piston and Hill and took a course from Gustav Holst, who was a visiting professor. Neither of his parents had been particularly musical, but the family had a player piano, and Elliott decided when he was in the third or fourth grade that he wanted to take piano lessons. He had broad intellectual interests and spent two years as a graduate student in English. He received his Master of Arts degree from Harvard in 1930, then spent three years in Paris studying with Nadia Boulanger. "The things that were most remarkable and wonderful about her," Carter remembered, "were her extreme concern for the material of music and her acute awareness of its many phases and possibilities." He met Stravinsky in Paris, "because he used to come to tea at Mlle. Boulanger's." Carter returned to the United States in 1935 and for two years was music director of the Ballet Caravan.

His approach to music reflects the scope and depth of his cultural background. He composed incidental music to Sophocles' *Philoctetes*, for a performance by the Harvard Classical Club in 1933 and has often returned to classical subjects. He wrote a comic opera, *Tom and Lily* (1934); an oratorio, *The Bridge* (1937); two ballets, *The Ballroom Guide* (1937) and *Pocahontas* (1939); a suite for four alto saxophones (1939); *The Defense of Corinth* (1942), after Rabalais, for narrator, male chorus, and two pianos; and his First Symphony (1942), performed in Rochester in 1944. A number of his early pieces are marked by a self-conscious classicism, and there are often Stravinskian characteristics. The early works are generally simpler in idiom, and Carter seemed to be getting out of his system a number of obvious debts to other composers. Most of these selections are diatonic, although *Pocahontas* uses a dissonant chromatic style. After 1939 Carter's music developed a surer quality. The exhuberant *Holiday* Overture demonstrating considerable ingenuity in rhythmic design, was written in 1944, and another ballet, *The Minotaur*, was performed in New York by the Ballet Society in 1947. By the end of World War II, Carter's attitude toward composition was changing a great deal. "For one thing," he said, "the whole Expressionist point of view had come...to seem as if it were part of the madness that led to Hitler. Indeed, some German expressionists did become Nazis, although many more left Germany, changed their styles, and so on."

But much of the transformation resulted from Carter's own search for his version of an American style. A major advance came in 1946 with the completion of his Piano Sonata, in which the composer achieved a powerful individuality. The piece has sweep and scale, drama and intensity, and carried forward Carter's exploration of irregular rhythm and shifted accents. With the Piano Sonata there is a new coherence, greater clarity and expressiveness. The composer introduced his principle of "metrical modulation," which has become a hallmark of his mature scores, in his sonata for cello and piano (1948). Here Carter passes from one metrical speed to another by shortening or lengthening the value of the basic unit note. He extends the principle even further with his First String Quartet (1951), in which changes of speed occur unsimultaneously in the four instruments, resulting in a constant variation of pulse. For this string quartet, the composer said, "I decided for once to write a work very interesting to myself, and to say to hell with the public and with the performers too."

Mellers considers Carter's First Quartet "among the handful of American masterpieces," and Richard Franko Goldman in 1957 proclaimed it "without doubt the most important and imposing accomplishment of American music in the last decade." The work spoke to the postwar American vanguard much as Stravinsky's *Sacre* spoke to progressive Europeans a half century earlier. Bartok influenced the piece, and Copland and Ives, but the totality is one of great originality and dark intensity. Each of the four instruments has its own personality and independence, yet Carter has achieved freedom without losing control, balancing the interchanges of material. Unlike *Tristan* or the *Sacre*, which ensnared so many later composers with their particular newness, the First String Quartet has seemed to serve as a liberating rather than a constricting influence on contemporary writers.

Carter's reputation was further strengthened by a comparatively relaxed sonata for flute, oboe, cello, and harpsichord (1952), the Variations for Orchestra (1956), his Second String Quartet (1959), a Double Concerto for harpsichord and piano with two chamber orchestras (1961), and a Piano Concerto (1965). In reviewing the Variations, Goldman said that the shadows of Bartok, Berg, and Schoenberg had dissolved into the background, becoming merely "the point of departure for a new, dominant, strong, and sure personality." All of Carter's works are stamped with urgency, while his later selections are distinguished by an increasing richness of texture. While the composer has used key signatures in none of his pieces since the Cello Sonata, his sense of tonal direction remains strong. A fastidious worker, Carter lavishes much time on each composition, choosing his language freshly for each one. He constantly seeks to combine new approaches with the traditional forms of Western music and professes impatience with repeating what he has already done.

Achieving a national expression has been important to Carter, although for those used to thinking of American music in terms of folk song, lively rhythm, and syncopation, this has not been readily apparent. "Actually, the professional cheerfulness of much Americana was a false note," Martin Boykan argues; "the poets have always thought of America as a haunted and tragic place. . . . It has been remarked that where English literature tends to precise and objective description, a dominant strain in American literature is the tortured confessional." Boykan therefore finds Carter's pathos and personal method of organization comfortably within the American tradition, especially in an age when isolation is no longer fashionable. Whereas Samuel Barber reflects a continuing American innocence, Elliott Carter represents an America come of age, possessing a truer vision of what and where his people are.

Western music between the wars was haunted by ghosts. Many composers consciously avoided whole areas of musical material simply because these were thought too conservative or too radical or represented the wrong ideology. This atmosphere inevitably led to artificiality. For Carter the antiromantic struggle is over, its issues dead. He has chosen from the whole range of musical possibilities. Some young composers in the 1920s and 1930s rushed to embrace one technical fad after another, as its leading proponents became well known. Most of the fads lasted only a few years, then were discarded in the race to something else. But Carter's innovations appear more permanent. "I do not consider my rhythmic procedures a trick or a formula," the composer has said, for all aspects of his compositions "are closely bound together."

Carter began serious composition fairly late, and since he comes from a well-to-do family, has been able to pursue his musical career a bit more leisurely than most. He has taught at various colleges and universities, including Yale, but his main occupation has been writing music. He received the Prix de Rome in 1953 and has held two Guggenheim fellowships. He admits that his music is difficult, both for listeners and performers. His style contains a psychological dimension, as various motives bubble up to the mind's surface. Mellers, in fact, finds an analogy between Carter's musical processes and the literary "stream of consciousness." At his height the composer's work is marked by aural imagination, rhythmic fluidity, dynamic power, and an individualistic self-reliance, combining a pioneer's energy with an artist's order.

Carter's conservatism, to be sure, is far more restricted than that of Deems Taylor, "the Eastman group," Piston, Sowerby, Barber, or Menotti. While Barber has evolved from neoromanticism, to a Stravinskian neoclassicism, to atonality, he comes nowhere near Carter's inventiveness, even at his most modern. Yet Carter has sought his way within conventional molds, has borrowed ideas from warring camps, and has created an American music that is distinctly his own. He is a traditionalist with an emancipated mind, a revolutionary loyal to his heritage.

CHAPTER

V

COPLAND AND GERSHWIN

Once jazz became the rage with Americans in the 1920s, it was merely a matter of time before art composers turned to the popular idiom in the hope of creating a truly national music. By the mid-1920s "symphonic jazz" was the fad, paralleling a diplomatic withdrawal from European affairs and the retreat into jingoism brought on by disillusionment over World War I. Although several young composers attempted to interpose a jazz motif into orchestral works and opera, two stood at the front: Aaron Copland and George Gershwin. Within two years of the same age, both were of Russian-Jewish descent. Both were born in Brooklyn and lived in New York, and in differing ways they each incorporated the sounds and confusion of the city into their music. While Gershwin's use of jazz was the more extensive, Copland went through a definite jazz period early in his career, often combining popular themes and rhythms with a modern French style he had formulated under Nadia Boulanger. Copland came to "symphonic jazz" after intensive training in serious composition at home and abroad, whereas Gershwin approached it as a Tin Pan Alley songwriter gone highbrow. Copland went on to develop his art in other forms, while Gershwin continued to deepen his work in the only style in which he felt comfortable.

Born amid drab surroundings, November 14, 1900, Aaron Copland stayed in Brooklyn for twenty years. His neighborhood, peopled largely by

Italians, Irish, and blacks, had "none of the garish color of the ghetto, none of the charm of an old New England thoroughfare. . . . It was simply drab." The family name had originally been Kaplan, but was changed somewhere during his father's migration from Russia to Scotland to the United States. In Brooklyn Aaron's father became a merchant and eventually the owner of a fair-sized department store. His mother also came from Russia, but neither of his parents were particularly interested in music. An older brother did play the violin and his three sisters the piano. On top of the family upright there were stacks of ragtime for relaxed moments, and Copland remembers "passable performances of potpourris from assorted operas." But the future composer heard little talk of music at home and did not attend a professional concert until much later.

When he was about eight and a half years old, Aaron came down with a mild case of typhoid. While he was sick, a sister-in-law sent him some cherries. To show his gratitude, the boy wrote a song for her, although this was more play than anything else. At eleven he had a few abortive piano lessons from sister Laurine, but not until he was thirteen did Aaron take music seriously. Then suddenly, on his own, he decided he wanted to become a musician. By the time he graduated from Boy's High School in 1918, he had studied with a number of teachers. Yet music as an art, Copland staunchly insists, "was a discovery I made all by myself."

None of his friends liked serious music, and at times the boy felt very lonely. He first tried to learn harmony through a correspondence course, then found a formal teacher. In the fall of 1917 he began private lessons in theory and composition with Rubin Goldmark, nephew of the composer of the opera *The Queen of Sheba* and later head of the composition department at Juilliard.

"I want to be a composer," the gangling, bespectacled youth told his new teacher.

Goldmark looked at him sternly and asked, "What for?"

Copland had trouble explaining his reasons, but impressed Goldmark with his industry and talent. What the teacher disapproved of was young Copland's inclination to experiment, for Goldmark had been trained in the conservative school and had no use for modern music. When the boy brought him a short, Debussy-like piano piece entitled *The Cat and the Mouse*, the teacher took one look and threw it aside.

"How do you expect me to criticize such music?" he asked in disgust.

"As far as I can remember," Copland maintains, "no one ever told me about 'modern music.' I apparently happened on it in the course of my musical explorations." So long as he studied with Goldmark, however, he found it wise to proceed with these explorations in private. Yet from Goldmark he received a solid grasp of the fundamentals of music, which the composer says spared him "the flounderings that so many American musicians have suffered through incompetent teaching."

Copland continued to work with Goldmark through the spring of 1921, uncovering new music literature—Scriabin, Debussy, Ravel—on his own. It was still a foregone conclusion that any American with serious pretensions as a composer must "finish" his studies abroad. For the postwar generation "abroad" meant Paris; Germany by then was considered old-fashioned. Copland read in a music journal that a school for American musicians was to be inaugurated in the Palace at Fontainebleau during the summer of 1921. He responded to the announcement immediately and became the school's first pupil. Copland left for France with money saved from helping out as a cashier at his father's department store and working summers as a Wall Street runner. He knew no one in Paris and spoke only high school French. At Fontainebleau he studied with Paul Vidal of the Paris Conservatory, whose approach was every bit as conventional as Goldmark's and whose peculiar patois the young American could scarcely understand. All summer Copland kept hearing ecstatic reports about a brilliant harmony teacher named Nadia Boulanger. "This news naturally had little interest for me," the composer recalls, "since I had long finished *my* harmonic studies." But he finally agreed to sit in on Mlle. Boulanger's class. That particular day she was explaining the harmonic structure of a scene from *Boris Godunov*. "I had never before witnessed such enthusiasm and such clarity in teaching," Copland wrote, and he knew then that he had found his teacher.

He had only one reservation. Who ever heard of studying composition with a woman? "Everyone knows that the world has never produced a first-rate woman composer," Copland explains, "so it follows that no woman could possibly hope to teach composition. Moreover, how would it sound to the folks back home?" Nevertheless, in the fall he found himself at 36 Rue Ballu, Boulanger's home and studio. He became her first fulltime American composition student. At last Copland was in his element, surrounded by a congenial group of young musicians interested in experimenting with new ideas. Paris was an exciting place in those days. Gertrude Stein was there; so were Ezra Pound, James Joyce, and Ernest Hemingway. Diaghilev and his ballet company were in the city, as were Stravinsky, Picasso, and Andre Gide. Copland met George Antheil there and later Virgil Thomson, visited the Left Bank bookshops, and heard the music of Honegger, Poulenc, Ravel, Satie, Milhaud, Bartok, Hindemith, Falla, and even Schoenberg. The pent-up artistic energies of the war years were being unloosed in Paris, and Copland later characterized the city as "an international proving ground for all the newest tendencies in music. Much of the music that had been written during the dark years of the war was now being heard for the first time."

Boulanger was about thirty-three years old when Copland began studying with her. He found her bright-eyed, eager-faced, full of feminine charm and wit. She had a consuming love for music, an encyclopedic knowledge of the literature past and present, and a unique ability to inspire pupils with confidence in their own creative powers. At Boulanger's insistence Copland spent the summer of 1922 in Berlin and the following summer in Vienna, obtaining some contact with the German musical tradition. But he wanted to write in an American idiom, and this Boulanger helped him work out, although the French influence was initially strong.

Under her guidance he composed four a capella motets, a passacaglia for piano, a rondino for string quartet, and "As It Fell Upon a Day" for soprano, flute, and clarinet. His earlier *The Cat and the Mouse* had been played at a student concert at Fontainebleau and was published in France. Copland received $25 for it from Jacques Durand, Debussy's publisher, and felt that he had "arrived." His most ambitious work undertaken in Europe was a one act ballet based on a German film—*Grohg*, written after the summer in Berlin.

The composer received additional funds from home and remained with Boulanger for three years. He also studied piano with Ricardo Vines, Poulenc's teacher. Meanwhile he attended the influential Concerts Koussevitzky at the Paris Opera and as much ballet as possible. He heard and discussed samples of the new music at Boulanger's class meetings and teas. "The watchword in those days," Copland says, "was 'originality.' The laws of rhythm, of harmony, of construction had all been torn down. Every composer in the vanguard set out to remake these laws according to his own conceptions." And this included Copland himself.

He returned to the United States, with baggage under his arm, in June, 1924. Before leaving France he had received a request from Boulanger to write a concerto for organ and orchestra. Walter Damrosch had invited her to come to America and appear as organ soloist with the New York Symphony, and she wanted to perform a contemporary American work. Copland accepted the commission, although he had only passing acquaintance with the organ and had written little in the larger forms. He spent the summer in Milford, Pennsylvania, working on the concerto and supporting himself by playing piano in a hotel trio. The orchestration for what ultimately became his Symphony for Organ and Orchestra was completed in New York the following fall. He played his *Cat and the Mouse* and Passacaglia for the League of Composers in November, and Boulanger and Damrosch introduced the organ piece in January, 1925. When the performance of the symphony was over, Damrosch turned to the audience and, referring to the composer's liberal use of dissonance, said: "If a young man at the age of twenty-three can write a symphony like that, in five years he will be ready to commit murder." While the press turned over that statement, Boulanger played the work again with the Boston Symphony Orchestra under Koussevitzky.

Impressed by the worth of the Symphony for Organ and Orchestra, Koussevitzky performed a new work by Copland every year until well into the 1930s. In 1925 Copland became the first composer to receive a Guggenheim fellowship and spent that summer at MacDowell's Peterboro Colony, working on a five-part chamber suite entitled *Music for the Theatre*. This was one of his earliest attempts to use jazz ingredients. The composer had come to feel that his symphony was "too European in inspiration." He wanted to write something that would immediately be recognized as American in spirit. "This desire to be 'American' was symptomatic of the period," he later admitted, but he frankly wanted "to adapt the jazz idiom" and see what he "could do with it in a symphonic way." But the jazz usage was closely bound up with patterns then fashionable in Paris, so that it now seems more nearly related to the jazz experiments of Ravel, Stravinsky, and Milhaud than anything particularly American. The piece was the first to win Copland wide attention, although conservative critics like W. J. Henderson heard it with misgivings. Henderson, reviewing the work for the New York *Sun* in 1926, dismissed it with the observation that the composer's "music betrays...a great anxiety to be modernistic while the modernist lamp holds out to burn." *Music for the Theatre* stands up, however, as something fresh and alive— brassy yet sensitive. Introduced by Koussevitzky in November, 1925, the piece is sophisticated and demonstrates remarkable craftsmanship. While it embodies many of the blues cliches of the 1920s, its form still makes them appealing.

Copland further developed the use of jazz in his next work, a Concerto for Piano and Orchestra (1926). Here he used not the "sweet," commercial style popular with the public, but free polyphony served up with the newest European stridencies of harmony. Already there were foreshadowings of the mature Copland. The concerto contains a formal balance and an economy in development. It was first performed by the Boston Symphony Orchestra, with the composer as soloist, in Boston and New York. The music proved too advanced for most of the public and many of the critics. Conservative Boston listeners were aghast at the audacity of the piece, and some even argued the conductor had no right to inflict such music on audiences. Several critics considered the concerto an example of the musical depravity of the day. "The dissonance habit," said one professional observer, "demands increased doses as do narcotics." Although Lawrence Gilman of the New York *Tribune* thought the work austere, he judged it "bold in outline and of singular power." In the musical circles of Boston and New York, Edward Burlingame Hill contended a few months later, "the concerto as a topic of conversation became taboo; the mere mention of it dulled sociability and even threatened to alienate friends." This would be Copland's last conscious experiment with symphonic jazz. "With the concerto," he said, "I felt I had done all I could with the idiom, considering its limited emotional scope." The composer acknowledged that jazz was an easy way to be American in musical terms and felt that jazz rhythms offered considerable potential. But "all American music could not possibly be confined to two dominant jazz moods—the blues and the snappy number."

Copland returned from France expecting to teach, but private patronage, the Guggenheim grant (renewed for a second year), and prize money enabled him to devote himself to composing. He won a $5000 award from RCA Victor in 1929 for his *Dance* Symphony, three movements extracted from the ballet *Grogh*. The *Dance* Symphony was initially performed by the Philadelphia Orchestra under Stokowski in April, 1931, and was later expanded into the *Symphonic Ode*, played at the fiftieth anniversary of the Boston Symphony. Although this *Symphonic Ode* lies at the juncture between two periods, it is perhaps the most compelling selection of Copland's early years. The French craftsmanship and the deep impression made by Stravinsky and Ravel remain clear, and there is still some aura of jazz syncopation. But the highly individual use of melody and polyrhythms make the work one of distinct musical depth.

The composer now began casting about for new materials. The trio *Vitebsk* (1929) was based on a Jewish theme, while his Piano Variations (1930), embrace much of the nervous energy of the big city and the brittle quality in a machine-oriented civilization. Copland treats the piano in the Variations in a sharply antiromantic way, almost Bartok-like in its percussive emphasis. Economy is the watchword, for the piece concentrates on a few notes. The theme is one of hard-edged grandeur, while the texture is so bare as to be almost skeletal. Mellers feels that the composer set out "from the broken bones of a disrupted culture" to question "whether anything of human worth could still be salvaged." He uses both elements of black blues and the declamatory leaps of Jewish synagogue music to represent modern man's uprootedness. Although highly controversial when it appeared, the Piano Variations survive as an invigorating composition—complex, but uncompromisingly honest.

At the MacDowell colony Copland met a number of young American composers interested in new things. Among these were Roy Harris and Roger Sessions; he already knew Virgil Thomson and Douglas Moore from Paris. Copland returned to Peterboro four or five times and found hearing other artists talk about their problems immensely stimulating. He shortly established acquaintances in New York and before long found the city alive with fresh ideas. After 1922 the League of Composers aided the American musician, and Koussevitzky was always a loyal friend. But Copland wished for more opportunities for the unrecognized American composer and with Roger Sessions arranged a series of concerts of contemporary music between 1928 and 1931. He later founded an American festival at Yaddo, in Saratoga Springs, New York. Copland was a lecturer at the New School for Social Research in New York City from 1927 to 1937, took over Walter Piston's duties at Harvard for a term in 1935, and after 1940 taught composition during summers at the Berkshire Music Center.

In his own work he continued the lean, abstract style of the Piano Variations through the *Short* Symphony (1933) and *Statements* (1934). The latter, written for orchestra, describes the rock-bottom nature of urban existence. It is bold, lonely music, sometimes savage in its hardness, yet vitally affirming the human spirit. The pattern consists of short phrases, serially related, almost cubistic in technique. But with the completion of *Statements*, Copland seemed to feel the need for wider communication. He therefore turned from such fiercely personal creations to music more easily understood, writing for radio, motion pictures, and ballet.

In 1932 the composer made a trip into Mexico, where he played his Piano Concerto with the Mexican Symphony Orchestra under Carlos Chavez. During this visit he fell in love with the country—thoroughly enjoying its easy-going life, picturesque villages, mild climate, beautiful mountain scenery, and especially its colorful, rhythmic music. Even the banal tunes of the Mexican night clubs fascinated him. Two years later he put his enthusiasm for Mexico on paper, composing *El Salon Mexico*, one of his most widely played pieces. Based on popular Mexican melodies and orchestrated in 1936, the work was named for a dance hall in Mexico City that the composer had visited. *El Salon Mexico* heralded a new, greatly simplified style for Copland, one in which he would focus on American folk material. Fragments of two Mexican tunes, for example, combine to form the final motif of *El Salon Mexico*, carrying the work to giddy heights and a brilliant conclusion. First heard in 1938 on a broadcast by the NBC Orchestra under Adrian Boult, the piece was an immediate hit with the public and convinced Copland that he had previously been working in something of a vacuum.

His opera *The Second Hurricane*, written in 1937 for high school students to perform, continued the new style. The delight of watching young nonprofessionals having fun making music further persuaded Copland that directness and simplification were worth striving for. "An entirely new public has grown up around the radio and phonograph," Copland observed, "and it made no sense to ignore them as if they did not exist. I felt that it was worth the effort to see if I couldn't say what I had to say in the simplest possible terms."

During the Depression-torn 1930s many of the artists who had been alienated in the decade before experienced a revived social conscience. A society in peril needed the talents of every individual, and the intellectual atmosphere of the times stressed the welfare of the nation as a whole. Esoteric experimentation in art was no longer fashionable; speaking to a mass audience was. This was the mood set by Franklin Roosevelt's New Deal, and this was the one that would continue through the war years ahead. Copland— like Roy Harris, Virgil Thomson, Marc Blitzstein, Douglas Moore, and others—joined in this concern for a broad public, forsaking during these times of crisis the personal artistic expressions which the prosperity and international tranquility of the 1920s had permitted. Instead the emphasis was on functionalism, traditionalism, the folk, the regional experience, and common heroes—with the hope of revitalizing a sense of security and a sinking optimism. "In all the arts the Depression had aroused a wave of sympathy for and identification with the plight of the common man," Aaron Copland wrote in 1967. "In music this was combined with the heady wine of suddenly feeling ourselves—the composers, that is—needed as never before."

In 1938 Copland was commissioned by the Ballet Caravan to write the music for Eugene Loring's *Billy the Kid*. With this score the composer's American folksong style became clearly defined. The work is highly effective theater and establishes a Western atmosphere through the fragmentary use of cowboy ballads. The Kid's story is used to symbolize the conflict between society and the outlaw. The mood is one of loneliness, for the Kid's life is lost in emptiness. Whereas society is seen initially as dignified and noble, it eventually becomes hardened and nasty, bent on the destruction of a tragic individual. The Kid emerges as part hero, having turned against a world responsible for destroying the basic human relationship (the killing of his mother). For Billy society spells turmoil and dishonesty, and so he has become an outsider, at peace only when alone in the desert. Billy's humanity is suggested by a forlorn waltz version of the tune "Come Wrangle yer Bronco," while "Bury Me Not on the Lone Prairie" is used in an idealized form to create a mood of pathos right before the Kid is shot. Society regains its dignity in the end, as the pioneers resume their march westward, led by the sheriff responsible for Billy's death.

Copland drew on cowboy tunes again for *Rodeo*, first presented by the Ballets Russes de Monte Carlo on October 16, 1942. This time he dealt with a comic version of the outsider theme, one which concluded happily. Although the score is simple and direct, the composer does not allow the limitations of his folk material to restrict him. Instead he intricately shapes the folksongs used into his formal design, as in the *Buckaroo Holiday* section. *Appalachian Spring*, commissioned for Martha Graham, followed in 1944 and proved the most beautiful and delightful of Copland's ballet scores. An orchestral suite from the work received the Pulitzer Prize the next year. The piece utilizes squaredance rhythms, revivalist hymns, country fiddler tunes, and the Shaker melody "'Tis the Gift to Be Simple." The opening bars constitute the utmost in simplicity, but what emerges is sheer poetry. Whereas *Billy the Kid* stresses loneliness, *Appalachian Spring* stresses love, the togetherness that can transform pastoral emptiness from a threat to a comfort.

With *Billy the Kid*, *Rodeo* and *Appalachian Spring*, Copland became established as America's foremost composer of ballet, and all three quickly found their way into the standard symphonic repertory, along with the highly colored *El Salon Mexico*. The declamatory style and the more fluid use of melody made these pieces far more popular than anything the composer had written during his avant-garde years. And yet to this Americana Copland brought a sophistication and polish that reflect his cosmopolitan training. Whether the composer was using a cowboy ditty, a New England hymn, or a Mexican rhythm there was always that distinct, unmistakable Coplandesque sound.

Folk material was also used in *Hear Ye! Hear Ye!* (1934), a ballet for Ruth Page, which included cabaret scenes and jazz touches. Unlike earlier, the composer now used jazz as a relatively small part of his American folk sources. *Music for Radio*, commissioned by the Columbia Broadcasting System in 1937 and written in New York City, was ironically given the subtitle *Saga of the Prairie* when members of the radio audience were asked to suggest names. In 1942, amid heavy Allied losses, conductor Andre Kostelanetz asked several composers to write selections that would "mirror the magnificent spirit of our country." Copland responded with *A Lincoln Portrait*, for speaker and orchestra, in which he used snatches of popular songs from the Civil War era and the folk ballad "Springfield Mountain." This is perhaps the most poignant piece the musician has written, concluding with the final lines of the Gettysburg Address, spoken by the narrator over a thinly scored orchestral background. *Fanfare for the Common Man* (also 1942) was composed in honor of the wartime homefront—the many who performed no deeds of valor on the battlefield, yet quietly shared the labors, sorrows, and hopes of those fighting for victory. *John Henry* was scored for small orchestra in 1940, while *Danzon Cubano* (1942) returned to Latin American themes.

Around this time Copland was writing a great deal of music for the movies. With *The City* in 1939, a documentary, he became the first established American composer of serious music to be courted by Hollywood. Later that year he took up partial residence in California and surprised motion picture producers with his dramatic scoring for the Hal Roach film *Of Mice and Men.* In 1940 he provided the music for the movie version of Thornton Wilder's *Our Town*, again proving that he could write plainly without forsaking art. The composer was working on Samuel Goldwyn's *North Star* at the same time he was writing *Appalachian Spring* and in 1947 delivered one of his best scores for *The Red Pony*, shortly turned into a *Children's Suite.* Three years later he won the Academy Award with his music for William Wyler's *The Heiress*, based on the Henry James novel *Washington Square.* Although he had begun as a concert hall musician guessing how his work would come out on the final celluloid print, by 1950 Copland had grown into a veteran screen composer, working in constant association with the film, able to make his point with seemingly no effort and without disturbing the verbal continuity. His film music is restrained and sincere, underlining the atmosphere of the drama effectively, but quietly. Highlights from these scores, however, stand up well in the concert hall; the *Our Town Suite* and *Music for the Movies* evidence that Copland was creating more than just movie background music.

By no means all of the composer's music during the 1940s was intended to be functional. The Piano Sonata (1941) was written in abstract form and saw a fusion of the integrity of the Piano Variations with the more relaxed style of Copland's popular works. Here the spirited phrases seem oddly wistful—suggesting, Mellers feels, "man's ant-like energy and his ineluctable loneliness." The melody creates an atmosphere more than anything else, at times taking on an almost religious air. There is considerable dissonance, yet the harmony is predominantly consonant. Sadness and restlessness are combined with a calm transfiguration, as the piece ends simply and serenely. The Violin Sonata (1943), composed in part at the Goldwyn Studios in Hollywood, takes up where the Piano Sonata leaves off, continuing the mood of quiet happiness. Its inner tension involves a cheery buoyancy rather than turbulence. There are still references to folk material, specifically a rarefied use of New England hymnody in the opening section, but in the final movement a neoclassical continuity appears in Copland's music for the first time.

The composer continued to lecture and published two books, *What to Listen For in Music* (1939) and *Our New Music* (1941), both addressed to the layman. He contributed articles to a number of influential magazines and music journals and became the ardent champion of his fellow American composers. He replaced Piston again at Harvard in 1944 and returned as the Charles Eliot Norton lecturer in 1951-52. As a person he had changed little since his Paris days. He still preferred the simple life, while loosely hung suits and unpressed neckties became his hallmark. Although his concern for democracy and the musical brotherhood was genuine, his personality stayed basically inward. He enjoyed travel, but remained deeply attached to New York. Unlike many others, he normally did not find the city hostile to creativity. Early in his career the composer discovered that his most productive working hours were late at night, when the commotion of the outside world had quieted down and there were fewer chances of interruption. "Music is largely a product of the emotions," he once insisted, "and I can't get emotional early in the day."

Copland did retreat to the isolation of Tepotzlan, Mexico, to begin his Third Symphony, completing it in a converted barn near Tanglewood. This was his first nonprogrammatic orchestral work since 1934 and marked the beginning of his return to abstract music on a larger scale. The war was now over, freeing the composer to pursue his art with less anxiety for the needs of society. The best known of his three symphonies, the Third consists of four lengthy, sustained movements, in contrast to the short episodes characteristic of so many of his previous pieces. First performed in October, 1946, by Koussevitzky and the Boston Symphony, the work proved less popular than the composer's ballet suites, but one of his strongest achievements. Virgil Thomson called the symphony "at once pastoral and heroic" and pronounced it the "work of a mature artist, broadly conceived and masterfully executed."

A delightful Clarinet Concerto (1948), commissioned by Benny Goodman, and the song cycle *Twelve Poems of Emily Dickinson* (1950) more or less brought Copland's middle period to an end. With the Quartet for Piano and Strings (later in 1950) the composer again took up the deeply personal serialism he had explored in the Piano Variations and attempted the twelve-tone technique for the first time. This experimentation reached new heights in the Piano Fantasy (1957), in which all the material is derived from the opening phrase. The pattern is one of dissection and reintegration, employing a virtuosic flair that is unusual for Copland. The piece stands as one of the composer's boldest efforts—expressive and intellectual, consistently fresh and imaginative. Although the music is difficult for the average listener, the Fantasy was a resounding critical success. Mellers considers it unquestionably the greatest of Copland's piano selections, for "it fuses the stark energy of the Variations with the still serenity of the Sonata's last movement." When William Flanagan reexamined the piece almost a decade after its premiere performance at Juilliard, he found it "one of those rare works that leave one wondering how in heaven's name they ever got composed."

An opera, *The Tender Land*, which Copland had worked on some years before, was staged by the New York City Opera Company in April, 1954. A product of his earlier style, *The Tender Land* is the story of a midwestern farm girl who leaves home to join a drifter she has fallen in love with. The work opens with soft, widely spaced chords, from which emerges a pastoral tune reminiscent of *Appalachian Spring*. The score is simple, full of folklike songs and dances. Although the opera was conducted by Thomas Schippers and staged by Jerome Robbins, it was not a success. Copland's vocal music, while theatrically effective, does not seem to ring true, and there is much sameness. For the production's second season at the City Center the composer made extensive revisions. Julia Smith, Copland's biographer and a musician herself, finds the opera significant, despite a weak libretto. "In my opinion," she contends, "what *Oklahoma!* contributed to the revitalization of the Broadway musical comedy, *The Tender Land* has achieved in the American opera theater."

But in the 1950s the composer was reassessing his style, having grown weary of musical directness, and began devoting himself more and more to twelve-tone experimentation. After *The Tender Land* new works by Copland came slowly. "I have to make a conscious effort," he said during his sixtieth birthday celebration, "not to write a piece that sounds too much like what I've done already." While *Nonet* for nine stringed instruments (1960) showed only faint traces of serialism, *Connotations for Orchestra* two years later was a completely twelve-tone work and carried the composer's exploration of serial consequences farther than ever before. Commissioned for the opening of Philharmonic Hall at Lincoln Center, *Connotations* was Copland's first orchestral piece since 1948. It marked a return to an austere style of sparse harmonies and jagged lines, and its noisy, brooding outbursts brought protests from many who would have preferred another *Rodeo* or *Billy the Kid*. The composer, however, found twelve-tone writing "especially liberating," forcing him to "unconventionalize his thinking" and "freshen his melodic and figurational imagination."

Music for a Great City, based on Copland's score for the film *Something Wild*, was introduced by the London Symphony in 1964. *Inscape* (1967), for orchestra, although quite advanced, was more tonal than *Connotations*. Copland considers himself largely in the Schoenberg line. "I think of twelve-tone music as having a built-in tenseness," he said; "I like to think that the way I use it, it has a certain drama about it." But the accusations continued that the composer had sold out to the twelve-tone power group currently in control.

An elderly woman once gave Copland some advice. "Aaron," she said, "it is very important, as you get older, to engage in an activity that you didn't engage in when you were young, so that you are not continually in competition with yourself as a young man." The musician took this advice to heart and found his new activity in conducting. He has conducted the New York Philharmonic, appeared often in England and Scotland, directed the Boston Symphony on its 1960 tour of the Far East, and was one of the first

Americans to lead a Russian orchestra in the Soviet Union. He has continued to lecture, served as musical ambassador on several occasions (particularly to Latin America), and been president of the American Composers Alliance, which he helped found. He has done a great deal of summer teaching, although he does not look upon teaching in the usual academic way. "What I try to do," he says, "is what I used to find valuable in Boulanger: I react. I try to point out what I think are the good things and where the piece seems to founder or not carry on or to get off the rails."

On the tour with the Boston Symphony the mayor of Adelaide, Australia, asked Copland how his city might achieve such a fine orchestra. Remembering the response an Englishman supposedly gave an American cousin regarding what it took to develop a proper British lawn, the composer replied, "All you need is lots of money and seventy-five years!" But Copland himself attained greatness in about half that time with lots of talent and dedication. At seventy-five he had been the recognized dean of American composers for nearly three decades. Always a slow, careful worker, his output in recent years has been small. "Strangely enough," he told an interviewer asking about his composing, "it doesn't get any easier." He remained sharply intelligent, urbane, articulate, living in a handsome hilltop home overlooking the lower Hudson. He wears his eminence well, sensitive about his lack of college background. His keen eyes continue to scan the world warily, his smile ready but cool. He is always eager to know what is going on in the musical world and ready to have a part in it. He is still disturbed by the general lack of interest in contemporary music and worries about those "sad and lonely figures walking around with unperformed music in their pockets."

Copland has been unusually successful in winning the respect of younger American composers without necessarily meeting them on their own ground. Unlike his own early attempts at writing distinctly American music, Copland realizes that what concerns the current generation of composers is an international movement. "They're all thinking about what startling things they can do next without any relationship to American music *or* its past." Although Copland sometimes wishes that young composers were more aware of their musical heritage and hopes more will become interested in writing for the orchestra, he insists that each generation must find its own way. "I didn't like people telling me what to do when I was younger," he says, "and I'm not going to start doing it myself. After all, we were rebels in the Twenties, too. A big pot was boiling. We were in a continual mood of 'We gotta show 'em.'"

Surely no American composer has been more varied in his approach than Aaron Copland, and few have kept the level of accomplishment so consistently high. Nor have many developed a style so strongly individual. As early as the boyish "As It Fell Upon a Day," there were strongly personal touches. While his music contains a normal amount of derivation, Copland has been able to work his way from folk tunes to atonality and still remain himself. He returned home from studying with Boulanger having absorbed the French concern for refinement, detail, sophistication, restraint,

sensitivity, understatement, and elegance. He brought these characteristics to
his jazz experiments and to the fierce, astringent "geometric" pieces that
followed. When Copland abandoned ivory tower abstraction for the gentler,
smoother, more accessible works of the Depression and war years, he brought
to them the same sense of craftsmanship and another kind of originality.
With his Americana he achieved what heretofore had been considered
impossible: success in the market place without losing the respect of
intellectual circles. With his movie scores he was able to achieve economic
freedom without damaging his integrity as an artist. "For the first time," the
composer said during those years, "democracy has entered the realm of
serious music." In later life he returned to abstract writing and the
uncompromising pursuit of his personal vision, the most highly paid serious
composer on the ASCAP roster.

"Aaron Copland's music," wrote Virgil Thomson in 1932, "is American
in rhythm, Jewish in melody, eclectic in all the rest." The Hebraic element,
even in his early works, was probably not that strong. A rhythmic excitement
has indeed been characteristic of Copland, but the eclectic quality persists
most clearly. Some of his compositions are full of tunes that one might
whistle; others are as indefinite as a Jackson Pollock painting. "I like to feel
free," Copland says, "I don't want to be tied down by anyone's system, not
even my own." Most important, Copland's music shows signs of lasting. And
in this regard he stands almost as alone in his generation as Ives did a half
century before. "A decade or so ago," Richard Franko Goldman said in 1961,
"one thought of Copland and perhaps a quartet of others as our
'representative' or 'leading' composers, but the last ten or fifteen years have
separated this group in more ways than one. And it is Copland's music that
has most effectively remained with us."

George Gershwin's music remains with us, too, but in a more specialized
way. His show tunes are classics of the Broadway genre, while his work in the
larger forms marks a triumph of the popular spirit in American art music.
Like Aaron Copland, Gershwin led something of a double life. But while he
kept one foot in Tin Pan Alley, the other in the concert hall, he always wrote
music of the people, for the people. "I am not ashamed of writing songs," he
declared, "as long as they are good songs." And he was convinced that the
public was deserving of sophistication. "I am one of those," Gershwin said,
"who honestly believe that the majority has much better taste and
understanding, not only of music but of any of the arts, than it is credited with
having. It is not the few knowing ones whose opinion make any work of art
great, it is the judgment of the great mass that finally decides."

He approached jazz from the viewpoint of the Tin Pan Alley tunesmith
rather than either the Mississippi delta improviser or the serious musician
experimenting with colloquial forms. He probed the commercial music that
became part of him, discovered hidden depths and shadings, and developed
his unique style into an art. "Jazz I regard as an American folk-music,"
Gershwin stated; "not the only one, but a very powerful one which is
probably in the blood and feeling of the American people more than any

other style of folk-music. I believe that it can be made the basis of serious symphonic works of lasting value, in the hands of a composer with talent for both jazz and symphonic music." And this Gershwin achieved simply by being himself—youthful, vibrant, gifted. More than anyone else he brought the American composer out of the garret and the academy and made him a frequent guest in the concert hall and the living room, both at home and abroad.

Born on September 26, 1898, Gershwin was the second of four children. His parents came to New York from St. Petersburg, before they were married. The family name was originally Gershovitz. Isadore, the oldest Gershwin child, eventually became known as Ira; Jacob, who soon favored the name George, came along two years later. Their father tried his hand at many jobs during those years, and the family moved dozens of times. After George was a few months old, they were back on the New York side of the river. The Gershwin brothers grew up playing on the sidewalks and streets, surrounded by a gang of city kids. George was especially athletic and in one neighborhood was the roller-skating champion. While Ira enjoyed reading, the outgoing, mischievous George preferred the company of playmates. He disliked school and found study an absolute nuisance. He had no particular fondness for music, although singing songs like "Loch Lomond" at school was all right, and there were always the street hurdy-gurdies grinding out their tunes, the strolling fiddlers struggling to be heard over the traffic, the mechanical music of the carousels at Coney Island, and the ragtime from the fancier saloons and honky-tonks. But for a boy to take piano or violin lessons clearly made him, in George's mind, a "little Maggie."

The Gershwins, however, were an immigrant family trying to make good in a new country. They were conscious enough of their social standing to have a maid and buy a piano when one of their relatives bought one. It might be a good idea, the elder Gershwins decided, for Ira to take lessons. The lessons lasted only a short while; Ira had just discovered a circulating library in back of a laundry that had lots of Wild West adventure stories. Meanwhile George took over the piano stool. Before long he was positively fascinated with the instrument. When he was thirteen, he asked if he might have a teacher.

A few years before, George had acquired a new friend at Public School 25. He was a Rumanian boy, who played the violin—Maxie Rosenzweig, later the violinist Max Rosen. He was the son of a local barber and a year younger than George. Maxie was to play for a school assembly, but George was so little impressed that he stayed away. He was out on the grounds kicking a ball, when he heard the strains of Dvorak's *Humoresque* floating through the window. "It was," Gershwin later said, "a flashing revelation of beauty. I made up my mind to get acquainted with this fellow, and I waited outside from three to four-thirty that afternoon, in the hopes of greeting him. It was pouring cats and dogs, and I got soaked to the skin." Soon the two boys were fast friends. They went about arm in arm, wrote notes to each other, wrestled, and talked about music. "Max opened the world of music to me," Gershwin insisted, but it was a world in which he immediately felt at home.

George's formal education in music was fairly spotty. He began taking piano lessons and quickly advanced to a diet of operatic potpourris. His first important teacher was the pianist-composer Charles Hambitzer, who introduced him to Chopin, Liszt, and Debussy. "Gershwin is just crazy about music," Hambitzer said, "and can't wait until it's time to take his lesson. No watching the clock for this boy! He wants to go in for this modern stuff, jazz and what not. But I'm not going to let him for a while. I'll see that he gets a firm foundation in the standard music first." And to a sister the teacher wrote: "I have a new pupil who will make his mark in music if anybody will. The boy is a genius." Under Hambitzer, Gershwin became conscious of harmony, although he never taught him harmony as such. Hambitzer first wanted to make a pianist of George; the idea of composing came later. "I was crazy about that man," Gershwin said when Hambitzer died at a young age, and he never again found a teacher who meant so much to him. He later studied theory and harmony with Edward Kilenyi, but much of his training Gershwin gained by himself.

Once, in discussing Irving Berlin's songs and ragtime with Hambitzer, Gershwin said: "This is American music. This is the way an American should write. This is the kind of music I want to write." At sixteen he quit school and took a job with J. K. Remick as a song plugger. He was assigned one of the private cubicles, where he hammered out melodies for clients from eight to ten hours a day. He deeply admired the work of Irving Berlin, whom he considered "America's Franz Schubert," and shortly fell under the spell of Jerome Kern. George studied all of Kern's songs and began trying to compose in the same vein. When he showed some of his tunes to Mose Gumble, his boss at Remick's, the older man pushed them aside. "You're paid to play the piano not to write songs," he said. "We've plenty of songwriters under contract."

Already his instinct for music was highly developed. He had the phenomenal ability of absorbing on slight contact many different kinds of musical knowledge and adapting that knowledge to his own artistry. Frequently he could not verbalize what he was doing in a textbook sense, but he learned about polyrhythms, ambiguous tonalities, and changing meters and used these consciously for a precise effect. He played the piano dexterously and was deepening his capacity to critique his own work. Gershwin's first tunes were catchy, but not particularly original. He spent hours at the keyboard in endless experimentation. Through trial and error he acquired an experience rules and lessons could never have taught him, for what he eventually achieved was a style and an enchantment all his own.

George stayed with Remick for more than two years, earning fifteen dollars a week. He learned much about public taste, but what had been exciting at first grew into drudgery. He left Remick early in 1917, convinced that the routine was smothering him. One of his songs had appeared in a Broadway revue, and he looked to the theater as a means for widening the scope of his talents. He played the piano briefly at Fox's City Theater on Fourteenth Street, where his job was to accompany the vaudeville acts during the supper hour, when the orchestra was on break. Then he was hired as rehearsal pianist for the Kern-Herbert show *Miss 1917*. His duties consisted of rehearsing the principals and ensemble numbers and coaching the chorus, for which he received thirty-five dollars a week. The show ran slightly more than a month.

George's work with the chorus drills and ensemble rehearsals had been so capable, however, that the producers decided to keep him on the payroll even after *Miss 1917* closed. During the show's run the cast gave Sunday night concerts, and it was part of George's duties to provide the accompaniment. On one of these occasions Vivienne Segal sang Gershwin's song "There's More To A Kiss Than the XXX," later incorporated into *La La Lucille*. Nora Bayes, the vaudeville headliner, gave George an even more substantial introduction to Broadway when she put "The Real American Folk Song" into her show *Ladies First*. Gershwin accompanied Bayes in some of her numbers. Oscar Levant remembered seeing the show and how impressed he was with Gershwin's playing: "After one chorus of the first song my attention left Bayes and remained fixed on the playing of the pianist. I had never heard such fresh, brisk, unstudied, completely free and inventive playing—all within a consistent frame that set off her singing perfectly." Bayes on the other hand found George's inventiveness distracting, constantly complained about it, and finally threatened to get somebody else.

About this time Max Dreyfus offered Gershwin thirty-five dollars a week just to write songs. "I feel that you have some good stuff in you," Dreyfus said. "It'll come out. It may take months, it may take a year, it may take five years, but I'm convinced that the stuff is there." The agreement involved no hours and no set duties, except that the tunes produced were to be submitted to T.B. Harms for publication. If the song was published, the composer would receive three cents for every copy of the sheet music sold. Meanwhile Gershwin continued working as a rehearsal pianist for Broadway shows. He still harbored hopes of writing purely pianistic pieces, as evidenced by the "Rialto Ripples" (1917), a rag somewhat in the style of Scott Joplin. On May 26, 1919, *La La Lucille* opened in New York, Gershwin's first complete score. Later that year, Al Jolson interpolated "Swanee" into his Winter Garden show *Sinbad* and made it a big hit. With that George's reputation as a Broadway songwriter was made; sheet music sales and Jolson's recording of "Swanee" sold into the millions.

In 1920 George White asked Gershwin to write the music for the second edition of his *Scandals*. The two had worked together on *Miss 1917*, and White had never forgotten the way Gershwin played the piano. The composer remained with *Scandals* through 1924, cranking out mostly mechanical songs; "Somebody Loves Me" and "I'll Build a Stairway to Paradise" were the exceptions. For the latter White provided a lavish background, consisting of a huge white stairway on which dancers in black cavorted up and down as the number was sung. For the *Scandals of 1922*, Gershwin offered an ambitious, little one act opera called *Blue Monday*. Paul Whiteman, who conducted for the *Scandals* that year, was excited about the work, and for Gershwin it represented a goal toward which he had been groping for some time. But White objected to the opera's somber theme and deleted it from the show after opening night. Although *Blue Monday* was little more than a series of popular songs held together by jazzlike recitatives, it pointed the way for things to come. The work was later revived under the name *135th Street.*

Gershwin left the *Scandals* because of the heavy demands the revue made upon him. Planning, creating the music for, and rehearsing a yearly edition left little time for the book musicals he was more interested in. *Lady Be Good*, the composer's first major Broadway success, opened in New York on December 1, 1924, featuring Fred and Adele Astaire. Its lyrics were written by brother Ira, who was working with George for the first time. The irresistible appeal of the title song, the exhilerating effect of the changing meters in "Fascinating Rhythm," and the insinuating melodic line of the "You Don't Know the Half of It Dearie, Blues" represented a new sophistication in commercial music. The show was a triumph in London two years later.

Tin Pan Alley had been humming about jazz since the Original Dixieland Jazz Band's engagement at Reisenweber's Restaurant. By the early 1920s Kern, Berlin, and others had become engrossed with the blues style and were busily turning out tunes with syncopation and rhythmic thrust. Several major songwriters of the time were concerned about originality and quality, but none more than George Gershwin. Even his early songs abound with subtle detail—adroit changes in harmony, the use of after-beats and staggered accents, an ingenious setting of one rhythm against another. Besides poignant emotion and caressing melody, a Gershwin song is unmistakably stamped with the composer's personal mannerisms. He was prone to inject a minor third suddenly into the melody or shift from one key to another without the normal harmonic transitions. So germane is his harmony to the melody that many of Gershwin's songs lose their charm when sung without accompaniment. The composer revised, refined, and edited his tunes until they became masterpieces in their own right. As Gershwin gained control of his means, his technique became increasingly complex and unorthodox— sufficiently so that his songs were often not immediately successful in terms of sales. Some of the best ones required the passing of several years before they won general acceptance.

Among more sophisticated listeners, however, the caliber of Gershwin's work was recognized as something unique, and the composer quickly became a darling of the intellectual world. In November, 1923, the Canadian mezzo-soprano Eva Gauthier presented a recital at New York's staid Aeolian Hall. Her program included songs by Purcell, Byrd, and Bellini, as well as such European modernists as Milhaud, Hindemith, Bartok, and Schoenberg. But she also included six popular songs—one each by Berlin, Kern, and Walter Donaldson and three by George Gershwin. As her accompanist for this portion of the program, Mme. Gauthier chose Gershwin. It was a daring move for a concert artist, and the press made much of the incident. Deems Taylor thought the Tin Pan Alley songs "stood up amazingly well, not only as entertainment but as music" and described at length Gershwin's "mysterious and fascinating rhythmic and contrapuntal stunts with the accompaniment." When the recital was repeated in Boston, Henry Taylor Parker of the *Evening Transcript* praised Gershwin's playing: "He diversified them [the songs] with cross-rhythms; wove them into a pliant and outspringing counterpoint; set in pauses and accents; sustained cadences; gave character to the measures wherein the singer's voice was still." Gauthier later claimed she and Gershwin had given "the program which established jazz as a genuinely American musical contribution." While this is stretching the point, her 1923 recital did link commercial jazz with art music and laid open the possibilities of treating the jazz idiom in a more serious way.

And so it was that Paul Whiteman asked Gershwin to write an extended jazz piece for symphony orchestra. Whiteman had never forgotten *Blue Monday*, and the success of the Gauthier recital had convinced the band leader to give a formal concert of his own. He wanted an original, symphonic jazz poem as the focal point. Gershwin at first refused the offer, feeling he did not have the necessary technique to compose a work for orchestra. Besides that, he was extremely busy with Broadway commitments and was putting the finishing touches on *Lady Be Good*. But Whiteman persisted, and Gershwin finally agreed. "I'll write it as a rhapsody," Whiteman remembered the composer's telling him. "We don't want to be bound down. We'll lay ourselves open to criticism if we do." Whiteman's jazz concert was moved up to February 12, 1924, since another musician had come up with a similar idea. Gershwin raced against time. "I had no set plan, no structure to which my music could conform," he later said. "The Rhapsody . . . began as a purpose, not a plan."

From age fifteen on, Gershwin had attended concerts whenever he could. Yet his formal knowledge of music remained tentative at best. It was decided that Ferde Grofe, Whiteman's arranger, would orchestrate the work; all Gershwin had to do was to come up with the basic substance. Fortunately the composer worked well under pressure. He was on a train, headed for the Boston opening of his show *Sweet Little Devil*, when the ideas for the *Rhapsody in Blue* began coming to him. The concert was a bare month away, and he had written nothing. "I frequently hear music in the very heart of noise," Gershwin explained. "And there I suddenly heard—and even saw on paper—the complete construction of the rhapsody, from beginning to end. . . . I heard it as a vast sort of musical kaleidoscope of America—of our vast melting pot, of our unduplicated national pep, of our blues, our metropolitan madness." By the time he reached Boston, Gershwin had a definite concept of the piece in mind.

The composer began putting the *Rhapsody* on paper at the family home on West 103rd Street. Songwriter Vernon Duke remembered sitting in the Gershwin living room listening often to that now familiar opening theme. There were dinners with Ferde Grofe to discuss the orchestration. Suddenly it was rehearsal time. Victor Herbert was there to supervise the *Suite of*

Serenades he had composed for the program. Carl Van Vechten and Gilbert Seldes drifted in to see what this jazz concert was all about; the music critics were there for an advanced hearing, along with many of Gershwin's Broadway friends. The concert, called "An Experiment in Modern Music," took place in Aeolian Hall. Whiteman's aim was to present jazz in all its varied facets, showing the evolution from "Livery Stable Blues" to Kern and Berlin and even Schoenberg. *Rhapsody in Blue* was next to the last selection. The polyglot audience had found the concert interesting, but little more. Then Russ Gorman's clarinet broke into a seventeen-note ascent that made history.

The wail of that clarinet captured much of the age—the hysterical, hyperthyroid aspect of the 1920s that sought frenetic pleasures, the defiance of convention, sophomoric hedonism, and a down-to-earth sophistication. It spoke to an era of flappers and hip flasks and Dorothy Parker witticisms, phrasing its message in the national dialect. Like the America just coming of age, the *Rhapsody in Blue* was full of bravura and shone with a dazzling light. Yet while there was gaiety, there was also emptiness, incoherence, and the melancholy of Gershwin's blues. Even more than a reflection of contemporary America, the *Rhapsody* suggests a self-portrait of the composer, summarizing what he knew about music and his comprehension of the world he lived in.

Outside Aeolian Hall it was snowing heavily; inside the *Rhapsody in Blue* held the premiere audience in its grip through the final explosive coda. "Somewhere about the middle of the score I began crying," Whiteman said later. "When I came to myself I was eleven pages along, and until this day I cannot tell you how I conducted that far. Afterwards, George, who was playing with us, told me he experienced the same sensation. He cried, too." At the end there was a spontaneous ovation lasting several minutes. The success of Gershwin's *Rhapsody* was far beyond anything even Whiteman had hoped for. Serious musicians and critics began discussing the piece as if it were an important composition! There was by no means a consensus, but even those not much taken with the work admitted that it certainly had "zip and punch."

Gershwin's shortcomings as a technician were obvious to many, yet his melodies proved exceptionally fine. Some found the piece "a Lisztian rhapsody, loosely constructed." More felt the slow section was reminiscent of Tschaikovsky. Still others compared the harmony with Debussy's and Chopin's. A few said the selection brought to mind Puccini and Rimsky-Korsakoff. Through the years critics have repeatedly complained that the *Rhapsody* is not an organic work, that it is diffuse and awkward, that its contrasts were achieved mainly through changes in tempo. Others have found this carping. "Why, in its every bar it breathes the same thing," Leonard Bernstein exclaims in *The Joy of Music,* "throughout all its variety and all its change of mood and tempo. It breathes America—the people, the urban society that George knew deeply, the pace, the nostalgia, the nervousness, the majesty." Gershwin surely fused his various elements into something wholly American in spirit—and into something personal, for the *Rhapsody in Blue* is a tricky piano piece reflecting the composer's own technique. Although the jazz effects now seem a bit stilted, the basic melodic and rhythmic material have remained fresh and exciting. For Bernstein, Gershwin's themes "are perfectly harmonized, ideally proportioned, songful, clear, rich, moving. The rhythms are always right. The 'quality' is always there, just as it is in his best show tunes." Unlike Stravinsky, Milhaud, Debussy, and even Copland, the jazz idiom for Gershwin was not an exotic venture. The commercial forms at least had been his citadel. "With Gershwin," Edmund Wilson wrote in 1925, "the idiom of popular music is a natural mode of expression, the medium in which he has always worked— not...a language deliberately adopted and overlaid on an academic training."

Gershwin left the *Rhapsody* in an arrangement for two pianos. Grofe's orchestration was a good, honest job, typical of the Whiteman concert jazz tradition. Whatever its weaknesses, and however far removed from the black music it supposedly embodied, the *Rhapsody in Blue* brought Tin Pan Alley syncopation permanently into the concert hall and went a long way toward breaking down the barrier between the "popular" and "classical" categories. The piece has outstripped any other contemporary orchestral work in frequency of performance and was largely responsible for Paul Whiteman's being crowned "the King of Jazz." "What underlay the symphonic ambition of *Rhapsody in Blue*," Irving Sablosky maintains, "was not middle class longing for respectability but the democratic conviction that what was popular could also be fine."

Overnight Gershwin became one of the most famous persons in New York. The *Rhapsody* was rearranged for dance bands and was shortly being played all over the country. Gershwin's musical *Sweet Little Devil* had opened at the Astor Theater, and the composer awoke to find himself much the center of attention, lionized by wealthy hostesses. He was handsome and charming and seemed supremely self-assured. At parties he rarely waited to be asked to play the piano, but would sit for hours improvising on his own tunes. "People were reborn when he played," Kay Swift remembered. "It was like getting a double shot of B12." He seldom attempted concert music, except certain Chopin preludes, for which he had no particular interpretive feeling. "Listening to him improvise and play was enough for me," Oscar Levant said. "He had such fluency at the piano and so steady a surge of ideas that any time he sat down just to amuse himself something came of it. Actually this is how he got most of his ideas—just by playing. He enjoyed writing so much because, in a sense, it was play for him—the thing he liked to do more than anything else."

Enthralled by the success of the *Rhapsody in Blue*, Walter Damrosch prevailed upon Harry Harkness Flagler, president of the New York Symphony Society, to commission Gershwin to write a work of symphonic proportions. The composer decided upon a piano concerto and signed a contract with Damrosch, specifying that he would make seven appearances with the orchestra as soloist—in New York, Philadelphia, Washington, and Baltimore. This time Gershwin was determined to do his own orchestration and with that in mind began studying with Rubin Goldmark, Copland's teacher. "I maintain that a composer needs to understand all the intricacies of counterpoint and orchestration," George told Ira, "and be able to create new forms for each advance in his work."

Gershwin wrote on the Concerto in F through the entire summer of 1925; the third movement was finished in late September. The orchestration took another four weeks. At rehearsals George sat at the piano with his derby on, smoking a cigar. The orchestra at first thought him brash. When he handed out cigars to the players, they resisted. But in time they came to love him. The piano concerto was first heard in Carnegie Hall on December 3, with Damrosch conducting. The audience was about evenly divided between conservative subscribers, curious intellectuals, and Gershwin admirers. Damrosch made a short speech in which he heralded the composer as the knight who had lifted jazz to the level of respectability. "He is the Prince," the conductor said, "who has taken Cinderella by the hand and openly proclaimed her a princess to the astonished world."

What Gershwin had actually done was to compose a conventional piano concerto using traits from American popular music. Broadway was all agog. Gershwin, the Tin Pan Alley tunesmith, had trod the hallowed ground of the New York Symphony! Most of the critics felt the Concerto in F was a considerable advance over the *Rhapsody*—more astute, less inclined to ramble, greater richness and variety. Yet Gershwin's freshness and natural charm remained. Virgil Thomson, however, thought the composer had minded his manners too much, perhaps in the hope "that if he was a good little boy and didn't upset any apple-carts he might maybe when he grew up be president of American music, just like Daniel Gregory Mason or somebody." True, much of the pseudo-jazz motif of the *Rhapsody* is absent from the Concerto, although Gershwin did use a Charleston in the opening, a blues for muted trumpet in the second movement, and frequent grace notes and harmonic colorations from the blues. Like the *Rhapsody in Blue*, the Concerto in F has become a staple of the symphonic repertory, unquestionably the most performed piano concerto written by an American. "When I die," the Peruvian contralto Marguerite D'Alvarez once said, "I want Gershwin's jazz concerto played over my grave."

In December, 1926, Mme. D'Alvarez included some Gershwin songs on a recital at the Hotel Roosevelt that featured French and Spanish art songs. The composer not only accompanied the singer in his music, but appeared as soloist as well. He opened the program with a piano solo arrangement of the *Rhapsody in Blue* and later in the concert introduced his Five Preludes for piano. Three of these are still frequently performed. Engaging though the Preludes are, they often seem a bit short of breath and not to follow through to any logical conclusion. Yet they are unpretentious and full of the composer's special appeal.

Meanwhile Gershwin was continuing to turn out Broadway shows, for he had no intention of concentrating on serious music exclusively. *Tip Toes* followed *Lady Be Good*. *Oh, Kay!*, with Gertrude Lawrence, opened in November, 1926, and contained two of Gershwin's finest songs, "Someone to Watch Over Me" and "Do, Do, Do." *Strike Up the Band* and *Funny Face*, again featuring the Astaires, followed a year later. Gershwin's flow of melody seemed endless; he had more ideas than he could possibly use. Once when he lost a sketchbook with material for more than forty songs, he remarked that he had too many other ideas to worry unduly about the loss. But he spent hours working out details, finding the proper mold, carving it into the right design, and giving each phrase the precise touch. He made five trips to Europe and appeared to be on top of the world. In 1927 he was America's most popular composer and not yet thirty, but he had only ten years more to live.

An American in Paris, Gershwin's next symphonic piece, was also written for Walter Damrosch and the New York Symphony. It was first heard at Carnegie Hall, December 13, 1928. Once more the composer captured much of the spirit of the 1920s. "The Machine Age has influenced practically everything," Gershwin wrote. "I do not mean only music but everything from the arts to finance. The machine has not affected our age in form as much as in tempo, speed and sound." And so he used four taxi horns in *An American in Paris* for musical effect. A happy walking theme opened the tone poem, with the angry automobile horns entering later to suggest the tangled Parisian traffic. There is a music hall tune, a Charleston melody, and several aspects of the blues. Gershwin's orchestration seems more sure, employing the full symphony—snare drums, cymbals, triangle, rattle, xylophone, wire brush, glockenspiel, celesta, wood block, and tom-toms. The mood is relaxed, sometimes humorous, consistently sparkling, so that the overall impact is fairly dazzling. "What is this and who are you, George, to have done this thing to us," Frederick Jacobi said after hearing the piece: "to have changed our world, to have made our ordinary comings and goings to become things unreal, light and sweet, and ourselves disembodied and carefree as a kite in air?"

The premiere audience was loud in its approval of *An American in Paris*, but the critics as usual were divided. The structure of the composition was again found faulty. Several deprecated the work as mainly a study in tunes, linked together with tricks borrowed from Ravel, Strauss, and others. Even Gershwin's friend Vernon Duke admitted "the themes sounded like 32-bar choruses bridged together with neo-Lisztian passages; of real thematic development there was but little, and the codas were either too lengthy or too abrupt." And yet what is good in the piece "is so good that it's irresistible," Leonard Bernstein argues. "It is trying so hard to be good; it has only good intentions."

Despite the adverse opinions *An American in Paris* quickly became a fixture in the symphonic repertory in the United States and abroad. Even Arturo Toscanini conducted it. Few of those who criticized Gershwin doubted his sincerity. "Talent," Virgil Thomson said, "is rather easier to admire when the intentions of a composer are more noble than his execution is competent." Perhaps Gershwin's orchestration *was* top-heavy, with too much doubling and padding, it was nevertheless becoming the general agreement that the Broadway songwriter was growing into an artist of stature. No one knew better than the composer himself that his larger material was taxing, at times overpowering his hastily acquired technique. Determined to overcome these limitations he began studying counterpoint with Henry Cowell and after 1932 orchestration with Joseph Schillinger.

On the surface Gershwin gave the appearance of being the impulsive, happy-go-lucky, conceited playboy, basking in his sudden success without a care in the world. He smoked cigars at a jaunty angle and had the vitality and bounce of an adolescent. He loved fast cars and sports and was himself of athletic build. In 1928 he moved into a huge penthouse apartment on Riverside Drive, overlooking the Hudson and the Palisades. There he had a gymnasium and surrounded himself with original paintings and beautiful women. His brother Ira, who now supplied the lyrics for most of his songs, lived just across the hall. The Gershwins' apartments became a central meeting place for musicians, poets, novelists, playwrights, stockbrokers, and old friends. Wherever he went, George was greeted by reporters and society hostesses. Elsa Maxwell was fond of him, and practically every move he made was covered in the press. Millionaires introduced him to their daughters, for besides fame Gershwin had an income well into six·figures.

He talked about his work constantly, giving many the impression of extreme immodesty. "Tell me, George," Oscar Levant once asked him, "if you had to do it all over again, would you fall in love with yourself again?" At parties he invariably seized the piano, regardless of the other musicians present, and he preferred to play with women clustered around him. A series of mistresses floated through his life, and according to one psychiatrist Gershwin's attitude on sex was comparable to that of an irresponsible teenager. He claimed sexual encounters stimulated him to compose and sometimes slept with two women at once.

But beneath this frivolous, sometimes hedonistic exterior was an ambitious, sensitive musician, tortured by a sense of inadequacy and bent on self-improvement. To the few who knew him well the boyish quality often vanished, and there were moments when he became the puzzled hypochondriac, complaining bitterly about his health. He hated loneliness, even feared it. He began reading a great deal and developed a considerable gift for painting. His most famous painting is a self-portrait, which he modeled by an arrangement of mirrors, and gives the illusion of four Gershwins instead of one. The composer is pictured in tails and top hat and seems to be looking at himself out of the corner of his eye as he paints. After Gershwin began studying with Schillinger, his piano and writing table were cluttered with exercises assigned by the teacher. "George, who always resembled a child with a new toy," wrote Vernon Duke, "now finally found a toy that was real fun and would also yield great dividends." Through Schillinger he began to understand much about harmony and counterpoint that had come to him instinctively. "You see, I never knew why I was doing all these things," the composer said; "I thought they were just parlor tricks. They always went great at parties. Now they'll go right into my music!"

Gershwin produced no orchestral works during 1929 and 1930, as he was deeply involved with several Broadway shows, most notably *Girl Crazy* and *Of Thee I Sing*. In 1931 George and Ira were invited to Hollywood to write the music for a Janet Gaynor film, *Delicious*. Later that year Gershwin expanded a five-minute sequence from the score into his Second Rhapsody, originally called "Rhapsody in Rivets," because of the hammerlike motif. "Nearly everybody comes back from California with a Western tan and a pocketful of moving-picture money," he said. "I decided to come back with these things— and a serious composition besides, if the climate would let me. . . . The old artistic soul must every so often be appeased." The Second Rhapsody was first performed on January 29, 1932, by the Boston Symphony Orchestra, with Koussevitzky conducting and Gershwin at the piano. The reviews were none too good, although the New York critics were kinder when the piece was introduced at Carnegie Hall a week later. While the Second Rhapsody represents a technical advance over the first, the vitality and inspiration of the earlier work are missing. These performances, however, left Koussevitzky one of Gershwin's foremost admirers. "The sweeping brilliance, virtuosity, and rhythmic precision of his playing were incredible," the conductor said, adding that "his perfect poise [was] beyond belief, his dynamic influence on the audience electrifying." And to Koussevitzky, Gershwin confided, "I've only one object—to be a great musician, and I mean great!"

With the premiere of the Second Rhapsody behind him, Gershwin left for a short vacation in Havana. While there he listened to a great deal of Cuban music and was particularly fascinated by the native percussion instruments and the rhythms of the Cuban dances. He returned to New York motivated to compose his *Cuban Overture*, initially called "Rhumba," in which he utilized a number of the exotic instruments he had brought back with him. He tossed the piece off in three weeks, during July and early August, and had it ready for an all-Gershwin concert at Lewisohn Stadium on August 16, 1932. The *Cuban Overture* is lighthearted music and among the composer's least pretentious orchestral selections. Gershwin had a special fondness for the number, however, and it is delightful, full of intoxicating rhythms. "Gershwin may not have considered the work a major effort," Frank Campbell observed after an examination of the musician's manuscripts, "but from the rapidly written full score to the brilliant sounds of its complex orchestra, it reveals a composer of superb orchestral technique, now capable of choosing more consistently those materials that express his own musical nature."

Eager to demonstrate his mastery of some devices he had learned from Schillinger, Gershwin conceived the witty Variations on "I Got Rhythm" for piano and orchestra, his last instrumental writing. The melody, of course, is from his show *Girl Crazy* and was one of Gershwin's favorites. The composer applied it deftly and ingeniously. Written mostly during a Palm Beach vacation in December, 1933, the Variations were first heard at a Boston concert the next month.

Gershwin's work with Schillinger was but one important source of his broadening horizon. He was becoming curious about many things, about music and himself. He entered psychoanalysis in an effort to reconcile the man and the image. And he began formulating the idea for something really important, a composition that would blend his skill at writing for the theater and his advancing orchestral technique. Ever since *Blue Monday* he had thought about composing a full opera. He enjoyed grand opera and was curiously impressed with Alban Berg's *Wozzeck*. Gershwin treasured a piano score of the Berg work and in 1931 journeyed to Philadelphia for the performance under Stokowski.

Some five years before the composer had read DuBose Heyward's novel *Porgy* and immediately thought the story had musical possibilities. He even discussed the matter with the author, but told Heyward that it would be several years before he would be prepared technically to write an opera. In March, 1932, Gershwin approached Heyward again, and an agreement was arranged. The author would deliver a libretto to Ira, who would edit the manuscript and supply whatever additional lyrics were needed. George would then set the text to music.

Porgy and Bess came at the height of Gershwin's restless search for answers to personal and creative problems, and it proved his masterpiece. Much of the preliminary work was done by mail, since the composer was tied to New York and Heyward did not want to leave his Carolina home. Gershwin and his cousin Henry Botkin, who was painting black subjects at the time, spent July and August, 1934, in South Carolina gathering material. Most of those months were spent on Folly Island, about ten miles from Charleston, living in a screen-porched shack near the waterfront. But they also visited black farms and churches and urban slum areas.

Altogether Gershwin spent about twenty months on *Porgy and Bess*—eleven months on the score, another nine on the orchestration. Part of that time he was living in Florida, part in upstate New York, part in New York City. He kept the score of *Die Meistersinger* constantly beside him, referring to it often as a guide for plotting the choral parts and for general principles in vocal writing, although there is no indication that the Wagner work influenced either his texture or sound. His studies with Schillinger, however, are much in evidence in the finished opera, particularly in the rhythmic patterns and such episodes as the fugal background for the crap game scene. "Get this," he said to Vernon Duke, "Gershwin writing fugues! What will the boys say now?"

Porgy and Bess was called a folk opera and produced by the Theatre Guild, with virtually an all-black cast. It was first performed at the Colonial

Theater in Boston, September 30, 1935. The composer listened to the orchestra rehearsal beaming with delight at the sound that emerged from the pit. "Get this!" he whispered. "Just listen to those overtones!" The Gershwin tunes were there, but so was a clear orchestral apparel, shining with a new brilliance. The Boston tryout went well and received prolonged ovations. When Sigmund Spaeth approached Gershwin on opening night, he had tears in his eyes. "Hey, look," George exclaimed to a friend, "we've got the old doc crying." The work was then taken to Broadway, where it opened at the Alvin Theatre on October 10. Professionals had trouble deciding whether *Porgy and Bess* was a highbrow musical comedy or a lowbrow grand opera. On the whole the drama critics were more positive in their verdict than the music critics.

With *Porgy and Bess* the two paths of Gershwin's career came together at last. The popular songwriter is clearly present in Sportin' Life's numbers "It Ain't Necessarily So" and "There's a Boat That's Leavin' Soon for New York." But the serious composer is also there in the expressive chromaticisms, the antiphonal choruses, the skillful atmospheric writing, and the effective use of counterpoint in the duets and final trio. Porgy's "Buzzard Song" is a true operatic aria, complete with high notes, whereas "Bess, You Is My Woman Now" is a love duet in the grand manner. Yet the popular and the serious are integrated with little sense of incongruity. Folk touches are admitted through the cries of the street vendors—the Honey Man, the Strawberry Woman, and the Crab Man. "Gone, Gone, Gone" is a mourning spiritual reflecting the call-and-response pattern, while "It Takes a Long Pull to Get There" is a mutation of a black work song.

Gershwin's opera ran three acts and nine scenes and in its original form is almost continuous music. The composer's melodies are among his best, and the various facets fuse into a theater piece of great vitality. Gershwin's famous blues idiom is right at home in the opera's setting. The work focuses on Catfish Row, a black tenement in Charleston, but the composer's Tin Pan Alley chromatics immediately link the community with New York City. In Mellers' interpretation of the opera, a world of spiritual innocence is destroyed by a new world of materialism and commerce. The scene opens on Clara, nursing her baby and singing of a dream Eden, where it is always "Summertime." There the "livin' is easy, fish are jumpin', an' the cotton is high" and "daddy's rich an' ma is good lookin'." But this life is invaded by Sportin' Life, a light-skinned black from New York who represents commerce, corruption, and vice. The crippled Porgy enters (Gershwin's favorite part of the score), symbolizing unsoiled twentieth-century man—broken and alienated. He sings against the world of material possessions and commercial exploitation.

I got plenty o' nuttin',
An' nuttin's plenty fo' me.
I got no car, got no mule.

I got no misery.
De folks wid plenty o' plenty
Got a lock on dey door,
'Fraid somebody's a-goin to rob 'em
While dey's out a-makin' more.
What for?

With Bess, Porgy glimpses happiness and renewed faith: "Two is strong where one is feeble." But to keep her, he is thrust into contact with the corrupt world and is taken off to jail. Bess, weary with having her dreams destroyed, gives up any hope of finding stability and meaning. Instead she substitutes another dream by accepting Sportin' Life's offer to come to New York, where she will find the good time and—through happy dust—a release from fear. In the last scene Porgy in part rejects the old life and goes off in his goat-cart looking for Bess. What will happen is uncertain. He will find neither Bess nor New York, but the rumba lilt of Porgy's final spiritual, "O Lawd! I'm on My Way," provides the semblance of a happy ending. "The opera thus states explicitly the theme which we have seen to be latent in the history of American civilization," Mellers concludes; "and it had specific personal implications for Gershwin himself in so far as he hoped that the element within him that was Porgy might one day come to terms with the element that was Sportin' Life."

While musicians like Virgil Thomson quarreled that *Porgy and Bess* was "crooked folklore and half-way opera," "falsely conceived and rather clumsily executed," Gershwin loved his opera, arranged a *Porgy and Bess Suite,* and would play the music over and over with his eyes closed, enchanted with what he had done. The initial production was not a financial success, but the work was revived in 1942, again a decade later, and in 1959 was made into a motion picture. The 1952 revival, which starred William Warfield and Leontyne Price, was sent by the State Department on a goodwill tour to Europe, which included triumphant performances in Moscow. The opera has been given in La Fenice, San Carlo, and the Vienna *Volksoper,* and Gershwin was the first American-born composer to be performed at La Scala. Many of the music critics that originally condemned the work later altered their opinion, while those who had approved all along came to deepen their appreciation with the passing of time. "With *Porgy* you suddenly realize that Gershwin was a great, great theater composer," Bernstein concludes. "Perhaps that's what was wrong with his concert music: it was really theater music thrust into a concert hall."

The opera convinced Gershwin that he had found his stride and was capable of writing significant music. But he needed a vacation and a break from serious composition. He accepted another Hollywood film offer and arrived on the West Coast early in August, 1936, to prepare the score for the Ginger Rogers-Fred Astaire musical *Shall We Dance?* He enjoyed working for the movies, appeared to be bubbling over with good health and very much the eternally youthful George. He seemed happier, more in command of himself than ever. He had a firm opinion on just about everything, could even be reckless in his judgments. He fell madly in love with Paulette Goddard, and the romance added a new aura of excitement. Yet friends saw him as a man at peace. He painted, played tennis (once with Schoenberg), swam, and took a daily six-mile walk through the Hollywood hills. He enjoyed visiting the homes of film stars and having celebrities over to his place. He liked the attention Hollywood gave him and delighted in the sight of beautiful women in bathing suits gathered around his pool.

Film music came easily for Gershwin. In 1937 he wrote the songs for another Fred Astaire picture, *A Damsel in Distress*, and signed a contract with Samuel Goldwyn to provide the score for *The Goldwyn Follies*. It was remembered afterwards that he grew a little more restless than usual and that occasionally his temper snapped. His affair with Paulette Goddard ended; acquaintances were never sure why. Meanwhile he began working on the music for *The Goldwyn Follies*. He refurbished "Love Walked In" for the picture, a song Gershwin thought had a "Brahms strain," and completed "Love Is Here to Stay." He had also gotten the idea for a string quartet, which he intended to start as soon as *The Goldwyn Follies* was finished. "It's going through my head all the time," he told Merle Armitage. "It's about to drive me crazy; I'm so damned full of new ideas!"

But the composer's strength was ebbing. He was often listless. There had been danger signs a few months before. On February 10, 1937, he had appeared as soloist with the Los Angeles Philharmonic on an all-Gershwin program. It was a gala performance, with a reception at the Hollywood Plaza Hotel before the concert. Gershwin played brilliantly, except that he fumbled an easy passage in the second movement of the Concerto in F and missed a note in the coda. Conductor Alexander Smallens noticed the errors and covered for him. "I was thinking of you when I made those mistakes," Gershwin told Oscar Levant backstage. To others he admitted that his mind had gone blank for a few seconds. The following night, while the composer was conducting, he was assailed by a splitting headache and the sensation of burning rubber in his nostrils.

No one had any idea Gershwin was seriously ill. The first doctors called in diagnosed his condition as a mild nervous breakdown. One morning early in June he collapsed at the Goldwyn studios. He began suffering inordinate pain. The morning hours were the worst. "I would go up to his room," Levant said, "and find him sitting between two beds, holding his head with his two fists—wracked with agony." He would remain in his bedroom for hours with the shades drawn, his eyes glazed, demanding absolute quiet. Slowly, with immense effort, he would emerge from his silence during the afternoon. By evening he almost seemed himself. He still went to parties, but it was noticed that he often dropped and spilled things. When he sat down at the piano, the old fire was gone. Finally he asked Vernon Duke to take over the score of *The Goldwyn Follies*.

On the morning of June 20, he awoke with the worst headache yet and was taken to Cedars of Lebanon Hospital for a complete check-up. A few days after his return home, he fell in the bathroom and was knocked unconscious. He was rushed to Cedars of Lebanon Hospital in a coma. There the truth became known. X-rays revealed that a tumor was growing on his brain. His condition was inoperable, but surgeons decided to operate anyway. Friends and relatives waited downstairs. The tumor was too deeply imbedded. Gershwin never regained consciousness. He was returned to his hospital room—his head bandaged, his breathing coming with increasing difficulty. He died the following morning, July 11, 1937, at the age of thirty-eight.

Gershwin's death occurred on a Hollywood Sunday—"not a day," F. Scott Fitzgerald once wrote, "but rather a gap between two other days." His body was sent back to New York in a sealed coffin. The funeral was held on July 15, at Temple Emanu-El on Fifth Avenue. Some 3500 people attended the service. Honorary pallbearers included Mayor Fiorello La Guardia, ex-Mayor Jimmy Walker, Walter Damrosch, George M. Cohan, and Edwin Franko Goldman. The flower-covered coffin left the temple to the sounds of the slow section of the *Rhapsody in Blue*. As the cortege proceeded to the cemetery, heavy clouds swept across Manhattan and a dismal rain fell.

Alive, Gershwin had become a symbol of his time, and he joyously reaped the benefits of the age he mirrored. Until the six months preceding his death, Oscar Levant affirmed, life for George had been "just one big, wild, marvelous dream come true." Dead, Gershwin became a legend. "Like a rare flower which blossoms forth once in a long while," Koussevitzky said, "Gershwin represents a singularly original and rare phenomenon." Arnold Schoenberg pronounced him "beyond doubt . . . an innovator," while George Antheil considered him "one of those rarest of composers, a composer of *ideas!*" No less a figure than Maurice Ravel had adored his piano playing, and when the French composer came to America for a concert tour, he requested—as a birthday present—to meet George Gershwin. "One had forgotten," Gilbert Seldes declared at the time of Gershwin's death, "that there still existed in the world a force so boundless, an exaltation so high, that anyone could storm heaven with cheers and laughter." Gershwin effused exuberance, sincerity, and—above all—style. "I'll never forget his bow the opening night of *Porgy and Bess*," Levant wrote. "It was a beautiful one."

What might he have done had his life not been cut short? He was planning a ballet based on *An American in Paris* with George Balanchine, and rumors of a second piano concerto were afloat. Lynn Riggs was writing the libretto of an opera for him. He wanted to compose a screen ballet, and there had even been talk of a collaboration with Ring Lardner on an American version of *Carmen*.

"My people are American," Gershwin said; "my time is today—music must repeat the thought and aspirations of the times." Certainly his own work made an indelible impression on American music and brought a new concept to the European-dominated world of high culture. Idiomatically

Gershwin was an American composer, whose music reflects the movement, excitement, and nervousness of the urban society he knew so well. That the musician represents only one phase of American life there can be little doubt, but it was the phase that came into predominance during the decade that brought him fame. "If I look back on what they now call 'the roaring Twenties,'" Eva Gauthier told Henry Levinger, "it is like looking at a rich tapestry of almost blinding color. So much happened in those years which were marked by abundant prosperity in America and a cultural liveliness which was breathtaking. Music of our time all of a sudden became a matter of general interest, and everybody felt like jumping on the bandwagon."

Gershwin's fame reached the extent it did largely because the radio, phonograph, and sound motion pictures were becoming vehicles of mass entertainment. His destiny, biographer David Ewen concludes, was "to write popular songs with the techniques and approaches of serious music, and serious music with the techniques and approaches of popular music." Young Gershwin reputedly was practicing some preludes and fugues from Bach's *Well-Tempered Clavier* one day in his cubicle at Remick's. "Are you studying to be a concert pianist, George?" a fellow song plugger asked. "No," Gershwin replied, "I'm studying to be a great popular composer." But as he progressed in maturity, his ability to sustain larger ideas and present them with subtle harmony, counterpoint, and orchestration developed to a creative level beyond the Broadway songwriter's dreams. No one was more surprised at his accomplishments than Gershwin, for he often asked people what it was that made his music different from others.

The language of Tin Pan Alley jazz was Gershwin's native speech, the foundation from which all else grew. "Jazz is music; it uses the same notes as Bach used," the composer said. "Jazz is the result of the energy stored in America.... Jazz has contributed an enduring value to America in the sense that it has expressed ourselves. It is an original American achievement that will endure, not as jazz perhaps, but which will leave its mark on future music in one way or another." But while the popular idiom was an organic part of Gershwin's spectrum, to Aaron Copland it was exotic and limiting. Unlike Gershwin, Copland did not play jazz and could never improvise in the jazz manner. His use of jazz, therefore, was fairly contrived, and he used the motif only a short while. Whereas Gershwin knew little about the larger musical forms and expanded his popular gifts into frameworks he mastered with difficulty, Copland approached jazz as a musician schooled in the serious traditions.

For years Copland has championed the cause of American music by writing profusely in its behalf, traveling to conferences, and composing works that are much admired. Gershwin furthered the cause mainly by being himself and writing approachable music that the public immediately loved. Copland has been primarily the artist; Gershwin was the man of the theater. Whereas Copland had his popular period, Gershwin had his serious side. Both were at the Samuel Goldwyn Studios in Hollywood within five years of the same time. Copland wrote his movie music skillfully, but devoted spare moments to working on more serious things, often late at night at the studio itself. "An air of mystery hovers over a film studio after dark," the composer remembered. "Its silence and empty streets give off something of the atmosphere of a walled medieval town; no one gets in or out without passing muster with the guards at the gates." This seclusion provided Copland with the quiet needed for writing such works as *Appalachian Spring* and the Violin Sonata. While Gershwin had serious thoughts in the movie capital, most of his nights were spent out on the town, playing the piano at parties, and enjoying the company of adoring women.

Although Copland is dedicated to the notion that musical ideas must be tested outside "in the big world," he is privately much more retiring than Gershwin was. These same characteristics are true of their music. Copland's work is far more introverted, sometimes equating emptiness with peace; Gershwin's is extroverted, his rhythms lively and amusing, divulging the perpetual youth's enjoying a success he never expected. "The European boys have small ideas," Gershwin once remarked, "but they sure know how to dress 'em up." Copland learned from Boulanger how to handle ideas with craftsmanship. His pieces are therefore better integrated, while the dimensions of his art are multiple. Gershwin's scope is smaller, although his total output is proportionately larger. Both were innovative, but in ways as different as their personalities. Gershwin considered himself a "modern romantic" and essentially remained such. Copland evolved from an early preoccupation with jazz to a use of serialism and atonality without losing his spare, lean style.

Gershwin was an exciting and gifted, charming and sympathetic composer. Although his art was developing rapidly, his desire to be both sinner and saint and his tendency to burn the candle at both ends probably retarded his technical advance. On the other hand his internal struggle may explain much of his humanity and warmth. Copland was more ordered, less a part of the world, and lived to become the patriarch of his field. Both composers had experienced the confusion of a polyglot industrial society, yet responded to it in reverse ways. Gershwin accepted the market place, enjoyed its fruits, and bought enough isolation and freedom to pursue his genius. Copland intellectually shut out the city, could be alone amid tension, and attained a personal calm that enabled him to pull together disintegrated fragments, internalize restless movement, and blaze new directions of art for their own sake.

1. "Flying Colors," Norman Bel Geddes Sketch (From the Norman Bel Geddes Collection at the Hoblitzelle Theatre Arts Library, the Humanities Research Center, the University of Texas at Austin, by Permission of the Executrix of the Norman Bel Geddes Estate, Edith Lutyens Bel Geddes)

2. Mary Garden (Courtesy of Albert Davis Collection, Hoblitzelle Theatre Arts Library)

3. Lily Pons as Lucia. (Courtesy of Albert Davis Collection, Hoblitzelle Theatre Arts Library)

4. Arturo Toscanini (Courtesy of Albert Davis Collection, Hoblitzelle Theatre Arts Library)

5. At Rehearsal of *Out of This World*. Left to right: Lemuel Ayers, Hanya Holm, Agnes DeMille, Arnold Saint-Subber (Courtesy of Hoblitzelle Theatre Arts Library)

6. George Gershwin (Courtesy of Albert Davis Collection, Hoblitzelle Theatre Arts Library)

7. Original Production of *Show Boat* (Courtesy of Hoblitzelle Theatre Arts Library

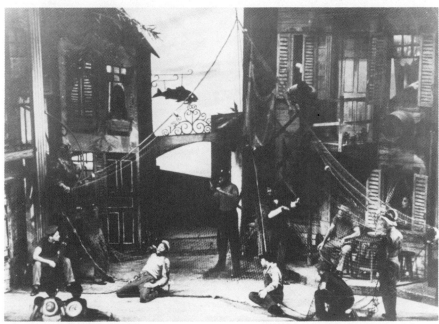

8. The Blevins Davis and Robert Breen Production of *Porgy and Bess* (Courtesy of Robert Downing Collection, Hoblitzelle Theatre Arts Library)

9. Left to right: Ruth Etting, Jack Pearl, Helen Morgan, Harry Richman (Courtesy of Albert Davis Collection, Hoblitzelle Theatre Arts Library)

10. Bing Crosby and the Rhythm Boys (Courtesy of Hoblitzelle Theatre Arts Library)

11. Rudy Vallee (Courtesy of Hoblitzelle Theatre Arts Library)

4 SAINTS IN 3 ACTS

GERTRUDE STEIN

FORTY-FOURTH STREET
THEATRE

12. Program Cover, *4 Saints in 3 Acts* (Courtesy of Hoblitzelle Theatre Arts Library)

13. Fred Fehl Photograph of the Rumble Scene from *West Side Story* (Courtesy of Hoblitzelle Theatre Arts Library)

14. Duke Ellington and His Orchestra (Courtesy of Hoblitzelle Theatre Arts Library)

15. Isham Jones and His Orchestra (Courtesy of Albert Davis Collection, Hoblitzelle Theatre Arts Library)

16. Sheet Music Cover. "This Is The Army, Mister Jones" (Courtesy of W.H. Crain Collection, Hoblitzelle Theatre Arts Library)

17. Sheet Music Cover, "The Hostess With The Mostes' On The Ball" (Courtesy of W. H. Crain Collection, Hoblitzelle Theatre Arts Library)

18. Elvis Presley (Courtesy of RCA Records and Tapes)

19. Loretta Lynn (Courtesy of MCA Records)

20. Loretta Lynn (Courtesy of MCA Records)

CHAPTER

VI

AMERICAN SCENE

COMPOSERS

Aaron Copland was by no means the only American composer to forsake an ivory tower approach to music for less abstract forms during the Depression and war years. In the early 1930s young intellectuals who had rarely given second thought to politics and economics before suddenly became vitally concerned with the plight of their country. Franklin Roosevelt's insistence that we "need not be frustrated by our misfortunes but could be masters of our future" stirred the patriotic instincts of artists in all fields. A new wave of nationalism and populism swept the land. The common, the historical, the regional, and the glaringly native not only found their way into art, but were often glorified to epic proportions. Themes of social protest and trade unionism were joined by sporadic outbursts from the left-wing. At the same time that Thomas Hart Benton, Grant Wood, John Steuart Curry, and others were recording the American scene, especially the rural Midwest, on canvases and post office walls, composers like Virgil Thomson and Roy Harris were rediscovering the American heartland in music. Whereas Edward Hopper depicted contemporary urban loneliness in his paintings, Marc Blitzstein lashed out at the injustices of capitalism in music for the theater. This collectivist temperament was stated with simplicity, aimed as it was at a large public. The strident progressivism of the 1920s gave way to broadly traditional styles, reflecting an America essentially isolated from Europe. "The time was not for novelty," Thomson later wrote. The times indeed were critical, when the country needed its heroes, its monuments, and its past. But most of all it needed the assurance that by sticking together and adhering to the democratic ideals its people could weather this crisis as they had those of times gone by.

Like the American Scene school in painting, composers began focusing on regional material in the mid-1920s, although the trend became far more pronounced after the Wall Street crash. Among the first to exalt the American landscape was Paul Whiteman's arranger, Ferde Grofe, the orchestrator of *Rhapsody in Blue*. Grofe was born in New York City, March 27, 1892, and came from a musical family. His father had been a professional singer, his mother a concert cellist. As a boy he studied piano, violin, and harmony with his mother and viola with his grandfather. At fourteen he ran away from home and supported himself for several years as a truck driver, a bank clerk, a bookbinder, an elevator operator, a patent medicine vendor, and by playing in dance halls. For a while he worked with a wandering cornetist who called himself Professor Albert Jerome. That lasted until the "Professor" ran out on him in a mining town in northern California, taking all the money and leaving Grofe with an unpaid board bill. "The only job I could get," he remembered, "was playing the piano in a sporting house... for two dollars a night. I didn't get corrupted, because I was in love with my landlady's daughter."

Around 1909 he became a violinist with the Los Angeles Symphony Orchestra, where his uncle was concertmaster. He remained with the orchestra for ten years, during which time his first composition was published—*The Elks' Grand Reunion March*, written in honor of an Elks' convention. He worked some with jazz bands and played banjo in one of the first ragtime groups heard in San Francisco. Eventually he formed his own band and began writing arrangements of the popular tunes of the day. When Paul Whiteman heard Grofe's outfit in 1919, he was so impressed by the novelty of their arrangements that he asked Ferde to join his orchestra as pianist and arranger. Grofe played his first engagement with Whiteman in 1920 at the Hotel Alexandria in Los Angeles. He continued studying and soon developed into a master of instrumentation, achieving unusual timbres and pungent effects in his jazz orchestrations that were new at the time. He left Whiteman in 1924, shortly after scoring Gershwin's *Rhapsody in Blue*, to become a freelance arranger and devote himself more fully to serious composition.

His first large work, *Broadway at Night*, did not attract much attention. But in 1925 his *Mississippi Suite* won him wide acclaim among serious music lovers. Two movements of the suite—"Huckleberry Finn" and "Mardi Gras"—became particularly popular. He wrote his most successful composition, the *Grand Canyon Suite*, in 1931. Although jazz techniques are used the work is basically not a jazz piece. Its five sections vividly describe various aspects of the Canyon. "On the Trail," the third and most famous section, contains a cowboy tune set against a rhythm denoting the jogging of a donkey. The *Grand Canyon Suite* has been widely performed, and even Toscanini conducted it. Grofe later wrote a *Death Valley Suite*, a *Hollywood Suite*, a *Hudson River Suite*, a *San Francisco Suite*, a *Niagara Falls Suite*, *Wheels* (a "Transportation Suite"), a *Symphony in Steel*, and an orchestral piece called *Knute Rockne*. To achieve musical reality he often introduces novel sounds like an actual typewriter, sirens, pneumatic drills, and the banging of carpenters. Many of his works have been written for specific occasions; in 1964, for instance, he was commissioned by the New York World's Fair to compose a *World's Fair Suite*.

Grofe made his debut as a conductor in Carnegie Hall in January, 1937, on a program of his own works. After that he was a frequent guest conductor with major symphony orchestras and from 1939 to 1943 taught composition and orchestration at the Juilliard Summer School. He made concert arrangements for Columbia and Victor and wrote music for several films. Like Morton Gould and Don Gillis, two younger American scene composers, Grofe devoted much of his time to radio.

Several of the musicians drawn to American subjects in the 1930s, however, came to these only after more esoteric experimentation. Virgil Thomson joined the ranks of the American scene composers by way of Nadia Boulanger and Paris and after a flirtation with Dada. Born in Kansas City, Missouri, on November 25, 1896, Thomson was of Scotch descent, the son of a tone-deaf father. The boy took his first music lessons from a cousin at the age of five and grew up listening to the gramophone and pumping a pianola. He studied piano, voice, and organ while attending public school and early demonstrated a keen intellect, a skill with words, and a love for paradox. When young Thomson heard Strauss' *Also Sprach Zarathustra*, it sounded to him "so much like Wagner that it might have been composed by Humperdinck." He graduated from Central High, but there was no money for college. The youth held various church positions, gave piano recitals, and toured regionally as an accompanist for singers. He acquired a good facility for sight-reading and learned much about the voice. A junior college opened up in Kansas City in 1915, and Thomson quickly enrolled. Peers considered him a man with a destiny, yet thought him eccentric, conceited, and a bit foppish.

He enlisted in the army in February, 1917, and about a year later was appointed to the School of Military Aeronautics at the University of Texas in Austin. When he arrived, it was discovered there were more cadets ready for pilot training than the airfields could handle. So he was sent to Columbia University for a course in radio-telephony. While in New York, Thomson managed on weekends to hear the Philharmonic under Josef Stransky and opera at the Metropolitan. After three months at Columbia, he was ordered to Lake Charles, Louisiana, for flying practice. He received his overseas orders in September, 1918, but the war ended before his troop ship was ready to sail.

He returned home with a reserve commission and resumed his courses at the junior college.

He moved to Boston in August, 1919, found a position as church organist, and that autumn entered Harvard. He majored in music, but supplemented this curriculum with courses in philosophy, Italian, German, and advanced English composition. Fellow students like Walter Piston and Randall Thompson remembered him as a model of industry and a dynamo of enthusiasm. He studied orchestration with Edward Burlingame Hill, advanced harmony with Archibald Davison, and later was assistant to both. After the first year he supported himself entirely by organ playing, concert engagements, and scholarships. He sang in the Harvard Glee Club, and in the spring of 1921, a year short of graduation, toured Europe with the group. In Italy Davison, the Glee Club's director, fell ill, and Thomson conducted a few concerts. When the boys returned to Harvard in the fall, Thomson remained behind, having received the John Knowles Paine Traveling Fellowship, and began casting about Paris for a teacher. A college friend introduced him to Boulanger, who agreed to take him on as an organ and composition student.

Thomson looked upon his stay in Paris as more than a rounding out of his musical preparation. He hoped it might prove the environment in which his emotional development could catch up with his intellectual advances. The city in 1921 was just beginning to fill with Americans. Some were there to escape prohibition, some were there for the fun of it, others were there to study. While Thomson did not share the expatriates' disaffection for the United States, he did feel some of their discontent. France gave him perspective, and if anything, strengthened America's hold on him. Yet he came to view his heritage in the light of cosmopolitan values. He reacted with some reserve to the Latin Quarter, seldom frequented the Left Bank bars, but was overjoyed with the Sorbonne, the antique shops, the book stalls, and the international restaurants. He practiced the organ daily at a church near the Parc Monceau and was inflamed by his lessons with Boulanger.

Emphasizing intuition and personal inspiration as much as scientific means, Boulanger insisted that so long as Thomson expressed what he had to say clearly and sincerely, his music would be worthwhile. She would look over his writing, point out the weak spots, and explain why she thought them weak—why something seemed to stop the flow or not to belong. She was invariably enthusiastic about what he was doing and gave him confidence in his own ideas. "Oh, you can do it!" she would say. "You can do it!" With Boulanger's encouragement he composed a Passacaglia and Two Preludes and a Christmas Pastorale, both for organ.

In the fall of 1922 Thomson reluctantly returned to Harvard to finish the work on his degree. Through Davison he obtained the position of organist at Boston's historic King's Chapel. He encountered the doctrines of disillusionment and despair then fashionable among young intellectuals, yet largely rejected them. That he had misgivings about the quality of American life is evident from a letter written shortly after his arrival in Cambridge. He confessed amazement at the nation's fabulous prosperity, but avowed he could "only say of her 'A poor thing but mine own.'" Still he remained convinced that ultimately his country would perceive her global destiny. At Harvard he composed Three Antiphonal Psalms and *Missa Brevis* for men's chorus. Upon graduation he received a Juilliard Fellowship and spent a year in New York, studying composition with Rosario Scalero at the David Mannes School of Music. He went back to Harvard as an assistant instructor, but grew bored and restless. In September, 1925, he left for Paris, remarking that if he was going to starve, he "preferred to starve where the food is good."

He would remain in Paris for the next fifteen years. He took up residence in his old quarters on the Rue de Berne and went to Boulanger for advice on how to proceed. He was determined to make his way exclusively as a composer. He ran short of money, but supported himself by commissions, obtaining temporary patrons, and borrowing. He spent practically nothing.

Four years before he had heard much about Dada, and there was evidence of that movement yet. Thomson had been charmed by Dada's iconoclasm and became enthusiastic about its offspring, surrealism. Dada was born in Zurich during the dark days of World War I and essentially represented a rejection of western civilization, a civilization that seemed to have degenerated into a tragic farce. To a world that seemed bent on destroying itself with bombs and poison gas, Dada added the weapon of ridicule. The Dadaists would hasten the extinction of a civilization gone mad by laughing at it, supporting the irrational and the incongruous. Unhinged by the collapse of their once-stable world, the Dadaists explored the possibilities of psychic escape, making use of Freud's ideas. They yearned to go back to their childhood and for their name took the French infant prattle word for hobbyhorse. At the same time they sought to free themselves from bourgeois values and the sham of traditional stereotypes. The creative process was reduced to pure impulse, while art became a compilation of the accidental.

Right before his return to Paris, Thomson wrote in *Vanity Fair* that satire was "an admirable corrective to pretense." Once you start poking fun at the other fellow, you wind up poking fun at yourself. "The movement known as Dada was exactly such a joke. 'Art is bunk,' announced the Dadaists. 'Music is bunk. Literature is bunk.'" By 1925 the Dadaists had fought among themselves, and the movement had splintered drastically. Surrealism emerged as its strongest survivor. And yet something of Dada infiltrated the music Thomson wrote at this time. He wanted to extend music's vocabulary and say fresh things by fresh means. The use of free impulse and the admission of incongruous material therefore appealed to him.

His *Sonata de chiesa* (1926), Thomson's first really important work, is a study in discord. The composer later referred to it as "my bang-up graduation piece in the dissonant neobaroque style of the decade." Translated into English, "Sonata for the Church" contains several elements of traditional church music. But while the first movement is written in an organ-prelude style, the second includes the popular dance rhythms of a tango, suggesting the impact of Satie and the younger French composers. Elsewhere there are indications that Stravinsky had made a firm impression. Composed for clarinet, trumpet, viola, horn, and trombone, the *Sonata de chiesa* achieves much of its effect through a deliberate misuse of formality.

Having mastered the use of discord, Thomson's interest in it dwindled. He sketched two movements of his *Symphony on a Hymn Tune* in 1926 and completed the work two years later. Again seeking to embrace a collage of incompatibles within a disciplined musical structure, the composer drew on melodies he remembered from childhood. The hymn tune is "How Firm a Foundation," although there are touches of "Yes, Jesus Loves Me" and even a bit of "For He's a Jolly Good Fellow." Yet unlike Ives' treatment of Americana, Thomson handled these tunes with the best Parisian rhetoric and syntax. "Square, inflexible revivalist tunes," Kathleen Hoover contends, "were slyly woven with buoyancy and wit into a symphony of impeccable structure. The result was a classic in musical satire, the first to convey through scholarly form the feel of rural America, evoking all the color and bustle of a Currier and Ives print." The whimsey of Dada is still present, but the method of communication has grown more direct. The harmony, according to Thomson, is "half-in and half-out of focus," while the mood is both homely and sophisticated. There is a nostalgia that perhaps is explained by the composer's self-exile. "I wrote in Paris," Thomson said, "music that was always, in one way or another, about Kansas City. I wanted Paris to know Kansas City, to understand the way we like to think and feel on the banks of the Kaw and the Missouri."

The composer met other Americans in Paris. Through James Joyce he came to know George Antheil, whose work he admired. A common interest in being contemporary and in getting their music performed drew Thomson and Antheil together. Early in 1926 Antheil was invited to pay a call on Gertrude Stein at her house on the Rue de Fleurus. He was becoming known among the inner circle as a budding genius, and Stein felt she should look him over. Antheil was a bit wary and took Thomson along for protection. "Naturally I went," the composer recalled. "Alice Toklas did not on first view care for me, and neither of the ladies found reason for seeing George again. But Gertrude and I got on like Harvard men."

Thomson's relationship with Gertrude Stein would prove one of the most decisive of his career. He had admired her work since college days and had vowed to meet her upon returning to France. Stein made no pretense at being a musical authority; Alice Toklas, in fact, knew considerably more about music than she. But she became quite excited about what Thomson was trying to do. "It's not at all banal," Stein said. "He frosts his music with a thin layer of banal sounds to put people off, but what's underneath is very pure and special."

The composer in return was strongly attracted to Stein's crackling word sequences. He read her writing, Hoover maintains, "as one watches a delightful circus, expecting it to make no sense but its own. And he saw it for what it was: a true literary cubism." *Susie Asado* (1926) was his first attempt to set a Stein text to music. The piece is extremely funny in a "dead-pan" way. A setting of Stein's *Capital, Capitals* followed in 1927. Then Thomson asked the author to write an opera for him. The two debated over subject matter and approach.

"What about the lives of the Saints?" Stein finally suggested.

"Fine," Thomson said. "But the Italian saints have been overdone, and the Renaissance racket isn't very fresh."

At last they decided on two Spanish saints—Saint Theresa of Avila and Ignatius Loyola. The opera was called *Four Saints in Three Acts*, although there were some thirty saints and four acts. The title was part of the general nonsense, while the stage directions proved as mixed up as the rest.

Stein worked on the libretto of *Four Saints* through the spring of 1927. Thomson by then had moved to a flat on the Left Bank. With Stein's help he had acquired an American patron, and by November was hard at work on their opera. He had also fallen in love with the British author Mary Butts. "She penetrated the Chinese Wall of his creative ego," Thomson's biographer says, "took him out of himself, opened his eyes to new values, gave him fresh perspectives." It was decided to use black singers in the opera, because the composer believed black artists sang more clearly and could better put themselves into the various moods demanded by the score. He also felt black singers could be satisfied with the sheer beauty of sound. They would consequently have no intellectual barriers to break through when the words spoken had no meaning; neither would they grow self-conscious.

Four Saints in Three Acts treats nonsense in terms of serious recitative and aria. The music incorporates elements from a variety of religious traditions, ranging from American folk hymnody to Gregorian chants. Thomson particularly enjoyed writing for the voice and allowed English to be sung naturally. His score is deceptively simple and has a pseudo-innocence about it, yet the music is full of subtleties, imagination, Parisian sophistication, and wit. Stein's fantasy emerged from the composer's hands wrapped in homespun, marked by rudimentary scales and early harmonic progressions. The original chamber orchestration is dominated by the sounds of an accordion. Still there are Spanish overtones, echoes of Elizabethan madrigals, and a Satie-like humor. The ultramodern libretto is treated in an antimodern way, while the prosaic is combined with the abstract, the irrational with the ordinary. Thomson solved the problem of handling Stein's text, void of literal meaning, by creating a musical scene that is crystal clear, giving the words speech inflections just as though their literal meaning were understandable. The mood of the music is serious, totally unambiguous, almost with no regard for the thing said. This is what gives the work its amusement and charm.

The opera was not performed until 1934, when it was staged in Hartford, Connecticut, on February 8, by the Friends and Enemies of Modern Music. It reached New York two weeks later. While some of Thomson's earlier pieces had been heard in Paris, he was practically unknown in the United States. *Four Saints in Three Acts* established his reputation. The premiere created a sensation in the press, and for a few months Thomson was the most talked about composer in the country. Lucius Beebe recorded the opening for the *Herald Tribune*'s society section, and most of the leading music and drama critics were on hand. Gershwin, then writing *Porgy and Bess*, attended Thomson's all-black opera. Relieved, he wrote DuBose Heyward, "The libretto was entirely in Stein's manner, which means it had the effect of a five year-old child prattling on." He was more impressed with the composer's music, because "it sounded early nineteenth century, which was a happy inspiration and made the libretto bearable—in fact, quite entertaining."

The public hardly knew whether to be amused or outraged by such lines as,

> *Pigeons on the grass, alas*
> *Pigeons on the grass alas*
> *Short longer grass short longer longer shorter yellow grass. Pigeons*
> *large pigeons on the shorter yellow grass alas*
> *pigeons on the grass.*
>   . . .

But pigeons on the grass became the best thing that had happened to headline and caption writers in many a day. The New York *Sun* got permission to reprint part of the libretto. Letters poured in, pro and con, as columnists and rewrite men suddenly burst into Steinian prose. Critics were confused, too, but most of them were favorable. Carl Van Vechten found *Four Saints* "as original in its conception as *Pelleas and Melisande.*" One reviewer called the work "delectable imbecility," while another thought it "a gorgeous piece of kidding." The opera defies analysis, and John Cage later wrote: "To enjoy it, one must leap into that irrational world from which it sprang, the world in which the matter-of-fact and the irrational are one, where mirth and metaphysics marry to beget comedy."

Thomson had come over from Paris to help select the cast and supervise the staging, but returned to France shortly after the four-week run. He had made an earlier trip to the United States in the fall of 1932. Meanwhile he had composed a violin sonata, a Second Symphony, two string quartets, and the *Stabat Mater*. Although he remained under the influence of Eric Satie and the Parisian "Six," he moved further away from ultramodern writing toward simpler forms of expression. Samuel Barlow found the string quartets "well made, vastly entertaining, and often lovely—like a seashell door stop." Thomson liked to think of himself as a neo-Romantic, a tendency that would continue as the composer rediscovered the American scene.

In 1936 Thomson was asked to write the score for the government documentary film *The Plough That Broke the Plains*. The text by Pare

Lorentz told of the destruction of the vast Southwestern agricultural region by wrong farming methods. It described the ploughing of the Plains, the droughts, the erosion of the soil, and finally the western migration of the "Okies."

> This is a record of land . . .
> of soil, rather than people—
> a story of the Great Plains.
> The 400,000,000 acres of
> wind-swept grass land that
> spread up from the Texas
> Panhandle to Canada. . . .
> A high, treeless continent,
> without a river, without streams. . . .
> A country of high winds,
> and sun. . . .
> and of little rain. . . .

The next year Thomson and Lorentz worked together again on *The River*, another government sponsored film, treating the floods along the Mississippi. The composer's score is concise and restrained and utilizes folk tunes and hymns with commendable craftsmanship. Thomson later drew orchestral suites from the scores of both films.

Like Copland, Thomson was now composing for a broad audience. His ballet *Filling Station* (1937), written for Lincoln Kirstein's Ballet Caravan, captures the flavor of the popular tunes of the Depression era and toured all over the United States and South America. The musician worked with the Federal Theater Project on two productions, *Walk Together, Chillun* and a black *Macbeth*, and wrote incidental music for Broadway productions of *Hamlet* and *Anthony and Cleopatra*. In 1937 he provided the score for another documentary film, *The Spanish Earth*, in collaboration with Marc Blitzstein. Thomson's music was versatile, his construction relaxed. Copland, who admitted that Thomson had influenced him, judged his colleague's work "plain and honest, with no fanciness for the sake of being fancy."

While the composer made frequent trans-Atlantic visits to the United States after 1932, he did not leave France permanently until 1940. Thomson in fact was one of the last Americans to get out of Paris. The exodus began in 1939, but the composer was reluctant to abandon the city he had loved so long. "Aren't you going to stick around and see the fun?" he asked Arthur Berger, the musician-critic, who was studying in France at the time. Thomson finally sent his paintings to a friend's chateau and with his manuscript scores in hand boarded a train for the south of France, about two days before the Germans entered Paris. He spent some two months with companions near the city of Pau and arrived in New York via Lisbon that fall.

Since his funds were exhausted, he accepted a position as music critic for the New York *Herald Tribune*, replacing Lawrence Gilman who had died the year before. He would remain at that post for fourteen years. His reviews were devastingly clever and urbane, and he would eventually publish five books. He also lectured extensively, did some guest conducting, and helped organize recitals of contemporary music. His personality remained part Kansas City, part Paris. On the one hand he manifested shrewd common sense, sentimentality, and a stubborn adherence to certain approved ethical values; on the other he exuded wit and sophistication. He took up residence in a top floor apartment of the old Chelsea Hotel, overlooking the southern part of New York. He entertained frequently, since cooking became a special hobby.

By carefully budgeting his time Thomson was able to continue his composing. He usually devoted mornings to his own work, writing in bathrobe and pajamas. "If I don't write music," he once said, "I get sick!" Altogether there are over a hundred *Portraits,* most of them for piano, a few for violin, and some for orchestra. These are done much as a painter would do a portrait, only notes are used instead of a brush. Among them are musical pictures of such notables as Picasso, Aaron Copland, Fiorello La Guardia, and Dorothy Thompson. *The Seine at Night, Wheatfield at Noon,* and *Sea Piece with Birds* were orchestral selections written between 1947 and 1952. A Cello Concerto was introduced by the Philadelphia Orchestra in 1950, while *Five Songs after William Blake* for baritone and orchestra were heard two years later. A concerto for flute, strings, and percussion premiered in Venice in 1954.

A second Thomson-Stein opera, *The Mother of Us All,* was produced at Columbia University in 1947. The drama deals with the suffragette leader Susan B. Anthony and proved Gertrude Stein's last completed work. *The Mother of Us All* is much less abstract that *Four Saints in Three Acts,* less extreme in its stylization, for the primary concern was communication. Much of the music sounds familiar because it evokes familiar things, yet there is only one quotation in the entire score—"London Bridge is Falling Down." "In *The Mother of Us All,*" John Cage maintains, "everything Americans feel about life and death, male and female, poverty and riches, war and peace, blacks and whites, activity and loitering, is shown to be real and true. It is everything an American remembers, if he remembers how it was at home on an evening when friends and relatives played and sang, how it was to hear a band playing in the park, a Salvation Army band on a corner, a soldiers' band going down Main Street, an organ when somebody was married or had died." The composer's music goes perfectly with the words, and often brings Charles Ives to mind, although Thomson did not know Ives' work then. But whereas Ives was dissonant and polytonal, Thomson writes mainly in consonances and is far more polished. Disregarding time and fact, the essentially plotless libretto includes such diverse characters as John Adams, Daniel Webster, Ulysses S. Grant, Lillian Russell, and even a "Gertrude S." and a "Virgil T." *The Mother of Us All* has been staged frequently by colleges, although the music is difficult for young voices, and was revived in 1967 by the Tyrone Guthrie Theatre in Minneapolis.

Thomson composed the score for Robert Flaherty's film *Louisiana Story* in 1948, a work of particular eloquence, from which he later fashioned an orchestral suite. *Louisiana Story* utilizes Acadian songs and dances from the bayou country, much as *The River* had drawn on white spirituals. The composer liked writing for the documentary film, Peggy Glanville-Hicks said, because its form "is epic, its themes deal with the general, the common ground of experience rather than the particular or the personal, and it is above all a poetic form whose poetry must work hand in hand with functionalism in the highest sense." The death of Gertrude Stein in 1949 prompted Thomson to write *A Solemn Music*, a piece of unexpected emotional depth—an elegy, Mellers says, "on her and Thomson's vision of a world new-made." He wrote incidental music for Truman Capote's play *The Grass Harp* in 1952 and produced his biggest work, *Missa Pro Defunctis* for chorus and orchestra, in 1960. *The Feast of Love* for baritone and orchestra was heard first at the Coolidge Festival in Washington, D.C. on November 1, 1964, while the composer broke new ground with a third opera, *Lord Byron*, set to a libretto by Jack Larson.

Virgil Thomson stands as one of the most original and controversial figures in American music. He himself is something of a paradox. His forebears were primarily farm people, and he grew up in a Baptist background. Yet there was an irreligious streak from an early age. Sunday school, the composer once confided, was bearable as a boy largely because his teacher was a grand niece of Jesse James, and he was charmed by the glamor of her ancestry. His long career as a church organist and choirmaster, however, impressed him deeply, for much of his music contains a religious atmosphere, and he has frequently used a revival meeting style. His work, nevertheless, possesses a fundamental elegance and an exquisite craftsmanship undoubtedly stemming from his years in France. "Thomson moves, unexpectedly but decorously, across the musical skyline like a baroque covered wagon," Samuel Barlow insisted. "More unexpectedly, there's a pioneer inside." France liberated the composer, gave him the perspective to formulate an international musical expression from regional and vernacular material. His exposure to Dada fired him with the courage to debunk old forms, pomposity, stuffiness, and the sham. What emerged was an idiom unique and personal, completely Thomson's own, for to him the eclectic approach is both profuse and real.

Unlike modernists all about him, Thomson's music—like his reviews— is simple and direct. His is the gift to be clear, and his works are marked by tremendous economy. His style is informal, unmannered, free, unpredictable, and easy. He loves a musical joke and has achieved imaginative writing through understatement. He objects to the neatly tied package and prefers music that is less relentless in its logic. While he has a definite technique, it is difficult to categorize or single out any detail of melodic, harmonic, or rhythmic procedure that is endemic. According to John Cage, Thomson "expresses only those feelings he really has; at the same time his attention does incline to move by means of joy and energy away from an inner emphasis to the outer world of nature, events, and people."

Thomson is looked upon as one of the more intellectual heads in the musical fraternity. Discussing what it felt like to be a musician, the composer wrote in his book *The State of Music*, "Mostly it is a feeling of being different from everybody." Of all the professional preparations, he argued, serious musical training is the most demanding. "Even medicine, law, and scholarship, though they often delay a man's entry into married life, do not interfere with his childhood and adolescence. Music does. No musician ever passes an average or normal infancy. . . . He must work hard indeed to learn musical matters and to train his hand, all in addition to his school work and his play-life."

During the Depression the composer not only worked on motion pictures, plays, and ballets, he even did some music for the WPA's Living Newspapers. Several of the projects he was associated with during those years might be considered propagandistic, but while Thomson's music for these is effective, it is in no way startling. Unlike those who depreciate the artistic climate of the 1930s, Thomson considers the period the definitive decade in American music. "After 1910," he claims, "everything led up to it, and after 1940 everything was different." The composer is not happy about the turn music has taken and feels that modern music is much too involved and pretentious. "The twelve-tone power group is so entrenched that it is an Establishment in itself," he complained. Many contemporary musicians, on the other hand, have dismissed Thomson as a dilettante. "I have always found it difficult to convince my fellow musicians that Thomson is a man to be taken seriously as a composer," Copland confesses. "They usually adopt the attitude that what he writes may be amusing, but essentially that is all it is."

Thomson depicts the American scene against a Continental fabric he has made intimately his own. In Meller's view, he "does not (like Ives) grow up from childhood, nor (like Barber) look back to it; he rather preserves the inconsequential spontaneity of a child into adult life." When he draws upon his midwestern musical legacy, he elevates it beyond the sentimental. Yet his American images are sketched without affectation and with no grandiose symphonic or operatic gestures, for his concern is with a less self-conscious America.

By the mid-1930s an expression had grown up in musical circles: "Every town in America has two things—a five-and-dime and a Boulanger pupil." Roy Harris, another of the American scene composers, arrived in Paris to study with Boulanger about five years later than Copland and Thomson. Like Thomson, Harris was interested in America's musical past; unlike Thomson, he did not absorb the Parisian sophistication and remained more aggressively American. His music is distinguished by a prairie spaciousness, it even has something of the rugged Whitmanesque quality of Ives.

Harris was born in a log cabin in Lincoln County, Oklahoma, on Abraham Lincoln's birthday, February 12, 1898. "The shadow of Abe Lincoln has hovered over my life from childhood," the composer wrote. He was christened LeRoy Ellsworth Harris by an itinerant preacher. His ancestry was part Scotch, part Irish, mostly Welsh. Grandfather Harris had been a Union officer and later became a Protestant circuit rider. His maternal grandfather was an enterprising hay-and-grain man in the Chicago suburbs and ran a small scale pony express line out West. The boy's parents had moved to Oklahoma by ox-cart during the Cimarron land rush. They staked out a claim near Chandler, felled the trees, built a cabin, and tilled the soil. Roy's father, Elmer Harris, was a powerful, big-boned man, who was a hard worker and found pleasure in almost everything. He had little education, but read much, could quote the Bible and Virgil in Latin, and knew quite a lot of history. He loved music, especially guitar playing and his wife's folk singing. But at heart Elmer Harris was a frontier pragmatist, believing in what could be measured. Later he would insist that Roy be an "honest-to-God farmer" instead of "chasing the rainbow and piddling around with music." Laura Harris, Roy's mother, painted a little, but was a hard-bitten fundamentalist, dedicated to doing the right thing at the right time. She rarely seemed to have a good time, the composer remembered, and could be "tougher than a boiled owl!" She once told her son, "Well, any woman who'll smoke will drink; and any woman who'll drink will do anything." Yet after she was eighty she practically lived on port.

Two of Roy's brothers died in Oklahoma of malaria. When his mother showed signs of failing, too, the family moved by wagon to Southern California. Roy was five at the time. Elmer Harris bought a piece of grazing land in the San Gabriel Valley and started farming again. Here Roy spent his boyhood. He showed an unusual fondness for books, reading everything from mail order catalogs to Shakespeare. As the boy grew older, he helped his father with the ploughing and the chores. Roy recalled how Elmer Harris would sing and whistle as he worked; one of his favorite tunes was the Civil War ballad "When Johnny Comes Marching Home." "He used to whistle it with jaunty bravado when he went to work on the farm in the morning," the composer said, "and with sad pensiveness as we returned at dusk behind the slow, weary plodding of the horses." One day when Roy was still a child, his dad brought home an Edison phonograph and a set of wax cylinders. After that the family spent evenings listening to the sounds that blared from the machine's gaudy horn. A little later the Harrises acquired a piano, the only one for miles around. Mrs. Harris could play by ear, and Roy soon followed suit. Eventually an itinerant teacher was found.

The youth attended the Covina Public Schools, was smart, tended to be introspective, and got into more than his share of playground fights. Roy was undersized for his age, and his father alternated between teasing and quiet sympathy. "My God!" Elmer Harris would exclaim. "It looks like the breed is running out." But when his son came home battered and bruised by a bully, he challenged him to a game of checkers, knowing that Roy would probably win. Determined to lose no more fights, young Harris took up sports and in high school distinguished himself in football, baseball, tennis, and track. He won the respect of classmates by breaking his nose and arm and badly injuring one of his fingers in a football game. He also learned to play the clarinet and to dance well. He played in the school band, discussed philosophy and world problems with friends, was taught to play chess, and went to Los Angeles to hear symphonies and operas that were there on tour.

At eighteen Roy started a farm of his own, growing berries and potatoes. But he had an inquiring mind, and while he worked his land, he also read Greek philosophy and continued playing the clarinet. During World War I he joined the army as a private. When he returned home, he had decided to quit farming and enter the University of California at Los Angeles. His father gave him ten dollars, and over his mother's tears, warned, "Don't come sucking around here for a square meal." Harris supported himself by driving a truck, delivering butter and eggs. He enrolled in evening classes at what was then the Los Angeles Normal School, studying harmony and reading Hindu theology. Meanwhile the San Gabriel Valley was changing. The grain fields gradually gave way to orange groves and irrigated farms. Soon even these disappeared, as speculators bought up the land and subdivided it into a network of country estates and small towns. The composer later claimed he had witnessed "the end of the pioneer days and the beginning of commercial, standardized America."

Disappointed with his course of study at college, Harris proceeded to tell the department chairman, Frances Wright, what he thought of her curriculum. "Well, what in the hell are you doing here then?" she asked. The young man explained that he wanted to be a composer. Looking back he remembered these years as "an extremely intense period in my life." On his own he read Ibsen, Shaw, Dostoyevsky, and Tolstoy and grew interested in sociology and history. Philosophy, he decided, was an "endless web of words modified by more words." He became convinced that "mankind is essentially an emotional organism, not a rational one; and that all progress is achieved out of the distress of necessity, not out of the obvious logic of reason." This belief led him ever more deeply into music. Since he could not afford to buy tickets for concerts, he ushered and for a brief while was music critic for the Los Angeles *Illustrated Daily News*. "Each new harmony, each new melody, each composer discovered," he said, "were a milestone for me."

Encouraged by Alfred Hertz, conductor of the San Francisco Symphony, Harris at twenty-four began studying composition with Arthur Farwell, who accepted him despite his slim musical background. Farwell recognized in Harris a young man of deep musical instinct and later remarked, "I was convinced that he would one day challenge the world." Harris worked with Farwell in Los Angeles for two years and under his tutelage wrote an Andante for orchestra, introduced by the New York Philharmonic at Lewisohn Stadium during the summer of 1926. The composer quit driving a truck, borrowed a hundred dollars, and hitchhiked to New York to hear the piece performed. Howard Hanson conducted a second performance of the Andante in Rochester.

Harris was given the opportunity to work at the MacDowell colony that summer and on the advice of Aaron Copland left for Paris in the fall to study with Boulanger. He remained in France for three years, holding a Guggenheim fellowship twice. At first he felt very much like an alien and feared being submerged by the European cultural tradition. Harris already had fixed ideas about music and considered it important for a composer to develop a technique through experience. Nadia Boulanger called him her "auto-didact" and largely let him go his own way. "She had the patience of an angel," Harris said. Through Beethoven's String Quartets he became "a profound believer in discipline and form." His concerto for string quartet, piano, and clarinet was played in Paris in 1927 and his Piano Sonata (with a scherzo reminiscent of "Turkey in the Straw") followed the next year. Then in 1929 Harris fell down the stone steps of his cottage outside Paris and fractured his spine. He partially recuperated in a French hospital, but soon returned to New York for surgery and then to California for recovery.

The composer wrote his First String Quartet flat on his back in a New York clinic. "In one short, concentrated period," he claimed, "I gained freedom from the room-with-a-piano-in-it which might have cramped my whole life." When he joined his family in California, he was asked time and again, "Well what are you going to do now?" It was expected that he would teach or maybe get a job as a piano salesman. A grant from some wealthy citizens of Pasadena, however, enabled him to continue his writing. By the early 1930s Harris had become an established figure among the young American school of composers. Arthur Farwell, paraphrasing Schumann's hailing of Chopin, announced his former pupil in *The Musical Quarterly*, January, 1932: "Gentlemen, a genius—but keep your hats on!"

Harris took the lead in the field of symphonic writing, and his compositions were performed in the concert hall, over radio, and recorded. His First Symphony was initially played by Koussevitzky and the Boston Symphony Orchestra on January 26, 1934, and repeated in New York. In the first movement Harris tried to achieve a mood of adventure and physical exuberance; in the second the pathos that seems to underlie human existence; and in the third the "positive will to action" that the composer deems a fundamental American characteristic. Koussevitzky found the work "unmistakably American," while Harris said it sounded even better than he had expected. "I mean to become a really great composer," he wrote a friend. The score of the symphony had nearly been lost, when a suitcase containing all the orchestral parts was stolen from a parked car while the composer was in New York. Eventually the discarded case with the music was found by police in a subway entrance and returned.

A Second Symphony appeared in 1936, but it was the Third which brought Harris wide and enduring fame. A relatively short work, in one continuous movement, the Third Symphony is powerful, well-integrated, compelling. First performed by the Boston Symphony Orchestra in February, 1939, the piece was a resounding success. Koussevitzky called it "the first truly great orchestral work produced in America." More than one critic said that "something of the crudeness and strength of pioneer America" had crept into the symphony. The manager of a baseball team supposedly wrote Harris after hearing the piece: "If I had pitchers who could pitch as strongly as you do in the symphony, my worries would be over." Not all listeners were so enthusiastic; pianist Alex Templeton, for instance, claimed the work sounded to him "like a lot of people moving furniture around." But the Third Symphony remains Harris' most popular, and perhaps best, selection and has been played repeatedly across the United States, as well as in Europe and Latin America.

The concert overture *When Johnny Comes Marching Home* is another of Harris' more frequently performed compositions, obviously built around the tune that was his father's favorite. Commissioned by the RCA Victor Company in 1933, the composer attempted to express in the selection "a gamut of emotions particularly American and in an American manner." The Piano Trio of 1934 was followed by a Prelude and Fugue for String Orchestra and the symphonic elegy *Farewell to Pioneers* (both 1936). The Symphony for Voices was written that same year for the Westminster Choir, is set to a text by Walt Whitman, and uses a three-movement pattern to be sung a cappella. The demands Harris makes on the singers in his Symphony for Voices are cruel, often are almost as difficult for the listener, and gives the work a somewhat stilted impression. A Piano Quintet appeared in 1936, while the Soliloquy and Dance for viola and piano and the Third String Quartet came along three years later.

Harris has been called "the most American of all our composers," and certainly his creative expression springs from his personal experience and background. He insists that music should be emotional rather than intellectual. To get the "feel" of America he once made a trip across the country sleeping in haystacks and on park benches; he paid his way doing odd jobs—once acting as gate-keeper for a rodeo. "It is natural for me to write music, and lots of it, and quickly," the composer wrote in 1946. "In other words, I am not a phony who has to go through strange experiences in his living, and tortuous effort in his writing, to produce music." He came to modernism as something of an American primitive. Copland claims Harris was born with a full-fledged style of his own. Melody comes to him easily, and he is known for long melodic lines. He contends that the rhythmic impulses of Americans are fundamentally different—less symmetrical—from those of Europeans, while his harmonic sense is thoroughly personal. Ornamentation as such seems not to occur to him. There is a slightly uncouth awkwardness in the composer's early pieces and a nervous restlessness, but these are part of the pioneer spirit. "Harris breathes his own musical air naturally," Arthur Farwell concluded, and in his best works the composer demonstrates both stamina and vision.

"America is desperately struggling to wrest social balance from her omnivorous industrialism," Harris wrote in the 1930s. "America is a nightmare of feverish struggling, a graveyard of suppressed human impulses." He was confident that the time was ripe for the development of serious music. Having much to share with the "common man," the composer illustrates the creative energy of the Depression era, at the peak of the nationalistic resurgence in the arts, when much of the country's aesthetic urge was consciously involved with its folk heritage. "How to serve society as a composer, how to become economically and socially recognized as a worth-contributing citizen, how to establish durable human contacts with individuals or groups is a harassing problem," Harris said. Yet his work is not diluted for the multitude, and the bulk of it stands on its intrinsic merits. "His music is of long days and short years," Patricia Ashley suggests, "and it starts when it starts and stops when it stops."

From 1934 to 1938 Harris headed the composition department of the Westminster Choir School in Princeton, New Jersey. The musician had met his first wife, a niece of George Bernard Shaw, in France and married her in Pasadena. She disliked the United States, however, could not see herself as an American housewife, and returned to England. In 1936 the composer married Beula Duffey, who changed her name to Johana. Johana Harris was a young concert pianist, who played the piano parts in a number of her husband's works. Although she continued an active professional life, the couple eventually had five children. Harris taught at Juilliard for a while, was composer-in-residence at Cornell University, and later was head of the music department at Colorado College. He organized broadcasts and festivals and was extremely active in music education.

The composer in middle age was tall, raw-boned, slightly slouched, and had never lost his drawling southwestern speech. He retained the habit of getting up early and maintained he did his best work before nine in the morning. He was a fount of physical vitality, liked to walk in the woods, play tennis and chess, and loved to speed on the highway. He had a sense of humor and enjoyed the artistic comradeship of fellow composers. He could be absent-minded, preferred simple dress, and favored steak and potatoes over fancier food. "Most people think of my husband as a good-natured easy-going Westerner," Johana Harris wrote. "And so he is. But he is many other people as well. To me he is a child—always eager, always ready to believe in everyone, always expecting miracles to happen, always being hurt and enraged by the social and economic injustices. And yet, he is an unquenchable optimist who loves beauty in every phase of living."

Harris continued his use of native material in his fourth symphony, the *Folk Song* Symphony, for chorus and orchestra. When the completed work was introduced by Artur Rodzinski and the Cleveland Orchestra in January, 1941, one critic said it was "like the American continent rising up and saying hello." The Fifth Symphony, which some consider Harris' finest, was composed in 1942 and dedicated "to the heroic and freedom-loving people of our great Ally, the Union of Soviet Socialist Republics, as a tribute to their strength in war." During his college years the composer had become deeply infatuated with Marxist theories, a trend that was fashionable in intellectual circles after the Russian Revolution. This early interest in Russian socialism surged again during the seige of Stalingrad toward the end of 1942. The Fifth Symphony, played by the Boston Symphony Orchestra under Koussevitzky, was radioed to troops at home and overseas and broadcast to the Soviet Union. Later Harris conducted the work in Tchaikovsky Hall in Moscow. The Sixth Symphony was also completed during World War II, first performed in Boston on April 14, 1944. The piece is another essay in musical Americana, based on Lincoln's Gettysburg Address, and dedicated to the United States Armed Forces.

During the war the composer engaged mostly in radio work as director of music for the Office of War Information. He wrote a number of pieces inspired by the armed conflict—notably *Ode to Friendship* (1941) and *March in Time of War* (1943). He composed *American Creed* for the Chicago Orchestra in 1940 and the next year *Cimmarron*, a symphonic overture for band. He also supplied the score for the documentary film *One Tenth of a Nation*, a study of black life in the rural South. *From This Earth*, a ballet for Hanya Holm, appeared in 1941, followed by *American Ballads* for piano in 1942 and the *Walt Whitman Suite* in 1944.

After World War II, Harris held another series of academic posts "with varying degrees of pleasure and success." He was composer-in-residence at Utah State College and Peabody College in Nashville, Tennessee, and taught at the Pennsylvania College for Women and Indiana University. His compositions during these years include a Concerto for Accordion and Orchestra (1946), a Concerto for Two Pianos and Orchestra (1947), a Mass for men's voices and organ (1948), a Concerto for Violin and Orchestra (1949), the *Kentucky* Overture (introduced in Louisville in 1949), and the *Cumberland* Concerto for orchestra (1951).

In 1952 the composer was executive director of the Pittsburgh International Contemporary Music Festival. During that time he became the brunt of an unfortunate witch hunt, incited by Senator Joseph McCarthy's current Red-baiting campaign. On August 7, 1952, a former FBI informer made allegations before a state convention of the American Legion against Harris' loyalty. In part this stemmed from the composer's interest in the plight of the common man, but more from his friendly attitude toward the USSR during World War II. In a speech before the Pittsburgh Optimist Club, Harris' accuser charged, "The infected tree of Communism has been cut down in Western Pennsylvania but some of the roots remain. There is more to be done." Before long it was being said that the composer's Fifth Symphony, slated to be performed at the Pittsburgh festival, had been dedicated to the Red Army. A justice of the Pennsylvania supreme court demanded the dedication be revoked before the November 26 performance by the Pittsburgh Symphony. When Harris refused, the judge asked that the audience refrain from applauding. The public, however, supported the composer by applauding long and loud. Yet from the radical right came cries that Harris be fired from the Pennsylvania College for Women, and eventually even Aaron Copland's name was brought into the fracas. The press exploited the affair, and there was irresponsibility from many quarters. Harris' case was examined by the American Legion, which ultimately acquitted him. Ironically the composer was putting the finishing touches on his *West Point Symphony* for band at the time.

Harris' Seventh Symphony (1953), commissioned by the Koussevitzky Foundation, was intended "as a declaration of faith in mankind." The work is impressive, although Mellers finds that the composer's rural music has acquired "an undercurrent of neurotic fury, incarnated not so much in harmonic tensions as in the piercing and most original orchestration." The Eighth Symphony (1962) was written to commemorate the fiftieth anniversary of the San Francisco Symphony, while the Ninth, subtitled *1963*, was commissioned by Eugene Ormandy for the Philadelphia Orchestra and inspired by the United States Constitution. Three more symphonies were yet to come.

Since 1961 Roy Harris had been composer-in-residence at the University of California at Los Angeles. He and his wife bought a house and garden outside the city, and in a way it was like coming home for him. He continued to compose a great deal and conducted many of his own works. A cantata for baritone and orchestra, *Give Me the Silent Sun*, was written in 1959, while *Epilogue to Profiles in Courage: J.F.K.* appeared five years later. A Concerto for Amplified Piano, Brasses, Percussion, and String Basses was first heard in December, 1968, with the composer's wife as soloist.

Harris' greatest popularity was in the middle 1930s, when he was looked upon by the intelligentsia as the best hope for epic American symphonism. Although his reputation has cooled since then, he remains among the more pronounced figures in American serious composition. At seventy Harris was still a man of great mental vitality, preferred driving a Toronado, and confessed that he "hates to be passed!" He had been elected to the Oklahoma Hall of Fame and initiated into the Ponca Indian tribe as Big Chief Music Maker. His personality continued to be contagiously enthusiastic, while he maintained an honest appreciation of his own work. "I have finished two movements of my Fifth Symphony," he wrote Nicolas Slonimsky in 1942, "and it is wonderful beyond my wildest hopes. I am sure that you will be happy about it." As a composer the septuagenarian was much what he had always been. He claimed he invariably heard music during his quiet hours, yet it was often music of an earlier time. His compositions tend to evoke a feeling of leisurely motion and rarely seem to hurry. He adheres to concrete forms, but approaches the problems of composition in a distinctly individual manner that results in music that is intensely American.

The composer has used themes from pioneer hymn tunes, considering them to possess "a simple direct beauty which is near to the spirit of

America," and there is frequently a primitive religious air about his work. Yet his music contains a more organic expression of the native character. His broad melodic lines give his compositions a spaciousness that is comfortably American, as are the angularity and very awkwardness of his style. His rhythm, particularly in fast sections, sometimes indicates a jerky, nervous disposition. There are crude passages with occasional yawps of sound suggestive of Whitman. The composer disliked coloration for its own sake and was little inclined toward impressionism. Form, he felt, should be determined by its content, growing along paths dictated by inner necessity. Harris has not always given the public music that is easily listenable, nor can his style be readily classified. He called himself a modern classicist. "Here is music of the bleak and barren expanses of western Kansas," *Modern Music* once concluded, "of the brooding prairie night, of the fast darkness of the American soul, of its despair and its courage, its defeat and its triumph, its struggling aspirations."

Harris was prolific and quite articulate about his aims as a composer: "History reveals that the great music has been produced only by staunch individuals who sank their roots deeply into the social soil which they accepted as their own." When writing programmatic music, he liked to do intensive collateral reading. "We are born into and surrounded by an age which thrives through deceit," he said. "Music can never be the mistress of duplicity." Although he developed a strikingly personal technique, he remained fundamentally a primitive. "Harris starts from the primitive identity between man and nature," Mellers observes, "and imaginatively re-enacts man's apparent conquest of nature and his achievement of civilization." The composer rejected the jazz idiom as an expression of the American spirit, considering it too frivolous and restricted in emotional range. "Our people are more than pleasure-loving," he insisted. "We also have qualities of heroic strength—determination—will to struggle—faith in our destiny. We are possessed of a fierce driving power—optimistic, young, rough and ready." And these are the traits Roy Harris tried to project in his music.

Whereas Harris emerged as a curiosity from the agricultural Southwest, William Grant Still came from the deep South, developing into the major spokesman of the American black in serious music. Born on a plantation near Woodville, Mississippi, on May 11, 1895, Still was the son of black school-teachers, both of whom were musicians. When his father died three months after the child's birth, his mother took the boy to Little Rock, where they had relatives. There William received his public education and began taking violin lessons. The lad listened while his maternal grandmother sang hymns and spirituals like "Little David, Play on Yo' Harp" as she worked about the house, and later his stepfather, a postal clerk with a fondness for opera, bought phonograph records of the standard masterpieces. William played these records over and over and enjoyed singing duets at home and occasionally in public. When he grew older, his family took him to musical programs and stage shows and frequently discussed music, plays, and books with him. As a youth he was torn between wanting to be a streetcar conductor, raising chickens, and being a composer.

Still grew up neither in wealth nor poverty, was aware he was a black and generally felt a feeling of pride. "[M]y association with people of both racial groups," he later said, "gave me the ability to conduct myself as a person among people instead of as an inferior among superiors." Eventually music became his first love, although he graduated from high school at sixteen as class valedictorian. He wanted to go to Oberlin Conservatory, but his mother was against a musical career for him. To please her he went to Wilberforce University, where he played the oboe and clarinet and joined the college band. Soon he became the leader and made arrangements for the group. He went into nearby Dayton for concerts and opera and bought music books and scores. He played with a college string quartet and even composed a few pieces that they performed.

William's mother wanted him to study medicine after college, a point over which they sharply disagreed. Four months before graduation he left Wilberforce, began earning his own living as a commercial musician around Columbus, Ohio, and was briefly married. For a time he worked with W. C. Handy in Memphis and discovered in the blues "an undeniable color and a musical atmosphere that stemmed directly from the folk." When he became twenty-one he inherited a small legacy from his father's estate and decided to enter Oberlin Conservatory. To supplement his funds he played in theaters, waited on tables, and worked as a janitor. After one semester he received a special scholarship. Meanwhile he studied violin, theory, and composition and came under the spell of Wagner.

In 1918 Still enlisted in the United States Navy and made his first visit to New York. He walked the streets until he was ready to drop, then boarded a streetcar. "Suddenly there in front of me was the Metropolitan Opera House!" A performance of *Rigoletto* was about to start. He bought a ticket up in the family circle and experienced the joy of a lifetime. Later he was assigned to a transport going overseas. Although he was supposed to wait tables during the crossing, he was invited to entertain officers at mealtime by playing the violin.

After the war he came back to New York, where he accepted a job from W. C. Handy as an arranger and member of Handy's traveling band. The group played the length and breadth of the South, and it was on this trip that Still first experienced real racial discrimination. "At home," he wrote, "I had been sheltered, and had moved in what I would consider enlightened social circles, but on the road with Handy and his orchestra, I found that the indulgence many people felt for Negro musicians did not extend to giving them much consideration for their ordinary needs." Later he played with Eubie Blake's orchestra for the popular black show *Shuffle Along*, which made an extended tour. While in Boston he filed an application at the New England Conservatory of Music and was accepted as a tuition-free student by George

W. Chadwick. After four months with Chadwick, Still returned to New York to take the position of recording manager of the Black Swan Phonograph Company.

He soon learned that Edgard Varese, the French modernist, was offering a scholarship in composition to a talented young black composer. Still applied for the scholarship and won it. He studied with Varese for two years, 1923-25. "He taught me to express myself," the black musician later said. "Before that I had just been groping." For a time Still wrote in a dissonant idiom patterned closely on Varese. "I was so intrigued by what I learned from Mr. Varese," he explained, "that I let it get the better of me. I became its servant, not its master." Gradually he developed an individual style that was neither ultramodern nor conventional.

At the same time he was studying with Varese, Still was receiving a different sort of education by playing in vaudeville, musical comedy, and night club orchestras, conducting for radio, and orchestrating for Broadway shows. He was essentially self-taught in the field of orchestration, and his experimentation with tone colors marked him as a pioneer. At various points in his career Still arranged for Earl Carroll, Sophie Tucker, Donald Vorhees, and Paul Whiteman, and he worked for both CBS and NBC radio networks. Artie Shaw's highly successful recording of "Frenesi" was arranged by Still. Later he went to the West Coast to work for the motion picture industry. He wrote several popular songs, two of which were published by Edward B. Marks under the pseudonym of Willy M. Grant. Still became convinced that from the rhythm, color, and fluency of jazz a great musical form could be built. "Real Jazz isn't cheap," he argued, "and it isn't haphazard. Most important of all is the fact that Jazz and its exponents have made friends for the Negro."

But he never considered commercial music an end in itself. There was much to be learned from it, he felt, but ultimately these lessons should serve a larger purpose. By the middle 1920s Still was ready to devote part of his talent to a treatment of black subjects in major compositions. *Darker America*, his first orchestral work, appeared in 1924 and was enthusiastically received after its premiere in Aeolian Hall two years later. The piece was intended to suggest the triumph of the American blacks over their sorrows through fervent prayer. It contained too much material, largely unrelated. The composer was clearly struggling with musical form, while the shadow of Varese looms large. *From the Land of Dreams* (1925) sounds even more under the influence of the Frenchman, and Still later called it a "lesson in what not to do!" He once described the piece as a "musical picture of an owl with a headache." *From the Black Belt*, written for small orchestra in 1926, is in a lighter vein, full of vigorous humor. The ballet *La Guiablesse* (1927) was produced by the Chicago Grand Opera Company in 1934, and there were several art songs. *Africa* (1929), a symphonic suite in three movements— "Land of Peace," "Land of Romance," and "Land of Superstition"—was Still's first important orchestral work, introduced by the Barrere ensemble in New York in 1930.

Among the composer's best known selections is his *Afro-American* Symphony, written in 1930 and performed first by the Rochester Philharmonic Orchestra under Howard Hanson the next year. Its four movements are subtitled "Longing," "Sorrow," "Humor," and "Sincerity," although the program was added after the piece was finished. The symphony was shortly played by the New York Philharmonic and the Philadelphia Orchestra under Leopold Stokowski. "There is not a cheap or banal passage in the entire composition," one critic said. It is full of melody, remarkably scored, and throbs with emotion. Still's high regard for the blues is demonstrated by the fact that the symphony is based on an original blues theme, one of haunting beauty. He later stated that he wanted to show how the blues, "so often considered a lowly expression, could be elevated to the highest musical level." The work is tonal with emphasis placed on a free flowing melodic line. The harmonies are basically simple, while rhythmic alterations play a significant role in the composer's thematic transformation. The overall style is fundamentally neoromantic, and the piece represents the first use of the banjo in a large symphonic work.

Still completed Symphony in G minor, subtitled *Song of a New Race*, in 1937. It is related to his *Afro-American* Symphony, a sort of extension of the latter with kindred themes. The composer states that "the purpose of the Symphony in G minor is to point musically to changes wrought in a people through the progressive and transmuting spirit of America." Whereas the *Afro-American* Symphony represents the blacks in the period after the Civil War, its successor represents American blacks during contemporary times. The work was introduced by the Philadelphia Orchestra under Stokowski and repeated in New York City a few days later.

Sahdji, a ballet laid in Africa, was presented in 1931, while *Kaintuck* for piano and orchestra was written in 1935 to express the composer's reaction to the shimmering sunlight on the bluegrass of Kentucky. He wrote *A Deserted Plantation* (1933) and *Three Visions* (1935) for piano and *Dismal Swamp* (1936) and *Lenox Avenue* (1937) for orchestra. *Blue Steel*, the composer's first opera, was finished in 1935. *Troubled Island*, based on a libretto by Langston Hughes, followed four years later, but was not produced until the New York City Opera Company staged it in April, 1949. This second opera deals with the struggle of the Haitian blacks to free themselves from the French and proved one of Still's most distinguished works. Although the musician is not a crusader, his cantata *And They Lynched Him to a Tree* (1940), for white and black choruses, is a strong plea for racial tolerance without bitterness. The next year he wrote the patriotic *Plain Chant for America*, a protest against Fascism, for baritone and orchestra.

In 1934 Still moved to Southern California, where he met and eventually married Verna Arvey, a concert pianist and writer. The late 1930s were unusually productive for him, and he twice received a Guggenheim fellowship. He spent from twelve to sixteen hours a day on his work, almost oblivious to time and the outer world. He composed slowly, constantly revising things he had written earlier. "[N]othing ever is," he contended, "it is always becoming." He preferred to live simply, enjoyed his family, and possessed a warm, well-rounded personality. He found relaxation in building furniture and toys for his children, but rarely allowed himself a vacation. Although he had grown into a dedicated artist, he refused to take himself too seriously and maintained a quick sense of humor and a deep humility. Above all he was a man of profound religious reverence, viewing God as the source of his inspiration.

He wrote the theme music for the New York World's Fair in 1939 and during World War II developed a strong social consciousness. From this came short compositions like *In Memoriam: The Colored Soldiers Who Died for Democracy* and *Fanfare for 99th Fighter Squadron*. In 1945 Still received a $1000 war bond for his *Festive* Overture, written for the fiftieth anniversary of the Cincinnati Orchestra. He also composed a *Poem for Orchestra* (1944), a Third Symphony (1945), *Archaic Ritual* (1946), and a Fourth Symphony (1947). The latter, called *Autochthonous*, was written in a combination of quasimodern, popular, and neoromantic styles, was intended to be descriptive of the American spirit, and speaks of the fusion of musical cultures in the United States. It was first performed by the Oklahoma Symphony Orchestra under Victor Alessandro in March, 1951.

Songs of Separation (1945) constitute a charming cycle of art songs set to poems by five black poets. *From a Lost Continent* (1949) is a suite for chorus, while the prize-winning *The Peaceful Land* (1961), also for chorus, is dedicated to the United Nations. Opera, however, remained the composer's great love. *A Bayou Legend* and *A Southern Interlude*, dating from the early 1940s, were followed by *Costaso* (set in Spanish colonial America), *Mota* (set in ancestral Africa), and *The Pillar* (centering around an American Indian theme). In 1958 Still completed another opera based on Minette Fontaine, a fictitious prima donna of the New Orleans opera company during the mid-nineteenth century. *Highway I, USA*, a one act opera dealing with contemporary America, was given its premiere at the University of Miami on May 13, 1963.

Much of Still's music has yet to be performed, although he is considered the "Dean of American Negro Composers." Certainly his musical path has achieved a breadth that exceeds any other black American's before him. Besides composing, Still was the first black to conduct a major symphony orchestra in the United States and the first black to conduct an all white orchestra in the deep South. Eventually the long hours of work took their toll on his eyes, and he was forced to accept a less demanding schedule. Nevertheless he was still writing in his seventies and continued to revise older compositions.

He discarded ultramodernism early in his career as a serious musician, preferring to elevate black idioms to a position of dignity in symphonic and operatic music. "This would have been extremely difficult," he said, "or even impossible, had I chosen the avant-garde idiom. Through experimentation, I discovered that Negro music tends to lose its identity when subjected to the avant-garde style of treatment." Later he leaned toward a more universal approach and evolved a more personal style reflecting a fusion of musical cultures. "Melody, in my opinion," he once wrote, "is the most important musical element." And he became strongly attracted to the exotic, causing him to spend many hours in research.

Concerned as he has been with propagating Afro-American traditions, Still professed impatience with the black militants of the late 1960s. "There is no substitute for keeping an open mind and for analyzing both sides of a question," he declared. For Still the American ties of his race are no less important than its African heritage. "For a long time," he said, "we Afro-Americans needed something like the fact that Black can be beautiful to give us identity and pride in our racial heritage. Now that has been accomplished. Most of us have come to realize that Black is indeed beautiful, but only as White, Brown, or Yellow are beautiful: when we make it so."

Unlike William Grant Still, who remained a calming voice in an age of campus and ethnic unrest, Marc Blitzstein emerged during the Depression Era as the angry young man, aggressive in his fight for social justice. Like the proletarian novels of the time, Blitzstein's theme was most often the class struggle. Music for him had a job to do—to energize propaganda, and he therefore wanted to be very clear in his message. Blitzstein began with a function, then discovered the appropriate language. To him the social questions of the 1930s were far more urgent than to Aaron Copland or any of the other major American scene composers, and he became considerably more left-wing in his enthusiasm. His concern was life in an industrial society, for in contrast to Thomson or Harris he was immersed in the present. Whereas Copland's work is latently involved with life in the city, Blitzstein's is vividly so.

Like Copland, Blitzstein was the child of the city, born in Philadelphia on March 2, 1905. He was also of Russian-Jewish parents and was raised amid affluent surroundings. Although no one in his family was particularly musical, Marc showed an interest in music early, began taking piano lessons at the age of three, gave his first concert at five, began composing at seven, and at fifteen was a soloist with the Philadelphia Orchestra. He attended the University of Pennsylvania and Curtis Institute, where he studied composition with Scalero. At the same time he commuted to New York to take piano lessons from Siloti. Meanwhile he had developed into a young man of great charm, with a wry sense of humor and a gallant manner. In 1926 he went to Europe, studying with Boulanger in Paris and Arnold Schoenberg in Berlin.

His first compositons were abstract and ultramodern—full of *"Donner und Blitzstein,"* one critic said. He returned to the United States and did some lecturing on music at Columbia University and the New School for Social Research. A Piano Sonata written in 1927 was played at a League of Composers' Concert and proved something of a scandal. The piece was written in sonata form, but "instead of being joined together," the composer said, "it was separated by pauses. There were in fact more pauses than notes; it was positively hysterical with them." Several of his songs were heard at the Copland-Sessions concerts, and his farce *Triple-Sec* was included in the *Garrick Gaieties* of 1928. Percussion Music for Piano (1929) was judged among his better modernistic pieces, although the composer later disowned all of his early efforts, calling them "wild, dissonant, percussive." Interestingly enough, a one act choral opera, *The Condemned*, was based on the lives of Sacco and Vanzetti, two men who repeatedly occupied Blitzstein's thoughts. Critics were hard on the work, however, and judged the central characters "remote and inhuman."

In 1930 the composer wrote a String Quartet and a ballet, *Cain*. A concerto for piano and orchestra followed the next year, along with an opera, *The Harpies*. Serenade for String Quartet appeared in 1932, and he wrote the music for several films. A set of Variations for orchestra was completed in 1934, while his *Children's Cantata* was produced a year later. Blitzstein grew increasingly interested in the stage and came to know a number of people connected with the theatrical world. In 1933 he married Eva Goldbeck, daughter of the light opera singer Lina Abarbanell and a writer of the radical left.

Soon after his marriage Blitzstein suddenly changed. The liberal political convictions he had held all his life now became evident both in his behavior and his work. He argued that "music must teach as well as entertain—must have a social as well as an artistic base; it should broaden its scope and reach not only the select few but the masses." When he ran into his friend and colleague Douglas Moore one afternoon in Times Square, he took in Moore's conservative dress and well-groomed appearance and observed critically, "You look like a banker." In 1934 Blitzstein wrote an article entitled "Coming, the Mass Audience!" and a piece for piano and speaker, *Send for the Militia*, composed shortly after the Spanish government had suppressed a revolt with bloody retribution.

At twenty-nine he put Schoenberg's modernism behind him and led by a burning social conscience turned largely to the theater. Tired of thrashing about in a void, he decided to hit out at things tangible through tangible means. The composer's parents had been staunch proponents of social democracy, and Blitzstein grew up with a strong personal integrity. As a young adult he had difficulty reconciling the sophisticated circle in which he found himself and his attraction for elegance with his concern for the oppressed. He resolved the conflict about the time the New Deal was enjoying its heyday by devoting his art to the plight of the working classes.

During the winter of 1935-36 the composer's wife became seriously ill. He remained with her constantly, permitting no one to relieve him. Upon her death he plunged into the writing of *The Cradle Will Rock*, finishing the work in six weeks. Blitzstein earlier had composed a song called "Nickel under the Foot," about a prostitute. When he showed the song to Bertolt Brecht, the latter suggested he write an entire opera centering around various kinds of social and economic prostitution. *The Cradle Will Rock* is a searing drama, composed at high intensity. Blitzstein wrote both the text and music. The story is set in Steeltown, USA, where Mr. Mister, the symbol of capitalism, and his Liberty Committee are attempting to prevent the steel workers from forming a union. The town's leading citizens—Dr. Specialist, Editor Daily, President Prexy, even Reverend Salvation—have all sold out to Mr. Mister. What opposition could not be bought has been crushed. Yet in the face of powerful and unscrupulous odds, Larry Foreman manages to organize the steel workers, promising that one day the bigoted forces "hiding up there in the cradle of the Liberty Committee" will rock. "When the storm breaks, the cradle will fall!"

Blitzstein's "play in music" appeared just as the big drive for industrial unionism was getting under way and captured much of that facet of the Depression-haunted 1930s. It was slated for production by the WPA Federal Theater Project, with its New York opening set for June 16, 1937, at the Maxine Elliot Theatre. John Houseman was the producer, Orson Welles the director, while Howard Da Silva was signed for the role of Larry Foreman. The Federal Theater had been under scrutiny since its creation in 1935, for there were many conservative congressmen who opposed the whole notion of government in the arts and were on the alert for signs of radicalism. While *The Cradle Will Rock* was in rehearsal, it became clear that some Washington officials considered the play dangerous. To make matters worse the opening coincided with a bitter clash between CIO organizers and "Little Steel." A WPA bigwig flew up to New York for a preview of the work and pronounced it "magnificent." But on June 13, Hallie Flanagan, the director of the Federal Theater Project, received a communication that effective immediately "no opening of new productions shall take place until after the beginning of the coming fiscal year, that is, July 1, 1937." The official explanation was that budget cuts and reorganization had become necessary.

Censorship in disguise was suspected immediately. Mrs. Flanagan, Archibald MacLeish, Virgil Thomson, and others interested in *The Cradle Will Rock* tried to get an exception to the ruling, but to no avail. Orson Welles flew to Washington, but the answer remained the same. Those associated with the play, however, were determined it should be heard. On the evening of June 16, the Maxine Elliot Theatre was sealed; neither the performers nor the audience gathered outside could enter. As Howard Da Silva and Will Geer, assigned to play Mr. Mister, entertained the audience in front of the theater, Houseman, Welles, and lighting expert Jean Rosenthal located a pick-up truck, a piano, and an available theater—the old Venice, twenty blocks uptown. Da Silva and Geer then led the audience and cast, augmented by some six hundred curiosity seekers, up Sixth Avenue and into the newly rented quarters.

Blitzstein sat in shirtsleeves at the upright piano. Since union regulations prevented the performers from appearing on stage, they sat scattered through the house. The composer began playing the opening music. Suddenly a woman's voice was heard from the lower left box singing the part of the Moll. A spotlight finally found her. Some minutes later Hiram Sherman as Reverend Salvation rose, nervously grasping pieces of paper folded to look like a Bible. Gradually as their cues came, most of the singers walked up to the edge of the stage to play their scenes, although Blitzstein had to fill in a few of the parts and occasionally made informal comments about the action taking place. It was a night that made theatrical history, the most spectacular moment in Marc Blitzstein's career. "[N]one of us who were there will ever forget it," Aaron Copland recalled.

Orson Welles had planned a rather elaborate production of the opera, with glass wagons illuminated from underneath and a finale in which the whole stage rocked, blinding lights shot up from below, and the steel workers' trumpets, fifes, and drums blared unexpectedly from loudspeakers located all through the theater. Since the sets and costumes belonged to the Federal Theater, in the initial presentation there was no scenery at all and singers appeared in regular street clothes. The simplicity of the performance seemed to add to the work's dramatic force and emotional impact. When it began a regular Broadway run on January 3, 1938, produced by Houseman and Welles' newly formed Mercury Theatre, *The Cradle Will Rock* was again given without scenery, costumes, or orchestra. It played about four months. Virgil Thomson called it "the most appealing operatic socialism since *Louise*." John Mason Brown considered it, "the most exciting propaganda *tour de force* our stage has seen since Clifford Odets' *Waiting for Lefty*." Others predicted Blitzstein's opera would become for America what Kurt Weill's *The Threepenny Opera* was to Germany. The composer himself judged the work a "mixed-up kind of musical theater—my kind!"

The Cradle Will Rock is a combination of wit, audacity, and sarcasm, as artistically brilliant as it was politically explosive. Blitzstein succeeded in creating an operatic idiom that sounds convincing when heard from the lips of the common man. The music is simple, yet in its own right is music of considerable subtlety and beauty. The structure is remarkably controlled, with every word of the sparse text seemingly set in place to enhance the theme. The composer specifically states his scorn of art devoid of moral persuasion:

> *Art for Art's sake,*
> *It's smart, for Art's sake,*
> *To part, for Art's sake,*
> *With your heart, for Art's sake,*
> *Be blind, for Art's sake,*
> *And deaf, for Art's sake,*
> *And dumb, for Art's sake,*
> *Until, for Art's sake,*
> *They kill, for Art's sake,*
> *All the art, for art's sake.*

Within the context of a serious musical drama, popular songs with catchy lyrics and ordinary speech are used to lighten the atmosphere. Speech passes easily into song. The result is not only an opera that is American in tone, but one that is superb theater.

The work is unmistakably tied to the Great Depression, however, while Blitzstein's belligerence and unswerving insistence on the greed and cruelty of the rich later seemed overdrawn. The opera was revived at the New York City Center in 1947 with Leonard Bernstein conducting a full orchestra on stage. It was performed again with orchestra in 1960 and given in Philharmonic Hall in April, 1964, much as it had been done originally, with Bernstein at the piano. Later that year Howard Da Silva directed a production for Theatre Four in New York, which was commercially recorded.

At the height of the furor over *The Cradle Will Rock*, Blitzstein was commissioned by the Columbia Broadcasting System to write a half hour radio opera, which he entitled *I've Got the Tune*. Almost an allegory on his own career, the message was that the modern composer has the obligation of writing music for the masses. The musician's second major work for the stage was *No for an Answer* (1937), an advance over *The Cradle Will Rock* in practically every way. There is more music, less spoken dialogue, yet fewer set numbers. The melodic line is generally straightforward, although the accompaniments may be fairly complex. The score is deceptively easy, while the choral sections are particularly exciting. The composer again showed an unusual gift for making words and music fit together, and he has panhandlers and taxi drivers singing songs that sound natural. *No for an Answer*, like *The Cradle Will Rock*, is almost a contemporary ballad opera based on the style of American popular song and the speech of the streets. The work is full of nervous energy, for Blitzstein often set his talky prose to short, clipped musical phrases. This time he expressly intended that the opera be staged without orchestra, scenery, or costumes.

No for an Answer tells the grim story of a group of Greek waiters victimized by big business. The work was introduced at Mecca Temple in New York on January 5, 1941. Shortly after the premiere city authorities prohibited further presentations of the production on the grounds that building violations made Mecca Temple unsuitable for operatic performances. Since the auditorium had been used many times before for this purpose, there were once again complaints of censorship. Blitzstein began thinking of himself as the most banned composer in the country. "The trouble is," he said, "I'm a great labor boy, and I put down everything I feel."

The composer joined the Communist Party in 1938. After Pearl Harbor he enlisted in the army and was eventually assigned to the Eighth Air Force. He was given various musician assignments during the war, among them the writing of the score for the documentary film *The True Glory*. In 1943, while musical director of the American broadcasting station in London, Blitzstein composed *Freedom Morning*, a symphonic poem dedicated to the black troops abroad. The piece was first heard at Albert Hall with 200 blacks in the chorus. The *Airborne* Symphony for speaker, soloists, men's chorus, and full orchestra was begun in England and dealt with the history of human flight from Icarus through World War II. Flight was viewed, in the composer's words, "as an agent of man's destruction of tyranny, as a device for building the better world." An especially moving section described the Allied cities laid low by Fascist bombs. The symphony was initially performed in April, 1946, by the New York City Symphony under the direction of Leonard Bernstein, with Orson Welles as narrator. Blitzstein was with the first contingent of the liberating forces that marched into Paris in 1944, a city he had not seen in eighteen years. On impulse he decided to visit the Rue Ballu to see if Mlle. Boulanger's apartment was still there. The Nazis had taken it over during the occupation, and she herself had gone to the United States. Boulanger's secretary opened the door; "*Monsieur Blitzstein!*" she cried, recognizing him despite the uniform.

The composer left the Communist Party in 1949. He wrote incidental music for an American Repertory Theater production of *Androcles and the Lion* and Lillian Hellman's *Another Part of the Forest*. But his most important undertaking after the war was *Regina,* an opera based on Hellman's *The Little Foxes.* Unlike his earlier works for the stage, *Regina* was nonpolitical, essentially a character study of great psychological dimensions. Musically it was more ambitious than *No for an Answer,* with broader dramatic range. It is full-fledged opera, with fewer of the conventions of popular music. Although *Regina* deals with the impact of commercial interests upon human decency, it does so on individual terms. The action centers around the money-grubbing machinations of the Hubbard family. Their corruption is related to the decaying Southern society in which they live, but the Hubbards stand out as singular characters rather than sociological types. Blitzstein's anger is less obtrusive, yet the themes of love and courage, which offset unprincipled power in his leftist dramas, have also softened. In total effect *Regina* marks a substantial step forward in the composer's creative development. It was produced by the New York City Opera Company in 1950, with Brenda Lewis in the title role, after a two-month run on Broadway.

Blitzstein conceived a ballet with Jerome Robbins, *The Guests,* staged by the New York City Ballet in 1949. He wrote incidental music for the Orson Welles production of *King Lear* in 1951 and the following year made a powerful adaptation of the Bertolt Brecht-Kurt Weill *Threepenny Opera,* which enjoyed a recordbreaking run in New York and on the road. Wanting to enlarge his vision, he produced the experimental *Reuben, Reuben* in 1955, a semiautobiographical musical play inspired by the Faust legend. Leonard Bernstein, in a tribute to Blitzstein, once said that he often thought of his friend as the "chief survivor of the welts of passion, the agony of commitment, of a long chain of beautiful work-failures." *Reuben, Reuben* was surely the classic work-failure. It contained much lovely music, but the libretto was so abstruse that the audience was left bewildered. The show tried out in Boston and closed after one week. The composer wrote *This Is the Garden*, subtitled "A Cantata of New York," for the Interracial Fellowship Chorus in 1956 and created a musical version of Sean O'Casey's *Juno and the Paycock* three years later, basing his score on Irish folk songs and dances. *Juno* opened at the Winter Garden Theatre in New York, but closed within two weeks.

In 1960 Blitzstein began work on another opera, *Sacco and Vanzetti*, commissioned by the Metropolitan Opera Company under a Ford Foundation grant. It was a subject dear to his heart and one that presented him with a number of agonizing problems. He had doubts that Metropolitan audiences would empathize with the trauma of the fishmonger and the cobbler, and the story was even spread that when Rudolph Bing was told the name of Blitzstein's opera, he thought Sacco and Vanzetti were lovers! The Federation of Music Clubs filed a formal protest because of the composer's political past. Artistically the musician was plagued by efforts to reconcile his affection for melody and harmony with the current vogue of modernism. He grew frustrated trying to balance his social concerns with the aesthetic demands of a stageworthy libretto.

Depressed, tired, and anxious for a change, he locked the unfinished score of *Sacco and Vanzetti* in the trunk of his car and left to spend the winter of 1963-64 swimming and working in the Caribbean. He took along two short stories by Bernard Malamud, "Idiots First" and "The Magic Barrel," which he wanted to set to music. Unable to ignore the contemporary idiom, he experimented in *Idiots First* with the serial technique. On the evening of January 21, 1964, Blitzstein had dinner with a friend in Martinique. Later he went out alone to join the crowds in a carnival. He was found about 3 A.M. lying in the street, robbed and badly beaten. Within a few hours he was dead. The half completed score of *Sacco and Vanzetti* was discovered several months later by a used car dealer in New York.

By the 1950s Blitzstein had become something of an anachronism. Although he was no longer satisfied to write in the style of the 1930s, neither could he embrace the abrupt shift in aesthetic philosophy that had occurred since World War II. His talent for writing for the stage had grown slowly, at times retarded by his desire to needle audiences and flaunt unpleasant truths. He remained close to the vernacular, more comfortable composing for singing actors than for trained voices. Blitzstein was nevertheless a gifted musician who developed into an able craftsman, with the added advantage of being able to write his own texts. He was a man of intelligence and a warm human being, who came to find himself in an era not wholly his own. For him the American scene was neither the untamed garden, the Dust Bowl, nor the Vermont village. His was an industrial America, corrupted by bigness and greed, but where the little man still represented hope. Post-war society in some ways passed him by, yet while he had trouble adjusting to the new, he was unwilling to deny the present.

Blitzstein's friend Douglas Moore was another New Yorker who wrote principally for the theater. Moore stands as a prime example of American conservatism, a twentieth-century romantic composing in a basically nineteenth century, Teutonic technique. When he turned to American subjects, as he frequently did, he colored them with a nostalgia for the past— the urbanite glorifying the parochial.

Born in Cutchoque, Long Island, August 10, 1893, Moore was descended from early American stock. His mother could trace her ancestry directly to Miles Standish, while his father's forebears arrived from England before 1640, joining the oldest English speaking settlement in New York. His parents later published *Ladies' World*, one of the first women's magazines. The composer remembered lying in front of the fire as a child, listening to his mother play the piano. He could also recall hearing his mother's choral club, as it rehearsed in the big music room of the family's Brooklyn home. The boy took piano lessons, but disliked scales and finger exercises and had to be coaxed into practicing. He was educated at Hotchkiss School, where he knew Archibald MacLeish, and graduated from Yale in 1915. He stayed on at Yale for two more years to take a degree in music, studying with David Stanley Smith and Horatio Parker. He wrote several college songs, among them the football favorite "Good Night, Harvard." He was interested in drama and drew his early musical inspiration from the romantics—Chopin, Grieg, Tchaikovsky—as well as Broadway composers like Victor Herbert, Rudolf Friml, and Jerome Kern.

After two years in the Navy, 1917-1919, Moore enrolled in the Schola Cantorum in Paris, where he worked with Vincent d'Indy and for a time was an organ pupil of Nadia Boulanger. He studied composition with Ernest Bloch in Cleveland, did some acting at the Cleveland Playhouse, and became Music Curator of the Cleveland Museum of Art. In 1925 he was awarded the Pulitzer Fellowship for study abroad and went back to Paris to work with Boulanger. Upon returning to the United States, he joined the music faculty of Columbia University and in 1928 was promoted to associate professor. Twelve years later he succeeded Daniel Gregory Mason as head of the department. In 1945 he was appointed MacDowell Professor of Music.

Some of his first songs were set to MacLeish texts, and he wrote a number of selections for piano and organ. His first work of importance was a set of Four Museum Pieces (1922), originally composed for organ but later scored for orchestra. The *Pageant of P. T. Barnum* (1924) was introduced by the Cleveland Orchestra and immediately achieved a wide vogue. The suite contains five episodes associated with Barnum's career: "Boyhood at Bethel," "Joice Heth," "General and Mrs. Tom Thumb," "Jenny Lind," and "Circus Parade." There are sounds of country fiddles, brass bands, black spirituals, and New England hymnody—evoking the sentimental atmosphere of mid-nineteenth century America. The symphonic poem *Moby Dick* was produced in 1929, followed two years later by a sonata for violin and piano and a short *Symphony of Autumn*. His *Overture on an American Theme* (1932) is a tonal portrait inspired by Sinclair Lewis' Babbitt, while *White Wings*, a three act opera after Philip Barry's play, was completed in 1935. *The Headless Horseman*, a high school operetta based on Washington Irving's "The Legend of Sleepy Hollow," with lyrics of Stephen Vincent Benet, appeared in 1937, as did *Simon Legree*, a setting of Vachel Lindsay's poem for male chorus and piano accompaniment.

Moore's interest in native lore ran a wide range, and he possessed an unusual feeling for the vernacular in American music. But writing for the opera house came to be his first love. "I've always liked setting words better than any other form of composition," he once said, "and I've always had a passion for the theatre." His one act *The Devil and Daniel Webster* was first produced in 1939 by the short-lived American Lyric Theatre. The libretto, adapted from Benet's short story by the author himself, moves from beginning to end with increasing dramatic momentum. The composer was keenly sensitive to dramatic values, so that his music almost becomes a play in sound. As with Moore's later operas, there is a unique combination of folk elements and Broadway refinement. *The Devil and Daniel Webster* has been frequently staged by professional opera companies across the country, in universities and opera workshops, and in 1959 entered the repertory of the New York City Opera Company.

The composer published two books, *Listening to Music* (1932) and *From Madrigal to Modern Music* (1942), and was a brilliant teacher. He continued to write chamber music, choral works, songs, music for documentary films, and another symphony. Yet his fame rests primarily on his operas drawn from the American scene. *Giants in the Earth* (1950), based on O. E. Rolvaag's novel, is a masterly score, straightforward and dramatic, and was awarded the Pulitzer Prize in music in 1951. Moore's most successful work, *The Ballad of Baby Doe*, centering around the controversial second marriage of silver king Horace Tabor, was appropriately premiered at the Central City Opera Festival in Colorado during the summer of 1956. It was given by the New York City Opera Company two years later with Beverly Sills and received the New York Music Critics Circle Award. *The Ballad of Baby Doe* is freshly scored and rich in melody. The composer temporarily abandoned folk idioms and regional nostalgia in *The Wings of a Dove*, taken from the Henry James novel, in favor of an American-European theme. He returned to an American subject, however, for his last opera, *Carry Nation*, commissioned for the centennial of the University of Kansas in 1966. Moore died in 1969.

The American Scene movement in serious composition, like its equivalent in painting and letters, came to a focus in the early 1930s. That was a time when artists and intellectuals all over the world were abandoning abstract forms, turning their talents to social ends, and attempting to communicate with the mass audience in a simplified language. While the creative mind is independent, it is after all a product of the age and society in which it grows to fruition. Younger artists particularly during the Great Depression and World War II years often became caught up in the political and economic destiny of their country and in the United States sought to reaffirm democratic ideals in their work. The degree of directness varied, although most of the younger generation of that time expressed the conviction that elitism in the arts was over and backed away from the more advanced techniques. Some drew patriotic valentines, beat their breasts, and were fired to speak in optimistic terms that had formerly been reserved for Rotary Clubs and staunch conservatives. Others saw hope only in radicalism and called for revolution. Many emphasized regionalism and the folk of yesteryear; a few zeroed in on the city and the industrial problems of the moment. Composers like Ferde Grofe wrote in tangible terms, delineating specific pictures; others, like Virgil Thomson, represented America by more circuitous means.

Unlike Farwell, Gilbert, and an earlier national school, most of the American Scene composers of the 1930s and 1940s were concerned less with the quotable hymn or spiritual than with a largeness that captured the American spirit envisaged by Whitman. It was a time of national predicament and action, when hopelessness gave way to determination. Some composers became so absorbed in propaganda, they neglected art; others were able to address the times in ways that had more universal implications. For many the American Scene approach was a passing fancy, and these either returned to or discovered more specialized themes after World War II. "I no longer feel the need of seeking out conscious Americanisms," Aaron Copland eventually wrote. "Because we live here and work here, we can be certain that when our music is mature it will also be American in quality. American individuals will produce an American music, without any help from conscious Americanisms." Others once squarely in the American Scene group later shifted gears or considerably altered their mood. A few stayed fundamentally the same, nostalgic for an America of spacious skies and heroic frontiersmen.

CHAPTER
VII

THE MODERNISTS

The years before and after World War I were turbulent ones for serious music both in Europe and America. While older composers tended to cling to established methods and command respect, many younger musicians became certain the Classic-Romantic tradition had reached a crisis point and badly needed revision. In Europe the nineteenth-century aesthetic had splintered shortly after the turn of the century into impressionism, expressionism, dynamism, and nationalism, and by 1920 the impact of futurism and Dada had been felt. Much of the resistance to formalism was violent, some less troubled, resulting in a multiplicity of moods and styles. Paris in particular was a cauldron of ferment, although so was Vienna, long a center of tradition. Originality was the goal for most of the younger generation, who for a time discarded the conventional laws of form, harmony, and rhythm. Dissonance became the order of the day, as a number of the rebels tried to outdo each other. The air was charged with various currents and crosscurrents of progressivism, while the public grew confused and spasmodically hostile.

The new music reached the United States at an especially strategic moment, for American composition had just developed to a point that a host of musicians were around worthy of serious attention. Nadia Boulanger, for instance, was convinced that American music was about to "take off," much as Russian music had done some eighty years before. Most of the composers that came to maturity between the end of World War I and the Wall Street collapse of 1929 were influenced by the progressive trends. That decade represented a time when young artists could spurn the achievements of older generations, a time of intellectual freedom when new music could flourish, as did innovations in art and literature. For some composers the flirtation with modernism was a passing fancy; for others it proved the bedrock of their later creativity.

These young composers often took an eclectic approach, since internationalism was a trend among the advanced guard. There were those who returned to the primitive and childlike, some who sought the boldly exotic, others who pursued a unique, personalized path. The more forwardlooking writers particularly had difficulty getting their music played, while conservatives howled that the new music was undermining everything that guardians of the genteel tradition had worked to accomplish during the past century. Daniel Gregory Mason, for example, called American music between 1914 and 1928 the "Music of Indigestion"—full of "rumblings and belchings," all "disastrously bewildering." Early in the 1920s the New York *World* sent a sports reporter to cover a modern music concert, not altogether amiss perhaps, since audiences sometimes responded violently. But the young generation of composers was a tenacious lot, determined to get their ideas before the public. They formed organizations, wrote about one another in major periodicals, and in 1929 formed the Cos Cob Press, to publish contemporary American works.

The new music was eclipsed in part when the Americana vogue hit during the Depression, although it by no means died out completely. Faced with hard times, the management of the nation's symphony orchestras became more resolved than ever to avoid difficult and unknown music, which meant even greater suspicion of modernism. In the late 1930s, however, a stream of distinguished European composers fled to the United States to escape Fascism, among them Stravinsky, Schoenberg, Hindemith, Bartok, Krenek, and Milhaud. The very presence of these avant-garde luminaries stimulated an interest in advanced writing, so that after World War II, as the American Scene school abated, the United States assumed a role of international leadership in the progressive currents of Western music. At the same time a fresh generation of composers was appearing in the United States and Europe who responded to a different intellectual climate, were unwilling to accept the rebellion of the 1920s as final, and demanded its own revolution in music.

Aside from Boulanger, the teacher responsible for training more creative American musicians than any other in recent times was Ernest Bloch, himself a distinguished composer. Born in Geneva, July 24, 1880, Bloch was a French Swiss of Jewish parentage, who migrated to the United States at the age of thirty-six. His father was a clock merchant; no one in the family demonstrated any special aptitude for music. Ernest, however, began taking violin lessons as a boy and by the time he was eleven had decided to become a composer, much to his parents' dismay. He studied in Brussels, Frankfort, Munich, and Paris, but returned to Geneva in 1904. Already he had written his First Symphony. He became a bookkeeper and salesman for his father's shop, doing his composing at night. He did some teaching at the Geneva Conservatory and conducted concerts in Lausanne.

Bloch's opera *Macbeth*, frequently considered his masterpiece, was produced at the Paris Opera Comique in 1910. The *Schelomo* rhapsody for cello and orchestra followed in 1915 and contains a wealth of color. An exuberant Jewish quality is present in much of Bloch's music, particularly in certain melodic and harmonic traits. This orientalism is fully assimilated into his style and in no sense is an exotic decor. His work is often sumptuous, grandiose, marked by directness and an intensity of feeling. Repeatedly expressed is the cry of human suffering, as in the *Hebrew Poems* (1913). Eventually he would write more as a solitary individual. Aware of the superhuman forces over which modern man has only limited control, Bloch infused his later music with violence, producing sounds that were ruthless and mechanical.

The composer came to the United States early in 1916, making an extensive tour of the country as conductor of the Maud Allen dance troupe. He directed programs of his own works with the Boston Symphony Orchestra and the Philadelphia Orchestra and in 1917 became a teacher of composition at the David Mannes School in New York. Three years later he was appointed director of the newly founded Cleveland Institute of Music. He held that post for five years, although he was never happy with teaching and especially disliked the political aspects of administration. In 1926 he went to California, where he headed the San Francisco Conservatory. He influenced a vast number of students, but resented the time away from his composition. A patron of the arts befriended him and arranged for an endowment fund, which enabled Bloch to devote himself wholly to writing from 1930 to 1940.

He composed an *Israel* symphony in 1917, and his suite for viola and piano won the Elizabeth Sprague Coolidge prize of $1000 two years later. A Violin Sonata appeared in 1920, followed by *Baal Shem* for violin and piano in 1923, a quintet for piano and strings in 1924, and the *Concerto Grosso* for piano and string orchestra in 1925. His epic rhapsody *America* was completed for orchestra in 1927. The impersonality of American life, its restlessness and confusion, intensified Bloch's pessimism and sense of a decaying culture that had begun in Europe. He went back to Switzerland for several years and rediscovered Jewish themes in *Sacred Service* (1934) and *A Voice in the Wilderness* (1937). A Violin Concerto (1938) used an American Indian idiom in the opening movement, whereas the Second String Quartet received the Music Critics Circle Award as the best chamber work for the 1946-47 season. The composer returned permanently to the United States in 1939, settling in a small town on the Oregon coast. For a time he taught summer classes at the University of California in Berkeley, but gradually isolated himself almost entirely. A *Scherzo Fantastique* for piano and orchestra was heard in 1950, and *Concerto Grosso No. 2* was introduced in 1953. At seventy he announced that he would compose no more, since he had said all that he had to say. He died in Portland, Oregon, in 1959.

Bloch's pupils composed thoughtfully, but differently. He was satisfied that nothing important could be taught, that students must essentially learn for themselves. Many of his proteges composed music that departed radically from Bloch's own. He never attempted a distinctive American style, nor to emulate fads or fashions considered "new." His aim was to be "'true' and to be human, in a general sense, though faithful to my roots." His technique, however, was basically modern. While the composer sometimes looked to past centuries, he also looked ahead, occasionally experimenting with quarter-tones.

Another foreign-born American modernist was Louis Gruenberg, who came to treat jazz themes in a Central European fashion. Born August 3, 1884, in Brest-Litovsk, Russia, Gruenberg was brought to the United States when he was two years old. His father was a violinist, and the composer later said he could remember nothing in his childhood not associated with music. He was educated in the New York public schools and studied piano as a young boy. Later he attended the National Conservatory of Music, met Edward MacDowell, and toured the Keith circuit as a child prodigy. In his spare time he wrote music. He returned to Europe in 1903, worked in Berlin with Ferruccio Busoni, and in 1912 became a master pupil at the Vienna Conservatory. He launched a career as a concert pianist, making his debut with the Berlin Philharmonic, yet continued to compose. He wrote *The Hill of Dreams*, a symphonic poem, and in 1913 a Violin Sonata. With the advent of World War I, he returned permanently to the United States, determined to focus on writing.

The Dumb Wife, an opera based on Anatole France's play, was finished in 1921, but not produced. The composer had failed to get permission to use the drama from France's executors and made three unsuccessful trips to Paris in an effort to gain the necessary rights. He grew vitally interested in the possibilities of jazz and wrote *Daniel Jazz* (1923), a *Jazz Suite* for orchestra (1925), *Jazzettes* for violin and piano (1926), and a number of smaller jazz pieces. His First Symphony also appeared in 1926, and he continued to compose a great deal of chamber music. *The Enchanted Isle*, another symphonic poem, was published in 1929, while his opera *Jack and the Beanstalk* was staged at Juilliard in 1931.

Convinced that writing for the stage was his special forte, Gruenberg began work on *The Emperor Jones*, based on Eugene O'Neill's one act play. The musician had just married Irma Pickora, and the couple took a house in the New England woods. Gruenberg worked on his new opera through the winter months, almost in total isolation, surrounded by bears and wild animals. His score is likewise savage and sinister, emphasizing the cumulative effect of terror. There are moaning, brooding sounds and bloodcurdling shrieks from the chorus. The composer built the atmosphere hoping audiences would respond with the same emotional impact he had experienced writing it. When *The Emperor Jones* was premiered at the Metropolitan in 1933, it was an emphatic success. The work rated frontpage reviews, while Gruenberg for the moment found himself the most discussed of modern composers. The opera was shortly staged with success in Chicago, Boston, San Francisco, and Los Angeles.

In 1934 Gruenberg composed a *Serenade to a Beauteous Lady* and became chairman of the Chicago Music College. Three years later the Columbia Broadcasting System commissioned him to write a radio opera; he chose as his subject W. H. Hudson's fanciful *Green Mansions*. In 1940 the musician moved his family to California, where he devoted more time to composing. He wrote two piano concertos, three new symphonies, a Cello Concerto, and a Violin Concerto for Jascha Heifetz, in which he used fragments from black spirituals and other bits of Americana. His later stage works include the opera *Volpone* (1951) and a mystery play, *The Miracle of Flanders* (1950). Gruenberg also established himself as a highly regarded film composer, producing scores for *The Fight for Life, Commandos Strike at Dawn, So Ends Our Night*, and *The Arch of Triumph*. He lived until 1964.

Gruenberg was a man of superior mental gifts, a blend of pessimism and geniality. He was an international artist, widely traveled, who worked in a number of styles. Like most moderns he placed little importance on thematic development, but his orchestral effects and rhythmic interests were many. As his musical convictions grew more defined, he came to believe that emotion was the only valid basis for artistic creation, since it was the essence of human experience. "A great work," the composer said, "must be done under compulsion. You must do it because you *have* to." The artist should seek new forms of expression, developing his individual resources. European music, he felt, was suffering from oversophistication; for America it was "the indefinable and at the same time unmistakable atmosphere...that must be youthfully interpreted in a new idiom, not merely exploited in a characteristic melody."

Far less meditative than Gruenberg, although quite intellectual, was Arthur Shepherd, whose music is often found to have an Anglo-Celtic flavor. Born on February 19, 1880, in Paris, Idaho, Shepherd was the son of English parents recently emigrated to the United States as converts to the Mormon religion. His family had deep musical interests, and as a boy he was given instruction first on the melodeon and later on the piano. Shepherd entered the New England Conservatory at the age of twelve, where he studied with George Chadwick, graduating with honors and as president of his class. He then moved with his parents to Salt Lake City, where he taught, performed as a pianist, played the organ in churches, conducted both a theater orchestra and the Salt Lake Symphony, and did some composing. His *Overture Joyeuse* won him the Paderewski Prize in 1902 and national acclaim. He was appointed to the faculty of the New England Conservatory in 1908, but some dozen years later settled in Cleveland. There he was assistant conductor of the Cleveland Symphony Orchestra, music critic for the *Cleveland Press*, and after 1927 chairman of the music division of Western Reserve University.

Shepherd's most widely played work, the orchestral suite *Horizons* (1929), is based partly on frontier ballads like "The Dying Cowboy," "The Dogie Song," and "The Old Chisholm Trail" and is full of the spaciousness of life on the Plains. Earlier the composer had won awards for his First Piano Sonata (1907) and his song "The Lost Child" (1909). His Sonata for Violin and Piano (1920) smacks strongly of Faure and d'Indy, while *Triptych* for high voice and string quartet (1927) and the Second Piano Sonata (1929) rank among Shepherd's best selections. He wrote three string quartets, two cantatas, a *Choreographic Suite* (1931), a Piano Quintet (1941), a *Fantasy on Down East Spirituals* (1946), and a Violin Concerto (1947). His Second Symphony was first performed in 1940 by the Cleveland Orchestra under the composer's direction. Shepherd fairly evenly divided his creative interests between the larger and smaller musical forms, for his work includes a number of short piano pieces and songs. He produced slowly and deliberately, cautiously refining every page he wrote. "I was never one to succumb to the American curse of speed," he said.

Considering his training it is surprising that Shepherd's music is not more shackled to late nineteenth-century Romanticism than it is. He was a lifelong friend of Arthur Farwell and Henry Gilbert, and their influence is evident in Shepherd's periodic efforts to write American music as such. Some of his first pieces, in fact, were published by the Wa Wan Press. An eclecticism always was characteristic of Shepherd's style, yet an independent trend and a probing for personal expression appeared early. He was a highly successful melodist, although there were idiosyncrasies here. He was criticized for cluttering up his scores with too many notes and falling into the mire of one particular tonality. Shepherd was by no means at the vanguard of the modernists, for he grew out of, rather than revolted against, tradition. He did, however, live in the present and gave close attention to composers more adventurous than himself. He continued to develop in expression and techniques and before his death in 1959 showed increasing concern for complex rhythms and a free contrapuntal texture.

Another composer who came to modernism leisurely was Roger Sessions, a student of Ernest Bloch. Although born in Brooklyn, on the same street as Aaron Copland, December 28, 1896, Sessions was a New Englander by heritage. Many of his ancestors were Protestant clergymen. His mother had studied piano at the Leipzig Conservatory, while his father sang in a chorus under Theodore Thomas. Shortly after Roger's birth, his family returned to Massachusetts, where the boy grew up. He was educated at the Kent School in Connecticut and graduated from Harvard in the spring of 1914. He had begun piano lessons at the age of four and at fourteen decided to become a composer, upon hearing his first opera—*Die Meistersinger* in Boston, conducted by Toscanini. In college he was editor of the *Harvard Musical Review*, for which he contributed many articles, several on Strauss, whose *Elektra* he greatly admired. He heard the Boston Symphony every week, spent a lot of his father's money on scores, and became aware of moderns like Stravinsky, Scriabin, and Schoenberg. He later admitted that the Harvard of his day was "training cultured gentlemen rather than musicians." Edward Burlingame Hill took a walk with Sessions during the boy's junior year and told him confidentially that "we are not in a position here to give you what you need. I won't go into the reasons why." Hill advised his student to go to Paris after graduation and study with Ravel.

World War I, however, ruled out any possibility of the youth's going to France, so he decided instead to study with Horatio Parker at Yale. Sessions was very shy at the time and knew nothing "about the musical world except what I had gotten from going to concerts." He found Parker's training extremely traditional and secondhand, but developed a lasting respect for the man, whom he considered sad and lonely. The general level was such, Sessions recalled, "that it would probably never have occurred to a teacher like Parker to give what he had it in him to give." At Yale he wrote a sonata movement for violin and began his First Symphony. He was appointed to the music faculty at Smith College in 1917.

Aware that he was floundering and needed further instruction, the young composer approached Ernest Bloch in New York and showed him some of his better efforts, including part of the symphony. The older musician treated him roughly. "He sat me down at the piano and made me play the first movement of my symphony, and then he stood behind me and shouted the name of all the composers that I was influenced by." Afterwards Bloch calmed down and said, "Look, after all, every young man is influenced by other composers. But the important thing is that *you* must be there too." As Bloch continued to talk, things Sessions had studied earlier suddenly began making sense. He traveled to New York frequently for lessons with the Swiss composer, and in 1921 moved to Cleveland as his teacher's assistant. He no longer studied with Bloch formally, but continued to show him his work. When the composer resigned as head of the Cleveland Institute of Music in 1925, over a quarrel with the directors, Sessions left in protest. He spent the next eight years in Europe. He went with a letter of introduction to Boulanger from Bloch, met Copland in Paris, but lived mainly in Florence, Rome, and Berlin. He received a Guggenheim fellowship, later a Carnegie grant, and the Prix de Rome.

Sessions demonstrated an amazing gift for languages, matured into a cosmopolitan personality, and learned to incorporate European elements without being absorbed by them. While abroad he finished the First Symphony (1927) and wrote Three Chorale Preludes for organ (1926), a Pastorale for flute (1929), a Piano Sonata (1930), and began a Concerto for Violin and Orchestra (1935). In the latter Sessions moved away from the neoclassicism of his previous works and began exploring the use of the tone row. In 1928 he expanded his incidental music to Leonid Andreyev's play *The*

Black Maskers, composed in 1923 for a production at Smith, into a symphonic suite. Although dedicated to Bloch, *The Black Maskers* also reflects the early influence of Schoenberg and Stravinsky. The suite was first performed in 1933 by the Philadelphia Orchestra under Stokowski and remains the composer's best known music.

He made periodic trips home, but did not return to the United States permanently until 1933. Five years before, on a visit to New York, he had helped found the Copland-Sessions Concerts, which lasted for three seasons. He taught composition at the Delacroze Institute in New York from 1933 to 1935, then joined the music faculty of Princeton University. He proved an extremely effective teacher, approaching his students with understanding and encouraging them to go their own way. In 1945 he was appointed Professor of Music at the University of California in Berkeley, but returned to Princeton eight years later. During a summer session at Berkeley the composer met Elisabeth Franck, made her his second wife, and the couple eventually had two children. In 1961 Sessions was chosen one of the four directors of the Columbia-Princeton Electronic Music Center. By then he had become recognized as the intellectual mentor of the academic wing of the advanced music movement.

Sessions insisted he had no desire to write so-called American music, nor was he intentionally trying to write modern music. "I am seeking always and only," he said, "the coherent and living expression of my musical ideas." He developed into a highly individual composer, yet had "no sympathy with consciously sought originality." He moved from the highly chromatic and expressionistic manner of the First String Quartet (1936) to the more chromatic, densely textured, almost serialized Second Piano Sonata and Second Symphony (both 1946). The latter, dedicated to the memory of Franklin Roosevelt, was initially played by the San Francisco Orchestra under Pierre Monteux. Critics found the symphony "fiendishly difficult" and austere, while Nicolas Slonimsky remarked that the dedication was appropriate, since Sessions' music "was as much a challenge to untutored ears as Roosevelt's political ideas were a challenge to horse-and-buggy minds." The composer considered the piece one of the key works in his career. "If you hear my Second Symphony next year, or the next," he explained, "it is possible it will have a different meaning to you than when you first heard it."

He composed far more after he passed the age of fifty, his creative energies in part stimulated by an evolving interest in the twelve-tone method. He wrote two operas: the one act *The Trial of Lucullus* (1947) and *Montezuma*, a huge, four act work about the Aztec emperor, produced in Berlin, April 19, 1964. He completed four more symphonies, a Piano Concerto, a Second String Quartet, an *Anglican Mass*, and an elaborate work for soprano and orchestra, *The Idyll of Theocritus*. There remained a certain stern, grim aspect to Sessions' music—"as if the pieces themselves dared you to like them," Copland said. "But it may well turn out that the quality that makes them not easily lovable may be the very quality that makes us return to them always, each time hoping to crack the nut they represent." Sessions slowly became aware of the twelve-tone system's resources, beginning with the Second Sonata, although by his Quintet in 1958 he was using it in a more thorough way than before.

The composer's music is difficult to classify. It is frequently stark, yet never seems to indulge in cacophony for the purpose of aggressiveness. It is sophisticated and European, yet at the same time is consistent with contemporary life in America. It has absorbed influences from Bloch, Stravinsky, Schoenberg, and others, yet emerges as something distinctly personal. It was written with painstaking craftsmanship, yet sounds full-blooded and robust. Despite his devotion to teaching, the musician considers himself "first and foremost a composer," with all of his ideas stemming from his "firsthand knowledge of a composer's psychology." Highly articulate in his views on aesthetics, Sessions has written several books, including *The Musical Experience of Composer, Performer, Listener* (1950) and *Reflections on the Musical Life in the United States* (1956). Revealed again are the composer's integrity, his philosophical nature, and his perfectionist standards, all evident in his art. "Sometimes it seems to me that Sessions writes his music for Titans," Copland concluded, "forgetting that we are, after all, only mortals with a capacity for lending our attention within definite limits."

Another of Ernest Bloch's students, who had studied earlier at Harvard with Hill, is Randall Thompson. Like Sessions, Thompson has assimilated a number of styles into a personal speech, although he has purposely sought an American idiom. He has combined elements of folk and popular music within a fairly conservative academic framework. His sound is forward-looking, yet seldom dissonant. Born in New York City on April 21, 1899, Thompson graduated from Harvard in 1920 and during the next year studied with Bloch in New York. He left for Rome in 1922, spending three years there at the American Academy. He later taught at Wellesley, the University of California, Curtis Institute of Music, the University of Virginia, Princeton, and Harvard.

Between 1925 and 1926 Thompson lived in Greenwich Village, ready to write anything to help earn a living. He supplied some tunes for the *Grand Street Follies* and was commissioned to set a patron's text to music. His early pieces include two tone poems, *Pierrot and Cothurnus* and *The Piper at the Gates of Dawn*, in an essentially romantic vein and several items in the jazz idiom. He demonstrated a grasp of choral writing, completed his First Symphony in 1929, and emerged as a composer of importance with a Second Symphony two years later. Making use of black folk material, Thompson's style in the Second Symphony is one of unaffected simplicity. There is a constant flow of melody and from time to time suggestions of humor. The piece is warm and intrinsically rhythmic.

Americana (1932) for mixed voices, piano, and orchestra was drawn from five of H. L. Mencken's articles in the *American Mercury*. Here Thompson's wit becomes almost slapstick, as he attempts to produce music that matches his texts. The words are easily understood, for the composer's score does not distort them or get in their way. The lines of *The Peaceable Kingdom* (1936), for a double a capella chorus, were taken verbatim from Isaiah. The composer temporarily put aside choral writing for a suite for oboe, clarinet, and viola (1940) and a String Quartet (1941). His radio opera *Solomon and Balkis*, based on one of Kipling's *Just So Stories*, was heard in 1942. An effective work of art, the little drama is full of charm and humor, at times making playful references to the melodramatic style of earlier opera. *The Testament of Freedom* (1943) utilizes four passages from the writings of Thomas Jefferson and was composed in honor of the two hundredth anniversary of the statesman's birth. Written for men's voices, piano, and orchestra, the selection was first performed at the University of Virginia, broadcast over the Columbia network, and later transmitted overseas to the armed forces.

A Third Symphony appeared in 1949. Critics found it neither oversophisticated nor ungrateful to the ear. An orchestral fantasy, *The Trip to Nahant*, was introduced by the Philadelphia Orchestra in 1955 and was pronounced "genuinely evocative and American in spirit." *Ode to the Virginia Voyage* (1957), set to a text by the seventeenth-century English poet Michael Drayton, commemorated the three hundred and fiftieth anniversary of the colony at Jamestown. A requiem for double chorus followed in 1959.

Noted most for his choral works, Thompson has an amazing proficiency for accenting words and setting them in a tempo appropriate to their meaning. He knows how to achieve a dramatic climax, startling contrasts, and create singable music. He has been inventive, yet is reserved in his dissonance. Simplicity and clarity are perhaps his most distinguishing characteristics. Thompson is a craftsman, Quincy Porter said, riding "eloquently through the present in the fine stagecoach of our ancestors." His work is contemporary in feeling, even though he has consistently shunned the more radical tendencies of contemporary music. Above all he has been true to his own ideals. "My hand has never been restrained from writing what I wanted to," Thompson maintains, "so long as what it wrote was the best I could write, written in the best way I could write it."

Paul Creston has similarly composed in a simple, direct, understandable manner. Like Randall Thompson, Creston was born in New York City, October 10, 1906. The younger musician, whose name was originally Joseph Guttoveggio, came from a poor, Italian family and attended public schools on the East Side. In his third year of high school he was forced to drop out and seek fulltime employment. He had begun piano lessons at the age of eight, but continued to practice before work and late at night. Sometimes he smoked ground coffee beans to stay awake. He enjoyed reading and for the most part taught himself harmony, theory, and composition. Creston matured into an active, fun-loving, aggressive young man, combining the artistic sensitivity of his Italian forbears with a typically American sense of enterprise.

Shortly before his twenty-first birthday, he married Louise Gotto, who at that time was a dancer in Martha Graham's company. Creston had written a few songs, but did not think of becoming a professional composer until almost five years after his marriage. He took a job playing the organ in a movie theater and for many years was organist at St. Malachy's Church in New York. In 1933 he submitted his Seven Theses for the Piano to the New Music Publishing Company, and Henry Cowell, the editor, agreed to publish them. Creston was awarded a Guggenheim fellowship in 1938, which was renewed the next year, and composed Two Choric Dances and his First Symphony. The symphony was performed in Carnegie Hall on March 23, 1943, by the Philadelphia Orchestra under Ormandy and was selected by the Music Critics Circle as the outstanding new American work of that season.

He wrote a number of chamber works, a Concerto for Saxophone and Orchestra (1941), a Fantasy for Piano and Orchestra (1942), a Second Symphony (1944), a Concerto for Piano and Orchestra (1949), *Missa Solemnis* for chorus (1949), and a Third Symphony (1950). There were also several songs, as well as pieces for piano and organ. The dominant characteristics of Creston's music have been melody and rhythm. He approaches composition from the abstract side rather than attempting to paint tone pictures or tell a story. He has innovated, but has proceeded cautiously. "I believe in evolution," Creston declared, "not revolution." He has been strongly influenced by dance, and much of his ingenuity has been expressed through his use of rhythms.

The composer spent long years directing radio programs and teaching composition, piano, and organ. He lived with his wife and two sons in the suburbs of Yonkers. When asked why he composed, Creston once replied that writing music for him was "a form of prayer," the art itself "a form of religion." While his construction has remained along conservative lines, his harmonic combinations are contemporary. "I strive to incorporate all that is good from the earliest times to the present day," he explains. "If modality serves the purposes of expression, I utilize it; and if atonality is called for, I utilize it with an equally clear conscience." He has made no special effort at being American but attempts to stay true to himself and is cosmopolitan by choice. His later works include a Concerto for Two Pianos and Orchestra (1951), a Fourth Symphony (1952), *A Dance Overture* (1955), the symphonic poem *Janus* (1959), and two concertos for violin (both introduced in 1960).

Resembling Creston in background and some aspects of his writing is Norman Dello Joio, another New Yorker of Italian extract. Born on January 24, 1913, Dello Joio grew up listening to grand opera and was given his first music lessons by his father, a composer and organist. At fifteen he studied the organ with his godfather, Pietro Yon, the distinguished organist of St. Patrick's Cathedral with whom Creston had studied. Later he attended the Institute of Musical Art and City College of New York. He began composing as a boy, although he loved sports and was good enough at baseball that the manager of a professional club once made him an offer to join his team. At fourteen Dello Joio held the first of several positions as church organist and choir director. He developed a strong feeling for Gregorian chants, frequently evident in his music, yet also became interested in jazz. For a time he even had his own band. He won a scholarship to the Juilliard Graduate School and between 1940 and 1941 studied at the Berkshire Music Center and Yale with Paul Hindemith, who urged the young composer to let his natural lyricism come out. He spent two years on a Guggenheim fellowship, then succeeded William Schuman as head of the music department of Sarah Lawrence College. He resigned from teaching in 1950 to devote himself to composition.

Dello Joio matured into a prolific writer of great lyric gifts, stamped by his Italianate family environment and his training under Hindemith. His Piano Trio won the Elizabeth Sprague Coolidge award in 1937, while his *Magnificat* for orchestra won the Town Hall Composition award six years later. He composed a concerto for two pianos and orchestra, four ballets, and the chorale *The Mystic Trumpeter*. He was musical director of the Dance Players for two years and like Paul Creston married a dancer. In 1944 the couple bought an English-style house in a wooded area not too far from New York, equipped with a picturesque studio for the composer's work. He made a trip to Europe in 1947, played concerts in Poland, and in 1950 completed his first opera, *The Triumph of St. Joan*. He has written in virtually every form, although opera ultimately became his favorite.

Among his most attractive and successful orchestral works is the one movement *Serenade* (1948), light in texture, transparent in sound. *A Psalm of David* (1950) and the *Song of the Open Road* (1952) are both for mixed chorus. *The Ruby*, a one act opera fashioned from Lord Dunsany's eerie play *A Night at the Inn*, was initially performed at the University of Indiana in 1955. The work was unashamedly theatrical—colorful, exciting, with touches of Puccini in its melodies. The composer returned to the subject of St. Joan, creating an almost new work, entitled *The Trial at Rouen*. Drawing upon the actual proceedings of Joan's trial, Dello Joio devised his own libretto and set it to music that moved quickly and decisively. The opera was given first on NBC television in 1956 and staged by the New York City Opera Company three years later under the original title, *The Triumph of St. Joan*.

After 1957 Dello Joio showed a renewed interest in chamber music and choral writing. His third opera, *Blood Moon*, was commissioned by the Ford Foundation as part of the general plan to encourage American composition. The work deals with interracial love in antebellum New Orleans and received its premiere in San Francisco in 1961. Critics found the libretto dramatically weak and much of the music banal. The score contains arias, duets, and ensembles that are melodious, deliberately conservative in harmony, and often blatantly romantic. The composer wrote incidental music for Shakespeare's *Antony and Cleopatra* (1960), the *Prayer of Cardinal Newman* for mixed voices and organ (1960), the score for the CBS television adaptation of Thackeray's *Vanity Fair* (1961), and *Fantasy and Variations* for piano and orchestra (1962).

"In a sense, all of Dello Joio's music is dance music," Robert Sabin once wrote. The composer's development has followed a path from experimental complexity in his early years to the relative accessibility of *Blood Moon*, although not always in a straight line. Simplicity, tenderness, and strength have been considered the major qualities of his music. He strives for directness and a lyric emphasis, "the feeling for line we find in Verdi." While his structure and contrapuntal texture are sometimes complicated, Dello Joio has been perfectly happy to work within the tonal system. Even when there are dissonance of harmony and unorthodox thematic materials, his music is basically melodious. Increasingly he has sought to communicate with a broad contemporary public rather than a select avant-garde. He has never considered himself "consciously a modernist" and has worried about the obsession in modern music with staying up-to-date.

Not only did William Schuman share Dello Joio's youthful enthusiasm for jazz, he launched his career in music as a Tin Pan Alley songwriter, arranger, and plugger. Two of his more successful popular tunes were "Waitin' for the Moon" and "In Love with a Memory of You," the latter featured by Rudy Vallee and both closely patterned after the sentimental formula. Born in New York City, August 4, 1910, and named for William Howard Taft, Schuman organized a thriving jazz band in high school. His early musical training was modest, although he grudgingly studied the violin and eventually learned to play MacDowell's "To a Wild Rose." He was a school athlete, excelling particularly in boxing and baseball. He heard his first concert as a high school student and from then on haunted the concert halls of New York. He began writing popular songs, but around nineteen developed more serious interests in music. He attended Malkin Conservatory and Columbia University and studied composition with Roy Harris, the decisive factor in shaping his career. He spent the summer of 1935 at the Mozarteum in Salzburg and timidly began his First Symphony.

He joined the music faculty of Sarah Lawrence College the following fall. He was a popular teacher and had the girls flocking to sing in his chorus, which the college newspaper called "the football team of Sarah Lawrence." One headline read, "They Had Knute, But We Have Bill." His Second Symphony and the *American Festival* Overture were both performed in 1939 by the Boston Symphony Orchestra. The former proved highly unconventional, with abundant dissonance and an independent construction. That same year Schuman was awarded a Guggenheim fellowship. He composed his Third Symphony in a neoclassical style, revealing a penchant for bitonality and polyharmony. This tendency was continued in his Fourth Symphony, first played by the Cleveland Orchestra under Rodzinski a few weeks after the bombing of Pearl Harbor.

He had married Frances Prince during his first year at Sarah Lawrence and momentarily returned to Broadway with a number for Billy Rose's revue *The Seven Lively Arts*. He wrote chamber music, including four string quartets, a concerto for piano and small orchestra (1942), *Prayer in Time of*

War (1943), a *Symphony for Strings* (1943), and the *William Billings Overture* (1944). The composer obviously enjoyed polytonality and used jazz from time to time—never as a foreign body, but as an integral part of his work. His orchestral colors already were bold and clear, while his melodies leaned toward the angular. His music tended to be warmer than Roy Harris', however, combining ruggedness with intensity and feeling. He wrote some choral works, two ballets for Martha Graham, and incidental music for a Broadway revival of *Henry VIII* (1944).

Schuman succeeded Carl Engel as director of publications for G. Schirmer, Inc. in 1945 and a few months later was appointed president of the Juilliard School of Music. He bought a home in New Rochelle, yet remained casual in appearance and full of energy, both in his personal life and in his composition. He was a man of great common sense, unassuming, looking neither like a conservatory president nor like a composer. He was ever the pragmatist, relatively free of psychic conflict, well read, generally attending between sixty and seventy concerts a year.

The composer finished a Violin Concerto in 1947 and his Sixth Symphony the next year. Whereas the Third Symphony had been judged the most brilliantly written piece of the musician's early period, the Sixth was hailed as the peak of Schuman's work to date. It contained formal logic and intellectual control, as well as grandeur and passion. The composer's love of baseball and theater merged in his opera *Casey at the Bat* (later retitled *The Mighty Casey*), first staged by the Hartt Music School in Hartford, Connecticut. Amusing and lighthearted, the work includes several tunes in a Broadway musical comedy style. A New York *Herald Tribune* reviewer suggested the opera be sent to Italy as *Cassio al Bastone*.

William Billings inspired two more of Schuman's selections, *New England Triptych* (1956) and *Chester* (1957). *Credendum* (1958) was composed for the United Nations, while *A Song of Orpheus* (1962) was commissioned for cellist Leonard Rose. The Seventh Symphony was initially heard in 1960, and the Eighth was introduced by the New York Philharmonic during its first season in Lincoln Center. The latter proved remarkably conservative, both in its concern with tonality and its handling of melodies. The composer left Juilliard in 1962 to become president of the Lincoln Center for the Performing Arts.

Unlike Gershwin, William Schuman eventually made a complete break with popular songs, devoting himself exclusively to serious music. An innovative teacher, the musician argued that a student must proceed naturally by cultivating his own interests rather than being forced to follow an accepted sequence of theory instruction. He composed several works for high school and college bands, like the *George Washington Bridge* (1950), and remained "at heart a teacher." "I can think of nothing more inspiring," he remarked, "than to have younger composers come to me and ask for advice."

Schuman is somewhat akin to Roger Sessions in spirit, and his early compositions particularly bear the influence of Roy Harris. "Fine!" Kousevitzky told the composer after conducting his *American Festival Overture*. "Now you must begin to hate Roy Harris." Schuman's rhythms, however, always tended to be more nervously athletic than his mentor's, his orchestration brighter and sharper. He developed an extensive use of cross rhythms and once argued that his "music is all melody." His big instrumental pieces especially lean toward the confidently epic, are subtle and free in tonal plan and emblazoned with rhythmic fire. He has brought a keen intelligence to the mechanics of his art and insisted that a "composer must create on his own terms." He contributed substantially to the American Scene school during the 1930s and early 1940s and returned to American themes from time to time later. But eclecticism is dominant in Schuman's music, for he has insisted on universality in taste and approach.

Leonard Bernstein's career in some ways has been the reverse of Schuman's and Gershwin's. Although he had played the piano with a jazz group as a boy, he began his professional life as a serious musician and found his way into the popular field only after his sensational debut as assistant conductor of the New York Philharmonic. Born August 25, 1918, Bernstein rapidly became known as the bright young man of American symphonic music—the result, he said, of "accidents, miracles, and coincidences." As a student at Harvard, he had studied composition under Edward Burlingame Hill and Walter Piston and later orchestration with Randall Thompson at Curtis Institute. He composed his first serious music for a Harvard production of Aristophanes' *The Birds*, conducting the orchestra for the performances himself. He wrote a Clarinet Sonata in 1942, full of charm and youthful freshness, but rather sprawling in form. The *Jeremiah* Symphony followed in 1944, first played by the Pittsburgh Symphony Orchestra with Jennie Tourel as soloist. Bernstein had worked on the symphony for nearly three years, and it proved far more complex than the Clarinet Sonata. The third movement in particular was lauded for its drive, poignancy, and dramatic strength. The composer described the middle section as "fitful...chaotic...brazen...seven minutes of wild rhythm." The orchestration was especially skillful, enough so that the *Jeremiah* Symphony won the Music Critics Circle Award for the best new American work of the 1943-44 season.

The musician completed a group of piano pieces in 1943, along with an amusing song-cycle, *Five Kid Songs: I Hate Music*. *Fancy Free*, commissioned by the Ballet Theater, was written in collaboration with choreographer Jerome Robbins. Working at a feverish pace, Bernstein composed the ballet partly on trains and through the aid of telephone conversations. It was initially performed in April, 1944. *Facsimile*, another ballet with Robbins, appeared two years later. Whereas *Fancy Free* is sparkling and gay, *Facsimile* is an introspective psychological study.

Despite his frequent use of jazz, **Bernstein** is by no means a conscious nationalist in his composition. "Those who try to write music that is deliberately American seldom succeed," he insists. He finished *Four Anniversaries* for piano and *La Bonne Cuisine*, another song-cycle, in 1948. His second symphony for piano and orchestra was introduced the next year by the Boston Symphony Orchestra under Koussevitzky, with Bernstein playing the piano part. Dedicated to the conductor and called *The Age of Anxiety*, the symphony was judged his most ambitious work to date, "at once sardonic and tender, at once violent and sentimental." The score was later made into a ballet and presented by the New York City Ballet at City Center. During the winter of 1949-50 Bernstein wrote incidental music for a new Broadway production of *Peter Pan* and composed a set of five pieces for brass ensemble, each dedicated to a dog belonging to one of the musician's friends or relatives. The last, for instance, is a fanfare for Koussevitzky's dog, Bima.

Bernstein's facility for writing music is amazing. "Things come to me in a kind of inarticulate flash," he confesses, "as if I might have known them in another world." *Trouble in Tahiti*, a one act opera, was given first at Brandeis University in 1952, produced on television, and later added to the repertory of the New York City Opera Company. The work, set to the composer's own libretto, combines the popular style with the operatic. *Serenade* for violin, strings, and percussion was introduced at the Venice Festival in 1954, under Bernstein's direction. A third symphony, the *Kaddish*, involving a soprano soloist, chorus, and narrator, was performed in 1964 by Charles Munch and the Boston Symphony Orchestra. Critics found the alternation between music and spoken text disturbing. Bernstein's *Mass*, which opened the John F. Kennedy Center for the Performing Arts in Washington, D.C., September 8, 1971, was conceived as a theater piece for singers, players, and dancers. The composer worked on the *Mass* for more than a year. It proved flamboyant, visually exciting, and varied, drawing from practically every musical idiom within reach. Critical opinion was divided, although many thought the work a disappointment—timely, even entertaining, but rarely profound.

Not since Gershwin has an American composer been so firmly entrenched in both popular and serious music. Bernstein's acclaim for his Broadway musicals has, if anything, been more spectacular than his success as a composer in the more cultivated forms. Yet he has never looked upon the two as disparate fields. Like Gershwin, Bernstein has attempted to fuse serious and commercial elements, injecting rock into his *Mass* and converting popular tunes into operatic duets and ensembles in *West Side Story*. His mosaic personality and background have allowed him to do this convincingly.

While Bernstein's technique has not been as advanced as many of the modernists, David Diamond began composing on the edge of atonality, but evolved in the direction of neoromanticism. Born in Rochester, New York, July 9, 1915, of Austrian-Jewish parents, Diamond became interested in music and composition during his public school years. He studied violin and harmony at the Cleveland Institute of Music and later composition with Bernard Rogers at the Eastman School of Music. He won a scholarship to the Dalcroze Institute in 1934, where he studied analysis and composition with Roger Sessions. He heard a great many concerts in New York and won a prize for his Sinfonietta. He spent a summer at the MacDowell colony at Peterboro and in 1936 studied composition with Boulanger at Fontainebleau. He loved Paris, met Ravel and Stravinsky, and over the course of three trips gained a standing in the city as one of the most gifted of the younger American composers. In France he composed *Tom*, a ballet based on a book by e. e. cummings, a Violin Concerto, a Psalm for orchestra, and a Concerto for String Quartet.

Diamond left Paris in 1939, with the outbreak of war. He returned to New York City short of funds and for two years played violin in the orchestra of the *Hit Parade* radio program. Meanwhile he continued writing, most notably his concerto for cello and orchestra and his First String Quartet. He won a Guggenheim fellowship twice and in 1943 the Paderewski Prize. He began his First Symphony at the retreat for artists in Yaddo, near Saratoga Springs, and the piece was introduced in 1941 by the New York Philharmonic under Mitropoulos. A cash prize from the American Academy in Rome enabled him to finish his Second Symphony. The musician felt certain that "tense world unrest" and "a certain amount of exterior emotional influence" affected the quality of the symphony, although it is by no means a programmatic piece. Initially performed by the Boston Symphony Orchestra under Koussevitzky, the work established Diamond at the front rank of the country's most original young composers.

He wrote a ballet, *The Dream of Audubon* (1941), a Second String Quartet (1943), and Rounds for Orchestra (1944), one of his most widely played numbers, full of freshness and energy. He contributed incidental music for Margaret Webster's production of *The Tempest* in 1945 and Tennessee Williams' *The Rose Tattoo* five years later. He did scores for two documentary films and the 1949 screen version of *Anna Lucasta*, starring Paulette Goddard. He composed several songs, some choral works, a number of piano pieces, a Third, Fourth, and Fifth Symphony, a Sonata for Violin and Piano, a Third String Quartet, and a Second Violin Concerto. *The Enormous Room* for orchestra, after e. e. cummings, appeared in 1948, followed two years later by a Concerto for Piano and Orchestra and a Quintet for Clarinet, Two Violas, and Two Cellos. A Fourth String Quartet was completed in 1951. Tenderness, passion, and strength consistently reigned among the composer's characteristics. His melodies had become straight-forward, supported by essentially tonal harmony.

Ahavah for narrator and orchestra was commissioned in 1954 by the National Jewish Music Council, while the Sixth Symphony was heard in 1957. *The World of Paul Klee* (1958), for student orchestras, was written under a grant from the Rockefeller Foundation. The Seventh Symphony (1962) was faulted for the composer's "old-fashioned modernism," whereas the Eighth employed an unorthodox twelve-tone technique. A setting of Lincoln's Gettysburg Address, entitled *This Sacred Ground*, for baritone, chorus, children's chorus, and orchestra was introduced in 1962 by the Buffalo Philharmonic under Lukas Foss. *Night Music* for accordion and string quartet and a Second Concerto for string quartet were finished that same year. Like the other modern composers, David Diamond has not always been understood. His work has been called "noisy and artificial," with "violent color changes." Most critics agree, however, that he has an imaginative style and a special talent for orchestration.

More experimental than Diamond is Alan Hovhaness, who has attempted to construct an American-Oriental music. Of Armenian and Scotch descent, Hovhaness was born in Somerville, Massachusetts, March 8, 1911. His father was a chemistry professor. Alan was composing by the time he was eight years old and wrote a religious opera for his class in junior high school. He took piano lessons and studied composition with Frederick Converse. Later he was given a scholarship to study at the Berkshire Festival with Bohuslav Martinu. He had written a profuse amount of music early, much of it bearing the mark of Sibelius, to whom he was slavishly devoted. Then in 1940 he announced his intention of destroying everything he had composed, which indeed he did. This supposedly included over a thousand works, among them two symphonies and several operas. Hovhaness felt he had not been sufficiently critical, and besides his interests were turning in other directions.

He had become spiritually attracted to the East and Middle East. The music of India first caught his attention, and he studied it eagerly. Next he grew curious about the music of ancient Armenia. He had become organist of an Armenian church in Boston, and his work there sparked his interest in Aramaic and Hebraic modal patterns. Although he did not attempt to incorporate Armenian melodies or folk material into his own compositions, he became intrigued by the modal simplicity of the archaic songs and chants and tried to integrate this into his writing. Gradually he developed a unique art, full of atmosphere and impressionistic exoticism.

Hovhaness began winning notice in Boston music circles in the early 1930s. He was a gaunt, pale man with dark eyes and hair. He was tall, walked with a slight stoop, and had a generally ascetic appearance. His maturation as a composer, however, really commenced with his contact with Eastern and ancient near-Eastern music. He came to regard Oriental expressions as a natural kind of music, closer to nature than most of contemporary Western music. These basic expressions, he concluded, exist without national boundaries. He also became fascinated with medieval monody and renaissance polyphony, yet showed practically no interest in the eighteenth or nineteenth centuries. Hovhaness deepened into a creative artist by going back in time, out in space. His music sounds modern in an uninhibited way, for he has discovered new methods for using archaic materials. He "writes no climaxes," Peggy Glanville-Hicks observed; "his music is designed to create and maintain an ecstatic peace, to define a period of tranquility and motionless joy." His work has won extraordinary favor with the public, and a report by Broadcast Music, Inc. in 1962 revealed that a total of 1080 performances of selections by Hovhaness had been heard during the previous year alone, a record matched by few living composers.

The musician has written nineteen symphonies, three *Armenian Rhapsodies, Vision from the Rock* (1955), *The Mysterious Mountain* (1957), and *Mountain of Prophecy* (1961)—all for orchestra. *Meditations of Orpheus*, for dancer and orchestra, and Variations and Fugue for orchestra were both performed in 1964. There are several Concertos, scored for a variety of instrumental combinations. *Sosi—Forest of Prophetic Sounds*, for instance, was written for violin, piano, percussion, and strings. A Concerto for Accordion was completed in 1960. The composer has amassed a long list of chamber pieces and a number of choral works, among them *The Thirteenth Ode of Solomon*. He has written a ballet, *Wind Drum*; incidental music for Odet's play *The Flowering Peach*; and three operas: *The Blue Flame* (1959), *The Burning House* (1962), and *Pilate* (1962). While Hovhaness' music is complex in ornateness, it is simple in feeling and extremely beautiful in melody. His works are pleasant to listen to and easily liked. At their best they bring delight and a relaxed calm to the listener.

Younger than Hovhaness by slightly over a decade is Lukas Foss, born in Berlin, Germany, on August 15, 1922. His father was a professor of philosophy, his mother an artist. The future musician moved with his parents to Paris in 1933, when Hitler came into power, and immigrated to the United States four years later. Foss began composing when he was seven and as a teenager studied at the Paris Conservatory. He worked with Rosario Scalero, Fritz Reiner, and Randall Thompson at the Curtis Institute, but his appetite for modernism was whetted by contact with Paul Hindemith during summers at Tanglewood. He continued his studies with Hindemith at Yale. In 1942 Koussevitzky appointed Foss pianist of the Boston Symphony Orchestra, and he became an American citizen the next year. He was awarded a Guggenheim fellowship in 1945 and the Prix de Rome in 1950.

Foss first attracted notice in 1942 with incidental music for a Theatre Guild production of Shakespeare's *The Tempest*. That same year the League of Composers presented some of his chamber works, and his Allegro Concertante was heard in Philadelphia and New York. But it was with a CBS radio performance of *The Prairie* in 1943 that Foss won wide attention. Inspired by Carl Sandburg's poem, the cantata impressed Artur Rodzinski so much that it was performed under his direction the following season by the New York Philharmonic and the Westminster Choir. The composer was then only twenty-two years old. He wrote his First Piano Concerto in 1943, an Ode for orchestra and his First Symphony in 1944, and *Song of Anguish* for baritone and orchestra in 1945. The latter, drawn from Isaiah, is unusual for Foss in its grim bitterness. His ballet *The Gift of the Magi* was featured by the Ballet Theatre in 1945, while the cantata *The Song of Songs* was introduced by the Boston Symphony Orchestra in 1947. The composer's work after *The Prairie* showed increasing growth and maturity of concept. His best pieces are marked by enthusiasm and a strong melodic instinct.

The Jumping Frog, a one act opera taken from Mark Twain's short story, was completed in 1949 and given four different productions within the next year. A Second Piano Concerto and another choral work, *Behold I Build a House*, followed in 1951. The oratorio *Parable of Death* was initially performed in New York in 1953, and *Psalms*, for chorus and orchestra, was introduced by the New York Philharmonic four years later. *Griffelkin*, another opera, was performed on NBC television in 1955, while *Introduction and Goodbyes*, to a libretto by Gian-Carlo Menotti, was first staged in 1960 at the Festival of Two Worlds in Spoleto. Whereas *Symphony of Chorales* (1959) is based on four Bach chorales, *Time Cycle* (1960) found Foss venturing into atonality. Scored for soprano and orchestra, *Time Cycle* designates improvisatory interludes between its four songs and was written in two different versions. The occasion and the size of the hall, the composer indicates, "will call for one or the other." *Echoi* (1963) is even more experimental, including barless, beatless notation, ensemble improvisation, and two prerecorded but uncoordinated tape tracks. Much is left to chance, and the composer intends that no two performances will ever be the same.

Foss has written great quantities—"trunksfull," he says, "but not all of it worth printing!" For a time he was on the faculty of the University of California at Los Angeles and appeared as guest conductor and piano soloist with several of the nation's leading symphony orchestras. In 1963 he was selected music director and conductor of the Buffalo Philharmonic.

Distinguished women composers have been few, although Peggy Glanville-Hicks has been among the more notable in recent times. Born in Melbourne, Australia, December 29, 1912, she came to the United States in 1939. She had previously studied with Ralph Vaughan Williams in London and with Boulanger in Paris. Glanville-Hicks has been an astute commentator on the American musical scene and has composed a *Concertino da Camera* (1945), a Harp Sonata (1950), a Sonata for Piano and Percussion (1951), *Letters from Morocco* (1953), an *Etruscan* Concerto (1956) for piano and orchestra, and a *Concerto Romantico* (1957) for viola and orchestra. Her operas include *The Transposed Heads* (1954), *The Glittering Gate* (1959), and *Nausicaa* (1961). She was commissioned by the Ford Foundation in 1963 to write another opera, *Sappho*, to a libretto by Lawrence Durrell.

While Lester Trimble's music is comfortably modern, it generally avoids the avant-garde. Born in Bangor, Wisconsin, August 29, 1923, Trimble studied at the Carnegie Institute in Philadelphia and later with Darius Milhaud and Arthur Honegger in Paris. He has been a critic for *The Nation* and the New York *Herald Tribune*, taught for a while at Bennington College, and in 1963 was appointed professor of music at the University of Maryland. Among his compositions are a Concerto for Winds and Strings (1956), a Symphony in Two Movements (1959), Five Episodes (1962) for orchestra, and

In Praise of Diplomacy and Common Sense (1965). *A Night View of Pittsburgh* (1958) stresses the orchestra's percussive resources in order to depict the steel factories of that city. *Four Fragments from the Canterbury Tales* (1959) is a cantata for soprano, harpsichord, flute, and clarinet, while *Boccaccio's Nightingale* is a three act opera based on a libretto by George Maxim Ross.

One of America's most effective operatic composers is Carlisle Floyd, who began writing shortly after World War II. Born in Latta, South Carolina, June 11, 1926, Floyd studied at Converse College in Spartanburg and took a master's degree from Syracuse University. He joined the music faculty of Florida State University in 1947. His first opera, the one act *Slow Dusk*, was completed in 1949, but not staged until the Opera Workshop of Augustana College presented it eight years later. *Susannah*, the work which established Floyd's reputation, was initially produced in 1955 at Florida State University. The composer proved an excellent dramatist, and his score is unstylized and moving. The opera is set among the present-day Tennessee mountain folk and deals with an innocent girl, suspected of immorality but ultimately seduced by an itinerant preacher who expounds the duty of saving her soul. The hymn singing of the congregation and Susannah's arias are particularly forceful. The work was produced by the New York City Opera Company in 1956 and was well received by the critics. Although Floyd is clearly aware of contemporary harmonic and rhythmic devices, his music is not widely dissonant and frequently depends upon unabashed lyricism.

Wuthering Heights, commissioned by the Santa Fe Opera Association and produced by the company in 1958, was less tightly integrated. Sometimes the composer's spoken word seemed at odds with his recitative and song. Floyd revised the work after the Santa Fe production, and in its new form *Wuthering Heights* was presented by the New York City Opera Company in 1959. *The Passion of Jonathan Wade*, set in North Carolina during the Civil War, was commissioned for the City Center opera company by director Julius Rudel under the Ford Foundation grant and premiered in 1962. Floyd claims to have used more polytonality in *Jonathan Wade* than in his previous operas, but there is little of the avant-garde about his score. Its construction is somewhat like Verdi's, consisting of arias, duets, trios, and ensembles. *The Sojourner and Mollie Sinclair* was written for television, but was staged in Raleigh, North Carolina, in 1964.

By no means has all of Floyd's work been limited to opera. Early in his career he composed a Theme and Variations for piano and a Nocture for soprano and orchestra. He later wrote *Lost Eden* (1951) for piano, *Pilgrimage* (1956) for voice and orchestra, a Piano Sonata (1959), and *The Mystery* (1960) for soprano and orchestra, subtitled *Five Songs of Motherhood*.

In the years since World War II the number of able composers turning out well made works has been bewildering, and select American writers have made solid gains in their quest for international recognition. The variety of styles has also been bewildering. More than ever before the social and intellectual milieu in the United States has been congenial to deviation and change. Individuality in the arts is greater than ever before, while eclecticism in serious music has run rampant. At the same time an international style has prevailed, a common, exportable language of interest to sophisticated listeners all over the Western world, subordinating the blatantly national themes of the Depression and war years. And yet even the more abstract works of the moderns are not necessarily less American simply because they are less conspicuously nationalistic. "If the composers will increasingly strive to perfect themselves in the art of music and will follow only those paths of expression which seem to them the true way," Walter Piston urged, "the matter of a national school will take care of itself." Most contemporary artists would agree.

Despite definite advances, modern music is still far from popular outside an exclusive group. With symphony orchestras and opera companies across the country faced with mounting economic problems, a cautious repertory remains essential to survival. The more progressive composers especially must content themselves with limited performances and an elite following. Foundation grants have helped tremendously, but many of the modernists have taken refuge in college music departments. While the major conservatories still offer the best training in the country, since 1945 the better endowed colleges and universities have increasingly assumed the function of teaching musicians, particularly beyond the eastern seaboard. Their programs often include artists and composers "in residence." College instrumental ensembles and opera workshops have time and again performed for a captive audience modern works that professional groups would have found financially ruinous. Whereas the academic environment in the late nineteenth and early twentieth centuries provided security for a few music professors who composed in addition to a heavy teaching assignment, in more recent times it has expanded into the protected province for composers who teach on a limited basis and are permitted the freedom to write. In an earlier age the university was the citadel for musical conservatism; it has lately become a haven for traditionalists and a growing avant-garde.

CHAPTER

VIII

THE EXPERIMENTALISTS

The post-World War I ideal of originality produced all sorts of experimentation. Dissonant counterpoint, syncopated rhythms, quarter-tone techniques, atonal excursions, emphasis on percussion, and music for mechanical instruments all became part of the "revolution" in musical expression. Barbs of satire and ridicule were part of the bombast against tradition, and the Futurists often included buzzers, screamers, hissers, exploders, and cracklers in their concerts. Eventually certain experimentalists began looking to oriental systems in the hope that some fusion might provide a way out of the impasse created by the exhaustion of tonal resources and revitalize the music of both the East and the West. In the 1920s Henry Cowell, Edgard Varese, and George Antheil represented modernity in America in its most advanced forms. But there were precursors like Charles Ives and Carl Ruggles not yet in the public eye.

Like Ives, Carl Ruggles was a New Englander, a creative mind, and a rugged individualist who arrived at his music essentially in isolation. Born on Cape Cod, March 11, 1876, in the town of Marion, Massachusetts, near Buzzard's Bay, Ruggles was descended from New England whalers. He was Ives' junior by only a year and a half and came to have a similar feeling for the vastness and mystery of the universe. As a child Carl lived for a while in the family home built in 1640, grew up in a musical atmosphere, and became something of a prodigy on the violin. The sea also made a deep impression on the boy, and he remembered well a lighthouse on Bird Island across the bay from the Ruggles' home. The lighthouse keeper was his friend and gave Carl his first real instrument. The boy soon played well enough that he was asked to entertain summer visitors who came to the Cape. Among these were President and Mrs. Grover Cleveland; Carl even played duets with Mrs. Cleveland.

The lad's dream, however, was to become a shipbuilder, and as a young man he went to Boston to study ship design. Shortly after arriving in the city he met a musician named Joseph Klaus, who taught at the Boston Conservatory. Ruggles persuaded Klaus to give him lessons in composition, and the teacher was so impressed with the display of talent that he soon encouraged the youth to go to John Knowles Paine at Harvard. "I have taught him all I can," Klaus wrote Paine. "Now I am sending him to you. He will either dash his brains out against a wall, or he will jump over the wall."

The academic environment quickly proved confining for Ruggles, and he left Harvard to pursue music on his own. He went West and in 1912 founded an orchestra in Winona, Minnesota. There he met violinist Christian Timner, who became his concertmaster and mentor. For over a decade Ruggles toured with his orchestra through Minnesota, familiarizing himself with the world's great music as he conducted it. Already he had embarked on his highly original composition, although this was not music that he later cared to preserve. In Minnesota he married Charlotte Snell, a young singer from Lawrence, Massachusetts, who often sang with her husband's orchestra. The couple had a son, Micah, and returned to New England in the early 1920s.

The composer's oldest surviving piece is a song to piano accompaniment called "Toys," written in 1919. His earliest orchestral work to be performed was initially entitled *Men and Angels* and was first heard in New York at a concert of the International Composers Guild on December 17, 1922. Originally scored for six muted trumpets, the piece is closely packed with dissonances, although it maintains an affinity with classical form. The response of the premiere audience was generally negative. "Terrible!" the man sitting next to Ruggles exclaimed. "What do they want to do a thing like that for?" The lines aspire to freedom both tonally and rhythmically, towards unbounded expressionism. The composition was later revised for strings and brass, retitled *Angels*, and stirred up a great deal of intellectual excitement when it was revived in 1949 on a program by the National Association for American Composers and Conductors. Like many of Ruggles' works *Angels* now exists in several versions.

Men and Mountains, the musician's second important orchestral work, was written in 1924, but has since been revised a number of times. When the piece was played by the New York Philharmonic-Symphony in 1936, there were again cries of "Terrible! Horrible! Terrible!" Ruggles took the title from Blake's line, "Great things are done when men and mountains meet." Suggesting the stern New England countryside, *Men and Mountains* is "roughhewn, unrelentingly harsh and thoroughly inspired." It is full of craggy formations of sound, which are juxtaposed, disintegrated, and built anew. "The violence of the harmony," Mellers maintains, "reminds us of the American axe in the wilderness, and of the savagery within the mind that it came to represent." The second section of the piece—*Lilacs*—is for strings alone and contains a curious sweetness. The composer's love of nature is obvious, as well as his attachment to old, familiar places and people. When Charles Ives ran across *Men and Mountains* in the 1928 volume of *New Music*, he was so enthusiastic about it that he ordered twenty-five copies.

As Ruggles developed, he turned more and more to counterpoint. In *Portals* (1926) the long chromatic, contrapuntal lines are woven into incredibly dense textures. Composed for small string orchestra, the selection was inspired by Walt Whitman and is alive in every phrase and rhythm. There are two themes—one intensely human, the other remote and floating. The themes come into conflict, producing grinding dissonances, then break off, unresolved. The growth process, Ruggles seems to suggest, is both natural and painful. The composer concentrates on strife, attempting to reconcile his individual consciousness with the ways of nature. His early pieces particularly possess an heroic quality, reaching a climax in *Sun-Treader*, often considered his masterpiece.

Scored for large orchestra, *Sun-Treader* lasts almost eighteen minutes, a long piece for Ruggles. The composer wrote on the selection for six years, finishing it in 1931. The work received its premiere in Paris on February 25, 1932, but was not heard in the United States until 1966, when the Boston Symphony Orchestra performed it under the auspices of Bowdoin College. Based on Robert Browning's tribute to Shelley—"Sun-treader, Light and Life be thine forever"—Ruggles formulated the piece virtually without harmony in the conventional sense.

After *Sun-Treader* the composer worked even more slowly. Each piece was written with tremendous care, polished to a gemlike hardness. Time and again the lines were recast in Ruggles' search for the sublime. His total output, despite an extremely long life, was small, fewer than a dozen pieces. All of these are compositions in miniature; *Portals*, for instance, is only four and a half minutes long. There was extraordinary growth, although disregarding superficial similarities to Schoenberg, Ruggles' music is almost impossible to locate in terms of historical progression or outside influences. Much of his early work precedes the first twelve-tone experiments to come out of Vienna.

Ruggles' form was mainly rhapsodic, while the sustained melodic line was of prime importance. His melodies are flexible, his rhythm subtly irregular and without lilt. The composer's music is more intensely conceived than Ives', more splendidly perfected. Like Ives, he refused to be popular and was content to remain an artist for artists. His titles and explanatory mottos tend to evoke mystical experiences and religious visions, spiritually relating man and nature. "What are those of the known but to ascend and enter the Unknown?" Ruggles' pieces are not only personal in content, but are constructed so that they seem capable of resisting wear and time, somewhat like Elliott Carter or Poe in letters. The composer frequently wrote on wrapping paper of varying sizes and colors, ruling off his own staff lines about an inch apart. His notes are grand and fat, most likely made with a colored crayon.

Crusty and full of "pith and vinegar," Ruggles was laconic and biting, yet effused excitement and passion. For the faint and weakhearted he had unbounded contempt; for the incompetent he had only scorn. For the gifted and great he had boundless admiration. He was the friend of many of the artists and writers of the 1920s and 1930s. Thomas Hart Benton painted him as "Sun-Treader." He knew Georgia O'Keeffe, Alfred Stieglitz, and eventually Jackson Pollock. Robert Frost was his neighbor, Carl Sandburg his friend. "She was some gal, that one that wrote poetry," he recalled, "you know, the one that lived at the Hotel Brevoort...what was her name...oh sure, Millay." In his early days he was closely associated with the International Composers Guild, and several of his works were played on the association's concerts. His intimate acquaintances there were Charles Ives, Edgard Varese, and later Henry Cowell and Wallingford Riegger.

Ruggles himself took up painting on a trip to Jamaica in 1935 and came to spend increasing amounts of time working on abstract pictures. "All art— music and painting especially," the composer once said, "overlaps and continues from one artist to the next. It is a steady stream; each person is a part of all that has gone before." In 1937 Ruggles was appointed to the music faculty of the University of Miami and remained there for many years. He was an instructor in modern composition, although he repeatedly argued, "Creative work can't be taught—you can only provide the tools, the fundamentals."

His permanent home, however, was Arlington, Vermont, where he and his wife lived for nearly four decades in a reconverted schoolhouse. The main schoolroom became the musician's studio, some forty feet square and twenty feet high. Here in this picturesque and homely dwelling, Ruggles honed his compact compositions. Henry Cowell told of visiting the composer's studio one morning and finding him at the piano, playing a single chord over and over. Finally Cowell shouted, "What on earth are you doing to that chord? You've been playing it for at least an hour." Ruggles replied, "I'm giving it the test of time."

The composer had always been fascinated by small towns and small townspeople. He might have dinner with the local traffic officer or village housepainter one night, a distinguished writer or artist the next. He spent hours at the corner store in Arlington, swapping stories. Friends found him irascible, lovable, honest, self-assured, intelligent, disrespectful, and splendidly profane. Some considered him downright lazy. But his bohemian lifestyle was cast in an individual mold, harmonizing well with the New England landscape.

He was a small man, with a curiously peaked head and clear blue eyes. If anything he grew more self-critical as the years went by, yet remained indifferent to current trends and changing fashions. He had little patience with the modern music movement as such. "Music is music," he declared. "It is no better than it sounds." Nor did he worry about failure. "Great facility is dangerous," Ruggles insisted. "Be glad of obstacles—if you don't run into them 'suspicion yourself.' Stumbling blocks should be steppingstones." When he was about forty, he was fortunate enough to find a patron, Hariette Miller, a wealthy New Yorker who provided Ruggles an annuity for life. Still he composed at his own deliberate pace, constantly doctoring pieces already performed or published. A work is never finished, he contended, but once written is something the composer must keep perfecting the rest of his life. And through it all Ruggles struggled to identify man with the immensity, beauty, terror, and cruelty of the natural world.

He wrote *Polyphonic Composition* for three pianos in 1940, followed by the song suite *Vox Clamans in Deserto*. His four chants for piano, the *Evocations*, were composed between 1937 and 1945, his only work for a solo instrument. Each one is short, grows to a single climax, and involves a minimum of repetition. The form is free, the design brilliant and ultimately sharp. The *Evocations* last about ten minutes, are abstract but never vague, concentrated rather than abbreviated. To the average listener, they are perhaps Ruggles' most accessible pieces. *Organum*, for orchestra, was completed in 1945 and ranks among the composer's more straightforward works. It is rich, full-blooded, neoromantic, urgent—only seventy-eight measures long. First performed by the New York Philharmonic under Stokowski in 1949, *Organum* achieved a popular success, much to the surprise of the composer. "Audiences have gained wide experience since the twenties," Henry Cowell explained, "when all dissonant music sounded alike and horrible to them."

Ruggles supposedly wrote another piano piece, *Flowers*, but there were no more published works after 1945. His unfinished one act opera to Gerhard Hauptmann's *The Sunken Bell* apparently was destroyed. Although the Metropolitan Opera had agreed to perform the work, the composer became convinced that he had no talent for the stage. Ruggles continued to paint, usually during the afternoon. As he advanced in years, he became even more the hermit. He papered the walls of his study with his own manuscripts and increasingly shut himself off from the turmoil of the contemporary scene. His hours were strictly kept: breakfast at seven, lunch at noon, dinner at six. Every morning he would work revising his handful of compositions. Mrs. Ruggles eventually put a sign on the front door: "No Admittance. Don't Knock Until One . . . Then Come In and Stay As Long As You Like."

The musical world of Carl Ruggles was clearly of his own devising. He occasionally gave lectures, scrawling them out in advance on butcher's paper. He was often outspokenly critical of American music and was not afraid of naming names. "I thought that music had reached the lowest possible point when I heard the works of John Alden Carpenter," he told a group at the Whitney Museum. "Now, however, I have been examing the scores of Mr. Henry Hadley!" (Mrs. Hadley happened to be in the audience.) But mostly Ruggles remained the sage of Arlington, Vermont, dressing in old clothes and rough boots and living a happy life that to him was deeply satisfying and meaningful. He liked to talk about music with friends who dropped by and argued for hours with Henry Cowell over matters like whether Tschaikovsky was a thirteenth- or fourteenth-rate composer.

Ruggles was achieving his unique style about the time that Ives was falling silent. Unlike most of the works by Ives, Ruggles' music contains no nostalgically familiar tunes. He wrote from sheer genius and inspiration pieces that are powerfully dissonant and frequently atonal. While Ruggles' mode of speech is of its times, it was nonetheless derived independently, belongs to no school, and leads to no one. The musician was always a loner, an essentially self-taught composer who did things his own way, fusing together without seams "the whole person of the separate soul." For John Cage, Ruggles is no experimentalist at all, but in a most sophisticated manner is "attached to the past and to art." His compositions are filled with magnificence and an expressionistic immediacy, yet his gift for texture probably stamped his music most strongly of all. Dedicated to the integrity of his own spirit, Ruggles sought freedom from the austerities of Puritanism, yet remained the very essence of village New England.

Unlike either Ives or Ruggles, Wallingford Riegger began as a romantic composer and did not start writing in the modern idiom until he was past forty. Still he stands as one of the first native-born champions of the twelve-tone system, although his music was shamefully neglected during most of his lifetime. Born in Albany, Georgia, April 29, 1885, Riegger was the son of highly literate and musical parents. His father had been the concertmaster of an orchestra in Indianapolis at the age of fourteen, while his mother was an accomplished pianist. When Wallingford was three years old, the family returned to Indianapolis, where the boy was soon given violin instruction and was found to have perfect pitch. He also had piano lessons and at an early age began experimenting with strange harmonies.

The family moved to New York in 1900, and it was decided that Wallingford should take up the cello, so that the family could have a string quartet. The youth received a scholarship to Cornell University in 1904, but left after one year, having decided to make music his career. He graduated from the Institute of Musical Art in 1907, then went to Berlin to study counterpoint, cello, and composition. He made his debut as a conductor with the Bluthner Orchestra in 1910 and returned to the United States to become cellist with the St. Paul Symphony Orchestra. He also married Rose Schramm, his high school sweetheart.

Riegger described the St. Paul experience as "a pioneer existence in more ways than one." By playing hotel and movie theater jobs he was able to get some extra money together and with his wife returned to Germany in 1914. He conducted opera in both Wurzburg and Konigsberg. Two years later he was appointed one of the regular conductors of the Bluthner Orchestra, but was forced to come home when the United States joined in the war against Germany. He made a guest appearance with the San Francisco Symphony in October, 1917, then accepted a position at Drake University in Des Moines, Iowa, as head of the theory and cello departments. "I was perfectly willing to take over the New York Philharmonic or the Philadelphia Orchestra," he later said. "I was even willing to *move* to Philadelphia if it was absolutely necessary. The orchestra managers, however, didn't see it my way." He taught at Drake for three years, then took an assignment at the Ithaca Conservatory of Music.

Meanwhile he was busily composing. His Trio for violin, cello, and piano, a thoroughly conservative piece, won the Paderewski Prize in 1921. His setting of Keats' *La Belle Dame Sans Merci*, for four solo voices and chamber orchestra, was written in 1923 and was performed at the Berkshire Festival the next year, with the composer conducting. Slowly a change was taking place in Riegger's style, as he attempted to resolve "the conflict between the old and the new." With the Rhapsody for orchestra in 1925, called by the name of Edna St. Vincent Millay's poem *Second April*, he began to write atonally. He wanted to develop a freer means for interpreting his creative ideas and gradually began to break loose from the conservatoirists' complexes and inhibitions. It was not until *Study in Sonority*, however, that the composer broke with the past by abandoning tonality altogether.

Written in 1927 for ten violins or any multiple of ten, the *Study in Sonority* was first played by the Philadelphia Orchestra under Stokowski two years later. The professional response was divided, although a large segment of the public was horrified and angry, and the piece was hissed by some of the box holders. Riegger confessed that he could not be too disturbed, since he himself had joined the audience in hissing Scriabin's *Poeme de l'Extase* after its Berlin premiere. But the *Study in Sonority* is imaginative and novel, employing a boldly dissonant harmonic scheme. The piece is animated, atmospheric, elaborate in contrapuntal design, airy in texture, powerful, and witty all at the same time. "Emotionally," Cowell maintained, "the work soars like the choiring of angels."

Dichotomy, finished in 1932, is based on two tone rows of eleven and ten notes, rather than the twelve-tones of Schoenberg. Actually Riegger knew little of Schoenberg's work at this time. While he later became an admirer of the Viennese composer and used twelve-tone rows, Riegger's approach to atonality remained essentially his own. Consistently he subordinated theory to expressive ends. *Dichotomy* reflects his fondness for melodies of angular, almost jagged contour and block harmonies of crushing dissonance. There is a wonderful sense of sonority and texture. First performed in Berlin under Nicolas Slonimsky the year of its completion, the piece has seldom been played in the United States.

Riegger's career reached a climax with *Dichotomy*. He moved his wife and three daughters permanently to New York City just about the time of the Wall Street crash. He got to know several of the pioneers in the modern music movement, among them Ives, Ruggles, Cowell, and Varese. He participated in a number of new music concerts and helped form the Pan American Association of Composers. "We had rejected the neoclassicism of war-weary Paris," Riegger said, "and struck out for ourselves, each in his own way." To help his financial situation, he took jobs editing, arranging, and proofreading.

He was introduced to the art of Martha Graham and "was drawn into a new sphere of creative activity." From 1933 through 1941 Riegger wrote almost exclusively for modern dance companies. *Frenetic Rhythms, Evocation,* and *Chronicle* were all composed for Martha Graham. *New Dance, Theater Piece,* and *With My Red Fires* were written for the Humphrey-Weidman group. The composer also produced scores for Hanya Holm, Helen Tamiris, and Eric Hawkins. His dance music is full of kinetic energy, yet is highly satisfactory to musicians. *New Dance* and *Chronicle* were later turned into concert selections. Most of these works involve themes of social protest, a fundamental concern at the time and one with which Riegger had great sympathy. Although he was little impressed by the prettiness of ballet, he found modern dance "vital and expressive"—an American product that he thought fascinating. "In my music for the dance," Riegger declared, "I found the twelve-tone technic entirely compatible with my own idiom."

The composer entered his most productive period about 1941, when his preoccupation with dance abruptly ended. He had already written his First String Quartet (1939), employing a twelve-tone system. A Second String Quartet followed nine years later, a piece of greater poise and maturity—one that is freely atonal, but does not use the twelve-tone idiom at all. Riegger composed four symphonies between 1944 and 1957. The Second is for high school orchestras, while the Third is a work of great power, in some ways a summation of Riegger's composition. It has vast intellectual appeal, yet is always vividly musical, using a delightful variety of instrumentation. The selection is by no means consistently twelve-tone, for only the first and fourth movements are based on a strict tone-row construction. Riegger's Fourth Symphony, presented by the Boston Symphony Orchestra in 1959, has both head and heart appeal. Its texture, critic Cyrus Durgin said, "ranges from free-flowing melody to grinding dissonance, with a good amount of mild and tonal harmony in between."

There were still occasional periods of unproductiveness—"due partly to my own maladjustment and partly to the need of earning a livelihood," the composer explained. He generally wrote slowly and revised extensively. He enjoyed fussing and landscaping at his summer place in Massachusetts and loved to play jokes on friends. He confessed to liking bridge and detective stories, which, he said, "supply a wonderful excuse for not getting at my composing." After 1948 he received a number of commissions for works and was invited to hold a series of visiting professorships. He finished his *Music for Brass Choir* in 1949 and his Cantata for chorus and orchestra and his Piano Quintet the next year. *Music for Orchestra* followed in 1951 and Variations for piano and orchestra in 1954. The Piano Variations abandon the tension of his symphonies, while the total effect of much of his later music is more relaxed. A Rhapsody for four cellos appeared in 1957, a *Festival* Overture in 1960, and ultimately an Introduction and Fugue for cello and symphonic winds.

Riegger was an outspoken champion of freedom. "As an artist," he said, "I feel impelled to continue my creative work, but I also feel, as an artist, that I must help oppose those forces which would deny humanity its heritage of culture and freedom." He was an ardent liberal and during the McCarthy era was accused of being a Communist or at least a sympathizer. "As an American," he told the Un-American Activities Committee, "I fear the loss of my self-respect if I answer you." The composer was announced to receive the Brandeis Award in 1961, but died a few days later as the result of a trivial accident. He tripped while walking on a side street near his home in the neighborhood of Columbia University. Brain surgery was decreed necessary, from which the musician did not recover.

Riegger was thirty-five years old when he wrote his first important composition. He grew from nineteenth-century Germanic roots and came to modernism only after he had mastered the methods of the past. Always he was a romantic who admired strict forms. He wrote some of the most advanced music of his day, but followed the dictates of his own personality. Yet there was some truth to the description of Riegger as "the common man's Schoenberg." He did not receive wide public recognition until his Third Symphony won the New York Critics Circle Award in 1948, when he was past sixty. Few composers have had the courage to change their style as completely as Riegger, and even after his conversion to atonality, his music did not adhere to any prescribed system. On the other hand, the Riegger stamp is always clear. The composer remained a quiet man, in an increasingly noisy world. He laid down no principles, but wrote music that made up in craftsmanship what it lacked in melody and placed content before size.

Another experimentalist who began a second life as a composer in middle age was Edgard Varese. Radically original, Varese explored new possibilities in percussion sounds, created many orchestral effects, brought contemporary symphonic composition to a fullness of power, and was consistently uncompromising in his modernism. Born in Paris, December 22, 1883, of French and Italian parentage, Varese did not come to the United States until the end of 1915. He spent much of his boyhood with his mother's family in Villars, a small village in Burgundy. He was greatly impressed by the Romanesque cathedral in nearby Tournus and later said that he wanted to write music with the power and strength of that church. In 1892 the boy was taken by his family to Turin, where he was enrolled by his father in the

Polytechnical Institute to study engineering. He rejected science and mathematics, but found the opera and concert life in Turin vastly exciting. He taught himself a little about music and was eventually given free instruction by the director of the Turin Conservatory.

Edgard's mother died when the boy was fourteen. His father, an engineer whom Varese described as "a kind of Prussian sergeant, the drillmaster type," staunchly opposed a musical career for his son and bullied the boy unmercifully. Antagonism between the two became unbearable. In 1903 Varese left his family and went to Paris, planning to become a musician. Despite a dearth of funds, he was admitted to the Schola Cantorum the next year, becoming a pupil of Roussel and d'Indy. Later he studied at the Paris Conservatory under Widor and received advice and guidance from Massenet, Debussy, Richard Strauss, Muck, and Busoni. Disappointed with the musical climate of Paris, he left for Berlin toward the end of 1907, spending most of the next six years there. He got to know Gustav Mahler and Hugo von Hofmannsthal, did some teaching, formed a chorus, and from time to time conducted. He composed a number of unusual late-Romantic tone poems, all of which have been lost or destroyed. "Varese's Old World career belongs to another era," Eric Salzman states, "the twilight of a golden age that was to be shattered by World War I."

Largely as a result of his relationship with his father, Varese grew to manhood hating authority. He met both Lenin and Trotsky and admired Rodin and Picasso. By the time he returned to Paris in 1913, he was already yearning to liberate sound from any control except that imposed by the conscious designer. He imbibed the conviction that musical composition must be unshackled from the limitations of the tempered system and traditional tonality. He was inducted into the French army in 1914, but was discharged after one year because of ill health. He had trouble breathing and suffered from claustrophobia. He was also finding the musical traditions of Western Europe smothering, grew increasingly restless and depressed, and departed for New York City on December 8, 1915.

Varese arrived in America a free man. His wife had recently left him to pursue her career as an actress, taking with her their child. All but one of the composer's manuscripts were lost, most of them burned in Berlin during the war. The surviving composition Varese himself destroyed in 1962. He knew no English when he arrived in the United States and had about ninety dollars in his pocket. He found the atmosphere of New York less confining and more sympathetic than either Paris or Berlin. He loved the city, its sounds and commotion, and enjoyed Americans. "The people here," he said, "have a sense of optimistic realism. In Europe they bellyache." Through Karl Muck he was introduced into the musical circles of New York, and on Palm Sunday, 1917, just as the United States was about to declare war on Germany, Varese conducted the Berlioz *Requiem* at the Hippodrome before an audience of five thousand. The occasion was to commemorate the dead of all nations, while the performance received rave notices.

The musician met Louise Norton, his second wife, that year and conducted a concert with the Cincinnati Symphony. The New Symphony Orchestra made its debut under Varese's direction in April, 1919, but he resigned shortly, when the board asked him to alter his programming. "Too many musical organizations are Bourbons who learn nothing and forget nothing," he told the press. With composer-harpist Carlos Salzedo, Varese formed the International Composers' Guild in 1921, devoted exclusively to new music. The composer began work on *Ameriques* around 1919 and completed it two years later. Written in sonata form, *Ameriques* is characterized by a new preoccupation with sound. "I dream of instruments obedient to my thought," the composer said, "and which, with their contribution of a whole new world of unsuspected sounds, will lend themselves to the exigencies of my inner rhythm." Scored for one hundred and forty-two instruments, *Ameriques* was not heard until 1926, when the Philadelphia Orchestra performed it under Stokowski. Fourteen rehearsals were necessary. The *Christian Science Monitor* judged the work "the first original score for grand orchestra that has been made in America since the twentieth century began."

Offrandes, a setting of two surrealist poems for soprano and small voice, followed in 1922. Melody no longer prevails over timbre, for the orchestra's balance has shifted, with the strings subservient to the percussion. "What we want is an instrument that will give us a continuous sound at any pitch," Varese told a reporter. "The composer and electrician will have to labor together to get it. At any rate, we cannot keep working in the old school colors. Speed and synthesis are characteristic of our epoch. We need twentieth-century instruments to realize them in music."

Varese was still looking for a New World of orchestral sound. *Hyperprism*, dating from 1923, is a short work scored for seventeen percussion instruments against nine melodic ones. Sometimes the composer uses percussion instruments alone, although he does not wholly ignore melody and harmony. First played at the Klaw Theater in New York, *Hyperprism* produced a near riot. At Salzedo's insistence the number was repeated, causing half of the audience to leave. When performed later under Stokowski's direction in Philadelphia and Carnegie Hall, critic Paul Rosenfeld claimed that "Varese undoubtedly has done as much with the aural sensations of contemporary nature as Picasso with the purely visual ones."

Octandre, for seven wind instruments and double bass, appeared in 1924 and became one of the composer's more widely played ensemble pieces. *Integrales*, the longest of his early works, was a daring tonal experiment, a collage of the noises of urban life, with sirens, automatic drills, and the din of traffic. These earlier compositions, Varese later observed, "were what I would call more architectonic. I was working with blocks of sound, calculated and balanced against each other. I was preoccupied with volume in an architectural sense, and with projection." *Arcana*, for 120 players and even more instruments, was introduced in 1927 by Stokowski, who later admitted that his musicians detested the piece. Evidently the audience did too, for hissing overwhelmed the applause. The critics, as usual, were divided, although one called *Arcana*, "a nightmare dreamed by giants." "You know," Varese said, "some critics think one is writing music only to annoy them!"

The composer insisted that the basis of music should be sound, pure and simple. He spoke time and again of "musical space as open rather than bounded," of "spatial projections," and of "throwing open the whole world of sound to music." He once argued that he was "the first composer to explore, so to speak, outer musical space." Although Varese's music has nothing in particular to do with America, it was almost as if his European training were merely a prelude to the work that lay ahead. The composer was strongly affected by the "futurist" school of percussionists, while his exposure to science led him to consider the actual materials of music. He experimented with sonorities almost as if he were a scientist in a laboratory. "I refuse to submit myself only to sounds that have already been heard," he said. Listeners in the 1920s were frequently horrified by what they experienced, but few could deny that Varese's music had strength, and certainly it exercised far-reaching influence on younger composers of that decade.

Around 1927 the musician began exploring the possibilities of creating a new electronic instrument with the acoustical research director of Bell Laboratories, one that would have a voice more consistent with the present age. He returned to Paris in 1928, remaining there for four years. In 1932 he applied for a Guggenheim fellowship to pursue work on his instrument for producing new sounds. Varese insisted he was never interested in tearing down, but in finding new means. "Unlike the dadaists," he said right before his death, "I was not an iconoclast."

He began work on *Ionisation* in 1930, the selection that was to bring him more fame and notoriety than any other. Conceived for percussion ensemble, the rhythms actually become the melodies. The music is static in the same sense that architecture is static, and there are all sorts of analogies to advanced geometry. The composer thought of musical space as a continuum not always broken up into fixed scales and measured time by the slow revolution of solid masses in space. *Ionisation* was conducted by Nicolas Slonimsky at Carnegie Hall in 1933, and according to *Musical Courier*, it "moved even earnest devotees of the musical esoteric to smiles."

With *Ionisation* Varese virtually disappeared from the musical scene for more than two decades. "In those days," he explained, "the situation really seemed hopeless. I'm afraid I developed a very negative attitude toward the entire musical situation." The 1930s and early 1940s were very bad years for avant-garde experimentation; even Stokowski practically stopped playing advanced music. But Varese refused to compromise. He was still absorbed with the idea of an instrument that would free music from the tempered system and did not quit composing altogether. "I kept working on a score that I called *Espace*," he said, "but I would tear up at night what I had written during the day or vice versa."

Between 1931 and 1954 he produced only one piece—*Density 21.5*, for unaccompanied flute, revealing a completely original, expressive conception of a single instrumental line. Written for George Barrere, 21.5 refers to the density of Barrere's platinum flute. The title seems to imply that the music is the aural reality of the metal. Varese and his wife had returned to New York in 1933 and, with the help of a patron, went to Santa Fe in 1937, where he taught several music courses. The next year he underwent a debilitating operation and grew profoundly depressed. He lived for a time in Los Angeles, but by 1940 was back in New York. He remained a personable man, who liked to cook, drink wine with his friends, and listen to new works by others. He organized the Greater New York Chorus, which specialized in early music. In 1948 he gave a seminar in composition at Columbia University and taught in Darmstadt two years later. He approached various firms and institutions for funds to support experimentation on his new instrument, but without success.

The composer reappeared from oblivion in 1954, with a work called *Deserts*, for orchestra and prerecorded tape. What he created might not be music, Varese admitted, "it's organized sound." First performed in Paris, *Deserts* was simultaneously broadcast over French Radio. Its American premiere followed in 1955, the same year that RCA's sound synthesizer was installed at Princeton University. The work proved impressive, almost frightening. The use of piercingly high sounds and growling low ones, coupled with extreme rhythmic dislocation, make the piece exceedingly difficult to listen to, although its searing dissonance is intended to reflect the violence of contemporary life. While there were strong protests, Varese's ideas and music were shortly being discussed again all over Europe and the United States.

In 1955 and 1956 the musician created the electronically organized sound for the *Good Friday Procession in Verges* sequence of the film *Around and About Joan Miro* and began work on *Poeme Electronique* at the Philips Radio Laboratories in Holland. The latter was presented during the 1958 Brussels World's Fair in the pavilion designed for Philips by Le Corbusier. Over four hundred loudspeakers projected the electronically generated sound from every point inside the continually curving building. The composer chose several auditory images, each different in character but simultaneously heard coming and going in different directions. The sound was recorded on a three-track tape and lasted for about eight minutes, during which its images turned and collided in transilient spatial encounters. Meanwhile Le Corbusier's visual effects were being projected across the irregular concrete walls of the pavilion. "In the *Poeme*," Varese said, "I heard my music—literally in space—for the first time."

The new possibilities offered by electronics brought Varese back to composition, although he was little impressed by most of the electronic music of his day, feeling it did not make full use of its unique potential. As civilization began moving more and more toward automation, nature was increasingly being taken out of the hands of men. The complexity of men and things entered into new relationships. Yet for Varese, "working with electronic music is composing with living sounds, paradoxical though that may appear." He found the whole twelve-tone approach limiting, overly disciplined, especially in its adherence to the tempered scale and its rigid pitch organization. But he was devoted to the notion that experimentation by the serious musician should result in art. "My experimenting is done before I make the music," he said. "Afterwards, it is the listener who must experiment."

Varese was gradually being discovered all over the world, and in October, 1959, he confided to a friend, "I am working a lot." An all-Varese concert was conducted by Robert Craft at New York's Town Hall in 1961. The composer was an impressive man in later life, with a great shock of white hair and bushy eyebrows over a craggy face. Many found him difficult, crotchety, uncompromising. He worked on *Nocturnal* for soprano, chorus, and orchestra and a second version entitled *Nuit*. He received the first Kousevitsky International Award and heard a performance of *Deserts* at a regular subscription concert of the New York Philharmonic in 1964. He underwent surgery for the removal of an intestinal obstruction, but died on November 6, 1965, in the New York University Medical Center. He had requested that his body be cremated immediately, without ceremony, and that his ashes not be preserved. "Farewell, Varese," Pierre Boulez said in a tribute. "Your time is finished and now it begins."

Although Varese approached his music with a scientist's precision, he was an emotional man who wanted his music to produce an emotional effect. Few composers have torn at his listeners as cruelly as he does. He began his attempt to give music greater freedom by using sirens in several of his scores and even in the 1920s wanted his sound to move in space. He desired to produce music in which shifting planes of sound masses took the place of linear counterpoint. "There will no longer be the old conception of melody or interplay of melodies," he wrote. "The entire work will be a melodic tonality. The entire work will flow as a river flows." He was convinced that mid-twentieth-century man could not live much longer by tradition and insisted that it was not art's function to prove an aesthetic dogma. "The very basis of creative work is irreverence!" he insisted. Yet he built on the great music of the past. "No matter how original, how different a composer may seem," he said, "he has only grafted a little bit of himself on the old plant." He crusaded for new instruments, and eventually found his liberating medium in electronics. But again he argued, "Electronics is an additive, not a destructive factor in the art and science of music." He was among the first to write directly for instruments, rather than making a piano sketch and later orchestrating it. Far more revolutionary, however, was his fundamental view of music in terms of sonoric and rhythmic balance.

By the last years of his life, Edgard Varese was regarded by young composers the world over as one of the major figures in new music. In the years immediately after World War I, Leo Ornstein—twelve years Varese's junior—raced onto the American scene as the bad boy of contemporary music, then almost faded from view. Another immigrant, Ornstein was born in Krementchug, Russia, on December 11, 1895. He enrolled in the Conservatory at St. Petersburg in 1904, but after two years there moved with his family to the United States. Amid revolutions and pogroms the Ornsteins found Russia unsafe for Jews and settled on the lower East Side of New York City. Leo attended the Institute of Musical Art, already revealing a disregard for rules. He made his debut as a concert pianist in 1911 and played a concert tour in Europe three years later. Meanwhile he wrote some compositions in a new form and was shortly hailed as one of the forerunners of the modern music movement. "All that I am attempting to do," he explained to his teacher, "is to express myself as honestly and as convincingly as I can at present."

While he often played pieces like Chopin's *Nocturnes* and Liszt's *Liebestraum*, he composed things like his *Wild Man's Dance*, full of barbaric, chaotic sounds and nervous energy. Then came a *Dwarf Suite* and his *Impressions of Notre Dame*. In the years around 1917, when Ornstein stood practically alone in the United States, his music was performed often and discussed at length. After one recital, where the composer played some of his own selections, a critic wrote: "An imbecile child escaped from an asylum into a room where a piano happened to be, and thumping upon it with all his might could not have produced madder music." Another observer said the composer's Piano Sonata sounded like "four separate spasms of mental anguish, too great to be borne." Others found his music to have intense power and purpose. For Paul Rosenfeld, Ornstein was "a mirror held up to the world of the modern city."

The musician denied that he purposely set out to create peculiar sounds, claiming that his music was the spontaneous reflection of certain mental images that came to the surface of his mind. Charles Buchanan, writing for the *Musical Quarterly* in 1918, considered him the most salient musical phenomenon of that day. "He is a salience just as Billy Sunday is a salience," Buchanan held. "You may experience extremities of admiration or abhorrence for these gentlemen, but you cannot ignore them." Ornstein remained a public curiosity into the 1920s, then was overshadowed by Varese and others who went much further in their musical experimentation, often with greater creative power. Time gradually dulled the shattering impact of Ornstein's dissonances. His imagination seemed to exhaust itself. He taught piano for several years at the Philadelphia Musical Academy and in 1940 became director of the Ornstein School of Music. Later he was on the faculty of Temple University.

But Ornstein did pave the way over which more gifted experimentalists could travel. One to follow hard upon Ornstein's heels was Henry Cowell, who in mid-adolescence composed a series of unprecedented piano pieces, using tone-clusters played by fists and forearms. Other selections called for the player's hand to pluck or sweep the piano strings with the damper pedal down, while some instructed the player to depress the keys with one hand, while reaching over and performing directly on the strings with the other.

Cowell was a native Californian, born in Menlo Park on March 11, 1897, of Anglo-Irish stock. His parents believed in complete intellectual freedom for their son and encouraged his interests in music. At four he learned to play a mandolin-harp and later the violin. He played Mozart and Beethoven sonatas on a few recitals, but at eight was forced to give up the violin because of ill health. The boy then decided to become a composer, which he felt would be more interesting and less strenuous. At eleven he wrote part of an opera based on Longfellow's *Golden Legend*. He was extremely sensitive to the sounds around him—the noise of the sea, the clatter of trains, singing games of Oriental children, his father's Irish songs, dissonant speech intonations. The family was too poor to own a piano, but Henry began to "practice" mentally several hours a day. He worked odd jobs and in 1911 bought a secondhand upright. The piano fascinated him, and he explored it inside and out. By plucking the strings he found he could achieve a sound something like the violin; he could create an eerie, windlike effect by running his fingers lightly over the strings. And it was through such experimentation that he independently hit upon his tone-clusters, which he felt expressed anger and strong emotions. He knew nothing yet of Ives or the European moderns trying similar things.

When he was fifteen, Cowell performed some of his music at a concert for the San Francisco Music Club. In one of these pieces, "The Tides of Manaunaun," he introduced the tone-cluster idea. Arthur Lewis, of the San Francisco Symphony, was impressed, but felt the boy needed formal instruction. Lewis took him to Charles Seeger, head of the Music Department of the University of California at Berkeley, who recognized Cowell as a bright and unusual talent. Seeger trained the youth in harmony and counterpoint without forcing him into a conventional mold. Meanwhile the young musician continued to turn out his unorthodox compositions.

During 1917 he enlisted in the army, where he directed a band in Allentown, Pennsylvania. After his discharge the next year, he enrolled in the Institute of Musical Art in New York City. He found the school conventional and exasperating and eventually asked for his money back. He next studied at the Institute of Applied Music and had a few lessons with Carl Ruggles. He made his debut as a composer-pianist in Europe in 1923 and played his first Carnegie Hall concert a year later, again offering a number of his own works. His music set off such heated controversy that Cowell became one of the most discussed of the new American composers.

He wrote his First Symphony in 1918, but mainly concentrated during that period on piano works and chamber music. Between 1919 and 1931 he devoted himself increasingly to exploring new concepts of rhythm and dissonant chromaticism. He wrote *Synchrony* for large orchestra in 1929-30, as well as a Piano Concerto. The latter is a fiendishly difficult piece, with a finale of great rhythmic complexity. His book *New Musical Resources* was written in 1919, but was not published until 1929, after some revision. Cowell made five European concert tours and in the late 1920s an annual tour of the United States. He stirred up controversy on both continents. One English reviewer congratulated the makers of the piano which had withstood the onslaught of the composer's tone-clusters, while a New York critic referred to a Carnegie Hall concert as a bout between "Battling Cowell" and "Kid Knabe."

The composer established the *New Music Quarterly* in 1927, which shortly published works by Ives, Ruggles, Varese, Copland, Harris, Riegger, Antheil, and others. He received a Guggenheim fellowship in 1931, enabling him to study comparative musicology at the University of Berlin. He grew deeply interested in Oriental music and learned to play some Eastern instruments. He became fascinated by the folk songs of the Appalachians and made a trip to a gathering of shape-note gospel singers at White Top Mountain. He wrote *Rhythmicana* (1931), utilizing a new instrument he had constructed called a rhythmicon, capable of performing multiple rhythms. He composed an *Orchestral Set* in 1932, *Old American Country Set* five years later, and a Second Symphony in 1938.

Cowell married Sidney Hawkins Robertson, an authority on folk songs, in 1941 and two years after that was appointed chief music editor of the Office of War Information, in charge of selecting the music used on propaganda broadcasts to foreign countries. Yet throughout the heyday of the American Scene composers, Cowell insisted that nationalism in music "has no purpose as an aim in itself." His own output from the mid-1930s through the late 1940s concentrated on the reworking of modal musical materials, Eastern as well as Western. He was still producing a great many chamber pieces, wrote several choral selections, a Violin Sonata (1945), and a Third, Fourth, and Fifth symphonies (1942-1948).

The list of Cowell's compositions is endless. By 1960 there were fifteen symphonies alone. The quantity of his music is in part explained by the fact that the composer preferred to move on to a new work rather than make revisions on something already done. His interest in Oriental music continued, and he spent a year between 1956 and 1957 in Asia listening firsthand to the music of various Asian cultures. Cowell's inquiries into Oriental and American folk music, like his probing of acoustical and instrumental resources, were undertaken to find intellectual justification for procedures he had begun to incorporate into his writing instinctively. He was looking for no personal style and was content to learn as he went along. The expansion of his vision continued through his entire life, for he once declared that he wanted "to live in the *whole world* of music!" The composer died at his home in Shady, New York, on December 10, 1965. He was working on his twentieth symphony at the time of his death.

Although the music of Henry Cowell would ultimately prove more significant and influential, the most scandalous American composer of the 1920s was George Antheil, the undisputed *enfant terrible* of that decade. Like

Leo Ornstein, Antheil would eventually become more traditional, but the Carnegie Hall performance of his *Ballet Mechanique* in 1927—using an airplane propeller, buzz saws, horns, and other mechanical sounds—set off an explosion in the world of serious music and brought snorts of laughter from a public that misunderstood the composer's whole intent. The piece was talked about as the ultimate in iconoclastic music.

Antheil was of German-Polish ancestry, mostly Polish. He was born in Trenton, New Jersey, on July 8, 1900. A year or so after George's birth, his parents moved across the street from the Trenton State Penitentiary. One of his first childhood memories was of looking out the front window to the brown wall and guard tower a few feet away. His first recollection of music came when two old maids moved in next door and proceeded to play the piano in shifts night and day. They played parlor melodies like "The Maiden's Prayer," "The Midnight Fire Alarm," and "Star of the Sea," to the growing disgust of George's parents. Then one night the playing stopped; the next morning the old maids were gone. So were sixteen prisoners from across the street! The incessant piano playing, it seems, had been a cover for the grating, crunching sounds of digging a tunnel from the cellar of the house next door to the prison yard.

The family moved again when Antheil was about five. By then he had begun studying the violin and the piano. When he was twelve, he invited his friends in to hear a piano "sonata" he had written, called "The Sinking of the Titanic." "It was a very stormy piece," the composer remembered, "with great rolling chords in the bass and a touching version of 'Nearer My God to Thee' as a grand finale." George eventually studied the piano in Philadelphia with Constantine von Sternberg, a pupil of Liszt, and later composition in New York with Ernest Bloch. At a Philadelphia Orchestra concert Antheil heard Stravinsky's *Petrushka*, which revolutionized his previous musical ideas. Under Bloch's guidance he wrote his First Symphony in 1920. "I wanted the symphony to express that part of America which I saw all around me," he said: "Trenton, the Delaware River, the people I knew, the sounds and emotions I felt."

He improved his piano playing and in 1922 went on a tour of Europe as a concert artist, making his debut in London. He was one of the few pianists of that period to end his concerts with a modern group, often a piece or two of his own. He delighted in the cacophonous works of Stravinsky, Schoenberg, Honegger, and Orstein and became the darling of the avant-garde. He played his first concert in Paris on October 4, 1923, almost causing a riot. Shortly he came to represent the antiromantic, antiexpressive, mechanistic aesthetic of the early twenties. "When I first went to Paris I was jealous of Antheil's piano playing," Aaron Copland confessed—"it was so brilliant; he could demonstrate so well what he wanted to do." Gradually Antheil lost interest in the concert field, as he became more and more smitten with composition. Shorter works like *Mechanisms, Sonata Sauvage*, and the *Jazz* Sonata were heard in Paris, and he shortly added an *Airplane* Sonata. "Concords or discords did not exist for me," he insisted; "I used one or the other with perhaps more brutality than people were then accustomed to, but I never used them...unless I needed just them, nothing else."

The Berlin Philharmonic performed Antheil's First Symphony. "I almost fainted with sheerest joy," he said, yet critics were hostile. He met Stravinsky in Berlin, but made Paris his home. He was very much the young man in a hurry. He played some of his compositions for Boulanger, made the acquaintance of Virgil Thomson, and in 1925 married Boski Markus. He had come to consider machines very beautiful and advised innovative artists to take a good look at them. His First String Quartet was given a salon performance in 1926 at the home of a French millionaire. Later that season *Ballet Mecanique* was heard in Paris, where it was largely a success, especially among the younger generation. The work was meant to be a warning of the simultaneous strength and danger of the contemporary world's growing mechanistic philosophy. The piece suggested a dream and was not intended to have anything to do with an actual description of factories or machinery. "As I saw it," Antheil wrote, "my *Ballet Mechanique*...was streamlined, glistening, cold, often as 'musically silent' as interplanetary space, and also often as hot as an electric furnace, but always *attempting* at least to operate on new principles of construction beyond the normal fixed...boundaries."

The piece was heard at Carnegie Hall the next year, in a greatly distorted context. Against the composer's wishes, the number of pianos used in the composition was doubled. Then to add to the visual effect, a real propeller was brought on stage at the last moment, and a propeller-sound machine was used behind it. A gigantic, tasteless curtain was hung against the back wall, giving the concert an air of complete charlatanism. The publicity surrounding the event was of the most sensational sort. On the morning of the performance, April 10, 1927, a cartoon appeared on the front page of one New York newspaper, showing a group of men in evening dress digging up a street with automatic picks and steam shovels, with a conductor directing them. At the concert itself Eugene Goossens led the orchestra in the best reading he could, but the handicaps were too great. The next day's headlines announced: "Forty million Frenchmen CAN be wrong!" The public considered the *Ballet Mecanique* brutal, hard-boiled, symbolic of the spiritual exhaustion that followed World War I. Antheil, who had come over for the occasion, returned to Paris heartsick and financially exhausted. "Nobody knows better than I," he later said, "what a fickle and all-demanding bitch Fame is."

With the *Ballet Mecanique* the composer felt he had said everything he had to say in this "dreamlike, ultraviolet-light medium." He ultimately considered the piece youthful, although by no means a mad prank. But the public persistently linked him solely with this one selection, until it frankly became his nightmare. *Transatlantic*, an opera centering around an American election, was finished in 1930 and staged that May by the German State Opera of Frankfurt. The work proved uneven, employed a jazz idiom, and contains probably the only operatic aria ever written which a lady sings in a bathtub. The premiere audience, however, received the production warmly, giving it twenty curtain calls.

Antheil lived in Germany from 1928 to 1933, when he went back to Paris. He found the city "as madly gay as the Riviera," while the Cafe du Dome was filled with German refugee artists. He returned to the United States on borrowed money, settling for a time in New York City. *Helen Retires*, his second opera, was given at the Juilliard School of Music early in 1934, but was a gigantic failure. The composer did a ballet for George Balanchine, then moved to Hollywood, where he wrote several movie scores. He and his wife bought a home at the upper end of Laurel Canyon shortly before their son Peter was born. In 1936 Boris Morros, music director of Paramount Studios, assigned Antheil to write the music for Cecil B. DeMille's picture *The Plainsmen*. The musician also worked on *The Buccaneer*, but was taken off a third DeMille film, the epic *Union Pacific*. Antheil later produced scores for *The Specter of the Rose*, *That Brennan Girl*, *The Plainsman and the Lady*, *Knock on Any Door*, *We Were Strangers*, and *Sirocco*.

Meanwhile he continued writing more serious compositions, although he found working on movie music all day and doing his own composing at night extremely difficult. "Symphonic writing is just too organic a process," he explained. A Fourth Symphony was completed in 1943, conducted by Stokowski over NBC radio a year later. Into this work, Antheil said, "had gone El Alamein, Stalingrad, *and* the *new* America I saw awakening. The feeling of it. You *can* put these big abstractions into music." A Fifth Symphony followed in 1945 and a Violin Concerto in 1947. The next season Pierre Monteux and the San Francisco Orchestra introduced the composer's Sixth Symphony. *Tom Sawyer, A Mark Twain Overture* appeared in 1950, along with a third opera, *Volpone*. There was also a great deal of chamber music, a song-cycle after William Blake, and *Eight Fragments from Shelley* for chorus. In addition the composer wrote several magazine articles and for a time a syndicated column for the lovelorn.

Gradually the "bad boy" who had once been so shocking with his "modernism-gone-berserk" simmered down to a fairly conventional frame of mind. "As I grow older," he confessed, "I find myself more and more finding my true musical happiness in the works of the great masters of the past— particularly Beethoven." He admitted that at heart he was probably a classicist, whereas *Ballet Mechanique* was "essentially a *romantic* work, breaking all the barriers, the rules, and thriving upon it." Yet after two decades even the *Ballet Mecanique* sounded less noisy, almost old-fashioned. "I've gone through many things," Antheil eventually said, "but now I know that there is only one thing that counts: to continue the great art of music. It must follow along the grand line." The notion of an "American school" of music, he considered, "the most unadulterated vicious nonsense." The composer died in New York on February 12, 1959. His cantata *Cabeza de Vaca* was posthumously performed over the CBS television network three years later. The work has color and warmth, along with melodic simplicity and directness.

Ballet Mecanique appeared at a time when the world of art was discovering machines, factories, and the staggering implications of the industrial complex. It was a time of questioning for intellectuals and aesthetics and a time for exploring new ways. While some experimentation continued into the 1930s, it was eclipsed by the fixation with the American scene and a tendency for artists to aim at communicating with a broad public through more traditional means. Yet the ground for a later revolution in music was being prepared during the Depression and war years by Varese and others and by the arrival of a number of the advanced guard from Europe. Arnold Schoenberg fled Berlin in 1933, arriving in the United States on the last day of October. He taught one year at the University of Southern California, but in the fall of 1936 was appointed Professor of Music by the University of California at Los Angeles, where his impact was tremendous. Schoenberg became an American citizen in 1941 and remained at UCLA until his retirement in 1944. Paul Hindemith came to the United States in 1937; Ernst Krenek returned to stay a year later. And there were others—Stravinsky, Milhaud, Martinu, Stefan Wolpe.

With the end of World War II, American music entered another period of rapid development and progressivism. By 1950 novelty had again come to the fore, while multiple-row and electronic composition represented the new left. As in the years after World War I, the experimentation of the 1950s and 1960s was sparked by a growing intellectual alienation and aided by a rising prosperity. Increased patronage from large industrial and philanthropic foundations invigorated the movement, most notably the Rockefeller and Ford Foundations. One group of innovators attempted to build a new musical structure based upon the tone-row; another was convinced Western music had not progressed far enough in breaking down the old tonal system. John Cage, the most discussed of the new avant-garde composers belongs to the latter.

Beginning in the late 1930s with his experiments with the "prepared piano." Cage ushered a neo-dadaism into American music. Like his European precursors a generation before, Cage's aim seems to be mainly destructive. Like Jackson Pollock's paintings, the composer's work is abstract, although there is more of Pollock in his art than there is of Cage in his. Cage insists that music must not be separated from life, yet stresses the irrationality of a tumultuous world—a world to which he has nothing to say, no message to give, since none is relevant. The world cannot be improved, he insists, and the reformer who tries will only make matters worse. Meaning for him exists only in expression and sound. Yet whereas Varese turned noise into music, one critic observed, "Cage turns music into noise."

Born in Los Angeles, September 5, 1912, Cage was strongly influenced by Varese and studied composition with both Schoenberg and Cowell. His father, who came to California from Tennessee, was an inventor—not a rich one, for he lacked business sense. John, an only child, learned to play the piano, but later admitted, "I wasn't very gifted....I disliked the technical exercises and all the physical aspects." He was lanky, had red hair and skin that freckled; he was both an activist and a thinker. He graduated valedictorian of his high school senior class and entered nearby Pomona College. Disgusted with what he considered the stifling of individual curiosity, he dropped out of school and traveled through Europe for a year and a half. He was interested in poetry, painting, and architecture, but music gradually became his great love. Cage returned to Los Angeles, studied briefly with Cowell, then convinced Arnold Schoenberg to give him free lessons. Later he attended Schoenberg's courses at USC and UCLA, supplementing his income by lecturing on contemporary music to neighborhood housewives. "Schoenberg was a magnificent teacher," Cage said, "who always gave the impression that he was putting us in touch with the musical principles." Eventually the youth rejected the European's serial techniques as too rigorous an approach to the organization of sounds. In Schoenberg's opinion, Cage was "not a composer, but an inventor—of genius."

The young musician had spent 1933-34 in New York City, where he studied with Adolf Weiss. He played bridge occasionally with Henry Cowell, talked a great deal about modern music, and spent at least four hours a day composing. Through Varese he became aware of the possibilities of percussion and at UCLA got interested in modern dance, composing a number of percussion pieces for a dance group there. Already he was experimenting with new sounds. He married Xenia Andreevna Kashevaroff, an art student, and in 1937 moved to Seattle, where he accepted a job as composer-accompanist for dance classes at the Cornish School, a progressive school of the arts. A student asked him to write the music for a *Bacchanale* of hers, and Cage responded to the request by inventing a whole new instrument, the prepared piano. It marked the turning point in his career. By placing a bolt or a large wood screw between two strings of a piano, every aspect of the sound was changed. "I soon had a whole new gamut of sounds," he said. "The piano had become, in effect, a percussion orchestra under the control of a single player."

Composer Lou Harrison arranged for Cage to work with the summer dance program at Mills College in Oakland, California, and the musician later taught at the School of Design in Chicago. He returned to New York in the early 1940s, quickly establishing himself as the most discussed young composer of the avant-garde. A concert at the Museum of Modern Art in February, 1943, thrust Cage into the midst of controversy, but won for him a number of influential friends, one of whom was Virgil Thomson. "Mr. Cage has carried Schoenberg's twelve-tone harmonic maneuvers to their logical conclusion," Thomson wrote after a prepared piano recital at the New School for Social Research. The composer made his living primarily by writing music for modern dancers, particularly Merce Cunningham, and by doing library research for his father. The elder Cage had moved to New Jersey during the war and was engaged in a top secret experiment for the government. Because of his assistance on the project, John was deferred from military service.

Cage became deeply interested in Zen Buddhism after hearing a lecture on Oriental religion at Columbia University later in the 1940s. He was especially impressed with the notion that there is music around us all the time, part of the Zen concept of perpetual reality. He began to study the wisdom of the Orient and the ideas behind Indian music. He grew convinced that art goes beyond individual self-expression and concluded that the purpose of music is to sober and quiet the mind. The composer felt that the musical ideas he was developing were more related to modern painting than to anything else, although he continued to work with dance companies.

He came upon Zen Buddhism during a time of severe stress in his personal life. He and his wife separated in 1945, whereupon Cage went to live on the top floor of a tenement building on the lower East Side. He had developed uncertainties about his ability to express himself musically. He tried psychiatry, but found more answers in Zen. "I had the impression that I was changing—you might say growing up," Cage said after two years exposure to Oriental philosophy. "I realized that my previous understanding was that of a child." He immersed himself in a long work for prepared piano—sixteen sonatas and four interludes, strongly influenced by the music of India and employing ragas and talas. The composer's aim was to express the various "permanent emotions" of East Indian tradition. Again the piano was "prepared" by inserting nuts, bolts, screws, hairpins, and bits of wood, rubber, or metal between the strings. The Sonatas and Interludes were performed at Carnegie Recital Hall by Maro Ajemian in 1949 and were received with occasional laughter, a few catcalls, but much applause.

Cage was now the center of much attention for his novel combinations of percussion instruments (like ox bells, tin cans, flower pots, automobile brake drums, electric buzzers, tubs of water, and anvils) as well as his compositions for prepared piano. One critic said that the last part of the musician's *The Perilous Night* sounded like "a woodpecker in a church belfry." Virgil Thomson reviewing a concert for two prepared pianos, spoke of the "gamut of pings, plunks, and delicate thuds," yet found these "both varied and expressive." Percussion music, Cage argued later, is "a contemporary transition from keyboard-influenced music to the all-sound music of the future." The composer actually feels the word "music" should be reserved for eighteenth- and nineteenth-century instruments; he prefers the term "organization of sound," which he claims is more meaningful. "A single sound by itself is neither musical nor not musical," he said. "It is simply a sound. And no matter what kind of a sound it is, it can become musical by taking its place in a piece of music." Eventually Cage favored abandoning all vestiges of control, no structure save what could be achieved through rhythm.

As early as 1937 Cage had declared: "I believe that the use of noise to make music will continue and increase until we reach a music produced through the aid of electrical instruments which will make available for musical purposes all the sounds that can be heard." Two years later he wrote the first of his *Imaginary Landscapes*, his initial attempt at electronic music.

Imaginary Landscape No. 2 (1942) combines percussion instruments, buzzers, and an amplified coil of wire, while *Imaginary Landscape No. 3* (later in 1942) combines percussion with audio-frequency oscillators, a buzzer, variable speed turntables, and variable frequency recordings—all of which was intended to suggest war and devastation.

Influenced by the *I Ching* or *Book of Changes*, the most ancient book of China, which had just been published in English translation, Cage sketched out the procedure for his *Music of Changes*. Notation for the piano piece was based on chance operations, while pitch, duration, and timbre were determined by tossing three coins six times. Since the selection lasts forty-three minutes, the number of coin tosses required was astronomical. Cage worked on the piece steadily for nine months. It was first heard at the Cherry Lane Theater in New York during the winter of 1952. In Cage's hands, Virgil Thomson wrote, "the use of chance in composition gives a result not unlike that of a kaleidoscope...all the patterns turn out to be interesting."

His *Imaginary Landscape No. 4* employed twelve portable radios, while his musical materials consisted of any sound picked up by turning the dials, including static and silence. Each radio was to be "played" by two performers—one working the volume and tone controls, the other the station selector. The process was "like fishermen catching sounds," Cage maintained. Only the wave lengths to be tuned in at a particular moment are indicated in the score. A conductor holds things together, yet clearly no two performances were intended to be the same. Much of the burden of structuring the piece is shifted to the audience, each person organizing the experience differently, according to his own consciousness. The first performance of the piece took place much later at night than had been planned, so that some stations had gone off the air. While many critics enjoyed a good laugh at a performance gone wrong, Cage insisted the "failure" was all part of his doctrine of music by chance. *Imaginary Landscape No. 5* (1952) was the composer's first score on tape. The work was made by fragmenting the sound of forty-three jazz records and rerecording the fragments on tape at random.

From *Music of Changes* onward Cage has become more and more concerned with silence. One of his most revolutionary pieces is *4' 33"* (1953), in which the pianist seats himself at the piano with a stopwatch nearby and, except for three motions with his hands to open and close the keyboard lid, simply sits there quietly for four minutes and thirty-three seconds. Cage's musical material in this case consists of all the sounds that are audible in the concert hall during that period. Since the audience makes most of the accidental noises, the spectators may be counted among the performers. The piece consists strictly of "nonintentional music." The implication is that anything is possible in art, including nothing at all. "I have nothing to say," Cage contends, "and I am saying it and that is poetry." The most agreeable art for the composer is not just like life, it *is* life.

Cage's Piano Concert (1958) consists of a piano part whose elements may be played in any order desired. In addition there is an orchestral part which may be realized by any number of players on any combination of instruments, including none. The performers play from pages of which any number may be used, including none. Again it is possible that the performance could result in complete silence. The composer explains that his "intention is to hold together disparities much as one finds them held together in the natural world—in a forest or a city street." Aria with Fontana Mix (also 1958), like several of Cage's more recent works, is notated on graphs and leaves many aspects of the performance undetermined. While a number of critics found the Aria laughable, others said it was drably depressing. Richard Franko Goldman labeled the Fontana Mix "truly intolerable, a scrap heap of taped sounds, with gurgles and grunts."

The composer has been greatly impressed with existentialism, but prefers living its principles to spinning existential theories. He is fond of solitary walks through the woods and has made an extensive study of mushrooms. Mystic, intelligent, and highly sensitive, Cage at the same time is a practical craftsman. As a young man, he could be stubborn and argumentative, frequently prone to silence and preoccupation with his own development. His acceptance of Zen Buddhism seemed to bring happiness, tranquility, and peace of mind. In social situations he became the man with the outgoing smile, joking easily and exuding youthful optimism. "Around him everyone laughs," Peter Yates observed. The musician has traveled extensively, made several trips to Europe, but lives alone in a small cottage in an artists' community about an hour north of New York City. He is remarkably well read, smokes cigarettes through a filter, drinks nothing stronger than wine, and objects to drugs on moral grounds. He thinks of himself as music's corrective, dissolving the whole of Renaissance and post-Renaissance tradition, and has been exceptionally articulate in elaborating these thoughts.

Cage taught at the New School for Social Research during the years from 1956 to 1958 and had already begun to father an avant-garde school of American composers, headed by Earle Brown, Morton Feldman, and Christian Wolff. His own work by then was becoming more valid as theatrical spectacle than as purely aural experience. Theatre Piece (1960) offers a set of eight parts for from one to eight musicians, dancers, and mimes, any of which may be used. Within a given time space, the performers are free to do what they please, although the composer makes suggestions. "I wanted to leave the performer free," Cage maintained. "I didn't want him to get involved in a situation that he wasn't willing to carry through." He began some pieces called Variations in 1958 and around 1960 began using contact microphones to amplify the sound made on any object to which they were attached. At one concert Cage even put a lavalier microphone around his neck, turned the volume up all the way, and drank a glass of water.

Atlas Eclipticalis for full orchestra was composed in 1962 by transferring the patterns of stars from an atlas to sheets of music paper. The work was performed by the New York Philharmonic under the direction of Leonard Bernstein two years later, much to the disgust of Philharmonic subscribers. Many of the composer's later pieces have moved out of the field of time altogether and into space. "It doesn't matter what sounds are coming up," Cage contends. "What's interesting is where they come from." In 1967 he began working with the University of Illinois on a four-and-one-half hour composition involving fifty-two tape machines, fifty-nine power amplifiers, fifty-nine loudspeakers, two-hundred eight computer-generated tapes, and seven harpsichords played by hand. Called *HPSCHD*, a six-letter version of the word *harpsichord* suited to computer programming, the work was produced in the University's 18,000-seat Assembly Hall on May 16, 1969. Visual effects were supplied by sixty-four slide projectors showing 6400 slides and eight moving picture projectors using forty films.

In his effort to achieve "indeterminate music," Cage has sometimes splattered a manuscript page with ink, although he prefers to use tables of random numbers in selecting musical elements such as notes. He has also employed the technique of taking a piece of music written on a number of pages and instructing the musician to drop the pages before the performance, so that the sequence of the pages played cannot be predicted. The composer acknowledges his debt to Varese and Ives and suggests that Cowell more than anyone else led to his experiments with the prepared piano. He has increasingly come to rely upon electronic music, claiming that his purpose is "to spread joy and revolution." For Cage the aim of music is neither entertainment, communication, nor the expression of the artist's ideas, but to help men and women attain a keener awareness of their own lives. "Everything we do is music," the composer repeats, yet he insists that the world is changing faster than most people realize. "One must be disinterested," he advises a displaced society, "accept that a sound is a sound and a man is a man, give up illusions about ideas of order, expressions of sentiment, and all the rest of our inherited aesthetic claptrap."

Few figures on the contemporary music scene have been so perennially controversial as John Cage. He has repeatedly been charged with being an incompetent and a fraud. Many have complained that his music relegates the composer to the role of page turner, yet others assert that he has "emancipated music from its notes." Some have found his experiments too burdened with theatrical effect for the intrinsic interest of his innovations to become fully apparent. Most would agree that the composer has created an atmosphere of spontaneity in his work more often associated with popular music and jazz. Aside from Jackson Pollock, Cage has most frequently been compared with sculptor Alexander Calder, although he is sympathetic with the ideas of Marshall McLuhan and has recently become greatly influenced by Henry David Thoreau. How one reacts to Cage's sounds is largely dependent upon one's personal temperament. "Those who envisage art as a bulwark against the irrationality of man's nature, and as a monument to his constructive powers," Copland concludes, "will have no part of the Cagean aesthetic. But those who enjoy teetering on the edge of chaos will clearly be attracted." The composer himself sees his position as profoundly humanistic—aimed at freeing man from the artificial barriers that entangle him. Until these barriers are destroyed, Cage remains convinced, the individual is incapable of experiencing life with reawakened sensitivity.

By the early 1950s the musician was forsaking works for the prepared piano and concentrating on chance procedures, patterned after everyday life. For Cage the use of random choices in writing music was a device that led out of the labyrinth of complexity presented by ordered multiple-row composition. Milton Babbitt, on the other hand, emerged as a strict and uncompromising twelve-tone writer, preferring to organize every aspect of his work. Babbitt stands as the apostle of total rationality; Cage is far more the antirationalist, consciously rejecting consciousness. If Cage has much in common with the abstract expressionists in painting, Babbitt is closer to the geometric abstractionists, who minutely delineate and control.

Four years younger than Cage, Milton Babbitt was born in Philadelphia on May 10, 1916, but was raised in Jackson, Mississippi. He displayed an aptitude for both mathematics and music and studied a great deal of logic as an undergraduate at New York University. He played the violin as a boy, but eventually specialized in reeds. He started composing at the age of ten and briefly performed in a jazz orchestra. He won a national popular song contest and, as a high school student, did some work for Harms. Babbitt claims to remember every popular song hit between 1925 and 1935 and continued to write commercial numbers himself until into the 1940s. At sixteen he saw his first Schoenberg score, which helped turn his interest to serious composition. He studied for a time with Roger Sessions at Princeton and in 1938 became an instructor there, teaching mathematics as well as music. Although twelve-tone writing was then an object of scorn, opposed even by the free-thinking Sessions, Babbitt decided to make the serial language his own.

Perhaps because of his mathematical training, the young composer saw in twelve-tone music not just a method, but a real system. For him the pitch row was not merely a series, but an ordered set in the true mathematical sense. By 1948 he had completed Three Compositions for Piano, Composition for Four Instruments, and Composition for Twelve Instruments. In the latter the musician integrated the pitch and durational components of the piece by deriving a durational set from the pitch set. His goal was to extend the serial techniques to all the fixed elements of a musical composition—rhythm, timbre, dynamics, instrumentation, as well as pitch. For Babbitt, Eric Salzman contends, "the twelve-tone material represents the totality of possible relationships inherent in every aspect of the musical material, and the actual unfolding of each piece is a process of permutation within which all these potential relationships are revealed."

It was this concept of "total serialization" that first won Babbitt wide recognition. He expanded Schoenberg's principles of order, writing twelve-tone music of unprecedented complexity. He sought to produce compositions that were "profoundly organized" and "structurally intricate." His works are intense, rich in multiplicity, brimming over with interweaving activity. "I want a piece of music to be *literally* as much as possible," Babbitt once stated. His compositions have been compared with James Joyce's *Finnegans Wake*, in which several stories are told at once, and the early films of Orson Welles, in which, the musician explains, "each event has many perceptual dimensions."

By the end of the 1950s Babbitt was working with the RCA Electronic Sound Synthesizer at the recently organized Columbia-Princeton Electronic Music Center. Dissatisfied with what happened to his pieces when played on ordinary instruments, he began experimenting with electronics, hoping to achieve precisely all the complicated effects he desired in a permanent form. His first electronic works include Composition for Synthesizer and Ensembles for Synthesizer, both composed directly on the RCA Mark 11 Synthesizer. His *Vision and Prayer* (1961), a setting of a Dylan Thomas text, was written for soprano and synthesized accompaniment.

The composer has continued to teach at Princeton, commuting each week from his apartment in New York, and in 1961 was appointed a director of the Electronic Music Center. He brings to music a scholarly, analytic, probing attitude more normally associated with pure science. He likes students, keeps in touch with many of them after they graduate and, despite his cerebral approach, is an extremely popular lecturer. His campus office is decorated with a Mondrian print and some enlarged *Peanuts* cartoons. He and his wife rarely travel to Europe, and Babbitt advises his students to go there for the food rather than for musical training. Although the composer feels no necessity of communicating with the layman, his ideas have exerted a tremendous influence upon younger musicians. Advanced music is no more comprehensible to the average man, Babbitt affirms, than advanced theories of astrophysics. Yet the composer's first obligation is to his art and the evolution of new concepts. "If not for Schoenberg," Babbitt confesses, "I would have gone into mathematics. Schoenberg hit upon a technique that made composition more interesting and challenging."

Philomel (1964) exploits the synthesizer's ability to produce unprecedented sounds. In the Greek legend of Philomel the maiden was ravished and her tongue torn out; then, through the mercy of the gods, she was turned into a nightingale. Babbitt's piece employs a live voice in combination with transformed recordings of that same voice. The result is stunning. The language becomes a form of musical expression, while the music is precise, almost articulate. The composer regards the synthesizer as a supplement to traditional instruments, however, rather than a replacement and has continued to write pieces like *Relata I* (1965) and *Relata II* (1968) for live orchestra. But he remains enthusiastic about the possibilities of electronic music: "I love going to the studio with my work in my head, realizing it while I am there, and walking out with the tape under my arm. I can then send it anywhere in the world, knowing exactly how it will sound."

Babbitt has become the recognized leader of the academic avant-garde, highly critical of the state of serious modern music in the United States. Whereas Cage emphasizes the unpredictable and the emotional experience, Babbitt's work is self-contained and ferociously intellectualized. Cage, the mystic, stands for unrestrained freedom; Babbitt, the positivist, stands for logic and order. Edgard Varese found Cage's approach too accidental, almost making the composer unnecessary. Babbitt he admired and respected, although Varese recognized that the younger musician's view of electronic music was very different from his own. "It seems to me that he wants to exercise maximum control over certain materials," Varese said, "as if he were *above* them. But I want to be *in* the material, part of the acoustical vibration, so to speak."

In Milton Babbitt's music the network of interlocked components are inseparable; they *become* the music. It is no longer meaningful to hear one, or speak of one, separate from the other. Ben Weber, another significant twelve-tone writer, stays much closer to the methods of Schoenberg. Weber does not, however, rigidly adhere to the tone row principle and often relies on intuition. "I feel that people respond more readily to intuitive things," he says. The composer admits to having something of a romantic temperament and, therefore, tends to use the tone row melodically. His rhythms are determined by his melody. For Babbitt the row is never a thematic thing; it is purely structural.

Born in St. Louis, Missouri, July 23, 1916, Weber was educated at the University of Illinois and DePaul University in Chicago. Bored by the routine of traditional music education, he explored atonality largely on his own and independently developed a serial technique characterized by such devices as recurring themes. The composer's originality, however, was less technical and conceptual than emotional and perceptual. His first pieces clearly took their departure from Schoenberg, but gradually moved toward a vocabulary allowing for more variety of texture and greater expansion of thought and passion. He moved to New York in 1945, where he devoted much of his time to composing. Most of his works are for chamber combinations, including two sonatas for violin and piano, two string quartets, and a Concertino for Violin, Clarinet, and Cello. A *Symphony in Four Movements on Poems of William Blake* (1952) for baritone and chamber orchestra is expressionistic and dramatic. The *Sonata da Camera* for violin and piano, one of Weber's most distinctive and moving pieces, is based on a tone-row throughout, yet allows for digressions and irregularities. The effect, however, is one. *Chamber Fantasia* was first played in New York in 1959, while Three Songs for soprano and string quartet was heard in 1962. Among the composer's relatively few works for large orchestra are a Concerto for Violin and Orchestra (1954), a Prelude and Passacaglia (1955), and a Piano Concerto (1960), written in memory of Dmitri Mitropoulos.

Although he has won an audience for his music slowly, Weber writes as directly as possible and consistently comes up with a poetic tone and a serious emotional comment. "Probably the process of introspection which governs most of my personal existence," he told Lou Harrison, "is very closely related to the impulses of perception which prompt me to write music." He rarely enjoys the act of composing itself, but writes "in order to accomplish emotional comfort."

Irving Fine also experimented with a serial method in several of his later works, but in his early pieces was much more influenced by Stravinsky and Hindemith. Born in Boston, December 3, 1914, Fine studied with both Walter Piston and Nadia Boulanger. Later he wrote in a highly rhythmic, contrapuntal manner that is quite melodious. Fine served on the faculty of the Berkshire Music Center at Tanglewood, taught at Harvard, and was composer-in-residence and chairman of the School of Creative Arts at Brandeis. His compositions include *The Choral New Yorker* (1944), a Violin Sonata (1946), a String Quartet (1950), *Serious Song* (1956), and a Symphony (1962), written for the Boston Symphony Orchestra under a Ford Foundation grant.

Lou Harrison stands roughly midway between Cage and Varese, interested both in quasi-Oriental sounds and in exploring the resources of pure percussion. His music has ranged from the reasonably conservative to the polytonal and atonal. Born on May 14, 1917, in Portland, Oregon, Harrison studied with Cowell and Schoenberg and has taught at Mills College, the University of California in Los Angeles, and Black Mountain College in North Carolina. He has been concerned with esoteric sonorities and in dividing the scale into intervals smaller than the semitone. His Canticle No. 3 is scored for percussion ensemble including six muted iron pipes, three wood blocks, five muted brake drums, and an ocarina tuned in quarter-tones. Concerto, for violin and percussion orchestra, calls for a double bass struck like a drum, flower pots, and several washtubs. Unlike most percussion composers, Harrison does not use noise unmelodiously for its own sake. He has also written a Mass for unison chorus, a Symphony in G, *Four Strict Songs* for eight baritones and orchestra, a Suite entitled *Seven Pastorales, Simfony in Free Style, Song of Quextecoatl* for percussion orchestra, and a short opera, *Rapunzel*, to a text by William Morris. *Pacifika Rondo* and *Nova Odo* both employ Oriental instruments, although Harrison has never envisioned Orientalism as a substitute for the Western tradition.

Other recent composers, like Harry Partch, have attempted an entirely independent musical system. Born in Oakland, California, in 1901, Partch was reared in Arizona. He developed his own theory of music, invented his own method of notation, and designed his own instruments. The composer's musical system divides the octave into forty-three tones, instead of the twelve of the tempered scale. Partch has also explored a concept of integrating music and speech in a new kind of musical theater, based on microtonal inflections of the vocal line.

Although forwardlooking musicians were becoming aware of the possibilities of electronics by the 1930s, electronic music and taperecorder music have developed considerably in the years since World War II. Otto Luening and Vladimir Ussachevsky, both professors at Columbia, began systematic work in tape music composition and in the fall of 1952 presented probably the first American tape music concert at the Museum of Modern Art in New York. Two years later the musicians produced *Rhapsodic Variations*, a work for tape recorder and symphony orchestra commissioned by the Louisville Orchestra. The RCA Electronic Sound Synthesizer was installed in the Columbia-Princeton laboratory in July, 1959, under the direction of Luening, Ussachevsky, Babbitt, and Sessions. Among the younger composers who have worked at the Columbia studio are Mario Davidovsky (born in 1934), an Argentinian now residing in the United States, and the former jazz pianist Mel Powell (born in 1923), later director of the Yale University electronic studio.

Related to electronic and tape recorder music is computer music, in which an electronic computer is programmed to generate music or material that can be transcribed into musical notation. The first serious attempts at computer composition were carried out by two composer-mathematicians at the University of Illinois, Lejaren Hiller and Leonard Isaacson. Their initial product appeared in 1956, a four-movement *Illiac Suite* for string quartet. A more sophisticated *Computer* Cantata—written with Robert Baker, for voice, instruments, and electronic tape—followed in 1963.

Post-World War II America has seen an extraordinary amount of musical activity along widely diverging lines. For many younger composers especially, the barriers were down, the old categories destroyed. Artists have felt free enough and adventuresome enough to go their own way, much as their counterparts in the 1920s did. Dissonance has gradually become accepted by the educated public, except for the most reactionary. By the 1960s a movement away from strict twelve-tone writing was already in evidence. Serialism was becoming academic, as composers began exploiting atonality by a great variety of methods and means, much of which puts unprecedented demands on performers. A great deal of the new music results in effects in space more than in time. Many advanced composers speak of "densities," "sound structures," or "sound objects," rather than "sonorities." Imaginative works by Roger Reynolds, like *The Emperor of Ice Cream* (1963) and *Blind Men* (1966), not only designate the spatial distribution of the performers, but indicate their movements from one area to another as well. And yet this new, expressionistic, asymmetrical architecture of sound in time and space is not without precedent in the modern American musical tradition, for ultimately it is related to the ideas of Ives and Carter and Cage and, most certainly, Edgard Varese.

CHAPTER

IX

FROM MUSICAL COMEDY

TO MUSICAL DRAMA

For the American musical stage the 1920s was a decade of luxury, a time when Broadway theaters were deluged with an array of shows. Since the prestige of foreign operettas was on the decline, the demands on native talent were greater than ever before. Writers of established reputations were incapable of meeting the annual need for material, so that promising young artists were given a hearing by producers. Not all of this proliferation was good, for the easy money of the middle 1920s resulted in a glut of productions that were ephemeral and tasteless. Even in the better shows little more was needed than popular stars, attractive melodies, spirited dancing, and eye-filling scenery and costumes. Contrived plots were seldom more than an excuse for offering songs, dance routines, and the speciality of performers. Characters were two-dimensional stereotypes, unrelated to everyday life. The purpose was exclusively to entertain, the formula nearly invariable. A chorus opened and closed each act, while songs and dances were interpolated at certain points in the story, with no particular regard for the stage situation. The comedian was essential to keeping things moving, but his humor remained closely patterned after vaudeville greats like Weber and Fields—characterized by outrageous puns, non sequiturs, mangled English, and unrestrained nonsense. In one episode, for instance, Fields decided to commit suicide. He left the stage brandishing a pistol, fired a shot, and returned. "Missed!" he caroled, laying onlookers in the aisles. Comedians on the musical stage continued much the same approach through the 1930s.

Audiences in the boom-rich 1920s wanted no more than to be amused, and they reveled in the banalities and spectacle Broadway producers set before them. Production costs had not yet risen in proportion to the increased national income, so that extravaganzas could be marketed at box office prices within the reach of the middle class. Lavish revues like the Ziegfeld *Follies*, George White's *Scandals*, and Earl Carroll's *Vanities* maintained their immense popularity, capturing much of the moonlight-and-honeysuckle mood of that generation, along with its sophistication and its almost hysterical restlessness. There were also the more intimate *Grand Street Follies* and *The Garrick Gaieties*, while in 1923 the Shuberts unveiled the first of their annual *Artists and Models* series, displaying more "nudity" than the Broadway stage had heretofore tolerated. In this show, chorus girls descended steps that were accessible to the auditorium, and ran up the aisles handing out noisemakers and appropriate souvenirs to a startled audience. In the 1924 edition the beauties were seen on stage reflected in a lily pond. Three years before, *Shuffle Along*, the first all-black revue in more than a decade made its appearance at the Sixty-third Street Theatre, creating a vogue for black shows that lasted through the Depression years. With lyrics by singer Noble Sissle and music by the former ragtime pianist and composer Eubie Blake, *Shuffle Along* contained the hit song "I'm Just Wild about Harry" and had Josephine Baker as one of its chorines. The show opened in the midst of the Harlem Renaissance and was followed in 1924 by Sissle and Blake's *The Chocolate Dandies*. Perhaps the most successful of all the black revues was *The Blackbirds of 1928*, which launched a series of seven *Blackbird* shows.

Even book musicals were still little more than a connecting thread for a series of songs and comedy routines. Songs were presented for their own sake and in practically any order, since they were rarely intended to fit a particular context. The main consideration for the composer was to provide so many fast numbers and so many slow ones. Lyricists were interested in supplying words that could be sung anywhere and wrote with an eye toward sheet music sales. The result was more an anthology than a score. Plots remained incredibly sentimental, while storybook characters were by no means limited to operetta. As the decade progressed, some of the cynicism of the period seeped onto the musical stage, and there were increasing topical themes, especially references to the idle Long Island rich and the problem of rum-running. Even the writers of operetta began evidencing some concern for fusing their songs and story. When *Rose Marie* opened in 1924, with music by Rudolf Friml and lyrics by Oscar Hammerstein II, the theater program noted: "The musical numbers of this play are such an integral part of the action that we do not think we should list them as separate episodes." Although many of these attempts at integration were awkwardly done, *Rose Marie* did herald a trend for the decades ahead.

But most musical comedies of the 1920s were simply pretty, tuneful pieces of froth, comfortably within the established mold. *Irene* (1919) had the appeal of a rags-to-riches success story and ran for an unprecedented 670 performances, the longest run for a story-line musical until *Oklahoma!* in the 1940s. *Irene*'s charm, however, came not so much from its plot as from its delightful score, especially the hit song "Alice Blue Gown." Composer Harry Tierney had studied at the Birgil Conservatory of Music in New York, had toured for a time as a concert pianist, but achieved his greatest success with *Rio Rita* in 1927, the first show booked into Florenz Ziegfeld's palatial Ziegfeld Theatre.

Good News, by the trio of De Sylva, Brown, and Henderson, concerned itself with college football and opened in 1927 during football season. The show's story was slight, but its collegiate atmosphere served to hold jokes about athletes, sororities, fraternities, and college life together. A youthful cast and much energetic singing and dancing made *Good News* spirited entertainment, while the score included the title song, "The Best Things in Life Are Free," and "The Varsity Drag." Like Harry Tierney, Ray Henderson had received formal musical training, principally at the Chicago Conservatory of Music. With lyricists B.G. DeSylva and Lew Brown he had earlier written "The Birth of the Blues" for the 1926 edition of the *Scandals*, along with the "Black Bottom" for Ann Pennington, who introduced a dance craze that swept the nation.

For audiences tiring of sedate operettas with exotic settings and about bygone aristocrats, the shows by De Sylva, Brown, and Henderson seemed like a breath of fresh air. They dealt with contemporary life, made references to current fads, were alive and rousing, and possessed a smartness and a sophistication that the youth of the 1920s much admired. *Hold Everything* in 1928 turned to the boxing game; *Follow Through* a year later looked at golf, country club life, and the business tycoon; while *Flying High* in 1930 cast Bert Lahr as a comic air pilot. Gradually the topical musical became the ruling type.

Vincent Youmans' *No, No, Nanette*, one of the decade's sensations, opened out of town in 1924. The show is filled with the flavor of the 1920s and reflects much of the buoyancy of flaming, middle class youth. Nanette's friends merrily insist that they are "flippant and fly and free" and only have time for "petting parties with the smarties." The girl's uncle is a wealthy publisher of Bibles with a weakness for pretty girls. Matters get out of hand when Uncle Jimmy takes three attractive misses under his protective wing, much to his wife's dismay. When caught red-handed, Uncle Jimmy explains by singing one of the show's best songs, "I Want to Be Happy," although "Tea for Two" proved even more captivating. *No, No, Nanette* lasted for a year in New York—an exceptionally long run in those days—and for almost two years in London. At one time seventeen road companies were on tour throughout the world. Youmans' score is deceptively simply but it earned him over a half million dollars.

The composer also enjoyed successes with *Wildflower* (1923), *Oh, Please!* (1926), and *Hit the Deck* (1927). The latter, about sailors and their girls, contained the songs "Hallelujah" and "Sometimes I'm Happy." Youmans' tunes are often characterized by a vigorous, driving rhythm. The effervescent "Eadie Was a Lady" and "Rise 'n' Shine," both of which he wrote for Ethel Merman in *Take a Chance* (1932), are cases in point. Youmans went to Hollywood in 1933, where he furnished the music for the Ginger Rogers-Fred Astaire film *Flying Down to Rio*. Besides the title number the *Rio* score included "The Carioca" and "Orchids in the Moonlight," all three of which struck the popular fancy. Youmans suffered from tuberculosis and died in 1946 an unhappy and dissatisfied man.

By present standards the story material for even the best of the 1920s Broadway musicals is practically worthless. And yet despite its cliches and simpering plots, the musical theater of that decade did bring to maturity a wealth of gifted composers who wrote memorable songs for shows that are otherwise undistinguished. Ragtime and later jazz had given musical comedy scores an undisputable national color, as well as a new dynamism and cogency. The more sophisticated of the young Broadway composers tapped creative resources formerly thought too complex for public consumption and lifted the jazz idiom into both a natural musical speech and an art. Stilted language was nudged out of the way by vernacular and slang expressions, yet at the same time lyrics became more inventive in rhyme scheme and rhythm, increasingly erudite in their references.

Between 1921 and 1924 Irving Berlin gained stature by producing the music for his annual *Music Box Revue*. The tunes George Gershwin wrote for the theater were freshly conceived and technically adventuresome, evoking a spectrum of emotions and capturing the pulse of urban America. Gershwin blithely murdered the standard musical formulas, adding uncommon melodic, harmonic, and rhythmic turns to his brother's ingenious lyrics. Not only did the composer's efforts revolutionize the musical theater, they made a lasting impact on Tin Pan Alley as well. "George's music gets around so much before an opening," George S. Kaufman once said, "that the first night audience thinks it's at a revival." While the songs for *Lady Be Good, Oh, Kay!*, and *Funny Face* in several cases proved immortal, the books—while considered first class in their day—soon appeared painfully dated. Nor was there much attempt to integrate the musical numbers into the plot. "Clap Yo' Hands" from *Oh, Kay!* is a delightful Gershwin tune, but it was wedged into the story by having the comedian ask a line of chorus girls, "Do you want to hear a Mammy song?" The girls scream that indeed they do not. "Very well, then," says the comic, "I'll sing you the song she used to sing to me." The number has absolutely nothing to do with the plot, yet the writers were foresighted enough to realize this and essentially made a joke out of the fact. Taken alone, the show's songs are generally exceptional, even by Gershwin standards. Ira's pithy lyrics are models of humanity, wit, and polish. Topical inferences, repetition of words and phrases, alliteration, and unexpected

unexpected shifts of emphasis are woven into an artistic whole.

But in 1927 the Gershwins with George Kaufman concocted a far more original musical comedy, *Strike Up the Band*. The show was a radical departure from anything the writers had done before, dealing with the subject of war with satiric brutality. The story finds Switzerland protesting the fifty percent American tariff on Swiss cheese. Horace J. Fletcher, owner of the American Cheese Company, uses high government influence to force Switzerland into war, promising to assume the financial burden so long as his country calls the struggle the Horace J. Fletcher Memorial War. The text frequently made stinging commentary on Babbittry, big business, and foreign relations, while Gershwin used his resources with a new deftness to underscore an acid remark, emphasize humor, or delineate nuances of a character. *Strike Up the Band* was a far more subtle and intellectual work than anything the composer had done for the theater earlier, but the show was so uncompromising that it folded on the road. Three years later the script was revised by Morrie Ryskind, who blunted the edges by having the action take place in a dream, changing the commodity taxed from cheese to chocolate, and stressing comedy over cynicism.

By then the budding master of satire on the Broadway stage, however, was Cole Porter, who preferred a fencing touch rather than the bludgeon. Porter avoided society's traumas, revealed almost no martial spirit, favored a sting that was momentary. His lyrics are sometimes tricky, involved, often suggestive, but always smart and urbane. He could do marvels with a catchy phrase and turn the ordinary innuendo into poetry. His music is exquisite, at times superbly classic. Unlike Berlin or Gershwin, Porter was independent of Tin Pan Alley, for he came from a wealthy family. He could experiment at his leisure, cared nothing for message, and judged his work strictly on its entertainment value. Yet he perfected his technique into something distinct and durable.

Born in Peru, Indiana, June 9, 1892, Porter graduated from Worchester Academy as valedictorian, made a trip to Europe, then entered Yale University. He was a debonair undergraduate, already an accomplished charmer. He liked to improvise on the piano for friends, wrote a couple of football songs and several numbers for the annual Yale Smoker. He was fond of poetry, especially Browning, read Homer in Greek, and became convinced that a song's words and music must be inseparably wed. He vowed early always to write his own lyrics. Porter's days at Yale were spent mainly with socialite acquaintances; one of his best friends in college was Monty Woolley, the actor. Upon graduation he entered the Harvard Law School, but shortly switched over to music.

Porter produced his first hit song, "An Old-Fashioned Garden," for Raymond Hitchcock's revue *Hitchy-Koo of 1919*. Then followed several years of little success. In 1923 the youth inherited a great deal of money from his grandfather, who had made a fortune on California gold and the purchase of West Virginia coal and timber lands. Associates repeatedly told Cole that his songs were much too highbrow for the general public and that he should consider them no more than a hobby. The composer lived abroad throughout much of the 1920s, something of a musical expatriate. He studied with Vincent d'Indy at the Schola Cantorum in Paris, yet avoided the literary crowd then so prominent in the city. He met F. Scott Fitzgerald, but found him a bore because of his drinking. Cole and his wife, a wealthy American divorcee, went on a two-month cruise up the Nile and, after his grandfather's death, leased a *palazzo* in Venice, where their parties were spectacular. "It was not what I really wanted," Porter said. "[W]hat I wanted more than anything was success on Broadway—but it was a reasonable facsimile of something to do."

The wealthy young man was looked upon by those who knew him as a gentleman-composer. In New York theater circles his name was scarcely recognized. But he wanted desperately to prove himself, as the entrepreneurs of his family had. On the surface Porter seemed the witty playboy, happily doing nothing of import; in truth, he worked very hard indeed. "I did everything and anything, from Egyptology to mah-jongg, to forget composition," he confessed, "though I could not escape from my regime of daily study." He familiarized himself with the cream of nineteenth-century art songs, particularly the *lieder* of Schubert and Schumann. He attended opera at La Scala and the small Italian provincial houses as well. He wrote a ballet for the Swedish Ballet company, but also made friends with a number of black musicians performing in Paris. Influenced perhaps by his black acquaintances, he began experimenting with jazz rhythms. Like F. Scott Fitzgerald, Cole Porter could never take seriously the high society of which he was a part. At moments he even hated it. Emotionally he was always detached, bringing to his work a wry objectivity.

He wrote the music for the *Greenwich Village Follies of 1924* and three years later was asked by producer E. Ray Goetz to do the score for an upcoming comedy called *Paris*, featuring Goetz's wife, Irene Bordoni. The production included the slightly suggestive song "Let's Do It" and was an instant success, so that from 1928 on Porter was in great demand. *Fifty Million Frenchmen* followed the next year, with such tunes as "You Do Something to Me" and "Find Me a Primitive Man" demonstrating the composer's smartness and his gift for making a satiric point on sexual relationships. *Wake Up and Dream* (also 1929) was a lesser show, but contained Porter's first unqualified song masterpiece, "What Is This Thing Called Love?" *The New Yorkers*, a more adventuresome musical which opened a year later, took audiences on a tour of both high and low life. The show introduced another Porter perennial, "Love for Sale," revealing the musician's free attitude on sex in an exceptionally sophisticated way. The song was initially sung by Kathryn Crawford, impersonating a prostitute vending her charms, and was easily the production's most talked about number. The New York *Evening World* found it "in the worst possible taste," while radio stations banned vocal versions for years. The idea for "Love for

Sale" came to Porter one night while he was strolling the streets of London. Its lyrics are uninhibited, haunting, starkly realistic, bitter, with wisps of literary naturalism.

Love for sale,
Appetizing young love for sale.
Love that's fresh and still unspoiled,
Love that's only slightly soiled,
Love for sale.
Who will buy?
Who would like to sample my supply?
Who's prepared to pay the price
For a trip to paradise?
Love for sale.
Let the poets pipe of love
In their childish way,
I know ev'ry type of love
Better far than they.
If you want the thrill of love,
I've been thru the mill of love,
Old love, new love,
Ev'ry love but true love.
Love for sale,
Appetizing young love for sale.
If you want to buy my wares,
Follow me and climb the stairs,
Love for sale.

Porter favored direct communication in music, but kept his standards high. His work stayed much the same throughout his lengthy career—full of melodic inventiveness, cultured wit, and glossy opulence. In many regards the composer symbolized the decade that brought him fame, most notably in his conflicting values, his unconventional views, his personal iconoclasm, his unpredictable moods and actions, his pleasure-seeking, his exhibitionist tendencies, his easy-come-easy-go facade, but also in his provocative accomplishments.

Just as daring were Rodgers and Hart, who began a twenty-three-year collaboration with *Fly With Me* in 1920. Richard Rodgers was the son of a physician, born in New York City, June 28, 1902. Lorenz Hart was seven years older, but also a native New Yorker. The two became partners, best friends, and creative equals, both craftsmen with a unique artistic stamp. Lyricist Larry Hart was especially fond of tricky rhymes, while his phrasing and figures of speech were tart and fresh. His allusions to people, places, and cultural watchwords gave his work a maturity and bite heretofore unknown on the Broadway stage. Richard Rodgers liked to set these verses to warm, innovative, but uncomplicated melodies. The songs Rodgers and Hart wrote were richly imaginative, solid in technique, unquenchably youthful. The team was the first composer-lyricist combination to receive matching billing, and they ultimately made a greater impact on the evolution of the American musical stage than anyone else of their day, surpassing even the Princess Theater shows in charm and invention.

Their first real success came in 1925 with *The Garrick Gaieties*, a new, more literate type of revue. Overnight Rodgers and Hart emerged from the ranks of the struggling unknowns to become two of the most sought after young songwriters along Broadway. The show, produced by the Theatre Guild, was impudent and spontaneous, while the Rodgers and Hart score, including the hit song "Manhattan," was coated with irreverence and originality. Later that year the partners were joined by Herbert Fields for their first book musical, *Dearest Enemy*. Set in revolutionary America, the story was based on an alleged incident wherein a New York woman artfully detained the staff of General Howe's army of occupation by inviting them to dinner, thereby giving General Washington time to withdraw his troops to a more tenable position. A footnote to American history was treated nostalgically and vivaciously, yet the gaiety was spiced with discreet salaciousness. There were duets, trios, choral numbers, and instrumental interludes, while the writers genuinely tried to make their songs fit the spirit of the time and place.

During 1926 Rodgers and Hart had three productions running on Broadway at one time—*Dearest Enemy*; *The Girl Friend*, a bright up-to-date show best remembered for the song "The Blue Room"; and the second *Garrick Gaieties*, containing the number "Mountain Greenery." Next came *Peggy-Ann*, an unusually mature musical for the time, in which almost all the action takes place in a dream. Peggy-Ann's love affair was not the perfumed, romantic kind, but a far more colorless one. The plot was built around the fantasies of its heroine, which occasionally became confused with reality. Modern dance and undisciplined lighting contributed to the sense of disorder, while songs were used intelligently to make satiric points. Rodgers and Hart dispensed with the opening chorus and, in fact, had no singing or dancing at all for the first fifteen minutes. Along the way most of the musical comedy rules got broken, and the finale was played in the dark, consisting of a slow comic dance.

A Connecticut Yankee in 1927, inspired by Mark Twain's farce, was the team's longest running show to date. Hart's lyrics blended the archaic speech of King Arthur's court with current slang expressions, much to the delight of the public. By the second act King Arthur's courtiers could be heard remarking, "Methinks yon damsel is a lovely broad," while the highways of Camelot were flanked with advertising slogans like "I would fain walk a furlong for a Camel." The score included some of Rodger's best writing, especially "Thou Swell" and the still beautiful "My Heart Stood Still." Although *Chee-Chee* (1928) offered music far more integrated into the stage action, it had the shortest run of any Rodgers and Hart show, thirty-one performances. Musical passages helped identify characters, heighten emotions, and accentuate pieces of stage business, but the story—about a eunuch—was boring. *Present Arms* (also 1928) and *Spring Is Here* (1929) fared better—the former highlighted by "You Took Advantage of Me," the latter by the ballad "With a Song in My Heart."

Even the finest of Rodgers and Hart's shows in the 1920s, however, were set to books that by today's standards are virtually unplayable. Although the writers consciously shied away from stereotyped boy-meets-girl themes and avoided the unreal emotions of operetta, their plots and characters nevertheless remained sketchy, with parts of the production more significant than the whole. The team had an uncanny knack for coming up with something fresh and novel, but the revolution in the musical theater, even in the hands of genius, was necessarily gradual. All around them Rodgers and Hart found vapid extravaganzas and the stale formulas of the past accepted and rewarded at the box office—a constant reminder that their more personalized approach was more curiosity than the norm.

To succeed on Broadway during the early 1920s Jerome Kern himself, the musical light behind the Princess Theater shows and the model for Gershwin, Rodgers, and other forwardlooking songwriters, was forced to adhere to more conventional methods. Kern's two big shows in the first half of the decade were *Sally* (1920) and *Sunny* (1925), the latter almost a carbon copy of the original. *Sally* had everything musical comedy audiences wanted in 1920 and made no pretense at subtlety. Kern had clearly forsaken the informality of the Princess Theater productions for big, old-fashioned, escapist theater. But commercially the show was a sensation. Florenz Ziegfeld produced it, and Marilyn Miller was the star. Sally is a dishwasher at a Greenwich Village restaurant, where Connie—actually the Grand Duke Constantine from one of the Balkan countries—is a waiter. Connie takes Sally to a Long Island garden party of a millionaire friend, at which she poses as a Russian ballerina. She naturally enchants the guests, gets an offer to appear in the Ziegfeld *Follies*, and eventually marries wealthy Blair Farquar, whom she met at the party. Along the way she has become a famous dancer and sung "Look for the Silver Lining." All in all this does not represent much of an advance over Victor Herbert's *Mlle. Modiste* fifteen years before. Indeed Herbert contributed part of the score. The show was a success largely because it was a veritable feast for the eye, with lavish sets and flaming colors, all of which served to frame the personality of Marilyn Miller, who sang and danced enticingly. Leon Errol as Connie added comedy and warmth to the proceedings, and Kern's songs were melodious. Certainly the plot held few surprises, and audiences knew practically from the start how the story would end.

Ziegfeld produced *Sunny* five years later, again for Marilyn Miller, paying her a reported $3000 a week. for several years the highest salary in American musical comedy history. Kern's score contained the standard love songs, specialty numbers, choruses, and the hit song "Who?"—although with no particular concern for how any of this fit into the story situation. The show featured Clifton Webb, was highly entertaining and elaborately staged, yet was cut from the same cloth as most of the other Broadway spectacles of the time.

But by 1927 Kern was established enough to risk boldness. With Oscar Hammerstein II he conceived *Show Boat*, based on Edna Ferber's novel, the great turning point in the development of the American musical theater. Its adult libretto shattered many of the musical comedy conventions, dealing with two unhappy marriages, one between a white man and a mulatto woman. The black is treated not with the customary sentimentality and humor, but with compassion. Music is used as an essential tool in telling the story. While there are strong elements of coincidence, even absurdity in the plot, delicate subject matter is handled far more realistically than ever before in a Broadway musical. The dramatic conflict, for a change, is strong enough to have been performed without music, yet Kern—always a sound craftsman—carefully selected his material so that the drama was enhanced and given deeper meaning. Each number was chosen for a definite purpose, always with the idea of advancing the story. Gone are the shreds and patches typical of musical comedy of that day, for with *Show Boat* Kern and Hammerstein made the play and the play alone the first and basic consideration.

In the story Magnolia Hawks, the innocent daughter of Cap'n Andy, the show boat operator, falls in love with the river gambler Gaylord Ravenal and soon marries him. Gaylord adores his wife, but cannot resist the gaming tables. Eventually Magnolia takes their child and sadly leaves him, although she is ill-equipped to make her own way. Earlier the show boat's star, Julie LaVerne, the tragic mulatto, has been driven from the river by authorities when her racial identity is made known. She leaves with Steve, her white husband, who shortly deserts her. Abandoned and barred from the friends who have meant so much to her, Julie sinks into alcoholism, keeping herself in liquor by singing. She appears at a rehearsal drunk, plaintively rendering the immortal "Bill," confirming her love for her worthless man.

But along came Bill,
Who's not the type at all,
You'd meet him on the street
And never notice him;
His form and face,
His manly grace
Are not the kind that you
Would find in a statue;
And I can't explain,
It's surely not his brain
That makes me thrill.

I love him
Because he's wonderful,
Because he's just old Bill.

When Magnolia interrupts this scene, looking for work as a singer, Julie walks out unnoticed by the girl, quits her job, and thereby leaves her place open for her beloved "Nolie." Eventually Magnolia and Ravenal are reunited in a somewhat bittersweet ending.

The rather sprawling plot is unified by the song "Ol' Man River," sung by Joe, a black dock worker. The lyrics mildly protest the hardness of American black life, contrasting the helplessness Joe feels with the might and indifference of the Mississippi. The melody captures some of the qualities of the black spiritual, while the words are simple, with few rhymes, yet portray an oppressed race with dignity. Part of the song is used earlier, chanted by black workers in the opening scene, as they carry bales of cotton on the Natchez levee and lament the drudgery of their back-breaking labor. Against this, the town dandies and their ladies come down to the river to sing the praises of another "Cotton Blossom," in this case Cap'n Andy's show boat. Other musical themes are quoted and skillfully developed in almost a Wagnerian *leitmotif* fashion. In one small section the audience is made to realize that, despite all his bravado, Gaylord really does love Magnolia, when he sings the lines "I let fate decide/If I walk or ride," repeating four measures that Magnolia has sung in their first duet, "Make Believe." A "misery theme" is used to underline Julie's unhappiness, foreshadowing in her second appearance, in the midst of a gay scene, her eventual disaster. Even Julie's first act blues number, "Can't Help Lovin' Dat Man," forewarns of her hopeless love and perhaps suggests her black origin.

Kern made much of his dramatic gifts, heightening immeasurably the emotional value of a complex book. No less remarkable are Oscar Hammerstein's lyrics. The grandson and namesake of the famous opera and vaudeville impresario, Hammerstein had worked on a number of highly successful operettas, among them *Rose Marie, The Desert Song*, and *New Moon*, but for him *Show Boat* was an even bigger departure than it was for Kern. He rose to the occasion masterfully, revealing the insights of a true poet. He gained atmosphere and borrowed words and phrases from Mark Twain's *Life on the Mississippi* and produced such beautiful verses that Kern said, "the music wrote itself." *Show Boat* is colorful in background, richly nostalgic, and contains its share of lovely tunes and haunting duets, like "You Are Love" and "Why Do I Love You," that link the show to the operetta tradition. But the writers dispensed with the rows of pert chorus girls, who in a more conventional treatment might have chirped endlessly about how it feels just dandy to be with Cap'n Andy.

Flo Ziegfeld produced the experiment, convinced at first that he had a white elephant. Time and again he procrastinated in getting the play on the boards, but the delay gave the writers time to work out details to their full satisfaction. In the end extravagant scenery and costumes were all subservient to the dramatic demands of the book. Although the production featured the dark-haired, soulful-eyed torch song singer Helen Morgan, who made the shadowy Julie the most interesting role in the show, the character remained an integral part of the totality. By the standards of the day, all of the characters are strongly drawn. The story deals with real people, real feelings, racial prejudice, and a forbidden subject—miscegenation. While it is romance, it is more than a fairy tale. There is tenderness and humor, but the plot is basically believable. More than anything else, *Show Boat* offers two things unknown in the musical theater of its day—an integrated score and dramatic truth.

Much to Ziegfeld's surprise, the venture turned out to be a box office delight, immediately establishing itself as the major musical show of the 1920s. It opened in Washington, D.C. on November 15, 1927, and later enjoyed a long New York run. *Show Boat* is the only musical of its decade still revived with any regularity. In 1954 it became the first Broadway musical to become part of the New York City Opera repertoire. The show represents an important milestone in the growth of the American musical stage, freeing musical comedy from its bondage to hackneyed ritual and setting it in the direction of a new art form, toward an American play with music. While the individual songs are superior, it is the totality that was revolutionary— possessing a realism that distinguishes it from old time operetta and set in a popular idiom that differentiates it from grand opera.

"If you were at all sensitive to music," Richard Rodgers later said, "Kern had to be your idol." The composer worked again with Oscar Hammerstein II on *Sweet Adeline*, an original story about the rise of a beer garden singer to musical comedy star, which they prepared for Helen Morgan. The book in this case was not particularly strong, but the turn-of-the-century setting did provide the writers great period charm and gave them the opportunity to produce two of Morgan's best remembered songs, "Don't Ever Leave Me" and "Why Was I Born?" *Sweet Adeline* premiered on Broadway five weeks before the Wall Street crash, offering relief from the worries of the months ahead. *The Cat and the Fiddle* (1931), on which Kern collaborated with Otto Harbach, was another unusual story, involving a jazz-crazy American girl who falls in love with a serious European composer. The show did away with production numbers, chorus girls, and comedy, directing all of its resources toward the development of plot and characters. *Music in the Air*, with another solid book by Hammerstein, opened in New York during the fall of 1932, followed the next year by *Roberta*. Although described as a "glorified fashion show," the latter contained one of Kern's mellowest scores, almost every song a hit: "Smoke Gets in Your Eyes," "The Touch of Your Hand," "Yesterdays," "You're Devastating," "Let's Begin," "Something Had to Happen," "I Won't Dance," and "I'll Be Hard to Handle." In the cast were veteran actress Fay Templeton and Bob Hope, in his first major role. *Roberta* was Kern's last Broadway triumph before he left for Hollywood, where he wrote many beautiful tunes for motion pictures.

Songwriters by the dozens began flocking to California in the early 1930s. The success of Al Jolson in *The Jazz Singer* in 1927 had demonstrated that sound motion pictures were feasible and set off a chain reaction among the major studios. With the movie mills working overtime to meet the demand, film producers were willing to pay composers tantalizing wages, as Hollywood entered its golden age of the musical extravanganza. Broadway on the other hand was hard hit by the Depression. Admission prices were forced down so sharply that several productions that had opened before the crash were pressed into a premature closing. Whereas there had been 423 musicals on Broadway in the decade from 1920 to 1930, there were only 179 between 1930 and 1940, a drop of nearly fifty percent. Meanwhile motion pictures flooded the screen, and because of relatively modest admission fees, after 1932 the industry found a voracious public and an effective means of mass distribution, doubtlessly cutting into the domain formerly held by the stage.

For Broadway, however, the effect was not entirely negative. The audience that remained loyal to the musical theater was more elevated in its tastes, so that the Broadway stage was free to cater to a sophisticated public rather than the masses. Producers quickly learned that if they were to outdo the motion picture moguls, they would be better off emphasizing intelligence and freshness rather than splashy production numbers which Hollywood could do better. They also discovered that subtlety and taste were often cheaper to execute. Only the better songwriters survived, while lyricists were expected to find words of more than two syllables and rhymes more inventive than the old *moon* in *June* scheme. Although the Depression and the movies were severe blows to Broadway, reducing it to a restricted corner of the entertainment industry and robbing it of an audience that never came back, from the standpoint of art the result marked a step forward. Writers and technicians were now forced to focus on their craft and quickly assumed a sneering attitude toward their West Coast colleagues.

Because of the hard times, artists in the 1930s were unusually interested in social and political problems, the common man, and crusades of all kinds. The giddy, inane shows of yesterday were out of kilter with much of the existing mood, so that writers for the musical stage began opening their eyes to the world around them as never before. Like the serious musicians and literary figures of the day, songwriters searched for answers, hoped for economic panaceas, and dared to speak of the times. America had lost some of its bumptious self-confidence and in certain areas became more questioning and serious minded. Part of the musical theater followed suit. During the 1920s a new generation of Broadway talent had grown more literate and stylish in their work; in the decade that followed the point was driven home to them that life could be less than a bowl of cherries. As the national climate sobered, the social conscience of this new crop of songwriters deepened, while they probed and made telling comments about the system at hand. Foreign topics held little interest, for the country was preoccupied with its own ills and sought its own salvation.

Yet by no means all of the musicals of the 1930s were satirical or thought-provoking. Most, in fact, were not. While social concern became a fashionable theme, another—just as important—was lighthearted escape. Many of the shows during the Depression years aimed at nothing more than sending audiences home smiling, maybe even whistling, their spirits rejuvenated. There was still lots of nonsense about bootlegging, and comedians continued their heyday. Old-fashioned revues with chorus girls and spectacle occasionally made an appearance, while *The Great Waltz* in 1934 harked back to vintage operetta. But scarce money limited such productions to a few. Although surrounded by frivolity, the new trend was in having something to say, toward a new theatrical form that pricked balloons and exposed foibles while it entertained.

George and Ira Gershwin's two big hits of the early thirties sum up these contrasting approaches on a high level. *Girl Crazy* (1930) is essentially a light-minded, old-style musical comedy, cheerfully poking fun at the Old West. *Of Thee I Sing* (1931) was much more in the caustic manner of *Strike Up the Band*, unorthodox in concept and full of subtle detail. Both made stage history. But *Of Thee I Sing* was a genuine play with music and became the first Broadway musical to win the Pulitzer Prize for drama—during a year when Eugene O'Neill's *Mourning Becomes Electra* was in the competition. It was the first American musical comedy to be published in book form and enjoyed the longest run of any Gershwin show.

Girl Crazy, on the other hand, takes place on a dude ranch outside Custerville, Arizona, where Danny, a Park Avenue playboy, has been sent by his father to get him away from the wine, women, and song of New York. The wealthy Danny arrives in a taxicab and proceeds to turn the ranch into a Broadway annex with chorus girls, liquor, gambling, and lots of music. But when he falls in love with Molly Gray, the local postmistress, he finally realizes the error of his ways. In the pit was the Red Nichols Orchestra, which included Benny Goodman, Gene Krupa, Glenn Miller, Jimmy Dorsey, and Jack Teagarden. The show featured Willie Howard and Ginger Rogers, fresh from her first Hollywood success. But the limelight was taken by a young singer making her Broadway debut—Ethel Merman, as Kate Fothergill, wife of the man who ran the gambling room at the ranch. Dressed in a lowcut red blouse and a tight black satin skirt slit to the knee, she stepped onto the stage and sang her first song, "Sam and Delilah." "Delilah was a floozy," she began, winning immediate favor. Then in "I Got Rhythm" she threw her big brassy voice wide open, holding a high *C* in the second chorus for sixteen bars, while the orchestra continued the melody. Not only the audience, but the entire theater was hers. "I knew that I'd stopped that *Girl Crazy* show," Merman remembered years later. Gershwin, who conducted the opening performance, told her, "Don't ever let anybody give you a singing lesson. It'll ruin you." Guy Bolton and John McGown had provided the sassy book, while the hits "Embraceable You," "But Not for Me," "Bidin' My Time," and "Boy! What Love Has Done to Me" were all in the score. The cast had youth and vitality, and their exuberance spilled across the footlights. Yet the show made no pretense at being more than delightful, beautifully packaged entertainment.

In *Of Thee I Sing*, however, individual moments are less significant than the total impact. Gershwin's music is as integral to the satire as the dialogue and lyrics. The score is more flexible, closely shaped to the book. "[T]here are no verse-and-chorus songs," Ira said, and the set pieces so important to *Girl Crazy* are gone. The text by George Kaufman and Morrie Ryskind castigates political conventions, the Presidency, Congress, the Supreme Court, bathing beauties, even motherhood, yet does so skillfully and amusingly, becoming neither heavy-handed nor exhortatory. The story centers on John P. Wintergreen's campaign for the Presidency. Wintergreen, an unqualified nonentity, glibly talking out of both sides of his mouth, is elected on the platform of Love. His Vice President, Alexander Throttlebottom, is a pathetic little man, whose name Wintergreen can never remember. Party banners in the torchlight parade that opens the show proclaim: "A Vote for Wintergreen Is a Vote for Wintergreen," "Vote for Prosperity — And See What You Get," and "Wintergreen—the Flavor Lasts." When the President-elect marries his faithful secretary rather than the winner of a beauty contest, as promised, the country is thrown into a diplomatic break with France, for the rejected girl turns out to be "the illegitimate daughter of the illegitimate son of the illegitimate nephew of Napoleon." Meanwhile Vice President Throttlebottom, played by Victor Moore, innocently tries to find out what his duties are, even joining a conducted tour so that he can see what the White House looks like. Wintergreen escapes impeachment when his wife announces that she is pregnant, for as Throttlebottom points out, the country "has never impeached an expectant President."

The show opened during the depth of the Depression and, with a crucial election near at hand, was appropriate to the mood of the time. Gershwin's ambitious score welds together the singing, dancing, and plot content, cogently underpinning the stage action by orchestral interludes that comment on a character or situation with telling strokes. There are glorious songs and a brilliant first act finale, but these are more maturely structured into the whole than in *Strike Up the Band* or any Broadway musical to date. The subject is highly American, while the speech is natural. *Of Thee I Sing* stands as a remarkable experiment both in form and content, the major advance in the direction of musical drama after *Show Boat*.

The writers tried to repeat their achievement in *Let 'Em Eat Cake* two years later, but had far less success. The sequel found Wintergreen and Throttlebottom losing the race for reelection, organizing a revolution, and setting up a dictatorship of the proletariat. After a baseball game settles a tense international dispute, the republic is restored with Throttlebottom as the new President. There were a few good moments, but the score seemed self-conscious and lacked spontaneity. Brooks Atkinson felt the authors had allowed their hatreds to triumph over their sense of humor.

Yet side by side with this sharpening social conscience was plenty of outright escapism. After spending much of their time in the early 1930s in Hollywood, Rodgers and Hart returned to Broadway in 1935 for the Hippodrome extravaganza *Jumbo*, complete with clowns, tightrope walkers, bareback riders, trapeze performers, jugglers, and wild animals. The interior of the giant theater was rebuilt to look like a circus tent. Jimmy Durante headed the cast, while Paul Whiteman's orchestra played from a tall platform upstage. The plot was pure sentiment, about a romance between a son and daughter of two rival circus owners. The spectacle played for nine months, but failed to revitalize the grandeur the Hippodrome had once known. The edifice was torn down three years later.

With *On Your Toes* in 1936 Rodgers and Hart really hit their stride, for the first time helping to write the book, in collaboration with George Abbott. A satire on ballet, the show not only fused text and music, but used dance as an essential part of the plot. Instead of the high kicks of earlier musical comedy, genuine choreography was devised by dance director George Balanchine to advance the story line, the most impressive of which was a ballet called "Slaughter on Tenth Avenue." There were also superior Rodgers and Hart songs; for example, "It's Got to Be Love" and "There's a Small Hotel."

Babes in Arms the next year continued the trend, its stunning score—including "My Funny Valentine," "Where or When" and "Johnny One Note"—tightly integrated into the play. "The Lady Is a Tramp" is the brazen confession of a nonconformist and demonstrates Hart's ability to turn a lyric into a thing of beauty, wit, and meaning. Its verses chide social pretensiousness, speak of recent events, laugh at current fads, and assume a gentle political stand. "I still like Roosevelt and think he's a champ," the girl sings. "That's why the lady is a tramp." Actually the young woman leads a very normal life; she simply refuses to do the silly and thoughtless things fashionable among her friends.

Rodgers and Hart's main political commentary, however, came later in 1937 with *I'd Rather Be Right*, a none too subtle lampoon on the New Deal administration. Unlike *Of Thee I Sing*, the later show named actual people and stuck closer to specific issues of the day. The book by George Kaufman and Moss Hart dealt with Roosevelt's attempt to alter the Supreme Court, the innumerable agencies created by Congress, mounting taxes, and a budget gone out of control. "The trouble with the country," George M. Cohan, as President Roosevelt, confessed, "is that I don't know what the trouble with the country is." The script's sharp-edged dialogue cut deeply: "Cummings— take a law," the President ordered his Attorney General. None of the songs reached the individual popularity of hits from other Rodgers and Hart shows, because they were all too intricately bound to the text. Among them were "A Little Bit of Constitutional Fun," "A Homogeneous Cabinet," "We're Going to Balance the Budget," and "Labor Is the Thing."

In *I Married an Angel* (1938) the writers returned to ballet. Since the production featured the Berlin-born Norwegian dancer Vera Zorina, in her

Broadway debut, George Balanchine could broaden the scope of his choreography, and his "Honeymoon Ballet" was ambitious indeed. *The Boys from Syracuse* a few months later was an adaptation of Shakespeare's *The Comedy of Errors* and proved one of Rodgers and Hart's more lasting books. Its two best songs are "Falling in Love with Love" and "This Can't Be Love," both used naturally within the situation of the play. Rodgers and Hart's shows had come to average about thirteen numbers, fewer than had been typical during the 1920s, allowing more time for the drama to unfold with plausibility.

The summit of the writers' collaboration was reached in 1940 with *Pal Joey*, a powerful play based on a series of sketches John O'Hara had written for *The New Yorker*. Its characters are thoroughly unpleasant, odious people. Nightclub entertainer Joey Evans is a tasteless, conniving, immodest, ignorant scoundrel, not hesitant to lie and cheat to get what he wants. He is set up in his own club by wealthy Vera Simpson, a hardboiled, pleasure-loving matron, who has no more scruples than Joey and is willing to pay for love. Rodgers and Hart's songs are appropriately unsentimental and sardonic. Vera makes it clear in "Bewitched, Bothered and Bewildered" that she has no false notions about Joey. She is a worldly society woman bored with her existence; he will relieve the dullness of her world for a brief while. There is no thought of permanent happiness. The constant repetition of the main musical theme of the song suggests the emptiness of Vera's life. Her love for Joey is almost entirely sexual.

> *Couldn't sleep*
> *And wouldn't sleep*
> *Until I could sleep where I shouldn't sleep.*
> *Bewitched, bothered and bewildered am I.*
>
> *I'll sing to him,*
> *Each spring to him,*
> *And worship the trousers that cling to him.*
> *Bewitched, bothered and bewildered am I.*
>
> *Vexed again,*
> *Perplexed again,*
> *Thank God, I can be oversexed again!*
> *Bewitched, bothered and bewildered am I.*

The score abounds with extraordinary words and music. The writers burlesque the kind of songs typically heard in cheap nightclub acts. In the number "Zip" they achieve a delightfully comic effect by combining opposites. Its melody and rhythm are raucous, while its words reveal that stripteaser Gypsy Rose Lee had only sophisticated thoughts as she unzipped her zippers. The show's songs are frequently cynical and callous, but are consistently realistic, a far cry from the material out of which Broadway musicals were normally fashioned.

Pal Joey marked a drastic shift in the structure of the musical theater. "It seemed to us," Richard Rodgers said, "that musical comedy had to get out of its cradle and start standing on its own feet, looking at the facts of life." Never before had a musical play been populated by such a mash of immoralists, and the writers made no concessions. The characters were depicted as three-dimensional human beings, not as cardboard figures, while Rodgers and Hart's score masterfully underlined the book's viewpoint. The leading roles were superbly enacted by Gene Kelly and Vivienne Segal, but the initial production opened to mixed reviews and had a relatively short run. The public was simply not ready for such a brutally honest approach from a musical. A decade later *Pal Joey* was revived with far greater success.

Certainly the American musical stage was acquiring a deeper personality, and by the mid-1930s the old-style musical comedy was beginning to look anemic. Even the revue was moving toward a more sober attitude. Arthur Schwartz and Howard Dietz, whose tightly knit, fast-moving *Little Show* had earlier represented important innovations in stagecraft and sleek professionalism, wrote *The Band Wagon* in 1931, establishing a new level of discernment. Their literate, urbane songs fit in perfectly with the flavor of the show, the most beautiful of which was "Dancing in the Dark." In reviewing *The Band Wagon* Brooks Atkinson said, "you need not check your brains with your hat." The *New Americana* revue in 1932 pictured a breadline, while Irving Berlin's *Face the Music* dealt with the general theme of the Depression, but also touched on police and political corruption. Moss Hart's text had Wall Street tycoons taking their meals at an Automat and singing "Let's Have Another Cup of Coffee," Albert Einstein earning his living in vaudeville, and the Roxy Theater offering four feature films and a room to attract customers. Berlin's music was a strategic part of the overall scheme. In 1933 the two writers teamed again for one of the liveliest, funniest revues ever staged, *As Thousands Cheer*. Concerned with political and social issues of the day, the show even took the format of a daily newspaper. In one sequence a black man has been lynched by a frenzied mob. Ethel Waters, playing his widow, sang "Supper Time," wondering aloud how she will tell her children of their father's death, as she set the table for dinner. In another scene she caused a sensation, singing the popular "Heat Wave," although "Easter Parade" proved the show's most perennial melody. The cast included Clifton Webb and Marilyn Miller, in her last Broadway appearance. She died in April, 1936.

But the most explicit comment on the Depression years came from *Pins and Needles*, produced in 1937 by the International Ladies' Garment Workers' Union. Harold Rome did the music, including such relevant numbers as "Sing Me a Song with Social Significance," "It's Better with a Union Man," "Doing the Reactionary," and the love duet "One Big Union for Two," all of which took a blatantly "leftist" position. Staged at the

Princess Theater, the revue was cast entirely from members of the garment workers' union, given with only a two-piano accompaniment ·and the simplest scenery possible. The intent was to propagandize for the trade-union movement and entertain union members at the same time. Yet because of the freshness of its satire, *Pins and Needles* became the surprise hit on Broadway, running for 1108 performances and was subsequently taken on tour. Encouraged by the show's success, George Kaufman, Max Gordon, and Moss Hart joined forces a year later in producing a similar revue, *Sing Out the News*. Harold Rome again was the composer, providing such songs as "My Heart Is Unemployed."

By no means were all of the better productions of the period absorbed with events of the day. Cole Porter continued to refine his idiosyncratic style, much as he had during the 1920s. The apolitical Porter cared little for social commentary and made few concessions to the common taste. "I wasn't trying to plumb any depths or interpret mass psychology of the times," the composer said. His shows basically adhered to the established musical comedy format, yet they were considered highly sophisticated and were immensely popular. *The Gay Divorce* in 1932 carried much of the glitter of the 1920s into the new decade and featured Fred Astaire, for the first time without his sister Adele. "Night and Day," the production's best number, was innovative in two respects. First, it was written in forty-eight bars, rather than the thirty-two bars, the tradition in popular music; second, Porter widened the range to four notes over an octave, thereby making the tune difficult to sing and reducing its sheet music sale.

Anything Goes (1934), one of the composer's very best shows, brought welcome relief to the grim conditions at hand, although it was set to a thoroughly modern book. Ethel Merman was teamed with Victor Moore aboard a trans-Atlantic liner. Merman played the part of a one-time evangelist turned nightclub singer, who momentarily combines her two selves in "Blow, Gabriel, Blow." Moore was cast as Public Enemy Number 13, who flees from police disguised as a Reverend. Besides the title song, the score contained "I Get a Kick Out of You," "All Through the Night," and "You're the Top." Although a love song, the latter made references to such superlatives as the Louvre Museum, Dante, the *Mona Lisa*, a Shakespeare sonnet, equating them with the great Durante, a Berlin ballad, and Mickey Mouse. The seemingly effortless rhymes are indissolubly wedded to the clipped melodic phrases, syllable by syllable. Part of the show's vitality and appeal stemmed from its debunking smartness, aided in no small measure by truly splendid music and lyrics.

Much less successful was *Jubilee* (1935), although that production did include two of Porter's finest songs, "Just One of Those Things" and "Begin the Beguine." *Leave It to Me*, three years later, starred Victor Moore as an American ambassador to the Soviet Union homesick for Topeka, Kansas, henpecked by his wife, Sophie Tucker. The spoof had Stalin dancing around in lively musical comedy fashion and Moore kicking the Nazi ambassador in the stomach. But it was a young lady from Texas who stopped the show night after night, doing an enticingly innocent striptease on a Trans-Siberian Railroad platform and singing "My Heart Belongs to Daddy." She was Mary Martin, making her Broadway debut.

Porter was unusually adept at writing for star personalities, sometimes without much regard for the logic of plot development. Merman was featured in several more of his shows. *Red, Hot and Blue* (1936) cast her with Jimmy Durante and Bob Hope and provided her with such songs as "It's De-Lovely," "Ridin' High," and the torchy "Down in the Depths of the Ninetieth Floor." *Du Barry Was a Lady* (1939) had Bert Lahr as a nightclub washroom attendant, secretly doting upon the club's star entertainer, Merman. In his dreams Lahr became the lecherous Louis XV of France, while Merman became a lusty Madame Du Barry. The production also offered Betty Grable in her first Broadway role; its score included "Friendship," "Do I Love You?" and "Well, Did You Evah!" The rambunctious *Panama Hattie* opened in 1940, while *Something for the Boys* (1943), set in and around an army camp, found Merman as a girl who could receive radio messages through the fillings in her teeth. The latter included the song "He's A Right Guy" and dance routines built on military formations. Cole Porter's shows abound in wit, melody, and glamor, for his goal was amusement above all else. He was seldom simple, however, never artless, and possessed the ability to remain genteel even when being suggestive.

Yet protest and serious musical plays with something to say were decided trends in the 1930s. Kurt Weill, who fled Germany the morning after the Nazis set fire to the Reichstag, found sanctuary in the United States, becoming one of the most dynamic figures writing for the American musical stage. His initial offering in this country, *Johnny Johnson* (1936) was a bitter diatribe against war. The composer brought to the theater solid German training and was one of the few musical comedy writers to orchestrate his own works, spending months at a time in New York putting color into the pit. While he wanted to speak to the masses, he was never willing to condescend to the public. With *Knickerbocker Holiday* in 1938 Weill enjoyed his first important American success. The show made a genuine effort to fuse Maxwell Anderson's philosophical book with songs relevant to the play's action. The writers spoke out boldly against the evils of Fascism and dictatorial rule, yet did so entertainingly by letting audiences draw their own parallels between the current situation in Europe and Pieter Stuyvesant's attempt to suppress the liberties of the people of New Amsterdam. Weill demonstrated a great feel for popular songwriting, while Anderson's lyrics were exquisite, especially in the classic "September Song." Written for Walter Huston, who played the role of Stuyvesant, the composer took the actor's vocal limitations into account when he constructed the melody with its unusual progressions. Huston had been signed for the part because the producers wanted to emphasize the dramatic content of the play. The story goes that Weill telegramed the performer in Hollywood: "What is the range

of your voice?" Huston is supposed to have wired back: "No range. Regards."
But his rendition of "September Song" was wonderfully touching, made all
the more poignant by the actor's rough, rasping voice.

In 1941 *Lady in the Dark* opened with Gertrude Lawrence and comedian
Danny Kaye. Moss Hart's play was an unusual one—profound for its day—
about a woman editor of a fashion magazine who undergoes psychoanalysis.
Kurt Weill's music was used to depict the patient's dreams and probe her
subconscious. Ira Gershwin wrote the lyrics, his first major assignment since
the death of his brother. The drama moved continually from the heroine's
real world to dream interludes in which song and dance were expertly
integrated into the basic structure. Gradually the dream sequences fit into the
plot narrative with greater clarity, ultimately achieving a unity of purpose.

Two years later Weill joined Ogden Nash for *One Touch of Venus*, the
show that brought Mary Martin to full stardom. The writers supplied the
singer with two beguiling numbers, "That's Him" and the more popular
"Speak Low." The composer produced the operatic *Street Scene* in 1947,
based on Elmer Rice's moving Pulitzer Prize winning drama about New York
tenement life. Weill's music intensified the passions surging through Rice's
play, bringing stronger emotional impact to the dramatic action. His last
Broadway achievement, *Lost in the Stars*, was unveiled in 1949. Adapted by
Maxwell Anderson from Alan Paton's novel *Cry the Beloved Country*, about
racial conflicts in South Africa, *Lost in the Stars* proved one of Weill's most
powerful plays, with music germane to the action. His choral writing
particularly attained a new level of artistic significance. The musician died
suddenly in New York City, April 3, 1950, having lifted Broadway standards
immeasurably.

"There are now a great many things to be thought about in our
musicals," John Mason Brown wrote in 1938. "They no longer permit us to
be pleasantly relaxed. They demand us to be jubilantly alert. Our laughter at
them is the surest proof that we are thinking." Broadway songwriters found
themselves called upon to be serious composers, capable of writing extended
musical passages. Light and serious music were moving closer together. In
the 1940s the musical play came fully into its own, growing increasingly
urbane and cosmopolitan, yet maintaining a distinctly American idiom.
Musical comedy was by no means displaced, for good entertainment still had
strong box office appeal. But that entertainment was becoming adult,
intelligent, experienced without losing freshness or verve.

The Second World War returned prosperity to the American theater. A
new ardor permeated Broadway, even though the total number of musical
productions for the 1940s was almost ten percent less than the decade before.
During the war years there were lots of shows with military themes, like Cole
Porter's *Let's Face It*, Irving Berlin's *This Is the Army*, and Leonard
Bernstein's *On the Town*. Although the latter was a carefree story, it was
among the more literate and original works of its day, enhanced by sprightly
tunes and an exceptional amount of fine choreography. For *Best Foot
Forward* (1941) George Abbott selected a young cast, the male actors all well

below the minimum draft age. *Follow the Girls* (1944) cast Gertrude Neisen as Bubbles La Marr, a stripteaser who gives up a burlesque career to spend her time in a canteen for servicemen. Neisen stopped the show with her ribald song "I Wanna Get Married," singing encore after encore, each successive verse becoming bawdier and funnier. Although revues by this time were rare, Harold Rome's *Call Me Mister* reflected the mood of the country right after the war, its unifying thread concerned with the problems of veterans readjusting to civilian life.

There was a momentary nostalgia for operetta, bringing about *The Song of Norway* (1944), a charming, if sentimentalized, look at the life of Edvard Grieg, with the Norwegian composer's melodies adapted into popular numbers. But experimentation and message remained a major consideration. Vernon Duke, who had studied at the Kiev Conservatory and under the name Vladimir Dukelsky had written serious music, created an attractive, well-integrated score for *Cabin in the Sky* (1940), set to a meaningful, adult book. The show told with sensitivity a black legend in which the forces of good triumph over evil and in a memorable moment had Ethel Waters singing "Taking a Chance on Love." Harold Arlen, who had written "Stormy Weather" for Miss Waters earlier, produced *Bloomer Girl* in 1944, treating both the feminist and the abolitionist movements, although putting its message across lightly. Arlen is best known for his blues and rhythm songs and would later compose the scores for *St. Louis Woman, House of Flowers, Saratoga,* and *Jamaica,* all in some way dealing with black subjects.

The most potent trend in the Broadway musical theater, however, was the continued growth of the musical drama. And the greatest milestone in that direction opened in New York on March 31, 1943, introducing a new partnership, the most successful in the history of the American musical stage, Richard Rodgers and Oscar Hammerstein II. The show, a genuine play with music, was *Oklahoma!*, the second musical to win the Pulitzer Prize for drama. For the first time an original cast recording was made of a "complete" score. *Oklahoma!* would eventually run for a record-breaking five years and nine weeks, a total of 2202 performances.

Rodgers and Hart had produced their last show, *By Jupiter,* the year before. Hart, always a strange, lonely man, had found writing increasingly difficult as the years went by. He drank heavily and would often disappear for weeks in the middle of preparing a new production, only to return as mysteriously as he had left. The more systematic Rodgers grew progressively frustrated with this and was finally urged by Hart to seek out another collaborator. A revival of *A Connecticut Yankee* opened in 1943, and despite failing health Hart worked to update the show, adding some new lyrics. During the opening night performance, the writer disappeared and could not be found. Two days later he was discovered sprawled across a hotel room bed, more dead than alive. Rodgers had him rushed to Doctors Hospital, where at the age of forty-eight Hart died of pneumonia, November 22, 1943, eight months after the premiere of *Oklahoma!*

When Rodgers and Hammerstein agreed to set Lynn Riggs' play *Green*

Grow the Lilacs to music for the Theatre Guild, they did not realize that they were entering a longterm partnership. But like the team of Rodgers and Hart, the team of Rodgers and Hammerstein was a coalition of equals. Whereas Rodgers wrote quickly, Hammerstein slaved over his lines until every nuance was right. With Hart the composer had supplied the music first; with Hammerstein the lyricist usually worked first. Hart's rhymes sparkle with brilliance and bite, while Hammerstein's possess a quiet glow and a poetic simplicity. Hammerstein's basic philosophy of life was more positive than Hart's, and he expressed this firmly in his verse. "I believe not that the whole world and all of life is good," he once said, "but I do believe that so much of it is good, and my inclination is to emphasize that side of life." Yet whether the lyric was written by Hammerstein or Hart, Rodger's songs seem to have been the product of a single mind, for the words and music are indivisibly fused with the other.

Oklahoma! was a different kind of show from the moment the curtain went up. The scene was a farm house with a woman outside churning butter. Then the unaccompanied voice of Curly is heard offstage, singing "Oh, What a Beautiful Mornin'." As he enters, the orchestra quietly begins to support him. The tune is bucolic, inspired by some lines in Riggs' original play. When Rodgers first saw the lyric, he was deeply moved. "I was a little sick with joy," he later recalled, "because it was so lovely and so right. When you're given words like 'The corn is as high as an elephant's eye,' you've got something to say musically." The rest of the songs grew out of the text, capturing the flavor of the American folk character and possessing a freshness, innocence, and vitality appropriate to a western setting. The complete score consists of only twelve numbers, but these are woven in and out of the story, sometimes in brief quotations, sometimes in altered shapes, sometimes as background for spoken dialogue, sometimes to serve as transition. The music is unpretentious, colloquial, direct. Chorus girls do not appear for about the first forty minutes and are used then for a definite purpose. More than any musical play before it, *Oklahoma!* employs ballet as an integral part of the drama. Its imaginative choreography by Agnes De Mille synthesizes formal ballet steps with square dance movements, yet requires an exacting technique from performers. The long "Dream Ballet" actually heightens the drama by revealing the subconscious desires and fears of the leading characters.

The first act of the show deals with little more than a girl trying to make up her mind whether Curly or Jud will take her to a dance. The villainous personality of Jud Fry adds much to the realism of the entertainment. As Hammerstein put it, Jud was "the bass fiddle to give body to the orchestration of the story." He is a complex individual—evil yet pitiful; understandable, if not likeable. In the "Poor Jud" number, he is seen as a somewhat comic figure, pathetically thinking of the tears that will be shed at his funeral. Eventually there is a scene in which Jud is murdered on stage, a revolutionary moment in the development of musical comedy. Before the opening predictions ran high that the show would fail. Except for Rodgers, everyone connected with *Oklahoma!* had experienced a string of disasters. But the production was popular with the public from the beginning and received the best notices since *Show Boat*. Some critics even referred to it as a folk opera. While *Oklahoma!* had realism, it was also hopeful, giving wartime audiences a chance to feel pride in a sunnier page from the country's past.

In *Carousel* (1945) Rodgers and Hammerstein permitted the turning point of the drama to take place in song. The happy-go-lucky carousel barker, Billy Bigelow, is a libertine and a hustler. When he learns of his wife's pregnancy, he chats gaily in his musical "Soliloquy" about the prospect of having a son. Then, realizing the child might be a daughter, his attitude changes; he becomes serious and responsible, determined to make for her a better life than he has known. "You can have fun with a son," he wistfully sings, "but you gotta be a father to a girl." As the tension mounts, Billy vows that he will do anything to get money enough to bring his daughter up properly.

> *I got to get ready before she comes!*
> *I got to make certain that she*
> *Won't be dragged up in slums*
> *With a lot o' bums like me.*
> *She's got to be sheltered*
> *And fed and dressed*
> *In the best that money can buy!*
> *I never knew how to get money,*
> *But I'll try,*
> *By God! I'll try!*
> *I'll go out and make it*
> *Or steal it,*
> *Or take it or die!*

The selection is a seven-minute narrative of operatic proportions, containing eight different melodies. It took Oscar Hammerstein two solid weeks to write the lyrics; Rodgers set them to music in less than two hours. The "Soliloquy" adds up to one of the most probing expositions of inner thought ever written for the musical stage. The blustery Billy reveals far more of himself than he could have reasonably done in speech alone, moving from boyish enthusiasm to tenderness to something approaching maturity.

Carousel is an adaptation of Ferenc Molnar's complex play *Liliom*, with the Hungarian setting changed to New England around 1873. Rather than the usual potpourri overture, the show begins with the expressive "Carousel Waltz," a piece of symphonic dimensions, requiring an orchestra almost twice the size of that normally found in the Broadway theater. The characters converse naturally in song, such as in the duet "You're a Queer One, Julie Jordan" early in the first act. Julie's melodies are compelling, but simple, appropriate for a shy young factory worker. Her personality is expressed perfectly in the number "What's the Use of Wond'rin'?" She is Billy's girl, and he is her feller, and "all the rest is talk." Halfway through the second act, Billy is killed in a desperate, stupid attempt to meet his forthcoming financial obligations. A note of hopefulness is injected at the end of the tragedy by the moving hymn "You'll Never Walk Alone," urging faith in mankind. The play's text encompasses greater depths of feeling than in *Oklahoma!*, while the musical horizon is expanded considerably. *Carousel* is one of Rodgers' most ambitious and tuneful scores and among his finest. Hammerstein's lyrics glow with humanity and compassion.

For nearly two years *Carousel* at the Majestic Theater and *Oklahoma!* at the St. James played across the street from one another in New York. *Allegro* (1947), Rodgers and Hammerstein's next show and their first original play, had a comparatively short run, although many of the critics liked it. The production was very avant-garde and had too heavy a message, however, to please the public. Directed by Agnes De Mille, *Allegro* detailed the life of a young physician from birth to his thirty-fifth year and explored the reasons why dedicated men sometimes lose their integrity after achieving success. In telling the story formal sets were eliminated, while a modern Greek chorus was used to comment on the action. The score was deliberately functional, with most of the important numbers assigned to relatively minor characters. There were also large choral episodes and an extended cantata for solo voices, chorus, and orchestra.

But two years later the team was victorious again with *South Pacific*, which opened in New York to the largest advance sale of any musical up to that time. Again the emphasis was on drama. The play is drawn from two stories in James Michener's *Tales of the South Pacific* and takes place during the Second World War. Its hero, Emile DeBecque, is a worldly, middle-aged Frenchman, in love with Nellie Forbush, a naive Navy nurse from Little Rock. All is well until the Arkansas girl discovers that her French planter is the father of two Eurasian children by his dead wife. Nellie, programmed by her background, reacts badly and for a time allows bigotry to overcome love. Both characters are flawed, both immensely human. Rodgers and Hammerstein's music develops naturally from the dialogue and captures something of the personality singing it. Nellie's songs are buoyant, uncomplicated, direct. She admits to being "stuck (like a dope!) with a thing called hope." Emile's music—"Some Enchanted Evening" and "This Nearly Was Mine"—is more mature, cultured, almost operatic.

The secondary plot involves a love affair between young Lieutenant Joe Cable and Liat, a Polynesian girl, which raises the racial issue squarely but tastefully. Liat's mother, Bloody Mary, has arranged the affair. Although Mary is aggressively opportunistic where the dollar is concerned, about her daughter she is genuinely sentimental. Her song "Bali Ha'i" is exotic and tender, full of haunting dissonance, capturing the romance of the South Pacific islands. Cable's "Younger Than Springtime" is a projection of his own youth and innocence, while in "Carefully Taught" he makes an eloquent plea for tolerance, explaining that people's hatred for other people is not born, but rather is the result of attitudes and prejudices we have learned from our society as children. Cable is ultimately killed on a daring mission mission with DeBecque, leaving his relationship with Liat unresolved.

While there is romance in *South Pacific*, there are also strong currents of realism. The idealized dream of "Bali Ha'i" is effectively contrasted with the Seabees' raucous "There Is Nothing Like a Dame," in which they divulge their single-minded desires. There are set pieces and hit tunes like Nellie's "I'm in Love with a Wonderful Guy," "I'm Gonna Wash That Man Right Outa My Hair," and "Honey Bun," among the most charming moments in all musical comedy, but none of these disturb the progress of the play. Consistent with the wartime setting, there is no formal choreography. The nurses and servicemen move in an ordinary way. Conversation and song flow one into the other. Take, for example, the scene in which Nellie first visits DeBecque's plantation home.

> Nellie: (speaking) "Want to know anything else about me?"
>
> Emile: "Yes, you say you are a fugitive. When you joined the Navy, what were you running away from?"
>
> The orchestra quietly enters here, giving a hint of her feelings.
>
> Nellie: "Gosh, I don't know. It was more like running to something. I wanted to see what the world was like—outside Little Rock, I mean. And I wanted to meet different kinds of people and find out if I like them better. And I'm finding out."
>
> Emile: "Would you like some cognac?"
>
> Nellie: "I'd love some."
>
> As DeBecque pours the brandy, Rodgers and Hammerstein take advantage of the lovers' momentary separation to allow them to sing a double soliloquy, in which the two can express their private thoughts.
>
> Nellie: "Wonder how I'd feel, living on a hillside, looking on an ocean, beautiful and still."
>
> Emile: "This is what I need, this is what I've longed for, someone young and smiling climbing up my hill!"
>
> Nellie: "We are not alike; probably I'd bore him. He's a cultured Frenchman—I'm a little hick."
>
> Emile: "Younger men than I, officers and doctors, probably pursue her—she could have her pick."
>
> Nellie: "Wonder why I feel jittery and jumpy! I am like a schoolgirl waiting for a dance."
>
> Emile: "Can I ask her now? I am like a schoolboy! What will be her answer? Do I have a chance?"

As the lovers stand facing one another, brandy in hand, the orchestra rises to a climax, telling the audience just how much in love they are, although they themselves are hesitant. A few more lines are spoken over music. Then Emile sings "Some Enchanted Evening."

In passages like this *South Pacific* comes close to the grandness of opera. The characters are portrayed realistically and at the same time, because of the music, are drawn larger than life. The big number does not come as a sudden jolt, for Rodgers and Hammerstein have masterfully prepared the way for it, heightening the drama all the while. And yet the score never *seems* operatic, for it is conceived in colloquial speech and popular song forms. The American musical theater had indeed come a long way. It had borrowed "this from opera, that from revue, the other from operetta, something else from vaudeville," Leonard Bernstein once said, but it had mixed "all the elements into something quite new,...something which has been steadily moving in the direction of opera."

Appropriately enough the original production of *South Pacific* featured the Metropolitan basso Ezio Pinza in the role of DeBecque, his first professional appearance outside the opera house. Nellie was delightfully played by Mary Martin, probably the finest performance of her career. Joshua Logan directed. While the message is clearly tolerance, the writers never make that their primary purpose. *South Pacific* is basically a love story, warmly and entertainingly told—one in which intolerance appears, but is overcome. The theme of brotherhood is simply a point of view; it is never allowed to stand in the way of good theater or burden a supreme musical achievement.

Many of the shows with less content in the 1940s demonstrated a professional polish and an integrity of story and music unknown twenty years before. Although Irving Berlin's *Annie Get Your Gun* (1946) is essentially musical comedy, its songs fit logically into the plot and are tailor-made for the characters who sing them. Jerome Kern had originally been engaged to write the score, but when he died, Berlin was asked to take over. The composer, still sensitive about his lack of training, was reluctant to commit himself to such an ambitious project, but producers Rodgers and Hammerstein prevailed. *Annie* proved the pinnacle of Berlin's career. Based on the exploits of Annie Oakley, the famous sharp-shooter of Buffalo Bill's Wild West Show, the musical has a folksy charm that the songwriter's music and lyrics complement beautifully. Few productions have offered such a concentration of hit tunes, among them "The Girl That I Marry," "Doin' What Comes Naturally," "You Can't Get a Man With a Gun," "I Got Lost in His Arms," "They Say It's Wonderful," "I Got the Sun in the Morning and the Moon at Night," "Anything You Can Do I Can Do Better," and the indomitable "There's No Business Like Show Business." All of these exude a warmth and a melodic lilt that are as fresh as Herbert and Dorothy Fields' book. *Annie Get Your Gun* provided Ethel Merman her greatest triumph and netted an average weekly income of $2500. A road company featuring Mary Martin was almost as successful, one of the finest touring productions ever. Like the original, it was carefully prepared, lavishly executed, with no expense spared.

Three years later Berlin worked with Robert Sherwood on *Miss Liberty* and a year after that with Howard Lindsay and Russel Crouse on *Call Me Madam*. The latter again starred Ethel Merman and enjoyed enormous popularity. This time Merman played a Perle Mesta-like lady ambassador, singing such befitting numbers as "The Hostess with the Mostes' on the Ball," "Washington Square Dance," and "Can You Use Any Money Today." *Call Me Madam* opened just as the build-up for the Presidential election of 1952 was getting underway and included the timely novelty "They Like Ike." More lasting were "It's a Lovely Day Today" and the duet "You're Just in Love," in which a show stopping intensity is reached when the song's two melodies are blended one on top of the other. Irving Berlin wrote little else for the next ten years. Then in 1962 he joined Lindsay and Crouse for another show, *Mr. President*, which opened to a large advance sale, but sustained only a modest Broadway run.

Cole Porter's masterpiece, *Kiss Me, Kate* (1948), followed a series of personal tragedies and professional disappointments. During the autumn of 1937 Porter had suffered a nearly fatal accident, when the horse he was riding reared and fell, crushing both of the composer's legs. After some thirty-five operations, one of his legs at last had to be amputated. Porter was in almost constant pain for nearly three decades, although he never seemed to grow old. He went on to write several more Broadway shows, like *Mexican Hayride* (1944), none of them quite equaling his earlier successes. The musical stage was changing, and Porter felt inadequate in the face of the more demanding style ushered in by *Pal Joey* and *Oklahoma!* Eventually he convinced himself that he was through.

Then came *Kiss Me, Kate*, a play within a play based on—of all things!—Shakespeare's *The Taming of the Shrew*. Sam and Bella Spewack wrote the book. The production ran for 1077 performances and contains some of the finest music Porter ever composed. His lyrics are highly intellectual, infinitely clever and yet human. Some of the words are taken directly from Shakespeare. There are glorious songs like "So in Love," "I've Come to Wive It Wealthily in Padua," "Were Thine That Special Face," and "Wunderbar," an echo from operetta. There are earthy comedy songs, such as "I Hate Men," "Always True to You in My Fashion," and the sunny "Brush Up Your Shakespeare." And there are big production numbers like "Too Darn Hot." While *Kiss Me, Kate* is musical comedy first and foremost, it is musical comedy on a high level, possessing a strong book, well-defined characters, sublime music, literate lyrics, and a production unity that *Anything Goes* or *Du Barry Was a Lady* never approached.

Porter later wrote the score for *Out of This World* (1950), which had an indifferent reception, *Can-Can* (1953) and *Silk Stockings* (1955), both considerably more successful. Toward the end of his life the composer was a crippled recluse, dividing his time between a cottage in Williamstown and an apartment in the Waldorf Towers. He died in 1964 at the age of seventy-three. Stephen Handzo noted in the Columbia University *Spectator* at the time of

Porter's death: "As Kern is the great romantic and Berlin is the great primitive, Porter remains the supreme sophisticate of American song."

But while an earlier generation of Broadway composers was coming to an end, a younger one was gaining prominence. Many of the newer songwriters after World War II differed from their predecessors in that they had received their basic professional training and achieved their first major successes not in Tin Pan Alley or on the musical stage, but in the Hollywood movie studios. Among these were Harold Arlen, Frank Loesser, and Jule Styne.

Loesser had enjoyed a happy introduction to Broadway in 1948 with the comedy hit, *Where's Charley?* Two years later he realized an even greater triumph with *Guys and Dolls* based on some Damon Runyan stories. In many respects the ideal musical comedy, *Guys and Dolls* contains a lot of debunking wit, while its characters are given lifelike dimensions, aided immeasurably by Loesser's songs. Sky Masterson, a self-centered professional gambler, identifies himself as such in "My Time of Day" and "Luck Be a Lady." Sarah, the prudish mission worker with whom Sky falls in love, eventually comes to see that her concept of life is narrow and unreal. She suggests her new sense of joy in "If I Were a Bell." Miss Adelaide, a nightclub performer, expertly played by Vivian Blaine, has been engaged to her gambler fiance, Nathan Detroit, for fourteen years. Every time she gets him near the altar, he runs off to the race track. In "Adelaide's Lament" her whole personality comes alive. The lyrics not only tell the audience how Adelaide feels and speaks, but imparts the nuances of her inflection. The song is both uproarious and pathetic, much like Adelaide herself. "I try to examine characters," Loesser maintained, "not events."

Jule Styne made his Broadway debut with *High Button Shoes* in 1947, a delightful piece of nostalgia featuring Phil Silvers and Nanette Fabray. *Gentlemen Prefer Blondes,* based on Anita Loos' book, came along two years later; the show skyrocketed Carol Channing to fame. The part of Lorelei Lee was ideal for Channing, who made the covetous blonde both adorable and musically exciting. She introduces herself as "A Little Girl from Little Rock" in the first act, but gets to the heart of her credo in the second with "Diamonds Are a Girl's Best Friend." Neither *High Button Shoes* nor *Gentlemen Prefer Blondes* made any pretense at being more than well-paced musical comedy, but Styne's score in each case was attractive and served the performers well.

The team of Alan Jay Lerner and Frederick Loewe would eventually do some work for Hollywood, but they began their collaboration on the musical stage. *Brigadoon* (1947), their first hit, was a fantasy about two Americans lost in the Scottish Highlands. Agnes De Mille did the choreography, while the Lerner and Loewe score included "Almost Like Being in Love," "Come to Me, Bend to Me," and "The Heather on the Hill." *Paint Your Wagon,* set in the California gold fields, followed in 1951. Its songs, most notably "They Call the Wind Maria" and "Wand'rin Star," project a flavor of genuine Americana, seeming more like expanded folk ballads than Broadway show tunes.

There were few successful revues after 1948, the year *Make Mine Manhattan, Inside U.S.A.,* and *Lend an Ear* all attracted large audiences. From then on television provided the public with more variety-type entertainment than they could absorb. Whereas an average of fourteen revues had been offered each season during the 1920s, by the 1940s there were only six. In the 1950s the seasonal average dropped to three. One of the most significant of these was *New Faces of 1952.* Off-Broadway revues, however, did continue to serve as a training ground for developing new talent. While there were fewer book musicals, too, in the 1950s, the average run of hit shows had greatly increased. A musical that lasted for 200 performances in the 1930s was considered a success; by the 1950s long-run shows frequently achieved well over 1000 performances. Despite mounting production costs, competition from other media meant that greater care must be given to all the component parts of a play if it were to appeal to the numbers desired. The appearance of longplaying records around 1951 resulted in more Broadway scores being recorded "complete," which in turn had a stimulating effect on the box office.

New York has never been the be all and end all of the American musical theater, although it has consistently dominated. The Los Angeles Civic Light Opera Association has become increasingly important since World War II and has introduced a number of hit shows in advance of their Broadway opening. The St. Louis Municipal Opera Association began in 1919, offering light opera and musical comedy in the gigantic outdoor theater in Forest Park in the summer seasons. Since these accommodations seat in the neighborhood of 12,000 people, the St. Louis "Muny" Opera has been one of the best-attended and most financially solvent summer theaters in the nation. The project was launched with a production of deKoven's *Robin Hood,* followed the next week by Balfe's *The Bohemian Girl.* For the first several years this was the pattern. American operettas like *El Capitan* and *The Wizard of the Nile* were alternated with European works ranging from *The Mikado* to *Die Fledermaus* to *Martha* or even *Cavalleria Rusticana.* Gradually new shows were added. *Gentleman Unafraid,* a Civil War story with music and lyrics by Jerome Kern and Oscar Hammerstein, was staged by the St. Louis company in 1938 for the first time anywhere. Although the operation for many years was essentially a local stock company, any number of performers who later became famous played there, among them Red Skelton, June Havoc, Pinky Lee, Irene Dunne, and Cary Grant, while Virginia Mayo spent a summer in the chorus. Jacob Schwartzdorf, subsequently known on Broadway as Jay Blackton, conducted the "Muny" Opera orchestra for six seasons, and Edwin McArthur, Flagstad's accompanist, was musical director for well over a decade.

The St. Louis Municipal Opera reached maturity around 1942, but did not employ the star system until 1957, when such luminaries as Eddie Foy, Jr., Dorothy Collins, and Mindy Carson came to Forest Park. *Show Boat* was revived the next year with Marion Marlowe, a St. Louis girl, as Julie and Andy Devine as Cap'n Andy. That same season Bob Hope returned to the role of

Huckleberry Haines in *Roberta,* his first appearance on the musical stage in nearly two decades. Attendance figures continued to grow, for the "Muny" Opera has always aimed at a popular following. Whereas similar ventures have either moved indoors or folded, the St. Louis company has remained alfresco. Various cooling systems have been tried from time to time, but the informal surroundings seem to be part of the charm. The management still prefers offering a different show every week and occasionally has shared productions with sister cities like Kansas City and Dallas. Current New York shows, with the original cast, have even been lured out for a brief run, mainly by the financial rewards of such a large theater.

The Dallas Summer Musicals began later and have never attained as much national recognition. Inspired in part by the success of the St. Louis Municipal Opera, the Dallas season was originally called the Starlight Operetta. Its organization was undertaken in 1941 by a committee of the State Fair of Texas, who felt that quality entertainment might attract more tourists into Dallas and appeal to the flood of wholesale buyers that came to town during the summer months. The twelve shows presented the first year, mostly vintage operetta, were managed and produced by J. J. Shubert, who worked with the State Fair on a profit-sharing basis. This arrangement lasted for only one season; by 1943 the company was an entirely local operation. The productions were staged in the Fair Park Casino, an outdoor bandshell near the midway and remained there for a decade. Unlike the "Muny" Opera, the Dallas management was attracted to the star system early. Dorothy Kirsten, Allan Jones, Vivian Blaine, Kenny Baker, Vivienne Segal, Ilona Massey, and Carol Bruce were all seen at the Starlight Operetta during the 1940s. Eventually the repertoire was freshened to include recent Broadway hits like *Up in Central Park, Bloomer Girl, Brigadoon,* and *High Button Shoes.*

In 1951 the musicals moved into the huge State Fair Auditorium and were renamed. Outdoors, rain had proved a problem, and the 1950 season closed with a substantial deficit. The year before an insect had gotten lodged in Nanette Fabray's costume, and the singer broke into hysterics on stage. The performance could not continue. With the move inside the number of shows was reduced to six a season, but the run of each was extended to two weeks. "Off beat" casting was attempted in an effort to fill the 4000-seat auditorium, usually with fairly curious artistic results. Cinema queen Arlene Dahl was brought in for *I Married an Angel;* Joan Blondell was given the Merman part in *Call Me Madam;* Lisa Kirk switched from Bianca to the title role in *Kiss Me, Kate;* Johnny Ray was seen as Sky in *Guys and Dolls;* and Liberace and his brother were offered in *The Great Waltz,* supported from behind in one scene by dancing waters rising and falling to the rhythm of "The Blue Danube," as multicolored lights played upon the cascading fountains. Featured performers were not always used so capriciously. Jeanette MacDonald was seen in *Bittersweet;* Gordon MacRae did *Carousel* before he made the movie version; Shirley Jones was an attractive Magnolia in *Show Boat;* and Janet Blair took the Mary Martin role in *One Touch of Venus.*

Lehman Engel conducted the Dallas Summer Musicals on numerous occasions, and the shows selected became increasingly modern. By the 1960s casting had grown more logical, although the presence of a star remained crucial for the box office. Juliet Prowse and John Davidson have returned for several productions, while road shows have frequently been imported to take some of the burden off the local company. Despite considerable success, the Dallas Musicals have never had the financial solidarity enjoyed by the St. Louis Municipal Opera.

While other cities have presented seasons of musical comedy, usually during the summer months, none of them have been particularly innovative. Even more have relied on touring companies and amateur groups to fulfill their community's theatrical needs. Except for an occasional West Coast production, Broadway continues to monopolize the new shows available, an out-of-town tryout still seems desirable, if often prohibitively expensive. Perhaps more than ever, New York dictates the nation's taste in musical theater, both production trends and stage techniques.

By the prosperous 1950s the emphasis on well-constructed librettos and dramatic integrity had become firmly established. Writers of musical plays no longer seemed afraid to enter the world of ideas. Social message was restricted largely to the theme of brotherhood, but that point was made frequently and with considerable impact. *Finian's Rainbow* (1947), with lyrics by E. Y. Harburg and music by Burton Lane, had dealt directly with the question of racial discrimination by using an interracial cast. The show combines fantasy and satire, joining Irish legends with contemporary American social and political problems. Left-wing socialism, prejudice in the South, share-cropping, corrupt legislation, and the idle rich are all touched upon without assuming a soapbox stance. The sting climaxes when a reactionary southern senator, who despises blacks, is turned into a black by a leprechaun. On the other hand, the leprechaun's love for a beautiful deaf mute who communicates by dancing reveals some of the play's tenderness. The score is highlighted by songs like "How Are Things in Glocca Morra," "Look to the Rainbow," "Old Devil Moon," and "That Great Come-and-Get-It-Day," all of which complement the story. *Finian's Rainbow* marvelously demonstrated that a show which is fundamentally musical comedy need not shy away from sturdy intellectual content.

Brotherhood continued to leaven the work of Rodgers and Hammerstein, but was especially prominent in *The King and I* (1951). The play focuses on two people from totally different environments who struggle to understand one another and come to realize that respect need not mean full agreement. Anna, an attractive English widow, is brought to Siam to teach the royal children the ways of the West. Her employer, the Siamese King, is tyrannical, incapable of admitting personal imperfection to others, although in "A Puzzlement" he expresses self-doubt to himself. Both characters are stubborn and proud, but ultimately find the humility to modify their views. Fundamental to their conflict is a contest between freedom and despotism and a different cultural perception of individual worth. While the show's setting is exotic, originally produced with sumptuous sets and costumes made of silks imported from Thailand, *The King and I* is a far cry from romantic operetta. Not only is there no traditional love interest between the two leading characters, the drama ends with the hero's death. There are sentimental moments, but these are treated tastefully, usually to reinforce the theme of tolerance.

Musically the play represented quite a challenge for Rodgers and Hammerstein. "I finally decided," Rodgers said, "to write a score that would be analogous in sound to the look of a series of Siamese paintings by Grant Wood." While his music is appropriate for the locale, the style is inescapably the composer's own. Action and musical continuity are combined more tightly than in any of his preceding work. Songs are interrupted with dialogue and then resumed, while instrumental music is extensively used to lend atmospheric support and to tie scenes together. Since the drama is nourished by an almost constant murmur of music, the transition from speech to song is made easily. A lengthy orchestral interlude, "The March of the Siamese Children," accompanies the entrance of the royal princes and princesses, its intensity growing proportionately with the increasing numbers of the children. The songs vary in color and texture, depending upon the characters singing them, and comprise some of Rodgers and Hammerstein's finest efforts: "I Whistle a Happy Tune," "Hello Young Lovers," "Getting to Know You," "We Kiss in a Shadow," "I Have Dreamed," "Shall We Dance?" and Lady Thiang's thoughtful "Something Wonderful." *The King and I* brought fame to actor Yul Brynner and marked the last performance of Gertrude Lawrence, who died of cancer during the play's run.

Me and Juliet (1953), a story about backstage life, found the team enjoying a change of pace. The show's most popular melody, "No Other Love," was drawn from Rodgers' mammoth score for the television series *Victory at Sea*. *Pipe Dream* (1955), based on the Steinbeck novel *Sweet Thursday*, with former opera singer Helen Traubel playing the part of a whorehouse madam, was as close as the songwriters ever came to failure. They were more successful three years later with *Flower Drum Song*, which lightly touched on the brotherhood issue. Primarily musical comedy, *Flower Drum Song* deals with Chinese and Chinese-Americans in San Francisco, but makes its strongest plea for understanding between generations.

The Sound of Music (1959), Rodgers and Hammerstein's last show, returned the partners to the top of their profession. Based on the career of the Trapp Family Singers and starring Mary Martin, *The Sound of Music* is set in Austria just before and during the Nazi occupation. While there are heavy, somber moments in the play, the mood is lightened by the Trapp children's discovery of joy as they come to trust and love their effervescent governess, Maria. Despite impending tragedy, the story radiates an infectious glow. Many of the songs—"My Favorite Things," "Do-Re-Mi," and "The Lonely

Goatherd," for instance—are winningly sentimental. Rather than with a formal overture, the show opens with a group of nuns singing an *a capella* "Preludium." The almost operatic "Climb Every Mountain," sung by the Mother Abbess, reaffirms the conviction Rodgers and Hammerstein had expressed in "You'll Never Walk Alone" that every man must have a faith or a dream to carry him through dark times.

Hammerstein knew during the rehearsals of *The Sound of Music* that he had abdominal cancer. Mary Martin met him coming into the theater one day. He pressed a crumpled piece of paper into her hand and said, "This is for you." The performer opened the paper and found written on it words she would later sing to the eldest Trapp daughter.

A bell is no bell till you ring it,
A song is no song till you sing it,
And love in your heart wasn't put there to stay,
Love isn't love till you give it away.

Hammerstein died on August 23, 1960. He had helped change the direction of the musical stage, having produced some of the warmest, most sincere lyrics ever written for the American theater. Rodgers and Hammerstein had brought more of their personal philosophy to the musical drama than anyone before them, lifted the American musical theater to a new artistic level, and proved the most influential force of their generation. They demonstrated that serious subjects could be effectively treated within the framework of light entertainment, bringing realism to the musical stage without surrendering sentiment. "What's wrong with sweetness and light?" Rodgers once asked. "It's been around quite a while. Even a cliche has a right to be true."

The composer continued writing, although the death of Hammerstein took its toll on his work. He wrote his own lyrics for his score to *No Strings* (1962), a play almost devoid of humor and with an unhappy ending. That same year he was made director of the New York Music Theatre at the Lincoln Center of the Performing Arts. He composed the music for *Do I Hear a Waltz?* in 1965, with Stephen Sondheim as lyricist, and in 1970 produced *Two by Two*, a musical setting of Clifford Odets' play about Noah's Ark. Much of the old spark seemed gone from Rodgers' music, although there were still those distinguishing traits, most notably the composer's penchant for suddenly introducing a note that is foreign to the scale in which the tune is written. While Rodgers claimed he never wrote for posterity, his best work contains a freedom of movement and an emotional impact that give his music the dignity of art. "Music lovers," he said, "should not cling to the belief that music is either too good to be popular or too popular to be good. What we need is more people who appreciate equally an Irving Berlin song and a Vivaldi concerto."

Other Broadway songwriters more deliberately aspired to serious art. Frank Loesser graduated from musical comedy to the musical play in 1956 with *The Most Happy Fella*, writing the text himself and creating a score of operatic proportions. Based on Sidney Howard's Pulitzer Prize winning drama *They Knew What They Wanted*, the show contains three acts rather than the usual two, almost three-quarters of which contain music in some form. There are hit songs, like "Standing on the Corner" and "Big D," but there are also arias ("Joey, Joey, Joey"), duets, recitatives, choral episodes, and instrumental interludes. To the best elements of the Broadway theater is added music of enormous emotional intensity. The characters speak and sing in an American idiom, and although *The Most Happy Fella* is conceived with craftsmanship and style, it does not become self-conscious in the way that many of the more formal attempts at American opera have. There is always a verve and a pace that reveal the show's vernacular roots.

Jule Styne achieve no such heights, but he did deepen his approach considerably for *Gypsy* (1959). He had written the score for *Hazel Flagg* in 1953, done a few songs for *Peter Pan* in 1954, and composed the music for the Judy Holliday vehicle *Bells Are Ringing* in 1956. But *Gypsy* was far more mature, its songs superbly congruous with the play. Derived from Gypsy Rose Lee's memoirs, the show offered Ethel Merman in one of her most dynamic performances, as the ambitious stage mother driving her daughters to success. Styne exhibited far greater gifts for dramatic writing than ever before, especially in "Everything's Coming Up Roses" and the powerful "Rose's Turn," both of which are star-tailored numbers, yet grow directly out of the story. The haunting "I Had a Dream" passage links several of the songs together, while the banal little tune "Let Me Entertain You" is used first as the two girls are auditioning for a vaudeville job, then reappears as the vulgar accompaniment for Gypsy's first striptease.

Fiorello!, a musical about New York's Mayor La Guardia, won the Pulitzer Prize for drama in 1959. The book was by Jerome Weidman and George Abbott, the lyrics by Sheldon Harnick, and the music by Jerry Bock, who had been introduced on Broadway three years earlier with *Mr. Wonderful*. *Fiorello!* begins with Mayor La Guardia reading the comic strips to children over the radio during the 1945 newspaper strike. Then, in flashback sequences, the career of the blustering iconoclast is traced from his law practice in Greenwich Village before World War I, through his term in Congress, to his election as mayor of New York. Along the way a rich panorama of the city's social and political life during those years unfolds, while Tom Bosley's faithful recreation of Mayor La Guardia was a marvel.

But perhaps the highest peak yet in the fusion of music, drama, and dance had appeared in New York on September 26, 1957, when *West Side Story* opened at the Winter Garden Theatre. A modernization of the Romeo and Juliet story, the drama deals with the clash between teenage gangs of native Americans and newly arrived Puerto Ricans and includes such novel touches as the Balcony Scene from Shakespeare played on a fire escape of a New York tenement. Instead of glamor *West Side Story* offers a look at life among the poverty stricken; rather than fantasy it probes the problems of juvenile delinquency and intolerance. When it turns to romance, it focuses on a hopeless love affair which concludes with the violent death of the male lead. There is a rawness and a naturalistic force to *West Side Story* that goes beyond the realism heretofore seen in the American musical theater, and yet there is a tenderness and an uneasy beauty that is tormenting.

Leonard Bernstein, who had had great success four years before with *Wonderful Town*, wrote the score, one of the most brilliant ever conceived for the Broadway stage. Stephen Sondheim did the lyrics. Since Jerome Robbins directed the production, in addition to creating the choreography, he could use dance with greater homogeneity of style. The "Jet Song" is part of a ballet, sung by the boys as they strut along the West Side streets. They belong not to society, they inform us, but to one another. Later "The Rumble" is entirely dance, savage and electrifying, yet serving to soften on stage a brutal ritual of the city slums. Graceful melodies like "Something's Coming," "Maria," and "Somewhere" take on added poignancy when sung against the squalor of the story's surroundings, amid the hatred and turmoil in which the lovers find themselves. "One Hand, One Heart" symbolizes their spiritual marriage, for they verbalize to one another emotions that are fine and true. There are lighter moments such as "The Dance at the Gym" and "I Feel Pretty"; there are ironic ones like "America" and especially "Gee, Officer Krupke!," a patter song explaining delinquency that is both wildly funny and heartbreaking. The "Tonight" quintet, counterpointing the love song against the gang's fury, is really an operatic ensemble, a dramatic and musically powerful conclusion to the first act. The full integration of music and drama comes with the scene in which Anita viciously confronts her friend Maria in song, with the rage of "A Boy Like That" eventually giving way to the triumph of love over hate with the gentle "I Have a Love."

West Side Story is a legitimate tragedy, steering a course between realism and poetry. The fierceness of the drama is eased by the ability of the city toughs to move in lyrical dance patterns, while their pent-up anger is offset by glimpses into their secret longings. The ugliness and vulgarity swirling beneath the city's surface is tempered by a fraternal chivalry and the realization that love can cross seemingly insurmountable barriers. Never before had the grim social problems of the present—racial, political, economic, and sexual—been handled musically with such uncompromising strength, yet these are treated in such a way that the questions raised speak of something universal. Bernstein's score is intelligent, full of subtlety, and reflects a serious composer's mastery of the popular idiom. Much of the music is fresh and lovely, although at times it becomes hard, nervous, dislocated. The cast—originally headed by Carol Lawrence, Larry Kert, and Chita Rivera—consists of thirty-nine members, with every person in the chorus playing a speaking part. With *West Side Story* the musical theater had become something truly vibrant—an indigenous, vital aspect of American art.

Even shows that were comfortably musical comedy had grown in

dramatic punch, tended to be based on sensible books, and often dealt with timely subjects. The plot of *The Pajama Game* (1954) revolves around labor problems in a midwestern pajama factory. The union is demanding a wage increase of seven-and-a-half cents an hour, and when the management of the Sleep-Tite plant refuses to approve the raise, the workers threaten to strike. The love interest centers around the factory superintendent and Babe Williams, head of the Union Grievance Committee. The emphasis, however, is less on employees' rights than on their fun and romantic complications. Certainly *The Pajama Game* has none of the social consciousness so blatant in *Pins and Needles*. Richard Adler and Jerry Ross, who wrote *The Pajama Game*'s music and lyrics, had begun their career as Tin Pan Alley songwriters, and their score contained its share of hits: "Hey There," "Steam Heat," "Hernando's Hideaway." The two repeated their success the next year with *Damn Yankees*, a story about a Washington, D.C. real estate salesman willing to sell his soul to see the Washington Senators win the pennant from the New York Yankees.

But the ultimate in post-war musical comedy was reached in 1956 with Lerner and Loewe's *My Fair Lady*, one of the most literary and coherent productions in Broadway history. Taken from George Bernard Shaw's *Pygmalion*, the text is incredibly witty; its characters become excitingly alive. Eliza, the Cockney guttersnipe, is believably transformed into a lady by a pompous and princely Henry Higgins. Julie Andrews and Rex Harrison gave virtuoso performances in these roles, aided by Moss Hart's brilliant staging. Each of the songs furthers the momentum of the plot, climaxing with the infectious "The Rain in Spain" number, in which all of the aspects of the musical stage come together in an inextricable unity. Some of the lyrics are drawn directly from Shaw's play; others, like "Why Can't the English?", are transformations of the original lines into a musical setting. The production was precisely timed and carefully synchronized so that its various elements contributed to one another and to the overall design. While pre-World War I London society is depicted romantically, the portrait conveys a feeling of authenticity with enchantment and charm.

The writers tried to match their achievement four years later with *Camelot*, casting Richard Burton as King Arthur, Julie Andrews as Guenevere, and Robert Goulet as Lancelot. Mounted with sumptuous sets and costumes, *Camelot* lacked the freshness and consistency of viewpoint that distinguished *My Fair Lady*. It nonetheless had a run of 874 performances. Shortly after the show closed, Frederick Loewe announced that he was taking a leave from Broadway for health reasons. Alan Jay Lerner soon began working with Burton Lane on *On a Clear Day You Can See Forever* (1965).

Far more old-fashioned than the musical comedies of Lerner and Loewe was Meredith Willson's *The Music Man* (1957), which aimed strictly at giving audiences a wonderful time. The composer had been known for years from coast to coast as a radio conductor and Hollywood songwriter. *The Music Man* was his first Broadway show. The fast-moving book, written by the musician himself, was an unashamedly sentimental story about an itinerant swindler's attempt to pad his pocket by organizing a boy's band in a small Iowa town. Willson had himself been a flutist in Sousa's band, although he later played with the New York Philharmonic. His score has a breeziness about it reminiscent of George M. Cohan, while its songs possess a homey quality that is hard to resist. *The Music Man* was a smash hit, in part because of Robert Preston's engaging portrayal of "Professor" Harold Hill. The composer was again successful with *The Unsinkable Molly Brown* (1960), but had less luck with *Here's Love* (1963), a musical version of the motion picture *Miracle on 34th Street*.

There were other productions in the 1950s intending little beyond sheer enjoyment. *Li'l Abner* (1956) was inspired by the comic strip; *Little Mary Sunshine* (1959) was a spoof on operetta; while *Once Upon a Mattress* (also 1959) combined light satire and fairy tale and set comedienne Carol Burnett on her way to stardom. *Kismet* (1953) was pure operetta, a fable about ancient Bagdad, with music derived from Alexander Borodin.

The Fantasticks, with music by Harvey Schmidt and lyrics by Tom Jones, opened on May 3, 1960, in a 150-seat theater in Greenwich Village and is still playing there nearly two decades later! Its mood is set by the wistful "Try to Remember," the show's most popular song. *Little Me* (1962), a Neil Simon play based on Patrick Dennis' book, is a musical burlesque on the familiar movie queen autobiography. *Bye Bye Birdie* (1963), the first Broadway show directed by Gower Champion, is a laughing look at a rock-and-roll singer, Conrad Birdie (obviously patterned after Elvis Presley), about to be drafted into the army. *A Funny Thing Happened on the Way to the Forum* found Stephen Sondheim writing music as well as lyrics, while the off-Broadway *You're a Good Man, Charlie Brown* was based on another favorite comic strip. *Sweet Charity* (1966), with Neil Simon again responsible for the book, served as a delightful romp for Gwen Verdon, while *George M!* (1968) revived the old Cohan tunes and found Joel Grey swaggering through the title role. By 1972 *Grease* could look back with some fun and some nostalgia at the teenage life style of the 1950s that *Bye Bye Birdie* had merely laughed at.

More and more Broadway musicals came to be based on material that had already proven itself in a different media. In part this resulted from the greater dependence on themes of substance; in part it grew out of increasing production costs and the need for assurance that the show stood a good chance of success. Robert Merrill, another Tin Pan Alley songwriter, was introduced in the theater by *New Girl in Town* (1957), a George Abbott adaptation of Eugene O'Neill's 1922 drama *Anna Christie*. Merrill's second musical, *Take Me Along* (1959), was derived from the O'Neill comedy *Ah, Wilderness*. N. Richard Nash's play *The Rainmaker* became *110 in the Shade* (1963), its music by Harvey Schmidt and lyrics by Tom Jones. *Cabaret* (1966) was based on the play *I Am a Camera* by John van Druten, while *I Do! I Do!* (also 1966) with Mary Martin and Robert Preston making up the entire cast, was inspired by Jan de Hartog's *The Fourposter*. *Mame* (again 1966) was a musical version of the book and later play *Auntie Mame*, offering Angela Lansbury in the role created by Rosalind Russell. *Two Gentlemen of Verona* (1971), with music by Galt MacDermot, was an updating of Shakespeare, and *Seesaw* (1973) was a revision of the play *Two for a Seesaw*.

Other shows were based on novels or satire. Betty Smith's *A Tree Grows in Brooklyn* was set to music by Dorothy Fields and Arthur Schwartz in 1951, with Shirley Booth taking the role of Cissy. Leonard Bernstein composed an excellent score for a dramatization of Voltaire's *Candide* (1956), although its initial production was a failure. Budd Schulberg's *What Makes Sammy Run?* became a musical in 1964, and Harold Rome collaborated with Jerome Weidman on an adaptation of the novelist's *I Can Get It for You, Wholesale* (1962), a story dealing with cutthroat competition in the garment trade. *I Can Get It for You Wholesale* was also the show that brought recognition to Barbra Streisand and Elliott Gould. *The Grass Harp* (1971) came from the Truman Capote novel of the same name.

Still other musical comedies, in a reversal of the usual trend, were based on films. Harold Rome, after two earlier book musicals—*Wish You Were Here* (1952) and *Fanny* (1954)—turned the classic western *Destry Rides Again* into a musical in 1959. *Carnival!* (1961), which had music by Robert Merrill and featured Anna Maria Alberghetti, was a musical treatment of the MGM film *Lili*. *Promises, Promises* (1968), with music by Burt Bacharach and a book by Neil Simon, was taken from the Academy Award winning movie *The Apartment*. *Zorba* (also 1968) was a remake of the Anthony Quinn film *Zorba the Greek*, while *Sugar* (1972) was patterned on the motion picture comedy *Some Like It Hot*.

Some shows owed their success almost exclusively to the presence of a single performer. *How to Succeed in Business Without Really Trying* (1961), despite a clever book and music by Frank Loesser, was a triumph largely because of the endearing antics of Robert Morse and a nostalgic appearance by Rudy Vallee. *Wildcat* (1960) survived almost entirely because of its star, Lucille Ball, vacationing from television, while *Tovarich* (1963) offered little besides the radiance of Vivien Leigh. Although *Funny Girl* (1964) had a score by Jule Styne, it depended heavily on the formidable talents of Barbra Streisand. The show, loosely based on the life of Fanny Brice, followed the established formula for Broadway musical comedy, and its songs, above all else, were vehicles for the featured personality. *Coco* (1969), which cost more than $900,000 to produce, would in all probability have been a disaster without the magnetism of Katharine Hepburn. When Hepburn left to make a movie and her role was assumed by Danielle Darrieux, the show closed quickly, although Darrieux in many ways was better suited to the part. *Applause* (1970) was based on a superior film, *All About Eve*, but the production owed its popularity first and foremost to Lauren Bacall as Margo Channing and secondly to her replacement, Anne Baxter, who as a young woman had played the title role in the motion picture.

Social consciousness on the musical stage of the 1960s was restricted primarily to the question of civil rights, particularly for blacks. *Golden Boy* (1964), an adaptation of the Clifford Odets play, changed the central character from a Jewish boy to a black. A dynamic performance by Sammy Davis was the production's main interest, but the score did contain bits of social commentary, particularly the song "Don't Forget 127th Street," with the classic line "There's no slum like your own." *Hallelujah, Baby!* (1967), featuring Leslie Uggams and music by Jule Styne, pictured the relationship between blacks and whites over the past sixty years. *Purlie* (1970), based on the play *Purlie Victorious*, touched upon the racial problem, although not as hard as *Raisin* (1973), a musical version of Lorraine Hansberry's *Raisin in the Sun*.

Four shows in the middle years of the decade reflect the major trends in recent musical theater: *Hello, Dolly!, Fiddler on the Roof, Man of La Mancha*, and *Hair*. All were triumphant box office successes. Two broke records for the longest-running Broadway musical, while the other two began as off-Broadway productions. Three were almost immediately made into motion pictures, while the fourth was considered mildly shocking. One was based on a distinguished American play. Another was taken from stories written by a Russian-American shortly after the turn of the century. The third was an adaptation of a Spanish classic. Only the fourth was an original conception. In three of the plays the pivotal character is well into middle-age; the youth so admired on the musical stage in the 1920s is accented only in the most experimental, the only one of the four without the presence of an established performer.

Hello, Dolly! (1964) is decidedly musical comedy, with emphasis on lively tunes, sprightly dialogue, wit, glorious production numbers, and the charm of a period setting. And yet the show's dramatic content is respectable, based as it is on Thornton Wilder's *The Matchmaker*. The mood is nostalgic without becoming offensively sentimental. The widow Dolly Levi, initially played by Carol Channing, is so outrageously aggressive that she becomes lovable. The role contains enough "put on" that the conniving aspects are eclipsed by enchantment, while it is sufficiently flexible that a seasoned performer can make the part her own. Dolly fondles a cash register and announces that she plans to marry its owner, the Yonkers hay and feed man Horace Vandergelder, yet makes it clear that she wants money only so that she and those around her can have a good time. Vandergelder, on the other hand, introduces himself with pride as a man who is "rich, friendless, and mean, which in Yonkers is about as far as you can go." Old lithographs are used as backdrops, while costumes abound in satins and ostrich plumes, supplying both atmosphere and glamor. Jerry Herman's melodies are attractive, especially the title song, popularized by Louis Armstrong, while Gower Champion's choreography was rich with crisp, yet sweeping ensemble dance patterns. Much of the credit for the production's appeal went to the staging and to Champion's imaginative direction. Dolly's entrance at the

Harmonia Gardens was built into one of the warmest moments in musical comedy.

The show is full of energy and glow, and the effect is sheer pleasure. *Saturday Review* called *Hello, Dolly!* one of the "zingiest musicals in some time," while *Time* magazine said there was "no handsomer way to visit Little Old New York." When Channing left the cast, the show continued merrily with Ginger Rogers, Martha Raye, Betty Grable, and Phyllis Diller in the title role. Eventually Pearl Bailey took the part, and *Hello, Dolly!* was given an all-black cast, causing the lines to form at the box office all over again. Before the production closed after its 2844th performance, Ethel Merman and a couple of new songs had added another dimension to its success, the only time Merman ever played a role not created by her. On the road the show barnstormed practically every town in the country, with Mary Martin, Eve Arden, Dorothy Lamour, Yvonne DeCarlo, and Virginia Mayo all heading companies at one time or another. There were even suggestions that Mae West or Liberace (in drag) take the part.

Fiddler on the Roof (also 1964), which enjoyed an even longer run, is substantial musical drama with an eye toward social realism, requiring an actor who can sing rather than a singer who can act. Inspired by some stories by Sholem Aleichem, who settled in the Bronx around 1906 having fled the Russian pogroms, the play takes place in Anatevka, an impoverished peasant village in Tsarist Russia, populated largely by Jewish families. Its people are simple, pious, close to the soil. They live by age-old laws, for without their tradition their lives "would be as shaky as a fiddler on the roof," trying to scratch out a simple and sensible tune without breaking his neck. Tradition enables them to keep their balance, so that everyone in Anatevka knows "who he is and what God expects him to do." Tevye, originally performed by Zero Mostel, is a poor dairyman with five unmarried daughters on his hands and a nagging wife. He improvises on the Scriptures, quips with God, expounds folk wisdom, sings like a frog, and dances like a bear. But he is "a good man," full of heart, ready to face his wife's ire and even social ostracism for his daughters' happiness. The eldest girl chooses to marry a poor tailor over the well-off butcher arranged by Yente, the matchmaker. The second follows a student-revolutionary to Siberia. The third marries a Gentile. In the end an edict comes ordering the Jews to sell their property and leave the land.

Certainly *Fiddler on the Roof* did not resemble the conventional Broadway musical. While there is humor, the story ends almost tragically, with only slight hope that the exiles will find a better life in a foreign land. Instead of spectacle the women wear peasant costumes, shawls and long skirts, while practically every man in the cast has a scraggly beard and is dressed in torn coats and battered black hats. But there is a wealth of common sense, valor without heroics, and a core of human truth. Lyricist Sheldon Harnick and composer Jerry Bock created words and music so natural to the people who sing them that the audience is scarcely conscious of the transition from speech to song. "If I Were a Rich Man" is an extension of Tevye's very being—cheerful in spirit, gentle, good-naturedly accepting a hopeless situation. Yet there are lovely melodies and beautiful lyrics, exemplified in the song "Sunrise, Sunset." The choreography by Jerome Robbins, who also directed, is consistent with the setting, but at times becomes energized to the point of frenzy, especially in the wedding dance, during which the male celebrants seem to be letting loose all their suppressed emotions. The show provides entertainment without ever losing sight of an underlying pain.

Man of La Mancha (1965) is musical drama of a different sort for the stress is not on social realism but on a climate of neoromanticism. A play within a play, the drama is sufficiently integrated that it was originally performed with no intermission. Miguel de Cervantes, the Spanish novelist and poet, has been thrown into prison for levying taxes against a monastery and must appear before the Inquisition. The dungeon in which he finds himself is inhabited by thieves, cutthroats, murderers, and prostitutes. Led by a criminal called "The Governor," the ruffians threaten to seize Cervantes' possessions, although these consist solely of worthless theatrical properties and an unfinished manuscript. Cervantes demands a trial, and reluctantly the convicts agree. The Governor will serve as judge. The writer asks to be allowed to present his defense in the form of an entertainment, with the prisoners playing roles.

Cervantes' play is about an aging country squire, Alonso Quijana, who having grown soft in the head, sallies forth into the world as the dauntless knight-errant Don Quixote de la Mancha, determined "to fight the unbeatable foe," "to right the unrightable wrong," "to reach the unreachable stars." Around him Quixote sees a "bleak and unbearable world," as "base and debauched as can be." Resolved that goodness and courage shall survive, he sets off with his faithful attendant Sancho Panza on his quest for the "impossible dream." At a nearby inn Quixote meets a serving girl and parttime trollop, Aldonza, a savage alleycat who despises all men for what they have done to her. The knight addresses her as "Sweet lady—fair virgin" and insists that she is Dulcinea, the lady of his dreams. But Aldonza, the hardened realist, is convinced that Quixote is a man who wants of her what every other man wants. She understands nothing of his mission—"Why do you give when it's natural to take?" She tries in vain to persuade the Don that she is not his Lady Dulcinea and pleads with him to take the clouds from his eyes and see her as she really is: "Born on a dung heap, to die on a dung heap, a strumpet men use and forget." Dr. Sanson Carrasco, a self-assured scholar and pragmatist, appears and attempts to convince the old man to give up his nonsense, explaining that there have been no knights, no castles, no chivalry for three hundred years. To this Quixote replies, "Facts are the enemy of truth." Carrasco returns disguised as the Knight of the Mirrors and forces Alonso to look into his multiple reflections. What he sees, of course, is not a gallant knight but an elderly fool dressed for a masquerade, and the old man is broken.

As Señor Quijana lies on his deathbed, Aldonza comes to him and begs him to "bring back the dream of Dulcinea," which she finds insufferable to live without. The drama concludes on a note of unmitigated romanticism. Quixote dies, but Aldonza, having caught the romantic vision, refuses to recognize his death. When approached by Sancho, she replies calmly, "My name is Dulcinea." Quixote, by seeing her throughout as an individual of depth and value, has in reality transformed her.

"When life itself seems lunatic," Cervantes had told the prisoners earlier, "who knows where madness lies?" As the author is summoned before the Inquisition, the Governor hands him his unfinished manuscript: "I think Don Quixote is brother to Don Miguel."

"God help us," Cervantes answers, "we are both men of La Mancha."

It is a moving experience, romance in a profound sense. The music and lyrics by Mitch Leigh and Joe Darion are sublime, ranging from simple ditties to dramatic soprano arias. Richard Kiley was eloquent in the title role, while Joan Diener sang Aldonza's difficult music with compelling nuances. Howard Bay's stage picture, dominated by a great drawbridge-staircase leading down into the subterranean dungeon, created an atmosphere appropriately stark so that illusion seemed far preferable to reality.

Hair (1968) is much less heroic in its romanticism. It is neither musical comedy nor musical drama, for it approaches life impressionistically, evoking moods rather than advancing a definite plot line. *Hair* is essentially a collage of hippie behavior contemporary to the late 1960s and attempts to induce a theatrical "happening." Like Don Quixote, its central characters are alienated from the society around them. But their quest is more personal, as suggested in the song "Where Do I Go?" They are seeking their own identity and searching for values and meaning in a community of people like themselves. The tribe is disgusted with the establishment, yet believes deeply in abstractions like brotherhood, peace, freedom, love, happiness—all good romantic ideals. And they see hope, evident in such songs as "Aquarius," "I Got Life," "Good Morning Starshine," and "Let the Sunshine In." Their optimism, however, is built on a plea for internal revolution. The old ways must go, so that life may be experienced to the fullest. This means a liberation of the emotions, sexual freedom, heightened awareness, relaxing discipline, and drugs.

The show was bold in several respects, both in form and message. It was the first rock musical, employing some twenty-six songs by Galt MacDermot, James Rado, and Gerome Ragni. It took the musical theater a step away from verbalism toward a multisensual experience. It rebelliously voiced words like fellatio, sodomy, and cunnilingus, hardly routine on the musical stage, and spoke of homosexuality and interracial sex. But *Hair* caused raised eyebrows most of all because of its nude scene, when for a brief moment at the close of the first act part of the shaggy-headed cast was seen naked from the front on a dimly lighted stage. The show offered a varied score, youth, and high spirits, yet its innocent, basically likable youngsters joyously "blew the mind" of the conservatives in New York, but even more so on the road.

Before *Hair* the musical stage had paid practically no attention to the rock revolution. Afterwards the popular lyric theater began to catch up with recent trends in American vernacular music. Shows like *Celebration* (1969) and *Godspell* (1971), based on the Gospel According to St. Matthew, used a rock idiom freely, while even period pieces like *Pippin* (1972) employed rock rhythms. *Hair* also prepared the way for a great deal of stage nudity, most immediately in the erotic revue *Oh! Calcutta!* (1969), in which the cast began the show by completely disrobing.

By 1970 it was obvious that the Broadway musical theater had produced a new genius—Stephen Sondheim. At one time a private pupil of Milton Babbitt, Sondheim had written a remarkable score for the experimental, but not particularly successful, *Anyone Can Whistle* in 1964. Then came *Company* (1970), perhaps the most mature musical yet. The realism of *Company* is far more intimate than anything the Broadway musical stage had offered before. The play is about human relationships, marriage, and personal growth. Robert, initially played by Dean Jones, is an attractive, intelligent, charming bachelor of thirty-five. His friends, five married couples, are ardently devoted to him and want the best for Bob. The men fix him up with dates they vicariously enjoy and give him advice from their experience. The women want to please him, mother him, and find him a nice girl, whom they will later reject as not good enough for him. Robert looks at these marriages and sees competition, boredom, the loss of individual identity, and the need to control. One couple is happy, for they have decided to divorce. Robert has fantasies about the girl somewhere waiting for him; she will be the best of each of the five wives. But he is kidding himself and continues living his carefree, somewhat empty life—a bit guarded, a little too cool, careful to stay emotionally uninvolved, painfully independent.

The second act begins with the rousing number "Side by Side by Side," which leads into "What Would We Do Without You," done by the cast in a vaudeville, hat-and-cane, tap dancing style. The five married couples are again expressing their admiration for Bob. He is everyone's best friend, seven times a godfather, and "such a cutie." Suddenly their praise is not as happy as it appears on the surface. While his friends get older, Robert always seems to stay the same. A fellow like Bob "doesn't have the good things, and he doesn't have the bad, but he doesn't have the good things." He always looks like he is keeping score. "Who's winning, Robert?"

One evening he is out with Joanne and Larry. Everyone is a little too drunk. Then Joanne proposes a toast, singing her bitchy "The Ladies Who Lunch," one of the most biting songs ever written for the commercial theater and marvelously delivered by Elaine Stritch. The life she pictures of American middle class women is comfortable but sterile. The girls who stay smart rush "to their classes in optical art," take in a Pinter play at a matinee, or perhaps hear a piece of Mahler's. Those who play wife keep house but clutch "a copy of *Life*—just to keep in touch." The ones who follow the rules "meet themselves at the schools—too busy to know that they're fools." And the girls who just watch ease their depression with a little jest, and maybe another vodka stinger, as they look for a "chance to disapprove," another "reason not to move." "A toast to that invincible bunch," Joanne concludes, "The dinosaurs surviving the crunch. Let's hear it for the ladies who lunch: Ev'rybody rise!" While Larry is paying the check, Joanne offers to take care of Bobby, who unthinkingly blurts out, "But who would I take care of?"

With the help of his "good and crazy" married friends, Robert at last discovers that commitment is part of growing up, that the woman he marries will make him happy and unhappy. In his final song, "Being Alive," he glimpses what life is really all about and knows that it is time for him to move on.

> *Somebody hold me too close,*
> *Somebody hurt me too deep,*
> *Somebody sit in my chair, and ruin my sleep, and make me*
>   *aware of being alive,*
> *Being Alive.*
>
> *Somebody need me too much,*
> *Somebody know me too well,*
> *Somebody pull me up short and put me through hell and*
>   *give me support for being alive,*
> *Make me alive,*
> *Make me alive.*
>
> *Make me confused,*
> *Mock me with praise,*
> *Let me be used,*
> *Vary my days,*
> *But alone is alone, not alive.*
>
> *Somebody crowd me with love,*
> *Somebody force me to care,*
> *Somebody make me come through,*
> *I'll always be there as frightened as you, to help us survive*
> *Being alive, being alive, being alive.*

Company is musical drama of the highest order, challenging audiences in an extraordinarily private way. Sondheim's score was among the most original, polished, civilized, and satisfying to come along in some time. Boris Aronson's modernistic Manhattan apartment-complex set, all steel and plexiglass, was an optical wonder of vertical shafts, elevators, and multiple playing areas. The show's emphasis, the composer explained, is on "looser, richer, freer forms" than in the so-called integrated musical. "In *Company* the songs are really outside the scenes rather than part of them. You can't guess so well in advance when the dialogue is building to a music cue." The play is a leaner, less cluttered approach than most previous musical dramas, developing the story line in terms of character.

In *Follies*, the next year, the concentration is again on character, and Sondheim's score is another rich one. There is much nostalgia, but it is a tearless, haunting kind of nostalgia. Among the show's original stars were Alexis Smith, Dorothy Collins, Gene Nelson, and Yvonne DeCarlo, while lesser roles reached back as far as Ethel Shutta and Fifi D'Orsay from silent movie days. The title literally refers to the golden era of the Weismann *Follies*, plainly meaning Ziegfeld, the epitome of show business magic from an innocent past. The production begins with breathtaking pageantry, lavish costumes, dazzling tunes, and the romance of yesteryear, a time when "everything was possible and nothing made sense." Weismann is having a reunion, before his theater is torn down. The band onstage begins to play, and the former *Follies* girls, a bit faded and some a good deal heavier around the middle, descend the staircase of their youth, as if time had stood still. Gradually it becomes apparent that despite its bright and beautiful appearance, *Follies* is not really about show business at all. It is about different forms of human folly, the crack right down the center of the gorgeous American dream.

While the show continues to operate on several levels at the same time, the foolishness of its middle-aged partygoers comes more clearly into focus. The black and white ghosts who lurk in the shadows grow more conspicuous amid the lushness of the celebration. Sally is married to Buddy, yet has continued to love Ben. She lives largely in the past, unable to return her husband's affection, so that he is driven to an out-of-town mistress. Ben is married to the queenly Phyllis, Sally's best friend from the *Follies* days. He is a wealthy foundation executive, but his success is hollow. Torn by conflicting values, Ben is disappointed with himself and runs from his guilt by drinking heavily and playing around with other women. Hostility has built between Phyllis and Ben through the years, so that she has resorted to affairs with younger men. Carlotta, another former *Follies* girl, became a film star and currently has a television series of her own. Mostly she has become an expert in survival, as she acknowledges in "I'm Still Here."

The turning point of the reunion is reached in the song "Who's That Woman?," for here the past and the present converge. Stella, played by Mary McCarty, coaxes the six women who used to back her up in the number to join her in resurrecting it. The routine is exhausting and now fairly ludicrous. The spell of magnificence and gaiety is broken, and a series of confrontations follows. Phyllis is unwilling to go back to the lie she and Ben have been living. Buddy realizes that he loves the wrong girl. Sally and Ben talk of running away together. The ghosts of the two unhappily married couples come out in the open. They look at each other and their younger selves at a time when choices were still open to them. The four become eight, in a cacophony of pain too intense to be viewed undiluted. At the peak of the anxiety, brightly colored curtains drop, creating a storybook setting. It is the *Follies* once more, but this time it is the follies of four people, their neuroses, and the unhappiness of their lives.

Buddy, wearing a toy car to represent his fatiguing life as a traveling salesman, is tossed between his loving mistress and the rejecting wife he adores. The curtains part again, and Sally is seen in a Jean Harlow gown, as she sings the torch song "Losing My Mind," probably the score's best number. It is all about her unrequited love for Ben. The repressed, dignified Phyllis lets down her hair to sing an ironic, but lively Porter-like ditty. Ben begins a Fred Astaire song and dance routine depicting a life of success. He breaks down, forgetting the lyrics of the lie. Suddenly he admits that he does not like himself and calls out for Phyllis. The nightmare of thirty years fills the stage in a variety of images. Sally is forced into the realization that there never was a Ben for her. The thing she has feared most—tomorrow—is here. Fortunately Buddy is there to help her. Phyllis allows her strength to conquer her despair, contending that "hope doesn't grow on trees—you make your own." The *Follies* have come to an end.

The show is a cruel, cynical look at life and people who know they have failed. Sondheim's music abounds in popular song styles from several eras, yet is full of irony and courageously serves the dramatic continuity. While *Follies* remembers the past, it always does so through the prism of the present.

A Little Night Music (1973), on the other hand, is set in Sweden at the turn of the century and has a score made up entirely of waltzes. Based on Ingmar Bergman's 1956 film *Smiles of a Summer Night*, the play is called "a fairy tale for adults." It is about people of leisure, whose most pressing concerns revolve around their past, present, and future love affairs. Sondheim's waltzes are catchy, but bittersweet. The show is scarcely fluffy operetta, for its nostalgia is again of the haunted variety. If Strauss comes to mind, it is not Johann but Richard; a motive from *Der Rosenkavalier* is even quoted near the close of the "Weekend in the Country" ensemble. The "Night Waltz" is reminiscent of Ravel's "La Valse" rather than *Die Fledermaus*. Sondheim's music once more shows a rare ability to delineate character and situation, as in the remarkable "Now/Later/Soon" trio, in which the dramatic tensions are intrinsic to the musical structure. The composer proves himself adept at creating diverse nuances of emotion, human ambiguity, as well as subtle, ironic wit. He possesses an unusual talent for droll verse and unexpected rhymes, which contribute greatly to the comic effect, and is a master at caustic understatement. The elaborate orchestrations, including harp and celesta, add much to *A Little Night Music*'s extraordinary atmosphere. Sondheim went on to develop in later shows; *Pacific Overtures* and *Sweeney Todd* were both complex musically.

In the early 1970s nostalgia became a dominant theme on Broadway, a good deal of it the plainly sentimental, less clouded genre. Shows like *Applause* were basically old-fashioned, emphasizing youth and romance, with the various characters all orbiting around its star. *1776* looked back on a heroic moment of America's past and the romance of a high ideal. Far more blatantly nostalgic was a rash of revivals from the 1920s. A rejuvenated version of *No, No, Nanette* in 1971, which brought Ruby Keeler and Patsy Kelly out of retirement, began the trend. One critic said the Youmans musical had an innocence that "makes *Oklahoma* sound like a Marxist tract in comparison." And yet it was an undeniable triumph, followed by *Irene* (1973) with Debbie Reynolds and *Good News* (1974) with Alice Faye and John Payne. Attempts to revitalize *The Desert Song* and *The Student Prince* were less successful. New shows like *Annie* and *On the Twentieth Century* benefited from the nostalgia craze.

By the middle of the decade, however, Broadway was beset by acute financial troubles. The producer almost invariably was now a businessman first, reluctant to take chances. Long-running musicals far outnumbered long-running legitimate plays, but costs were spiraling at such fantastic rates that most productions had to run at least a year before the show netted a profit. The movies and later television had made the road undependable, greatly reducing the number of touring companies, although original cast recordings continued to sell. When veteran director George Abbott was asked in 1973 what he thought was wrong with the theater, he said, "There's nothing wrong that a lot of beautiful girls with a lot of beautiful voices wouldn't cure." Certainly Broadway directors in many instances had abused the privilege of using actors with little ability to sing. Other seasoned observers, like Brooks Atkinson, argued that the quality of music had deteriorated into a standard monotone, as if composing for the stage were more a job than a pleasure. The range of music had become narrow, Atkinson claimed, "the themes mechanical, and the melodies tight and introverted." Everything sounded alike, "as if the times were too stereotyped for individuality." Still others, like Lehman Engel, maintained that what the contemporary musical theater lacked primarily was feeling.

Younger voices like Stephen Sondheim remained far more optimistic, insisting that new talents with fresh ideas and enthusiasm would come along, bringing different approaches to the musical stage. "There is no end in sight," Sondheim insisted, "as long as there are new challenges. There's always content lying around, and there will always be forms invented by inventive people to suit the content." Many would agree that while there are fewer musicals on Broadway, the most ambitious ones are superior even to the classics of years gone by. Their books are more literate, their lyrics make a point, their characters are understandable, their music is at home in the dramatic context, their direction sharper in every department. Gone are the interpolated songs, the shopworn cliches, and most of the trite sentiment that once was the very essence of the Broadway theater. While the better modern musicals still offer good tunes, they must begin with an idea and develop it to a meaningful conclusion.

"Out of our natural musical theatre," Leonard Bernstein once said, "which is wholly an outgrowth of our culture is emerging our opera, intelligible to all." Any number of distinguished musicians and critics have suggested that true American opera, that which genuinely speaks to us and reflects the American way of life, has come from Broadway. The hybrid nature of the American musical drama is part of its strength, for in the Broadway musical the nation's cultivated and vernacular artistic traditions have combined with authenticity and force, forming something unique. Within recent years the American musical theater has become an international institution. *Man of La Mancha* has been given in Spanish and French, *My Fair Lady* in Turkish, *Fiddler on the Roof* in Japanese. All three contain elements that are distinctly American, yet each offers something universal. From indigenous roots an exciting new art form has evolved, one that has probably won the United States more recognition abroad than all of her accomplishments in "serious" music. Beyond question the Broadway musical stage has won global attention and ranks among the nation's foremost cultural achievements.

CHAPTER

X

THE EVOLUTION OF JAZZ

In the summer of 1922 Louis Armstrong was working in New Orleans with Papa Celestin's Tuxedo Brass Band. On the afternoon of July 8, they played for a funeral over in the town of Algiers, across the river. Trombone player Eddie Vincent had lost his father. As the body was brought out of the house to march to the cemetery, Celestin's band rendered the hymn "Free As a Bird," bringing tears to the eyes of mourners. It was a swelteringly hot day, and the musicians nearly smothered in their uniforms. When they returned to the lodge house, someone came up to Louis with a telegram. It was from Joe Oliver. He had a place for his protege in his band in Chicago and wanted Louis to come at once. Papa Celestin and the boys in the Tuxedo Brass Band did their best to talk the youth out of going, but he rushed home, packed, and within a matter of hours was at the Illinois Central Station ready to catch the seven o'clock train north. His sister and the whole band came down to see him off and wish him luck.

Around ten o'clock the next evening the twenty-two year-old Armstrong pulled into the old LaSalle Street Station in Chicago. He grabbed his bag and took a cab to the Lincoln Gardens, where King Oliver's Creole Jazz Band was the reigning sensation. As he opened the door to the large dance hall, Joe Oliver was standing in front of his band, blowing his head off. Suddenly,

Louis felt a little frightened. This was his big chance, and he stood there in his derby hat and country clothes, wondering how he was going to make out. He walked over to the bandstand, and there were some of the guys he had known back home—the Dodds brothers, trombonist Honore Dutrey, bassist Bill Johnson. They were all glad to see him, and Papa Joe was tickled to death. Louis sat in with the band, playing second cornet.

Chicago was now the jazz center that New Orleans had been earlier. The Lincoln Gardens, formerly the Royal Gardens, was on Thirty-first and Gordon Streets on Chicago's South Side and catered to both black and white audiences. It was a huge place, with a big balcony all around and a canopy that ran from the doorway to the street. Scrolls were cut in the stone of the sharply peaked gable, while two round arches hung over the entrance. At first glance the lobby seemed "a block long" to the young cornet player fresh from the bayou country. The hall was dimly lit and filled with tobacco smoke. Glasses of bootleg liquor were on the tables, while a large mirrored ball revolved slowly over the center of the dance floor, reflecting rays of colored light from the hidden lanterns trained on it. Every night that floor came alive with pleasure-seekers who bounced and shuffled to the rhythm and the melodies of the Creole Jazz Band. Joe Oliver had formed the group in 1920, soon afterwards taking it to California. He had returned to Chicago and had been booked into the Lincoln Gardens shortly before sending for Armstrong.

From the moment Louis arrived and began playing with Oliver, their bandstand was the focus of Chicago's interest in jazz. Their "breaks" rolled out of their two short horns fiercely and flawlessly and were discussed all over town. Transfixed audiences crowded around the bandstand, unable to understand how the two cornetists could play together so effortlessly, without anything written down, without even looking at one another. They never clashed on a single note. The whole team inspired each other, encouraged one another to soar to new heights, working with infallible instinct. The two cornetists would pile up choruses, Eddie Condon remembered, "with the rhythm section building the beat until the whole thing got inside your head and blew your brains out." Numbers like the "Snake Rag" grew into classics overnight. The management was fairly relaxed about admitting teenagers, and Lincoln Gardens became a hangout for white high school boys who had gotten turned on to this new thing called jazz. Side by side with these novices would be professionals from the commercially successful white orchestras, hoping to pick up a few gimmicks from the black musicians. Whenever Paul Whiteman, Art Hickman, or Paul Ash were in town, they would visit the Gardens, while their arrangers, pad in hand, tried to write down what the Creole Band was playing.

During and after the First World War thousands of blacks moved north, lured by the wages to be made in the major industrial cities and an atmosphere less blatantly racist than that in the South. Chicago attracted more of the black migration than any other city in the upper Mississippi Valley. Within a five-year period the black population of the South Side, between Twelfth and Thirty-first Streets, doubled—most of it congested into flimsy, unkempt tenements. Along with the stockyard and factory workers came black musicians, so that the city's black belt became the new jazz paradise. Many southern whites came north, too, for except for a brief post-war depression, there was lots of loose money. Chicago was notorious for its resistence to Prohibition, and hundreds of speakeasies operated openly. Amid rapid changes, gambling and prostitution enjoyed a heyday. Hoodlums from dozens of gangs made enormous profits from vice and the distribution of illegal liquor. The dance halls, saloons, cabarets, and cafes they supplied needed entertainment, and singers and musicians of all sorts were in demand. On the South Side particularly this meant opportunities for jazzmen, and while conditions there were violent and uncertain, the high salaries served as a sufficient magnet to draw musicians up from the Delta. Many of those who came found life in the black metropolis lonesome and impersonal. They longed for old friends, familiar cooking, the sounds and smells of "down home." Yet with work plentiful, few went back. Besides, black poet Langston Hughes recalled, on the South Side there was "excitement from noon to noon. Midnight was like day."

These are the surroundings Louis Armstrong acquainted himself with as the summer of 1922 wore on. The Creole Jazz Band continued its success at the Lincoln Gardens, with Oliver and Armstrong hypnotizing crowds with their combined cornet work, peeling off notes listeners had never heard before. "[T]here was a tone from the trumpets," Eddie Condon noted, "like warm rain on a cold day." The band was shortly rejoined by Lillian Hardin, a slender, pretty, lightskinned, Memphis-born pianist, who had studied music at Fisk University. She had first played for Oliver at seventeen; she was now nineteen. She and Louis hit it off from the beginning, and early in 1924 she would become Armstrong's second wife. When its winter engagement at the Lincoln Gardens was over in April, 1923, King Oliver took his band on a tour of Illinois, Indiana, and Ohio, playing one-night stands in ballrooms. At Richmond, Indiana, they made some recordings for the Gennett Company, Louis' first experience with records. Persuaded largely by Lil, Armstrong left Joe Oliver in 1924, performing next as featured soloist with Ollie Power's group at the Dreamland Cafe in Chicago. That September he went to New York to join the Fletcher Henderson Orchestra, one of the most famous of the big Harlem dance bands.

By then the Creole Jazz Band had split up. Oliver formed a larger group, the Savannah Syncopators, and recorded a number of sides for Vocalion. Time passed, but Papa Joe changed very little, either in his playing or his lifestyle. He remained the horn player from the South, eating a big plate of hominy for lunch and, now that he could afford it, a half dozen hamburgers, topped off with a quart of milk. Legend has it that he once ate twelve pies at a sitting. The King continued to play various spots around Chicago. He had an offer to open the Cotton Club in New York, but turned it down, preferring to stay in the Midwest. Gradually he faded. After a decade of failing health and sinking spirits, Joe Oliver died in Savannah in 1938, having spent his last years as the janitor of a pool hall.

At the height of his Chicago fame King Oliver's principal competition came from a white band calling themselves the New Orleans Rhythm Kings, which held forth at Friar's Inn. The Inn was a gangster-run speakeasy, slightly more select than the Lincoln Gardens, but a dim, smoky dive nonetheless. The Rhythm Kings consisted of eight members, about half of whom came from New Orleans. The group featured clarinetist Leon Rappolo, a veteran of Storyville. Trumpet player Paul Mares and trombone player George Brunies were also from the Crescent City, as was bassist Steve Brown, the oldest of the group at thirty-three. The band maintained a smooth, relaxed New Orleans style, and its most important members still could not read music. At Friar's Inn the Rhythm Kings earned as much in one month as they had in a full year back home and got so heady with success that they "wouldn't go round the corner without catching a cab."

Like the Lincoln Gardens, Friar's Inn became a gathering place for youngsters and professional musicians interested in the new music. Teenagers barred from entering would stand in the parking lot up against the rear wall of the Inn. The bandstand was just inside, and the music came out through the exhaust of a wall fan, located right over the performers' heads. There were young cornetists like Jimmy McPartland and Muggsy Spanier. There were aspiring reedmen like Bud Freeman and Frank Teschmaker, guitarists and banjo players like Eddie Condon and Dick McPartland, Jimmy's slightly older brother. And there were novice drummers like Davey Tough and George Wettling. Don Murray, one of the musicians who used to crowd into Friar's Inn, recalled Rappolo "riding high on his clarinet with one foot braced high up on a pillar alongside the stand,...so full of marijuana he could scarcely move out of his chair at the finish of a set."

If the high school kids could not come up with the money to go to Friar's Inn, they often met at a West Side drugstore known as the Spoon and Straw, where they listened to the Rhythm King's records. Eventually some of the youngsters decided to form their own jazz band, closely copying the work of the New Orleans musicians they had come to idolize. In 1922 five white boys from Chicago's Austin High School got up a group which included Jimmy McPartland, Frank Teschmaker, and Bud Freeman. Its instrumentation consisted of cornet, clarinet, banjo or guitar, piano, and six saxophones. The Austin High Gang called themselves the Blue Friars and began playing for high school fraternity dances and at the homes of fellow students, in a style of extraordinary freshness and verve. Later on, Eddie Condon sat in with the Austin High Gang and still later Gene Krupa.

In the fall of 1923 another local group, the Wolverines, was organized, and with them a distinct Chicago style really began. The group also produced the most distinguished of all the Chicago jazzmen, cornetist Bix Beiderbecke, whose unorthodox playing was considered perhaps the most beautiful, original, and sensitive of that decade. Born in Davenport, Iowa, March 10,

1903, Leon Bismarck Beiderbecke was the son of a well-to-do lumber merchant. Riverboats occasionally went as far as Davenport with their bands, and Bix grew up familiar with ice cream parlor ragtime. Although his family environment was reasonably musical, he never took a lesson on the cornet and was never more than fair at reading music. A handsome young man whose parents were full of college plans for him, Beiderbecke was sent in 1921 to Lake Forest Academy in the northern Chicago suburbs. Already he had heard the records of the Original Dixieland Jazz Band and was much impressed by the trumpet style of Nick La Rocca. In Chicago he listened to Oliver and Armstrong, but was probably most influenced by Paul Mares of the New Orleans Rhythm Kings. He was especially fond of the old Dixieland Jazz Band tunes and began playing piano and later cornet for school dances.

He spent more and more of his nights hanging around the speakeasies and cabarets listening to the jazz masters, less and less of his time on school work. Eventually he began jobbing around the city and playing on excursion boats with several different groups. Self-taught, he followed his own instincts in fingering the horn and raised all of the parts written for the cornet from B-flat to the piano key of C-major. Yet his playing was lyrical and precise, and he gradually developed a biting, easy, belltoned style completely his own—tasteful and controlled, much less forceful and dramatic than Louis Armstrong's.

Bored with school, he grew determined to quit. The Wolverines, which Beiderbecke helped form, an offshoot of the Chicago-Michigan City excursion boat band, secured an early booking at the Cascades, a neighborhood ballroom on the Chicago North Side. Their first great notoriety came from an engagement at the Stockton Club, a roadhouse near Hamilton, Ohio, on New Year's Eve, 1923. A gangland war broke out during the event, and to cover the clamor the band furiously improvised on "China Boy" for more than an hour, amid flying dishes and crashing bottles. All but one of the Wolverines were college men, and the group shortly became popular at Midwestern university dances. They also got a fair number of bookings at theaters, dance halls, and ballrooms around Indiana, Ohio, and Kentucky. At the University of Indiana the band proved such a sensation they played ten weekends in a row, impressing many, most notably Hoagy Carmichael, who was an undergraduate there. Soon they began to record, and the Beiderbecke legend was on its way.

The Wolverines continued to barnstorm the Great Lakes area through most of 1924, bringing live jazz for the first time to many midwesterners. That fall the group went to New York, playing at the Cinderella Dance Hall on Broadway. After a short while there, Beiderbecke left the band and returned to Chicago, doing some freelancing. In his best work he was not so much imitating the black idiom as he was inspired by it. Beiderbecke took jazz seriously enough to make it personal. Critics sometimes found his style too sweet and sentimental, but few denied his clear, plaintive, romantic sound or his emotional dedication. "To me, Bix, well, that was it," Jimmy McPartland said. "What beautiful tone, sense of melody, great drive, poise, everything!" Hoagy Carmichael remembered hearing him rehearse: "The notes were beautiful, and perfectly timed. The notes weren't blown—they were hit, like a mallet hits a chime, and his tone had a richness that can only come from the heart." Beiderbecke sat in with Louis Armstrong lots of times in Chicago. "His tone—phrasing—his sense of harmony was the most marvelous thing anybody wants to hear," Armstrong recalled. "All my life I had been listening to music," Eddie Condon wrote. "But I had never heard anything remotely resembling what Beiderbecke played. For the first time I realized that music isn't all the same, that some people play so differently from others that it becomes an entirely new set of sounds."

Bix became the greatest of the Chicago jazz virtuosos, the embodiment of the Chicago style. His artistry had greater refinement than that found in New Orleans, while his ensemble work was fused with subtle tints and shades. The Chicago tempo tended to be faster than that characteristic of New Orleans. Rather than the relaxed, flowing line typical in the South, the Chicago style was more jagged, harsh, tense, and driving—reflective perhaps of the hectic industrial complex that gave it birth. Chicago jazz was also more highly arranged, although bands sometimes faked group improvisation.

Early in 1925 Beiderbecke was playing with Charles Straight's band at the Rendezvous Cafe on North Clark Street in Chicago. Straight himself was not much interested in the hotter forms of dance music, but after the leader left, around midnight, the band played what they wanted until closing time. Bix still spent a great deal of time at the black night spots on the South Side, listening to local favorites like Jimmy Noone, and he adored Bessie Smith, who had just come to town. He returned briefly to Iowa, enrolling for formal courses in music at the State University in Iowa City. He took up residence at the Beta Theta Pi fraternity house, and for one semester was a full-fledged college student. In September he received an offer to play with Frankie Trumbauer and left for St. Louis, where Trumbauer was engaged for a year at the Arcadia Ballroom. Beiderbecke had grown fond of symphonies and especially liked modern music—Debussy, Ravel, Stravinsky. While he was working in St. Louis, he nearly wore out a recording of the *Firebird Suite* and discovered in Trumbauer a companion who shared his interest in the modern classics. When Trumbauer's band broke up in the middle of 1926, both Frankie and Bix moved into Jean Goldkette's Orchestra. This marked a real step up in prestige, for Goldkette was a shrewd businessman, and his orchestra was well known, on top of the best commercial market. Beiderbecke joined the Goldkette forces mainly for financial security, but also he had a vague desire to come to grips with "composed" music.

Younger jazz enthusiasts like drummer Gene Krupa were meanwhile gigging around Chicago, happy to land any job that paid. Born on the South Side in 1909, Krupa was of Polish-Catholic descent. He dropped out of high school and began working some of the small Chicago clubs, beer joints, and an occasional party—much to his family's dismay. He came along too late to hear the Rhythm Kings and missed Oliver and Armstrong at the Lincoln Gardens. The Austin High Gang became his idols, for he found them very much "the real, noncommercial thing." Because he needed money Krupa began playing with a number of classy bands, like the Hoosier Bell Hops, the Seattle Harmony Kings, and the Benson Orchestra of Chicago. Their leaders were all afraid of "hot pollution," and Gene considered their public "square." After these commercial engagements Krupa and his friends would meet at the Three Deuces, a speakeasy opposite the Chicago Theatre on State Street, where they would jam for the rest of the night. While the practice of after hours "sitting in" had been widespread in New Orleans, the Chicago jam sessions were much less orderly affairs, with any combination of instruments blaring away in a determined effort to seize the spotlight and gain the attention of the crowd.

By the mid-1920s Chicago harbored more night spots than any other city in the country, and most of them employed musicians. It was a city of varied personalities, and the music that grew up there reflected this. Certainly the postwar hysteria and disillusionment found their way into the hyperthyroid jazz style that was emerging. The rowdier places, those most closely associated with vice and corruption, preferred hot music. Nightclub musicians learned to expect the unexpected. One band returned to the stand from an intermission to find their instruments shot full of holes. "We would see those rods come up and duck," drummer George Wettling recalled. The boss at the Triangle Club was shot in the stomach one night, but the musicians kept on playing. "At one place we worked," trumpeter Marty Marsala said, "Capone would come in with about seven or eight guys. They closed the door as soon as he came in. Nobody could come in or out. Then he gets a couple of hundred dollar bills changed and passes them round to the entertainers and waiters. His bodyguards did the passing. They got five or ten bucks just for playing his favorite numbers." Against this background Chicago jazz was bound to develop a different sound than what had come up from New Orleans—on the one hand tougher and more bitter, on the other more commercial and sentimental.

Around 1922 there were two kinds of jazz bands. One was the small unit of five or six men, featuring piano, banjo, drums, tuba, cornet and C melody saxophone or clarinet. This is the sort of combination of instruments that made up the New Orleans Rhythm Kings and the Original Creole Band. The other type was the production outfit of fourteen or more players, emphasizing more brass and lots of saxophones. The latter tended to move further away from improvised playing toward the more commercial forms and worked the better night spots, hotels, cafes, and showrooms. They appealed to a more sedate crowd and were more closely tied to formal entertainment. The smaller groups supplied the music for the cabarets and dance halls and sometimes brothels thinly disguised as eating and drinking places. Black musicians tended to dominate the South Side, but the white bands were more important in the area around the Loop.

As time went on and the number of jazzmen increased in the city, there was considerable resentment between the local musicians and those coming up from the South. Since the local jazzmen had the support of the musicians' union, they often made it difficult for outsiders to get jobs. Musicians from New Orleans were frequently barred from the musicians' union on the basis that they could not read music and had to demonstrate this ability before an examining board. "I can read them notes," Wingy Manone protested, "I just can't separate 'em—five flats look like a bunch of grapes to me." Many distinguished southern jazzmen—Kid Ory and Eddie Garland among them— could not read music until after they came to Chicago. Ory said he took lessons from a German musician who played with the Chicago Symphony.

There was also a jazz piano style in Chicago known as boogie-woogie, which flourished on the South Side a decade or so before it was discovered by the rest of the country. Boogie-woogie emerged from the blues, borrowed heavily from the barrel-house sounds of the South, and was marked by a steady, rocking rhythm. The left hand repeated a brief rhythmic pattern throughout the piece, while the right hand created the melody. Jimmy Yancy had played boogie-woogie at Chicago rent parties before World War I, but it was not until Clarence "Pinetop" Smith recorded in the late 1920s that the style received national attention. Boogie-woogie did not become really well known for another decade, when it was greatly commercialized and reduced to a formula.

But for many observers jazz was jazz and by definition suspect. More than most decades, the 1920s was an age of insecurity and social conflict. America's rapid emergence as a world power, her increased industrialization, the sudden emergence of a significant white collar class, newly gained freedom for women, a growing sophistication in the cities, and the failure of basic traditional values combined to produce uneasiness in most aspects of life. World War I and the shortcomings of the Paris Peace Conference served merely to dramatize the inadequacies of conventional thinking. Middle class youth particularly were restless and often seemed eager to flaunt the standards inherited from their parents. The press fanned their anxiety into wanton revolt. Many young people, in Chicago and elsewhere, found in jazz not only a meaningful esthetic experience, but a way through which to voice their protest. Eventually the new music became the symbol of rebellion, and as that happened it was condemned by conservatives with a vehemence bordering on fanaticism. In their attempt to find comprehensible explanations for far-reaching problems, educators, clergymen, and reactionary politicians sometimes spoke as if jazz—and jazz alone—was responsible for the deterioration of the nation's morals.

"I can say from my own knowledge," an official of the state hospital at Napa, California, declared, "that about fifty percent of our young boys and girls from the age 16 to 25 that land in the insane asylum these days are jazz-crazy dope fiends and public dance hall patrons." Jazz combinations, dope fiends, and public dance halls—for him—were all the same. "Where you find one, you will find the other." Disturbed by conditions in Chicago, the New York *American*, January 22, 1922, reported:

> Moral disaster is coming to hundreds of young American girls through the pathological, nerve-irritating, sex-exciting music of jazz orchestras, according to the Illinois Vigilance Association.
>
> In Chicago alone the association's representatives have traced the fall of 1,000 girls in the last two years to jazz music.
>
> Girls in small towns, as well as the big cities, in poor homes and rich homes, are victims of the weird, insidious, neurotic music that accompanies modern dancing.

And in a speech before several hundred teachers, the Kansas City, Missouri superintendent of schools warned, "This nation has been fighting booze for a long time. I am just wondering whether jazz isn't going to have to be legislated against as well."

As the new music spread across the country by traveling bands, phonograph records, radio, and motion pictures, conservative fears mounted. James T. Farrell, in his novel *Studs Lonigan*, pictures a Catholic priest during the late 1920s lashing out with equal fire at atheism, free love, birth control, and jazz. "These and similarly miscalled tendencies," he insisted, "are murdering the souls of youth." Many contended that jazz appealed to the primitive instincts and evoked man's baser nature. Dr. E. Elliot Rawlings, a New York physician, explained: "Jazz music causes drunkenness...[by sending] a continuous whirl of impressionable stimulations to the brain, producing thoughts and imaginations which overpower the will. Reason and reflection are lost and the actions of the persons are directed by the stronger animal passions." Others condemned jazz as "nigger music" and "whorehouse music," arguing that its "jungle" sounds would return American society to the level of barbarism. When white clarinetist Milton Mezzrow openly renounced his ties with the white world and moved into a black community, these suspicions were simply intensified.

It was pointed out that jazz had grown up with vice, while the unconventional behavior of many of its players was made much of—everything from their experimentation with drugs to their own complex argot. The new dances were found sensuous and therefore indecent; some even compared them with the orgies before the fall of Rome. The motions, the *Catholic Telegraph* of Cincinnati complained, "are such that as may not be described with any respect for propriety in a family newspaper." There were frequent claims that the new dancing was responsible for an increase in illegitimate births. And the lewd lyrics of jazz singing were no better.

Professional critics and serious musicians almost uniformly deplored jazz as a doggerel music, which—like the newspaper comic strip—represented America's taste at its lowest. "To condemn a lover of music to sit through a concert of such stuff," Daniel Gregory Mason wrote, "is to closet

Shelley with the schoolboy for a whole evening. . . . There are people who seem to think there is something shocking about jazz. Ah, if there only were! It is its blank featurelessness, its unrelieved tepidity, that are so pitiless." Jazz violated a traditionalist concept of idealism that implied a nobility and an esthetic perfection derived from God. Art in this sense demanded restraint and discipline. Rather than being confined by formal techniques, jazz musicians improvised and indulged in a freedom of emotional expression. *Musical Courier* denounced "this Bolshevistic smashing of the rules and tenets of decorous music," while *The Musical Quarterly* suggested that "jazz may be destined ever to play the court fool in the kingdom of music, irritating and yet amusing us by the sardonic quality of its jest." Less lofty publications likewise considered jazzmen incompetent, dismissing their music as so much noise. "If Beethoven should return to earth and witness the doings of [a jazz] orchestra," the *Ladies Home Journal* bemoaned, "he would thank heaven for his deafness."

Yet while the jazz arena was being labeled a disaster area by many, others saw hope. Perhaps in the right hands this lowly music could be spruced up a bit, tamed, and have its rough edges knocked off. At the same time that Americans in the 1920s were growing alarmed by what they deemed a rising degeneration of the youth, they were also busily searching for a national identity. For some jazz held the potential for becoming the distinctly American music the country had wished for so long. By 1926 *Harper's Magazine* admitted that it had become fashionable to hail jazz "as the only truly American contribution to music and to acclaim it as Art." But this was jazz that had been pruned of its primitive beat and earthy lyrics, jazz that had been housebroken and brought within the pale of the genteel tradition.

The mid-1920s found the push to make jazz a lady well underway, although the impulse had begun earlier. As long as jazzmen were content to work the bordellos and underworld dives, they could play practically anything they liked. But when they began seeking respectability and acceptance by polite society, changes and dilution were clearly essential. By 1922 the classy bands were not the only ones playing commercial music; some of the smaller groups, like the Original Dixieland Jazz Band, had discovered that there was more money in emphasizing fox trots and a more subdued sound. Black musicians in the North shortly succumbed to pressures both within the black community and from the white middle class, as they began moving into the majority lifestyle to an extent that would have been impossible in the South. Within a social environment radically different from that in which jazz had been formed, much of black jazz became sublimated, as its interpreters adapted an increasing number of traits from the popular music of the dominant culture. By the end of the decade black jazzmen in Chicago were starting to invade the all-white cabarets and theaters of the Loop, where they were expected to be well behaved and play a softer, more "legitimate" music than they had played on the South Side. Meanwhile white musicians like Eddie Condon and his combo continued to resist commercialization, sticking close to a pure Dixieland style, but the trend toward larger orchestras was undeniable.

Jazz by then had grown into a national phenomenon, played in all the black ghettos of the North, as well as in southern cities like New Orleans and Memphis. White bands and hotel orchestras had carried the jazz idiom into many areas from coast to coast where black musicians would not have been welcome. Even small towns in the interior often boasted a ballroom with live music at least on weekends, and resort and amusement centers up and down both coasts and across the country from Atlantic City to Los Angeles offered a ready market for dance orchestras. In the whistle stops a vacant store was sometimes taken over, fixed up with a bandstand, and turned into a dance hall by throwing a little powdered wax on the floor. Around 1925, however, Chicago began losing out to New York as the country's jazz capital. Once jazz became part of the organized entertainment industry, more and more of the bands looked to New York for out-of-town bookings, and the city was still the center of the music publishing business. Many of the national broadcasts emanated from there, and it was the location of the major recording companies' headquarters. Increasing numbers of jazzmen were lured to New York City largely because that was where the big money was.

But the New York style from the beginning was a different sort of thing from what jazz had been in either New Orleans or Chicago. It was farther both in time and geography from jazz's origin, while Harlem, where much of the city's black music was played, had already grown sophisticated enough to concern itself with middle class values and the cult of respectability. New York jazz therefore tended to be more genteel and from the outset was something of a captive of the commercial music business. By the latter twenties even the hotter bands had begun enlarging their personnel in an effort to look more impressive, while both white and black bands increasingly came to reject the tunes of jazz's degraded past in favor of the more socially acceptable songs of Tin Pan Alley.

The first of the refined black bands in New York was the Fletcher Henderson orchestra, which in 1923 and 1924 was playing mostly downtown, at places like the exclusive Club Alabam on Forty-fourth Street and the Roseland Ballroom on Broadway. Henderson was a black pianist from Georgia, with a degree in chemistry from Atlanta University. He arrived in New York in 1920, working for several months as a song-plugger and an administrator who organized recording dates for Black Swan Records. Later he toured as accompanist for the popular blues singer Ethel Waters. Henderson's ten-piece orchestra was thoroughly rehearsed, played from written arrangements, and alternated a smooth, well coordinated ensemble with solo improvisation. Don Redman, Henderson's arranger, was a conservatory graduate who wrote for the rhythm, reed, and brass sections as if they were the individual instruments of a small band. The next few years after Henderson's success produced a number of notable black orchestras in New

York, among them those led by Jimmie Lunceford, Chick Webb, Andy Kirk, Erskine Hawkins, and Cab Calloway.

Among the first of the large white dance bands was Jean Goldkette's, which hit the Roseland Ballroom in 1927 like a tropical storm. More pretentious was the Paul Whiteman orchestra, which combined some of the simpler rhythmic patterns of jazz with melodic and harmonic shadings from the blues, adding to these a quasisymphonic orchestration. Trained as a serious musician, Whiteman arrived in New York from the West Coast in 1921, bringing with him a nine-piece band and the urge to arrange dance tunes "symphonically." He wanted to filter out the "primitive" elements of jazz that traditionalists deemed offensive and by adding violins and saxophones produce a sweeter, lusher, more sentimental sound. After 1924 he headed a large ensemble, sometimes augmented into a small concert group, which played mainly glossy arrangements of Tin Pan Alley songs, light classics, and overblown attempts at "symphonic syncopations." His musicians dressed in tuxedos and played from written scores, approximating the appearance of a symphony orchestra.

But even the sophisticated Whiteman wanted an occasional "hot" element in his music, at least one good jazzman to carry the featured solos. For this reason he hired Bix Beiderbecke in 1927. Well paid and highly respected by his colleagues, Beiderbecke was free to improvise during spotlighted moments, but found Whiteman's overall approach confining and frustrating. By then Bix was recognized as one of the jazz masters, greatly admired even by serious musicians. French composer Maurice Ravel supposedly made a special trip to New York just to hear him. Through the years Beiderbecke's golden tones had grown richer, and he played with a lovely unhurried warmth. His phrasing seemed increasingly easy, his attack practically flawless. But Bix had developed a drinking problem, which eventually forced him out of the Whiteman orchestra. In 1931 he was dead at the age of twenty-eight. Despite a high fever he had driven to Princeton University in an open car for a dance engagement. What had been a severe cold turned into a fatal case of pneumonia. Immediately he became the tragic, baby-faced symbol of the 1920s, second only to F. Scott Fitzgerald. Like James Dean later, Beiderbecke passed into legend, his premature death adding a macabre luster to his memory. Much of his cornet style he had worked out for himself, and he possessed an integrity, an artistic consistency, and a musical innocence that never left him, even though he was more and more surrounded by commercialism. Above all Beiderbecke brought a lyric sensibility to jazz that had a profound effect on subsequent development.

Perhaps the single most important event in the flowering of New York jazz was the opening of the Cotton Club in 1927, during the midst of the "Harlem Renaissance." Intellectuals after World War I, as their faith in traditional values waned, had become enthusiastic about black culture and had begun frequenting Harlem night spots like Connie's Inn and Small's Paradise, which offered jazz as a specialty. Once such dignitaries as Carl Van

Vechten, Eugene O'Neill, Dorothy Parker, Theodore Dreiser, Fanny Hurst, and Heywood Broun were known to have enjoyed the Harlem night clubs, the fashionable set followed suit. Before long even the upper crust was attending the black cabarets and speakeasies, looking for the exciting entertainment they heard was all the rage. For the well-to-do to mix with the regular Harlem customers in the smaller clubs, to have experienced this raw life, unspoiled by middle class restraints and pretensions, became a mark of sophistication. The pseudo-African floor shows were viewed as exotic and delightfully daring, especially in their open attitude toward sex. The noise of jungle drums and the uninhibited jazz combos was found a refreshing change from the salon orchestras, tea ensembles, and large dance bands typical of the Broadway area.

When the Cotton Club opened, it immediately became known as "the aristocrat of Harlem." Limousines would be parked outside nightly, with chauffeurs waiting until three or four o'clock in the morning to take wealthy white customers back downtown. The best black bands played at the expensive club, auspiciously beginning with the Duke Ellington Orchestra. Ellington had come to New York in 1922 from Washington, D.C., where he was born in 1899. He came from a comfortable middle class black home and knew nothing of the squalor and violence that Louis Armstrong and Bessie Smith had experienced. Although he had little formal training, Edward Kennedy Ellington began playing ragtime piano professionally as a teenager. Already he had earned the nickname "Duke." By the time he was twenty he was a part-time band leader, supplementing his income as a soda fountain clerk at the Poodle Dog Cafe. His first New York jobs were with theater orchestras, but by 1924 he had taken over the six-piece Elmer Snowden band and was soon booked into the Kentucky Club on Broadway, as well as making recordings. He was also doing some arranging and rapidly coming to the attention of a number of prominent people in show business and music.

When Ellington's band opened the Cotton Club on December 4, 1927, it had been increased to eleven men. This was the turning point of Ellington's career, for his orchestra broadcast from the club over the CBS radio network and immediately attracted a nationwide following. The floor shows at the Cotton Club were more lavish than at any of the other Harlem night spots, and Ellington eventually began writing some of the tunes for them—songs like "Echoes of the Jungle" and "Jungle Nights in Harlem." "Saturday night was the big night for people to come up to Harlem," the musician explained. "They expected the horns to blow loud and the girls to look wild. When a girl began to wiggle and shake to the throb of that great tom-tom Sonny Greer was beating, they thought she was in the throes, and that the spirit of Africa was upon her." Ellington's band played with a "jungle" growl that audiences came to hear, but from the beginning he endeavored to create a personal style in the tradition of more formal music.

While Ellington started out comfortably within the jazz format, he gradually came to terms with Tin Pan Alley, blending the "reality" of the folk idiom with the "artistry" of commercial music without violating his integrity. Ellington after all was a man of the big city; as such it would have been virtually impossible for him to turn his back on the market place. His orchestra achieved some of the most polished ensemble playing of any dance band in the country, for it contained an impressive number of quality soloists. He imposed an organization that was formal and melodic and through instrumentation and impressionistic harmony created a delicate atmosphere consistent with his own personality, full of muted colors and mystery. Ellington proved an arranger of exceptional ability, and he became the first jazz musician since Jelly Roll Morton habitually to compose his own tunes. His songs are sophisticated and clever, unmistakably influenced by the popular styles. The titles of his early "jungle" numbers reflect more the work of his white booking agent, Irving Mills, than the nature of Ellington's compositions. Later came "Misty Mornin'," "Creole Love Call," "Mood Indigo," "Solitude," "I'm Beginning to See the Light," and "Sophisticated Lady," although his eventual theme song, "Take the 'A' Train," was written by arranger Billy Strayhorn.

Cab Calloway was later one of the major attractions at the Cotton Club, with his famous "Minnie the Moocher" routine, and Jimmie Lunceford's Orchestra played there, with Adelaide Hall as the star and Lena Horne a featured performer. Ethel Waters sang there, and Ellington returned for an extended engagement in 1937. The Cotton Club shows were lurid affairs, and the club itself was a gaudy place full of jungle decor. Most of the white crowds that came "slumming" to the Harlem night spots, however, were unsophisticated enough to be satisfied with these transparent shams. Harlem blacks hated the club on Lennox Avenue, for except for celebrities like Bojangles, black visitors were told that the tables were all reserved, even though the place might be half empty. But the Cotton Club's success was sufficiently great that rivals, such as the Plantation, were not long in coming, while the less exclusive Savoy Ballroom, built in 1926, did a steady business, offering a dance floor big enough for 2000 couples.

With the whites moving in on Harlem so fast and demanding popular music, local black musicians were never free to develop an indigenous jazz style. Ellington and most of the other band leaders had learned about jazz mainly from theater orchestras, and their approach always leaned toward the white tradition. The big bands flourishing downtown in the Broadway section were even more subdued, playing the smart tunes cafe society wanted to hear, in a slick style that undergraduate Babbitts and their dates could readily understand.

By 1927 jazz in New York had become so commercialized that a revolution was almost inevitable. When the revolt came, it appeared not on the East Coast, but out in Kansas City, although a number of "territory" bands spread the rebellion over the Southwest. Kansas City in the late 1920s was a wide open town, dominated by political boss Tom Pendergast. Like Chicago, Kansas City had its gang rule and a network of nightclubs, speakeasies, cabarets, and gambling dens, creating another boom market for musicians. Even after the Wall Street Crash, night life continued to prosper in Kansas City, and when Prohibition ended, the racketeers simply changed over to legitimate means of distribution without losing a day's business. The main strength of the city's jazz revolution came from the blacks, and the best bands played in the black district, between Twelfth and Eighteenth streets. Kansas City's black population had increased at a rapid rate since 1900, proportionately more than the white, and was far less sophisticated than New York's Harlem. Since the Missouri city was isolated from the main stream of popular culture in America, it was possible for a new jazz style to grow up there.

Kansas City jazz was savored to its fullest in some thirty-odd cabarets— the Mayfair Club, the Yellow Front Saloon, the Panama Club, the Boulevard Lounge, the Cherry Blossom, the Old Kentucky Bar-B-Que, but especially the Reno Club. Operated by a member of the Pendergast syndicate, the Reno Club was a long, narrow barn of a place on Twelfth Street between Cherry and Locust, catering to both black and white customers. A divider ran down the center of the club to discourage racial mixing. There was a separate bar and dance floor for each group. The white-owned Sunset Club at Eighteenth and Highland became one of the first and most popular places to jam, for its black manager, Piney Brown, was a jazz enthusiast. Occasionally a tall, young bartender who worked at the Sunset would burst into song. His name was Joe Turner. After hours, musicians drifted from club to club, checking out the action. Since a good jam session attracted customers, many of the club owners hired a house rhythm section to encourage guest musicians to drop in and sometimes supplied them with free drinks.

The first major Kansas City band was led by ragtime pianist Bennie Moten. Born and raised in the city, Moten opened with a six-piece combo at the Panama Club in 1921 and recorded for Okeh sometime before 1923. His early recordings show much of the ragtime piano style and demonstrate how, even at this late date, pure ragtime was converted into an orchestral medium. The band proved exceptionally popular, while the ragtime influences were gradually shorn off. Around 1926 the ensemble was expanded to ten pieces. When the Blue Devils, an Oklahoma territory band, broke up in 1933, some of its personnel went over to the Moten Orchestra, giving Bennie just about the cream of the crop in the Kansas City area, including clarinetist Buster Smith, saxophonist Lester Young, and pianist Count Basie.

Competition by then was very keen, although Moten's chief rival over the years was George E. Ewing. George Lee and the Paul Banks Orchestra were other contemporaries. Compared with the Chicago style, the Kansas City sound was much simpler, almost a country cousin. Most Kansas City jazzmen were never comfortable playing in more than three or four keys; Bennie Moten played everything in B-flat, although he could read in other keys. In contrast with Ellington and the Harlem musicians who moved toward elaboration, Kansas City jazz began as a grass roots movement and maintained an earthy, colloquial character to the end. It groped its way erratically, accumulating its language bit by bit, drawing primarily from folksong and ragtime. There were heavy doses of the blues, both the old country blues and the more recent urban variety. While there was refinement over the years, the Kansas City musicians retained much of their aggressively provincial sound, speaking comfortably to the community at hand. With constant jamming Kansas City jazzmen grew more self-reliant, experimenting with phrases sometimes bizarre, even disturbing. Solo work was far more important than it had been elsewhere, to the point that ensembles became merely a base, allowing players to get a firm grip on the melody, harmonies, and rhythmic pattern before launching forth on their own. The long melodic line became characteristic, backed by a persuasive beat.

With Kansas City the focal point, territory bands sprang up all over Texas, Colorado, Arkansas, Kansas, New Mexico, Oklahoma, Nebraska, Iowa, and Missouri. Eventually a Southwestern style was discernible, marked at its height by an intense drive that was at the same time relaxed. Rather than hitting a note directly on the beat, it might be played just before or just after, while phrasing was simple. Industrial development meant that many towns in the Southwest had gained population rapidly since World War I, and the recent arrivals from the rural areas wanted a plain-spoken music they could identify with. Dancing audiences insisted on a heavy diet of instrumental blues. Most of the territory bands worked from a home base, played the outlying districts, but never attained a national reputation. The bigger bands were booked into hotels, ballrooms, nightclubs, and outdoor amusement parks, while the smaller ones worked the cheaper clubs and played for school dances. Black groups held forth in the black sections of the larger towns. Barnstorming leaders who drifted into the region often recruited local talent, creating bands of more than ordinary distinction. Texas, because of its size, yielded the greatest number of these musicians, most of whom were more closely acquainted with the blues and even boogie-woogie than with ragtime. The influence of New Orleans jazz was not strongly felt, and outside Kansas City, the black theater circuits did not penetrate the Southwest until the 1920s.

The Blue Devils, which operated out of Oklahoma City, used lots of saxophones and had a bright, honeyed sound. The most polished and successful of the Texas bands was the Alphonso Trent Orchestra, which broadcast and played long engagements at the Hotel Adolphus in Dallas. But there were also the Blues Syncopaters, the Deluxe Melody Boys, and Terence T. Holder and His Clouds of Joy. Art Bronson's Bostonians worked out of Salina, Kansas, while Clarence Love led some good groups in and around the Tulsa area. Jumps of 800 miles or more between engagements were not uncommon, and an entire band might cram into a single automobile. The Depression broke up most of the territory bands, although many of their sidemen wound up in Kansas City, where times continued to be good until the middle 1930s.

While the nation at large heard echoes of Kansas City jazz through broadcasts by Coon-Sanders and others from the Hotel Muehlebach, Bennie

Moten's orchestra remained the most important in the evolution of the Kansas City style until Moten's sudden death in 1935. The band had just begun an engagement of several weeks at the Rainbow Ballroom in Denver, one of the major dance halls in the West. Bennie had stayed behind to undergo a much-postponed tonsillectomy. The surgeon was an old friend of Moten's, and the two of them spent the night before shooting pool and visiting cabarets until a late hour. The next morning there was a mishap on the operating table. Somehow the knife slipped, and thirty-nine year-old Moten was dead.

It was a blow both to his band and to the whole development of jazz in the Southwest. Bus Moten, Bennie's brother, under whose leadership the orchestra had gone to Denver, tried to keep things going, but the old fire was burning out. Before long younger groups were usurping prime engagements, and sidemen began to defect. Then William "Count" Basie, who had been playing with Moten's band, alternating at the piano with Bennie, formed a small combo and took it into the Reno Club. Like Moten, Basie was a ragtimer, although one trained on the East Coast. Born in Red Bank, New Jersey, Basie was greatly influenced by Fats Waller and the Harlem school of jazz piano playing. His success at the Reno Club was immediate, and he soon began broadcasting live from the club. Much of Moten's style survived intact under Basie's leadership, most obviously his simple, direct approach. Basie took more from the blues than Moten did, however, and his music was always melodic, with an easy, flowing rhythm—tastefully and imaginatively delivered. The Count himself was a confident technician, clean in phrasing, yet he did not play merely to show off his technical prowess.

While Count Basie was working at the Reno Club in 1936, young musicians used to congregate in the small balcony directly over the orchestra shell. Others stood in the paved area out back, listening to the band play. Frequently among them was fifteen year-old Charlie Parker, who idolized Basie's saxophonist, Lester Young. This is where the jazzmen took their traditional ten minute break between sets, mingling with fellow musicians and hangers-on. The area behind the club was also a soliciting place for prostitutes, who turned tricks at the going rate of two dollars in rooms over the Reno, reached by a private stairway. Marijuana cigarettes, known locally as "sticks of shit," were vended by individuals who procured their supply from a neighborhood woman called simply the "Old Lady." Three joints sold for twenty-five cents; a Prince Albert tobacco can of marijuana could be had for from three to five dollars. After hours, jazzmen still floated about the district, sitting in on one jam session or another. Jam sessions at the Reno began about five in the morning, after Count Basie and his boys had played the last floor show and had time to grab a bite to eat at a nearby lunch wagon or bar.

Basie gradually enlarged the size of his band to fifteen pieces and introduced his Kansas City jump style to New York late in 1936, arousing both interest and controversy. He played first at the Roseland Ballroom and later at the Famous Door on West Fifty-second Street. Solo talent abounded in the band, which alternated riffs with the ensemble. Much of the informality, spontaneity, and verve from the Kansas City days was retained, while Basie's revolutionary piano playing grew increasingly polished. Unlike other jazz pianists, he believed in an economy of notes, improvising without undue embroidery. By 1940 Count Basie's orchestra had elevated the Kansas City sound to new heights, swinging the blues with an inherent spirit that tempered the magnitude of the direct ensemble attack with precision and sensitivity.

Yet with the exception of Kansas City, the jazz scene across the country was unequivocally changed by the stock market collapse of 1929. Suddenly the flamboyant aspect of the 1920s seemed gone, as the mood of the nation slowed down and settled into something more solemn. With the onset of the Depression the public generally seemed to want only quiet, soothing dance music. Unsophisticated jazz might be played in the black districts and at rent parties and the tougher ginmills, but the majority culture favored a sweeter, lusher sound, such as might be heard in the country clubs of their dreams. The trend toward big bands continued, while the saccharine tones of Rudy Vallee, Guy Lombardo, Wayne King, Fred Waring, and Isham Jones became the rage—all of whom did a great deal of broadcasting. Society bands like Meyer Davis' remained fashionable, along with sentimentalists like Paul Whiteman, but many of the smaller groups went under. The preferred style was mildly "peppy," although even up-tempo tunes emphasized muted instruments, shaded colors, and a general pianissimo. With Rudy Vallee's success the crooning vocalist became popular, while the recording of authentic jazz all but stopped. A nation searching for security wanted romance and fantasy in its dance music, full of violins and saxophones, lots of sugary phrasing, and slick arrangements. And so, during the worst of the Depression years, the country eased its tensions by listening to the murmurs of Vagabond Lovers and gently tapping its feet to what has been called "the businessman's bounce."

Some of the hotter jazzmen escaped this scene by going to Europe for a while. Louis Armstrong went to England in 1932, right after his divorce from Lil Hardin, and Duke Ellington made his first European tour a year later. Jazz combos, including the Original Dixieland Jazz Band, had been heard in London and Paris before 1920. A Russian whom George Antheil met in Berlin around 1922 was enthusiastic about an American black orchestra he had recently discovered in France, telling the composer that the group played "some of the most exciting music I've ever heard in my life." But from 1932 on, the jazz picture became more and more international, with indigenous jazz orchestras springing up all over England and the Continent.

By the mid-1930s the Depression in the United States had begun to subside, as the New Deal administration instilled hope into the hearts of the American people. Whereas sentimental music, with its emphasis on fantasy and self-pity, had appealed to the public during the black years following the crash on Wall Street, the country—particularly the young people—by the middle of the decade were ready for joy and happiness and a more intense form of dance music. A new age, called the "Swing Era," was born on the night of August 21, 1935, with Benny Goodman's triumphant engagement at the Palomar Ballroom in Los Angeles. Goodman was a Chicago clarinetist, born into slum conditions, May 30, 1909, who at sixteen had joined Ben Pollack's Orchestra on the West Coast. He formed his own band in 1934, which played at Billy Rose's Music Hall, a New York nightclub, attracting few people except musicians. When the coast-to-coast Saturday night radio program "Let's Dance" was booked for twenty-six weeks beginning in the latter part of 1934, Benny Goodman's orchestra was one of the featured bands, but its option was not picked up. Things indeed seemed to be going downhill for the Goodman aggregation—until that night at the Palomar. With his band on notice, Goodman reportedly told his men: "No sweet tunes tonight. No mush. No goo. Go out there and play every killer-diller in the book. Blow those bastards off the floor."

The band did just that, and somehow clicked as never before. Goodman's success not only started the "Swing" craze, but brightened the spotlight on the big bands for more than a decade. The trip back from California was wild. The Congress Hotel in Chicago, known in the music business as a "dead room," held the Goodman orchestra over for eight months. They were engaged for a prime radio spot on the "Camel Caravan" and became a national phenomenon. Before long a new generation—of jitterbuggers and bobbysoxers—had found *their* special music, as dances like the Lindy Hop, the Big Apple, and the Shag swept the nation.

Goodman's orchestra numbered twelve players and for some time included Harry James on the trumpet and Gene Krupa on drums. They played a clean, crisp, hard-driving, rolling kind of music that was both exciting and easily understood. Benny himself was a superior musician, who projected a great deal of personal charm through his horn. "Swing" depended upon technically brilliant arrangers and virtuoso performers who could alternately improvise in solo passages (or play with enough freedom of invention that it sounded as if they were improvising) and work from strict notation during harmonized ensembles or when supplying arranged backgrounds. This meant endless rehearsals and high-level teamwork. The degree of commercialization in "Swing" was high, its reliance upon Tin Pan Alley heavy. The new music was brought to the attention of the public at large by all the high-pressure tactics known to modern publicity—talked about in the press, played on jukeboxes and over the radio, and performed in ballrooms, on the stage, and at the movies. But it returned some of the original vitality to jazz, at the same time expanding its repertoire and vocabulary. Whereas the collective improvisation of the Original Dixieland Jazz Band had sounded unrestrained and confused to traditionalists, the Goodman orchestra seemed far more dignified—smoother, fuller, more flowing and appealing.

The late 1930s found big "Swing" dance bands appearing everywhere.

The Casa Loma band (later Glen Gray and His Casa Loma Orchestra) and the Dorsey Brothers band both preceded Goodman. The Dorseys split in 1935, when Jimmy set a too-fast tempo on "I'll Never Say 'Never Again' Again" at the Glen Island Casino outside New York City and Tommy stomped off the stand. Jimmy retained the original orchestra, while Tommy took over Joe Haymes' group. But they were soon joined by the forceful Dixieland of Bob Crosby, the purer blues sounds of Texas-born Jack Teagarden, the dulcet strains of Jan Garber, the mellow tones of Artie Shaw, the flowery piano of Eddy Duchin, the soft, moaning saxophone of Freddy Martin, and the highly commercial swing of Glenn Miller. Most of these groups were built around their leader, and the big band craze quickly turned into something of a personality cult. Gene Krupa, who had exuded all sorts of stage charm for Benny Goodman, went on his own in 1938, capitalizing on his expressive movements and dark, trim, romantic appearance as much as his playing. Eventually gimmick bands became popular, and there were several all-girl orchestras, the most successful of which was led by Ina Ray Hutton.

The big band era also saw the rise of the jazz vocalist. Among the first of the dance orchestra singers to bridge the gap between jazz and popular music was Mildred Bailey, who was featured by Paul Whiteman. Mildred was part Indian, while her voice—in contrast to Bessie Smith's dark power—was light and high, almost like a child's. During the early 1930s she incorporated blues and jazz phrasing into commercial singing and used her delicate equipment intelligently and with considerable heart.

Next to Bessie Smith, probably the strongest single influence on jazz vocalists was Billie Holiday, the most noted of the 1930s blues singers. Born in 1915, Billie spent her childhood in a Baltimore ghetto, where she was raped as a young girl. She moved to New York City, still living in squalor, and grew up listening to Bessie Smith and Louis Armstrong records. For a while she was a prostitute, then began singing in Harlem. She was a beautiful girl with a sad, moody voice. She sang popular ballads rather than the classic blues numbers, in a sophisticated, mannered style, improvising on the melody and underplaying her words. No one in the business could project hopelessness, despair, or regret as intensely, with such dignity, or with such bitter matter-of-factness and courage as Billie Holiday. She became Count Basie's first female vocalist, playing the Savoy Ballroom with him. Later she toured with Artie Shaw.

A fresh white gardenia in her hair became her trademark, and she was known as Lady Day. While her range was admittedly small, Billie sang with perfect poise and rhythm. Her special musical talent was an ability to find beauty and emotion in essentially banal material. "Nothing was more perfect than what she was," Imamu Baraka maintains. "Nor more willing to fail." Gradually she became bitter and personally estranged, a hopeless heroin addict. "It wasn't long before I was one of the highest paid slaves around," Billie wrote. "I was making a thousand a week—but I had about as much freedom as a field hand in Virginia a hundred years before." In later life she was still beautiful, although her appearance was ravaged by drugs and loneliness and the inner pain that had tormented her since childhood. Eventually even her voice began to fray, perhaps—as Martin Williams suggests—"from a deeply suppressed sob which, if she ever let go, would bring tears she might never be able to stop." She died tragically in 1959, already a legend.

Ella Fitzgerald, who began singing with Chick Webb's band in 1934, at the age of sixteen, idolized Billie Holiday. Her style leaned more toward the popular approach than toward the blues, although most of her work was buoyed with jazz nuances. Ella had been raised in an orphanage in Yonkers; the first time she fronted Webb's band, they had to borrow a dress for her from the leader's wife. She sang with control, precise pitch, and impeccable rhythm. Her voice had body and color, but while she could improvise with abandon, she preferred singing her songs straight, with none of the harsh tones and displaced accents of the blues.

Sarah Vaughan later proved one of the most remarkable voices in the jazz field, as did Carmen McRae and Dinah Washington. Peggy Lee won her first recognition as Benny Goodman's vocalist, whereas Helen Forrest at different times worked for Goodman, Shaw, and Harry James. Jo Stafford sang with Tommy Dorsey, Helen O'Connell with brother Jimmy. Perry Como started the climb to fame with Ted Weems, while Doris Day appeared with Les Brown. Kay Starr, Rosemary Clooney, Dick Haymes, Betty Hutton, Dale Evans, and Betty Grable all fronted big bands before establishing themselves in their own right.

But of the white vocalists from the Swing era, none had greater impact than Frank Sinatra. In 1939 Sinatra was singing with Harry James, but was released from that contract so that he could join Tommy Dorsey. He stayed with Dorsey for two and a half years. "Working with a good band in those days," Sinatra explains, "was the end of the rainbow for any singer who wanted to make it in this profession." He was noted early for his easy phrasing and later said he learned his technique mainly by listening to "the way Tommy Dorsey breathed and phrased on the trombone." He liked the strings which Dorsey had added by 1942, particularly as vocal background, and made more skillful use of the microphone than anyone before him.

Besides the leader the person most responsible for a band's sound was the arranger. He was the one who gave it whatever originality it had. Glenn Miller's success was based largely on his own arrangements, although he later turned over some of the writing chores to Jerry Gray and Bill Finegan. Billy May also did some arranging for Miller, while Paul Weston worked for Tommy Dorsey. Henry Mancini wrote for Tex Beneke, Nelson Riddle for Charlie Spivak, David Rose for Ted Fio Rito. The average dance band needed a library of at least forty or fifty arrangements to get through an evening without repeating too much.

The band's schedule was determined by a manager or booking agent, who would try to break up long jumps with one-night stands. Eventually the musicians' union limited the distance between engagements to 400 miles. Since planes and trains were too expensive and inflexible, traveling was done mostly by chartered buses and private cars. A band would often arrive at a ballroom or dance pavilion just in time to wash up and change clothes in a dingy dressing room or men's rest room before playing. After something quick to eat, the musicians would climb back onto the bus and attempt to catch some sleep while they rode to the next engagement. They would try to spend every other night in a hotel. Longterm bookings into places like the Aragon Ballroom in Chicago or the Blue Room of the Hotel Roosevelt in New Orleans were coveted engagements and offered considerably more comfort. Still, most sidemen stopped playing around age thirty, mainly because of the strenuous travel.

By the late 1930s there were hundreds of dance bands playing in hotels, ballrooms, movie theaters, nightclubs, and gymnasiums across the country. The three major record companies—Columbia, Decca, and RCA Victor— were all issuing "Swing" releases, and the airways were filled every night with the sounds of the big bands. Young people especially followed the bands closely, knew all of their latest hits, could identify most of the players and recognize their favorites after hearing only a few measures. Within a short while "Swing" classics like Benny Goodman's "Sing, Sing, Sing," Tommy Dorsey's "Opus One," Artie Shaw's "Begin the Beguine," and Glenn Miller's "In the Mood" had won a lasting place with the American public. At dances, if a band were communicating exceptionally well with its audience, couples would crowd around the bandstand as close as possible. Behind them, others would continue dancing, joined later by the onlookers, as the band lapsed into a mellower mood.

American entry into World War II, however, brought problems. Gasoline rationing and rubber shortages made travel difficult, and out-of-the-way clubs like the Glen Island Casino were forced to close down. A twenty percent amusement tax hurt, as well as a midnight curfew. Many places cut out live music to avoid what jazzmen called "the cabaret tax." The draft soon decimated the personnel of dance bands, so that new men were constantly coming in. "We were rehearsing more than we were playing," Gene Krupa said. By the end of 1942 Artie Shaw had joined the Navy, Eddy Duchin received a Navy commission, and Glenn Miller became an Air Force captain. Clyde McCoy's band enlisted as a unit; two months later Ted Weems and six of his men signed up for the Coast Guard. As sidemen became scarce, leaders were forced into the position of bidding against one another; hard feelings resulted. Gradually women began moving into the homefront bands, filling seats even in the brass sections, but mostly in the strings. The manpower shortage was further aggrevated by the fact that the size of dance bands continued to grow. A nation at war seemed to want loud, full music on the upbeat side. Some leaders, like Jan Garber, previously associated with a sweet approach, converted to a "Swing" style.

The hotels, nightclubs, and ballrooms that stayed open during the war did a turn-away business, yet despite boom conditions, the obstacles for entertainment remained great. The big bands, like other forms of music, suffered in 1942 from the recording ban. Death claimed a number of key jazzmen. Fats Waller died in 1943, Charlie Christian the year before. Glenn Miller met his untimely end in a transport plane over the English Channel in 1944. Suddenly the vocalist seemed more important than the band as a whole. After the war television, taxes, and rising prices killed most of the nightclubs, while fewer and fewer radio stations were employing staff orchestras.

Times were clearly changing. The free-spending and reckless abandon of the war years vanished, as returning servicemen grew serious about buying homes and cars and appliances, once they became available. Benny Goodman signaled the end of an era in music by dissolving his band in 1944. A few months after the Japanese surrender, Jan Garber returned to the sweet sound he had played before the war, setting the example for others. Artie Shaw quit the music business, attempting a writing career for a while, later operating a shooting range in Connecticut. By the summer of 1946 one name band after another had gone under, and within a few months "Swing" was little more than a memory. A few perennials, like Duke Ellington and Count Basie, held on. The Dorsey brothers were reunited in the spring of 1953, but they never approached the popularity they enjoyed before and during World War II.

Ray Anthony, who had worked for Glenn Miller and was much influenced by his style, returned from leading a service band in the Pacific during the war to form one of the fastest rising post-war orchestras. Bill Finegan and Eddie Sauter, both distinguished arrangers, put together a "new sound" band in the early 1950s, creating a stir for a time. The Sauter-Finegan Orchestra offered both dance and "mood" music, but soon proved too complex for the general public. Recording companies attempted to create successful bands, giving consecutive releases a heavy build-up, then sending the group on the road for a series of one-night engagements. The RCA Victor publicity office made arranger Ralph Flanagan a name band leader before he ever played a job and tried to repeat its success a bit later with Buddy Morrow. Capitol had good luck with Billy May, while Mercury was the promotional force behind Ralph Marterie. But these ventures were abandoned after a few years.

By the late 1950s Lawrence Welk stood practically alone as a reminder of the big band era. Welk had been a band leader since 1925 and became a favorite among polka fans in the early 1940s. A decade later he won a nostalgic place with middle-age Americans through a Saturday night television program. Welk's was the only band in the 1950s actually to increase its drawing power. His "champagne music" had all the subtlety of a used car salesman and practically no imagination, but the organization men and suburban housewives of a placid decade, looking for clean, wholesome, Rotarian entertainment, found it satisfying.

Jazz during the "Swing" era came out of the dives and speakeasies and entered the ballroom, gaining the acceptance of middle class America along the way. Successful band leaders, concerned with their orchestra's image, encouraged responsible and respectable behavior from their musicians. Players sat on the bandstand smartly dressed, projecting an aura of relaxed dignity that audiences admired and emulated. Although Benny Goodman had broken the color line by bringing black pianist Teddy Wilson into his band at the Congress Hotel, the "Swing" bands had increasingly come to be dominated by whites. Improvisation decreased, as arrangements became more intricate, giving dance orchestras the semblance of greater refinement and bringing jazz closer to the standards for music inherited from Europe. Many of the big band sidemen were formally trained, while virtually all of them could read music. By 1938 Benny Goodman was presented on a concert-lecture series at Town Hall in New York, playing between explanatory remarks by John Erskine, president of the Juilliard School of Music. Goodman also gave a Carnegie Hall concert that year. Classes were being devoted to jazz, while serious musicians at home and abroad were discussing its merits. There were still adversaries, like Professor H. D. Gideonese of Columbia University, who argued in the early 1940s that "swing is musical Hitlerism." But the complaints for the most part had disappeared. Most Americans had come to support jazz ardently, and there were some who even spoke of it as a popular art form.

As jazz came above ground, it suffered a loss of vitality. "Swing" at its best represented a synthesis of the older jazz forms and the sweeter music of Tin Pan Alley. For purists it became entirely too polite and subdued. "The flash, the bite, the sporting house phrasing had been replaced by a sentimental accent," Stephen Longstreet contends. "It had the face but not the body." Lyrics, once earthy and frank, became inoffensive and honeyed, while the jazzmen themselves came to look like the boy next door. The musicians often realized they were playing trash, but resigned themselves to the situation, realizing that dilution was essential to keeping a wide following. "Sure it stinks," Artie Shaw summed up the feelings of his band members, "but it pays good dough so the hell with it." Black jazzmen resented the fact that during the "Swing" era the major publicity and the best jobs went to the white orchestras, even though the black bands often played with superior musicianship. "Swing" early became the establishment's jazz, backed by white money and listened to by genteel audiences.

The time was ripe for another revolt. It came in the 1940s from two directions. The more conservative rebellion attempted to take jazz back to its New Orleans beginnings, and for a time Dixieland enjoyed a substantial revival. Small combos were recruited from the larger orchestras, while older jazzmen were brought out of retirement. A San Francisco trumpet player, Lu Watters, had formed a New Orleans-style jazz band as early as 1939, although it had broken up during the war. Watters tried it again in 1947, enjoying considerably more success. He played a faithful imitation of the King Oliver type of music and won national attention for the New Orleans renaissance. Twenty year-old recordings by Kid Ory, Jelly Roll Morton, and Bunk Johnson were soon rediscovered, and during the war boogie-woogie had gained a new lease on life. Much of the new Dixieland music was played by young white musicians, but by 1947 even Louis Armstrong had broken up his big orchestra and gone back to a combo format. The next year Pee Wee Hunt formed a Dixieland combination and put out a recording of the "Twelfth Street Rag." Hunt meant for it to be humorous, but much to his surprise a new generation found his hackneyed approach delightful. A Tennessee player, John Maddox, even put ragtime piano on the jukeboxes for a time. Suddenly more and more Dixieland groups appeared on the scene, reflecting a growing nostalgia for the 1920s. Before long Americans were again dancing the Charleston and rummaging through attics for their parents' raccoon coats.

From an esthetic standpoint, however, the Dixieland revival was a mere sideshow. A more forwardlooking rebellion had begun during World War II as a *sub rosa* movement within the mainstream of "Swing." Known first as "rebop," then "bebop," and finally just "bop," this controversial music was exceedingly modern. Because of its experimental nature, it was played by small groups, with much solo work. From the beginning "bop" was protest music, representing an attempt on the part of black musicians to give jazz back to the black. Its formulators stressed its antiestablishment nature by wearing berets, goatees, and dark glasses (even in the darkest clubs), speaking "hip" language, and by flaunting "weird" behavior, including the use of drugs.

The "bop" revolution was born around 1941, principally in after-hours jam sessions at Minton's Playhouse in Harlem. Minton's was a drab place in the Hotel Cecil on 118th Street, with a faded green awning and a marquee in front. It was poorly lighted, attractively priced, and out of the way—the sort of place jazz musicians liked to frequent, particularly on Monday nights when lots of them were not working. Henry Minton himself was black, and Teddy Hill, a former bandleader, ran the club. Jazzmen looking for action would stop by after their last set, much as some of them had done in Kansas City earlier. Enthusiasts bored by the commercialism of "Swing" began dropping in to listen to the innovators as they tried out new harmonies and rhythmic variations. The emerging style placed the emphasis on individual expression, although solos were built upon a rich, percussive foundation. In terms of harmonic evolution, "bop" was to jazz roughly what the period between Wagner and Debussy had been to serious music.

Although Charlie Christian, a black guitarist from Oklahoma who had played in Kansas City and later worked with Benny Goodman, was one of the pioneers of "bop," he died at the age of twenty-three, before his efforts really bore fruit. The greatest figures in the formulation of "bop," therefore, became Charlie Parker, Dizzy Gillespie, and Thelonious Monk.

Parker was born in Kansas City, Kansas, August 29, 1920, but grew up across the river in Missouri. He began playing the saxophone, early developing an eccentric style and a penchant for blowing strange notes. Right before World War II he joined the Jay McShann Orchestra, a rough, spirited Kansas City band, reminiscent of Moten and George Lee. Nineteen year-old Parker quickly became the band's principal soloist and idea man. He acquired the name "Yardbird," shortened to "Bird," while traveling with McShann in Nebraska, when the car in which he was riding ran over a chicken. Parker retrieved the fowl from the road, carried it into the next town, and had it for dinner. In 1941 the McShann Orchestra played the Savoy Ballroom and the Apollo Theater in New York, and it was during this time that Parker discovered the half dozen or so Harlem clubs, taverns, and chili parlors where jazz experimentation was taking place. He found Minton's packed night after night, and the bandstand there became one of his favorite haunts. When Parker left McShann in July, 1942, he was already saddled with a chronic narcotics problem.

In a real sense "Bird" brought the Kansas City sound to New York, shaping it in his personal way. For several months after leaving McShann, he deserted organized music altogether, disappearing into the anonymity of Harlem. Rapidly he became a legend in the jazz underground there. Then in December, 1942, veteran bandleader Earl Hines was dragged uptown by his vocalist, Billy Eckstine, to hear Parker's alto saxophone. "Bird" played with Hines' orchestra for nearly a year, working with trumpeter Dizzy Gillespie. Nineteen year-old Sarah Vaughan joined the band as a singer during April, 1943. When Eckstine left Hines to form his own orchestra, both Parker and Gillespie went with him. Parker, tired of big bands, quit in August, 1944. He wanted the freedom of a small combo and preferred to work exclusively in New York. He and Gillespie soon formed their own group and began playing some of the Fifty-second Street clubs. West Fifty-second Street at that time was "The Street" so far as the jazz world was concerned, and Gillespie and Parker became its most controversial and exciting attraction.

They worked places like the Three Deuces, setting off tremors that were felt across the nation. The press disliked the new music, and while some of the critics tried to be fair, few of them succeeded. "[T]he artificial absurdities of the so-called 'bebop' style," Sigmund Spaeth declared, "must be fairly obvious even to the casual listener." Even professional musicians failed to understand "bop" and regularly put it down. "Bebop has set music back twenty years," Tommy Dorsey said. But the "boppers" found such remarks hilarious, took delight in quoting one another the latest put-down, and pulled more and more into their own world. Hipster terms and expressions like "gone," "flip your wig," and "pad" reflected a conscious attempt to exclude the uninitiated, confuse the "square," and strengthen the inner group.

Parker spent sixteen months in California and upon returning to New York in 1947 formed his own quintet. The jazz scene had changed a great deal. The cool sounds and galvanic rhythms of "bop" had achieved a dramatic breakthrough, winning the enthusiasm of the under-thirty crowd in the urban ghettos. The larger East Coast and upper midwestern cities all had jazz clubs modeled after those on Fifty-second Street. Parker was reaching the zenith of his career, his time of greatest creativity and influence. He was vitally concerned with expanding the emotional intensity of jazz, especially in the impromptu portions, and recorded numbers like "Parker's Mood" are full of blues passion that is both agonized and ecstatic. No one could match him for the power and clarity of his tone. After playing with him, Sidney Bechet once said to "Bird": "Man, those phrases you make!" The tunes Parker played had no names or numbers. He simply played tunes; the names came later. Customers at the clubs he worked never glimpsed a sheet of music paper, nor did they hear so much as an arrangement. Parker rephrased black music without altering its fundamental truth and purity. The revolutionary quality of his approach was unmistakable, and for urban blacks "Bird" became a cultural hero.

But Parker was leading a hopelessly disorganized life, the victim of his own passions. He got up around dusk and began preparing for his opening set. The first order of business was to put on his "shades," then pick out a promising combination of pills, dissolving them in a Dixie cup and drinking off the contents. If he was on the needle, he would prepare to give himself an injection, using a necktie to bind off the veins of his left arm. After that it was time to think about eating. Defiance of the establishment was implicit in his whole lifestyle. His debts to local pushers kept him low on funds. He changed addresses often and meandered through strange beds. His clothing generally looked as if it had been slept in, as indeed it frequently had. Sometimes his saxophone was in hock, so that he had to play on a borrowed horn. As he probed the depths of chaos, he oscillated between opposites, passing from moments of gentleness to moments of suspicion and rage. Yet his music maintained the image of wholeness—subtle and complex, satiated with fresh, liberated feeling and unending invention.

By 1950 Parker's idiosyncrasies were legion. He grew heavier, wearing a swollen mask of disillusionment. Behavior once mildly bizarre twisted into something genuinely tragic. When he was not on drugs, he drank and eventually attempted suicide. He dropped by to visit Edgard Varese one day, finding the avant-garde composer packing for a trip to Europe. "He was like a child," Varese remembered, "with the shrewdness of a child. He possessed tremendous enthusiasm." Parker asked, as he had before, to study with the composer. "I want structure," he told Varese. "One instrument is not enough. I want to write for a lot of instruments, voices, a symphony or an opera." Varese was encouraging. "Of course, Bird," he replied. "I always told you I was willing. But you must promise to show up."

He never did. The disintegration of his life gradually began to take its toll on his music. By 1951 Fifty-second Street was no longer the center of the new jazz forms. Its cellar restaurants and bars were giving way to larger places on Broadway. Parker worked the Blue Note in Philadelphia in 1954 and spent ten days in the Psychiatric Division of Bellevue Hospital. A few months later he played Birdland, a Broadway club named after him. It was his last engagement. Parker died, March 12, 1955, in the Stanhope Hotel in New York. He was thirty-five. His effect on jazz had been as total as Armstrong's had been a generation before.

Whereas Parker became the tragedy of the "bop" style, his associate Dizzy Gillespie was more the clown, ready to laugh at or show off for the society he rejected. Gillespie was witty, verbal, extroverted, sunny. His domestic and social life was basically tranquil. Yet his wonderfully improvised trumpet was passionate, full of vitality, specked with fantastic pyrotechnics, and he played with a harmonic understanding so advanced that many of his contemporaries thought the notes he hit were mistakes. "Gillespie could find freedom in a dizzy game," Wilfrid Mellers contends; "Parker could find freedom only in death."

Born in Cheraw, South Carolina, October 21, 1917, Gillespie was the son of a bricklayer. As a teenager he followed his family north to Philadelphia and soon began playing with jazz groups. During World War II he was living in Harlem, at a time when a Mohammedan cult waxed strong there. Some of its members adopted Mohammedan names and began dressing in turbans and African robes, while a few even studied Arabic. Several of the early "bop" musicians joined this cult, and *Life* magazine published a picture of Dizzy Gillespie "bowing to Mecca." His visored beret, heavy smoked glasses, and goatee became imitated by young hipsters all across the country, as Gillespie established himself as "bop's" high priest. Milt Shaw recalled Parker and Gillespie playing together at the Three Deuces. "Dizzy would take a bebop solo and Charlie would stand off and watch him," Shaw said. "Then Charlie would take one and Dizzy would watch. Then, I swear to God, they'd just *look* at each other and take off on a long unison passage that would scare the daylights out of you—something neither had ever dreamed of before!"

Thelonious Monk, the third member of the "bop" triumvirate, was a heavy, bearlike man, who never appeared without his "shades" and had a penchant for wild hats and wild chords. Monk was a pianist and had begun his career playing with a gospel group. He was an original, self-made talent, a master of shaded delays and displaced accents. His work was marked by rhythmic virtuosity and a sense of emotional completeness. Monk's playing was filled with imagination, spontaneity, unresting melodic and harmonic explorations. "His greatest importance," according to Martin Williams, "lies in the fact that Monk is an artist with an artist's deeply felt sense of life and an artist's drive to communicate the surprising and enlightening truth of it in his own way."

New York jazz had heretofore been mainly functional music, geared to the theater and social dancing. "Bop" on the other hand was undanceable and was most at home in a barroom atmosphere. While the beginnings of "bop" can be traced way back in the "Swing" era, the new style seemed to appear with considerable suddenness, in part because of the recording ban in effect during the early years of the war. By 1946 the "bop" influences could be heard in many of the commercial dance bands, particularly in a greater chromaticism. The orchestras of Earl Hines and Billy Eckstine were the first to absorb "bop" sounds, simply because Gillespie and Parker had been members of those groups. Of the big white bands Woody Herman's Herd used more "bop" coloring in its arrangements than any other, although there was never the free improvisation of the real thing.

By the late forties "bop" itself appeared to be branching off in two directions. On the one hand emerged "Progressive" jazz, a commercial adaptation to large white bands; on the other was "Cool" jazz, a cerebral approach emphasizing a non-emotional involvement. The "Progressives" went in for dissonance, atonality, and abstraction. They wanted lots of percussion and blaring, precise brass. The "Progressive" bandleaders often hired arrangers to write modernist harmony, producing a jazz equivalent of Stravinsky and Shostakovich. Dance was forsaken in the interest of sound, yet critics found their work empty and pretentious. Most of the leading "Progressives" came from a "Swing" background, although they quickly picked up on "bop" ideas. Among these were Boyd Raeburn, Earle Spencer, and especially Stan Kenton.

Kenton himself admitted that his incorporation of new technical devices directly contributed to the decline of the dance bands. Born in Colorado, Kenton was raised in California. He began playing the piano in high school and was soon taking jobs around the Los Angeles area. At one hamburger joint he played for fifty cents a night, tips, and all the hamburgers he could eat. He started working with dance bands in the early thirties, also doing some experimental arranging on the piano. In 1936 he got a job traveling with Gus Arnheim, who had won a substantial reputation in the 1920s at the Los Angeles Cocoanut Grove. Kenton later did some motion picture scoring, worked briefly with the house band at NBC, and in 1939 played in the pit orchestra for Earl Carroll's *Vanities* in Los Angeles. He had tried out a number of ideas in his writing and already knew that there was a definite sound he wanted. Hoping to achieve that sound, he organized his first band in 1941.

Competition at that time was fierce. Toward the end of the year Kenton's band was booked into the Hollywood Palladium, one of the classiest ballrooms in the country. The sound was controversial from the beginning, but the first few days of the war brought the group national recognition. Kenton built up a considerable following on the West Coast and by 1944 had invaded the East. The Kenton orchestra was reorganized several times, although a wall of loud brass, relentless intensity, a metallic sounding rhythm section, discipline, and polish were invariably characteristic. The band really came into its own around 1946, when the smoky voiced June Christy was the featured singer. Stan Getz played with the orchestra, while Shelly Manne for years was the drummer. Pete Rugulo, who had studied with French composer Darius Milhaud, did a lot of arranging for Kenton; so did Shorty Rogers and Bob Graettinger. Graettinger was an eccentric genius, who wrote electronic music for traditional instruments. His major work was an innovative, four part suite called *City of Glass*, which practically no one understood. More typical concert pieces included Kenton's *Opus in Pastels*, *Concerto To End All Concertos*, and the Kenton-Rugulo collaboration *Prologue Suite*. In ballrooms, hotels, and theaters, Kenton performed more popular material, but played dances only when necessary. "Eager Beaver" was one of his perennial numbers, while "Artistry in Rhythm" became his theme song.

Kenton got into "Progressive" jazz about 1948, performing at Carnegie Hall in New York City, Symphony Hall in Boston, the Philadelphia Academy of Music, and the Chicago Civic Opera House. His dream was to bridge the gap between serious music and jazz. With that in mind, he formed Innovations Orchestra consisting of forty pieces, sixteen of which were strings. Kenton himself was an aggressive personality, with tremendous drive and an extremely analytical mind. His music was consistently criticized, as being synthetic and lacking the emotional center essential to jazz, although few could deny its power and precision. The "Progressive" style was especially championed by college students and young executives whose affluent tastes caused them to view the protest element in "bop" with suspicion. After 1958 Kenton became an important force in the music clinic movement, working in colleges and universities across the nation.

"Cool" jazz, the other form coming out of "bop," appeared around 1949 and was again listening music. If "bop" reflected the tensions of World War II, especially the bitterness of urban blacks, the "cool" approach captured much of the middle-of-the-road psychology sweeping middle class America in the early 1950s. Charlie Parker was one of the idols of the "cool" adherents, but rather than the explosive, torrential outbursts characteristic of "bop," "cool" jazzmen preferred a relaxed, flowing line. Whereas "bop" contained a fundamental rawness, the "cool" style revealed a kind of Bauhaus purity. Percussion instruments, in addition to providing rhythm, sometimes became the major carriers of melody. "Cool" solos caught the essence of individual disengagement, almost completely devoid of excitement and smooth to the point of blandness. Critics frequently belittled the "cool" sound as an exercise in boredom, while others insisted that the new style ran contrary to the very nature of jazz.

The "cool" movement may almost be seen as a musical counterpart of Beatnik literature. Both celebrated the virtues of withdrawal and passivity in a cold war society grown fearful, even paranoid, and doting on leaders like Dwight Eisenhower, Joseph McCarthy, and Norman Vincent Peale. Each confined emotional expression to a very limited range and saw "dropping out" the only feasible means of rebellion for alienated young whites. Musically the "cool" style represented a more or less conscious attempt to "whiten" jazz, to "bleach out" its Afro-American origins. Much of this activity took place on the West Coast, where the jazz tradition was less cemented—particularly in Los Angeles, but to a lesser degree in the San Francisco Bay area.

But the West Coast by no means had a monopoly, and a few of the "cool" jazzmen were black. Trumpeter Miles Davis, who had studied at Juilliard and played in the Charlie Parker Quintet, was among the style's pioneers. Born in 1926, Davis made his first "cool" recordings in 1949 for Capitol, later brought together in an album called *Birth of the Cool*. The chamber ensemble included such unusual instruments for jazz as French horn and tuba and played sophisticated arrangements by Gil Evans. Solo work by "bop" standards was pale and thin. Davis shortly became Mr. Cool, outwardly unemotional and indifferent. On the stand he was motionless, unsmiling, unshowmanly, sometimes turning his back on customers. He dressed nattily in tailored British tweeds, drove an imported sports car, and played with a gentle lyricism, in what seemed like as white a style as it was possible for any black man to play. Inside, however, he seethed with hostility. For a time he was a heroin addict, but later broke the habit. "I got hooked," Davis said, "after I got back from the Paris Jazz Festival in 1949. I got bored and was around cats that were hung. So I wound up with a habit that took me over four years to break. I broke it because it was too damn much trouble." His work during that period was uneven. Early in 1954 he experienced something of a musical rebirth, discovering an intense, passionate, often ravishing trumpet sound. Eventually he broke with the "cool" convention, manifesting a pride in his black roots and evolving in a more blues-oriented direction.

One of the members of Davis' group was John Lewis, another trained musician, who in 1952 organized the Modern Jazz Quartet. Its sound was delicate, while its style borrowed from contrapuntal devices like canon and fugue. The Quartet used material based on Elizabethan virginal music, Bach, and even traditional Christmas carols. Lewis, who had earlier worked for Dizzie Gillespie, played the piano and also did some composing. Yet opponents repeatedly found his efforts too consciously arty.

The virtually all-white West Coast school leaped into prominence soon after Miles Davis' success. Shorty Rogers, initially from Massachusetts, left the trumpet section of Stan Kenton's band, settling in Los Angeles and quickly becoming an exponent of the "cool" style. Gerry Mulligan came from New York City to distinguish himself as one of the leading California jazzmen. His Quartet originally consisted of Chet Baker on trumpet, Chico Hamilton on drums, and Bob Whitlock on bass; Mulligan himself played the saxophone and did most of the arranging. But California "cool" jazz reached its height with pianist Dave Brubeck. Brubeck had studied with both Milhaud and Schoenberg and made no secret of the fact that he wanted to bring jazz closer to the classical fold. He was particularly noted for his use of Baroque counterpoint and later broke out of the traditional 4/4 meter of jazz, playing works in 5/4 and 7/4 time. The Brubeck Quartet was greatly enhanced by the presence of alto saxophonist Paul Desmond, often featured in long, improvised solo work.

Other "cool" musicians included blind pianist Lennie Tristano, saxophonist Stan Getz, and arranger-saxophonist Jimmy Giuffre. Veteran jazzman Lester Young was a supporter of the "cool" movement, occasionally spoken of as the Cezanne of modern jazz. Later would come George Shearing, the Jay Jay Johnson-Kai Winding Quintet, Ramsey Lewis, and black flutist Buddy Collette. By 1955 the "cool" trend had hit its peak. Most of the style's representatives were brilliant, technically assured musicians, whose work was often highly self-conscious and sometimes strained to be genteel. Tonally the "cool" sound remained ambiguous, almost dreamy, while harmony at times was nonexistent. Gone were the "dirty" tones of jazz; in their place had come mellow sonority that was part of the ambiguity. While instrumentation grew more subtle, a basic beat was sometimes left out altogether. Unlike Parker or Gillespie, the "cool" musicians worked in close cooperation with arrangers, who supplied them material that would stimulate improvisation. "The cult of the Cool," Mellers argues, "must of its nature involve order, control, and therefore composition, of a more 'externalized' form than was manifest in Parker's subtly organized but intuitive heat."

European jazzmen and college-aged Americans embraced the "cool" approach enthusiastically, but many black musicians looked upon it as a denial of their heritage. By the 1950s jazz had generally become so middle class and respectable that blacks were having trouble identifying with it. Since the end of nightclubs, jazz had been more and more restricted to the concert hall and festival grounds. The first international jazz festival, which Louis Armstrong attended, was held in 1948 at Nice, France. Armstrong by then had practically become the country's number one cultural ambassador, although Duke Ellington ran him a close second. Some 25,000 people turned up for the 1955 Newport Jazz Festival, whereas several of the old Kansas City bands would be assembled at the Monterey Jazz Festival in 1971. Yet for many Americans of the late 1950s clarinetist Pete Fountain, a graduate of the Lawrence Welk orchestra, was the epitome of the New Orleans tradition.

By then, too, jazz had formed strong alliances with the older, more time-honored arts—poetry, ballet, symphonic music, and theater. Highbrow composers like Gunther Schuller, who had worked professionally in the jazz world, attempted to launch a "third stream," combining jazz and classical materials. The "third stream" writers generally leave spaces in their compositions for improvisation and have tried to introduce group improvisation into symphonic works. Ellington earlier had written several serious compositions (*Harlem, Night Creature, Such Sweet Thunder*), and a jazz opera, entitled *Opera Without Banners* and dedicated to Charlie Parker, would have its premiere in Kansas City in 1966. A number of television shows and movies, like *Streetcar Named Desire* and *The Man With the Golden Arm*, used jazz as background music, while jazz societies had sprung up in most of the major cities. To the avant-garde all of this sophistication of jazz spelled esthetic bankruptcy, and the way was paved for another revolution.

The insurgence that erupted was closely linked with black nationalism. Known first as "hard bop," then as "funky," and still later as "soul," the new style was a purposeful rejection of the "cool" technique. Its formulators wanted to take jazz back to its emotional roots, thereby communicating with urban blacks. The movement began in the mid-1950s, drawing its major inspiration from "bebop," but intensifying the emphasis on the blues. Instead of the complex structure and the advanced counterpoint, harmonies, and melodies contrived by the "cool" jazzmen, the "hard bop" musicians returned to passionate improvisation and the more direct, vital statement. Miles Davis sounded the call to arms in 1954, when he recorded "Walkin'," a blues number addressed to the ghetto. Theolonious Monk, bassist Charlie Mingus, pianist Horace Silver, and drummer Art Blakey contributed to the development of "hard bop," combining the chromaticism, phrasing, and sharp punctuation of the "bebop" style with the earthiness of classic New Orleans jazz. The result was a tough, angular music—fervent and powerful. Blakey had made several trips to Africa after World War II, where he studied the polyrhythms of tribal music, and in the late 1950s recorded several albums using African percussion. His approach was relentless and fiery, yet contained a subtle display of African passion and beauty.

The later term "funky" was an old Afro-American colloquialism for "smelly," with sexual implications, and clearly meant earthy and fundamental. Within the black community, to describe a musician as "funky" was to offer praise; similarly, "bad" is often used by urban blacks to mean "good." The compliment is all the greater when spoken in specifically black terms. "Funky" was succeeded by the name "soul" in part simply because the black subculture prizes verbal agility, and there is ordinarily a rapid turnover in ghetto argot. "Soul" had also become an inclusive reference to the Afro-American experience. The "funky-soul" trend in jazz occurred during the time that the civil rights movement was heating up, and many of the black jazzmen made this point explicit by using African-derived titles.

While the revolt against "cool" jazz was spearheaded by veterans like Davis, Silver, and Blakey, the front ranks of the rebellion were soon taken by a number of younger men from the northern cities—most of them coming from solid musical backgrounds, well educated in modern theory and harmony. One was tenor saxophonist Sonny Rollins, from New York, who was among the first horn players in jazz to improvise extended solos with thematic development and cohesion, without loss of freedom and ease.

But perhaps the most important of the "hard bop" musicians was John Coltrane, another saxophone player, who had worked with Gillespie, Monk, and Davis. Born in Philadelphia, Coltrane left the Miles Davis Quintet in 1961 to go on his own. His tone tended to be hard and harsh, while he lacked the varied coloration of Parker. He had extended the range of his instrument unbelievably, however, and expanded the texture of the sound he could evoke from it. "[A]t times he seemed prepared to gush out every possible note," Martin Williams recalls, "find his way step-by-step through every complex chord, careen through every scale, and go even beyond that prolixity by groping for impossible notes and sounds on a tenor saxophone that seemed ready to shatter under the strain." Gradually he was influenced by African and Oriental music, giving his compositions names like "Africa/Brass" and "Dahomey Dance." He was not politically a black nationalist, although there were aspects of the movement that interested him. Asked *why* he had incorporated rhythmic instruments from Africa and the Middle East into his work, Coltrane replied, "it's just something I feel." "Hard bop" musicians, he felt, looked "all over" for inspiration. "And inside." Coltrane's sudden death in July, 1967, robbed the younger generation of one of its most influential jazz figures. He was not yet forty-one.

Around 1961 there was a new avant-garde movement gathering in jazz, called "the new thing" or "free jazz." To a younger group of black musicians the "funky" style had become too formal, so that opportunities for imaginative expression were limited. The new music began in lofts and small bohemian clubs in Los Angeles, Chicago, and especially New York's Lower East Side, reflecting a growing restlessness within black society. In form, timbre, and spontaneity it represented a move away from European rigidity toward a greater expression of self and both the individual and collective Afro-American spirit. In the fall of 1964 a series of avant-garde jazz concerts, publicized as "the October Revolution," were held at the Cellar Cafe in New York City. By then the civil rights movement had passed beyond the phase symbolized by Martin Luther King and the Little Rock school integration crisis and was headed in the direction of the more militant black nationalistic stance of Malcolm X and the Black Panthers. Simple affirmation that "black is beautiful" was being replaced by negation of the white-dominated status quo. The music heard at "the October Revolution" concerts mirrored the anger of urban blacks. In it were the sounds of the ghetto—jagged squeals from the clarinet, eerie shrieks and deep explosions from the saxophone, stately lamentations from the trumpet.

At the vanguard of this new, freer jazz was Ornette Coleman, who appeared in New York late in 1959, bursting with creative energy. Coleman was from Fort Worth, Texas, born March 19, 1930. He grew up playing rhythm-and-blues and jazz; as a teenager he worked some of the more disreputable black night spots in town. Although he had read about Dizzy Gillespie and Charlie Parker, he was more familiar with Cab Calloway and Billy Eckstine. In 1948 he became the alto saxophonist in Red Connors' band, playing his first all-white club, and toured the South with Clarence Samuels' rhythm-and-blues group a few months later. He spent nine years in Los Angeles, initially playing a cross between rhythm-and-blues and bebop. He began jamming with some young musicians who agreed that certain basic changes had become necessary in jazz. He eventually formed his own combo, triggering as much controversy when he arrived in New York as Gillespie and Parker had fifteen years before.

The bearded Coleman played with great abandon, influenced both John Coltrane and Sonny Rollins, and soon became a walking myth. Intonation in his style is free, while blues inflections are elevated to the point that they encompass white-influenced melodic lines. Improvisation triumphs over all other aspects of jazz structure and for the first time is based on a general thematic outline. His form heeds no meter. The drummer and the bass, for instance, may be playing entirely different rhythms at the same time. Soloists maintain no relationship with what other musicians in the group may be doing, producing what to the uninitiated often sounds like chaos. Analogies between Coleman's approach and procedures in East Indian music are obvious. His work has been called raw, shrill, provocative, irreverent, but seldom boring. It is always extremely personal. Coleman gave a concert in Town Hall during the winter of 1962 and later received a fellowship from the Guggenheim Foundation.

Another of the "new thing" exponents is Cecil Taylor, the most controversial jazz pianist since Thelonious Monk. Taylor had studied at the New England Conservatory and developed a truly formidable style. His music has fire and energy, balancing improvisation and composition. Taylor has led a revolt against the white entrepreneurs who dominate the music business, asking black musicians to boycott all jazz clubs in the United States. Among other things he feels it is a demoralizing experience for a jazz artist to present his music in nightclubs. Archie Shepp, who studied and worked with Taylor, shares his mentor's bitterness toward the white establishment. "We are only an extension of that entire civil rights—Black Muslims—black nationalist movement that is taking place in America," Shepp said. "That is fundamental to music." His growling, raspy saxophone simulates the vocal patterns of the black ghetto, the essence of what might be heard on the streets of Harlem, Philadelphia, Detroit, Chicago, and elsewhere.

Trumpeter Don Cherry, who had come to New York with Coleman, is still another of the jazz iconoclasts. Born in Oklahoma in 1936, Cherry grew up in Los Angeles, where his father was a bartender at the Plantation Club. Saxophonist Albert Ayler was the same age. Raised in Cleveland, Ayler was among the most creative of the recent innovators, finally playing only his own music. He was found dead in the East River in November, 1970. Bass clarinetist Eric Dolphy was also a prominent avant-garde jazzman who died young. Like Coleman, Dolphy was the complete individualist, playing without regard for tempo, key, or accompaniment. Other recent left-wing jazz artists include trumpeter-composer Bill Dixon, pianist Sun Ra, and saxophonist Pharoah Sanders.

The contemporary jazz scene illustrates that there is indeed a black subculture in the United States, separate and apart from the mainstream. Both "hard bop" and the new avant-garde jazz, in differing ways, have sought to reaffirm black values and produce an art that black musicians can know to be their own. But the new music serves as a sociopolitical weapon as well, reinforcing the black-white division within urban society and thereby complicating the debate over the music's esthetic worth. The freeform jazzmen attempt to invoke the cadences unique to the lives of city blacks and depict the struggles and tensions of the Afro-American through searing expressionism. Jazz, Albert Ayler once commented, is "not about notes anymore. It's about feelings!" To the back-to-the-roots emphasis and rhythmic intensity of "hard bop" have been added Afro-Asian elements and the hostility of militant black nationalism. One of Archie Shepp's early pieces was entitled "Rufus," which dealt with a lynching, while the wailing sounds of the avant-garde musicians indicate the pain of an awakening minority. While the diversity of styles seems endless, the movement is unified by the theme of revolution. As in most revolutions, concern for human freedom is at times overshadowed by outrage, so that the avant-garde approach has yet to gain a wide popular following.

On the other hand, no form of modern jazz has been popular with the public at large. Beginning with "bop," jazz has been too sophisticated and esoteric for general acceptance. Forwardlooking jazzmen may be followed by a dedicated cult, but they are no longer household words in the sense that Armstrong, Beiderbecke, and Goodman once were. Jazz, like any of the popular arts, has had difficulty steering that tenuous path between substance and commercialism, between the rarity appreciated by an elite in-group and the banality preferred by the crowd. Whenever jazz has become too far removed from the ghetto, it seems to have lost heart. When it has grown too respectable or consciously arty, its inner verve has repeatedly suffered. Mellers feels that the neurotic element in traditional jazz was balanced by innocence. Now only the neurosis is left, while what was once vitality has become hysteria. Its later growth has come not from a harmonious relationship between the individual and society, but out of protest and rejection. Rather than communicate with the public, jazz artists prefer to play in small combos for themselves as outsiders. "They would accept the fact," Mellers concludes, "that the only vitality they could encompass was the nervous frenzy of a jungle turned to asphalt. Their music was their religion in that they put into it all the skeletonic truth they knew. Having played it, they died of consumption, drink, drugs or mental breakdown."

Jazz began as the music of a minority, moved north and west with that minority, became one of America's major cultural gifts to the world, and in its more advanced forms returned to the minority from whence it came. Along the way it was rejuvenated time and again by black innovators. Young white musicians interested in popular music are still frequently knowledgeable about current happenings in jazz, and jazz concerts continue to draw reasonably well in the larger cities and on college campuses. But jazz, as a living expression, has ceased to be a national craze primarily because as dance music it became too closely associated with the establishment, while in its experimental forms it grew too complex, too uncompromising. And so it reviewed its origins, took stock of the ghetto to which its promulgators had moved, and again became an essentially black music, speaking thoughts and feelings at odds with the institutional framework to which it had once been spectacularly wed.

CHAPTER
XI

POPULAR SONGS

The finest and most innovative popular songs have traditionally come from the theater. After World War I, however, the better products of Tin Pan Alley grew in sophistication, so that the division between theater music and the best popular songs was less marked. By the end of the 1920s writers from both fields found a common ground in the musical film, and within a short time songs for motion pictures were only slightly less polished than those for the stage. During the years between the wars commercial music in the United States enjoyed an unprecedented boom, aided by radio and the phonograph and achieving a wide international following.

The most lasting songs of the opulent twenties were nonetheless written by the current giants of the musical theater: Kern, Gershwin, Porter, Berlin, Rodgers and Hart. What many authorities consider George and Ira Gershwin's best song—"The Man I Love"—had surprisingly little success on the stage. Originally intended for *Lady Be Good,* it was dropped from the production before opening night in New York. The song was later included in the first version of *Strike Up the Band,* but again withdrawn. Gershwin decided that it was not a production number, since it allows for "little or no action while it is being sung." Curiously enough, "The Man I Love" became popular in London and Paris before it caught on in the United States. Part of the reason for the song's slow appeal may indeed be its complexity, particularly its chromatic pitfalls and the fact that it is not easy to sing without accompaniment. The main melody consists of a six note progression, which achieves poignancy through a contrapuntal background of a descending tonal scale. Both lyrics and music treat the love dream with irony and compassion, transforming a stock theme into something fresh and mature. Mellers considers "The Man I Love" the most moving popular song of recent times. "The girl has grown in the course of the piece," the musicologist concludes, "and we have grown with her. . . . The music tells us that. . . the joy of love can survive the fallibility of human nature, and the girl knows that, even before the love has happened to her." Gershwin caught the prevalent mood of the moment, as he did characteristically in his best works, crystallized it, stamped it with his own personality, and lifted it toward immortal heights.

Many of the classic Irving Berlin songs outlived the Broadway shows of which they were initially a part. "What'll I Do?" and "All Alone" were interpolated into the *Music Box Revue* in 1923, for the then unknown Grace Moore. Neither "Always" nor "Remember," written in 1925, were conceived as show tunes. The versatile Berlin became one of the top money-makers in Tin Pan Alley, with songs like "All By Myself" selling a million copies of sheet music, more than 150,000 piano rolls, and over a million records within a seventy-five week period. In 1927 he wrote "Blue Skies" and "The Song Is Ended," both masterpieces of economy and clarity. "How About Me?" followed the next year. A number of Berlin's songs tend to be self-pitying, suggesting repeatedly that love will hurt.

But there was a brighter side to the songs of the 1920s, many of them owing much to the evolving jazz tradition. Jazz orchestrations came into vogue during the decade, with key arrangers becoming exceptionally skillful. Gradually jazz lyrics mirrored less of the black subculture and more of the jubilant, hedonistic stereotype of the decade. Such latter-day minstrels as Al Jolson and Eddie Cantor pranced up and down the stage singing "Swanee" and "Makin' Whoopee" with joyful abandon, while in the 1927 edition of the Ziegfeld *Follies* Ruth Etting recalled the happy Southland image in the Irving Berlin rhythm song "Shaking the Blues Away." As the jazz band grew increasingly important in making songs popular, the beat and accent were often emphasized more than the melody. Numbers like "The Big Butter and Egg Man from the West" served as a Louis Armstrong vehicle, but its lyrics reflected the free-spending of the times. Some of the jazzmen were prolific composers. Fats Waller, for instance, wrote "Honeysuckle Rose" and "Ain't Misbehavin'," while Spencer Williams emerged as a major songwriter in the Dixieland tradition, producing perennials like "Basin Street Blues" and "Twelfth Street Rag." Fred Fisher's "Dardanella" had an almost boogie-woogie beat, while Zez Confrey's syncopated piano pieces included "Stumbling" and "Kitten on the Keys."

Eventually everything from "The Star-Spangled Banner" to Chopin's "Funeral March" received a jazz treatment. Tin Pan Alley began turning out jazz lyrics that were as sentimental and synthetic as the old ballads had been. Frequently the weakness lay not only in what was said, but the way in which it was said. Banalities were spoken in tones of great seriousness, in language affectedly poetic. Jazz singers increasingly came to lapse into fantasy, yearning and dreaming for ideal mates, as reverie replaced action in the commercialized lyrics. Male-female relationships were seen through rose-colored shades, synonymous with lasting happiness, while love was viewed as a heavenly magic by which lovers transcend ordinary experience. "When You're Smiling" suggests that the world's problems can be dissolved in a smile, whereas the prosperity of the decade is reflected in "My God, How the Money Rolls In," which in its revived form, changed the line "My father he fiddles for gin" to "My father sells bootlegger gin."

Some of the economic exuberance and superficial recklessness of the 1920s was expressed in the current dances. After Gilda Gray, Bea Palmer, and Ann Pennington had made the shimmy famous on Broadway, Tin Pan Alley glorified the dance in such songs as "Indianola" and "I Wish I Could Shimmy Like My Sister Kate." By 1923 the shimmy was pushed aside by a new dance craze—the Charleston, introduced in the black revue *Runnin' Wild*, along with a tune of the same name. With rolled stockings and bobbed hair, many a "flapper" kicked frantically and criss-crossed her hands over silken knees to the big Charleston number "Yes, Sir, That's My Baby." Within three years the dance had been superseded by the even more extreme Black Bottom, the movements of which suggested the dragging of feet through a muddy river bed. Since the ragtime era most popular songs have needed to be danceable, yet the uninhibited steps of the 1920s demonstrate the restlessness of that age. The first dance marathon was held at the Roseland Ballroom in New York in 1923. Marathon dancing grew in popularity during the early Depression years, but in 1933 was declared illegal.

In their quest for escapism, white middle class Americans of the 1920s looked to blacks and especially Harlem as a psychic release from the fetters of Puritanism. In nightclubs with a jungle motif or replicas of southern plantations, downtown Babbitts could thrill at watching bronze "primitives" revert to nature in erotic dances, while white matrons might vicariously enjoy a hot lover boy in the form of a sexy black strutter, decked out in his best city clothes. Irving Berlin captured this high-stepping strutter in his 1929 song "Puttin' on the Ritz." At the Harlem clubs white Americans could lose themselves in an exotic atmosphere, amid infectious music with an unrelenting drive, and in the darkness even join in the "jungle dances" themselves. As Nathan Irvin Huggins pictures the scene in his fine account of the Harlem Renaissance: "Heads swaying, rolling, jerking; hair flying free and wild; arms and legs pumping, kicking, thrusting—going wherever they, themselves, would go—chasing the bass or drum or cornet; clenched eyes and teeth, staccato breath, sweat, sweat — bodies writhing and rolling with a drum and a beat as they might never with a woman or a man."

But there were other indications of exotic dreams. The tango enjoyed a revival after Rudolph Valentino magnetized American women with his dancing in the silent film *The Four Horsemen of the Apocalypse*. Earlier

"The Sheik of Araby" had become a popular song, and Ramon Novarro later made a hit of "The Pagan Love Song." Hawaiian songs, like "On the Beach of Waikiki" and "Song of the Islands," had been in vogue during World War I, but afterwards "Japanese Sandman," "My Isle of Golden Dreams," "Russian Lullaby," and Lecuona's "Siboney" all contained wishes for far away places. In *Ramona* love was glamorized into Spanish romance, with the peal of mission bells, the fragrance of flowers, and the gentle California climate as additional lures.

And there were sheer nonsense ditties like the popular "kid" song "I Faw Down an' Go Boom." A nation with a recent rural past sang voraciously of "Horses."

> *Horses, Horses, Horses!*
> *Nutty over Horses, Horses, Horses!*
> *Goofy over Horses, Horses, Horses!*

The verses were intended as pure silliness and did not pretend to make sense. An even greater hit was "Yes! We Have No Bananas," written in 1923 by Frank Silver and Irving Cohn, about a Greek fruit store owner. "Barney Google" was inspired by a newspaper comic strip, while "Digga, Diga, Doo" had no other purpose than fun for fun's sake. Helen Kane, the "boop-a-doop" girl, a cute, pert vaudeville performer, won fame by inserting meaningless syllables into songs like "Button Up Your Overcoat" and "I Wanna Be Loved By You."

It was a high-spirited age that could laugh at itself, but it was also an age in need of heroes. There were songs celebrating Lindbergh's flight, and "Babe Ruth, He Is a Home Run Guy" appeared in 1923. Shortly after the death of Valentino came the mournful "There's a New Star in Heaven Tonight." The Scopes trial was discussed in song, while the spirit of Freud entered such titles as "My Suppressed Desire." The growing importance of the city was reflected in "Chicago" and "Manhattan Serenade," whereas the decade's sophistication was revealed by such lyrics as "A Farewell to Arms" (inspired by Ernest Hemingway's novel) and "Strange Interlude" (referring to the Eugene O'Neill play). Interestingly enough, when Fanny Brice sang "Second Hand Rose," she used a Yiddish accent; when Barbra Streisand recorded the song in the 1960s, both the accent and the more Jewish lines were gone.

The success of "Three O'clock in the Morning" in 1921 indicated that the waltz still had a foothold in the jazz age. There was a rash of bird songs, most notably "Follow the Swallow Back Home," "When the Red Red Robbin Comes Bob Bobbin' Along," and "Bye Bye Blackbird." Far more titles bore girls' names: "Dinah," "Sweet Georgia Brown," "Mah Lindy Lou," "Margie," "Sweet Lorraine," "Sweet Sue," and the more rampageous "Hard Hearted Hannah." Although the mass of love songs in the 1920s were delicate and sentimental, some possessed a frankness, a realism, and an earthiness that the older generations found shocking.

The ballads of the "torch singers" sublimated the raw blues feeling of Ma

Rainey and Bessie Smith. Libby Holman, whose voice possessed a husky, throaty quality, really began this approach, which lamented life in an orgy of self-pity. The torch singers appeared in cabarets, nightclubs, and Broadway shows late in the decade, specializing in such numbers as "Moanin' Low" and "Am I Blue?" Ruth Etting, married to mobster "Gimp" Snyder, sang ballads that echoed the toughness of her life. She approached sex obliquely in songs like "What Wouldn't I Do for That Man?"—usually refined by a soft saxophone, violin, and piano accompaniment. Despite a growing promiscuity, the social ethic still insisted that sex, if not in marriage, must be part of a romantic love affair. "Ten Cents a Dance," put into Rodgers and Hart's *Simple Simon* for Etting, was a bitter tale of a dance hall hostess:

> *Seven to midnight I hear drums,*
> *Loudly the saxophone blows,*
> *Trumpets are tearing my ear-drums,*
> *Customers crush my toes.*

But the queen of the torch singers was Helen Morgan, who sang with doleful eyes, clutching a handkerchief, in a voice that sounded as if she had seen it all. "Why Was I Born?" served as one of her vehicles, containing a sincerity of expression that avoided artificial phrases. Morgan's own life was far from happy, and she died penniless.

On the whole popular songs during the 1920s became more intricate, less banal, and more musically complicated, breaking from the thirty-two bar prison that had confined Tin Pan Alley's efforts for so long. While the great Broadway composers paved the way, there were distinguished songsmiths outside the theater that helped turn American commercial music into a miniature art. Hoagy Carmichael, a talented, inventive, jazz-oriented craftsman, attempted writing for the stage only once, a venture from which nothing lasting emerged. Carmichael's most famous song is the classic "Star Dust" (1929), although "Washboard Blues" was his first great success and "Rockin' Chair" became the hallmark of blues singer Mildred Bailey.

Bandleader Isham Jones wrote a number of durable songs, including "Swingin' Down the Lane," "I'll See You in My Dreams," and "It Had to Be You." Richard Whiting, whose World War I triumph, "Till We Meet Again," had sold over five million copies by the time of the Armistice, added "Sleepy Time Gal" and "She's Funny That Way" in the 1920s. Walter Donaldson, who would compose a string of unforgettable melodies for Hollywood, won distinction with "My Buddy," "Carolina in the Morning," "My Blue Heaven," "At Sundown," and "Love Me or Leave Me," another Ruth Etting favorite. Harry Ruby established himself with tunes like "Who's Sorry Now?" and "Thinking of You," while Fred Ahlert produced such standards as "I'll Get By" and "Mean to Me." Harold Arlen, who would later write many songs for the Cotton Club *Parade* and whom Ethel Waters once called "the Negro-ist white man" she had ever known, caused a sensation in 1929 with "Get Happy," which won him a contract with a publishing subsidiary of Remick. Arlen's approach to music was pragmatic and down-to-earth, although much of his work has an undertone of melancholy.

The 1920s marked the final golden years for Tin Pan Alley. Most of the music publishers by then had moved uptown as far as Forty-second Street, again following the theaters. The reduced size of sheet music, made necessary by the paper shortage during World War I, proved more practical and continued permanently. ASCAP, which paid its first sums to members in 1921, grew in strength and won a number of strategic court battles. Sheet music sales, however, were on the decline, since fewer people were making their own music. The parlor piano was rapidly being replaced by the handcranked, mahogany phonograph. The recording industry began gaining momentum after 1910, with some discs selling a million or two million copies. Whereas a song's popularity had once been measured in terms of sheet music sales, in the mid-1920s a more important yardstick had become the number of records sold. Several publishing firms even went out of business and by 1928 mergers were the order of the day.

In 1921 Americans were spending more money on phonograph records than any other form of recreation. Acoustical recording, reproduced by an exterior horn, still could not capture the sound of a full orchestra with anything like its full frequency range, and drums presented special problems. By 1924, however, an electrical method of recording had been developed, enhancing the quality of sound, with the result that the phonograph industry prospered even more. Before long no middle class home was complete without copies of the latest hit records. Dancers at private parties moved to the mechanically reproduced strains of "Tip Toe Through the Tulips" or "If I Could Be with You," and the family musician strummed along on his ukulele as the phonograph turned out "Five Foot Two, Eyes of Blue."

Before 1925 a successful song was expected to sustain public interest for about sixteen months. The phonograph lessened this, but the advent of radio shortened it even more. With radio a new song could be sung in a New York theater or nightclub one evening and be recognized as a coast-to-coast hit the next. The 1920s was an age doting on fads, when it became a mark of sophistication to know not the old tunes, but the very newest ones. Songs were sometimes made into a hit by a single broadcast, then quickly forgotten. Radio also created new singing stars, who because of electrical amplification needed less lung power. By the end of the decade the "crooner" had become popular—a vocalist who sang in a soft, caressing, almost whispering manner. Nick Lucas, Gene Austin, and Russ Columbo were among the original "crooners," but Rudy Vallee made a far bigger splash after his first radio appearance in 1928. Broadcasting with his own band, the Connecticut Yankees, from the Heigh-Ho Club in New York, Vallee gained immediate recognition, while his radio greeting, "Heigh-ho, everybody, this is Rudy Vallee," became nationally famous. A society striving to be less provincial found the singer's collegiate ways and Ivy League background particularly appealing, and his theme song, "My Time Is Your Time," almost became an American institution. Radio also influenced orchestration and in time affected songwriting.

Motion pictures, even in the silent days, played an important role in making songs popular. "Charmaine," a waltz interpolated into the 1926 film *What Price Glory*, was the first movie theme song to become an overnight hit. Erno Rapee, who wrote the music, also supplied "Diane" for *Seventh Heaven* in 1927 and "Angela Mia" for *Street Angel* in 1928, all with words by Lew Pollack. But when Al Jolson sang some of his specialties in *The Jazz Singer* in 1927, basically a silent picture, it was evident that the screen had found a voice. The dewy story—about the son of a synagogue cantor who wants to become a jazz singer—was brought to its poignant conclusion with Jolson speaking a few words and emoting the indomitable "Mammy." At a time when the film industry was suffering temporary reverses, movie producers were not long in realizing the financial advantages of sound.

Suddenly musicals of all kinds began bursting out of the major studios. Nacio Herb Brown, a native Californian who worked almost exclusively with the movies, wrote two hits for the *Hollywood Revue of 1929*, "You Were Meant for Me" and "Singin' in the Rain." A total of seventy screen musicals was produced that year, and *The Broadway Melody* won the Academy Award for the year's best motion picture. Meanwhile Tin Pan Alley acknowledged the innovation of sound with the song "If I Had a Talking Picture of You," included in the Janet Gaynor film *Sunny Side Up*. By then Hollywood studios were beginning to swallow up the New York music publishing houses. Warner Brothers bought out three major firms, Harms, Witmark, and Remick, paying a combined ten million dollars and assembling these assets into a single unit called Music Publishers Holding Corporation. Metro-Goldwyn-Mayer followed suit by acquiring Leo Feist, Robbins, and a couple of lesser companies, thereby gaining a backlog of songs from which production numbers could be drawn. After 1930 Tin Pan Alley, as a street and a commercial entity, was no more.

Soon one well known songwriter after another was pouring into Los Angeles, attracted by a new challenge and high salaries. Rodgers and Hart were among the first to be called, although they did far from their best work for films. First National paid them each $50,000 to write the songs for two pictures. Both musicians came to hate Hollywood, but they did produce a few good numbers there. For *Love Me Tonight* in 1932 the team wrote "Lover" and "Isn't It Romantic?" *Hallelujah, I'm a Bum*, an Al Jolson vehicle released in 1933, contained the ballad "You Are Too Beautiful," although the picture itself was a box office failure. "Blue Moon," the only Rodgers and Hart song not part of a show score, was probably written in 1932 for Jean Harlow in the *Hollywood Revue of 1933*, but not used. New lyrics were added, and the melody was sung by Shirley Ross in the 1934 picture *Manhattan Melodrama*, under the title "The Bad in Every Man." Later that year, with yet another lyric, the song was copyrighted under the name "Blue Moon."

The Gershwin's had written for the movies as early as 1931, but returned for a more extended stay in 1935. Paradoxically, while George Gershwin's "serious" compositions were growing more complex, his last songs were actually *less* complicated. Vincent Youmans and Jerome Kern shortly arrived on the West Coast. Kern came in 1934 to do the score for the RKO production *I*

Dream Too Much, starring the Metropolitan coloratura Lily Pons. He quickly fell in love with the California climate and by 1936 was convinced that most of his work thereafter would be concentrated on motion pictures. Unlike Rodgers and Hart, Kern did some of his most inventive writing for films. "Lovely to Look At" was introduced in the movie version of *Roberta* in 1935, while "The Way You Look Tonight" and "A Fine Romance" were both composed the next year for *Swing Time*.

Irving Berlin's flirtation with Hollywood was even longer. Since the late 1920s Berlin had been in something of a creative impasse. This was broken in 1932 when "How Deep Is the Ocean?" became a best-seller. Then began his cavalcade of screen triumphs, starting with *Top Hat* in 1935, which featured Ginger Rogers and Fred Astaire. The Berlin score included the ballad "Cheek to Cheek," earning the composer over $250,000 in royalties from the initial sheet music sale. Cole Porter's first work for motion pictures came in 1936 with *Born to Dance*, an M-G-M film starring Eleanor Powell and James Stewart, and had as its finest numbers "Easy to Love" and "I've Got You Under My Skin." *Rosalie*, a year later, offered the title song and "In the Still of the Night." As with his Broadway efforts, Porter's lyrics were as distinguished as his music, exuding gloss and poise.

Harold Arlen wrote his first Hollywood songs in 1933 for the motion picture *Let's Fall in Love*. Six years later he did the score for *The Wizard of Oz*, one of the peaks in the flowering of the musical film. Here the composer contrasted what he called "lemon-drop songs," such as "We're Off to See the Wizard" and "Ding-Dong! The Witch Is Dead," with the rich, arching melody of "Over the Rainbow." Written for the poignant voice of young Judy Garland and touched with traces of the blues, "Over the Rainbow" spun dreams to which listeners in the troubled Depression days could respond. The number not only became immensely popular, but won the Academy Award for the best original movie song of 1939.

Richard Whiting also worked on the West Coast, supplying the superb "Too Marvelous for Words" for the 1937 film *Ready, Willing and Able*. Burton Lane's first well known song, "Everything I Have Is Yours," was composed in 1931 for the picture *Dancing Lady*, and Arthur Freed and Nacio Herb Brown wrote the haunting "Temptation" for *Going Hollywood* two years later. In 1934 "The Continental" by Con Conrad and Herb Magidson, introduced by Ginger Rogers and Fred Astaire in *The Gay Divorcee*, became the first song to win an Academy Award. Harry Warren and Al Dubin, already established song kings in Hollywood, captured the Oscar the next year with "Lullaby of Broadway," the big number from *Gold Diggers of Broadway*. Three years before the partners had done much to revitalize the movie musical with *Forty-Second Street*, a tightly scripted comedy about putting on a show. The film featured Ruby Keeler and Dick Powell and introduced all sorts of novel camera angles. Its best number, "Shuffle Off to Buffalo," typified Hollywood sophistication, danced by a young couple in pajamas on their honeymoon train to Niagara Falls. Warren and Dubin had three major song hits in 1934: "The Boulevard of Broken Dreams" from *Moulin Rouge*, "I'll

String Along with You" from *Twenty Million Sweethearts*, and "I Only Have Eyes for You" from *Dames*.

After the initial shock, movie attendance was up during the Depression. Hollywood offered all sorts of escape, but the film musical was among the most profitable. Audiences wanted to forget their cares when they sank into seats at the movie palace, and by 1932 Technicolor added to the screen fantasy world. Busby Berkeley, the choreographer-director who dramatized many of the Warren and Dubin songs, had a penchant for kaleidoscoping girls. *Fashion Follies of 1934*, for instance, opened with girls as petals forming flowers. On another occasion he had girls plucking harps made of more girls. His work abounded in leggy, shimmering dance routines and soft-voiced ballads. Several of the early sound pictures succeeded because of their songs, and by the end of the 1930s the movie industry controlled over three quarters of the nation's commercial music. As more and more music publishers became offshoots of the major studios, film executives began to rely increasingly on their own songwriters, dictating the type of material needed for a particular production. While good songs still came out of Hollywood, most of the efforts became pretty banal. Producers bought the rights to Broadway musicals and operettas, but much of the original work suffered from the heavy demands made on writers and severe regimentation.

The crooner remained popular both on radio and the screen. Rudy Vallee revived old songs and made new ones, like the sentimental "Goodnight, Sweetheart," familiar. Bing Crosby became a big success on the airwaves in the fall of 1931, having earlier been one of Paul Whiteman's Rhythm Boys. Crosby's singing seemed natural and effortless, although rather than Vallee's high-pitched voice, his was a more manly baritone. Women and men alike loved the soft caress of Crosby's sound, while his clean-cut appearance stood him well when he made his first motion picture, *The Big Broadcast*, in 1932. The foremost lady crooner was Kate Smith, whose fame spread quickly over radio, becoming known as the "Song Bird of the South." Like Rudy Vallee and Bing Crosby, Kate Smith had a relaxed approach, but also a down-to-earth, homey quality.

By 1930 radio had taken over the role once filled by vaudeville in plugging popular songs, although broadcasting was responsible for selling far more phonograph records than sheet music. Most of the smaller stations across the country soon began using records as a basic part of their programming, which in turn sent listeners scurrying to record shops for the latest hits. In 1929 the Radio Corporation of America took over the Victor company, making the union between the two media more tangible. By then the National Association of Broadcasters had created a code of ethics which black-listed material considered suggestive. "How Could Red Riding Hood Have Been So Very Good and Still Keep the Wolf from the Door?" was reputedly the first song banned from radio. "Dancing on the Ceiling," a hit tune of 1930, was forbidden because the word "bed" occurs twice in the verse and again in the refrain. For years Cole Porter's "Love for Sale" was permitted only as an instrumental, and many of the great theater songs had to be rephrased for the airwaves. "Today," music publisher Edward B. Marks lamented in 1934, "songs are made hits in a week and killed off in sixty days. The public hears so many songs it has long ceased to distinguish among them. ... More songs are produced than ever before, but nobody profits from them—except the broadcasters."

Your Hit Parade, a program which for twenty-five years presented the "top ten" tunes of the week, began on April 20, 1935. Based on frequency of playing and record and sheet music sales, the program's charts provided a fairly accurate barometer to popular taste and came to be looked upon as absolutely authoritative. On its first broadcast the number one song was Jerome Kern's "Lovely to Look At," followed by Kern's "I Won't Dance," Warren's "Lullaby of Broadway," and Gershwin's "Soon." The program was heard every Saturday night, and its format eventually became as familiar and reassuring as a church service. Through the years the ritual was sponsored by Lucky Strike cigarettes, which punctuated its commercials with the cries of tobacco auctioneers and hammered the public with phrases like "I've smoked Luckies for nigh onto forty-five years" and "Lucky Strike green has gone to war." Besides the "top ten" songs, listeners also heard Lucky Strike "extras," which the announcer called "all-time all-timers," but which rarely seemed worth remembering. Toward the last segment of the broadcast the atmosphere grew more tense, as the "three top songs of the week, clear across the nation" were introduced with harp glissandos and much fanfare.

Record sales, like movie attendance, had fallen off sharply in the early years of the Depression, but began to pick up again around 1933. The popularity of the big bands helped invigorate the recording industry, and in 1934 Decca, a new firm backed in part by British money, instituted a policy of providing a quality disc at a moderate cost, initially thirty-five cents. The company succeeded in signing Bing Crosby, the Dorsey brothers, Guy Lombardo, the Mills brothers, and other major artists and by 1938 sold over 300,000 copies of the novelty tune "A-Tisket, A-Tasket," unprecedented at the time. Victor quickly followed Decca's lead, issuing its Bluebird series as an economy label. Victor also marketed a turntable that could be attached to a radio set, began advertising its records in radio trade journals, and in 1939 had its own best-seller in "Beer Barrel Polka."

The record revival was stimulated by the success of the jukebox, which with the end of Prohibition found its way into practically every drugstore, bar, and diner in the country. A nickel in the slot and the punch of a button could produce for patrons their favorite song hit from a big, gaudy Seeburg jukebox. At cheap night spots and honky tonks, where there were lots of customers, the stubby, chrome machines provided dance music for a fairly nominal fee per person. It was estimated that in black taverns jukeboxes outdrew their counterparts in equivalent white clubs by a ratio of three to one. By 1939 there were almost 225,000 jukeboxes in the United States, playing something like 13,000,000 records a year.

In time ASCAP was successful in forcing payment from radio stations, just as it had been earlier with motion picture theaters using songs for silent films. With the advent of sound Warner Brothers negotiated a contract whereby they would pay ASCAP $125,000 annually for the right to use their choice of the works owned or controlled by the society's members. Publishers not absorbed by the Hollywood studios took offices either in Radio City or in the Brill Building at Forty-ninth and Broadway. Many of them bolstered their business by putting out albums with a popular performer's name and photograph on the cover. The collection would contain the words and music of a few recent hits, but was filled out with tunes on which the copyright had lapsed. Since no royalties were required on the latter, the publisher could recover some of the company's original investments.

Hughson F. Mooney, in his stimulating study for the *American Quarterly* (1954), concludes that American popular songs between 1895 and 1925 tended to be abandoned and unorthodox; from the late 1920s into the 1940s they leaned toward the negative and the morbid. Mooney calls the latter mood the "Old Rockin' Chair's Got Me" period and feels that it was a direct outgrowth of the emotional and social impact of the Depression. Although the popular music of the 1930s was subdued, relaxed, and sweet, it spoke of quiet despair, disillusion, and resignation. The Depression years, Mooney argues, were dominated by perennials like "Stormy Weather," "Mood Indigo," and "Deep Purple"—all quite passive. Equally meek were the radio crooners and the pretty stylings and "highbrow" orchestrations of the big dance bands.

Certainly by 1930 the nation had suffered a loss of confidence. "Brother, Can You Spare a Dime?"—from the short-lived 1932 revue *Americana*—captured much of the spirit of the day, as did Rodgers and Hart's "I've Got Five Dollars," which spoke of debts "beyond endurance on my life insurance." "Let's Have Another Cup of Coffee" looked to the simpler pleasures of life, while Joan Blondell sang of "My Forgotten Man" in the Hollywood film *Gold Diggers of 1933*. The materialism of the decade was humorously indicated by "If Love Makes You Give Up Steak and Potatoes, Then I Don't Want Love," whereas a bigger song hit suggested that since there was no more money in the bank, "let's turn out the light and go to bed." "Life Is Just a Bowl of Cherries" became a success in 1931, and "Happy Days Are Here Again" was soon used as a theme song by the victorious Democratic party, but both seemed more dreams than reality. "In a Shanty in Old Shanty Town" conveyed some optimism, as did "I Found a Million Dollar Baby in a Five and Ten Cent Store," yet they saw poverty against visions of wealth and palaces. From Walt Disney's *Three Little Pigs* came "Who's Afraid of the Big Bad Wolf," while *Snow White and the Seven Dwarfs* contained "Whistle While You Work." Although these two tunes were outwardly happy, one dealt with calamity, the other with subsistence.

But there were still hopes and fantasies and the desire for escape. "Just a Cottage Small by a Waterfall" combined the humble with the picturesque. "Some Day My Prince Will Come" was another song from *Snow White*, and Richard Whiting collaborated with serious composer W. Franke Harling on "Beyond the Blue Horizon." "I've Got a Pocketful of Dreams" in 1938 was followed by "Wishing" a year later. There were airy thoughts of "Blue Hawaii," "South of the Border," and "Red Sails in the Sunset." "Underneath the Harlem Moon" again found the black as an escape mechanism, while "Stars Fell on Alabama" cast a misty aura over the Southland. "Is It True What They Say about Dixie?" was an Al Jolson favorite. Singers longed for "Moonglow," "September in the Rain," "East of the Sun," but especially "Pennies from Heaven."

The Depression years witnessed a Latin influx, beginning with "The Peanut Vendor" in 1931 and continuing through "La Cucaracha." Americans took up the rumba, and by 1937 Cuban bandleader Desi Arnaz had introduced the conga. At a time when midwestern painters Thomas Hart Benton and Grant Wood were lauding the American heartland, popular songs like "Wagon Wheels" and "Tumbling Tumbleweeds" glorified the frontier West. The later 1930s particularly had their share of nonsense tunes— "Three Little Fishes," "Scatterbrain," "Jeepers Creepers"—and such lively ones as "It's a Sin to Tell a Lie" and "The Music Goes Round and Round." But there were also songs of self-pity, among them "You've Got Me Crying Again," "Willow Weep for Me," and "When Your Lover Has Gone." And the ubiquitous love ballad was far from forgotten: "Prisoner of Love," "Don't Blame Me," "I'm in the Mood for Love," "You Go to My Head," "That Old Feeling."

The big bands fulfilled a major role in popularizing songs during their heyday. "Under a Blanket of Blue" was featured by Leon Belasco and His Orchestra, "I'm Gettin' Sentimental Over You" became Tommy Dorsey's theme song, while "Moonlight Cocktail" was introduced later by Glenn Miller. Name bandleaders supposedly received gratuities from the large publishing companies, much as vaudeville headliners had earlier. Broadcast time was the surest way for a band to gain national distinction, and a radio signature helped a group become immediately recognizable. Ben Bernie had begun this practice back in the 1920s, when he made "My Buddy" his theme song. Benny Goodman used "Let's Dance," Artie Shaw "Begin the Beguine." Several of the more successful bands were sought out by Hollywood. Glenn Miller, for instance, played "At Last" and "Serenade in Blue" in the film *Orchestra Wives,* helping both numbers to become hits.

New songwriters of promise appeared during the 1930s and early 1940s, while more established ones developed. Vernon Duke wrote "April in Paris" in 1932, followed two years later by "Autumn in New York"—both for Broadway shows. Harold Arlen added to his growing reputation with "I Gotta Right to Sing the Blues," "It's Only a Paper Moon," "Come Rain or Come Shine," "I've Got the World on a String," "Last Night When We Were Young," and "Blues in the Night." Hoagy Carmichael, who did a lot of work for films, came along with "Lazybones," "Two Sleepy People," "Heart and Soul," and "Skylark."

Among the younger writers was Jimmy McHugh. Two of his first and best known songs, "On the Sunny Side of the Street" and "Exactly Like You," were written in 1930 for *Lew Leslie's International Revue.* He later did "I'm in the Mood for Love," "Where Are You?" and "I Feel a Song Comin' On" for films. Jimmy Van Heusen, soon a mainstay of the movie industry, showed up in 1938, producing songs like "Darn That Dream" and "Imagination." Englishman Ray Noble, whose band toured all over the United States, composed "Goodnight, Sweetheart," "Love Is the Sweetest Thing," and "I Hadn't Anyone Till You." Rube Bloom, originally a piano player, wrote such standards as "Day In—Day Out" and "Don't Worry 'Bout Me." Johnny Green, who had grown up admiring George Gershwin, much as Gershwin had admired Kern, copyrighted his first big song in 1930—"Body and Soul," interpolated into the Broadway revue *Three's a Crowd*. Green spent most of his career composing and orchestrating film scores, but he did manage to write popular numbers like "I'm Yours" and "I Cover the Waterfront." More recently he has become an active concert conductor.

On Armistice Day, 1938, a few months before Nazi bombs fell on Poland, Kate Smith introduced over radio a patriotic song freshly fashioned by Irving Berlin. It was destined to become almost a second national anthem. The song was "God Bless America," written shortly after Berlin's return home from a trip abroad, during which he had seen the shadows of Fascism lengthening across Europe. The melody had originally been intended for the World War I soldier show *Yip, Yip, Yaphank*, but had been put aside unused. Berlin supplied new lyrics and presented the song to Kate Smith, who sang it time and again during the dark years ahead. With America's entry into World War II, Berlin began work on *This Is the Army*, which opened in New York on July 4, 1942. The show had a cast of some 300 soldiers, later toured all over the United States, and was eventually made into a screen musical by Warner Brothers. Its score borrowed "Oh, How I Hate to Get Up in the Morning" from *Yip, Yip, Yaphank*, but also included new songs like "I Left My Heart at the Stage Door Canteen" and "This Is the Army, Mr. Jones," two of the more popular war songs.

Successful war songs, however, were none too plentiful, despite the War Department's constant striving to encourage another "Over There." Unlike earlier wars, World War II was much more mechanized, impersonal, and thoroughly reported. It was a total war, in which the destruction far surpassed that of World War I, and it was a war Americans were not at all sure they would win. The bombing of Pearl Harbor had dramatized the bloodshed and grimness of the conflict from the outset, making the romantic sentiments of previous wars seem out of place. American soldiers marched off to World War II not with a holiday air, but with the awareness that they might not return. The homefront felt more anxiety and duty than excitement, for this they knew was a war for survival.

Yet while World War II was not essentially a singing war, there were attempts to provide songs that would stimulate morale. A lot of silly titles appeared early in the war, like "Goodbye Mama, I'm Off to Yokohama," "You're a Sap, Mr. Jap," "Let's Put the Axe to the Axis," "Put Another Nail in Hitler's Coffin," and "Der Feuhrer's Face." Gradually there were better efforts. Britain's struggle was commemorated in "The White Cliffs of Dover," while "My Sister and I" paid tribute to the fallen Holland. More lasting was "The Last Time I Saw Paris" by Jerome Kern and Oscar Hammerstein II. From Germany came "Lili Marlene," perhaps the song most closely associated with the war. "When the Lights Go on Again" appeared in 1942, followed the year after by "There's a Star Spangled Banner Waving Somewhere," a surprise hit from the hillbilly field. "Bell Bottom Trousers" became the unofficial song of the Navy, whereas "Comin' In on a Wing and a Prayer" pictured the hazards of the Army Air Corps. Servicemen glorified "Dirty Gertie from Bizerte," while women at home lamented "They're Either Too Young or Too Old." Other homefront songs with a wartime flavor included "I'll Walk Alone," "Goodnight Wherever You Are," "Say a Pray'r for the Boys Over There," "Saturday Night Is the Loneliest Night of the Week," and the revived "I'll Be Seeing You."

Aside from Irving Berlin, the most distinguished composer of World War II songs was the newcomer Frank Loesser. Before the war Loesser had written only lyrics. Stunned by the Pearl Harbor disaster, he began casting about for a suitable song. Suddenly he remembered the words Chaplain William Maguire of the United States Navy supposedly said at the height of the bombing: "Praise the Lord and pass the ammunition." From this remark Loesser created a stirring war song, writing both words and music. "Praise the Lord and Pass the Ammunition" was recorded by Kay Kyser and became the first war song to make the "Hit Parade" charts, selling over a million records. Loesser later wrote "What Do You Do in the Infantry?" and "The Ballard of Rodger Young," both possessing the homespun quality that had made "Praise the Lord" such a success. Rodger Young was a twenty-five year-old soldier who had sacrificed his life to save his buddies by attacking a Japanese pillbox in the Solomons. Yet even poignant war songs like "The Ballad of Rodger Young" lacked the innocence and naive idealism that songwriters a generation before had found so attractive and rewarding. In war and the ensuing peace the great impersonal machine had taken over, encouraging sentimentality to make way for cynicism.

But escapism was not yet dead. Romantic love, with its inevitable losses and frustrations, continued at the heart of popular music, as neurotic and long-suffering as ever. "I Don't Want to Walk Without You" was a theme heard time and again, as was "I'll Never Smile Again" and "I'll Get By"—"as long as I have you." Still the need to laugh was great, and war-torn America gave nonsense and novelty songs high priority: "The Hut-Sut Song," "The Woodpecker Song," "Mairzy-Doats," "Mister Five by Five," "Swinging on a Star," "Shoo-Shoo Baby," and "Rum and Coca-Cola." The craze for western numbers persisted with "You Are My Sunshine," "Deep in the Heart of Texas," "Pistol Packin' Mama," and "Jingle, Jangle, Jingle." "Don't Fence Me In" even found the urbane Cole Porter playfully venturing west.

The music business, however, was having its problems. Among the early casualties of the war in the Pacific was shellac, a vital commodity for the recording industry. Then in August, 1942, the American Federation of Musicians went on strike, insisting that records could not be used in jukeboxes and by radio stations without proper payment to the artists involved. For nearly two years no recordings were made except by performers outside the orbit of the musicians' union.

Several months earlier ASCAP had demanded more money from broadcasters for the privilege of using selections in the ASCAP catalogs. The major networks refused and monitored their shows so that no ASCAP tunes were used. Eventually the percentage demanded by ASCAP was appreciably lowered and harmony restored, but not until the radio interests had come up with the idea of establishing a rival licensing agency. Broadcasters put up around $400,000 and in the autumn of 1940 began Broadcast Music Incorporated. At first BMI received songs only from those writers who had somehow failed to make the grade with ASCAP, which included a vast number of hillbilly and gospel tunes. The agency steadily broadened its listing, and within a decade BMI had become an effective and well-respected organization. It would later control a great deal of the rock and roll material.

During the nine months that ASCAP and the broadcasters were quarreling over royalties, several tunes by Latin American composers were introduced. Before long there was a Mambo craze, and in the middle 1940s Carmen Miranda brought in the Samba from Brazil. By 1946 the rage for Latin American rhythms had reached such proportions that Betty Garrett begged for mercy in the Broadway revue *Call Me Mister*, singing "South America Take It Away." The "jitterbug," which had emerged with the Swing era, remained popular with young dancers, who invented their own slang and doubletalk. By the war, Swing had become known as "jive," while "hepcats" were those who "grooved" the scene. Those who disapproved were "squares." The "zoot suit" came in, and fast dancing was "cutting a rug."

Within the big bands a revolution was already taking place. The vocalist, who had once been content to sing along with the ensemble in a simple, almost colorless way, suddenly began to stand out. The shift really occurred in 1943 with the success of Frank Sinatra. A thin, gangly, not particularly handsome young man, Sinatra had sung with both Harry James and Tommy Dorsey. He was essentially a crooner, who had listened to and obviously absorbed much from the casual Crosby. He left Dorsey in the fall of 1942 to go on his own and early the next year was a tremendous sensation at the Paramount Theater in New York. He broke attendance records wherever he sang, as adolescent "bobby-soxers" went wild, screaming and "swooning" at the sound of his voice. "I shiver all the way up and down my spine when you sing," one girl wrote Sinatra. "Just like I did when I had scarlet fever." Some have explained his phenomenal popularity as a byproduct of the war, suggesting that young women turned to Sinatra as compensation for the absence of their sweethearts. Others add that the skinny figure with the hollow cheeks and bow-tie, almost hidden behind the microphone, looked irresistibly like the kid next door. He joined *Your Hit Parade* in February, 1943, and stayed until January, 1945. Meanwhile Frankie became the idol of the American schoolgirl, who listened to his records in a quivering hush.

Although Sinatra's climb to fame was accompanied by much ballyhoo, it was evident from the beginning that his was no ordinary talent. He had early shown a sensitivity to changing vocal colors, while his phrasing had much in common with jazz singers like Billie Holiday and Ella Fitzgerald. He had a special feeling for words, and no one in the business knew how to use the microphone as he did, treating it almost as an instrument. The result was a new approach to singing, one in which the emotional content was greatly deepened. Above all, Sinatra possessed an original musical intelligence that enabled him to turn popular styling into an art.

As the big bands began to fade toward the end of the war, their former vocalists took advantage of the opportunity to become stars in their own right. The public now seemed to prefer singers, especially those with an individual technique. Vocalizing moved from the soft, passive styling of the 1930s toward more unique, dynamic approaches, while large, string-dominated orchestras merely provided accompaniment. Most of the male singers followed Sinatra's lead by assuming an unaffected, nice guy image and capitalized on their good looks and intimate voice. Perry Como, Dick Haymes, Andy Russell, Nat "King" Cole, Mel Torme, and Vaughn Monroe all knew their craft and had accurate intonation, although none generated quite the hysteria that Sinatra did. Of the female vocalists Dinah Shore, Peggy Lee, Ella Fitzgerald, Jo Stafford, Sarah Vaughan, and Doris Day were among the more important. Each offered her own special style, ranging from Peggy Lee's sexy whispering to Jo Stafford's almost "belting" manner. Arrangements and interpretation became the thing, sometimes even more important than the song itself. Not only had the world of popular music become primarily a singer's world, both on records and radio, but popular music was also becoming separated from jazz and fragmented within itself.

Despite problems the music industry had boomed during the war, as had the motion picture business. An increasing number of the better popular songs were coming from screen musicals, and some of the master songwriters actually seemed to prefer Hollywood over Broadway. Irving Berlin's classic "White Christmas" was introduced in the movie *Holiday Inn* in 1940, eventually achieving a financial success unequaled by any of the musician's earlier hits. Jerome Kern continued to work for films, composing "Dearly Beloved" for *You Were Never Lovelier* in 1942 and "More and More" for *Can't Help Singing* two years later. One of Kern's very finest songs, "Long Ago and Far Away," was written with Ira Gershwin for *Cover Girl* in 1944, a picture that featured Rita Hayworth and Gene Kelly. In this song the composer daringly restates his major theme a minor third higher after just eight measures. The piece sold more sheet music in a single year than anything else Ira Gershwin had done. Kern's last original screen score was for *Centennial Summer* in 1946, highlighted by "In Love in Vain" and "All Through the Day."

Cole Porter contributed several more songs to films, including "You'd Be So Nice To Come Home To" from *Something to Shout About,* which struck a responsive note with millions of war-separated couples. Rodgers and Hammerstein wrote perhaps the best original screen score ever for *State Fair* in 1944. The picture contained "It's a Grand Night for Singing," "That's for Me," and the Academy Award-winning "It Might As Well Be Spring." *State Fair* has much of the sweet and simple flavor of *Oklahoma!*, while its songs are sheer poetry. Johnny Mercer joined Harold Arlen in writing "That Old Black Magic" for *Star-Spangled Rhythm* in 1942 and also collaborated with Arlen on "One for My Baby" for Fred Astaire in *Sky's the Limit* and "Accentuate the Positive" for Bing Crosby in *Here Come the Waves*. For *Cabin in the Sky* (1943) Arlen composed one of his most distinctive songs, "Happiness Is a Thing Called Joe."

Harry Warren split with Al Dubin in 1939, but the musician went on to write "You'll Never Know" for Alice Faye in *Hello, Frisco, Hello* and "On the Atchison, Topeka, and the Santa Fe" for Judy Garland in *The Harvey Girls*—both of which won an Academy Award. Warren had two hits from the Betty Grable film *Diamond Horseshoe*, "The More I See You" and "I Wish I Knew," but considers *The Barkleys of Broadway* (1948) his best score. The latter reunited Ginger Rogers and Fred Astaire and contained such songs as "My One and Only Highland Fling" and "You'd Be Hard to Replace." Both had lyrics by Ira Gershwin. *The Shocking Miss Pilgrim* in 1946, another Betty Grable picture, offered a score of heretofore unpublished George and Ira Gershwin numbers, the most delightful of which were "Changing My Tune" and "Aren't You Kind of Glad We Did?" Jimmy Van Heusen did something like twenty scores for Bing Crosby movies, including the *Road* pictures. From *Road to Morocco* came "Moonlight Becomes You." Dorothy Lamour sang "Personality" in *Road to Utopia,* while "But Beautiful" was from *Road to Rio.* "It Could Happen to You" was another Van Heusen song, from *And the Angels Sing.* Ralph Blane and Hugh Martin had tremendous success with the film *Meet Me in St. Louis* in 1944. "The Trolley Song" was an almost perfect vehicle for Judy Garland, while "The Boy Next Door" became their best known song.

Kurt Weill teamed with Ira Gershwin on the numbers for an interesting picture called *Where Do We Go from Here?*, while Hoagy Carmichael wrote both words and music for "Ole Buttermilk Sky," introduced in the western *Canyon Passage.* Frank Loesser did "I Wish I Didn't Love You So" for films, although the Dinah Shore recording really made the song popular. Loesser won an Oscar in 1949 for "Baby, It's Cold Outside" from the M-G-M extravaganza *Neptune's Daughter.* Esther Williams and Ricardo Montalban first sang the tune seriously, after which Betty Garrett and Red Skelton gave it a comedy treatment. Jay Livingston and Ray Evans had good luck with "Buttons and Bows" from *The Paleface* in 1947 and the year before had worked with Victor Young on the title song for *Golden Earrings.* Sammy Cahn and Jule Styne provided Doris Day with her first screen hit in "It's Magic" from *Romance on the High Seas,* whereas "I Should Care," played by Tommy Dorsey in *Thrill of a Romance,* had found Cahn joining forces with

Axel Stordahl and Paul Weston. One of the most lasting songs to come out of Hollywood is the Johnny Mercer-David Raksin theme melody for the Twentieth Century-Fox mystery *Laura,* while Herman Hupfeld added a permanent piece of motion picture nostalgia when he penned "As Time Goes By" for the Warner Brothers film *Casablanca.*

But many of the tunes that made the *Hit Parade* listings were from neither the screen nor the Broadway stage. "Tonight We Love" was appropriated from Tchaikovsky's First Piano Concerto, and several other melodies were taken from the classics, particularly during the strike against ASCAP in 1941. "Till the End of Time" came from Chopin's Polonaise in A-flat, whereas "Full Moon and Empty Arms" was borrowed from Rachmaninoff. "Paper Doll" was an early Frank Sinatra specialty, while "I've Heard That Song Before" and "Don't Get Around Much Any More" emerged from the big bands. Peggy Lee and her husband wrote "Manana," an engaging novelty number, and Frank Loesser scored a popular hit with "On a Slow Boat to China." "Tico Tico" was an instrumental popularized by Ethel Smith on the Hammond organ. But there were also "Sentimental Journey," "Symphony," "Near You," "Linda," "The Old Lamplighter," "Tenderly," "A Tree in the Meadow," "Now Is the Hour," "Ballerina," "Serenade of the Bells," "Civilization," "I Can Dream, Can't I," "Riders in the Sky," and "Red Roses for a Blue Lady." By the late 1940s popular music seemed to be moving from introspection toward greater warmth and heartiness. In the midst of cold war old values were exonerated, accompanying a yearning for the status quo. There was a trend toward homey numbers, sometimes deliberately "corny," containing more simplicity and vigor than originality—songs like "Sunflower," "Dear Hearts and Gentle People," "If I Knew You Were Comin' I'd Have Baked a Cake," "Hear Them Bells," and "Home Cookin'." And there were quasi-folk tunes like "Goodnight, Irene" and "On Top of Old Smokey," which paved the way for the advent of "country music."

By the end of World War II the pivotal figure in promoting a song to success was the radio disc jockey. Since the late 1930s the disc jockeys had made deeper and deeper inroads into popular music, but during the 1940s the link between these radio announcers and the record companies had become well established. By giving the public intimate glimpses into the personality of certain performers and plugging their numbers, the seemingly easygoing disc jockey could create recording stars and hit records almost overnight. Soon the recording became more important in the music business than the song itself, and record companies began courting the disc jockeys lavishly, since they could make or break an item almost at whim. With the coming of television more and more local radio stations shifted to the spinning of records between news and weather reports, taking requests telephoned in by listeners. In 1960 there would be something like 3000 disc jockeys operating on 3500 stations across the nation. By then the disc jockey had become the single most important force in directing taste in popular music.

An example of the kind of power the disc jockey had is the story behind the revival of "I'm Looking Over a Four-Leaf Clover" in 1948. The song had been written by Mort Dixon and Harry Woods in 1927, but was later recorded by bandleader Art Mooney in an accelerated arrangement. As usual, copies of the record were sent out to the leading disc jockeys. One announcer in Salt Lake City had a jazz program, and although he personally disliked the number, he played "I'm Looking Over a Four-Leaf Clover" all afternoon, while he read a book. The incident was carried by the wire service, with the result that sales on Mooney's version of the song began to soar. The tune made the *Hit Parade* charts and ended up on that year's "top-ten" list.

Rivalry between the disc jockeys themselves became tremendous, as stations attempted to secure advertisers. After the war record production was greatly expanded, so that the most important disc jockeys by the late 1950s might receive as many as 300 new releases a week, although the average was about half that. Whereas 45,000,000 popular records had been sold in 1939, this figure had tripled a decade later. Major disc jockeys like Martin Block of "Make Believe Ballroom" in New York and Al Jarvis in Hollywood became the keys to creating hits and keeping them before the public. It was essential that a recording company somehow obtain a solid "in," if it were to succeed in the frantically competitive market.

By the mid-1950s the music business had proliferated all over the country, although New York, Philadelphia, Chicago, Detroit, Nashville, and Los Angeles represented the leading citadels. By then the sale of sheet music had unquestionably lost out to Record Row as the barometer of public taste, for a sale of 250,000 copies was considered exceptional. The Brill Building continued to house dozens of publishers ranging from gigantic concerns like the Mills Music Publishing Company to one room operations hoping for their first hit. The three biggest record companies—Victor, Columbia, and Decca, all of which were based in New York—were joined by Capitol and M-G-M in Los Angeles, Mercury in Chicago, and scores of small, independent firms. The magnetic tape-recording process meant high level performances at lower costs, while the seven-inch 45 rpm record was a great boon to sales. Teenagers, who had more money than ever before, had become popular music's best customers, with the result that songwriters aimed at a considerably younger audience than had been the case before World War II. A popular tune was now expected to endure for only a few weeks, even if it sold close to a million records. The disc jockeys and the recording industry seemed content to exploit a number in a big way as quickly as possible, then let it drop into oblivion. The constant demand for new material meant that few songs were of the quality to enter the permanent repertoire built up by Tin Pan Alley.

While the music business was no longer the closed corporation it once was, there was still considerably more to having a hit record than a pleasant song and a catchy rendition. Popular musicians in the 1920s had had to get along with the gangsters, since much of their efforts were used by the night spots which the bootleggers and racketeers controlled. In the 1950s the underworld element was less obvious, yet the presence of powerful syndicates, both on the local and national level, could not be denied.

The vocal pendulum continued to swing from the gentle crooners to the hard "belters." Frankie Laine arrived on the scene in 1946 with "That's My Desire," ushering in an era of more dramatic singing. He perpetuated the trend with "Jezebel," "Mule Train," and "Your Cheatin' Heart." Tony Bennett added an almost hysterical quality to songs like "Rags to Riches," whereas Johnnie Ray screamed and sobbed his way through a number called "Cry." Far less demonstrative were Eddie Fisher, Julius LaRosa, and Pat Boone. Perhaps the foremost female "belter" was Rosemary Clooney, who established herself with "Come On-a My House," backed by a jazzy harpsichord. But Teresa Brewer, Georgia Gibbs, Jo Stafford, and Kay Starr had their own brand of vocal muscularity. Gimmick voices like Joni James, Eartha Kitt, and Kitty Kallen were popular, while Patti Page was a smash success with such songs as "The Tennessee Waltz" and "Doggie in the Window." Arrangements and novel accompaniment grew increasingly important, and Mitch Miller at Columbia created all sorts of refreshing sounds and odd combinations. He brought in French horns to back Guy Mitchell, employed a vocal group with Johnnie Ray, and (before he left Mercury) used wood blocks to simulate a snapping bull whip on Frankie Laine's version of "Mule Train." Multiple recording became fashionable, reaching a height with Les Paul and Mary Ford.

Current songs were becoming more and more the property of individual performers, who stamped them with their personal artistry. A number recorded by one singer was rarely done effectively by another, since it was a special styling that counted. Records were now produced for their own sake; no longer did a performer recreate in the studio what he had been doing nightly in public appearances. If a recording was a success, the singer might then highlight the song in a personal appearance or on television, but the studio rendition, often with all sorts of electronic effects, echo chambers, and overdubbing, generally came first. With so much emphasis on performance, the quality of the songs themselves was almost bound to slip.

This point became evident on *Your Hit Parade*, which made the transition from radio to television in 1950. First of all, the shenanigans devised to present the songs visually week after week were ludicrous. But singers like Dorothy Collins and Snooky Lanson simply could not do the specialized material of other performers with much conviction. In their attempt the limitations of the writing itself became painfully obvious. The *Hit Parade* format was never the same on television, and in 1953 the program was forced to withdraw.

Hughson Mooney, in his analysis of American songs since 1890, contends that popular music around 1950 entered a "May the Good Lord Bless and Keep You" period and was aimed largely at reaffirmation. Dwight Eisenhower reflected the prevailing mass mood with his "new conservatism," while Congress in 1954 voted to add the phrase "under God" to the pledge of allegiance and a year later made "In God We Trust" mandatory on United States currency. The "top ten" charts for 1953 included Les Paul and Mary Ford's "Vaya con Dios," June Valli's "Crying in the Chapel," and Frankie Laine's "I Believe." In the heyday of Senator McCarthy's particular brand of Americanism songs like "Oh, My Papa," "This Ole House," "I See the Moon, the Moon Sees Me," and "Heart of My Heart" found their way onto the *Hit Parade* listings, all of them blatantly orthodox in sentiment and structure. Such ditties, Mooney argues, "partake of that warm, folksy, often reverent quality captured in the childlike primitives of Grandma Moses as well as in the robust, earthy, thoroughly American voices of Guy Mitchell, Rosemary Clooney, Champ Butler, Rusty Draper, Doris Day—a simple wide-eyed extroverted delight in the familiar."

Patti Page's "Cross Over the Bridge" (1954) was another song with a spiritual message, and the singer could be heard two years later praising "Allegheny Moon." Others found pleasure in "Sweet Violets," insisted "Little Things Mean a Lot," implored "Dance with Me, Henry," called on "Mister Sandman," dreamed of "Dungaree Doll," and concluded "Whatever Will Be Will Be"—all of which seemed to suggest that it was indeed "A Marshmallow World," full of "Candy and Cake." "The Yellow Rose of Texas" and "The Ballad of Davy Crockett" indicated a certain nostalgia for the old, but "The Rock and Roll Waltz" brought even the new under control. The "belters," almost Ayn Rand-like figures in a society of "organization men," continued to bombard the public with personalized messages like "Botch-a-Me," "Kiss of Fire," "Wheel of Fortune," "Please, Mr. Sun," and "You Belong to Me." Groups had a field day harmonizing on "Undecided," "You, You, You," and "Sincerely," while Julie London defied the "belting" trend by seductively breathing "Cry Me a River." Sinatra returned to popularity, now something of the "grand old man" of popular music, enjoying such hits as "Young at Heart," "Witchcraft," and "All the Way."

There was a variety of successful instrumental numbers during the 1950s: "Ebb Tide," "Blue Tango," "Delicado," "The Poor People of Paris," "Canadian Sunset," "Cherry Pink and Apple Blossom White," "Autumn Leaves," "Quiet Village." Part of the superficial tranquility of the decade was captured in the penchant for longplaying records of mood music—the quiet, syrupy sounds of Mantovani, Jackie Gleason, and the Melachrino Strings.

A fair percentage of the current tunes still came from the Broadway stage. Eddie Fisher's recording of the title song from *Wish You Were Here* stayed on the "top ten" charts for twenty weeks and sold over a million copies, while Rosemary Clooney made a big hit of "Hey There" from *Pajama Game*. Unfortunately when theater music was successfully recorded by a popular singer, later performers in outlying productions tended to emulate the recording star, often wrenching the number from its dramatic context and violating the mood of the play. A few songs, like "Let Me Go, Lover," originated on television, while "Love and Marriage" was introduced in a video version of *Our Town*. One of the finest musicals especially written for television was

Rodgers and Hammerstein's *Cinderella,* which in its initial form featured Julie Andrews and Edie Adams.

But new releases were more consistently tied to motion pictures, as Hollywood was finding a popular title tune almost a prerequisite even for dramatic films. "Three Coins in the Fountain," "High Noon," "My Foolish Heart," "Love Is a Many-Splendored Thing," "Ruby," "It's a Woman's World," "April Love," "The High and the Mighty," "Anastasia," "The Tender Trap," "Friendly Persuasion," "Around the World in Eighty Days," and "Gigi" were all songs from movies of the same name. There was the "Song from Moulin Rouge," "The Third Man Theme," "Unchained Melody," and the "Theme from A Summer Place." "Secret Love" was a Doris Day hit from the screen musical *Calamity Jane,* whereas "Something's Gotta Give" was from the Fred Astaire picture *Daddy Long Legs.* Nat "King" Cole recorded "Mona Lisa," "Because You're Mine," and "Blue Gardenia" specifically for Hollywood, and Mario Lanza had good commercial results with "Be My Love" and "The Loveliest Night of the Year," both from movies in which he starred. Burton Lane and Alan Jay Lerner wrote "Too Late Now" for *Royal Wedding,* Frank Loesser did "Anywhere I Wander" and "No Two People" for *Hans Christian Andersen,* while Cole Porter had his last success with "True Love" from *High Society.* Harold Arlen collaborated with Ira Gershwin on "The Man That Got Away" for *A Star Is Born,* sung in the film by Judy Garland with all the yearning and anguish that had already made her a legend.

Even in the late 1950s, with "rock" dominating the popular field, there were songs in an older style. Two tunes entitled "Young Love" made the "top ten" list in 1957—one recorded by Tab Hunter, the other by Sonny James. Pat Boone revived "Love Letters in the Sand," and Perry Como made a hit of "Catch a Falling Star." "Volare," "It's All in the Game," "A Certain Smile," "Mack the Knife," and "The Three Bells" all became successes without yielding to the new idiom.

Foreign elements colored the contemporary repertory. The Mambo remained in vogue, superseded by the Cha-Cha-Cha. Harry Belafonte brought calypso songs to a new level of artistry, recording hits like "Matilda, Matilda" and "The Banana Boat Song." Gospel singers, particularly Mahalia Jackson, became fashionable. Miss Jackson had grown up in New Orleans and was forced to sneak Bessie Smith records into her home, since her parents, like many blacks of that time, were ashamed of the blues. At her height the gospel star possessed a powerful voice, added all sorts of embellishments, and broke practically every rule of the concert singer. She sometimes garbled phrases, took a breath in the middle of a word, but her full-throated expression was celestial.

Folk singing by the end of the decade had become the rage, especially on college campuses. Burl Ives had established himself earlier, and in 1950 a unit called the Weavers made a big hit of Lead Belly's "Goodnight, Irene." The Weavers had a left-wing past, yet sang with great sincerity, influencing many of the group's that came later. In 1958 the Kingston Trio, three young fellows right out of college, had great success with a recording of "Tom Dooley," and the rush to folk singing was on. Coffee houses sprang up in Greenwich Village and San Francisco, while groups like the Gateway Singers, the Brothers Four, and later the Limeliters became the "in" thing.

Popular songs in the 1960s continued a life apart from "rock and roll," but the margin between had become considerably less. Songs like "Blue Velvet," "The Second Time Around," and "Strangers in the Night" had little in common with the new beat. "I Left My Heart in San Francisco," as sung by Tony Bennett, was an old-fashioned ballad, while Herb Alpert and the Tijuana Brass played "A Taste of Honey" in a modified big band style. Frank Sinatra gave a masterly reading of "It Was a Very Good Year," and Peggy Lee brought her special worldliness to "Is That All There Is?" Ramsey Lewis briefly revived cool jazz with "The 'In' Crowd," whereas Stan Getz helped make a fad of the bossa nova with "The Girl from Ipanema." There were novelty numbers like "Alley Cat" and "The Stripper" and blatantly nostalgic ones like "Winchester Cathedral" and "Those Were the Days."

A few of the current hits, such as "Hello, Dolly!" and "I'll Never Fall in Love Again," were outgrowths of the theater. Many more came from films: "More," "Call Me Irresponsible," "The Look of Love," "The Shadow of Your Smile," "Jean," "Chim Chim Cher-ee," "The Windmills of Your Mind." Motion picture title tunes had by then become perennial, among them "Never on Sunday," "A Man and a Woman," "Born Free," "Goldfinger," "Georgy Girl," "Star," and "To Sir, with Love." And there was "The Exodus Song," "Lara's Theme" from *Doctor Zhivago,* the "Love Theme from *Romeo and Juliet,*" and "Elvira" from *Elvira Madigan,* based on Mozart's Piano Concerto No. 21.

Nonrock singing stars still commanded the attention of the public, especially Andy Williams, Connie Francis, Robert Goulet, Lainie Kazan, and the decade's superstar, Barbara Streisand, a vocalist with superb natural equipment. Teenage idol Bobby Darin had been strongly influenced by Frank Sinatra, while Sinatra himself kept the respect of young listeners. Arrangements for the individual performer had become more crucial than ever, and instrumental inventiveness in accompaniment grew extremely significant. Recording costs had spiraled, so that a Sinatra "single" around 1964, on which he was backed by a large orchestra, might reach $3000. The average cost per release was about half that.

Of the younger songwriters two of the most ingenious have been Henry Mancini, who often worked with Johnny Mercer, and Burt Bacharach, who has collaborated consistently with Hal David. Mancini was born in Cleveland, Ohio, April 16, 1924, and grew up listening to the big bands. He was particularly fond of Artie Shaw and Glenn Miller. After the war he played the piano and made arrangements for the Tex Beneke orchestra, did odd jobs for nightclub singers and jazz combos, and supervised the music for countless motion pictures, among them *The Glenn Miller Story* and *The Benny*

Goodman Story. In 1958 he wrote the score for the *Peter Gunn* television series and had his first song hit three years later with "Moon River" from *Breakfast at Tiffany's,* a movie that won him two Academy Awards. "Days of Wine and Roses" and "Charade" followed shortly. Mancini has composed the music for many other films, including *The Pink Panther, Hatari,* and *Soldiers in the Rain* and has continued to produce quality songs with exquisite melodies.

The handsome Bacharach hails from Kansas City, but his cosmopolitan musical education was highlighted by studies with composers Darius Milhaud and Henry Cowell. For a time he conducted and arranged for Marlene Dietrich and later worked closely with singer Dionne Warwick. He has done scores for the movies *What's New, Pussycat?, Casino Royale,* and the remake of *Lost Horizon,* while the list of Bacharach song hits seems endless: "Wives and Lovers," "Walk on By," "What the World Needs Now Is Love," "Close to You," "This Guy's in Love with You," which Herb Alpert recorded for his vocal debut. "Alfie" and "The Look of Love" were both nominated for an Academy Award, while "Raindrops Keep Fallin' on My Head" won the Oscar in 1969. A composer of great ability and charm, Bacharach perhaps comes closest to being the modern heir to the Berlin-Kern-Gershwin-Porter-Rodgers legacy. His writing is imaginative, intelligent, direct if frequently complex. He is given to unusual harmonic patterns, irregular meters, and especially surprises in melodic direction. Hal David's lyrics are sharp, devoid of cliches, and have a strength that is equal to Bacharach's music.

By 1970 the old categories of current music—jazz, the commercial ballad, folk, country and western, rock, and the blues—had blurred appreciably, as a merging of styles and cross-fertilization seemed the wave of the future. Bobbie Gentry's "Ode to Billy Joe" was in the spirit of a folk tune, whereas Glen Campbell songs like "Wichita Lineman" and "By the Time I Get to Phoenix" and John Denver compositions such as "Leaving on a Jet Plane," "Rocky Mountain High," and "My Sweet Lady" are rooted in the country tradition. There were still pretty numbers, like "We've Only Just Begun," sung by the Carpenters, and "My Love" by Paul and Linda McCartney. Roberta Flack's work—"The First Time Ever I Saw Your Face" and "Killing Me Softly with His Song" is reminiscent of the jazz singers, while Diana Ross' is colored with the blues. Lyrics, however, tended to be more realistic, and even wistful songs like Diana Ross' hit rendition of "Touch Me in the Morning" express sentiment without wallowing in sentimentality.

> *Touch me in the morning.*
> *Then just walk away.*
> *We don't have tomorrow,*
> *But we had yesterday.*

A goodly share of the nonrock hits still came from motion pictures. "The Morning After" from *The Poseidon Adventure* won the Academy Award for the best movie song of 1972, while Barbra Streisand made a big success of the title number from *The Way We Were* a year later. "Where Do I Begin" from *Love Story* was particularly effective as an instrumental, as was the theme from *Summer of '42* by Michel Legrand, who has composed many quality scores for films.

But the decline of the Hollywood musical has undoubtedly had an effect on popular music. In 1942 seven of the year's "top ten" songs were from films; three decades later there might be one. The motion picture industry certainly gave work to hosts of quality writers and allowed them a fair amount of time to do their work. While there were lots of banal efforts, the movie tunesmiths did produce a remarkable repertory of lasting songs, so that the years between 1935 and 1950 saw a flowering of American popular music. Like the radio crooners, Dick Powell and other stars of the early screen musicals tended to be clean-cut kids, whose singing was sleepy and colorless. Motion picture directors in the early 1930s were still struggling to achieve a three-dimensional illusion both in dance routines and sound pickup. As radio and Hollywood recording techniques passed their infancy, more flexible ranges could be encompassed, paving the way for more complex songs.

Yet the maturation of American popular music was not only dependent on technical improvements, it had to await the intellectual and emotional growth of the consumer market. In the 1920s, 1930s, and 1940s the public clearly wanted sophisticated songs about moonlight and shadows, Indian summers, slumming on Fifth Avenue, blossoms on Broadway, penthouse serenades, and—above all—dreams and strange enchantments. Some of the morbidity and gloom of the nineteenth century remained, and the death-wish even crept into numbers like "The Last Roundup" and "There's a Gold Mine in the Sky." Love was still seen in misty-eyed, ethereal terms, linked to an uncertain, almost desperate search for security and contentment. The naivete of the American public was reflected in popular songs, as it was in other areas of mass culture, and sentiments tended to swing from one extreme to another. On the one hand was what might be called the "My Isle of Golden Dreams" pole; the opposite could be termed the "Willow Weep for Me" pole. Curiously enough, the two were intimately related. Having fabricated dreams and papier-mache romances that could never be realized, it was a matter of time before the fantasy seekers felt rejected, disillusioned, and inadequate. The low self-image, from which they had sought escape, was reinforced, manifesting itself in self-pity, the actual desire for unhappiness and perhaps even death. This excessive melancholy also involved an attempt at control, was a plea for attention, and demanded sympathy. And so Americans danced their way through the jazz age, the Depression and war years, and into the cold war era with tears in their eyes, neurotically hoping to feel better by feeling sad.

The attitudes expressed were in large measure thoroughly middle class, since middle class adults were then doing most of the buying of phonograph records and sheet music. By the 1930s popular music had seen a blending of the immigrant tradition (largely a composite of Jewish, Viennese operetta, and middle-European cafe music) with the jazz of the American blacks. But even when infused with jazz, popular tunes were still dominated by a European tone and often orchestrated like symphonic poems. The best of these songs, however, were polished, urbane, full of tricky rhymes, and witty turns of phrase. After 1920 popular numbers more often sought to evoke a mood than tell a story. Yet until World War II, most white Americans were singing and listening to the same melodies, those played on the jukeboxes and heard on all the radio stations. There was no youth market, no special programming for older adults. Besides a race division and a hillbilly audience, the public generally was of a similar taste.

The emergence of Sinatra, however, in a time of affluence, when many adults were taken up with the war effort, found the youth playing a more dynamic role in shaping the popular music business than ever before. The appeal was now more and more to the nascent libido of the American teenager. By the late 1950s even the preadolescent market had become a substantial one, so that suavity was replaced by cheapness and lack of refinement, as the number of records sold rose to almost 200,000,000 a year in 1963. A song that was a hit one day was often gone within a month. Should a new idea prove successful, it was immediately copied by dozens of imitators. Already there were songs like "Rose and a Baby Ruth" and "Venus in Blue Jeans."

> *She's Venus in Blue Jeans*
> *Mona Lisa in a ponytail*
> *She's a walkin' talkin' work of art*
> *She's the girl who stole my heart*
> *My Venus in Blue Jeans.*

With the arrival of television, more animation was needed from singers, further explaining why the pallid approach of the radio crooners went out of vogue. The personality cult came into prominence, along with novel arrangements and unusual sounds. The quality of the songs themselves was mainly forgotten.

But by the mid-1960s rock, the special delight of teenage and collegiate listeners, showed signs of maturing. While a barrage of simple-minded numbers still poured from the commercial firing line (something like ninety-five percent of all records produced failed to become hits), others actually had something to say. In an age when sex was viewed more casually, chivalric love and the sentimental ballad declined in popularity. Romance still existed, but it was not cloaked in the bourgeois prettiness heretofore expected. The whole concept of love changed to include feelings about mankind and the need for tenderness and intimacy. The problems of life were looked at squarely in songs often written by the singers themselves, drawn from personal experience and pain. In performance honesty and conviction were frequently placed before polish. Musically popular tunes became less melodious, more crudely arranged, but they were no longer confined by the old formulas. As the music business began catering to an even wider public, especially the working class and the lower class blacks, the influence of the urban middle class diminished. Current hits became less pretentious, less genteel, more realistic and straightforward. There were protests against the establishment in songs like "Ticky Tacky Houses," as popular musicians grew vitally concerned with the quality of life. Nonwestern musicial traditions were explored, and the essential humanity of all races was affirmed time and again.

Among the few constants in American popular music has been change, for substantial turnovers have taken place every four or five years. Today's youth look back with snickers on the modal personalities admired by their grandparents—the Crosby's and the Como's who dressed in tweeds, smoked pipes, and sang between golf games. The older generation is just as prone to cringe at the incessant sounds that come from the wild-haired rock musicians worshipped by their children or grandchildren. And yet the current music scene is a complex one. Whatever has been *is*. All kinds of popular music still have a following, and the best of this assortment is still revived and enjoyed—not only in this country, but all around the globe. Popular songs, perhaps more than any other type of music, tend to associate themselves with special moments, a time in a person's life when he was either in love or extremely happy or unhappy. Songs, therefore, frequently take on a meaning that is altogether personal. For most adults memories immediately come floating back on the strains of a familiar song. A young girl in love may adore a tune that is positively wretched if judged on its own merits, although she will probably never recognize this in her lifetime. A lonely person may wince at a melody that reminds him of happier days or smile at its bittersweetness. In the last analysis popular songs often become so colored with nostalgia that their impact has little to do with esthetics. Most people will proclaim, and defend with vigor, that the best in popular music is that which just happened to be in vogue when they were young. Lifelong favorites may come along later, but few will ever match the songs surrounding school-day experiences, when the world was verdant and the future eternal.

C H A P T E R

XII

COUNTRY MUSIC

American country music evolved out of the reservoir of Anglo-Celtic ballads and folk songs brought to North America by colonial immigrants, absorbed influences from other musical expressions, and emerged as a hybrid from the social peculiarities of the rural South. In their determination to preserve an agricultural society, southerners resisted the industrialization and urbanism growing in the North, with the result that traditions once the common heritage from Maine to Georgia endured in the South long after they had been lost elsewhere. The British ballads and folk songs once sung all through the American colonies were perpetuated in the South, contributing to the formation of a dynamic regional music.

While changes took place in this inherited body of songs and additions were made, the religiously conservative, ethnically homogenous southerners held on to traditional patterns and a common style of music far longer than the rest of the nation, in part because of the South's cultural isolation. Even as the rural inhabitants began moving into southern cities in search of better jobs, they continued to render their music in a "country" manner, although the song might describe an urban event, so that the rural attitudes and backwoods style persisted. At first these folk singers either performed for their own enjoyment or for a few relatives or close friends. Public performances were rare. Gradually the more accomplished singers gained a local reputation and were asked to perform at various social functions, usually with great embarrassment. With the acquisition of instruments a rudimentary string band was formed, as an individual performer was joined by some of his neighbors.

Rural southerners seemed to prefer mournful ballads, in large measure stemming from a religion that emphasized otherworldly attitudes and depicted this life as a tearful plight. Dozens of religious songs, such as "This World Is Not My Home," became favorites in the southern backwoods, indicating the tendency to look toward life beyond the grave for the ultimate consolation. Hundreds of songs suggested that only death could bring solace to a heart broken by unrequited love. Slowly popular elements from the vaudeville stage and Tin Pan Alley began to infiltrate the music of the rural South, so that commercialization was present before 1920. After that the commercial exploitation of southern country music increased rapidly.

The discovery of southern country music came as part of the general communications revolution that gradually broke down rural isolation. The automobile, the phonograph, but especially the radio brought southern country music to the attention of the general public. Southern broadcasting stations featured hours of live country music almost from their beginning. Performers began to modify and refine their approach, wishing to please as many listeners as possible. Soon hillbilly performers were traveling throughout the South, playing to packed houses. The country music industry was launched in 1923, when Fiddlin' John Carson became the first hillbilly performer to have selections recorded and marketed on a commercial basis. On April 19, 1924, WLS in Chicago initiated the first hillbilly radio show to gain national attention, the National Barn Dance, at first popular with rural and smalltown listeners throughout the Midwest, but shortly expanding its listening range to include most of the United States. In November, 1925, Station WSM in Nashville aired a barn dance, initially with only two entertainers appearing before the circular carbon microphone. The show's popularity was immediate, and in 1926 announcer George D. Hay gave it the name Grand Ole Opry. The program followed NBC's Musical Appreciation Hour, conducted by Walter Damrosch. When the serious music was over, Hay announced, "For the past hour we have been listening to music taken largely from grand opera, but from now on we will present 'The Grand Ole Opry.'" The name proved so popular with listeners that it became official, and the Opry was soon a Saturday night institution, the oldest continuing radio program in America. Before long fiddlers, banjo players, guitarists, and singers swarmed to the station wanting an opportunity to perform on the air, while whole families poured into Nashville by car and bus to attend the shows being broadcast.

Although the early Grand Ole Opry string bands offered vocal numbers along with instrumental, none of them had a featured vocalist. The first singing star of the Opry was Uncle Dave Macon, a portly, jovial banjo player with a mouthful of gold teeth, calling himself the Dixie Dewdrop. Uncle Dave had been a Tennessee farmer and did not become a professional musician until he was forty-eight years old. He joined the Opry eight years later, in 1926, after performing country music with medicine shows and having made several records. When he sang, he wore a double-breasted black jacket, striped pants, and a wide-brimmed black felt hat. Many of his songs he had learned before 1900 from both white and black laborers. His music was rooted in reality and dealt simply and frankly with love, grief, and other basic emotions. His energetic performances balanced an earthiness with an unquestioning faith and sense of moral purpose. Like many rural southerners he was suspicious of the encroachments of technology and uncertain about "progress." His songs are significant for their social commentary about a changing South in the decades following the Civil War.

Another of the early hillbilly vocalists was Bradley Kincaid, known as "the Kentucky Mountain Boy." Born in the foothills of the Kentucky Mountains, Kincaid was determined to sing only the native songs of his people, including British ballads like "Barbara Allen." One of the most respected string bands of the early period eventually became known as the Skillet Lickers, which at first offered a repertoire primarily of lively traditional tunes, essentially instrumentals, suitable for dancing. Riley Puckett, who played guitar for the group, soon won acclaim as a singer on a number of commercial recordings, often showing considerable black influences. By 1931 the Skillet Lickers were borrowing heavily from jazz and popular music.

Even more successful on records was Vernon Dalhart, from the bayou region of east Texas, whose best recordings sold several million copies apiece during the late 1920s. Dalhart recorded under several pseudonyms, while "The Prisoner's Song," which he recorded for a dozen or more companies, and "The Death of Floyd Collins" became two of his biggest sellers. He had sung light opera early in his career, but through his recordings he helped nationalize hillbilly music after 1925. Like most early country singers, Dalhart was unashamed of being nostalgic and sentimental, and his lyrics were more sincere than refined. Secularization, urbanization, and political liberalism were frequently decried in country music, and one of the numbers Dalhart recorded was "The John T. Scopes Trial." In it he sang, "Mr. Scopes' house was built on sand," then went on to praise "the folks of Tennessee, they're as faithful as can be," and ended with the refrain, "the old religion's better after all."

A trio called the Carter Family was formed in 1926, singing first for church affairs and local social gatherings in the Virginia mountain area. Headed by A. P. Carter, the group included A. P.'s wife Sara and her cousin, Maybelle Addington, who married A. P.'s brother Ezra J. Carter. The Carters established a style for singing close harmony and knew hundreds of tunes, ranging from religious songs to lively instrumental numbers to the sentimental ballads of the nineteenth century about blind orphans and dying mothers. Sara Carter took most of the solos, while Maybelle provided the alto and was the guitar soloist. A. P. sang bass and occasionally lead. Their rhythmic style, largely the product of Maybelle Carter's unique guitar style, influenced most of the folk musicians that came after them. The group began recording in 1927 and traveled all through the southeastern United States. Mother Maybelle recalled playing in schools and theaters by lamplight on one of their early tours in the late 1920s.

By far the biggest country singing star to emerge during the decade was Jimmie Rodgers, "the Singing Brakeman," who began recording the same year as the Carters and shortly became a household name in thousands of rural and smalltown American homes, particularly in the South. Possibly more than any other country singer, Rodgers understood what the poor southerner wanted to hear, because he had been one of them. Born in Meridian, Mississippi, on September 8, 1897, James Charles Rodgers was the son of a section foreman on the Gulf, Mobile, and Ohio Railroad. His mother died when he was four, so that he grew up in the switch-shanties, freight yards, and boardinghouses of the South. At fourteen his schooling ended, when he went to work for his father as an assistant foreman. Later he was hired as a brakeman on the New Orleans and Northeastern line between Meridian and the River City. He generally carried along a banjo or mandolin, for he enjoyed singing to his friends on the crew. The influence of black music was strong on Rodgers, and it was from snatches of black work songs and laments that he later fashioned his famous "blue yodels."

He married in 1920, became the father of a daughter the next year, but was often separated from his family, working railroad jobs in Colorado and Utah. Rodgers' health was fragile at best, and by 1924 the onset of tuberculosis had become evident. He temporarily left railroading and joined a medicine show, playing a banjo in blackface throughout Kentucky and Tennessee. During 1926 he worked as a brakeman on the Florida East Coast Railroad, but continued singing in boxcars and railway stations on lunch and rest breaks. When the damp climate proved disastrous to his health, the family moved to Tucson. Rodgers worked for a short time on the Southern Pacific, but doctors warned him that the rigorous railroad life was too much for a man in his weakened condition. Desperate for funds, he served for a while as a special officer on the Ashville, North Carolina, police force and for one winter was a janitor in an apartment house there.

In Ashville he organized the Jimmie Rodgers Entertainers and by May, 1927, was being heard three times a week over Station WWNC. The Entertainers developed a local following and later barnstormed through the Southeast. Late in July, 1927, Ralph Peer, who was then supervising hill-billy recordings for Victor, came south and signed Rodgers to a contract. After a slow start his popularity on records began to mount, augmented by vaude-ville, tent show, and radio appearances throughout the South. His tuberculosis persisted, curtailing his performing activities and forcing Rodgers to seek a permanent home in the drier region of central Texas. In

1929 he built a $50,000 mansion there called "Blue Yodeler's Paradise," near Kerrville. Before his death in 1933, mounting medical costs forced the family to move to a more modest home in San Antonio.

Although Rodgers drew much of his material from traditional sources, he wrote a large number of songs and imposed his own personality and unique approach on the music he sang, including his freight train whistles and lyrical yodels, usually uttered at the end of a stanza. He recorded practically every type of song familiar to rural southerners, but his blues numbers created the greatest interest, and he continued to borrow words, phrases, and techniques from black vocalists. While he was virtually unknown in the North, his popularity in the Southwest, particularly Texas, became tremendous. At the depth of the Depression Rodgers' records sold over 20,000,000 copies, exceeding the sale of Enrico Caruso and even most of the current popular performers in the Victor catalogue. Legend has it that customers of general stores in the rural South would approach the counter and say, "Let me have a pound of butter, a dozen eggs, and the latest Jimmie Rodgers record." With songs like "The Yodeling Cowboy" he did much to cement the romantic image of the West into country music, so that Rodgers is often credited with starting the "singing cowboy" trend. "My cowboy life is so happy and free," he sang, "out where the law don't bother me," a stereotyped view of the West held by many easterners.

With Jimmie Rodgers country music took a more commercial, star-oriented turn. He mingled the southern mountain ballad, the black blues, and the cowboy song into a whole new genre. While his success came largely from his individualistic approach, both to his songs and his audiences, his technique was more polished and professional than the country singers who had preceded him. He introduced a sweet crooning style that was markedly different from the nasal mountain sound of earlier performers. Although the fiddle would remain an important instrument in country music, the guitar and banjo were coming to the fore. But perhaps most important of all, Rodgers helped shift the stylistic center of country music from the Southeast to the Southwest.

By 1930 few of the hillbilly singers derived their material from folk sources, as newly written songs and commercial arrangements of older tunes gradually edged the traditional ballads aside. After Jimmie Rodgers, performers tended to be more polished and self-conscious about their professional status. Throughout the Depression years country music became increasingly urbanized by "city-billies," urban performers who nonetheless employed some of the songs and instruments of the rural culture. Record companies continued building their country catalogues, while more and more radio coverage was given hillbilly music, as advertisers during the 1930s began to realize the expanding popularity of country programs. One of the first companies to use country music in their advertising on a national basis was the Crazy Water Crystals Company of Mineral Wells, Texas, but soon Garrett Snuff, Light Crust Flour, Stevens Work Clothes, and other businesses marketing products popular with country people began sponsoring hillbilly bands on radio and then sending the groups on tour through the area where they seemed most popular. By the late thirties personal appearances had become increasingly common with successful country performers, as promoters began to appear to handle the careers of hillbilly talent.

In the dissemination of hillbilly music throughout the United States, the powerful Mexican border stations played an important role. Operating just across the American border in Mexico, these stations broadcast on a wattage sometimes two or three times greater than the maximum limit in the United States, so that they were heard throughout much of the United States and often could be picked up quite clearly in Canada. Generally these stations were owned by American businessmen, who aimed their transmitters toward the United States. Dr. J. R. Brinkley became the first of these border entrepreneurs when he moved to Del Rio, Texas, after his radio license was revoked in Kansas. Brinkley advertised his own medical remedies, as well as other American products, while listeners in the hours after midnight were deluged with right wing politicians, religious evangelists, and old-time hillbilly singers.

Before the 1930s the term "western" had seldom been used in connection with the commercial country music developing in the United States. Following the success of Jimmie Rodgers, however, connotations of the West and the cowboy could be heard frequently in the songs of hillbilly singers, and country performers began to don cowboy boots and gaudy western clothing, first in Texas, Louisiana, and Oklahoma. The romantic adulation of the cowboy, which had grown more intense as Americans moved farther away from the cowboy past, perhaps made the emergence of the western image in country music inevitable, eventually superseding the earlier mountain image. The southwestern states had mainly been populated by former residents of the Southeast, so that the values, traditions, and evangelical Protestantism of the older country music in large measure survived the transition westward.

By the mid-1930s "western" music had definitely become dominant, acquiring many of the commercial techniques of show business, as country music grew into a national phenomenon. Scores of singers modeled themselves after Jimmie Rodgers, and even young hillbilly singers from the deep South and the southeastern mountains became involved in perpetuating the cowboy image, singing tunes like "Out on the Texas Plains." Youthful Hank Snow, from far off Nova Scotia, dressed in cowboy attire and called himself "the Yodeling Ranger." While Ernest Tubb sang few cowboy songs, he nevertheless wore cowboy boots and a ten-gallon hat. The first performer to gain any real recognition for country music in New York was "Tex" Ritter, who was born in deep East Texas (far from any cowboy activity), attended the University of Texas, and for one year was enrolled in the Northwestern Law School. Ritter began singing on KPRC in Houston in 1929, but after an unsuccessful tour went to New York. In 1931 the Theatre Guild gave him a role in *Green Grow the Lilacs,* and during the fall of 1932 he was the featured singer with the Madison Square Garden Rodeo. His thick Texas accent and storehouse of cowboy lore made him a sensation. To New Yorkers Ritter became the embodiment of the Texas cowboy, while his radio program, "The Lone Star Rangers," was one of the first western programs to be broadcast from New York City.

Interest in western music became so great during the 1930s that Tin Pan Alley songwriters responded to the western theme, producing songs like "Gold Mine in the Sky," "I'm an Old Cowhand," and especially "The Last Roundup," by a Boston-born composer Billy Hill, which really awakened the general public to the romantic West. Most of these tunes were written by tunesmiths who had never seen a cowboy, yet were capable of creating songs that captured the public's imagination and were sung by both hillbilly and popular performers. During a time when the American heartland was being pictured in literature and by American Scene painters and serious composers, it is understandable that the American West would be discovered by commercial songwriters as well, particularly since the western image offered a comforting contrast to the Depression then gripping cities and agricultural areas alike. The social and economic flux of the thirties created a confusion of values and a yearning for stability. Many of the old social values were idealized, while the security symbols of the past were often reinforced in commercial country and western music.

Western country music broke into two major elements: the singing cowboy and western swing. Gene Autry, who continued the "romantic westernizing" begun by Jimmie Rodgers, made his first records for Victor in the fall of 1929, billed by the company as "Oklahoma's Singing Cowboy." Born on a tenant farm in Tioga, Texas, Autry had been exposed to little of the cowboy heritage growing up in northeast Texas. His early style was a soft, nasal tenor, much like that of Jimmie Rodgers, and he perfected a reasonable facsimile of Rodgers' yodeling style. For a brief time Autry had a fifteen minute radio show in Tulsa and by 1930 had been featured on the WLS Barn Dance in Chicago, where he was an immediate success. He recorded a number of hillbilly melodies in vogue at the time, had a tremendous hit with "Silver Haired Daddy of Mine," but rarely sang anything that could be considered western. His songs and style were basically in the southern rural tradition. Then in 1934 he signed a Hollywood contract, was given singing parts in western movies, and soon emerged as the "Nation's Number One Singing Cowboy."

Autry's whole repertory shifted, in keeping with films that romanticized the cowboy and helped stereotype western music through endless songs about the lonesome prairie. By the mid-1930s the "horse opera" had become a staple of the American film industry, and studios were turning them out in a steady stream. Autry's success encouraged rival movie companies to find their own versions of the singing cowboy, and studio executives began combing the ranks of hillbilly radio programs for likely candidates.

"Tex" Ritter signed a film contract in 1936, but Roy Rogers, born Leonard Slye in Duck Run, Ohio, became Autry's most formidable competition. Originally the lead singer for the Sons of the Pioneers, Rogers left the group in 1937, when he signed a contract with Republic Studios. The Sons of the Pioneers appeared in a number of his pictures, singing their close, smooth harmony. Many of their best songs, like "Tumbling Tumbleweeds" and "Cool Water," were composed by Bob Nolan, a gifted songwriter from Canada.

Hollywood tried to present its singing cowboys as modernizations of the nineteenth-century cowboys, who often sang on the range and supposedly quieted herds on bed ground at night with the sound of their voices. Much of the singing of the real cowboys probably came from loneliness and the need for something to kill time. Authentic cowboys often sang to familiar airs or voiced things they liked or hated or concerned them in a monotonous tune repeated to themselves, unaware that they were singing at all. Many of the traditional songs found among the cowboys had nothing to do with life on the range and might well be mountain songs or sentimental ballads they had known since childhood. "Jack" Thorp, who traveled through Texas and New Mexico around 1890 collecting authentic cowboy songs, claimed he never heard a cowboy with a really good voice. "If he had one to start with," Thorp insisted, "he always lost it bawling at cattle, or sleeping out in the open, or tellin' the judge he didn't steal that horse." Unlike the romanticized Hollywood variety, the original songs from the range were fairly realistic when depicting life among the cowboys and cattlemen. The "Cowboy's Lament," something of a classic, deals with the death of a sinner, who is filled with remorse for the anguish his dishonorable life has brought upon his family. The ballad of "Sam Bass" is a forthright example of frontier realism, sympathetic to the outlaw gang and hostile to the Texas Rangers and other law enforcement agencies. "Little Joe" depicts a boy who has left home to escape his stepmother's abuse, finds a job on the range, but is killed when his horse falls into a ravine during a stampede.

Clearly the life pictured in authentic cowboy songs was less pretty than that glorified by the Hollywood counterparts. Whereas the cowboys themselves had sung rough language in simple rhymes that seldom matched very well, the film stars sang far more refined lyrics, in voices beautiful enough to win them recognition. Synthetic though their approach might be, the singing cowboys of the 1930s made a tremendous impact on country music and a whole generation of youngsters who grew up spending Saturday afternoons at the movies. Dewey Groom, a Dallas country singer who traded a bull calf for his first guitar at age fourteen, grew up with Gene Autry as his idol and slavishly copied the Autry style in his early days. It was not until after he had been in the service during World War II that Groom was able to break away from his hero's influence and establish his own professional identity.

While Autry remained Dewey Groom's number one idol in the years before he was drafted, Bob Wills ran a close second. Born in Limestone County, Texas, Wills emerged as the king of western swing, revolutionizing the country dance business in the process. Operating for a time out of Fort Worth, where he advertised Light Crust Flour, Wills moved his center to Tulsa in 1934, where he and his Texas Playboys broadcast over KVOO. They also played at Wills' own ballroom and appeared in dance halls throughout the listening range of their noontime radio program. Wills himself played the fiddle, although his group occasionally used brass, would eventually add the steel guitar, and still later used drums. While Bob Wills and the Texas Playboys continued to draw from traditional rural music, the influence of jazz, particularly the swing orchestras popular at the time, was strong. Mexican mariachi music also contributed to western swing, along with black country blues. Bob Wills' group played with a distinctive heavy beat, and while they made records and even movies, the dance hall was their natural habitat.

Honky-tonks had sprung up all over the South with the repeal of prohibition, and dance music, either live or on the "juke box," became an essential part of the honky-tonk atmosphere. But when country music entered the dance hall, changes became necessary both in lyrics and style. Songs like "The Old Country Church" and "Poor Old Mother at Home" were clearly out of place in the honky-tonk environment and were replaced by songs about the new society in which rural southerners found themselves living. A steady, persistent beat was needed for dancing, while amid the laughter and noise of the dance hall, the music became louder, particularly as the electric guitar came into vogue. Unsophisticated at best, these saloons sometimes became so rowdy that the musicians occasionally put chicken wire in front of the bandstand to keep from being hit by flying beer bottles.

As southerners who had suffered from the hard times of the Depression demanded lyrics that spoke to them of their difficulties, protest songs appeared more frequently in commercial country music. The textile mills and Kentucky coal mines spawned a large number of socially conscious hillbilly songs, while the Dust Bowl and labor unions provided common themes for country songwriters. Woody Guthrie emerged as a major spokesman for this heightened folk consciousness, although he became more identified with the urban folk than with the rural. Born in Okemah, Oklahoma, Guthrie left home when his parents became impoverished in 1929, took odd jobs in the Texas Panhandle to make a living, and began singing in the small towns of Oklahoma and Texas in a style comfortably within the southern hillbilly tradition. The dust storms and economic hardships of the 1930s inflamed his social consciousness almost to the point of open rebellion. Guthrie moved to California, where he found a job singing for a Los Angeles radio station, but as the West Coast became deluged with homeless migratory workers his anger at the system he felt had caused their misfortunes found its way into his protest songs. In 1938 he moved to New York, where he became a leader of the urban proletarian movement. Later he sometimes worked with Pete Seeger, who came to typify the working class intellectual in the leftist cause.

Country musicians continued to write about contemporary events during the hectic years of World War II, patriotic songs like the immensely popular "There's a Star-Spangled Banner Waving Somewhere" and the poignant "Gold Star in the Window." The great demand for entertainment of all kinds among servicemen resulted in country music being played both in training bases at home and behind the battle lines all through Europe and the Pacific. By 1943 the Special Services Division of the European Theater of Operations included some twenty-five hillbilly bands, while the Grand Ole Opry had organized a traveling unit for servicemen called the "Camel Caravan." The mingling of city residents and country folk in the Army barracks created a new amalgamation of the American population, as did the migration of country people into northern and west coast cities to work in defense plants. Many southerners who had never before been more than a few miles from home, marched off to training camps or moved into industrial centers carrying their musical preferences with them. Country music was transported all over the country by professional singers and amateur bands formed by servicemen themselves. Dewey Groom remembers singing for troops in Australia and getting a standing ovation practically every time he sang the Bob Wills number "San Antonio Rose."

While the appeal of country music broadened and its foothold in the entertainment world improved, commercialization also increased. "You Are My Sunshine," written and initially sung by Jimmie Davis, was recorded by popular favorite Bing Crosby in 1941 and became "the taproom and tavern classic of the year." Likewise "Pistol Packin' Mama," "Smoke on the Water," and "Steel Guitar Rag" became great popular successes. When Bing Crosby recorded "San Antonio Rose" in 1941, it sold over 84,000 copies in the month of January alone. Gradually some of the city dwellers developed a tolerance for country music, and a few even came to like it. In 1944 the USO polled servicemen in Europe to determine the most popular singer, and surprisingly enough country singer Roy Acuff's name led the list.

Still a strong prejudice against country music remained, in part because of its performers' lack of sophistication and in part because of the untrained quality of the country singing voice. Most country musicians as late as the 1940s could not read music and knew only a few basic chords on the guitar, perhaps only a three chord progression. An old maxim in country music came in response to the question, "Can you read music?" Often the musician being querried would answer, "Not enough to hurt my playing." Many listeners who enjoyed country music were afraid of being caught listening to it, fearing that their social standing might suffer. Fred McCord, who came from a family of merchants, played for Station WRR in Dallas as a young man and can remember walking down the railroad tracks to work so that people would not see his guitar.

Certainly the honky-tonks that had appeared in the decade before expanded in popularity during World War II, exercising a powerful role in country music. Many singers emerged out of the honky-tonk atmosphere, but none proved more influential than Ernest Tubb. Born on a farm near Crisp, Texas, Tubb gained his greatest success during the war and the years just after. Essentially he carried the Jimmie Rodgers tradition into the 1940s, fusing western swing with the country vocal style. Tubb was among the earliest bandleaders to use an electric guitar on a regular basis, in response to the complaint by honky-tonk operators that it was difficult to hear his music after business picked up at night. Known as the Texas Troubadour, Tubb became Decca's most successful country performer during the 1940s, and his own composition, "Walking the Floor Over You," became a national hit, eventually recorded by Bing Crosby.

By 1944 more than six hundred hillbilly radio programs could be heard on stations throughout the United States. Although Chicago's WLS National Barn Dance continued to grow in popularity and later barn dances, like Shreveport's "Louisiana Hayride" and Dallas' "Big D Jamboree," experienced financial success, it was obvious that Nashville's Grand Ole Opry was emerging as the "king" of country music shows. In 1941 the Opry was moved into Ryman Auditorium, a converted tabernacle with a seating capacity of over 3500 persons, and even though an admission was charged the show played to capacity audiences. Built in 1892 Ryman Auditorium had narrow pointed windows, curved wooden church pews, primitive dressing rooms, but excellent acoustics. The Grand Ole Opry grew into the city's largest tourist attraction, as hillbilly artists began migrating to Nashville, aware that an appearance on the Opry at whatever fee meant prestige bookings across the country. In October, 1947, a Grand Ole Opry unit headed by Ernest Tubb became the first country group to appear in concert at Carnegie Hall. Meanwhile promoters had become aware of the financial possibilities of country music and expanded the personal appearance field into a profitable business.

Although many singers earned national popularity on the Grand Ole Opry during the war years, Roy Acuff emerged as the Opry's leading star of that period, the first major singing star since Uncle Dave Macon. A mountain boy from East Tennessee, Acuff attracted tremendous crowds not so much because of the excellence of his high tenor voice, but as a result of his showmanship. Accompanied by his string band, "The Smoky Mountain Boys," he performed sacred songs and traditional mountain melodies in a plaintive and sincere manner. His first recording, "The Great Speckled Bird" in 1936, was the number with which he remained most strongly identified. Later he recorded "The Wabash Cannon Ball." His success as a "mountain" singer came when the majority of country singers were discarding traditional tunes and accepting "western" styles and approaches. At a time when country music fans were being deluged with the new vogue, Acuff offered a refreshing musical alternative. In late 1942 he became half owner of the powerful Acuff-Rose Music Publishing Company, an exclusively country music house and the first based in Nashville. By 1943 Acuff was earning $200,000 a year and was the recognized "King of Country Music."

During the late 1940s Eddy Arnold approached Acuff's dominant position, although he later changed into almost a popular singer, moving toward a vocal style as appealing to businessmen and bankers as to laborers and farmers. Buck Owens, Rose Maddox, and Webb Pierce became familiar to fans during country music's surge of popularity in the postwar years, while Red Foley seems to have been the first country star actually to record in Nashville. Cousin Minnie Pearl, a comedienne who first appeared at the Grand Ole Opry in 1940, evolved into sort of the grand old lady of the show. Born Sarah Ophelia Colley in Centerville, Tennessee, Minnie Pearl ironically graduated from Ward Belmont, a fashionable finishing school in Nashville, and taught drama for a while before eventually deciding to become a country comedienne.

The diminution of ASCAP's power and the formation of Broadcast Music Incorporated parallels the commercial rise of country music, paving the way for the recognition of country songwriters. With the emergence of BMI hillbilly composers began to receive greater protection and increased profits through the performance rights of their songs. Tin Pan Alley became increasingly sensitive to country music after the Cole Porter number "Don't Fence Me In" became an overnight sensation in 1944, so that even the conservative ASCAP publishers began to realize that they stood to lose money if they did not get on the bandwagon. A few publishers sent staff members down to Nashville to find out what the ingredients were that made country music so appealing, and gradually dilutions of hillbilly sounds began pouring out of the major New York firms.

By 1946 country music was ready for another period of national expansion. The war had freed much of America's rural population, especially in the South where impoverished white and black sharecroppers and tenant farmers had left their meager farms and moved into urban areas in search of more lucrative employment. The migrations had affected not only the growth of southern cities, but reached industrial centers like Chicago, Baltimore, and Detroit as well. After the war country music flourished in these cities, as transplanted southerners, still rural in their values and attitudes, demanded a familiar music in the churches they attended and the taverns they frequented. Juke box operators soon found it advantageous to supply hillbilly selections to taverns drawing a heavily southern clientele. The West Coast, which had been the destination for the Okie migration in the mid-1930s, reported a tremendous growth in country music's popularity, as southerners continued to pour into the area. Amid the postwar economic boom the urban migrants were prosperous enough to go out frequently, buy recordings of their own, and eventually want more of their own music on radio and television. "Urbanization," according to historian Bill Malone, "did not kill country music, it merely transformed it. And the country musicians, placed in an urban atmosphere, performed their traditional music and adopted the newer styles and instruments that struck their fancy."

In many instances country people who moved to town became more attached than ever to country music, in an attempt to hold on to at least part of the heritage they had left behind. As the old security patterns seemed to be decaying and with the breakup of home, family, and church relationships, urban migrants often grew nostalgic for the country and found comfort in songs that reminded them of home and a vanishing past. Other urban dwellers who had never cared for hillbilly music before found that with repeated exposure the country songs offered a warmth and simplicity that were appealing, particularly in rapidly changing times.

During the late 1940s and early 1950s a number of songs with a country flavor faired well in the popular market. The Weavers, a folk group with a hybrid style, gained wide attention with "Goodnight, Irene" and "Kisses Sweeter Than Wine," while Marty Robbins' "A White Sport Coat" and Sonny James' "Young Love" scored high on the popular charts. "Sixteen Tons," written by Merle Travis in the late 1940s, was recorded by Tennessee Ernie Ford in 1955 and turned into a national success. Rawer hillbilly tunes, such as "It Wasn't God Who Made Honky-Tonk Angels," "If You've Got the Money, I've Got the Time," and "Cigarettes, Whiskey and Wild, Wild Women," became familiar with noncountry audiences, while lyrics like "Slipping Around" seemed to offer an honesty seldom found in Tin Pan Alley songs. As the big publishers and record companies turned more attention to the growing country music craze, numbers like "Mule Train," "Riders in the Sky," "High Noon," and "Cry of the Wild Goose" were drummed into commercial favorites, each recorded by a popular singer with lush accompaniment. "The Tennessee Waltz," released in 1948 strictly as a hillbilly song, was recorded in 1950 by popular vocalist Patti Page and became the nation's number one song of that year. More than any other single factor, "The Tennessee Waltz" was responsible for country music's great commercial boom and assured its future integration into the mainstream of America's popular music.

The individual who most clearly bridged the gulf between country and popular music was Hank Williams, who became the symbol of country music's postwar upsurge. Born on a tenant farm near Mt. Olive, Alabama, in 1923, Hank Williams grew up singing the country blues, probably deriving much of his style from black sources. At age twelve he won an amateur night contest at the Empire Theatre in Montgomery, singing his own composition, "The WPA Blues." A year later he had formed a band called "The Drifting Cowboys" and begun performing in local honky-tonks. By 1937 he had obtained a job on a Montgomery radio station, singing songs that were realistic depictions of the southern culture from which he came.

Williams fused the old with the new, reflecting the southern rural values as well as the forces undermining them. Although he remained basically a rural singer, he had the ability to create compositions acceptable to those outside the rural tradition. He possessed a light, small voice, but one capable of all sorts of twists and turns. His repertoire included blues numbers, religious melodies, love songs, and fast novelty tunes, all of which he sang with utter sincerity. He became emotionally involved with the songs he sang and could communicate his feelings to his listeners, so that each member of his audience felt the songs were being directed to him or her.

The key to Hank Williams' success as a writer lay in his honest simplicity. He had emerged from the common folk of the South and never tried to be anything else. His emotions, whether joy or anguish, were straightforward in his music, stated so that almost everybody could identify. "I'm So Lonesome I Could Cry" became one of his greatest successes, surpassed only by "Your Cheatin' Heart." "Hey, Good Lookin'" was another solid hit, while "Cold, Cold Heart" decidedly broke the pop barrier when Tony Bennett recorded it in 1951. "Kaw-liga" emerged as a big novelty song a year later, while Jo Stafford put "Jambalaya" high on the popular charts.

Williams appeared on the Louisiana Hayride, enjoying a great success with "Lovesick Blues," and joined the Grand Ole Opry in June, 1949. Minnie Pearl, who worked with him often, was immediately impressed by the tall, mournful looking young man. "Especially his eyes," she said. "He had the most haunting and haunted eyes I'd ever looked into. They were deepset, very brown, and very tragic." As a performer he possessed real animal magnetism, and his stage style was about as natural as could be. "He destroyed the women in the audience," Minnie Pearl insists.

But Williams had become a heavy drinker while still in his mid-teens, and the free-wheeling life of the honky-tonk musician did nothing to help. There were also serious emotional deficiencies, perhaps stemming from the fact that his family had moved around so much during his early years. He grew up gaunt, lonely, and insecure. While his songs were models of honesty, Williams found himself incapable, even at an early age, of dealing with the problems of his own life in a straightforward fashion. And so he drank, missing lots of performances because of instability and drunkenness. He also had a weakness for women and big cars. In 1950 he bought a green Cadillac with fish tails and all sorts of gadgets and accessories. But fame and money did not make him happy, and as the pressures built, he kept himself private and drank more and more. By 1951 it was obvious he was in deep trouble and that his career was awash in whiskey.

Audiences, however, often felt that Williams had the same problems they had and tried to be sympathetic, but there were embarrassing moments. Finally he was fired from the Grand Ole Opry. He appeared at the Louisiana Hayride one night obviously drunk. When he tried to sing, he stumbled, and the crowd taunted him. It became harder for him to get jobs, but he landed a show date for New Year's night, 1953, in Canton, Ohio. On the way to the engagement his chauffeur stopped the car to check on Williams' condition and found him dead in the back seat of his Cadillac. He was twenty-nine years old. Officially he died of a heart attack, although there have always been suggestions of a drug overdose.

At the theater in Canton where the singer was scheduled to appear a spotlight was thrown on the empty stage, as a record of Williams singing "I Saw the Light" was played. The audience stood and sang with the record. All across the country his recordings were suddenly in great demand, especially his current hit, "I'll Never Get Out of This World Alive."

New singers like Ray Price and George Jones received their inspiration directly from Hank Williams. Others like Marty Robbins preferred the softer, crooning style made popular by Eddy Arnold. But the most successful country singer in the years right after Williams' death was honky-tonk singer Webb Pierce from Monroe, Louisiana. Country performers by then consciously sought recognition from popular audiences and worked to place their songs on the popular music charts, adapting their styles to fit the more sophisticated urban tastes.

Decca set up recording facilities in Nashville during the late 1940s, and Capitol Records in 1950 became the first major company to base its country director there. Columbia and RCA soon built studio facilities on the city's Record Row, so that within a few years Nashville had become the third largest recording center in the country, only a step behind New York and Los Angeles. The concentration of booking agencies in the city sharply increased, as more and more music publishers located there. BMI opened a Nashville office in 1958 and six years later moved into a beautiful new building on Music Row.

With the arrival of the rock-and-roll phenomenon, triggered by Elvis Presley, the country music industry first flirted with the rock sounds, forming a hybrid known as rockabilly, and then settled into a rather bland compromise between the popular and folk styles identified as "country pop." Recording executives and performers discovered that the major obstacle in the acceptance of country music by popular audiences was its instrumentation. The hillbilly fiddle and the wailing steel guitar offended the musical sensitivity of many popular listeners, creating a rural or honky-tonk image that urban dwellers often sought to avoid. Once these instruments were replaced with the more conventional accompaniment offered by strings, piano, and drums, country singers were far more acceptable to general audiences, providing the nasal quality did not become too pronounced. Even brass and reeds came to be used in country and western arrangements, and vocal backup groups added to the slick sound. By the mid-1950s the Grand Ole Opry employed a cast of around 120 individuals, including singers, sidemen, and comedians, and opera singer Helen Traubel had even appeared on the show. Along the way country music had acquired increased respectability, something country performers had long yearned for.

While honky-tonk music fared miserably during the late 1950s, an older style known as bluegrass, featuring unamplified string instruments and a repertoire consisting heavily of traditional country and mountain tunes, actually gained in popularity. A direct descendent of the hillbilly string bands of the 1920s, especially the Carter Family, bluegrass evolved out of the style played by Bill Monroe and his Blue Grass Boys between 1944 and 1948. It achieved its widest popularity through the success of Flatt and Scruggs and their Foggy Mountain Boys. Guitarist Lester Flatt and banjoist Earl Scruggs had both been members of Bill Monroe's Blue Grass Boys, but left in 1948 to form their own band. Although their largest following was always in the rural areas, by the late 1950s their music was taking the cities by storm and became even more popular during the urban "folk revival" of the early 1960s. Bluegrass reached its widest audience as background music for the popular television series *The Beverly Hillbillies*, while Flatt and Scruggs' recording of the show's theme, "The Ballad of Jed Clampett," hit the top of the popular charts.

In the 1960s, as metropolises grew into megalopolises, a deepening disenchantment with the rootlessness, impersonality, standardization, and loneliness of urban life helped make rural attitudes and country music more appealing than ever before. The Kingston Trio created an interest in folk music on high school and college campuses in 1958 with their recording of "Tom Dooley," an old North Carolina murder ballad, so that a rash of Kingston Trio imitators appeared on the scene, groups like the Brothers Four and the Chad Mitchell Trio. Peter, Paul, and Mary added an element of protest, as America's youth began to have doubts about accepted urban-industrial values. Singers like Conway Twitty and Jerry Lee Lewis moved successfully from rock-and-roll back to mainstream country music, and even the honky-tonk sound was revitalized by a number of musicians like Ray Price, who skillfully blended a sense of tradition with superior musicianship.

The recording of country music had become increasingly sophisticated, as electronics and echo chambers came into frequent use. Country music styles generally grew more refined during the 1960s, as popular, and even classical, influences continued. Electric instruments were becoming more widespread, so that it was common to find electric fiddles and electric string basses providing accompaniment. The old cowboy songs were rarely sung, and except for the bluegrass bands, the mountain melodies were completely gone, but country music continued to reflect the changing patterns of American society. Country songs by the 1960s were less romantic and nostalgic, more open in dealing with the problems of infidelity, divorce, drink, and personal unhappiness in simple expressions easily understood by the average person. Despite having grown into a worldwide phenomenon, popular in Europe and the Orient, country music continued to be largely southern music, a reflection of its southern writers and performers. The song-writers, especially those catering to the honky-tonk style, remained predominantly southerners who had grown up in small towns or had once lived on farms.

In part because of the humble origins of so many of the country music performers, the glamor of Nashville became associated with the American dream, symbolizing the climb from rags to riches. Loretta Lynn, born and raised in the coal-mining hills of eastern Kentucky, rose from poverty to the height of success during the 1960s in a field that until recently had been almost exclusively dominated by men. Except for Kitty Wells, who emerged as country music's first female superstar around 1952, and Patsy Cline, whose spectacular career was tragically cut short in 1957, males had monopolized country music much as they had dominated southern rural society, relegating women to the status of fans or minor performers. Loretta Lynn not only broke the pattern, but sang in a direct, feisty way about cheating, hell-raising men and made it clear in her lyrics that she was tired of being pushed around. In two or her biggest hits, "Don't Come Home A-Drinkin' " and "Your Squaw Is on the Warpath," the line was firmly drawn, as the female vocalist threatened to leave her man rather than accept further abuse. A mother at fourteen and a grandmother at twenty-eight, Loretta Lynn could sing her hit song "The Pill" with solid conviction. In her private life she managed to balance a family and a career, femininity and feminism, new ideas and old sentiments. She somehow was able to sing with a sassy attitude and not appear threatening to the men in her audience, so that she became popular with rural and blue-collar society, as well as with more sophisticated urban circles.

Tammy Wynette, on the other hand, employed a style more obviously influenced by popular singers like Patti Page and Doris Day, while her view of women amounted to almost a "doormat" attitude. Her biggest hit, "Stand By Your Man," contrasted the unhappy fate of the wife waiting faithfully at home with the good times her husband is having elsewhere and urged forgiveness. Written by a man, Billy Sherrill, the number proved highly controversial at a time when women's liberation was a heated issue.

Johnny Cash became another 1960s success story, remaining comfortably within the country music tradition, yet including enough of a rhythmic element to attract the rock-and-roll audience. Born during the dark days of the Depression on a small farm near Kingsland, Arkansas, Cash sang in a mournful style that suggested the honky-tonk influence of Hank Williams and Ernest Tubb. There was a soulful quality about Cash's music, whether he was singing about the land, the pastoral ideal, mother, home, or unrequited love, that undoubtedly reflected his own suffering and his own struggle against adversity. Two of his songs, "Folsom Prison Blues" and "San Quentin," are about prison, and in the late 1960s, after an arrest on a drug charge, Cash himself came off a seven year pill jag with a more mature outlook on life. His more serious attitude, the development of his road show, and his prime time television show won him mass acceptance.

Television had become a major force in popularizing country music and in winning it respectability with middle class audiences. Glen Campbell came from genuine country roots although, like Johnny Cash, he watered down his approach for his weekly television series. On even more thorough-going country shows like *Hee Haw*, the steel guitar remained off camera or disappeared altogether, so as not to offend middle class viewers. Immensely popular was the Porter Wagoner Show with Dolly Parton, which offered precision, smoothness, and technical proficiency, at the same time retaining a country feel.

Among Nashville's most talked about songwriters has been Tom T. Hall, who began his parade of hits with "Harper Valley PTA," a song about hypocrisy, based on an angry mother in Hall's hometown who had told off a group of school authorities who were critical of the way she was raising her daughter. Recorded by Jeannie C. Riley, "Harper Valley PTA" sold over 4,500,000 copies within the first six months. Most of Hall's lyrics have been about people he has known or events he had experienced. Of the newer breed in Nashville the most successful writer-performer has been Kris Kristofferson. Born in Brownsville, Texas, and a Rhodes scholar, Kristofferson added the theme of sexuality to country music, frankly discussed and openly endorsed. His songs have often dealt with the importance of honest, uninhibited personal relations, as in "Help Me Make It Through the Night," and freedom, as in "Me and Bobby McGee." Mel Tillis, from Florida, has written a number of timely songs, demonstrating his considerable versatility, but remaining loyal to the hard country tradition. "Detroit City," which Tillis wrote with Danny Dill, is a poignant expression of the bewildered southerner struggling with the complexities of the industrial North. "Ruby, Don't Take Your Love to Town" depicts a crippled Vietnam war veteran no longer able to satisfy his restless young wife.

The more sedate, stylized country pop music coming out of Nashville recording studios became identified during the 1960s as the "Nashville Sound." The sound is characterized by a loose, relaxed feeling, an easygoing beat, and an instrumentation differing greatly from early country music. Rather than old-time fiddles and steel guitars, electric guitars supply a catchy beat much like rock-and-roll, while the piano often provides a cool, urbane quality, and a couple of dozen violins woo the easy-listening audience. Vocally the Nashville Sound was marked by background choruses and an absence of the old honky-tonk aura. Studio sidemen, most of whom still could not read music, moved freely from one recording session to another, improvising for country, pop, and rock-and-roll artists as a matter of course. If any one person could be credited with creating the Nashville Sound, it would be Chet Atkins, Victor's powerful Artist and Repertoire man and one of the most respected musicians on Music Row.

By 1970 over 300 record labels were home-based in Nashville, most of them subsidiaries of the major companies. Some 300 country performers worked out of the city, 900 songwriters lived in the Nashville area, and 390 publishers were either headquartered or represented there. The Country Music Association, which convened first in 1958, emerged as the industry's biggest booster organization, dedicated to publicizing and marketing country music on a worldwide scale. Market analyses conducted during the mid-1960s indicated that the industry's consumers were by then predominantly urban centered.

As independent agencies grew more influential, the Grand Ole Opry no longer dominated the booking of country artists. Nevertheless, the Opry, according to manage Bud Wendell, was still "the end of the rainbow." When the new Opryhouse was opened in 1974, President Richard Nixon flew to Nashville for the dedication. The new $15,000,000 hall at Opryland is ultra-modern in design, mostly glass and concrete, and has a seating capacity of 4400. By the early 1970s country music was an industry worth an estimated $100,000,000 a year to Nashville alone.

But a "Nashville West" had also come into prominence—Bakersfield, California, where both Merle Haggard and Buck Owens set up their operations. Bakersfield and Hollywood had blossomed as centers for the recording, packaging, and promotion of country talent during the mid-1960s, benefiting from the influx of country people who had earlier gravitated to the area. Haggard himself was a Bakersfield native, from a working class family that had moved to California from Oklahoma during the Dust Bowl days. Imprisoned for armed robbery as a youth, Haggard did some growing up in San Quentin. "The trouble with me," he once said, "was that I started taking the songs I was singing too seriously. Like Jimmie Rodgers, I wanted to ride the freight train. As a result, I was a general screw-up from the time I was fourteen." His "Okie from Muskogee" strongly lambasted the most visible attributes of the contemporary counterculture and reaffirmed the superiority of small-town values. In "The Fightin' Side of Me" Haggard spoke of squirrely draft dodgers, while "Workin' Man Blues" stated eloquently the plight of the modern urban workers, determined to stick it out and raise his family in the city.

Texas-born Buck Owens helped build a West Coast style and, like George Jones, contributed significantly to the honky-tonk resurgence. Employing a heavily accented, fast-tempoed brand of instrumentation, Owens remained close to the southern rural tradition with songs like "Dust on Mother's Bible," "Let the Sad Times Roll On," and "I've Got a Tiger by the Tail."

During the late 1960s Austin, Texas emerged as a country music center, successfully mating cowboy culture and the counterculture in a style known as "progressive country" or "redneck rock." The fusion began at Threadgill's Bar, where middle class youths looking for musical idols other than rock stars mingled and drank cans of Lone Star beer with country "kickers." After 1970 the cavernous Armadillo World Headquarters became a favorite haunt for the city's counterculture and the headquarters of progressive country music. Singer Willie Nelson, after a long Nashville career, relocated in Austin, becoming the focus around which the union of country music and rock would take place. Waylon Jennings often performed in the city, while Jerry Jeff Walker, Kinky Friedman, Doug Sahm, and a California swing band called Asleep at the Wheel all became identified with the Austin Sound. At its height the entire central Texas hill country seemed alive with the sound of progressive country music, serving as a melting pot for diverse types searching for a low-pressure environment and the freedom to pursue new musical directions. Jerry Jeff Walker recorded an album in the old dance hall at Luckenbach, while Dripping Springs and Kerrville had annual festivals. On the Drag opposite the University of Texas campus in Austin, street musicians played and sang for nickels and dimes, while the city's clubs were filled with progressive country's exponents. "In a sense," Chat Flippo wrote for *Texas Parade*, "the Hill Country sound evolved around musicians who were more or less misfits in the eyes of Nashville, California, or New York."

The color barrier had been broken in country music by 1967, when black singer Charley Pride was introduced at the Grand Ole Opry, the first black to perform there as a headliner. Pride, a tall, powerfully built man, the son of a Mississippi sharecropper, had been discovered four years before singing in a Montana honky-tonk and persuaded by veteran country entertainer Red Sovine to try his luck in Nashville. Despite its reputation as America's "whitest" music, country music had always borrowed heavily from black musicians. Charley Pride grew up singing along with Opry stars Ernest Tubb and Roy Acuff on radio, but sings mostly ballads in a voice more modern than the nasal tones of most of the older performers.

The first Chicano to achieve stardom in country music was Johnny Rodriguez, sometimes called the Chicano Charley Pride. Born in South Texas, Rodriguez has essentially rejected his ethnic musical genre in favor of a predominantly Anglo form, singing bilingual renditions of country standards. Young and billed as a sex symbol, Rodriguez has managed to develop a universal appeal, yet has remained solidly country in his approach.

As the country music industry began to place greater emphasis on youth than ever before, teenage Tanya Tucker arrived as a superstar, bringing in a new, younger audience. Although "Delta Dawn" has proved her biggest hit to date, her songs are often strongly sexual. "Would You Lay With Me" and "Satin Sheets" suggest the roadhouse chanteuse rather than a robust teenager. Then emerging in the mid-1970s as country music's reigning *femme fatale* came Dolly Parton, whose blonde wigs and natural endowments produced innumerable jokes and even comparisons to Mae West. Musically she has run the gamut from songs with an almost Elizabethan flavor to commercial successes like "Here You Come Again," aimed at the popular audience.

The meteoric rise of Dolly Parton summarizes the commercial expansion of country music since World War II and the growing preoccupation of country performers with respectability. Country music has increasingly adopted the manners and styles of the city, responding to the demographic integration of the nation and the proliferating impact of the media. Gradually it has taken on an urban sound, a greater diversity, and new messages, as regional accents and attitudes have softened. Yet despite these changes, country musicians have maintained much of their traditional frankness and tend to be less insulated from their audiences than more sophisticated entertainers. Although they have developed a keen sense of professionalism, the best country artists still avoid pretense, continuing the honesty and sincerity of the old hillbilly songs. With all its modernization country music remains rooted in the soil, expressing a populist view of life, commenting on the realities of a discontented society, and often providing a means of rationalizing failure without actually denying the American dream itself.

CHAPTER

XIII

ROCK AND SOUL

What emerged in the 1950s as rhythm and blues was far from new. Its roots went back into the musical heritage that included work chants, gospel songs, ragtime, and jazz. But mixed in with this earlier black music was the strident feeling of the big cities, the loneliness and alienation spawned by the ghetto life of the post-World War II American black. Whereas classic blues, ragtime, and early jazz all reflected the leisurely tempo of life in the remote areas and villages of the rural South, the aggressiveness and hard edge of rhythm and blues came from the city. Although the transition from the traditional blues evolved slowly, the Second World War acted as a catalyst, as the black migration to industrial centers snowballed. During the late 1940s rhythm and blues really began to take shape, giving expression to the tangible, pressing realities of the ghetto experience.

Since the appeal was almost exclusively to a black market until late in the decade, rhythm and blues was at first known as "sepia" or "race" music. In the early 1950s a growing number of white and black teenagers were made aware of the new sounds by black disc jockeys who began featuring "race" records on their radio programs, often aired late at night. In Cleveland an enterprising, young disc jockey named Alan Freed secured a radio program on WJW, adopting the name "Moondog" and originating in July, 1951, the first white show devoted to rhythm and blues. Before long white youngsters started buying what in Texas were known as "Cat" records in black bars and stores, secretly delighting in the knowledge that their parents were horrified. Like jazz three decades before, rhythm and blues was initially considered by most whites to be a low, degraded music, not to be heard by respectable people—an opinion often shared by middle class blacks. Yet teenagers found the accented beat appealing and the raw lyrics a welcome alternative to the sentimentality of the current Hit Parade favorites. Rhythm and blues records gradually were smuggled into gyms for sock hops, frequently bringing protests from watchful chaperons. In 1952 a riot occurred in Cleveland when 25,000 people showed up for a rhythm and blues dance held in a hall with a capacity of 10,000.

As record sales mounted, executives of the rhythm and blues labels began making regular trips into the South looking for black talent. Two pioneers were the Chess brothers, Leonard and Phil, who formed a recording company in Chicago in the late 1940s, eventually signing Chuck Berry. Through the early 1950s the independents dominated the field, usually limiting their distribution to a handful of cities or to one region of the country. Don Robey, who operated a club called the Bronze Peacock in Houston, began the Peacock label and eventually recorded Bobby "Blue" Bland. Aladdin, Specialty, Supreme, and Exclusive all recorded mainly on the West Coast, while Savoy Records operated out of Newark, New Jersey. Apollo and Imperial grew in size and stature, but it was Atlantic, based in New York, that by 1953 came to dominate the rhythm and blues scene.

In 1949 Ruth Brown, who had grown up singing gospel songs and the blues, recorded "So Long" for Atlantic and enjoyed an immediate success. She followed it with "5-10-15," "Mama, He Treats Your Daughter Mean," and a whole string of hits. Atlantic also promoted Joe Turner, whose "Shake, Rattle and Roll" became a classic in the field, Clyde McPhatter and the Drifters, and the Clovers, whose "One Mint Julep" proved perhaps the biggest of the early rhythm and blues successes.

From out of the honky-tonks of Louisiana came Fats Domino, who wrote, sang, and played piano for a series of hits. Earl Bostic, an alto saxophonist from Oklahoma, produced a searing, vibrant version of "Flamingo," creating the mood of after hours dancing in a dimly lit bar, while Lloyd Price won attention with "Lawdy Miss Clawdy." Willie Mae "Big Mama" Thornton had a smash hit with "Hound Dog," a full three years before the song was taken over by Elvis Presley. Especially controversial was "Sixty Minute Man," its erotic lyrics describing a delayed orgasm. The number was recorded in 1951 by the Dominoes on the King label and quickly sold 2,500,000 copies. Three years later the Midnighters, led by songwriter Hank Ballard, recorded "Work with Me Annie," its sexual content blatantly obvious, and followed it up with the equally shocking "Annie Had a Baby." Sometimes lyrics became downright filthy, as in the Penguin's "Baby Let Me Bang Your Box," so that the records were banned by white radio stations.

Clearly the loud, uninhibited approach was aimed at the ghetto dweller. Most of the early groups were small bands, usually five or six pieces, that belted out unpretentious songs free of the mushiness of most contemporary white music. While rhythm and blues was generally vocal, it was music for dancing. Since the places where the musicians worked were seldom noted for peace and quiet, electric amplification became necessary. Besides, as Arnold Shaw put it, "The tensions of life in the ghetto seemed to demand the shrillness, the distortion, the intensity, and the decibels of electricity." The electric bass gave a deep, throbbing power to the music, while the tenor sax added a raucous, honking quality. The lead voice was often played against several background voices, although as rhythm and blues recording progressed, the background vocals grew increasingly prominent. By the mid-1950s a gospel feel had been reinstated into the rhythm and blues style, producing the trend that would eventually be termed "soul." But basically rhythm and blues was music that boiled out of the big urban environment filled with blacks who were tired of prejudice, discrimination, second-rate schools, and third-rate citizenship, yet who still tended to mask their frustration and bitterness in fun music suitable for dancing, drinking, and having a roughhouse good time on Saturday nights.

As the rhythm and blues singers and songwriters tried to satisfy the newly discovered white market, a bleaching process began. In an effort to make themselves more acceptable to white listeners, who after all represented something over ninety percent of the country's buying power, many black groups cleaned up their lyrics and began to rely heavily on more genteel love songs. Soon strings were added, as rhythm and blues progressed toward sweeter harmonies, slicker arrangements, and more refined sentiments. Gradually white disc jockeys came to refer to this new music as rock-and-roll, the term supposedly coming from the old blues lyric, "My baby rocks me with a steady roll."

Early in 1954 a group called The Crows recorded a number entitled "Gee," which became the first rhythm and blues record to break into the national charts for best-selling popular songs. By July of that year the original version of "Sh-Boom" by The Chords, issued on the Cat label, a subsidiary of Atlantic, reached the top ten after three weeks on the charts. A white group called The Crew Cuts then recorded the song for Mercury, and their cover was released during the week the original version scored on the popular charts. Whereas The Chords had blended the vocal and instrumental portions of the song, using the voice, as the early jazz singers had, like an additional musical instrument, The Crew Cuts separated the instrumental background from the lyrics into parts more easily perceptible. The Crew Cuts clearly enunciated the words, individualizing or precisely unifying their voices, and while some of the original beat was preserved, the spontaneity of The Chords' rendition was lost. The cover version sounded simpler, was easier to listen to, but radically altered the stylistic character of the music. Just a week after The Crew Cuts' popularized version of "Sh-Boom" was issued, however, it entered the top ten on popular record charts, and the handwriting was clearly on the wall.

By 1955 the Moonglows' "Sincerely" had been taken over by the McGuire Sisters, LaVerne Baker's "Tweedle Dee" had been recorded by Georgia Gibbs, and "Blue Velvet," "Hearts of Stone," and "Earth Angel" had all been covered by white singers on major labels and turned into popular successes. Since the promotion and distribution facilities of the larger record companies were far greater than those of the independents, the tendency was for the popular cover to outsell the original. Also in 1955 The Platters, who had recorded a number of hits on the King label, moved over to Mercury, becoming the first rhythm and blues group to make the switch to a major recording company. The Platters quickly invaded the popular charts with "The Great Pretender" and "Only You," a hackneyed tune that could have dated from the big band era.

Yet not all black singers showed this inclination to adapt to a mass audience. Some clung tenaciously to the roughness of rhythm and blues. The purity that rock-and-roll was abandoning so quickly in the mid-1950s was maintained in the Chicago blues, by men like B. B. King, Muddy Waters, Howlin' Wolf, Bo Diddley, and others. Popular mainly within the black community, particularly among the youth, these singers represented a pride in being black and a determination to be accepted on their own terms. B. B. King, although he came from Mississippi and worked in Memphis, sang of the northern ghetto and his attitude was tough and cynical. His concerns were specific, deeply personal, and had little to do with social protest. His lyrics suggest that male roles in the contemporary black community had become confused, anxiety-laden, and in need of redefinition.

Muddy Waters, among the earliest of the delta bluesmen to add the ghetto tension and electricity to country blues, arrived in Chicago in 1946 and won a large black following first in the bars and clubs of the South Side. Later he appeared at the Ashland Auditorium and the Regal Theatre and recorded for Aristocrat Records. His lyrics were down-to-earth, frequently dirty, and brought back memories of the South without forcing listeners to identify themselves as lower class, rural types. Waters' stance was boastful, yet in respects compensating and defensive. Howlin' Wolf grew up in rural Mississippi, worked the cotton fields, but emerged as a leading exponent of the raw urban blues. The idiom typified by Muddy Waters and Howlin' Wolf was soon copied by young white Chicagoans, most skillfully and sensitively by Paul Butterfield and Elvin Bishop.

Bobby "Blue" Bland, another of the major urban bluesmen, was a Memphis boy who began his career before he was drafted in 1952 and soared to popularity later as a singer of great charisma. Time and again his lyrics dealt with the basic male-female conflict in black society, with often a plea that the relationship not fall apart as so many others had before. There is repeatedly a feeling of helpless desperation, growing out of a matrifocal pattern in which the male is expected to be the stud, the rogue, the unfaithful wanderer.

Whereas most of the classic blues singers had been women, the urban blues artists were mainly men, since by the post-World War II period the black male was most out of adjustment with living conditions in the ghetto. The lyrics generally told a story, as opposed to the country practice of simply stringing together phrases on a general theme. Consistently the bluesmen seemed more interested in freedom and self-respect than in integration and even appeared a little afraid of absorption into the white mainstream. Most of the urban blues singers assumed a heightened masculine image, the proto-type of the virile, no-good hustler, who knows what life is all about and sings about sex in a "gutbucket" way. Often the singing was done in falsetto, a carry over from the practice in Africa where falsetto singing was considered the very essence of masculine expression. Clearly lower class black culture held a different concept of manhood from that of the white middle class. The ideal in the black ghetto was not the head of a household who held down a steady job, but the man who dressed well, spent his money freely, and was great in bed. This was the image that preoccupied most urban bluesmen, although they also suggested that there were problems with the instability and interpersonal conflicts that came from acting out this ideal. Yet amid the shifting values of a bewildering, seemingly hopeless situation, the urban blues became both an individual and a group catharsis.

One of the more raucous, sometimes ribald, performers was Bo Diddley, who recorded for the Chess label in Chicago and originated the swiveling hip motions that would later be identified with Elvis Presley. Like John Lee Hooper, Bo Diddley used electric guitars and amplified sound, but remained close to the roots of rhythm and blues, at the same time setting a precedent for much that followed.

Serving as a connecting link between black audiences and white was Ray Charles, since he enjoyed wide popularity with both. His music embodied the essentials of the Afro-American tradition, yet was accepted intact by vast numbers of white listeners. Born in Georgia and brought up in Florida, Charles was blind from the age of six. Self-taught, he played and sang the blues-rooted material he had heard as a child, was strongly influenced by gospel music, but eventually reached out to embrace modern jazz as well, writing most of his own music and lyrics. Not only did he join black audiences with white, he also bridged the generation gap. His "I've Got a Woman" became a rhythm and blues hit early in 1955, establishing Charles as a major force for the next two decades.

Chuck Berry, who became one of the finest of the rock-and-roll performers, was nurtured in the Chicago blues style. Born in California, Berry grew up in St. Louis, where he eventually became a hairdresser and did weekend work with his own trio in clubs across the river in Illinois. Handsome, with wavy, oily hair, the flamboyant showman not only sang and played the guitar, but also wrote several of his own songs. In the spring of 1955 he arrived in Chicago and immediately went to see Muddy Waters on the South Side. Waters let the young hopeful sit in for a set, was impressed by

Berry, and sent him to see Leonard Chess, who signed Berry to a recording contract. Beginning with "Maybellene" Berry wrote and recorded a series of hits with strong teenage appeal: "Roll Over Beethoven," "Rock and Roll Music," "School Days," "Johnny B. Goode," "Sweet Little Sixteen," and in 1959 "Almost Grown." Musically, Berry's guitar penetrates his lyrics, frequently responding to given lines, so that voice and guitar join equally in making the total impact. His songs are open endorsements of good times, fun, and happiness, while there is a naivete as well as a natural vitality to his music.

More exhibitionistic in approach was Little Richard, who played piano and screamed in a freak voice that seemed tireless and indestructible. He embroidered his phrases with squeals and whoops, demonstrating a drive and a stamina that appeared limitless. Reared in Georgia, Little Richard first scored big with his recording of "Tutti Frutti" in 1955, following it up with "Long, Tall Sally" and "Lucille," both of which sold over a million records.

But the single most important event in bringing rock-and-roll into the mainstream of American popular music and turning the old rhythm and blues sounds into big business was the appearance in 1955 of "Rock Around the Clock," recorded earlier by Bill Haley and his Comets, but reissued when the number was used as the background theme for the film *Blackboard Jungle*. The record almost immediately sold over three million copies, reaching the top of the popular charts both in the United States and England. It stayed in the top spot eight weeks, with sales eventually reaching fifteen million. Haley brought the general public a distinctly rock style, an integration of popular and rhythm and blues elements, as opposed to the diluted cover versions of earlier black records. Although he was born in the suburbs of Detroit, the paunchy, baby-faced Haley was a former hillbilly singer. His group had originally called themselves the Saddlemen. For the "Rock Around the Clock" recording session he had added drums, tenor saxophone, and an electric guitar.

The popularity of *Blackboard Jungle* was largely responsible for the record's phenomenal success, and "Rock Around the Clock" might never have caught on had it not been for the film. Actually the number had been written in 1953 by two white, middle aged, part-time songwriters in Philadelphia. When the movie opened, teenagers danced in the aisles, ripped up theater seats, got into fights, and destroyed whatever was in sight, as Bill Haley's music pounded at them over the titles. The combination of the film's image of delinquent youth plus the raucous, driving sound of Bill Haley and the Comets confirmed what the establishment had already concluded—that rock symbolized rebellion. While Haley became rock-and-roll's first superstar, most Americans still felt that the new music was a passing fad.

But the younger generation was clearly in a mood for its own music, much as the youth of the 1920s had welcomed jazz. Repeatedly there was the criticism that rock was being forced on the public by the disc jockeys. Adults complained that the music was primitive and crude, that its lyrics made no sense, that its singers used poor grammar and improper enunciation, but the youth smiled with delight. By the mid-1950s almost half of the American population was under twenty-five years of age. With more spending money than ever before, teenagers became the primary consumers of entertainment and the nation's leading record buyers. Even more than during the 1920s the youth became the pacesetters in dress, hair styles, current expressions, social attitudes, dance, and fashions in music.

Whereas "Rock Around the Clock" had been the only rock-and-roll song to make the year's top ten records in 1955, by the end of 1956 eighteen of that year's top forty-two songs were rock-and-roll. Of the fifty top songs of 1957, thirty-one were rock-and-roll. As the demand for new sounds and lyrics expressing new values became increasingly evident, all of the major record companies jumped on the bandwagon, signing young performers that could help the record labels compete with one another. The 45-rpm record contributed to the spread of rock, as well as the portable radio, which middle class teenagers now deemed a necessity.

Any hopes that the rock-and-roll craze might soon blow over were dashed early in 1956 when Elvis Presley erupted onto the scene with his recording of "Heartbreak Hotel." For the first time rock-and-roll had a singer who embodied the ideals of the youth. He was young, charismatic, and sexy. He also sang well. But perhaps most important of all, he was controversial. Parents took one look at Presley's tight pants, swaying hips, and long sideburns and immediately condemned him, making the young singer all the more attractive to their sons and daughters. Quickly he became known as "Elvis the Pelvis," and wherever he sang girls squirmed and screamed as their counterparts had in the early days of Frank Sinatra. When he first appeared on television, Presley created a crisis for executives. After one debacle cameramen were ordered to photograph him only from the chest up. Even so there were those who considered Presley's lidded eyes, lopsided grin, and twitching gyrations obscene.

Born on January 8, 1935, in Tupelo, Mississippi, the son of poor whites, Presley had grown up in a holy-roller church, exposed to both country and western and blues singing. Upon graduation from high school he went to work driving a truck for an electrical contractor. By then his family had moved to Memphis, where he heard the urban bluesmen and began doing some singing of his own. He worked local nightclubs and performed on the small time southern circuit, mainly country fairs and school dances. Eventually he appeared on the Louisiana Hayride, so green that he dressed in his stage clothes before driving down from Memphis. He sang country songs with a beat, yet had much of the black sound and the black feel. Already he sang in an animated style, which he did even privately, and was a big hit with the crowd. He signed a year's contract with the Hayride, commuting each weekend to Shreveport from Memphis. Under the management of Colonel Tom Parker he began recording for Sun Records, a Nashville label, essentially singing in a rockabilly style. By 1955 Presley had gained enough of a reputation that RCA Victor bought his contract, paying Sam Phillips, owner of Sun Records, the sum of $40,000.

"Heartbreak Hotel" earned Presley his first Gold Record, although it sold enough for two. Soon he was receiving up to ten thousand fan letters a week. Following his initial appearance on the Ed Sullivan television show, RCA released seven of his records simultaneously. The volume of his sales shook up the entire industry. His records reached the top of all three charts: popular, country and western, rhythm and blues. Whereas other rock stars had enjoyed sporadic acclaim, Presley became rock's first consistently spectacular artist. "I Want You, I Need You, I Love You," "Don't Be Cruel," "Hound Dog," "Blue Suede Shoes," "Love Me Tender" all repeated the success of "Heartbreak Hotel." Presley remained king for almost ten years, within that time selling 100 million records. Gradually critics came to realize that his sensual voice had an expressive range, and while he moved more and more toward a popular styling, he always showed moments of folk inspiration.

Still the controversy over Elvis remained heated for some time, as civic and religious organizations campaigned against him. In Syracuse, New York, a women's group circulated petitions demanding that he be barred from television. In Romeo, Michigan, a high school student was expelled for refusing to cut his Elvis-like sideburns. The singer was burned in effigy in St. Louis, while in Nashville a disc jockey smashed and burned six hundred Presley records in a public park. Peter Potter, master of ceremonies of the Hollywood *Juke Box Jury*, even argued, "All rhythm and blues records are dirty and as bad for kids as dope." A noted psychiatrist from the Institute for Living in Hartford, Connecticut, called rock-and-roll "a communicable disease" and pronounced it "a cannibalistic and tribalistic" form of music.

Then in 1957 Presley was drafted, leaving his fans drooling for more. Somehow his patriotism and impeccable army record made him more respectable, so that his appeal broadened. Shortly after getting out of the army he married, and suddenly he seemed more saintly than menacing. Gradually he shifted more toward standard pop crooning, singing numbers like "Crying in the Chapel" and "It's Now or Never." He also launched an extensive movie career, starring in over thirty films. While he received something like a million dollars for each of his pictures, Presley maintained his country boy image, meekly asking actress Carolyn Jones for advice on how to play scenes and addressing directors he knew well as "Sir." By the 1960s even journalist Hedda Hopper, who had taken repeated pokes at Elvis during the 1950s, seemed to love him, devoting several columns to saying what an all-American boy he had become.

Soon there was a whole rash of Presley imitators—Ricky Nelson, Fabian, Frankie Avalon. By creating a larger middle class audience, Elvis opened the door for other rock stars. From Lubbock, Texas, came Buddy Holly, who had a smashing success with "Peggy Sue" in 1957, but was killed in a plane crash two years later. Like Holly, the Everly Brothers represented a fusion of country and western music with rhythm and blues. Their second hit, "Wake Up, Little Susie," was considered daring in 1957, since it was apparent that little Susie had slept in her boyfriend's company beyond the time when she should have been home. Tommy Sands and Pat Boone, on the other hand, projected the clean-cut image, while their rock-and-roll renditions were considerably watered down. Connie Francis emerged as one of the successful female singers, of which there were understandably few since most of the teenage record buyers were girls. Many of the songs dealt with teenage trauma ("Teenager's Prayer"), school ("Graduation Day"), cars ("Dead Man's Curve"), personal finances ("Get a Job"), or clearly reflected the teenage culture: "Teenage Crush," "Ballad of a Teenage Queen," "Lipstick and Candy," "A Rose and a Baby Ruth." Verbal content was generally sacrificed in the demand for a driving dance beat, as lyrics often became merely nonsense syllables used for their sound.

With millions of young people following rock-and-roll, disc jockey Alan Freed moved to New York, taking an evening slot on WINS and making it the top-rated program in the city. The power of disc jockeys to make hits grew tremendously all across the country, as radio audiences increased by leaps and bounds. By the late 1950s the most popular vehicle of all for rock-and-roll was a television dance party called *American Bandstand* telecast nationally from Philadelphia for two hours every weekday afternoon. Its host after 1957 was Dick Clark, a former disc jockey, who became about the most powerful man in the industry. Clark was the neatly groomed type, around thirty years old, who assumed a sympathetic older brother stance. He played records, while his television audience danced awkwardly. Occasionally this pattern was broken by short interviews or the appearance of guest performers who lip-synced their records.

American Bandstand helped popularize a whole series of new dances. When rock began, the dancing that accompanied it was most often know as the Bop. But in the late 1950s rock dances changed overnight. There was the Duck, the Pony, the Swim, the Woodpecker, the Monkey, the Chicken, the Mashed Potato, the Watusi, the Loco-Motion, and by the early 1960s, the Twist. Partners casually faced one another without making physical contact, showing little concern for what the other was doing, but feeling great personal involvement with the music. As the number of dances multiplied, the quality deteriorated, with the best unrealized revivals of earlier dances like the Charleston, the Eagle Rock, and the Lindy. By 1959 good rock-and-roll was conspicuous by its absence. Groups often produced one record that had momentary success with the teeny-bopper public, then disappeared altogether. By the end of the decade it was becoming evident that a lean period had set in and that the first phrase of rock's popularity was drawing to a close.

In the midst of this dearth came the payola scandals which shook the popular music scene during 1959 and 1960. Close on the heels of the television quiz scandals, a Congressional investigation revealed that record companies and music publishers were paying disc jockeys for playing their material on their programs. Alan Freed, the self-appointed "father of rock-and-roll," was indicted on charges of accepting money to push records and on charges of income tax evasion. Although these charges were eventually dropped, Freed's career became the major casualty of the payola probe. Driven off the air in 1960, Freed died five years later at the age of forty-three. Even Dick Clark's name became unfavorably connected with the scandals, and while Clark was never convicted of having accepted bribes, the hearings did bring out the extraordinary extent of his commercial enterprises, some of which represented a conflict of interests. Eventually 255 disc jockeys were found guilty of accepting either cash or expensive gifts. Clearly a few highly influential disc jockeys in key cities had maneuvered songs with gibberish lyrics and an infantile tune into positions of public acclaim by constantly playing them, reaping a harvest from this success. While some saw payola as an extension of the traditional practice of song plugging, others felt it represented a general degeneration of moral and ethical values.

For those who had hated rock all along, payola was proof that the music had been forced upon the public and had exerted a bad influence, causing corruption within the music business and encouraging juvenile delinquency. For several months it seemed that the rock era was over. Disc jockeys began playing the older jazz-oriented singers again, and folk music came in for a revival, most conspicuously led by the Kingston Trio. Then after the first Newport Folk Festival in 1959, Joan Baez gave the folk revival a considerable boost, singing in the dulcet tones of Appalachia, as folk recordings were issued in greater and greater numbers. The Brothers Four enjoyed their vogue, while Peter, Paul, and Mary had a whole string of hits, some of them serious efforts at social commentary.

By 1962 Bob Dylan had emerged as an important force in this folk revival, evolving within the next three years a style known as "folk rock." Born Robert Zimmerman in Duluth, Minnesota, on May 21, 1941, Dylan was influenced by rhythm and blues, blues singers like Big Joe Williams, and especially folk singer Woody Guthrie. He came from a Jewish background, but was on the road traveling a hobo's life at age eighteen, playing the guitar and writing poems. He changed his name in honor of his favorite modern poet, Dylan Thomas, and in 1961 went East, performing in Greenwich Village and sitting at the bedside of the dying Woody Guthrie.

In 1962 he recorded "The Ballad of Emmett Till," about a black youth who was lynched in Mississippi for having whistled at a white woman. Adopting a "talking blues" format, Dylan sang personal statements about war, prejudice, the nuclear threat, the law, the federal government, the shallowness of ordinary boy-girl relationships, and the dilution of Christian values. Dylan proved the sensation of the 1963 Newport Folk Festival and soon became the mouthpiece for the discontent of the youth all over the world. He seemed to spring from nowhere, used words beautifully, and had a vivid feel for imagery. Unlike the banalities of most rock-and-roll, Dylan's lyrics really meant something. "The Times They Are A-Changing" was one of his early hits, while "Blowin' in the Wind" became the first anti-war song ever to make the popular charts. He performed with an acoustic guitar and harmonica until the Newport Festival of 1965, where he added a set of electric guitars, only to be jeered from the stage. Then he returned in tears to sing "Mr. Tambourine Man," one of his greatest songs, regaining the support of his audience.

But in February of 1964 mainstream rock had been dramatically revitalized when four young men from England visited New York, touching off what was quickly diagnosed as Beatlemania. Dressed in mod clothes and each sporting a mop of hair, the Beatles completely took the United States by storm, twice appearing on the Ed Sullivan show and creating the biggest furor since the Elvis Presley telecasts eight years before. The Beatles' first record, "I Want to Hold Your Hand," was also released in this country in 1964, selling over a million copies within the first ten days. It rose to the number one position on the popular charts in just two weeks. Wherever the group appeared teenagers dissolved in hysterical rapture, but the Beatles proved far more creative than any of their predecessors in the rock field. Within fifteen months of their first American appearance, they had sold over thirty million records in the United States alone.

Born in Liverpool of working class parents, the Beatles had gravitated toward music because the nightclubs and dives of the tough port city offered plenty of employment. John Lennon was studying art when he met Paul McCartney and George Harrison in 1956, both students at Liverpool Institute at the time. Late in 1962 Ringo Starr joined the group on the drums. They played a club called The Cavern in Liverpool, then in 1960 took off for Hamburg, playing at a strip joint in that city's red-light district. In 1961 they were discovered by Brian Epstein, a dynamic young businessman who successfully guided their career until his accidental death in 1967. By 1963 Beatlemania was sweeping both England and the Continent.

The Beatles offered youth and love, but also wit and happiness and the sheer joy of living. They openly shunned adult values and had an honesty and an endearing ability to laugh at themselves. Their early songs were deliciously romantic, yet it was romanticism with a hold on reality. Even in the earliest Beatles songs there were hints of musical complexity, but their work soon showed an astonishing growth. The Beatles were the first rock group to sing sophisticated lyrics. Despite all of the riotous behavior of their fans, it was clear that the musicians themselves were intelligent and masters of the smart remark. Their approach was drawn from black rhythm and blues, country and western material, the popular folk idiom, and the traditional ballad style, although their strongest sympathies were with the best of recent rock. Specifically they had been influenced by Bill Haley and Elvis Presley. As Paul McCartney later said, "Every time I felt low I just put on an Elvis [record], and I'd feel great, beautiful."

In April, 1964, twelve Beatles records were on the list of the one hundred best selling records, five of them holding the top five positions. Their first songs, composed by Lennon and McCartney, had the driving beat of rock, but also a discernible melody. Hard rock numbers like "She Loves You" and "A Hard Day's Night" were among their early hits, as well as the lovely ballad "Yesterday" and the beautiful love song "Michelle." Bob Dylan became one of the great influences on the Beatles, evident in "Nowhere Man" and "Paperback Writer," songs that tended to "tell it like it is." Gradually this social awareness increased until "Eleanor Rigby" dealt with the loneliness of a wasted life in images that were haunting and powerful. George Harrison became vitally interested in Indian music, studied with Ravi Shankar, the great sitar virtuoso, and helped give rise to so-called raga-rock. In 1965 the Beatles introduced a sitar motif on their recording of "Norwegian Wood." Always the group succeeded in not repeating themselves, so that each new Beatles record had a fresh and distinct impact, even borrowing from the world of baroque and classical music.

By 1967, after the emotional turmoil had simmered down, the aesthetic contribution of the Beatles was beginning to be properly evaluated. Gradually their combination of sophistication and ecstacy was recognized. By then the group had immersed themselves in Eastern mystical theology and had frankly experimented with psychedelic drugs. In 1967 they won tremendous critical approval for their unique album *Sergeant Pepper's Lonely Hearts Club Band,* in which they seemed to speak in an existential way about the loneliness, terror, hypocrisy, and absurdity of modern life. Their music, full of dissonant sounds and electronic effects, had assumed a complexity and a profundity far beyond their early efforts, and they created a gallery of unforgettable characters. In perhaps their finest song, "A Day in the Life," the Beatles expressed their conviction that man cannot live without illusions, and yet the sustained, blurred orchestral chord at the end offered no easy resolution. Using between thirty and forty musicians to back up some of the segments, the album was four months in the making and cost over $56,000. *Sergeant Pepper* evolved into more than just twelve songs bundled together. It was an overall concept, achieving a symphonic unity.

"Hey Jude," a single which sold three million copies during a few months in 1968, contained several melodic changes and different rhythmic patterns, while "Strawberry Fields Forever," with its four separate meters and freewheeling modulations, was more complex and ominous, offering a psychedelic retreat from uncertainty. But as the Beatles' music grew more challenging, they began to lose some of their younger fans. The teenagers who had been the original Beatlemaniacs had themselves grown older, and many of them appreciated their idols mature work on a less hysterical level. But the teeny-bopper crowd much preferred groups like the Monkees, who blatantly aped the cuteness of the earlier Beatles. Faced with the dilemma of continuing their musical growth at the expense of losing their mass following, the Beatles after 1968 went back to an earlier, simpler rock form, then disbanded altogether.

In the wake of the Beatles unprecedented success, the American record market was flooded with English rock groups during the mid-1960s. There were Gerry and the Pacemakers, Herman's Hermits, the Animals, and the Dave Clark Five, many of whom were influenced by American black singers. Like the Beatles, several of these groups had gained their first recognition at The Cavern Club in Liverpool, and for a time American groups tried to imitate the unified smoothness of the British style, what became known as the Liverpool or Mersey sound. Of the English groups only the Rolling Stones offered a consistent challenge to the Beatles. Musically, the Stones were strongly loyal to the black rhythm and blues tradition, while alienation from society emerged as a pervasive subject in their lyrics. Mick Jagger, who as lead vocalist more or less set the image for the group, emphasized a rough and sensuous style of singing and, unlike the Beatles, an aloofness from the public. "Satisfaction" became a hit during the summer of 1965, holding the number one spot for a month. Later that year "Get Off My Cloud" provided the group with another number one hit, while "Mother's Little Helper" and "Nineteenth Nervous Breakdown" were both antiestablishment songs in a nonpolitical way. Often the Rolling Stones lashed out in blind rage at the adult world and what they considered plastic values.

Native to America was the surfer scene, which by 1965 had spread from southern California clear across the country, accompanied by its own music. Beginning in the early 1960s, the Beach Boys propelled the surfer sound into a national phenomenon. Consisting of three brothers, a cousin, and a local boy soprano, the Beach Boys all lived in Hawthorne, California, where they went to school and rode the waves. Drawing on the California sun cult for their personal image, the group came to symbolize all the pleasures of the beach world—casual dress, girls, surf boards, and hot rods. Their songs described this world in detail: "Fun, Fun, Fun," "Surfin' U.S.A.," "Surfer Girl," "Catch A Wave." The surfer sound was pure rock-and-roll—simple, direct, and exuberant, much like the rock around 1956. From the start the Beach Boys' style was based on recording studio techniques, requiring electronics and multiple tapes. "Good Vibrations" and "Do It Again" marked the climax of their development, and while their music remained linked to the past, it demonstrated a high quality and proved more than a passing fad.

Inspired by Bob Dylan, a number of important rock singers followed their social conscience in the mid-1960s, protesting especially against war and prejudice in lyrics that were meaningful, probing, and often poetic. Folksinger Barry McGuire's "Eve of Destruction" in 1965 damned violence, hatred, and death and suggested that mankind was on the brink of nuclear annihilation. Suddenly the old troubadour tradition seemed reborn, as young lyricists across the land became performers, singing their poetry rather than reading it. "There's something happenin' here," sang the Buffalo Springfield. "What it is ain't exactly clear. There's a man with a gun over there tellin' me I've got to beware. I think it's time we stop, children, what's that sound? Everybody look what's goin' down."

Paul Simon and Art Garfunkel consistently pursued a social consciousness in which the message was a popularized existentialism. Their favorite concerns were the loneliness, isolation, breakdown of understanding, and inability to communicate brought on by the crush of contemporary urban life. "Dangling Conversation," one of their finest lyrics, is full of images of noncommunication: "You read your Emily Dickinson, and I my Robert Frost." "I Am a Rock" and "Sounds of Silence" both dealt with the communication block in a blend of romance and realism. "Like a poem poorly written," the young musicians sang, "we are verses out of rhythm, couplets out of rhyme." Simon and Garfunkel harmonized particularly well together, in a gentle, charming manner, while their words and music were always a close marriage. Although they were critical of the times, their outlook was more positive than Dylan's. Simon and Garfunkel's songs were ironic and wistful, but usually hopeful.

Much harsher were the Mothers of Invention. Taking comic Lenny Bruce as their hero, the Mothers' approach to music and society was fierce and satirical. While they stood out as one of the seedier looking groups in the rock field, they were also among the truly skilled. Most of the folk rock groups were concerned with the war in Vietnam: "A time for peace, I swear it's not too late," the Byrds, one of the more vital and imaginative of the groups, sang. And most felt that communication, understanding, and love could save the world. "Don't you want somebody to love?" the Jefferson Airplane asked, while Bob Lind spoke of "the bright elusive butterfly of love." The Mamas and the Papas, whose intricate vocal blend gave them a sound all their own, sang of "a chance for folks to meet, there'll be laughin', singin' and music swingin', and dancin' in the street!"

After 1965 a scene developed in San Francisco that gradually affected the entire nation, signaling a return to the romantic squalor of the bohemian communities of the years surrounding World War I. By 1967 the hippie cult was in full flower in San Francisco's Haight-Ashbury district, as young people from all over the country began arriving by the truckload. Some came for just weekends, others for their vacations, while still others ran away from home and came with the idea of staying. The new youth culture condemned the duplicity, hyprocrisy, and supermaterialism of the older generation, favoring instead communal living, nonviolence, plain speaking, equality, and inner beauty. Out of the hippie movement came a harder form of rock, accompanied by drugs and psychedelic light shows.

The Grateful Dead, Country Joe and the Fish, the Door, Moby Grape, and the Grand Funk Railroad all emerged as leaders in what became known as acid rock. Each of these groups experimented with electronics, although the California sound itself had no real homogeneity except for its hippie association. There was a great deal of emphasis on mind-expanding drugs, liberation, the search for inner experiences, and sexual freedom. Rock bands poured into the San Francisco area, playing their emotion-charged music among the youth of Haight-Ashbury and Berkeley in any number of unofficial places. As live rock became one of the common bonds holding the youth movement together, San Francisco came to be called the Liverpool of the West. Although they were remarkably free from prejudice, the rock musicians migrating into Haight-Ashbury, unlike the early jazzmen, were not ashamed of being white and made little attempt to join the black culture or become part of it.

Much of the San Francisco rock became highly sophisticated. The Jefferson Airplane was the first Bay area group to gain national prominence and remained an advanced exponent of the West Coast sound, aided by the considerable talents of vocalist Grace Slick. An especially pretty girl, Grace Slick not only sang with a foghorn voice, but also wrote some exceptionally potent songs, including "White Rabbit," which propelled the group into the top ten on the popular charts. The number was one of the few hardcore drug songs to gain real popularity. A play on the *Alice in Wonderland* idea, "White Rabbit" describes several drug-induced visions and urged others to join in the fun.

Another of the San Francisco groups to achieve distinction was Big Brother and the Holding Company. With Janis Joplin as their lead singer, the group exploded nationally at the Monterey Pop Festival during the summer of 1967. When Joplin finished the last notes of Big Mama Thornton's "Ball and Chain," the stunned audience at Monterey suddenly went berserk, and the singer was big time. Although Big Brother folded in 1969, Janis Joplin went on to become perhaps the most exhilarating of the hard rock vocalists.

Raised in Port Arthur, Texas, Joplin ran away from home at seventeen to find her way as a singer. She attended the University of Texas for a while, working with several country music bands in Austin, then went to San Francisco at the height of Haight-Ashbury. She had grown up listening to Bessie Smith on records and remained a powerful exponent of the black blues, which cut right into her own tormented heart. Later she was influenced by Otis Redding and Tina Turner. Joining Big Brother and the Holding Company in 1966, she sang with forceful energy, sending out waves of nervous excitement and giving the impression she would rip her throat out with each song. Dressed in resplendent costumes, she laughed, jumped, and danced onstage, alternately clenching her fists and breaking them open to clap, her eyes and body never still. Her wild brown hair often covered her chubby face, until swept back by a hand with rings on each finger, while on her wrists were dozens of bracelets. From time to time she would pause to swig from a bottle of Southern Comfort, and she often uttered lewd comments before returning to sing "Piece of My Heart" or Gershwin's "Summertime" with an intensity that seemed to compress all her energy into a single moment. "Her voice had nuance and stretch from every shriek, moan, and shudder," Myra Friedman writes in her biography. "She pounded on through the rockers, roaring like a hopped-up carburetor about to explode in its heat."

But the singer's personal life became prey to her primitive, unbridled impulses. She drank too much and fell into periods of excruciating despondency. Gradually the liquor began to affect her voice, so that later on she sang with a rasp. Still she came on emotional and sexy, a wailing rainbow of sound. Her devotion to the exploration of the moment endeared her to the hip generation, but underneath all the commotion was a hurt, empty heart that wanted to belong. She used drugs to deaden the terror and guilt, overdosing at least six times. A heroin overdose finally killed her in October, 1970.

The same Monterey Festival that saw the coronation of Janis Joplin also brought Jimi Hendrix to prominence. Born in 1943 in Seattle, Washington, Hendrix had been influenced by rhythm and blues during his teens and spent his youth playing the guitar on the back porch and imitating the records of Muddy Waters. He left home to launch a career in music, playing the blues guitar with several rhythm and blues shows. By 1967 he had largely abandoned the blues in favor of a highly amplified acid rock. The Jimi Hendrix Experience became noted for huge gobs of chords, spiced with feedback, fuzz tone, and whatever other distortion Hendrix could muster from his guitar. He died in London two weeks before Janis Joplin, also of a heroin overdose.

One of Hendrix's most dramatic appearances was at the Woodstock Music and Art Fair in August, 1969, during which he performed his powerful version of "The Star-Spangled Banner." The three-day event in upstate New York brought together almost a half million people, who slept in the open, smoked dope, and bathed together in the nude, but otherwise behaved amazingly well. Woodstock marked the zenith of the youth culture. From that point on the hippie ghettos began to break up. What communities remained moved out to smaller cities like Boulder, Colorado, or Taos, New Mexico. Some of the young people moved to the country, exerting an influence on country rock, while others found themselves married with children and bills and the need for steady employment. But as 1969 faded into 1970, the memory of Woodstock lingered as a symbol of the youth culture and psychedelic rock.

With rare exceptions the music of the hippies was of little concern to the black, since blacks of the 1960s were faced with the task of defining their own unique culture. During the middle of the decade "soul" music became a vital expression of black society's self-conscious search for values and identity. Growing out of rhythm and blues, soul evolved into a popular style, shaped by singers like Ray Charles, James Brown, Lou Rawls, and Nina Simone. At least three different sounds entered into the makeup of soul, each resulting from a different record company located in a different city. There was the Atlantic or Harlem sound, the Memphis sound, and, most important, the Detroit or Motown sound.

The formative figure in the emergence of soul was undoubtedly Ray Charles, who became the embodiment of the soul approach long before the term came into use. Then by 1956 James Brown had appeared on the scene, offering a more primitive soul that spoke primarily to black audiences and to the very young. Gradually Brown earned the title of "The King of Soul," basically without the support of whites, who found his music funky and unrefined. White audiences much preferred the sophisticated smoothness of the Detroit sound, groups like the Four Tops and the Miracles. Popular also with whites were Booker T. and the M. G.'s and Sam and Dave, both representative of the Memphis sound, yet communicating something of the black experience.

But Motown made the biggest impact on the culturally integrated American middle class, in large part because it was polished and soft spoken, containing pleasant, if sometimes innocuous, lyrics and a firm, simple beat that was highly danceable. "It's less wild than most of the big beat music you hear today," Diana Ross, then lead vocalist with the Supremes, observed, "but it still has feeling to it. We call it sweet music." The most successful of all the Motown groups, the Supremes began singing together in high school, achieving national attention around 1964 with their recording of "Where Did Our Love Go." The original three members—Diana Ross, Florence Ballard, and Mary Wilson—all grew up in Detroit's Brewster Housing Project, within walking distance of one another. Their neighborhood, they recalled, had three things: rats, roaches, and music. Later they voiced some of the problems of the ghetto. In "Love Child," the number one record of late 1968, the Supremes sang of the shame of having been abandoned by one's father and being raised with the stigma of illegitimacy. "I'm Livin' in Shame" tells of a young girl who goes to college, marries well, and completely turns her back on the mother who wore rags and scrubbed floors to put her through school.

Under the guidance of Berry Gordy, Motown Records became a major power within the recording industry, one completely controlled by blacks. Stevie Wonder, blind from birth, proved the most gifted of the Motown artists, while Gladys Knight sang the best blues. But Marvin Gaye, the Jackson Five, Smokey Robinson, the Temptations, and Martha and the Vandellas all contributed to the Motown sound, retaining their black identity despite a large white following.

In 1965 Wilson Pickett had his first major record, "In the Midnight Hour," which placed him on the national charts. Later that year Otis Redding released the original version of "Respect," a song he had written himself. The number was soon taken over by Aretha Franklin, a former gospel singer from Detroit, who won the title of "Lady Soul." A minister's daughter, she had grown up in a large house, but the sounds and troubles of the ghetto were just minutes away. Possessing the strongest voice in the soul field, Aretha Franklin sang with emotional involvement, infinite sweep, and a chilling ferocity. In the late 1960s she headed the charts with numbers like "Chain of Fools," "See Saw," and especially "Think." Her only possible rival was Tina Turner, whose approach was sexier, while Dionne Warwick introduced soul into a basically popular repertoire.

Whereas the black soul singers dealt with defining their own culture in broadest terms, white rock artists continued their fragmentation of musical styles. Sonny and Cher grew their hair long and affected the dress of dissent, but avoided the poetry and philosophic heaviness of Bob Dylan and his followers. Commercially it was a successful format, and "I Got You Babe" became one of the biggest hits of the mid-1960s. Creedence Clearwater Revival rose to popularity in 1969, keeping hard rock alive with numbers like "Green River" and "Bad Moon Rising." Elvis Presley continued to place records on the charts; "In the Ghetto" was a hit in 1969, as "Suspicious Minds" was a short time later. Jazz rock made its appearance in bands like Blood, Sweat, and Tears, Santana, and Chicago, while Carole King and Carly Simon proved popular, yet created little more than entertainment. By 1970 rock seemed to have gone into another decline. At least there was nothing to compare with the truly great moments earlier in the decade.

Yet at the very time that rock seemed to be growing less creative as popular music, two rock operas appeared from England that added a new and ambitious dimension to rock culture. The first, *Tommy*, was recorded by the Who in 1969, written by Peter Townsend, the group's lead guitarist. The theme of the opera is alienation. Tommy is a deaf, dumb, blind boy who grows into the best pinball player in England. Playing pinball machines is the only way the boy can express himself, and in time he develops into a messianic cult hero. A year later the original recording of *Jesus Christ Superstar* was released, complete with eighty-five-piece orchestra, eleven rock singers, three choruses, additional jazz and rock musicians, and a Moog synthesizer. Composed by Andrew Lloyd Webber, with a libretto by Tim Rice, *Jesus Christ Superstar* used a variety of rhythmic forms and proved that the dramatic range of rock was enormous. Above all Webber's score is distinguished by melody. Jesus emerges from the opera doubting his own work, a man full of questions, a superstar surrounded by manipulators and exploiters. Judas is not the hazy betrayer of the New Testament, but a throbbing human being, tormented by confused emotions. The drama is full of power and feeling, while the lyrics are rich in contemporary wisdom. When Mary Magdalene sings "I Don't Know How to Love Him," the bewilderment, pain, and melancholy love she feels is exquisitely conveyed and touches deeply. While Christ is capable of vanity, his agony at Gethsemane is poignantly depicted. "I'm not as sure as when we started," Jesus announces to God, adding, "You're far too keen on where and how and not so hot on why." Both operas were eventually staged and turned into motion pictures. *Jesus Christ Superstar* was lavishly mounted on Broadway, while *Tommy* has been staged by a number of regional opera companies.

Although there have been notable exceptions, rock in the 1970s has not measured up to what was produced during the decade before. The breakup of the Beatles almost seemed to prophesy the deterioration of the whole rock movement. All four Beatles have subsequently had hits on their own, but the creative flow was no longer present. George Harrison's "My Sweet Lord" did very well early in the 1970s, and Paul McCartney had success with "My Love" a bit later, yet there was nothing to equal the creative depth of *Sergeant Pepper's Lonely Hearts Club Band*. Stevie Wonder continued with the Motown sound, producing quality songs like "You Are the Sunshine of My Life," while John Denver popularized country rock with hits like "My Sweet

Lady" and "Rocky Mountain High" and Chuck Mangione kept the jazz rock trend alive. The Carpenters won awards for their gentle versions of "We've Only Just Begun" and "Close to You," and Roberta Flack lent a touch of soul to "Killing Me Softly with His Song" and "The First Time Ever I Saw Your Face."

Kenny Loggins and Jim Messina consistently gave meaning to words in an easy rock-and-roll style, and while their approach was a bit sentimental, their ability to communicate happiness was particularly appealing. Fleetwood Mac won a wide following with a mellow rock sound, enjoying a lasting success with "Dreams." Peter Frampton's unpretentious rock-and-roll proved popular, especially "I'm in You" and his rendition of Stevie Wonder's "Signed, Sealed, Delivered." Billy Joel had a big hit in 1978 with "Just the Way You Are," almost a throwback to the old Tin Pan Alley days. Joel was from a middle class, suburban background, and his premium was clearly on melody and form, sometimes at the expense of emotion and rhythmic force. Gino Vannelli also preferred an easy, jazzlike approach, placing "I Just Wanna Stop" high on the popular charts. Vannelli's delivery was passionate enough that he was considered by many a white singer with soul. Of the women Linda Ronstadt proved the best of the soft rock vocalists, with an almost country rock style.

Led by David Bowie, glitter rock became a trend midway through the decade—so-called because of the almost effeminate dress and heavy use of eye make-up. Alice Cooper went in for a wilder kind of attire and added a comic grotesqueness to hard rock. Cooper assumed the stance of the last great juvenile delinquent, seemed to care little about either competent musicianship or good taste, and appeared to advocate anarchy. Later there was funk rock, groups like the Freedom Machine, and toward the end of the decade punk rock, bands like the Cars, ACDC, the Sex Pistols, the Clash, Kiss, and Cheap Trick.

Reminiscent of the 1950s idea of rebellion, the punk rock groups delighted in bad taste and vulgarity. Kiss, for example, indulged in blood spitting, platform shoes, wild make-up, and references to grimy sex. The Sex Pistols purposely set out to shock audiences by being sick onstage, sticking pins in their noses, and engaging in other forms of self-multilation. The Clash, the most intellectual and political of the New Wave bands, produced perhaps the fiercest, most challenging sounds in current rock, communicating kinetic, imperative anger more violently than any other group. From England, the Clash spoke for a generation of working class kids cut off from the social mainstream and disaffected from the cushy sound of most contemporary rock.

Basically the 1970s proved a time of sentimental escapism, and disco music fit this general mood with the thumping regularity of its beat and the silly, partying attitude of most of its songs. By the mid-1960s the discotheque, a nightclub where patrons danced to records, had replaced the cocktail lounge and the jazz club for teenagers and young adults. Amid a melange of vibrating colors, blinding strobe lights, and deafening music, young people danced until closing time, then often moving to an afterhours club so that the frenzy could continue. By the mid-1970s a distinct disco sound had been identified, characterized by high, piping voices that could be heard through the dense synthesizer or string texture of the disco songs and made a giddy contrast to the highly boosted, bass-oriented rhythm of the records. Despite the fact that disco trends were often set in homosexual clubs, most of the disco stars were women. Thelma Houston, who emerged from the Motown tradition, had a big disco hit with "Don't Leave Me This Way," while Gloria Gaynor won success with "I Will Survive." But it was Donna Summer who became the queen of the disco singers, going a long way toward satisfying male fantasies with the eroticism of such numbers as "Love to Love You, Baby." Possessing a large, strong voice, Summer was heard to good advantage in "Last Dance" and the ambitious "MacArthur Park Suite," yet on other songs, like "I Feel Love," it was the production work more than the singer's voice that captured the attention.

Not all of the disco singers were women. Notable exceptions were K. C. and the Sunshine Band, who had big hits with "Shake Your Booty," "Keep It Comin' Love," and "I'm Your Boogie Man," and more recently the Village People, who gained attention with "Macho Man" and "Y.M.C.A." Disco reached its height, however, with the John Travolta movie *Saturday Night Fever*, and the Bee Gees, who supplied most of the music for the film, were suddenly catapulted back to fame, enjoying tremendous hits with "Stayin' Alive," "How Deep Is Your Love," "Night Fever," "You Should Be Dancing," and "More Than a Woman." Yet the Bee Gees and many of the other male disco singers made heavy use of falsetto, which added up to males imitating females.

Like jazz, rock has gone through its creative periods and its flabby periods, but it has dominated American popular music for over two decades, proving flexible enough to grow and change with the times. Along the way it has become a truly international expression, since current rock hits can now be heard in metropolitan discos around the world. Consistent with an impersonal, computerized society, rock artists have come to rely on magnetic tape, echo chambers, variable speeds, and electronics to produce their explosion of sound. If some of the rock songs seem like frivolous nonsense, others possess genuine beauty. After all, even the age of Gershwin, Kern, Berlin, and Porter produced its "Hut Sut Song," "Three Little Fishes," and "Mairzy Doats." And while the generation that was young during the big band era remembers that music with nostalgia, most of the big band tunes were as trivial as any batch of current rock hits. The bulk of the popular music of any generation is soon forgotten, leaving behind either the best songs or those most typical of a given era. Even the worst songs reflect basic values of the generation that made them popular and serve to document attitudes of a particular moment in history. Like it or not, the overdubs and electronic reverberations of today's disco sounds are as revealing about contemporary life in the United States as the psalms were about colonial Puritanism or the patriotic tunes were about young America. Stephen Foster eased the tensions of urban dwellers before the Civil War, much as Barry Manilow soothes the nerves of residents crammed into the megapolis during the years after America's involvement in Vietnam, speaking old sentiments with new inflections.

Conglomerate living, dwindling natural resources, inflation, lack of leadership, and spiritual inertia all portend an uneasy future, one that America's music is certain to reflect, even when it helps us escape the problems that worry us. But while American music will change to satisfy new tastes and keep pace with new vogues, our musical heritage remains for the world to share, comforting us in the face of uncertainty, giving us identity as we move ahead, reminding us of our national past, and evoking images from our individual lives—times when we were happy, times when we were sad, times vivid enough for us to remember and know that we were alive.

BIBLIOGRAPHICAL NOTES

CHAPTER I. SYMPHONY ORCHESTRAS, CONCERT LIFE, AND A DEMOCRATIC SOCIETY

As a comprehensive study, John H. Mueller, *The American Symphony Orchestra: A Social History of Musical Taste* (Bloomington, Ind., 1951), is excellent. Other valuable general works include David Ewen, *Music Comes to America* (New York, 1947), and Cecil Smith, *Worlds of Music* (Philadelphia, 1952), while Quaintance Eaton (ed.), *Musical U.S.A.* (New York, 1949), offers brief historical summaries for each major city. Significant data may also be found in Harold C. Schonberg, *The Great Conductors* (New York, 1967); Hope Stoddard, *Symphony Conductors of the USA* (New York, 1957); and David Ewen, *The Man with the Baton* (New York, 1936).

Jacques Barzun, *Music in American Life* (Bloomington, Ind., 1956), and Roger Sessions, *Reflections on the Music Life in the United States* (New York, 1956), both take broad interpretative approaches, while Paul S. Carpenter, *Music: An Art and a Business* (Norman, Okla., 1950), is especially important in its analysis of the commercial aspects of the art. William J. Baumol and William G. Bowen, *Performing Arts—the Economic Dilemma* (New York, 1966), and a Rockefeller Panel Report entitled *The Performing Arts: Problems and Prospects* (New York, 1965) point out the economic situation facing the arts in contemporary America, and Alan Rich discusses the music business as it affects the young artist in *Careers and Opportunities in Music* (New York, 1964). Frederick P. Keppel and R. L. Duffus, *The Arts in American Life* (New York, 1933), is an interesting survey, containing a chapter on music and dance.

Herbert Kupferberg, *Those Fabulous Philadelphians: The Life and Times of a Great Orchestra* (New York, 1969), is a readable, solid account, while Edward Arian, *Bach, Beethoven, and Bureaucracy: The Case of the Philadelphia Orchestra* (University, Ala., 1971), is a penetrating look at the economic and administrative difficulties that harass a major orchestra. Robert C. Marsh's *The Cleveland Orchestra* (Cleveland, 1967), John K. Sherman's *Music and Maestros: The Story of the Minneapolis Symphony Orchestra* (Minneapolis, 1952), and Hubert Roussel, *The Houston Symphony Orchestra, 1913-1917* (Austin, 1972) are all capital, whereas John Erskine's *The Philharmonic-Symphony Society of New York* (New York, 1943) is thin and dated. Fortunately that story is adequately brought up to date by Howard Shanet in *Philharmonic: A History of New York's Orchestra* (Garden City, N.Y., 1975). Much regarding concert life in New York may be gleaned from Ethel Peyser, *The House That Music Built—Carnegie Hall* (New York, 1936), and Richard Schickel, *The World of Carnegie Hall* (New York, 1960). H. Earle Johnson, *Symphony Hall, Boston* (Boston, 1950), contains a great deal on the Boston Symphony Orchestra, and the early Berkshire Music Festivals are recounted by M.A. DeWolfe Howe in *The Tale of Tanglewood* (New York, 1946). A detailed account is William Barry Furlong's *Season with Solti* (New York, 1974), which probes the Chicago Orchestra.

Brief, yet well worth consulting is John K. Sherman, *Music and Theater in Minnesota History* (Minneapolis, 1958). More complete is Howard Swan, *Music in the Southwest, 1825-1950* (San Marino, Calif., 1952). Lota M. Spell, *Music in Texas* (Austin, 1936), remains a fine local history, while Mint O. James-Reed, *Music in Austin, 1900-1956* (Austin, 1957), serves as a case study for the cultural life of a smaller inland city. Scattered data will be found in E. Clyde Whitlock and Richard Drake Saunders (eds.), *Music and Dance in Texas, Oklahoma and the Southwest* (Hollywood, Calif., 1950); Herbert Elwell, "Metamorphoses in the Grass Roots, 1940-1955," *Musical Courier*, CLI (February 1, 1955), 50-53, although short, provides relevant information.

Moses Smith, *Koussevitzky* (New York, 1947), has been controversial, but is definitely worth examining. Hugo Leichtentritt, *Serge Koussevitzky: The Boston Symphony Orchestra and the New American Music* (Cambridge, Mass., 1947), and Aaron Copland, "Serge Koussevitzky and the American Composer," *The Musical Quarterly*, XXX (July, 1944), 255-269, are both excellent. Ranking high among the Toscanini portraits are Howard Taubman, *The Maestro: The Life of Arturo Toscanini* (New York, 1951); Samuel Chotzinoff, *Toscanini: An Intimate Portrait* (New York, 1956); David Ewen, *The Story of Arturo Toscanini* (New York, 1951); George R. Marek, *Toscanini* (New York, 1975); and Robert C. Marsh, *Toscanini and the Art of Orchestral Performance* (Philadelphia, 1956). John Briggs, *Leonard Bernstein: The Man, His Work, and His World* (Cleveland, 1961), is the most rounded look at that musical phenomenon, although young readers will enjoy David Ewen, *Leonard Bernstein* (Philadelphia, 1960). Mark A. Schubart, "Triple-Note Man of the Music World," *New York Times Magazine* (January 28, 1945), 18 and 39, illustrates Bernstein's early acclaim. On Pierre Monteux, Doris G. Monteux's *It's All in the Music* (New York, 1965) is interesting, as is Bruno Walter's autobiography, *Theme and Variations* (New York, 1946). Helpful and entertaining is Charles Reid, *Thomas Beecham: An Independent Biography* (New York, 1962). A number of biographical sketches are included in Charles O'Connell, *The Other Side of the Record* (New York, 1947), while Claire R. Reis, *Composers, Conductors, and Critics* (New York, 1955), will supply random information.

Abram Chasins' *Speaking of Pianists* (New York, 1961), contains biographical material on several artists, whereas *The Van Cliburn Legend*

(Garden City, N.Y., 1959), by the same author, deals with a contemporary sensation. The careers of other concert performers are related in Louis P. Lochner, *Fritz Kreisler* (New York, 1951); Robert Magidoff, *Yehudi Menuhin: The Story of the Man and the Musician* (Garden City, N.Y., 1955); Artur Schnabel, *My Life and Music* (New York, 1963); and Joseph Szigeti's reminiscences, *With Strings Attached* (New York, 1967). Charles Seeger, "Music and Class Structure in the United States," *American Quarterly,* IX (Fall, 1957), 281-294, and Stuart Levine, "Some Observations on the Concert Audience," *American Quarterly,* XV (Summer, 1963), 152-166, are both important, while Ray Ellsworth, "The Concert Scene of the Twenties," *HiFi/ Stereo Review,* XV (October, 1965), 53-58, is highly entertaining. Although mainly on dance, S. Hurok's memoir, *Impresario* (New York, 1946), in collaboration with Ruth Goode, adds an essential dimension to the story of the nation's concert life. More general are Alvin Toffler, *The Culture Consumers* (New York, 1964), and Vineta Colby (ed.), *American Culture in the Sixties* (New York, 1964).

Erich Leinsdorf, *Cadenza: A Musical Career* (Boston, 1976), and Halina Rodzinski, *Our Two Lives* (New York, 1976), are among the newer autobiographies, while H. L. Kirk, *Pablo Casals* (New York, 1974), is a definitive portrait. William F. McDonald, *Federal Relief Administration and the Arts* (Columbus, Ohio, 1969), is an exhaustive probing of the New Deal efforts to stimulate the arts, while Ashley Pettis, "The WPA and the American Composer," *The Musical Quarterly,* XXVI (Jan., 1940), 101-112, is more specialized and lacks the benefit of perspective. An attempted summary of a fairly complex subject is Thomas Johnson, "American Orchestras and American Music," *American Composers Alliance Bulletin,* II (June, 1963), 2-4.

CHAPTER II. THE DIFFUSION OF GRAND OPERA

Irving Kolodin's *The Metropolitan Opera, 1883-1966* (New York, 1966) is still the definitive study, although John Briggs' *Requiem for a Yellow Brick Brewery* (Boston, 1969) is a more readable record and Quaintance Eaton's *The Miracle of the Met* (New York, 1968) is an interesting informal account. More recent developments are chronicled in Stephen E. Rubin, *The New Met in Profile* (New York, 1972). Of the pictorial histories of the Metropolitan, *The Golden Horseshoe,* compiled by the editors of *Opera News,* is the most lavish; however, Mary Ellis Peltz's *The Magic of the Opera* (New York, 1960) is a more intimate picture memoir. A fascinating glimpse behind the scenes may be found in Helen Noble, *Life with the Met* (New York, 1954). Quaintance Eaton, *Opera Caravan* (New York, 1957), chronicles the Metropolitan on tour, 1883-1956.

Edward C. Moore, *Forty Years of Opera in Chicago* (New York, 1930), is a personalized record, written by the longtime critic for the Chicago *Tribune*, while Ronald L. Davis, *Opera in Chicago: A Social and Cultural History, 1850-1965* (New York, 1966), is a more recent effort. Claudia Cassidy, *Lyric Opera of Chicago* (Chicago, 1979), is a fascinating commemoration of the Lyric's first twenty-five years. Arthur J. Bloomfield, *The San Francisco Opera, 1923-1961* (New York, 1961), is a solid critical analysis, and the Works Progress Administration's two-part *History of Opera in San Francisco* (San Francisco, 1939) contains a wealth of material. Sections on Chicago, San Francisco, Dallas, Santa Fe, Central City, New Orleans, and San Antonio may be found in Ronald L. Davis, *A History of Opera in the American West* (Englewood Cliffs, N.J., 1965).

A superlative general volume is Mary Jane Matz, *Opera: Grand and Not So Grand* (New York, 1966). Thomas Matthews, *The Splendid Art: A History of the Opera* (London, 1970), includes interesting tidbits on the American scene, while Robert Lawrence, *A Rage for Opera* (New York, 1971), has some valuable observations on recent developments. Worth consulting for random data are David Ewen, *Music Comes to America* (New York, 1947), and Quaintance Eaton (ed.), *Musical U.S.A.* (New York, 1949). An important reference source is Julius Mattfeld, *A Handbook of American Operatic Premieres, 1731-1962* (Detroit, 1963). Although clearly outmoded, H. W. Heinsheimer, "Opera in America Today," *The Musical Quarterly*, XXXVII (July, 1951), 315-329, still merits looking at, but Ray Ellsworth, "The 1,950 Operas America Forgot," *HiFi Stereo*, XIII (October, 1964), 95-99, is more interesting than informative.

Herbert Graf's *Producing Opera for America* (Zurich, 1961), *Opera for the People* (Minneapolis, 1951), and *The Opera and Its Future in America* (New York, 1941) are all excellent. The economic problems surrounding the production of grand opera in the United States are discussed in the Rockefeller Panel Report, *The Performing Arts: Problems and Prospects* (New York, 1965), and William J. Baumol and William G. Bowen, *Performing Arts—the Economic Dilemma* (New York, 1966), and summarized by Ronald L. Davis in "The Glorious Pauper: the Financing of America's Opera," *Arts in Society*, III (Fall, 1964), 25-31.

Giulio Gatti-Casazza's *Memories of the Opera* (New York, 1941) offers useful insights, while the reminiscences of Rudolf Bing, *5000 Nights at the Opera* (Garden City, N.Y., 1972), are both prickly and discerning. Among the best of the singers' memoirs are Mary Garden and Louis Biancolli, *Mary Garden's Story* (New York, 1951); Grace Moore, *You're Only Human Once* (Garden City, N.Y., 1944); Lotte Lehmann, *My Many Lives* (New York, 1948); Marjorie Lawrence, *Interrupted Melody* (New York, 1949); Marian Anderson, *My Lord, What a Morning* (New York, 1956); James McCracken and Sandra Warfield, *A Star in the Family* (New York, 1971); and Robert Merrill's remarkably honest, highly introspective *Once More from the Beginning* (New York, 1965), written with Sandford Dody. Key biographies include

Edwin McArthur's *Flagstad* (New York, 1965), Kyle Crichton's *Subway to the Met: Rise Stevens' Story* (Garden City, N.Y., 1959), George Jellinek's *Callas: Portrait of a Prima Donna* (New York, 1960), Kenn Harris, *Renata Tebaldi* (New York, 1974), and Russell Braddon's *Joan Sutherland* (New York, 1962). Henry Wisneski, *Maria Callas: The Art Behind the Legend* (Garden City, N.Y., 1975), and especially John Ardoin and Gerald Fitzgerald, *Callas* (New York, 1974), are strong photographic studies.

Recent information in this chapter was gleaned from contemporary music journals, especially the Metropolitan Opera Guild's *Opera News*.

CHAPTER III. BALLET AND MODERN DANCE

The most readable, balanced survey of serious dance in the United States is Walter Terry, *The Dance in America* (New York, 1956), although Olga Maynard, *The American Ballet* (Philadelphia, 1959), and George Amberg, *Ballet in America* (New York, 1949), are both useful. John Martin, *America Dancing* (New York, 1936), is an early study of the background and personalities of modern dance, by one of America's first dance critics. *John Martin's Book of the Dance* (New York, 1963) is worth examining, while his *The Dance* (New York, 1946) includes pictures and text. Important information may be gleaned from Margaret Lloyd, *The Borzoi Book of Modern Dance* (New York, 1949); *Merle Armitage Dance Memoranda* (New York, 1946), edited by Edwin Corle; Paul Magriel (ed.), *Chronicles of the American Dance* (New York, 1948); Walter Sorell (ed.), *The Dance Has Many Faces* (Cleveland, 1951), a collection of writings by dancers; and Irving Deakin, *At the Ballet* (Toronto, 1956).

Arnold L. Haskell, *Ballet Russe: The Age of Diaghilev* (London, 1968), deals mostly with Europe and an earlier period, but serves as a good preface to recent developments. Anatole Chujoy, *The New York City Ballet* (New York, 1953), is heavy on detail, while Lincoln Kirstein, *The New York City Ballet* (New York, 1973) contains marvelous photographs. Mary Clarke, *The Sadlers' Wells Ballet* (New York, 1955), is an interesting look at the major English company, including its American tours. Individual dancers are treated in Lillian Moore, *Artists of the Dance* (New York, 1938), Walter Terry, *Star Performance* (Garden City, N.Y., 1954), and Olga Maynard, *American Modern Dancers: The Pioneers* (Boston, 1965). Ted Shawn provides a terse account of the years 1927-1959 in *Thirty-three Years of American Dance* (Pittsfield, Mass., 1959). Merle Armitage (ed.), *Martha Graham* (New York, 1966), is essential, while LeRoy Leatherman's *Martha Graham* (New York, 1966), contains gorgeous photographs by Martha Swope. Excellent are Walter Sorell, *Hanya Holm: The Biography of an Artist* (Middletown,

Conn., 1969), and Selma Jeanne Cohen, *Doris Humphrey: An Artist First* (Middletown, Conn., 1972). Biographies of ballerinas include A. E. Twysden, *Alexandra Danilova* (New York, 1947), and Anton Dolin, *Alicia Markova: Her Life and Art* (New York, 1953). *Nureyev* (New York, 1963) is an engaging autobiography with pictures, while John Percival, *Nureyev: Aspects of the Dancer* (New York, 1975) is a more recent treatment.

Agnes De Mille has written several important books, the most autobiographical of which is *Dance to the Piper* (Boston, 1951). *The Book of the Dance* (New York, 1963) offers a great deal of historical information, while *To a Young Dancer* (Boston, 1960) is a handbook. Also of interest is De Mille's *And Promenade Home* (Boston, 1956). S. Hurok's *S. Hurok Presents* (New York, 1953) is a significant memoir of the dance world, although his earlier volume, *Impresario* (New York, 1946), written in collaboration with Ruth Goode, is worth consulting. Essential is Bernard Taper, *Balanchine (New York, 1963)*.

Ruth Anderson Radir, Modern Dance for the Youth of America (New York, 1944), a text for high school and college teachers, suggests some of the early methods in dance education, while the Rockefeller Panel Report, *The Performing Arts: Problems and Prospects* (New York, 1965) discusses recent financial problems. Contemporary material has been drawn from assorted periodicals, the foremost of which is *Dance Magazine*.

CHAPTER IV. TRADITIONAL COMPOSERS

General works of merit on recent American art music include John Tasker Howard, *Our Contemporary Composers* (New York, 1941), Claire R. Reis, *Composers in America* (New York, 1947), David Ewen, *American Composers Today* (New York, 1949), Madeleine Goss, *Modern Music-Makers* (New York, 1952), Aaron Copland, *The New Music, 1900-1960* (New York, 1968), and Nicolas Slonimsky's more comprehensive *Music since 1900* (4th ed., New York, 1971). Particularly valuable is Benjamin Boretz and Edward T. Cone (eds.), *Perspectives on American Composers* (New York, 1971). Still significant is Henry Cowell (ed.), *American Composers on American Music* (Palo Alto, Calif., 1933), as is Gilbert Chase's updated version, *The American Composer Speaks* (Baton Rouge, La., 1966). An occasional insight may be gained from Harold Morris, *Contemporary American Music* (Houston, Texas, 1934), a pamphlet published by Rice Institute, while David Ewen's *Composers since 1900: A Biographical and Critical Guide* (New York, 1969) serves as a useful reference tool.

Although badly out of date, John T. Howard's *Deems Taylor* (New York, 1927) remains the most complete study of that composer-critic. An interesting chapter on Taylor may be found in Katherine Little Bakeless, *Story-Lives of American Composers* (New York, 1941). Burnet C. Tuthill,

"Howard Hanson," *Musical Quarterly*, XXII (April, 1936), 140-153; Martha Alter, "Howard Hanson," *Modern Music*, XVIII (March-April, 1943), 84-89; Robert Wykes, "Howard Hanson: 25 Years of Progress," *Musical America*, LXX (April, 1950), 37 and 50; and Patricia Ashley, "Howard Hanson," *HiFi/Stereo Review*, XXII (June, 1968), 47-55, are all worth consulting. Glimpses into Hanson's own views on contemporary American music may be gleaned from his "A Forward Look in American Composition," *Papers and Proceedings of the Music Teachers' National Association* (Hartford, Conn., 1926), and *Music in Contemporary American Civilization* (Lincoln, Neb., 1951). Hanson discusses his Eastman School of Music colleague in "Bernard Rogers," *Modern Music*, XXII (March-April, 1945), 170-175, but David Diamond, "Bernard Rogers," *Musical Quarterly*, XXXIII (April, 1947), 207-227, is a fuller treatment. Important background information is provided in Charles Riker's *The Eastman School of Music: Its First Quarter Century, 1921-1946* (Rochester, N.Y., 1948).

Essential are Israel Citkowitz, "Walter Piston, Classicist," *Modern Music*, XIII (Jan.-Feb., 1936), 3-11; Elliott Carter, "Walter Piston," *Musical Quarterly*, XXXII (July, 1946), 354-375; and Klaus George Roy, "Walter Piston," *Stereo Review*, XXIV (April, 1970), 57-67. Burnet C. Tuthill, "Leo Sowerby," *Musical Quarterly*, XXIV (July, 1938), 249-264, is still the major article on that composer. Nathan Broder, *Samuel Barber* (New York, 1954), offers solid analysis, supplemented by Broder's "The Music of Samuel Barber," *Musical Quarterly*, XXXIV (July, 1948), 325-335. Also helpful are Robert Horan, "Samuel Barber," *Modern Music*, XX (March-April, 1943), 161-169, and especially Eric Salzman, "Samuel Barber," *HiFi/Stereo Review*, XVII (October, 1966), 77-89. Bernard Stambler, "Robert Ward," *American Composers Alliance Bulletin*, IV (1955), 3-6, is a concise picture. Superb is Richard Franko Goldman, "The Music of Elliott Carter," *Musical Quarterly*, XLIII (April, 1957), 151-170, while Abraham Skulsky, "Elliott Carter," *American Composers Alliance Bulletin*, III (1953), 2-16, and Martin Boykan, "Elliott Carter and the Postwar Composers," *Perspectives of New Music*, II (1964), 125-128, contain pertinent observations. An interesting conversation with Elliott Carter has been published by Allen Edwards as *Flawed Words and Stubborn Sounds* (New York, 1971).

The most up-to-date material discussed in this chapter has been drawn from current periodicals, particularly *Saturday Review*, the *New Yorker*, *Theatre Arts*, and *Time* magazine.

CHAPTER V. COPLAND AND GERSHWIN

The two major biographies of Aaron Copland are Arthur Berger's *Aaron Copland* (New York, 1953) and Julia Smith's *Aaron Copland* (New York, 1955). The composer's autobiography in his *The New Music, 1900-1960* (New

York, 1968) is also important, as is the interview with Copland in Benjamin Boretz and Edward T. Cone, *Perspectives on American Composers* (New York, 1971). Valuable are Richard Franko Goldman, "Aaron Copland," *Musical Quarterly*, XLVII (Jan., 1961), 1-3; Arthur V. Berger, "The Music of Aaron Copland," *Musical Quarterly*, XXXI (Oct., 1945), 420-447; Frederick W. Sternfeld, "Copland as a Film Composer," *Musical Quarterly*, XXXVII (April, 1951), 161-175; and William Flanagan, "Aaron Copland," *HiFi/Stereo Review*, XVI (June, 1966), 43-54. Young readers will enjoy A. Dobrin, *Aaron Copland: His Life and Times* (New York, 1967).

Edward Burlingame Hill, "Copland's Jazz Concerto in Boston," *Modern Music*, IV (May-June, 1927), 35-37, and John Kirkpatrick, "Aaron Copland's Piano Sonata," *Modern Music*, XIX (May-June, 1942), 246-250, analyze specific compositions. A concise treatment of Copland may be found in Madeleine Goss, *Modern Music-Makers* (New York, 1952), while Virgil Thomson's "Aaron Copland," *Modern Music*, IX (Jan.-Feb., 1932), 67-73, is badly dated. Glimpses of the composer in more recent times may be gathered from Eric Salzman, "Dean of Our Composers at 60," *New York Times Magazine* (November 13, 1960), 51, 61, 63, 64, 66, 68; Lester Trimble, "Profile at 60," *Musical America*, LXXX (November, 1960), 13, 36, 73; "Copland Now," *Harper's Magazine*, CCXXII (April, 1961), 109-112; "American in London," *Newsweek*, LXIII (June 8, 1964), 88-89; John M. Conly, "Aaron Copland Looks Ahead," *The Reporter*, XXXIII (August 12, 1965), 54-56; and Robert Evett, "The Brooklyn Eagle," *Atlantic Monthly*, CCXXIV (Oct., 1969), 135-136. Well worth looking at is Copland's *Music and Imagination* (Cambridge, Mass., 1952), his Charles Eliot Norton lectures in published form.

The fullest portraits of George Gershwin are David Ewen, *A Journey to Greatness: The Life and Music of George Gershwin* (New York, 1956), and Robert Payne, *Gershwin* (London, 1960). More recent treatments include Charles Schwartz, *Gershwin: His Life and Music* (Indianapolis, 1973), and Robert Kimball and Alfred Simon, *The Gershwins* (New York, 1973). Shorter and less balanced accounts include Edward Jablonski, "George Gershwin," *HiFi/Stereo Review*, XVIII (May, 1967), 49-61; Isaac Goldberg, *George Gershwin: A Study in American Music* (New York, 1931); Edward Jablonski and Lawrence D. Stewart, *The Gershwin Years* (Garden City, N.Y., 1958); Merle Armitage (ed.), *George Gershwin* (New York, 1938); and Merle Armitage, *George Gershwin: Man and Legend* (New York, 1958). Highly significant are Vernon Duke, "Gershwin, Schillinger, and Dukelsky: Some Reminiscences," *Musical Quarterly*, XXXIII (Jan., 1947), 102-115, and Frank C. Campbell, "The Musical Scores of George Gershwin," *Library of Congress Quarterly Journal of Current Acquisitions*, XI (May, 1954), 127-139. Young readers will find David Ewen's *The Story of George Gershwin* (New York, 1943) interesting.

A chapter in Leonard Bernstein's *The Joy of Music* (New York, 1959), entitled "Why Don't You Run Upstairs and Write A Nice Gershwin Tune?"

is both entertaining and informative. Invaluable insights into Gershwin may be found in Oscar Levant's books, *A Smattering of Ignorance* (Garden City, N.Y., 1942) and *The Memoirs of an Amnesiac* (New York, 1965), while Henry W. Levinger's interview with Eva Gauthier, "The Roaring Twenties," *Musical Courier*, CLI (February 1, 1955), 42-44, contains a few consequential remarks. Outdated and therefore of limited use are Virgil Thomson, "George Gershwin," *Modern Music*, XIII (Nov.-Dec., 1935), 13-19, and Frederick Jacobi, "The Future of Gershwin," *Modern Music*, XV (Nov.-Dec., 1937), 3-7.

Wilfrid Mellers, *Music in a New Found Land* (New York, 1965), contains a thought provoking discussion of both Copland and Gershwin, and the author's interpretation of *Porgy and Bess* is particularly strong. Sketches of the two composers are included in Katherine Little Bakeless, *Story-Lives of American Composers* (New York, 1941), and John Tasker Howard, *Our Contemporary Composers* (New York, 1941). Excerpts from their own writing number among the selections in Henry Cowell (ed.), *American Composers on American Music* (Palo Alto, Calif., 1933), and Gilbert Chase (ed.), *The American Composer Speaks* (Baton Rouge, La., 1966).

CHAPTER VI. AMERICAN SCENE COMPOSERS

The major published sources on Virgil Thomson are Kathleen Hoover and John Cage, *Virgil Thomson: His Life and Music* (New York, 1959), and the composer's own *Virgil Thomson* (New York, 1967). Significant also are Harold C. Schonberg, "Virgil Thomson: Parisian from Missouri," *HiFi/Stereo Review*, XIV (May, 1965), 43-56; Eugene Cook, "Virgil Thomson: The Composer in Person," *HiFi/Stereo Review*, XIV (May, 1965), 58-61; Peggy Glanville-Hicks, "Virgil Thomson," *Musical Quarterly*, XXV (April, 1949), 209-225; and Samuel L. M. Barlow, "Virgil Thomson," *Modern Music*, XVIII (May-June, 1941), 242-249. The musician's own outlook on the contemporary music scene may be found in " Music in the 1950s," *Harper's Magazine*, CCXXI (Nov., 1960), 59-63, and "America's Musical Maturity: A Twentieth-Century Story," *Yale Review*, LI (Autumn, 1961), 66-74.

Important articles on Roy Harris include Patricia Ashley, "Roy Harris," *Stereo Review*, XXI (December, 1968), 63-73; Nicolas Slonimsky, "Roy Harris," *Musical Quarterly*, XXXIII (Jan., 1947), 17-37; Walter Piston, "Roy Harris," *Modern Music*, XI (Jan.-Feb., 1934), 73-83; and Arthur Farwell, "Roy Harris," *Musical Quarterly*, XVIII (Jan., 1932), 18-32. Robert Bartlett Haas (ed.), *William Grant Still and the Fusion of Cultures in American Music* (Los Angeles, 1972), is excellent, while *William Grant Still* (New York, 1939) by Verna Arvey, the composer's wife, has the advantages and disadvantages of proximity. Joan Peyser's "The Troubled Time of Marc

Blitzstein," *Columbia University Forum*, IX (Winter, 1966), 32-37, despite its brevity, is extremely useful. Jane DeHart Mathews, *The Federal Theatre, 1935-1939: Plays, Relief, and Politics* (Princeton, N.J., 1967), contains an interesting discussion of the original presentation of *The Cradle Will Rock*, whereas Blitzstein himself expresses some general opinions on the direction of serious music in "Towards a New Form," *Musical Quarterly*, XX (April, 1934), 213-218. Otto Luening, "Douglas Moore," *Modern Music*, XX (May-June, 1943), 248-253, remains among the better items on that composer.

Sketches of one or more of the American Scene composers are available in John Tasker Howard, *Our Contemporary Composers* (New York, 1941); Katherine Little Bakeless, *Story-Lives of American Composers* (New York, 1941); Claire R. Reis, *Composers in America* (New York, 1947); David Ewen, *American Composers Today* (New York, 1949); Madeleine Goss, *Modern Music-Makers* (New York, 1952); Aaron Copland, *The New Music, 1900-1960* (New York, 1968); and Virgil Thomson, *American Music since 1910* (New York, 1970), including a chapter by Victor Fell Yellin on "The Operas of Virgil Thomson." Writings by the musicians themselves are represented in Henry Cowell (ed.), *American Composers on American Music* (Palo Alto, Calif., 1933), Gilbert Chase (ed.), *The American Composer Speaks* (Baton Rouge, La., 1966), and Elliott Schwartz and Barney Childs (eds.), *Contemporary Composers on Contemporary Music* (New York, 1967).

CHAPTER VII. THE MODERNISTS

Much of the material on Ernest Bloch suffers from age, but among the better printed sources are Roger Sessions, "Ernest Bloch," *Modern Music*, V (Nov.-Dec., 1927), 3-11, and Guido M. Gatti, "Ernest Bloch," *Musical Quarterly*, VII (Jan., 1921), 20-38. Paul Rosenfeld includes an analysis of individual pieces by the composer in *Musical Portraits* (New York, 1920) and *Musical Chronicle* (New York, 1923). The information on Louis Gruenberg is also dated; A. Walter Kramer, "Louis Gruenberg," *Modern Music*, VIII (Nov.-Dec., 1930), 3-9, heads the better articles. The musician explains some of his own views in "For an American Gesture," *Modern Music*, I (June, 1924), 26-28. William S. Newman, "Arthur Shepherd," *Musical Quarterly*, XXXVI (April, 1950), 159-179, is excellent, while Denoe Leedy, "Arthur Shepherd," *Modern Music*, XVI (Jan.-Feb., 1939), 87-93, is only fair.

Published material on Roger Sessions is more abundant. Probably the finest article on him is Mark A. Schubart, "Roger Sessions: Portrait of an American Composer," *Musical Quarterly*, XXXII (April, 1946), 196-214, although Mark Brunswick, "Roger Huntington Sessions," *Modern Music*, X (May-June, 1933), 182-187, and Roy D. Welch, "A Symphony Introduces Roger Sessions," *Modern Music*, IV (May-June, 1927), 27-30, are useful. Nicholas Slonimsky has a brief section on the musician in "Composers of New England," *Modern Music*, VII (Feb.-Mar., 1930), 24-27.

Outstanding is Elliot Forbes, "The Music of Randall Thompson," *Musical Quarterly*, XXXV (Jan., 1949), 1-25, while Quincy Porter, "Randall Thompson," *Modern Music*, XIX (May-June, 1942), 237-242, remains of value. The major item on Paul Creston is Henry Cowell, "Paul Creston," *Musical Quarterly*, XXXIV (Oct., 1948), 533-543. Edward Downes, "The Music of Norman Dello Joio," *Musical Quarterly*, XLVIII (April, 1962), 149-172, is by far the most penetrating study of that composer, but Robert Sabin, "Norman Dello Joio," *Musical America*, LXX (Dec. 1, 1950), 9, 30, sketches the subject attractively.

Flora Rheta Schreiber and Vincent Persichetti, *William Schuman* (New York, 1954), and Nathan Broder, "The Music of William Schuman," *Musical Quarterly*, XXXI (Jan., 1945), 17-28, are both superb. Also worth consulting are Alfred Frankenstein, "William Schuman," *Modern Music*, XXII (Nov.-Dec., 1944), 23-29; Ronald F. Eyer, "William Schuman," *Musical America*, LXIV (Jan. 25, 1944), 8, 25; and Leonard Bernstein, "Young American— William Schuman," *Modern Music*, XIX (Jan.-Feb., 1942), 97-99.

The fullest biography of the ubiquitous Bernstein is John Briggs, *Leonard Bernstein: The Man, His Work, and His World* (Cleveland, 1961), although juvenile and teenage readers will enjoy David Ewen, *Leonard Bernstein, A Biography for Young People* (Philadelphia, 1960). *The Private World of Leonard Bernstein* (New York, 1968) contains a text by John Gruen and engaging photographs by Ken Heyman. Oliver Daniel, "Alan Hovhaness," *American Composers Alliance Bulletin*, II (Oct., 1952), 3-7, continues as a serviceable introduction to that career.

Collective accounts of modernists may be found in Aaron Copland, *The New Music, 1900-1960* (New York, 1968), Madeleine Goss, *Modern Music-Makers* (New York, 1952), David Ewen (comp.), *American Composers Today* (New York, 1949), Claire R. Reis, *Composers in America* (New York, 1947), and John T. Howard, *Our Contemporary Composers* (New York, 1941). Benjamin Boretz and Edward T. Cone (eds.), *Perspectives on American Composers* (New York, 1971) includes a particularly strong interview with Sessions, while a number of the moderns are represented in Gilbert Chase (ed.), *The American Composer Speaks* (Baton Rouge, La., 1966) and Henry Cowell (ed.), *American Composers on American Music* (Palo Alto, Calif., 1933). Reactions to the more recent works on these musicians may be gleaned from music journals and popular periodicals like *High Fidelity*.

Chapter VIII. THE EXPERIMENTALISTS

Background for understanding the ideas of the various American avant-garde composers may be found in books like Joan Peyer's *The New Music* (New York, 1971), Peter Yates' *Twentieth Century Music* (New York, 1967), Eric Salzman's *Twentieth-Century Music: An Introduction* (Englewood Cliffs, N.J., 1967), and William W. Austin's *Music in the 20th Century* (New

York, 1966). The subject is treated fleetingly by both Virgil Thomson, *American Music since 1910* (New York, 1970), and Aaron Copland, *The New Music, 1900-1960* (New York, 1968), in each case revisions of earlier works, while individual sketches are contained in Madeleine Goss, *Modern Music-Makers* (New York, 1952), David Ewen (ed.), *American Composers Today* (New York, 1949), Claire R. Reis, *Composers in America* (New York, 1947), and John Tasker Howard, *Our Contemporary Composers* (New York, 1941). Relevant facts occasionally appear in Nicolas Slonimsky's chronicle, *Music since 1900* (New York, 1949).

Charles Seeger, "Carl Ruggles," *Musical Quarterly*, XVIII (Oct., 1932), 578-592; Lou Harrison, *About Carl Ruggles* (Yonkers, N.Y., 1946); and Eric Salzman, "Carl Ruggles," *HiFi/Stereo Review*, XVII (Sept., 1966), 53-63, are all fundamental. Richard F. Goldman, "The Music of Wallingford Riegger," *Musical Quarterly*, XXXVI (Jan., 1950), 39-61, heads the secondary material on that composer, although Goldman's "Wallingford Riegger," *HiFi/Stereo Review*, XX (April, 1968), 57-67, is a more human portrait. Worth consulting are John J. Becker, "Wallingford Riegger," *American Composers Alliance Bulletin*, IX (1960), 13-14, and Henry Cowell, "Wallingford Riegger," *Musical America*, LXVIII (December 1, 1948), 9, 29. Fernand Ouellette, *Edgard Varese* (New York, 1968), is an excellent study, well supplemented by Louise Varese's *Varese: A Looking-Glass Diary*, I (New York, 1972), covering the years 1883-1928. Eric Salzman, "Edgard Varese," *Stereo Review*, XXVI (June, 1971), 56-68, includes an interesting personal account by Frank Zappa, "Edgard Varese: Idol of My Youth," while Henry Cowell, "The Music of Edgard Varese," *Modern Music*, V (Jan., 1928), 9-17, suffers from age. Most of the information on Leo Ornstein is badly dated: Charles L. Buchanan's "Ornstein and Modern Music," *Musical Quarterly*, IV (April, 1918), 174-183; Frederick H. Martens' *Leo Ornstein* (New York, 1918); and the sections in Paul Rosenfeld's *Musical Portraits* (New York, 1920) and *Musical Chronicle* (New York, 1923).

Superlative is Hugo Weisgall, "The Music of Henry Cowell," *Musical Quarterly*, XLV (Oct., 1959), 484-507, whereas Richard Franko Goldman, "Henry Cowell (1897-1965): A Memoir and an Appreciation," *Perspectives of New Music*, IV (Spring-Summer, 1966), 23-28, is a valuable eulogy. George Antheil's autobiography, *Bad Boy of Music* (Garden City, N.Y., 1945), is fascinating—chatty, colorful, informative. Useful are Randall Thompson, "George Antheil," *Modern Music*, VIII (May-June, 1931), 17-27, and Aaron Copland, "George Antheil," *Modern Music*, II (Jan., 1925), 26-28, while Ezra Pound, *Antheil and the Treatise on Harmony* (New York, 1968, revised edition), is far more specialized.

Anyone concerned with the more recent developments in serious American music would be advised to look at Walter H. Rubsamen, "Schoenberg in America," *Musical Quarterly*, XXXVII (Oct., 1951), 468-489. Perhaps the best printed source on John Cage is Calvin Tomkins, *The Bride and the Bachelors* (New York, 1965), although Richard Kostelanetz, "The

American Avant-Garde: John Cage," *Stereo Review*, XXII (May, 1969), 61-69, and Peggy Glanville-Hicks, "John Cage," *Musical America*, LXVIII (Sept., 1948), 5, 20, have strengths. Michael Kirby and Richard Schechner, "An Interview with John Cage," *Tulane Drama Review*, X (1966), 50-72, contains insights, but Cage's own writings are an indispensable storehouse: *Silence* (Middletown, Conn., 1961), *A Year from Monday* (Middletown, Conn., 1967), and "Diary: How to Improve the World," *Paris Review*, X, No. 40, 52-68. *John Cage* (New York, 1962) is a catalog of the composer's works, assembled by Robert Dunn. Richard Kostelanetz, "The American Avant-Garde: Milton Babbitt," *Stereo Review*, XXII (April, 1969), 61-69, is a fine summary, enriched by a comparative essay by Eric Salzman, "Milton Babbitt and John Cage: Parallels and Paradoxes." Anthony Bruno, "Two American Twelve-Tone Composers," *Musical America*, LXXI (Feb., 1951), 22, 170, contrasts Babbitt and Ben Weber. One of the few articles on the latter is Frank O'Hara's "About Ben Weber," *American Composers Alliance Bulletin*, V (1955), 3-9, whereas Peter Yates' "Lou Harrison," *American Composers Alliance Bulletin*, IX (1960), 2-6, ranks among the better items on Harrison.

Elliott Schwartz and Barney Childs (eds.), *Contemporary Composers on Contemporary Music* (New York, 1967), Gilbert Chase (ed.), *The American Composer Speaks* (Baton Rouge, La., 1966), and Henry Cowell (ed.), *American Composers on American Music* (Palo Alto, Calif., 1933), all contain sections on experimentalists, while Benjamin Boretz and Edward T. Cone (eds.), *Perspectives on American Composers* (New York, 1971), is particularly strong on Varese. Harry Partch, *Genesis of a Music* (Madison, Wis, 1949) is worthwhile, and two articles by Virgil Thomson—"The Abstract Composers," *Bulletin of American Composers Alliance*, II (June, 1952), 9-10, and "America's Musical Maturity: A Twentieth-Century Story," *Yale Review*, LI (Autumn, 1961), 66-74—each distill germane thoughts.

Electronic music is dealt with in Lejaren A. Hiller, Jr. and Leonard M. Isaacson, *Experimental Music* (New York, 1959), and Otto Luening, "Some Random Remarks about Electronic Music," *Journal of Music Theory*, VIII (Spring, 1964), 89-98. Highly technical explanations of computer music are available in Harry B. Lincoln (ed.), *The Computer and Music* (Ithaca, N.Y., 1970), Max V. Mathews, *The Technology of Computer Music* (Cambridge, Mass., 1969), and Heinz Von Foerster and James W. Beauchamp (eds.), *Music by Computers* (New York, 1969).

Chapter IX. FROM MUSICAL COMEDY TO MUSICAL DRAMA

Among the more comprehensive histories of the American musical theater are Cecil Smith, *Musical Comedy in America* (New York, 1950), Stanley Green, *The World of Musical Comedy* (New York, 1960), David

Ewen, *The Story of America's Musical Theater* (Philadelphia, 1961), and
Lehman Engel, *The American Musical Theater* (New York, 1967). Brooks
Atkinson's *Broadway* (New York, 1970) contains valuable insights, while Abe
Laufe's *Broadway's Greatest Musicals* (New York, 1969) and Leonard A.
Paris' *Men and Melodies* (New York, 1959) are both useful. Wilfrid Mellers,
Music in a New Found Land (New York, 1965), includes a provocative section
on the musical stage, and Leonard Bernstein has an interesting chapter in his
book *The Joy of Music* (New York, 1959) on the evolution of the Broadway
musical. Worth consulting is Paul Kresh, "I Remember Musicals!,"
HiFi/Stereo Review, XIX (Dec., 1967), 79-86, whereas Lehman Engel's
Words with Music (New York, 1972) is an informative account from the
production standpoint. Useful as reference tools are J. Walker McSpadden,
Operas and Musical Comedies (New York, 1946), particularly on the earlier
years, and David Ewen, *Complete Book of the American Musical Theater*
(New York, 1958).

Robert Kimball and William Bolcom, *Reminiscing with Sissle and
Blake* (New York, 1973), gives a good look at some of the black revues, while
Stanley Green, *Ring Bells! Sing Songs* (New Rochelle, N.Y., 1971), focuses on
the Broadway musicals of the 1930s. Marvin E. Holderness, *Curtain Time in
Forest Park* (St. Louis, Mo., 1960), is a detailed profile of the St. Louis
Municipal Opera from its beginnings through 1958.

Katherine Little Bakeless, *Story-Lives of the American Composers* (New
York, 1941), offers sketches of Irving Berlin and Jerome Kern. A fuller portrait
is David Ewen, *The World of Jerome Kern* (New York, 1960), although young
readers will enjoy Ewen's *The Story of Irving Berlin* (New York, 1950).
Michael Freedland's *Irving Berlin* (New York, 1974) is only fair. Books on the
Gershwins include Ewen's *A Journey to Greatness: The Life and Music of
George Gershwin* (New York, 1956), Edward Jablonski and Lawrence D.
Stewart, *The Gershwin Years* (Garden City, N.Y., 1973), Charles Schwartz,
Gershwin, His Life and Music (Indianapolis, 1973), and Robert Kimball and
Alfred Simon, *The Gershwins* (New York, 1973). Among the better Cole
Porter biographies are Richard G. Hubler, *The Cole Porter Story* (Cleveland,
1965), George Eells, *The Life That Late He Led* (New York, 1967), Charles
Schwartz, *Cole Porter* (New York, 1977), and Robert Kimball and Brendan
Gill, *Cole* (New York, 1971). Vernon Duke's *Passport to Paris* (Boston, 1955
is an engaging autobiography, whereas Edward Jablonski's *Harold Arlen,
Happy with the Blues* (Garden City, N.Y., 1961) is the finest study of that
composer. David Ewen, *Richard Rodgers* (New York, 1957) is excellent, as are
Deems Taylor, *Some Enchanted Evenings: The Story of Rodgers and
Hammerstein* (New York, 1953), and Stanley Green, *The Rodgers and
Hammerstein Story* (New York, 1963). Invaluable are Samuel Marx and Jan
Clayton, *Rodgers and Hart* (New York, 1976), and especially Richard
Rodgers' autobiography, *Musical Stages* (New York, 1975). John Briggs,
Leonard Bernstein: The Man, His Work, and His World (Cleveland, 1961),
includes solid discussions of Bernstein's involvement with musical comedy,

while Howard Dietz, *Dancing in the Dark* (New York, 1974), is another choice autobiography.

Sophie Tucker's *Some of These Days* (Garden City, N.Y., 1946), Ethel Merman's *Who Could Ask for Anything More* (Garden City, N.Y., 1955), Merman's later book with George Eells, called *Merman* (N.Y., 1978), and Mary Martin's *My Heart Belongs* (N.Y., 1976) number among the major autobiographies by performers, while Richard Stoddard Aldrich recalls his wife in *Gertrude Lawrence as Mrs. A* (New York, 1954). Charles Higham's *Ziegfeld* (Chicago, 1972) is an enchanting biography, whereas Craig Zadan's *Sondheim and Company* (New York, 1974) is a pioneering study of that Broadway talent.

Material on the more recent plays has been taken from reviews in such periodicals as the *New Yorker, Saturday Review, High Fidelity*, and *Time* magazine. "Stephen Sondheim Talks to Paul Kresh about the Future of America Musical Comedy" in *Stereo Review*, XXVII (July, 1971), 73-74, is significant. The newer Sondheim musicals are treated in Arlene Croce, "Stephen Sondheim's *Follies*," *Stereo Review*, XXVII (July, 1971), 110-111, and Royal S. Brown, "*A Little Night Music*—Musical Theater at Its Finest," *High Fidelity*, XXIII (July, 1973), 70-73.

Chapter X. THE EVOLUTION OF JAZZ

The best comprehensive history of jazz is still Marshall W. Stearns, *The Story of Jazz* (New York, 1956), although Gunther Schuller, *Early Jazz: Its Roots and Musical Development* (New York, 1968), is excellent on the period of the early 1930s. Barry Ulanov, *A History of Jazz in America* (New York, 1952), and Rudi Blesh, *Shining Trumpets: A History of Jazz* (New York, 1958), are both good surveys, while Wilfrid Mellers, *Music in a New Found Land* (New York, 1965), contains several highly interpretative chapters on jazz.

Early jazz histories include Henry O. Osgood, *So This Is Jazz* (Boston, 1926); *Hot Jazz* (New York, 1936) by Frenchman Hugues Panassie; Wilder Hobson, *American Jazz Music* (New York, 1939); Winthrop Sargeant, *Jazz; A History* (New York, 1964, revised ed.); Hugues Panassie, *The Real Jazz* (New York, 1942); *Jazz from the Congo to the Metropolitan* (Garden City, N.Y., 1945) by Robert Goffin of Belgium; Dave Dexter, Jr., *Jazz Cavalcade: The Inside Story of Jazz* (New York, 1946); and Sidney Finkelstein, *Jazz: A People's Music* (New York, 1948). Among the later accounts are Rex Harris, *The Story of Jazz* (New York, 1955); Stephen Longstreet, *The Real Jazz Old and New* (Baton Rouge, La., 1956); Andre Hodeir, *Jazz: Its Evolution and Essence* (New York, 1956); Woody Woodward, *Jazz Americana: the Story of Jazz and All-Time Jazz Greats from Basin Street to Carnegie Hall* (Los Angeles, 1956); Iain Lang, *Jazz in Perspective* (London, 1957); Francis

Newton, *The Jazz Scene* (London, 1959); Andre Hodeir, *Toward Jazz* (New York, 1962); and Dave Dexter, Jr., *The Jazz Story from the '90s to the '60s* (Englewood Cliffs, N.J., 1964). Especially important is Martin Williams, *The Jazz Tradition* (New York, 1970). Pictorial histories include Dennis Stock, *Jazz Street* (Garden City, N.Y., 1960), and Orvin Keepnews and Bill Graner, *A Pictorial History of Jazz* (New York, 1955). Juvenile readers will find Langston Hughes' *The First Book of Jazz* (New York, 1955) and *Famous Negro Music Makers* (New York, 1955) interesting.

Also of value are William L. Grossman and Jack W. Farrell, *The Heart of Jazz* (New York, 1956); Sinclair Traill, *Concerning Jazz* (London, 1957); Martin Williams (ed.), *The Art of Jazz* (New York, 1959); John F. Mehegan, *Jazz Improvisation* (New York, 1959); Leroy Ostransky, *The Anatomy of Jazz* (Seattle, Wash., 1960); Sidney Bechet, *Treat It Gentle* (New York, 1960); George T. Simon, *The Feeling of Jazz* (New York, 1961) with excellent drawings by Tracy Sugarman; and Lillian Erlich, *What Jazz Is All About* (New York, 1962). Less useful are Ernest Borneman, *A Critic Looks at Jazz* (London, 1946); George S. Rosenthal (ed.), *Jazzways* (New York, 1947); Ralph de Toledano, *Frontiers of Jazz* (New York, 1947); Rex Harris, *Jazz* (Harmondsworth, 1952); Eddie Condon and Richard Gehman (eds.), *Eddie Condon's Treasury of Jazz* (New York, 1956); Alun Morgan and Raymond Horricks, *Modern Jazz: A Survey of Developments since 1939* (London, 1956); Sinclair Traill and Gerald Lascelles, *Just Jazz* (London, 1957); Ralph J. Gleason (ed.), *Jam Session: An Anthology of Jazz* (New York, 1958); John S. Wilson, *The Collector's Jazz: Traditional and Swing* (Philadelphia, 1958); Whitney Balliett, *The Sound of Surprise* (New York, 1959); Nat Hentoff and Albert J. McCarthy (eds.), *Jazz* (New York, 1959); Andre Francis, *Jazz* (New York, 1960), translated by Martin Williams; Peter Gammond (ed.), *The Decca Book of Jazz* (London, 1960); Nat Hentoff, *The Jazz Life* (New York, 1961); and Burnett James, *Essays on Jazz* (London, 1962).

The black role in jazz is emphasized in Eileen Southern, *The Music of Black Americans: A History* (New York, 1971), and Leslie B. Rout, Jr., "Economics and Race in Jazz" in *Frontiers of American Culture* (Lafayette, Ind., 1968), edited by Ray B. Browne, Richard H. Crowder, Virgil L. Lokke, and William T. Stafford. A more biographical approach is taken by Frederic Ramsey, Jr. and Charles Edward Smith (eds.), *Jazzmen* (New York, 1939); David Ewen, *Men of Popular Music* (Chicago, 1944); Nat Shapiro and Nat Hentoff (eds.), *Hear Me Talkin' To Ya* (New York, 1955); Nat Shapiro, *The Jazz Makers* (New York, 1957); Benny Green, *The Reluctant Art* (New York, 1963); and Rudi Blesh, *Combo: USA* (Philadelphia, 1971).

Louis Armstrong's books, *Swing That Music* (New York, 1936) and *Satchmo: My Life In New Orleans* (Englewood Cliffs, N.J., 1954), are both informative, as are Robert Goffin, *Horn of Plenty: The Story of Louis Armstrong* (New York, 1947); Albert J. McCarthy, *Louis Armstrong* (New York, 1961); Hughes Panassie, *Louis Armstrong* (New York, 1971); and Larry L. King, "Everybody's Louie," *Harper's Magazine*, CCXXXV (Nov., 1967),

61-69. Barry Ulanov, *Duke Ellington* (New York, 1946); Peter Gammond (ed.), *Duke Ellington, His Life and Music* (New York, 1958); G. E. Lambert, *Duke Ellington* (New York, 1961); Stanley Dance, *The World of Duke Ellington* (New York, 1970); and Dance's "Duke Ellington," *Stereo Review*, XXIII (Dec., 1969), 69-80, are among the better portraits of that jazzman. Ellington's own account, *Music Is My Mistress* (Garden City, N.Y., 1973), is interesting, while Billie Holiday's autobiography, *Lady Sings the Blues* (Garden City, N.Y., 1956), is candid and poignant.

Eddie Condon tells his story in *We Called It Music* (New York, 1947), with the aid of Thomas Sugrue, whereas Charles H. Wareing and George Garlick's *Bugles for Beiderbecke* (London, 1958), is a serviceable study of trumpeter Bix Beiderbecke. Ralph Berton, *Remembering Bix* (London, 1974), is also worth consulting. Paul Whiteman records his thoughts on the more commercial jazz forms in *Jazz* (New York, 1926), with Mary Margaret McBride, and Rudy Vallee does the same in *Vagabond Dreams Come True* (New York, 1930) and the more comprehensive *My Time Is Your Time: the Story of Rudy Vallee* (New York, 1962), the latter with Gil McKean. Several of the decade's jazzmen are discussed in Richard Hadlock's *Jazz Masters of the Twenties* (New York, 1965).

The 1920s controversy over jazz is intelligently analyzed by Neil Leonard in *Jazz and the White Americans: the Acceptance of a New Art Form* (Chicago, 1962). Chadwick Hansen's "Social Influences on Jazz Style: Chicago, 1920-30," *American Quarterly*, XII (Winter, 1960), 493-507, and Gilbert Osofsky's "Symbols of the Jazz Age: The New Negro and Harlem Discovered," *American Quarterly*, XVII (Summer, 1965), 229-238, are both excellent. Contemporary attitudes toward jazz may be gleaned from Newman Levy, "The Jazz Formula," *Modern Music*, I (June, 1924), 24-25; Edwin J. Stringham, "'Jazz'—An Educational Problem," *Musical Quarterly*, XII (April, 1926), 190-195; Don Knowlton, "The Anatomy of Jazz," *Harper's Magazine*, CLII (April, 1926), 578-585; Aaron Copland, "Jazz Structure and Influence," *Modern Music*, IV (Jan.-Feb., 1927), 9-14; and Paul Fitz Laubenstein, "Jazz—Debit and Credit," *Musical Quarterly*, XV (Oct., 1929), 606-624. Louis Harap, "The Case for Hot Jazz," *Musical Quarterly*, XXVII (Jan., 1941), 47-61, is a later observation.

The finest exposition of the Kansas City renaissance is Ross Russell's *Jazz Style in Kansas City and the Southwest* (Berkeley, Calif., 1971), although sections of Raymond Horricks' *Count Basie and His Orchestra* (London, 1957) may prove helpful. George T. Simon, *The Big Bands* (New York, 1967), is the most balanced look at the "Swing" era, while Leo Walker, *The Wonderful Era of the Great Dance Bands* (Berkeley, Calif., 1964), and Albert McCarthy, *The Dance Band Era* (Philadelphia, 1971), are attractive complements. Marshall and Jean Stearns, *Jazz Dance: The Story of American Vernacular Dance* (New York, 1968), is by no means limited to the 1930s and 1940s, but it does contain a great deal of information on the big dance bands. Excellent is George T. Simon, *Glenn Miller and His Orchestra* (New York,

1974). Benny Goodman and Irving Kolodin, *The Kingdom of Swing* (New York, 1961, revised ed.), is an intriguing first-hand account, supplemented by D. Russell Connor and Warren W. Hicks, *B G—on the Record: a Bio-discography of Benny Goodman* (New Rochelle, N.Y., 1969). Other items of interest for record buffs include Stephen F. Bedwell (comp.), *A Glenn Miller Discography* (London, 1956), and Howard J. Waters, Jr., *Jack Teagarden's Music: His Career and Recordings* (Stanhope, N.J., 1960). Rex Stewart, *Jazz Masters of the Thirties* (New York, 1972), is a fairly personalized narrative. Definitely worth consulting are Stanley Dance (ed.), *Jazz Era: The 'Forties* (London, 1961), Paul L. Specht, *How They Became Name Bands: the Modern Technique of a Danceland Maestro* (New York, 1941), and Alberta Powell Graham, *Strike Up the Band: Bandleaders of Today* (New York, 1949).

Leonard Feather, *Inside Be-bop* (New York, 1949), is a good, general chronicle, but Ross Russell's biography of Charlie Parker, *Bird Lives!* (New York, 1973), is a more solid profile of the "bop" revolution. Also significant are Robert George Reisner, *Bird: The Legend of Charlie Parker* (New York, 1962), Max Harrison, *Charlie Parker* (New York, 1961), and Michael James, *Dizzy Gillespie* (London, 1959). Ira Gitler, *Jazz Masters of the Forties* (New York, 1966), sketches several of the major "bop" personalities.

Carol Easton, *Straight Ahead: The Story of Stan Kenton* (New York, 1973), is a fascinating portrait of the leading "progressive" jazzman, whereas Michael James, *Miles Davis* (New York, 1961), deals with one of the pioneers of the "cool" movement. Despite its militant edge, Frank Kofsky's *Black Nationalism and the Revolution in Music* (New York, 1970) nevertheless provides the best insights into recent developments in jazz. Biographies of four current jazz artists, including Ornette Coleman and Cecil Taylor, are contained in A. B. Spellman's *Black Music* (New York, 1970). Not to be overlooked are LeRoi Jones, *Black Music* (New York, 1970), Pauline Rivelli and Robert Levin (eds.), *The Black Giants* (New York, 1970), and Addison Gayle, Jr. (ed.), *The Black Aesthetic* (Garden City, N.Y., 1971). Of less certain value are Joe Goldberg, *Jazz Masters of the Fifties* (New York, 1965), Martin Williams, *Jazz Masters in Transition, 1957-69* (New York, 1970), and Albert McCarthy, *Jazzbook, 1955* (London, 1955).

Although considered thoroughly establishment by the avant-garde, the fortnightly magazine *Down Beat* is still the major publication in the jazz field. Guides and bibliographies include Robert George Reisner (comp.), *The Literature of Jazz: A Preliminary Bibliography* (New York, 1954); Alan P. Merriam, *A Bibliography of Jazz* (Philadelphia, 1954); Hughes Panassie and Madeleine Gautier, *Guide to Jazz* (Boston, 1956); Leonard Feather, *The Book of Jazz: A Guide to the Entire Field* (New York, 1957); Barry Ulanov, *A Handbook of Jazz* (New York, 1957); Charles Fox, Peter Gammond, Alun Morgan, and Alexis Korner, *Jazz on Record: A Critical Guide* (London, 1960); Joachim E. Berendt, *The New Jazz Book: A History and Guide* (New York, 1962); Samuel Barclay Charters, *Jazz: New Orleans, 1885-1963* (New York,

1963), an index to the black musicians of New Orleans; Leonard Feather, *The Encyclopedia of Jazz in the Sixties* (New York, 1966); and Donald Kennington, *The Literature of Jazz: A Critical Guide* (London, 1970).

Chapter XI. POPULAR SONGS

The most analytical volume on the recent accomplishments of Tin Pan Alley songsmiths is Alex Wilder's *American Popular Song: The Great Innovators, 1900-1950* (New York, 1972). Also important is Max Wilk, *They're Playing Our Song* (New York, 1973). Readable and basically solid are the books by David Ewen, especially *Panorama of American Popular Music* (Englewood Cliffs, N.J., 1957), *The Life and Death of Tin Pan Alley* (New York, 1964), and *Great Men of American Popular Song* (Englewood Cliffs, N.J., 1970). Sigmund Spaeth's *A History of Popular Music in America* (New York, 1948) is still valuable, as is Isaac Goldberg's *Tin Pan Alley: A Chronicle of American Popular Music* (New York, revised ed., 1961). More superficial are Ian Whitcomb, *After the Ball: Pop Music from Rag to Rock* (New York, 1972), and John Rublowsky, *Popular Music* (New York, 1967), although both make interesting points. Worth consulting is Larry Freeman, *The Melodies Linger On* (Watkins Glen, N.Y., 1951), while Volume VI of Mark Sullivan's *Our Times* (New York, 1936) contains a rather lengthy section on the popular music of the 1920s. *Great Songs of the Sixties* (Chicago, 1970), includes an extensive sampling of the tunes of that decade, along with an excellent introduction by editor Milton Okun.

Two articles by Hughson F. Mooney—"Songs, Singers and Society, 1890-1954," *American Quarterly*, VI (Fall, 1954), 221-232, and "Popular Music since the 1920s: The Significance of Shifting Taste," *American Quarterly*, XX (Spring, 1968), 67-85—are strongly interpretative. Also quite good are Gene Lees, "The Decline of the American Popular Song," *HiFi/Stereo Review*, XII (Jan., 1964), 59-63, and Owen Lee, "America's Changing Tastes in Popular Music," *High Fidelity*, XXII (Oct., 1972), 62-71. David Dachs, *Anything Goes: The World of Popular Music* (Indianapolis, 1964), stresses the economic aspects of the recent music scene, as does Hazel Meyer, *The Gold in Tin Pan Alley* (Philadelphia, 1958). Isidore Witmark and Isaac Goldberg's *From Ragtime to Swingtime* (New York, 1939 is the inside story of one of the major music publishing companies, whereas Roland Gelatt's *The Fabulous Phonograph* (New York, 1965) is a more objective and comprehensive history.

Among the works by and about specific songwriters are Hoagy Carmichael, *The Stardust Road* (New York, 1946); Hoagy Carmichael and Stephen Longstreet, *Sometimes I Wonder: The Story of Hoagy Carmichael* (New York, 1965); Sammy Cahn, *I Should Care* (New York, 1974); Edward

Jablonski, *Harold Arlen: Happy with the Blues* (Garden City, N.Y., 1961), and "American Songwriter Harold Arlen," *Stereo Review*, XXXI (Nov., 1973), 54-65; Tony Thomas, *Harry Warren and the Hollywood Musical* (Secaucus, N.J., 1975); and Gene Lees, *"Henry Mancini: Hollywood's New Master of Melody," Hi Fi/Stereo Review*, XVI (June, 1965), 39-44.

Biographies and autobiographies of major singers include Ethel Waters and Charles Samuels, *His Eye Is on the Sparrow* (Garden City, N.Y., 1951); Pearl Sieben, *The Immortal Jolson: His Life and Times* (New York, 1962); Rudy Vallee and Gil McKean, *My Time Is Your Time: The Story of Rudy Vallee* (New York, 1962); Bing Crosby, *Call Me Lucky* (New York, 1953); Ted Crosby, *The Story of Bing Crosby* (Cleveland, 1946); Barry Ulanov, *The Incredible Crosby* (New York, 1948); E. J. Kahn, Jr., *The Voice* (New York, 1946), about Frank Sinatra; Earl Wilson, *Sinatra* (New York, 1976); Eartha Kitt, *Thursday's Child* (New York, 1956); Arnold Shaw, *Belafonte: An Unauthorized Biography* (Philadelphia, 1960); Gerold Frank, *Judy*, (New York, 1975), far and away the best portrait of Judy Garland; and Rosemary Clooney and Raymond Strait, *This for Remembrance* (New York, 1977). Three of the better collective biographies are Edward B. Marks, *They All Sang: From Tony Pastor to Rudy Vallee* (New York, 1934), David Ewen, *Men of Popular Music* (Chicago, 1944), and Katharine Bakeless, *In the Big Time: Career Stories of American Entertainers* (Philadelphia, 1953).

David Ewen's *Popular American Composers from Revolutionary Times to the Present* (New York, 1962) is a convenient biographical guide, as is *The ASCAP Biographical Dictionary of Composers, Authors, and Publishers* (New York, 1966), compiled and edited by the Lynn Farnol Group, Inc. Useful are Peter Fammond and Peter Clayton, *Dictionary of Popular Music* (New York, 1961), John H. Chipman (comp.), *Index to Top-Hit Tunes, 1900-1950* (Boston, 1962), and American Society of Composers, Authors, and Publishers, *Thirty Years of Motion Picture Music* (New York, 1960). Julius Mattfeld, *"Variety" Music Cavalcade, 1920-1969* (Englewood Cliffs, N.J.), is a chronology of vocal and instrumental music popular in the United States, while Norman Charles, *Social Values in American Popular Songs (1890-1950)*, is an important Ph.D. dissertation, written at the University of Pennsylvania in 1958. Recommended background reading for this chapter and the preceding one is Nathan Irvin Huggins, *Harlem Renaissance* (New York, 1971).

Chapter XII. COUNTRY MUSIC

The definitive study on the evolution of country music is Bill C. Malone's *Country Music, U.S.A.: A Fifty-Year History* (Austin, 1968), although *Stars of Country Music* (Urbana, Ill., 1975), edited by Malone and Judith McCulloh, serves as an excellent supplement, covering the sweep from

Uncle Dave Macon to Johnny Rodriguez. Other general histories include Robert Shelton, *The Country Music Story* (Secaucus, N.J., 1966), Paul Hemphill, *The Nashville Sound* (New York, 1970), John Grissim, *Country Music: White Man's Blues* (New York, 1970), William R. McDaniel and Harold Seligman, *Grand Ole Opry* (New York, 1952), Linnell Gentry, *A History and Encyclopedia of Country, Western, and Gospel Music* (Nashville, Tenn., 1969), and Irwin Stambler and Grelun Landon, *Encyclopedia, Country, and Western Music* (1969).

Among the best of the biographies and autobiographies are Woody Guthrie's *Bound for Glory* (New York, 1943), Roger M. Williams' life of Hank Williams, *Sing A Sad Song* (Garden City, N.J., 1970), Loretta Lynn's *Coal-Miner's Daughter* (New York, 1970), and Charles R. Townsend's *San Antonio Rose: The Life and Music of Bob Wills* (Urbana, 1976). Valuable shorter accounts include John Greenway, "Jimmie Rodgers—A Folksong Catalyst," *Journal of American Folklore*, LXX (July-Sept., 1957), 231-234; Greenway, "Woody Guthrie," *The American West*, III (Fall, 1966), 24-30, 74-78; and Robert Windeler, "Loretta Lynn" and "Charley Pride," *Stereo Review*, XXVIII (Jan., 1972), 67-70.

For information on authentic cowboy songs see John A. Lomax (comp.), *Cowboy Songs and Other Frontier Ballads* (New York, 1923), and N. Howard ("Jack") Thorp, *Songs of the Cowboys* (New York, 1966), the latter edited by Austin E. and Alta S. Fife. Important on folk music of protest and the American left are John Greenway, *American Folksongs of Protest* (New York, 1960), Ray M. Lawless, *Folksingers and Folksongs in America* (New York, 1960), and S. Serge Denisoff, *Great Day Coming* (Urbana, 1971).

D. K. Wilgus, "An Introduction to the Study of Hillbilly Music," Archie Green, "Hillbilly Music: Source and Symbol," Norman Cohen, "The Skillet Lickers: A Study of a Hillbilly String Band and Its Repertoire," and L. Mayne Smith, "An Introduction to 'Bluegrass' " all appeared in the *Journal of American Folklore*, LXXVIII (July-Sept., 1965), 195-203, 204-228, 229-244, 245-256 respectively, and are all worth consulting. Paul DeMaggio, Richard A. Peterson, and Jack Esco, Jr., "Country Music: Ballad of the Silent Majority," and Jens Lund, "Fundamentalism, Racism, and Political Reaction in Country Music," are both part of *The Sounds of Social Change* (Chicago, 1972), edited by R. Serge Denisoff and Richard A. Peterson.

Charles Portis, "That New Sound from Nashville," *The Saturday Evening Post*, CCXXXIX (Feb. 12, 1966), 30-31; 34-38; John Cohen, "Country Music Outside Nashville," *Sing Out!*, XVI (Feb.-Mar., 1966), 40-42; Gene Lees, "Nashville: The Sounds and the Symbols," *High Fidelity Magazine*, XVII (April, 1967), 57-61; John Greenway, "Country-Western: The Music of America," *The American West*, V (Nov., 1968), 32-41; Mike Reagen, "The Pious Rhetoric of Country Music," *Music Journal*, XXVII (Jan., 1969), 50; 67-70; Peter Thorpe, "I'm Movin' On: The Escape Theme in Country and Western Music," *Western Humanities Review*, XXIV (Autumn, 1970), 307-318; Christopher S. Wren, "Country Music: The Great White Soul

Sound," *Look*, XXXV (July 13, 1971), 11-13; Noel Coppage, "Whatever Happened to Nashville?" *Stereo Review*, XXVIII (Jan., 1972), 60-66; Chet Flippo, "Hill Country Sound," *Texas Parade*, XXXIV (April, 1974), 16-23; Garrison Keillor, "Onward and Upward with the Arts: At the Opry," *The New Yorker*, L (May 6, 1974), 46-70; "Lord, They've Done It All," *Time*, CIII (May 6, 1974), 51-55; and Florence King, "Red Necks, White Socks, and Blue Ribbon Fear," *Harper's Magazine*, CCXLIX (July, 1974), 30-34, number amount the hundreds of recent articles.

Insights into the local country music scene were gleaned from interviews conducted in Dallas by Stephen R. Tucker for the Southern Methodist University Oral History Project on the Performing Arts, especially sessions recorded with Dewey Groom, Bob Sullivan, Hermes Nye, Fred McCord, Jim Boyd, Roy Newman, and Marvin Montgomery during the spring of 1974.

CHAPTER XIII. ROCK AND SOUL

Carl Belz's *The Story of Rock* (New York, 1971) is probably the best general history of rock, although Arnold Shaw's *The Rock Revolution* (New York, 1969) is a close rival. Also important are Nik Cohn, *Rock from the Beginning* (New York, 1969), Mike Jahn, *Rock from Elvis Presley to the Rolling Stones* (New York, 1973), and Jonathan Eisen (ed.), *The Age of Rock* (New York, 1969). Michael Lydon, *Rock Folk* (New York, 1971), Irwin Stambler, *Guitar Years: Pop Music from Country and Western to Hard Rock* (Garden City, N.Y., 1970), and Bruce L. Chipman (ed.), *Hardening Rock* (Boston, 1972) are more specialized, but definitely worth consulting. Several valuable interviews are included in Arnold Shaw, *The Rockin' '50s* (New York, 1974), while R. Serge Denisoff and Richard A. Peterson (eds.), *The Sounds of Social Change* (Chicago, 1972), and Ray B. Browne (ed.), *Popular Culture and the Expanding Consciousness* (New York, 1973), both contain articles of significance.

Charles Keil's *Urban Blues* (Chicago, 1966) is a marvelous study, placing the blues within the socio-economic setting of the black ghetto, while Arnold Shaw's *The World of Soul* (New York, 1970) gives a solid overall view. Worth noting is Yannick Bruynoghe's *Big Bill Blues* (New York, 1955), an interesting study of Big Bill Broonzy.

The better biographies on rock singers include Jerry Hopkins, *Elvis: A Biography* (New York, 1971), Hunter Davies, *The Beatles: The Authorized Biography* (New York, 1968), Myra Friedman, *Buried Alive: The Biography of Janis Joplin* (New York, 1973), and David Dalton, *Janis* (New York, 1971). Peggy Caserta's *Going Down with Janis* (Secaucus, N.J., 1973) is highly sensationalized.

Insights into the 1960s rock scene may be obtained from Joan Peyser, "The Music of Sound or, The Beatles and the Beatless," *Columbia University Forum*, X (Fall, 1967), 16-22; Al Carmines, "The Beatles: Troubadours of the New Kingdom," *Motive*, XXVIII (Oct., 1967), 17-19; Morgan Ames, "Simon and Garfunkel in Action," *High Fidelity*, XVII (Nov., 1967), 62-66; Gene Lees, "Rock," *High Fidelity*, XVII (Nov., 1967), 57-61; Ralph J. Gleason, "Like a Rolling Stone," *The American Scholar*, XXXVI (Autumn, 1967), 555-563; Burt Korall, "Of Times That Are A-Changin'," *Saturday Review* (Aug. 26, 1967), 76-77; and "The Messengers," *Time*, XC (Sept. 22, 1967), 60-68. Of major importance is Wilfrid Mellers, *Twilight of the Gods: The Music of the Beatles* (New York, 1973). *Rolling Stone* continues to be the best journal on current rock happenings.

Index